CASES
IN
MARKETING
MANAGEMENT

2nd edition

CASES IN MARKETING MANAGEMENT
Issues for the 1990s

Charles L. Hinkle
University of Colorado

Wesley J. Johnston
Georgia State University

Esther F. Lanigan
College of William and Mary

PRENTICE HALL, Englewood Cliffs, New Jersey 07632

Library of Congress Cataloging-in-Publication Data

Hinkle, Charles L.
    Cases in marketing management : issues for the 1990s. -- 2nd ed. /
  Charles L. Hinkle, Wesley J. Johnston, Esther F. Lanigan.
       ·p.   cm.
    Includes bibliographical references.
    ISBN 0-13-116351-5
    1. Marketing--Management--Case studies.   I. Johnston, Wesley J.
  II. Lanigan, Esther F.   III. Title.
  HF5415.13.H57 1992
  658.8--dc20   91-32550
                                                              CIP

Aquisition Editor: *Jennifer Young*
Production Editor: *Edith Pullman*
Copy Editor: *Sally Ann Bailey*
Cover Designer: *20/20 Services, Inc.*
Prepress Buyer: *Trudy Pisciotti*
Manufacturing Buyer: *Bob Anderson*
Supplements Editor: *Lisamarie Brassini*
Editorial Assistant: *Ellen Ford*

© 1992, 1984 by Prentice-Hall, Inc.
a Simon & Schuster Company
Englewood Cliffs, New Jersey 07632

Printed in the United States of America

10 9 8 7 6 5 4 3

ISBN   0-13-116351-5

Prentice-Hall International (UK) Limited, *London*
Prentice-Hall of Australia Pty. Limited, *Sydney*
Prentice-Hall Canada Inc., *Toronto*
Prentice-Hall Hispanoamericana, S.A., *Mexico*
Prentice-Hall of India Private Limited, *New Delhi*
Prentice-Hall of Japan, Inc., *Tokyo*
Simon & Schuster Asia Pte. Ltd., *Singapore*
Editora Prentice-Hall do Brasil, Ltda., *Rio de Janeiro*

CONTENTS

Preface, ix

The Purposes and Processes of Case Analysis, ix
The Marketing Audit, x
A Simplified Planning Model, xi
Data Analysis, xiii
Preclass Case Preparation Sessions, xiii
Responsibilities of Preclass Preparation Leaders, xiii
Preparing Written Analyses, xiv

Acknowledgments, xv

Case Topics, Text References, and Sequence of Contents, 1

PART I   ROLE OF MARKETING IN STRATEGIC PLANNING

Case   1   Hewlett-Packard Company, 5

Case   2   Pacific Coast Greetings, Inc., 13

Case   3   American Box Company, 31

v

Case 4   Eastern Downs, 43

Case 5   Sears, Roebuck and Company (A), 59

Case 6   Sears, Roebuck and Company (B), 72

Case 7   Cormark and the Ontario Psychiatric Association (A), 87

Case 8   Cormark and the Ontario Psychiatric Association (B), 91

PART II   STRATEGIES AND TACTICS:
DESIGNING, ASSEMBLING, AND IMPLEMENTING
THE MARKETING MIX

Product

Case 9   Celestial Seasonings, Inc. (A), 107

Case 10   Celestial Seasonings, Inc. (B), 126

Case 11   Measurement Research and Development, Inc., 152

Case 12   Digital Products Corporation, 164

Case 13   Robinson Associates, Inc. (A), 171

Case 14   Robinson Associates, Inc. (B), 183

Price

Case 15   A. Poe Designs, Inc., 202

Case 16   DeLorean Motor Company, 211

Case 17   Eclipse Films, 225

Case 18   Omni Automated Systems, 239

Place

Case 19   The Chinook Bookshop, 253

Case 20   YMCA/USO of the Pikes Peak Region (A), 270

Case 21   YMCA/USO of the Pikes Peak Region (B), 301

Case 22   Semester at Sea, 318

Promotion

Case 23   Compassion International, 331

Case 24   Julie Research Laboratories, 355

Case 25   The Monster That Eats Business, 387

Case 26   Mary Kay Cosmetics (A), 405

Case 27   Mary Kay Cosmetics (B), 434

Case 28   Time Inc./Seagram, 454

PART III   INTEGRATING AND ADMINISTERING MARKETING AND CORPORATE STRATEGIES

Case 29   Coke Tries to Counter the Pepsi Challenge, 463

Case 30   Fidji, 485

Case 31   Western Bell Yellow Pages, 521

Case 32   Kmart Stores, 533

Extra-Length Cases

Case 33   General Motors at the Industrial Divide, 556

Case 34   Liberty National Bancorp, Inc. and Liberty National Bank and Trust Company, 572

Case 35   Bolter Turbines, Inc. (A): Product Development in Industrial Marketing, 609

Exercise

Case 36   Bolter Turbines, Inc. (B): Negotiation Simulation, 648

PREFACE

**THE PURPOSES
AND PROCESSES
OF CASE ANALYSIS**

The authors hope that using this volume will help you to enrich your perspective on the so-called "real world" of business, one in which perhaps you and many of your group are already experienced. As you examine, study, and discuss these cases, developed in organizations being tested daily in the crucible of the marketplace, these four learning objectives, at least, seem reasonable:

1. To understand how managers' backgrounds and values affect their contributions to and views of policies and procedures.
2. To understand the impact of different management policies and practices upon various types of organizations and to distinguish between effective and ineffective policies under differing circumstances.
3. To grasp how marketing and the different functional areas of business (e.g., finance and production) are interrelated.
4. To understand both the theoretical and applied aspects of information decision systems for marketing management and to use various standard and special sources of data for analyses.

A principal goal of using case studies in management education is to stimulate direct involvement in the process of finding, defining, and analyzing issues and problems, which may be stated directly or merely implied in the case narrative, and developing recommendations and programs for the organization. Tackling real business problems is viewed as an excellent means of developing practitioners in the art of management. The approach has several implications for your preparation and participation, among them the following:

1. You increase your learning benefits with thorough preparation efforts before class and through participation in class discussion.
2. You develop problem-finding and analytic skills in a critical, although usually not hostile, atmosphere. The process helps to build both a willingness to risk stating conclusions and an ability to overcome fears of making and admitting mistakes.
3. You sharpen the capacity to recognize management's assumptions and to develop your own, in real situations presented in case formats.
4. You learn and teach along with the instructor whose central mission is to orchestrate the group's interaction, to stimulate ideas, and to guide discussion—in other words, to help you develop your ideas.

THE MARKETING AUDIT

As you examine the case—skimming first for highlights and then reading it thoroughly, preferably twice, for understanding—and list the principal features relating to what you see as the central issues, several tentative solutions may evolve.

The following suggestions are intended to help you examine the case, to pinpoint problem areas, and to devise solutions and recommendations:

1. Examine the firm's management, services, financial structure, and general and specific goals. Remember that companies do not do things; people do. Consider the managers' value systems, and estimate their impact upon objectives, policies, and strategies.
2. Take the customers' viewpoints and try to understand such factors as the following:
   a. **Who** are the customers? Classify them according to pertinent socioeconomic, demographic, and marketing characteristics.
   b. **What** products and services do they use?
   c. **Where** do they buy these products and services? Consider market geography, regional differences, and types of companies patronized.
   d. **When** do they buy? What is the frequency of use? Time of the day and week? Are there seasonal (cyclical) influences?
   e. **How** do they buy? Is help required to make the purchase? Do customers seek advice because of their lack of experience? Does personal selling play an important role?
   f. **Why** do they buy? You may not be able to infer motivations, but you can consider related literature, findings of the behavioral sciences, and your experiences that pertain to the product and/or service and to the circumstances in the case.
3. Define the nature of the product-service.
   a. What are its similarities to, and differences from, competitive offerings?
   b. After carefully evaluating how people choose and use the products and services, ask the question, "How can the firm's marketing system adapt its product-service capabilities to the requirements of the buying/using system?"
4. Given the composition of markets and the company's product-service capabilities, what seem to be the most desirable ways to close the gap between company and customers?

    a. What marketing elements—services, research, advertising, personal selling, publicity—are available?

    b. Will marketing operations provide adequately for the outgoing flow of the product-service, and the incoming flow of money and information?

5. By now you should be able to define, and rank order by urgency, the problems facing the firm. List all those issues that are important; pay particular attention to those that are critical.

6. Lay out a proposed program, maintaining an acceptable cost-price-profit relationship. Justify your preferred solution. Balance the risks and potential returns in keeping with corporate policies and available resources.

This section suggests but one way of approaching the tasks of case analysis; it is not intended as a formula to be followed by rote. You will wish to alter techniques for different situations. In developing analyses and solutions, make assumptions that you consider to be necessary and that are reasonable.

Since perfect information is never available, you might wish to seek case-related information, but *it is preferable to deal with the study as it is presented rather than to acquire postcase data on the company.* Perfect answers are hard to come by, and since there may be two or more acceptable solutions to a case problem, not only the solution itself but also the manner in which it is derived is important.

By objective, systematic, and thorough diagnosis, analysis, and preparation, you will be able to defend your ideas and enhance your skills. This will contribute to the learning of others in the class as well.

A SIMPLIFIED PLANNING MODEL

Exhibit 1 portrays conceptually the phases of planning, which can be used for a one-year budgeting cycle or expanded to embrace a long-term perspective, beginning with articulating (or examining it if there already is one) the organization's statement of purpose, its mission. The situation, or strengths-weaknesses/opportunities-threats (SWOT), analysis should be considered for almost every case in this book.

Leaping to judgments before examining the fundamentals of a situation often leads to unwarranted conclusions, and the recommendations based on such a superficial examination can instigate egregious circumstances. Before jumping into a business strategy for a going concern, develop an idea of what the current strategy is and how well, overall, the organization is doing. If possible, infer from the case information a mission statement; in short, try to answer the question, "What business are they in?" Expressing an answer to this query is an excellent starting point from which to go about the tasks of evaluating the firm's past, present, and future. However, if it is a fledgling enterprise, such as A. Poe Designs, or just a concept, such as Eclipse Films, and no history exists, a suitable starting task would be to draft your version of a mission-and-role statement for the entrepreneur. Following that, it may be worthwhile to consider a basic set of policies to guide management.

The goals and objectives of a business ideally are governed by its policies and implemented through planned practices. Policies and courses of corporate action might include a code of ethics, a plan for expanding into new territories, an approach to advertising and publicity, attitudes toward employees, viewpoints on promotion,

Exhibit 1

Phases of Planning

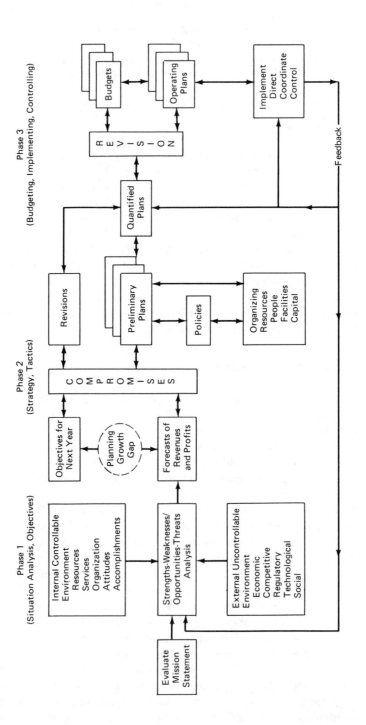

Source: Charles L. Hinkle.

and many other variables. Policies are ideas, attitudes, and philosophies, as distinguished from procedures or methods.

Management policies are the responsibility of the owner or board of directors, and in many organizations these policies are developed and approved by an executive committee of the board and put into effect and interpreted by the chief executive officer. In some organizations, the CEO develops the policies as a means of communicating intent and fundamental directions.

For an example of how one large and very successful company views this matter of philosophy, policies, and objectives, you might wish to review the Hewlett-Packard case, which indicates how one firm has approached developing general objectives.

DATA ANALYSIS

When analyzing the quantitative data in a case, remember that the words "figure" and "fictitious" both derive from the same Latin infinitive, *fingere*. Temper conclusions drawn from the superficial appearance of data with good judgment, being aware that even more important than the actual numbers is what management will believe or distrust about them. Some of the case studies you will analyze in this text provide large amounts of information, qualitative and quantitative, but do not require its use. That choice is up to you. A combination of analytical tools and personal judgments is often necessary.

PRECLASS CASE PREPARATION SESSIONS

Unless you spend the time and effort necessary to study a case before the class session, the classroom experience will not provide maximum returns for you, and others will not receive the benefit of your ideas. Small-group preparation periods allow time for "teams" to go over the case in a preliminary fashion before the whole class convenes. Everyone should read the case before a prep session. In these "warm-up" get-togethers, a number of erroneous ideas and solutions can be filtered out, bringing each person to a greater level of understanding before the entire class gets into the act, thus accelerating the learning process. Rather than arriving at a consensus, it is expected that members of prep groups will interact constructively with each other and come out with conclusions that, while based principally on independent thinking, will have the benefit of others' thoughts.

Intellectual income for you will be directly related to the thoroughness of your individual study and the intensity of your involvement in preliminary sessions and classroom discussions.

RESPONSIBILITIES OF PRECLASS PREPARATION LEADERS

In getting ready for the case prep session, the discussion leader

1. Thoroughly reads and analyzes the case
2. Develops thought-provoking questions to focus group attention upon important pros and cons in the case situation

During the discussion, the leader

1. Helps group members to get organized for the work session
2. States the basics of the problem
3. Encourages reticent members to participate
4. Discourages private conversations
5. Focuses and guides discussion
   a. Maintains logical progression, pushing toward solutions
   b. Summarizes key points

In directing and coordinating case preparation activity, the attitude that you display will significantly influence results. So employ your helpful traits—be dynamic, genial, interested, and responsible.

PREPARING WRITTEN ANALYSES

Your instructor will have his or her own special evaluation procedure for critiquing your written analyses, so these criteria are offered as preliminary guidelines only. We would suggest, however, that you check your analysis of each case for coverage of the following:

1. Key institutional strategic issues
2. Key marketing management strategic issues
3. Facts in the case, plus your own assumptions
4. Other functional areas (finance, production, etc.) when appropriate to the situation
5. Priorities for action
6. Plan for implementing recommendations
7. Alternatives and recognition of shortcomings of recommendations
8. Concepts presented by authors in course textbook, if any, and of ideas and frameworks developed in class discussion
9. Exhibits and appendices to aid the reader

Attention to writing—grammar, spelling, mechanics, and flow of ideas—is essential in ordinary text.

We wish you the best of luck in deconstructing these cases designed to challenge your skills in articulating significant strategies to be applied to marketing decisions in the 1990s.

Charles Hinkle
Wesley Johnston
Esther Lanigan

ACKNOWLEDGMENTS

Some cases in this volume were drafted by contributing writers who are acknowledged here under "primary authorship," indicating that the person being recognized was responsible in a substantial way for that particular write-up. Following that, recognition is given to individuals in various organizations who collaborated with the authors by orchestrating visits, arranging interviews with key persons, and providing resource materials. It will become clear to the reader, by quotations and references in the studies, that substantial credit is owed to many individuals who made this collection possible.

PRIMARY AUTHORSHIP

American Box Company and *Sears, Roebuck and Company*   Published with permission of Dryden Press. Both cases first appeared in *Cases in Marketing Management and Strategy* by Roger D. Blackwell, Wesley J. Johnston, and W. Wayne Talarzyk.

A. *Poe Designs, Inc.*   Susan Maples, president, Maples Enterprises, a management consulting organization, and instructor in marketing at Metropolitan State College, Denver.

Bolter Turbines (A)   Michael A. Jones and William S. Bishop, managers, Solar Turbines International, Division of Caterpillar Tractor, Inc., and John L. Graham, associate professor, Department of Marketing, University of California, Irvine.

Bolter Turbines (B)   John L. Graham, associate professor, Department of Marketing, University of California, Irvine, with permission of the *Journal of Marketing Education*. First published in 1984 as "Bolter Turbines, Inc.: Negotiation Simulation," pp. 28–36.

The Chinook Bookshop   Marshall Sprague, author-historian and well-known chronicler of the West.

Coke Tries to Counter the Pepsi Challenge   Dhruv Grewal, under the direction of Dr. Larry D. Alexander, associate professor, Department of Management, Virginia Polytechnic Institute and State University.

Compassion International   Stephen Sorenson, author and editor and public relations manager of the subject organization.

Cormark and the Ontario Psychiatric Association (A), (B)   David Large and Assistant Professor Julia Bristor, School of Business Administration, University of Western Ontario.

Eastern Downs   Dr. Richard Parker, associate professor of marketing in the School of Business, Glassboro State College, New Jersey.

Fidji   Helen Chase Kimball, research associate, under the supervision of Professor Christian Pinson, associate professor, INSEAD.

General Motors at the Industrial Divide   Dr. Jerry M. Calton, assistant professor of management, College of Business, Montana State University.

Julie Research Laboratories   Artist Dick Hafer, the cartoonist who helped to develop the booklets used as centerpieces of this study.

Kmart Stores   John L. Little, doctoral student in strategic management, and Larry D. Alexander, assistant professor of strategic management, Department of Management, Virginia Polytechnic Institute and State University.

The Monster That Eats Business   Artist Dick Hafer, who prepared and wrote the book for Joseph Sugarman, president and creative director of JS&A Group, Inc.

Sears, Roebuck and Company (A), (B)   Arthur P. Ismay and J. Alex Murray of Wilfrid Laurier University. The case was first published under the title of Sears World Trade, Inc.

Semester at Sea   Dr. Lloyd Lewan, director of academic affairs, Institute for Shipboard Education, University of Pittsburgh.

YMCA/USO of the Pikes Peak Region (A), (B)   Dr. Robert Knapp, a member of the Business School faculty, University of Colorado, Colorado Springs.

COLLABORATIVE SUPPORT

DeLorean Motor Company   Mike Knepper, director of public relations, and Carol Winkler, administrative assistant to John Z. DeLorean.

Eclipse Films   Benjamin C. McWhorter III, a consultant to the motion picture industry.

Hewlett-Packard Company   John Riggen, general manager of the Colorado Springs Division of Hewlett-Packard.

Julie Research Laboratories   Pamela Spencer, administrative assistant to Loebe Julie.

Mary Kay Cosmetics, Inc. (A)   Dick Bartlett, vice president of marketing; Dean Meadors, director of public relations; and J. Eugene Stubbs, chief financial officer.

Omni Automated Systems   James Gogan and Steve Imeye, both graduates of the University of Southern California M.B.A. program.

Pacific Coast Greetings, Inc.   Claudia Warne, president of the company.

Robinson Associates, Inc. (A)   The firm's president, Patrick J. Robinson.

Semester at Sea   James Gogan, a graduate of the University of Southern California M.B.A. program.

Time Inc./Seagram   Dr. Robert Schreiber, director of research, Magazine Group, Time Inc.

Western Bell Yellow Pages   John Gould, associate professor of business communications, University of Southern California.

DISCLAIMER

All case studies are intended to provide a basis for classroom discussion; none purports to illustrate correct or incorrect, appropriate or inappropriate, management policies and practices.

CASES
IN
MARKETING
MANAGEMENT

CASE TOPICS,
TEXT REFERENCES, AND
SEQUENCE OF CONTENTS

TWO REFERENCE TABLES

The first of the two tables in this introductory material outlines the marketing subject matter contained in the cases and provides other taxonomic descriptors. The second table presents references to related chapters in Philip Kotler's *Marketing Management,* seventh edition, published by Prentice Hall, and frequently adopted for upper-division college courses in marketing strategy and for M.B.A. marketing management courses. If you wish to investigate chapters in other textbooks, the headings of Table 1 provide useful leads.

SEQUENCE OF CASES

Since the majority of these case studies spans more than one of the listed core topics of marketing management, labeling them uniquely was, in some instances, necessarily arbitrary. Several cases could fit under one rubric as easily as under another.

The first major division of the book embraces the role of marketing, strategic planning and marketing management, and evaluation of market opportunities. Unavoidably overlapping this portion is the next major division related to strategies and tactics—designing, assembling, and implementing the mix: product, price, distribu-

Table 1

CASE CATEGORIES AND MARKETING TOPICS

	CONSUMER	BUSINESS-TO-BUSINESS	TANGIBLE (PRODUCT)	INTANGIBLE (SERVICE)	PRODUCT/SERVICE DECISIONS	PRICING	ADVERTISING/PUBLIC RELATIONS	PERSONAL SELLING	SALES MANAGEMENT	LEGAL, SOCIAL ISSUES	MARKETING RESEARCH	PLACEMENT (CHANNELS)	RETAILING	CORPORATE STRATEGY	MANAGEMENT VALUES	INTERNATIONAL	NOT FOR PROFIT
Hewlett-Packard Company			X	X	X				X					X	X	X	
Pacific Coast Greetings, Inc.	X		X		X	X			X					X		X	
American Box Company			X	X				X						X		X	
Eastern Downs	X				X	X	X	X			X						
Sears, Roebuck and Company (A)	X			X	X	X							X	X			
Sears, Roebuck and Company (B)		X			X	X						X	X	X		X	
Cormark and the Ontario Psychiatric Association (A)	X				X			X				X					X
Cormark and the Ontario Psychiatric Association (B)		X			X	X						X					X
Celestial Seasonings, Inc. (A)	X		X		X			X	X	X	X		X		X		
Celestial Seasonings, Inc. (B)	X		X				X				X			X	X		
Measurement Research and Development, Inc.			X	X				X	X		X			X			
Digital Products Corporation			X	X				X	X	X				X	X		
Robinson Associates, Inc. (A)			X	X					X			X		X	X		
Robinson Associates, Inc. (B)			X	X					X			X		X	X		
A. Poe Designs, Inc.	X		X		X	X			X			X	X	X			
Delorean Motor Company	X		X		X	X	X				X	X		X	X		
Eclipse Films			X	X			X	X						X		X	
Omni Automated Systems			X	X	X	X			X	X							
The Chinook Bookshop	X		X		X			X	X	X		X	X	X			
YMCA/USO of the Pikes Peak Region (A)	X				X	X	X					X	X	X	X		X
YMCA/USO of the Pikes Peak Region (B)	X				X	X	X				X	X	X	X			X
Semester at Sea	X				X			X	X			X		X	X	X	X
Compassion International	X				X				X			X		X	X	X	X
Julie Research Laboratories			X	X				X	X	X	X			X	X		
The Monster That Eats Business	X		X		X			X	X	X		X		X	X		
Mary Kay Cosmetics, Inc. (A)	X		X					X	X	X		X			X		
Mary Kay Cosmetics, Inc. (B)	X		X		X				X		X			X	X		
Time, Inc./Seagram		X					X	X			X						
Coke Tries to Counter the Pepsi Challenge	X		X		X							X		X		X	
Fidji	X		X		X	X	X					X	X	X			
Western Bell Yellow Pages		X			X		X			X	X					X	
Kmart Stores	X		X	X									X	X			
General Motors at the Industrial Divide	X	X	X								X			X	X		
Liberty National Bank				X	X	X	X	X	X		X			X			
Bolter Turbines, Inc. (A)			X	X	X				X	X	X						
Bolter Turbines, Inc. (B)			X	X	X	X			X	X							

tion, and promotion (including advertising, personal selling, and sales management decisions and programs). In the final group of cases, we are back full circle to developing and integrating marketing and corporate strategies and tactics, with emphasis on evaluating internal strengths and weaknesses of the organization and assessing opportunities and threats—forces largely beyond management's control—in the external environment.

Table 2

CROSS REFERENCES TO CASES AND CHAPTERS IN KOTLER, (SEVENTH EDITION), PRENTICE HALL, *MARKETING MANAGEMENT*

CASE	CHAPTERS
Hewlett Packard Company	1, 2, 7 11, 25, 26
Pacific Coast Greetings, Inc.	3, 5, 6, 8, 9, 11, 12, 17
American Box Company	7, 15, 16, 18, 24, 26
Eastern Downs	3, 9, 10, 21 22, 23
Sears, Roebuck and Company (A)	2, 5, 6, 13, 14, 20, 25, 26
Sears, Roebuck and Company (B)	2, 3, 7, 9, 12, 15, 17, 20
Cormark and the Ontario Psychiatric Association (A)	1, 4, 5, 17, 21
Cormark and the Ontario Psychiatric Association (B)	1, 4, 5, 17, 22, 25, 26
Celestial Seasonings, Inc. (A)	2, 5, 6, 11, 16, 19, 21
Celestial Seasonings, Inc. (B)	3, 5, 6, 11, 18, 20, 21
Measurement Research and Development, Inc.	4, 5, 7, 8, 9, 13
Digital Products Corporation	3, 7, 12, 13, 24
Robinson Associates, Inc. (A)	2, 4, 7, 11, 12, 17
Robinson Associates, Inc. (B)	4, 7, 18, 21, 26
A. Poe Designs, Inc.	5, 6, 9, 11, 12, 18
Delorean Motor Company	1, 2, 3, 8, 11, 12, 14, 25
Eclipse Films	3, 12, 15, 17, 18, 24
Omni Automated Systems	7, 8, 11, 14, 24
The Chinook Bookshop	6, 10, 20
YMCA/USO of the Pikes Peak Region (A)	1, 2, 3, 4, 5, 6, 12, 17, 25
YMCA/USO of the Pikes Peak Region (B)	1, 2, 3, 4, 5, 6, 12, 17, 25
Semester At Sea	1, 2, 3, 6, 10, 11, 17, 21
Compassion International	1, 4, 15, 17, 21, 22
Julie Research Laboratories	5, 7, 17, 21, 22, 23
The Monster That Eats Business	1, 5, 6, 7, 23
Mary Kay Cosmetics, Inc. (A)	3, 6, 10, 16, 19, 23, 24
Mary Kay Cosmetics, Inc. (B)	3, 6, 12, 16, 19, 23, 24
Time, Inc./Seagram	4, 17, 21, 22, 26
Coke Tries to Counter the Pepsi Challenge	4, 6, 8, 11, 14, 21, 22
Fidji	3, 4, 6, 8, 10, 11, 12, 15, 16, 18, 22
Western Bell Yellow Pages	5, 7, 17, 21, 22, 24
Kmart Stores	6, 8, 10, 11, 14, 19, 20
General Motors At The Industrial Divide	1, 2, 3, 6, 7, 13, 14, 25, 26
Liberty National Bank	3, 8, 11, 13, 17, 18
Bolter Turbines, Inc. (A)	7, 8, 18, 24
Bolter Turbines, Inc. (B)	7, 8, 18, 24

1

HEWLETT-PACKARD COMPANY

In 1939 Hewlett-Packard (HP) had one invention, an audio oscillator designed by Bill Hewlett, that was sold by engineers to other engineers to solve practical electronic measurement problems. The direct descendant of that original company business became an instrument line comprising over 3,000 products, still sold in the same manner—head-to-head discussions and problem-solving sessions with customers. There was a noticeable difference, however: for many years, formal marketing functions were not explicit parts of the organizational structure. In contrast, for fiscal year 1981, the company spent 15 cents of every sales dollar on marketing functions related to selling business and scientific computers, analytical and measuring instruments, electronic medical equipment, components, and hand-held calculators. The company began advertising on prime-time television, and its advertising placements in popular business periodicals steadily increased as corporate technological advancements expanded dramatically and planners began examining a wider array of potential markets.

In 1981, HP had more than 200 sales and service offices in over 80 cities throughout the United States and in 30 foreign countries. It sold through a network of 80 distributorships in certain countries where there were no company sales or service offices. There were 50,000 industrial and commercial customers, numerous educational and scientific institutions, and a variety of medical organizations doing business with the company. Virtually all products were sold directly through HP's

5

own sales force, with marketing operations supported by approximately 3,300 field sales engineers as well as 14,000 individuals providing field service and administrative support. Orders originating outside of the United States accounted for 48 percent of total company orders in fiscal 1981.[1]

New products were seen to be the keys to growth. In them, HP invested more than 9 cents of every sales dollar in 1981. This funding level was traditional at the company, placing it among the top U.S. industrial organizations ranked by proportion of sales invested in product development. It may not seem surprising, then, that about 70 percent of total 1981 orders were for products developed after 1977.[2]

Noted for its ability to innovate by nurturing small entrepreneurial units—an apt term might be "corporateurs"—while undergoing extraordinary growth, the company achieved total sales of $4.25 billion in the year ended October 31, 1982.[3] Although the firm's rapid growth might occasionally collide with its entrepreneurial spirit,[4] basic policies and objectives continually evolved at HP to guide the corporation's directions and behavior. A summary of these principles is presented in this case study to afford a framework for examining the implications of corporate philosophy and operating objectives for designing marketing policies and strategies.

HEWLETT-PACKARD: STATEMENT OF CORPORATE OBJECTIVES[5]

Distributed to many requesters annually, both inside HP and to outsiders, and considered by many observers to be an excellent model for formulating principles and general objectives, the pamphlet on which this section is based was endorsed in January 1982, by David Packard, chairman of the board, William R. Hewlett, chairman of the executive committee, and John Young, president and chief executive officer.

> The achievements of an organization are the result of the combined efforts of each individual in the organization working toward common objectives. These objectives should be realistic, should be clearly understood by everyone in the organization, and should reflect the organization's basic character and personality.
>
> If the organization is to fulfill its objectives, it should strive to meet certain other fundamental requirements:
>
> First, there should be highly capable, innovative people throughout the organization. Moreover, these people should have the opportunity—through continuing programs of training and education—to upgrade their skills and capabilities. This is especially important in a technical business where the rate of progress is rapid. Techniques that are good today will be outdated in the future, and people should always be looking for new and better ways to do their work.
>
> Second, the organization should have objectives and leadership which generate

---

[1]Hewlett-Packard Company Form 10-K, fiscal year ended October 31, 1981.

[2]1981 Annual Report.

[3]1982 Annual Report.

[4]"Can John Young Redesign Hewlett-Packard?" *Business Week*, December 6, 1982, pp. 72–78.

[5]HP publication, distributed both inside and outside the company, upon which this entire section is based, Palo Alto, California, 1982.

enthusiasm at all levels. People in important management positions should not only be enthusiastic themselves, they should be selected for their ability to engender enthusiasm among their associates. There can be no place, especially among the people charged with management responsibility, for half-hearted interest or half-hearted effort.

Third, the organization should conduct its affairs with uncompromising honesty and integrity. People at every level should be expected to adhere to the highest standards of business ethics, and to understand that anything less is totally unacceptable. As a practical matter, ethical conduct cannot be assured by written policies or codes; it must be an integral part of the organization, a deeply ingrained tradition that is passed from one generation of employees to another.

Fourth, even though an organization is made up of people fully meeting the first three requirements, all levels should work in unison toward common objectives, recognizing that it is only through effective, cooperative effort that the ultimate in efficiency and achievement can be obtained.

It has been our policy at Hewlett-Packard not to have a tight military-type organization, but rather, to have overall objectives which are clearly stated and agreed upon, and to give people the freedom to work toward those goals in ways they determine best for their own areas of responsibility.

Our Hewlett-Packard objectives were initially published in 1957. Since then they have been modified from time to time, reflecting the changing nature of our business and social environment. This booklet represents the latest updating of our objectives. We hope you find them informative and useful.

1. Profit

Objective   To achieve sufficient profit to finance our company growth and to provide the resources we need to achieve our other corporate objectives.

Commentary   In our economic system, the profit we generate from our operations is the ultimate source of the funds we need to prosper and grow. It is the one absolutely essential measure of our corporate performance over the long term. Only if we continue to meet our profit objective can we achieve our other corporate objectives.

Our long-standing policy has been to reinvest most of our profits and to depend on this reinvestment, plus funds from employee stock purchases and other cash flow items, to finance our growth.

Profits vary from year to year, of course, reflecting changing economic conditions and varying demands for our products. Our needs for capital also vary, and we depend on short-term loans to meet those needs when profits or other cash sources are inadequate. However, loans are costly and must be repaid; thus, our objective is to rely on reinvested profits as our main source of capital.

Meeting our profit objective requires that we design and develop each and every product so that it is considered a good value by our customers, yet is priced to include an adequate profit. Maintaining this competitiveness in the marketplace also requires that we perform our manufacturing, marketing and administrative functions as economically as possible.

Profit is not something that can be put off until tomorrow; it must be achieved today. It means that myriad jobs be done correctly and efficiently. The day-to-day performance of each individual adds to—or subtracts from—our profit. Profit is the responsibility of all.

2. Customers

Objective   To provide products and services of the highest quality and the greatest possible value to our customers, thereby gaining and holding their respect and loyalty.

Commentary   The continued growth and success of our company will be assured only if we offer our customers innovative products that fill real needs and provide lasting value, and that are supported by a wide variety of useful services, both before and after sale.

Satisfying customer needs requires the active participation of everyone in the company. It demands a total commitment to *quality*, a commitment that begins in the laboratory and extends into every phase of our operations. Products must be designed to provide superior performance and long, trouble-free service. Once in production, these products must be manufactured at a reasonable cost and with superior workmanship.

Careful attention to quality not only enables us to meet or exceed customer expectations, but it also has a direct and substantial effect on our operating costs and profitability. Doing a job right the first time, and doing it consistently, sharply reduces costs and contributes significantly to higher productivity and profits.

Once a quality product is delivered to the customer, it must be supported with prompt, efficient services of the same high quality.

Good communications are essential to an effective field sales effort. Because of our broad and growing line of products, very often several sales teams will be working with a single customer. These teams must work closely to assure that the products recommended best fulfill the customer's overall, long-term needs. Moreover, HP customers must feel that they are dealing with one company, a company with common policies and services, and one that has a clear understanding of their needs and a genuine interest in providing proper, effective solutions to their problems.

3. Fields of Interest

Objective   To build on our strengths in the company's traditional fields of interest and to enter new fields only when it is consistent with the basic purpose of our business and when we can assure ourselves of making a needed and profitable contribution to the field.

Commentary   Our company's growth has been generated by a strong commitment to research and development, and has been accomplished in two ways—first, by providing a steady flow of new products to markets in which we are already well established and, second, by expanding our technology into fields that are new but related to our traditional ones. The evolution of the HP product line is a reflection of this two-dimensional growth.

Our first products were electronic measuring instruments used primarily by engineers and scientists. In time we extended our range of products to include solid-state components and instrumentation for the fields of medicine and chemical analysis. Recognizing our customers' needs to gather and assimilate large quantities of measurement data, we developed a family of computers to complement HP measuring devices. By linking measurement and computational technologies, we gained added strength in our traditional, technically oriented markets and began to serve the broader needs of business and industry.

Today, the interactive capabilities of Hewlett-Packard instruments and systems enable our customers—decision makers in business as well as in technical fields—to gain ready access to essential information, to put it into meaningful form, and to use it effectively in improving the productivity of themselves and their organizations. Helping these customers achieve better results is the unifying purpose of our business. The areas we serve build on each other to add strength to our company and provide additional values to our customers. This guides our interests, our organization and our marketing philosophy.

The broad scope of HP technology often provides opportunities for our company to expand into new fields. Before entering a new field, however, we must satisfy ourselves that it is consistent with our business purpose and that it affords us the opportunity to make a significant *contribution*. This requires that we have not only the technology to create truly innovative and needed products, but that we also have the capability to manufacture and market them effectively and at a reasonable profit.

4. Growth

Objective   To let our growth be limited only by our profits and our ability to develop and produce innovative products that satisfy real customer needs.

Commentary   How large should a company become? Some people feel that when it has reached a certain size there is no point in letting it grow further. Others feel that bigness is an objective in itself. We do not believe that large size is important for its own sake; however, for at least two basic reasons, continuous growth in sales *and* profits is essential for us to achieve our other objectives.

In the first place, we serve a dynamic and rapidly growing segment of our technological society. To remain static would be to lose ground. We cannot maintain a position of strength and leadership in our fields without sustained and profitable growth.

In the second place, growth is important in order to attract and hold high-caliber people. These individuals will align their future only with a company that offers them considerable opportunity for personal progress. Opportunities are greater and more challenging in a growing company.

5. Our People

Objective   To help HP people share in the company's success which they make possible, to provide job security based on their performance, to ensure them a safe and pleasant work environment, to recognize their individual achievements, and to help them gain a sense of satisfaction and accomplishment from their work.

Commentary   We are proud of the people we have in our organization, their performance, and their attitude toward their jobs and toward the company. The company has been built around the individual, the personal dignity of each, and the recognition of personal achievements.

Relationships within the company depend upon a spirit of cooperation among individuals and groups, and an attitude of trust and understanding on the part of managers toward their people. These relationships will be good only if employees have faith in the motives and integrity of their peers, supervisors and the company itself.

On occasion, situations will arise where people have personal problems which temporarily affect their performance or attitude, and it is important that people in such circumstances be treated with sympathy and understanding while the problems are being resolved.

Job security is an important HP objective. Over the years, the company has achieved a steady growth in employment by consistently developing good new products, and by avoiding the type of contract business that requires hiring many people, then terminating them when the contract expires. The company wants HP people to have stable, long-term careers—dependent, of course upon satisfactory job performance.

Another objective of HP's personnel policies is to enable people to share in the company's success. This is reflected in a pay policy and in employee benefit programs that place us among the leaders in our industry.

There is also a strong commitment at HP to the concept of equal opportunity and affirmative action, not only in hiring but also in providing opportunities for advancement. Advancement is based solely upon individual initiative, ability, and demonstrated accomplishment. Since we promote from within whenever possible, managers at all levels must concern themselves with the proper development of their people and should give them ample opportunity—through continuing programs of training and education—to broaden their capabilities and prepare themselves for more responsible jobs.

The physical well-being of our people has been another important concern of HP's since the company's founding. With the growing complexity and diversity of our research and manufacturing processes, we must be especially vigilant in maintaining a safe and healthful work environment.

We want people to enjoy their work at HP and to be proud of their accomplishments. This means we must make sure that each person receives the recognition he or she needs and deserves. In the final analysis, people at all levels determine the character and strength of our company.

6. Management

Objective To foster initiative and creativity by allowing the individual great freedom of action in attaining well-defined objectives.

Commentary In discussing HP operating policies, we often refer to the concept of "management by objective." By this we mean that, insofar as possible, each individual at each level in the organization should make his or her own plans to achieve company objectives and goals. After receiving supervisory approval, each individual should be given a wide degree of freedom to work within the limitations imposed by these plans and by our general corporate policies. Finally, each person's performance should be judged on the basis of how well these individually established goals have been achieved.

The successful practice of "management by objective" is a two-way street. Management must be sure that each individual understands the immediate objectives, as well as corporate goals and policies. Thus a primary HP management responsibility is communication and mutual understanding. Conversely, employees must take sufficient interest in their work to want to plan it, to propose new solutions to old problems, to stick their necks out when they have something to contribute. "Management by objective," as opposed to management by directive, offers opportunity for individual freedom and contribution; it also imposes an obligation for everyone to exercise initiative and enthusiasm.

In this atmosphere it is important to recognize that cooperation between individuals and between operating units is essential to our growth and success. Although our operations are decentralized, we are a *single* company whose overall stength is derived from mutually helpful relationships and frequent interaction among our dispersed but interdependent units.

It is important, as well, for everyone to recognize there are some policies which must be established and maintained on a company-wide basis. We welcome recommendations on these company-wide policies from all levels, but we expect adherence to them at all times.

7. Citizenship

Objective   To honor our obligations to society by being an economic, intellectual and social asset to each nation and each community in which we operate.

Commentary   All of us should strive to improve the environment in which we live. As a corporation operating in many different communities throughout the world, we must make sure that each of these communities is better for our presence. This means identifying our interests with those of the community; it means applying the highest standards of honesty and integrity to all our relationships with individuals and groups; it means enhancing and protecting the physical environment, building attractive plants and offices of which the community can be proud; it means contributing talent, time, and financial support to worthwhile community projects.

Each community has its particular set of social problems. Our company must help to solve these problems. As a major step in this direction, we must strive to provide worthwhile employment opportunities for people of widely different backgrounds. Among other things, this requires positive action to seek out and employ members of disadvantaged groups, and to encourage and guide their progress toward full participation at all position levels.

As citizens of their community, there is much that HP people can and should do to improve it—either working as individuals or through such groups as churches, schools, civic or charitable organizations. In a broader sense, HP's "community" also includes a number of business and professional organizations, whose interests are closely identified with those of the company and its individual employees. These, too, are deserving of our support and participation. In all cases, supervisors should encourage HP people to fulfill their personal goals and aspirations in the community as well as attain their individual objectives within HP.

At a national level, it is essential that the company be a good corporate citizen of each country in which it operates. Moreover, our employees, as individuals, should be encouraged to help in finding solutions to national problems by contributing their knowledge and talents.

The betterment of our society is not a job to be left to a few; it is a responsibility to be shared by all.

2

PACIFIC COAST GREETINGS, INC.

"Some days are just busy, but today is absolutely crazy," thought Claudia Warne, of Pacific Coast Greetings, Inc. (PCG). After waking up to the sound of her beeper at 6:30 A.M. and racing to the Los Angeles Airport to correct a problem of missing luggage, her day had only become more hectic.

Managing her own company with 17 employees in five offices in five cities was challenging for Claudia. After a full day of handling calls from customers and employees and developing a sales brochure for the conference she was attending in two days, Claudia finally had time to do some longer-term planning. She was using the evening to analyze possible marketing opportunites for her company.

Claudia thought back to simpler days when she was on her own. Her only worries were getting to the airport on time to greet clients and writing customized welcome packets. As her business grew, however, so did the importance of her decisions. Facing her now was what to do with the new research that sat on her desk. It was a proposal written by an independent consultant she had hired. The proposal was titled, "Four Alternatives for Growing PCG."

COMPANY BACKGROUND

Pacific Coast Greetings, Inc., is a service provider in the tour and travel industry. The company arranges services and accommodations for chartered group tours and individual travelers from Europe to the West Coast of the United States. It has been in operation since 1984.

PCG is contracted by foreign tour operators to be a "receptive agent." As the title implies, the company "receives" the group at the destination city. PCG is responsible for ensuring that each traveler enjoys a worry-free vacation.

PCG develops customized itineraries for the inbound travelers, contracts hotel space, and gives presentations about the destination city and any planned activities. PCG renders customized services as requested by the tour operator. The following are some of the services provided by PCG:

> Airport greetings
> Transfers (ground transportation to and from airports)
> Welcome orientation briefing
> Welcome information packet
> Hospitality desk/hotel visits
> Hotel room bookings and billings
> Sightseeing tours
> Representation on chartered city bus tours
> Customized excursions
> Step-on guides and group escorts
> Multilingual staff
> Lei greeting (Hawaii)
> Office and administrative support
> 24-hour emergency phone contact

When large tour operators in Europe arrange a vacation package, they contract PCG to take care of the group or individual travelers during their stay. When the group or individuals arrive, on a chartered flight or scheduled service flight from Europe, the PCG representative's job is to familiarize them with their holiday destination. The representative also ensures that the services purchased via the original tour brochure are provided as scheduled.

The company arranges the services and events and charges the tour operator the cost plus a fee. With this arrangement, PCG's contracts are written for and paid by the foreign tour operator. The company's day-to-day services, however, are provided for the individual travelers who purchased the vacation package from the tour operator.

PCG's headquarters are in Redondo Beach, California, 5 miles from Los Angeles International Airport. It also has offices in Honolulu, Las Vegas, San Diego, and San Francisco. The company employs 7 full-time staff and 10 seasonal representatives.

INITIAL START-UP

Claudia Warne grew up in southern California after her parents emigrated from Germany in the late 1950s. She had an inherent love for travel and a special interest in working in the travel industry.

Fresh out of college in 1980, she started her career in the travel business as a flight attendant for Lufthansa, the German airline. A year later she took the position of airport and hotel coordinator for the Los Angeles office of Jetsave Travel, Inc., a major British tour operator. In this position, Claudia was in charge of scheduling all the company's hotel and airport representatives (i.e., the staff who greeted clients at the airport and gave presentations about attractions in Los Angeles). Within a year she became manager of Jetsave's Los Angeles office.

In 1983 Jetsave's director of customer services in London left the company to form Poundstretcher, a tour operator and wholly owned subsidiary of British Airways. Poundstretcher's business was developing and marketing charter tour packages. He asked Claudia to be the Poundstretcher's receptive agent in the United States, but she declined to continue at Jetsave.

In the fall of 1984, Poundstretcher General Manager Alan Fyfe convinced Claudia to become its representative for travelers inbound from the United Kingdom to Los Angeles and San Francisco. A contract was signed for calendar year 1985.

Claudia took no start-up money. She worked out of her home and the business grew very slowly. The first services provided were those for inclusive tours. As an inclusive tour agent, she set up the whole vacation: ground transportation, hotel accommodations, and local sightseeing. Another important part of the service was that she was the emergency phone contact when there were any problems. She was responsible for the clients from the time they landed until they departed for London.

Her initial costs were her labor in contacting airport shuttle service, booking city tours, making presentations at the hotels, and greeting the tours when they arrived at the Los Angeles airport.

Claudia's major contract was serving as Poundstretcher's receptive agent for all the flights into Los Angeles. This contract gave her a steady stream of incoming groups and individuals who arrived on a weekly basis from the United Kingdom. The travelers normally stayed for two weeks. Claudia's responsibilities were greeting the clients; arranging the hotel accommodations, ground transportation, and sightseeing tours; and giving a presentation (briefing) about Los Angeles upon the travelers' arrival.

PCG has served as the receptive agent for Poundstretchers's Program of Summer Charter Flights since 1985. It has also expanded to serve as a receptive agent for other tour operators' regularly scheduled charter programs and for individual travelers.

CONTINUED GROWTH

As the needs of Poundstretcher grew, PCG grew and diversified. PCG also added a second account, Premier Holidays. The new business forced Claudia to hire part-time help in Los Angeles and San Francisco. PCG provided airport greetings, hotel briefings, optional sightseeing administrative support, and a "welcome packet." No money was spent on advertising. New customers were added by referrals.

PCG's specialty was in customizing contracts for the tour operators based on their needs. This service provided an advantage over other competing receptive agents who offer a single package of services, with no variation.

By 1990, PCG had nine contracts. Of the six largest wholesale tour operators in the United Kingdom, four had contracts with PCG. The company also obtained contracts in France and Australia. Only one contract had been lost since the beginning of operation.

Contracts with tour operators were negotiated annually. The sales cycle started at the POW WOW convention in a different U.S. city each year. This is a huge convention for the trade, where tour operators from around the world bring in their vacation plans and look for rates (hotels, airlines, greeting companies). The convention allows tour operators and receptive agents to make contacts and to plan future business relationships.

The final contracts are usually negotiated at the tour operator's site overseas. To prepare, Claudia must know the economic situation in the tour operator's country, her own costs, and the tour operator's volume and the quality of their operation. (Different tour operators have different reputations for quality of service.)

PCG has a cyclical income period. May to October are the busy months operationally. The other months are spent finding new business and planning next year's season.

MARKET NICHE

PCG's main competitive advantage was its friendly and competent staff. The company had earned a reputation as the most reliable and courteous receptive agent. Many competitors offer the same services, sometimes even at lower cost. But PCG had developed a level of trust with its customers through past performance.

Another strength was PCG's ability to customize contracts for the incoming travelers. The company was able to offer any specialized services the travelers sought. This became an important differentiator because it made the vacations especially memorable for the passengers. This satisfaction was always noticed by the tour operator.

Finally, PCG was contracted with a variety of hotels in major cities in Arizona, California, Hawaii, and Nevada. It handled all bookings and billings for room and tax and all special requests. The company had a knack for choosing the appropriate accommodation for each arriving group. This service also saved tour operators from having to deal with many hotels and having to establish credit with the hotels.

Assumptions About the Clients

Claudia had observed that the British usually took their holiday in the summer. Their first trip would often be to Spain; their next trip was to the United States, usually Florida. The second visit to the United States usually involved going to New York. By the third trip to the United States, the West Coast was a favorite destination.

Claudia thought that most U.K. tour operators sent 10 to 20 times as many people to Florida compared to California. The other cities Poundstretcher serviced were New York, Los Angeles, San Francisco, Las Vegas, and Honolulu. Competition was more fierce in Florida where the costs were generally lower than in California. With lower margins, volume was the key to profitability in these markets.

Claudia knew that travel to California was different. The traveler had probably already been to the East Coast. The traveler was probably more affluent and was looking for additional servicing and better accommodations. She knew that PCG was uniquely positioned to handle this clientele. The staff was professionally trained to be courteous, to provide quality service, and to pay attention to detail.

Current Marketing Programs

PCG promoted its business by attending tour and travel conferences like POW WOW and World Travel Market. It also generated new business by referrals from current customers and the associations to which it belonged. PCG's memberships included

> Travel Industry Association of America
> Greater Los Angeles Convention & Visitor's Bureau
> Anaheim Area Convention & Visitor's Bureau
> San Francisco Convention & Visitor's Bureau
> San Diego Convention & Visitor's Bureau

The company used a small brochure in mailings to qualified prospects. PCG had a mailing list of tour operators in the United Kingdom and France, but it had not experimented with any direct-mail campaigns.

Claudia considered advertising, but felt that her potential customers were already familar with PCG. Travel magazines, trade journals, and local newspapers were used for advertising by other firms in the industry. Exhibit 2.1 provides a list of magazines and newspapers and their rates.

Exhibit 2.1

ADVERTISING RATES, BLACK AND WHITE COPY

Publication	Yearly Frequency	One-Time Rate (¼ page)	1-Inch	2-Inch
Endless Vacation	8	$2,500		
National Geographic Traveler	6	5,100		
Travel & Leisure	12	3,900		
Travel/Holiday	12	2,750		
Travel Trade Gazette	4	925		
Los Angeles Times, Sunday travel section	52		$310	$620
San Francisco Examiner	52		275	550

Competition

Claudia knew of several firms on the West Coast who also served as receptive agents for foreign tour operators. These firms were her major competition for contracts each year. She was familiar with most of the principals of these firms, after seeing them at conventions and working with them before starting PCG.

Claudia felt that the services offered by her competition were quite similar to those of PCG. Some of the competitors offered standardized services at standardized rates. These were the larger companies that had more market presence. As a smaller company, she knew that PCG's advantage was its ability to customize its services to the needs of the tour operator and the particular package vacation it was offering.

GROWTH OPPORTUNITY

Holding contracts with four of the biggest six London tour operators, Claudia was interested in expanding the business. She hired an independent consultant to write a study defining several alternative methods of growth.

The following are excerpts from the consultant's report.

Alternative 1. Adding offices in Florida and New York

Explanation

An obvious method of expanding your business would be to continue moving into markets served by your current customers. Your biggest customers offer many more tours to Florida and New York than to California. You estimate that Poundstretcher, for example, sends 20 times as many people to Florida as it does to Los Angeles. It sends about 10 times as many people to New York as Los Angeles. These huge markets could provide much more business for PCG.

Exhibits 2.2 through 2.4 provide information on the top states and destinations preferred by foreign travelers. Exhibit 2.5 lists the average hotel room rates in selected cities.

Benefits

This alternative has several benefits:

1. It is the same business that you currently do. Your services don't need to change, and your existing personnel can continue doing the same work with which they are familiar.
2. Your current contracts with the major tour operators and the reputation you have developed would provide an easy entry into the market. Your customers will be the same people you currently deal with. They know you and are familiar with your services and capabilities. They may be satisfied enough with your current performance to help you get started in the new market by paying your start up costs or guaranteeing your contract for the first year. On the other hand, they may be satisfied with the receptive agent they currently use in each location. This would make it tougher to break into the market.

Exhibit 2.2

TOP STATES RANKED BY GROWTH IN FOREIGN VISITORS, 1985–1989 ESTIMATE

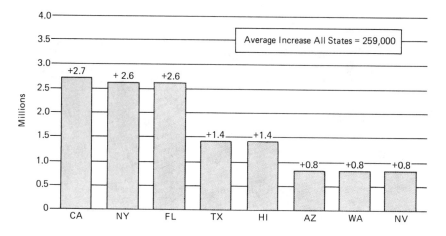

Source: U.S. Travel and Tourism Administration, June 1990.

Exhibit 2.3

TOP SIX STATE VACATION DESTINATIONS
POTENTIAL PLEASURE TRAVELERS ARE INTERESTED IN VISITING

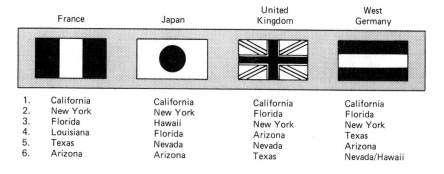

	France	Japan	United Kingdom	West Germany
1.	California	California	California	California
2.	New York	New York	Florida	Florida
3.	Florida	Hawaii	New York	New York
4.	Louisiana	Florida	Arizona	Texas
5.	Texas	Nevada	Nevada	Arizona
6.	Arizona	Arizona	Texas	Nevada/Hawaii

Source: U.S. Travel and Tourism Administration, February 1990.

Exhibit 2.4

TOP SIX MISCELLANEOUS VACATION DESTINATIONS
POTENTIAL PLEASURE TRAVELERS ARE INTERESTED IN VISITING

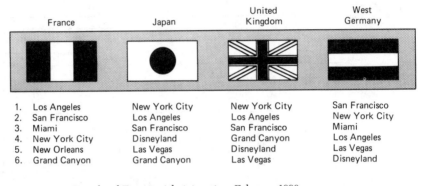

	France	Japan	United Kingdom	West Germany
1.	Los Angeles	New York City	New York City	San Francisco
2.	San Francisco	Los Angeles	Los Angeles	New York City
3.	Miami	San Francisco	San Francisco	Miami
4.	New York City	Disneyland	Grand Canyon	Los Angeles
5.	New Orleans	Las Vegas	Disneyland	Las Vegas
6.	Grand Canyon	Grand Canyon	Las Vegas	Disneyland

Source: U.S. Travel and Tourism Administration, February 1990.

Exhibit 2.5

AVERAGE HOTEL ROOM RATES IN
SELECTED LOCATIONS, 1989–1990

	1989	1990
Arizona	$70.79	$ 75.89
California	67.08	70.56
Florida	71.46	77.48
Hawaii	96.57	100.87
Illinois	57.75	59.72
Nevada	50.35	50.29
New York	93.14	98.71
Washington	46.57	49.74

Source: American Hotel and Motel Association.

3. The sheer size of the market makes it seem very profitable. Your current business has been quite successful in a limited market. The opportunity for a much greater volume could help your business grow substantially.

<u>Problems</u>

Two possible problems accompany this change in volume:

1. The profit margins are much lower in these markets compared to the West Coast market you currently serve. Rates for hotel accommodations in Orlando, Florida, for example, are much lower than are those in Los Angeles. Average airfare from London to Miami is $855. Average airfare from London to Los Angeles is $1,000. Thus, in Florida profit margins are much lower than in Los Angeles.

   In New York City, rates for hotel accommodations are approximately the same as those in Los Angeles. Average airfare from London to New York is $763. Thus, profit margins in New York are also lower than in Los Angeles. The accompanying table shows average airline rates (excluding taxes) from London's Heathrow Airport on July 13, 1990:

London to	7-Day Advance	30-Day Advance
Miami	$1,276	$ 855
New York City	1,254	763
Los Angeles	1,728	1,000

   In these East Coast markets, much greater volume is needed to maintain your current level of profitability.

2. Your company's ability to handle a large volume with the same quality of service may be a problem. To maintain your competitiveness, considering the lower profit margins in these markets, you will need to do a larger volume. This may change the scope of your business and your mission. Your biggest asset and your differentiator in the market is your quality of service. It is very hard to double your business volume without adding considerably to cost (i.e., hiring and training new employees).

Strengths/Weaknesses

The following summarizes the basic strengths and weaknesses of this alternative:

Strengths

+ The business is familiar to you. You can offer the same services you currently offer.
+ You can use your current contacts at the tour operators.
+ You can leverage your reputation to add additional business.

Weaknesses

− Low margins mean that volume must be increased.
− Volume increases may lead to sacrificing quality of service.
− The distance away from your headquarters may make your business much more complicated to manage.

Alternative 2. Increasing Domestic Business

Explanation

Another market in which PCG could excel is domestic travel. Your company could market its current services to U.S. tour operators. Thousands of chartered groups and individuals visit the cities where you currently have offices from other parts of the United

States. This alternative uses your current resources and talent, but opens your business up to a larger market.

The only start up costs involved in this alternative would be for marketing and advertising. No initial outlays are needed for personnel, office space, or new equipment. The only costs will be to research the market, develop contacts with tour operators in the United States and develop a marketing plan to obtain the additional business.

Benefits

Some of the benefits of this alternative are as follows:

1. It allows you to use your existing offices. These offices (Honolulu, Las Vegas, Los Angeles, San Diego, San Francisco) are strategically located tourist destinations. They are favorite spots for vacations, conferences, and corporate meetings for United States as well as foreign travelers. This will keep your costs down as you can depend on your current representatives to handle the additional business or hire temporary representatives on demand.
2. You will be able to offer the same receptive agent services you currently offer. This will save the cost of retraining employees or establishing new contacts with ground travel companies, entertainment locations, and hotels.
3. One marketing channel which may be efficient is attending domestic tour and travel conferences similar to POW WOW and World Travel Mart. This would be a good use of your existing resources since you have experience attending these shows and your booth could be used for both the foreign and domestic conferences.
4. Your boilerplate contract information which states the services offered and all contractual information could be reused with minimal changes. Since the contracts reside on your computer, very little administrative work is necessary in editing the contract for domestic tour operators.

Problems

The following are some of the problems PCG may encounter if it chooses to pursue this option:

1. You will need to spend some time researching the new market to find out which domestic tour operators offer vacations to cities where you maintain offices. Since you do not currently have contacts with domestic tour operators, you will need to allow time to develop relationships and a reputation with the new prospective customers.
2. PCG has done very little marketing in the past. The company has relied on word of mouth (referrals) to attract new business and the game of marketing will be new for you. While the rewards could be substantial, this is a very competitive business. Therefore, I would suggest adding a part-time marketing manager to plan the marketing strategy and develop an advertising plan that works within your budget.

Strengths/Weaknesses

Strengths

+ You can use your current offices.

+ The business is familiar to you. You can offer the same services you currently offer.
+ You can use your existing conference booth and contract boilerplate.

Weaknesses

− The market is new, and you will have to spend time researching it and developing contacts.
− It may take some time to break into the new market and establish a reputation.
− Since marketing is not a large part of your current business, you will probably need to hire a person with more experience in this area.

Alternative 3. Marketing to Tour Operators in Canada; the Pacific— Australia, New Zealand, Japan; and Eastern Europe[1]

Explanation

Marketing your current services to tour operators in other areas of the world is a promising direction for PCG. By including tour operators in Canada, Australia, New Zealand, and Eastern Europe as your market, you would open the door to a large volume of potential contracts. This alternative offers many of the advantages of alternative 2. It is also a fast-growing market. The projected increase in foreign visitor arrivals for key markets in 1990 and 1991 are shown in Exhibit 2.6. The U.S. Travel and Tourism Administration stated that total foreign tourism to the United States has increased 50 percent in the last four years.

These data indicate that California is the number one vacation destination for potential visitors from France, Japan, the United Kingdom, and West Germany. Los

---

Exhibit 2.6

FOREIGN VISITOR ARRIVALS, 1989–1991

Origin	1989 (000)	% CHANGE			
		1989–1988	1989–1985	1990–1989	1991–1990
Australia	406	21%	69%	13%	11%
Canada	15,366	18	27	11	8
France	654	6	95	5	4
Germany	1,076	−7	111	1	2
Japan	3,080	22	106	12	18
New Zealand	199	21	69	13	11
United Kingdom	2,222	22	158	9	7

Source: U.S. Travel and Tourism Administration, June 1990.

---

[1]No data were available for the expected travel of people from Eastern Europe. The U.S. Travel and Tourism Administration projected growth in travel receipts from these countries as a result of recent social and economic events.

Angeles, San Francisco, Disneyland, and Las Vegas are also among the top six miscellaneous vacation destinations for potential travelers from these countries. The data show that California has the highest growth (2.7 percent) of all states in inbound travel from abroad.

All the trends point to significant growth in these markets. The benefits, problems, strengths and weaknesses for this alternative are essentially the same as those for alternative 2. From the data that were available, I predict stronger growth in this international market than in the domestic market.

One large factor for the growth of this market is the exchange rate. Obviously, deflation of the dollar versus other currencies would lead to more foreign travel in the United States. Fluctuations in the exchange rate are difficult to forecast. Exhibits 2.7 and 2.8 present information regarding U.S. travel receipts and payments.

Benefits

The benefits are basically the same as those for alternative 2 except that inbound travel from international locations seems to be growing more rapidly than domestic travel. This may be due to a relatively weak dollar in the international currency market in recent years.

Problems

The problems are the same as those for alternative 2 except that the exchange rate will play a major role in the growth of this market. The exchange rate experiences regular fluctuations, and this makes planning more difficult.

Exhibit 2.7

U.S. INTERNATIONAL TRAVEL RECEIPTS AND PAYMENTS: THE BREAKTHROUGH, 1985–1990

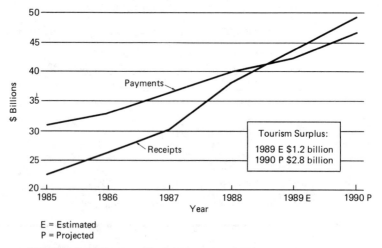

E = Estimated
P = Projected

Source: U.S. Travel and Tourism Administration, June 1990.

Strengths/Weaknesses

Same as those for alternative 2 except for the differences just described.

Alternative 4. Selling U.S. Originating Airline Seats

Explanation

The fourth growth alternative I investigated was selling airline tickets on chartered flights from Los Angeles International Airport to foreign destinations. From recent conversations with you, I detected your interest in expanding in this direction.

This alternative would allow you to start slowly and continue growing as demand rises. You could begin by working as a broker for licensed agents and selling seats for the chartered tours for the summer season (June–August). PCG is already closely associated with the summer chartered flight programs of two large tour operators.

As you become established in this new marketplace, you could easily add services such as hotel accommodations and entertainment packages. The possibilities are endless for this arm of your business to grow into a complete tour operator service.

The following table shows average airline ticket prices (including tax) from Los Angeles International Airport on July 13, 1990:

Los Angeles to	7-Day Advance	21-Day Advance
London	$1,474	$1,038
Paris	1,328	1,080

Exhibit 2.8

SOURCES OF U.S. INTERNATIONAL TRAVEL RECEIPTS, 1989 ESTIMATES

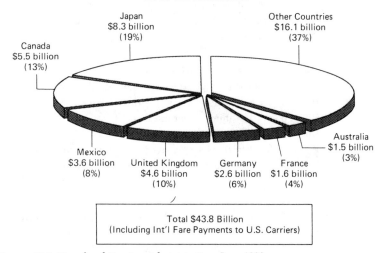

Source: U.S. Travel and Tourism Administration, June 1990.

Current Method for Airline Ticket Distribution

Airlines who service the LAX-to-U.K. route such as British Airways, Pan Am, and TWA sell their tickets through travel agents and their own reservation services. However, the carriers have a method for selling the seats when they don't feel their own reservation system will do the job. At roughly six weeks before departure, the carriers discount the seats and sell them to tour operators. Any additional tickets are sold to "consolidators" (companies in the business of selling only airline tickets).

You mentioned that the average profit margins on these tickets were between 10 percent and 12 percent.

Target Market

Summer is when demand is greatest for flights to the United Kingdom. Most people take their vacations in the summer. College students will be a large percentage of the target market because of the many travel opportunities (youth Eurail passes, youth hostel lodging, study abroad, and discounts provided by universities) for this segment of the market.

Competitors

Travel agencies and consolidators are your major competitors in this market. I sent a survey to seven of your current competitors to find out if any were tapping this market. Of the three responses, two reported selling outbound seats. The questions asked in the survey were as follows:

> Please provide a brief description of your business. (What is your main business? receptive agent? inclusive tours? outbound airline ticket sales? tour operator?) <u>If you have a brochure describing your business, it would really help me to see it.</u>
> How did you get started in this business?
> How are you different from a retail travel agent?
> Do you target a specific market? (the U.K., domestic) If so, which one?
> What method of marketing/advertising do you use? (trade journal ads, visitor's bureaus, conventions, word of mouth)
>
> **For companies who sell airline tickets:**
> How and when do you get the seats? (allocated from the airlines?)
> How do you sell them once you get them? (advertise?)
> How do your last minute seat sales work?
> How did you get your start in seat sales?
> Was it difficult to start? Expensive? How did you get your start up money?
> Is the seat sales business risky? How do you avoid the risk?

The following is a summary of the responses:

- All three targeted charter travel exclusively to and from Europe. The specific markets were London, Holland, Western Europe, and The Alps.
- All three claimed to have a special interest in traveling. One reported starting the business because of a "personal desire to travel to Europe at an economical price."

- Two of the owner-operators were originally from Europe.
- Both outbound seat sellers reported selling mainly to retail travel agents, with very few sales directly to clients.
- The methods of advertising they used were word of mouth, direct mail, trade shows, trade advertising.

The companies that sell outbound airline tickets reported

- Getting seats through contracts with the airlines and additional seats on a "space-available" basis through the airlines.
- Selling seats to travel agents using word of mouth, brochures, and some advertising.
- Having a rough time starting this business. They mentioned "hard work, long hours, good contracts, and few profits" at the beginning.
- Finding that the business is risky. One respondent said, "We try to avoid risk by selling more than one airline's seats."

Benefits

Some of the benefits I identified under this alternative are the following:

1. Since you mentioned this option in our meetings, I know that you have a special interest in moving into this market. Your attitude toward pursuing any of the options may be the biggest reason for making it work.
2. This alternative makes PCG less vulnerable during fluctuating exchange rates. Adding this business will alleviate your dependency on a weak dollar (which leads to more inbound travel) in the world currency market. When the dollar is strong, travel abroad by U.S. tourists will increase. When the dollar is weak, travel from your current markets will be strong.
3. You would be able to sell the round trip tickets in Europe. Your contacts with ethnic groups like Council of British Societies and corporations who have steady traffic flowing back and forth from LA to London provides you with a ready market.
4. The work is simple. The only services provided are being courteous on the phone, sending the tickets to buyers, and having contingency plans if problems occur.

Problems

Current

1. Although acquiring a group of tickets from the airlines is a relatively simple process for you, selling them may be time consuming. Selling large quantities of tickets for each flight may alleviate this problem. But, if you end up selling to individuals and having to advertise to make the sale, this option may cause more headaches than it is worth. Furthermore, to make a profit, under this scenario, you may have a volume problem similar to the one discussed in alternative 1, problem 2.
2. This alternative may offer great rewards once the process is in place, but you run a risk of buying tickets and then not being able to sell them.
3. Starting in a new market means that you will need to start from scratch in defining

and identifying your target market. You will have to develop a customer list and advertising methods. Obtaining information in a new market is hard. It may take a summer for you to determine how to price the tickets.

4. The U.S. Travel and Tourism Administration estimated that payments by out-bound U.S. Travelers grew only 37 percent from 1985 through 1989.

Future—as you grow this business

1. When this business becomes established and you wish to increase your volume, you will need the appropriate licensing. The two licenses you will need and their costs are:

ARC (Airline Reporting Corporation) license[2]	$ 500/year
IATA (International Air Transport Association) membership	$1,000/year

2. As you add services, you will need to establish contacts with hotels, subcontrac-tors for ground transportation, receptive agents, and so on, in the U.K.

Strengths/Weaknesses

Strengths

+ You seem to have a special interest in moving into this market.
+ It makes PCG less vulnerable during fluctuating exchange rates.
+ You have established contacts with travel agencies and prospective customers.
+ The new business, if it works appropriately, requires little servicing.

Immediate Weaknesses

− PCG is not equipped to handle large volume.
− This business involves a relatively large degree of risk.
− You need to plan on spending time to develop some expertise in this new market, including how to price your product.
− Travel by U.S. citizens to foreign countries is growing more slowly than is travel from foreign countries to the United States.

Although the consultant's alternatives were not mutually exclusive for PCG, Claudia was determined to choose only one. Her resources were limited, and she had decided to continue on a path of slow, steady growth.

Claudia wanted to choose the alternative that offered the biggest benefit and least risk over a time frame of three years. The notes she sketched comparing the four alternatives are included as Exhibit 2.9.

---

[2]The following restrictions apply for obtaining an ARC license: (1) the business must have a safe vaulted to the floor of its office, (2) the business must be bonded to $2,000, (3) special forms must be ob-tained, and (4) special filing methods are required.

Exhibit 2.9

PCG'S ALTERNATIVES

1. Opening Offices in New York and Florida

Revenues	New York City	Orlando
Year 1 (one representation contract in each city with a large tour operator.)	$ 20,000	$20,000
Year 2 (one additional contract plus services)	50,000	40,000
Year 3 (one additional contract plus services)	100,000	80,000

This information is based on volume in the new markets from your top three current customers. It assumes that you begin with volume from Poundstretcher the first year and add one new contract in each of the next two years. This assumes that revenue from each existing contract grows each year—as has been the case historically. Inflation is not considered.

Costs	New York City	Orlando
Year 1		
Representative (part time)		
Salary and benefits	$20,000	$15,000
Office Rental	12,000	5,000
Fax Machine (one time)	3,000	3,000
Telephone system	5,000	5,000
Office furniture (one time)	15,000	15,000
Total cost	55,000	43,000
Loss year 1	−35,000	−23,000
Year 2		
Representative (full time)		
Salary and benefits	28,000	22,000
Office rental	12,000	5,000
Telephone system	5,000	5,000
Total cost	45,000	32,000
Profit year 2	5,000	8,000
Year 3		
Representative (full time)		
Salary and benefits	38,000	30,000
Office rental (work out of home)	12,000	5,000
Telephone system	5,000	5,000
Total cost	55,000	40,000
Profit year 3	45,000	40,000
Total profit	**$15,000**	**$25,000**

These items are based on the costs you recorded of opening your San Francisco Office.

Exhibit 2.9 (Cont.)

2. Adding Domestic Business

Revenue

Year 1	$20,000
Year 2	40,000
Year 3	60,000

Based on adding one new account each year.

Costs per year
Developing a marketing plan
Advertising budget
  Trade journal space/month: $ 5,000
  Part-time marketing specialist: $22,000

Profit

Year 1	$ − 7,000
Year 2	13,000
Year 3	33,000
Total	**$41,000**

3. Marketing to Other Countries

Same as 2.

4. Selling Outbound Airline Tickets

	Profit
Year 1	
(sell 10 tickets per weekly charter on two airlines = 20 tickets/week.)	
12 week season = 240 tickets	
Average cost per ticket = $500	
Markup = 11%	
Average price per ticket = $500	
Revenue per ticket = $50	
Total revenue	$12,000
Administrative costs	2,000
Marketing costs	1,000
Total profit	9,000
Year 2	
Total revenue (sell 30 tickets/week × 12 weeks × $50)	$18,000
Administrative costs	3,000
Marketing costs	1,500
Total profit	13,500
Year 3	
Total revenue (sell 45 tickets/week × 12 × $50)	$27,000
Administrative costs	4,500
Marketing costs	3,000
Total profit	19,500
Total Profit, Years 1–3	**$42,000**

3

AMERICAN BOX COMPANY

Sam Smith, founder and president of ABCo, sat at his desk thinking of the decision he and the board had to make about ABCo's entry into the Icelandic market with fluid-box products. In addition to deciding whether or not to enter the market, ABCo's executives had to decide how to enter the market if they made a "go" decision. There were three possible ways: (1) simply export fluid-boxes to Iceland, (2) make a direct investment in production facilities in Iceland, or (3) set up a licensing agreement with an Icelandic firm.

BACKGROUND

In the autumn of 1945, S. S. Smith bought a small corrugated box business in Columbus, Ohio. At that time, the company had only 25 employees and sold only $250,000 worth of boxes annually. Almost immediately, the company acquired a new building with a 50,000-square-foot production facility and a 20,000-square-foot warehouse. Six years later, the square footage had increased to 78,000 square feet.

In 1953, a Huntington, West Virginia, facility was opened in order to manufacture boxes from the corrugated sheets made in Columbus. The Columbus plant was expanded to 118,000 square feet in 1956 and increased to 165,000 square feet by 1962. The importance of the Columbus plant to the community was recognized when the city renamed the street passing the plant Corrugated Way.

ABCo now has Fluid-Box, Bag-in-a-Box, and FilmCo divisions, in addition to the original corrugated operation.

THE FLUID-BOX CORPORATION

During 1961, the company began pilot production of plastic bags inside boxes. Used mainly by the dairy industry, the bag-in-a-box quickly supplanted the traditional 5-gallon milk can. Fluid-Box Corporation, a subsidiary, was set up to manufacture and sell the new product. By 1962, Fluid-Box introduced a disposable 10-quart bag-in-a-box with its own dispensing valve. Designed for home delivery routes, the milk dispenser grew in popularity. Its acceptance led the company into manufacturing additional products. By 1963, the Fluid-Box subsidiary had 20,000 square feet of production facility in Columbus and an additional 20,000 square feet leased in Dallas, Texas. A 10,000-square-foot addition in 1964 was devoted to corporate and Fluid-Box offices, and the other half was devoted to advanced research and development laboratories.

In 1967, to assure itself a regular supply of container board, the company built a paper mill in Hawesville, Kentucky. The ownership of the plant and its 300-ton daily output was shared by ABCo and another company. Later in the same year, the Fluid-Box division began blow-molding a polyethylene 10-quart dispenser to replace the bag-in-a-box version. Called Handi-tap, the new product was an instant success in test marketing. Blow-molding facilities were opened in Worthington, Ohio; Springfield, Massachusetts; Waukegan, Illinois; Los Angeles, California; Houston, Texas; and Orlando, Florida. Because the company was growing both in the variety of its products as well as in size, it adopted the more generalized name ABCo, Incorporated in 1968. (Exhibit 3.1 shows the location and type of facilities ABCo owns.)

In 1969, at its Worthington plant, Fluid-Box began blow-molding 1-gallon bottles in addition to the handy-tap dispenser. In the meantime, the company opened more blow-molding facilities for the gallon bottles at Baltimore, Maryland; Kansas City, Missouri; and Camden, New Jersey. Early in 1970, ABCo opened its fifth corrugated box plant in Grand Rapids, Michigan. The company continued its expansion by moving the Columbus and Dallas operations of Fluid-Box to a new facility in Ashland, Ohio. A few months later, the bag-in-a-box operation of Weyerhaeuser was acquired. This purchase allowed ABCo to enlarge the bag-in-a-box applications to include containers for battery acid and edible oils, thus broadening the product line even more.

THE BAG-IN-A-BOX

The uses of a bag-in-a-box were almost unlimited. Some of the first uses were for milk and ice cream mix. Then the firm began packaging items like food flavoring, condiments, citrus concentrates, hot foods, and, recently, wine. The plastic film that goes into the bag is also used for such items as disposable bags for kidney dialysis, inflatable bags for dunnage, and trashcan liners. One of the common problems in the

Exhibit 3.1

ABCo FACILITIES

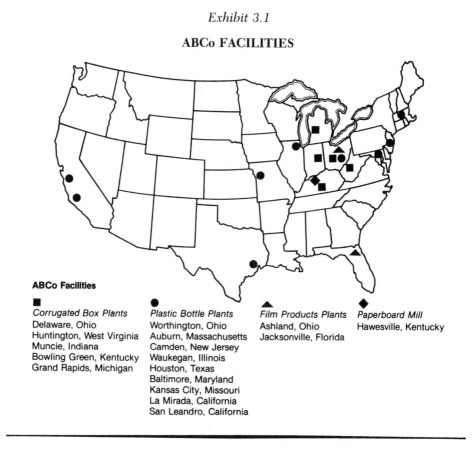

ABCo Facilities

■	●	▲	◆
Corrugated Box Plants	*Plastic Bottle Plants*	*Film Products Plants*	*Paperboard Mill*
Delaware, Ohio	Worthington, Ohio	Ashland, Ohio	Hawesville, Kentucky
Huntington, West Virginia	Auburn, Massachusetts	Jacksonville, Florida	
Muncie, Indiana	Camden, New Jersey		
Bowling Green, Kentucky	Waukegan, Illinois		
Grand Rapids, Michigan	Houston, Texas		
	Baltimore, Maryland		
	Kansas City, Missouri		
	La Mirada, California		
	San Leandro, California		

industry was leakage. ABCo was able to solve the problem by introducing a double-lined bag, which was actually a bag inside a bag. According to ABCo, the biggest advantage of its bag is the seal for the filler tab. Many of ABCo's competitors are unable to manufacture and design a seal able to withstand heavy use. It is common for their seals to tear out of the bag when they are being filled.

The bag-in-the-box is composed of three parts; the bag itself, the box that goes around the bag, and the seal and tube that are attached to the bag.

Equipment for Bag-in-a-Box

ABCo makes the machines to perform the packaging of the bag-in-a-box. The first machine is the sealer, which seals the plastic bags and installs the tap. ABCo also offers a model 620 bulk filler, which fills the bags with the desired liquid and seals a box around the bag. To companies that prefer to use their own machines to seal the boxes, ABCo offers two different models of fillers—the C2B and C2T bulk fillers. The capacity of each machine is shown in Exhibit 3.2.

The major problem ABCo has experienced with the machines is that they frequently need tuning. When ABCo sells machines to overseas affiliates, it usually trains its engineers for four weeks on the machines' uses and capabilities. ABCo will also send its engineers to a foreign facility to solve any mechanical problems its customers' engineers cannot.

Exhibit 3.2

ABCo BULK FILLERS

	OUTPUT PER HOUR	
Machine	For 2½-Gallon Container	For 5-Gallon Container
Sealer	840 bags	840 bags
Filler and boxer		
(620 bulk filler)	300 boxes	300 boxes
C2B	500 bags	300 bags
C2T	1,000 bags	600 bags

BULK LIQUID FILLING: THE SYSTEMS

Model 620 Bulk Filler—The Machine

This unique filling machine automates the most difficult hand operations common to other methods, ends tugging and snapping of bag, and eliminates undue shipping and storing stress to the bag because this machine precisely orients the bag seams to the box. This is an efficient one-person operation since filling and insertion are separate and simultaneous operations. As for speed, it is possible to fill and seal 300 bags per hour with the 620. Use with the LiquiForm and the LiquiSeal. Consider the accuracy of filling: computerized and guaranteed to within three-tenths of 1 percent.

Specifications

230-volt, single-phase power
80–125 pounds per square inch air supply
60″ wide, 78½″ front to back, 79″ high (on 15″ conveyor take-off)

C2B and C2T Accurate Bulk Fillers

Here's the way to fill bag-in-a-box packages using a proven machine with the most modern production techniques:

- self-driven filling meter with guaranteed accuracy of one-third of 1 percent
- easily cleaned stainless steel
- use it to fill 3,000 to 25,000 gallons in 8 hours

Exhibit 3.2 (Cont.)

- designed compactly to fill only 3 by 4 feet of space
- have it with either single or double filling heads
- use it for table-top or in-the-box filling

You can operate these machines with one filling head idle. Or change the fill volume easily if you like. The calibrated counter control will watch it for you.

Specifications

standard 240-voltage, single- or three-phase, 60 cycles per second
80–120 pounds per square inch air supply @ 1.0 cubic foot per minute
solid-state counters

FILM PRODUCTS

The company's capacity for extruding plastic film opened the way for a new division—FilmCo—in 1973. This division makes and sells a variety of film items, including custom sheets and tubes, bags for packaging bottles, shrink bundling, and trash-can liners.

In mid-1974, ABCo transferred its Columbus corrugated container facility to Delaware, Ohio. The new plant's capacity exceeded the capacity of the old one by 50 percent. In the same year, the company also opened its second film plant, in Jacksonville, Florida.

As a result of this expansion, the company that S. S. Smith started grew to a company with 17 plants, more than 700 employees, and sales of over $42 million.

FINANCIAL PERFORMANCE

ABCo's sales increased almost $20 million from 1987 to 1990, and its net income rose $1.2 million. Earnings per share increased by $1.30 during this time, and ABCo's cash dividends doubled (see Exhibit 3.3). During this time, ABCo's assets grew by about $2.5 million, and its ratio of total debt to equity was about 1:2 (Exhibit 3.4).

International Planning

The company has long considered entering foreign markets. The main reasons are the fear of a gradual saturation of the American market and management's desire for new ventures.

Since ABCo concentrates its products mostly in the dairy sector and most of the products are new even to the American market (most of ABCo's current products have been developed since 1986), it planned to look for new markets mostly in countries which had arrived at as sophisticated a dairy industry as in the United States. It

Exhibit 3.3

ABCo FINANCIAL DATA, 1987–1990

	1990	1989	1988	1987
Operations				
(in thousands, except per share data)				
Net sales	$48,617	$42,031	$33,679	$29,109
Costs and expenses				
Selling, administrative, and general	5,175	4,487	3,643	3,501
Depreciation	1,664	1,469	1,457	1,217
Interest expense	748	496	546	559
LIFO adjustment	1,808			
Other cost of sales	34,923	32,175	25,469	22,169
	$44,318	$38,627	$31,115	$27,446
Income before income taxes	$ 4,299	$ 3,404	$ 2,564	$ 1,663
Income taxes	1,985	1,717	$ 1,168	570
Net income	$ 2,314	$ 1,687	1,396	$ 1,093
Per share of common stock				
Net income	$ 2.37	$ 1.73	$ 1.40	$ 1.07
Cash dividends	$ 0.70	$ 0.45	$ 0.36	$ 0.35
Other Financial Information				
(in thousands, except per share data)				
Cash flow	$ 4,462	$ 3,466	$ 2,982	$ 2,648
Working capital	6,931	4,534	3,143	2,411
Current ratio	2.8	2.2	2.2	1.8
Long-term debt	$10,275	$10,946	$ 6,735	$ 7,315
Shareholders' equity	$13,262	$11,641	$10,404	$ 9,920
Return on shareholders' equity	18.6%	15.3%	13.7%	11.4%
Market price of stock				
(approximate bid range)	$11–16	$12–16	$13–16	$10–16
Cash dividends payout percentage	29%	26%	26%	33%

was feared that allocations of money for improvement in less developed countries had to go to sectors of the economy which needed improvement more urgently; furthermore, the advantages of ABCo's products (short-time, large-scale filling and emptying, and safe transportation) could not be used to their full extent by such countries. Therefore, in search of foreign operations, ABCo considered only countries with considerable similarities to the United States. Management had set forth some criteria which it thought countries should meet in order to be considered for ABCo's international activities. These criteria were

1. Strong dairy sector
2. High level of technology
3. High percentage of disposable income
4. Much use of plastic

Exhibit 3.4

CONSOLIDATED BALANCE SHEET FOR ABCo AND SUBSIDIARIES

ABCo, INC., AND SUBSIDIARIES
CONSOLIDATED BALANCE SHEET
DECEMBER 28, 1990 AND DECEMBER 29, 1989

	Dec. 28, 1990	Dec. 29, 1989
Assets		
Current assets:		
Cash	$ 133,000	$ 428,000
Short-term investments at cost (which approximates market)	1,500,000	700,000
Accounts receivable		
Trade	4,441,000	3,946,000
Other	117,000	162,000
	$ 4,558,000	$ 4,108,000
Less: Allowance for doubtful accounts	(36,000)	(22,000)
	$ 4,522,000	$ 4,086,000
Inventories	$ 4,244,000	$ 2,544,000
Current portion of advances to 50%-owned affiliate	400,000	400,000
Other current assets	64,000	32,000
Total current assets	$10,863,000	$ 8,190,000
Investment in and advances to 50%-owned affiliate	$ 3,356,000	$ 3,627,000
Cash surrender value of life insurance, net loans of $426,000 and $411,000	$ 57,000	$ 46,000
Property, plant, and equipment, at cost		
Buildings and leasehold improvements	$ 5,021,000	$ 3,074,000
Equipment and vehicles	16,410,000	14,082,000
Less: Accumulated depreciation	(8,430,000)	(7,401,000)
	$13,001,000	$ 9,755,000
Construction in process	$ 290,000	$ 678,000
Land	636,000	443,000
Funds held by trustee for construction of new plant	470,000	4,212,000
	$14,397,000	$15,088,000
Deferred charges and other assets	323,000	373,000
Total assets	$28,996,000	$27,324,000
Liabilities and Stockholders' Equity		
Current liabilities:		
9% note payable, bank	—	$ 300,000
Accounts payable, trade	$ 1,954,000	1,285,000
Dividends payable	137,000	124,000
Accrued expenses:		
Salaries and wages	548,000	454,000
Taxes, other than income taxes	230,000	308,000
Interest	127,000	121,000
Accrued income taxes	266,000	484,000
Current installments on term debt and lease obligations	670,000	580,000
	$ 3,932,000	$ 3,656,000

Exhibit 3.4 (Cont.)

Long term obligations (net of current maturities)		
Term debt	$ 3,000,000	$ 3,500,000
Long-term lease obligations	7,275,000	7,446,000
Allowance for future costs	500,000	150,000
Deferred income taxes	641,000	754,000
Deferred investment tax credit	386,000	177,000
Commitments		
Stockholders' equity		
Common stock and additional capital, $2 stated value		
Authorized: 2,000,000 shares		
Issued: 1,042,283 shares	$ 7,983,000	$ 6,653,000
Retained earnings	6,108,000	5,805,000
Less: Treasury stock: 65,274 shares and 65,660 shares at cost	(829,000)	(817,000)
Total stockholders' equity	$13,262,000	$11,641,000
Total liabilities and stockholders' equity	$28,996,000	$27,324,000

Having had business contacts through exports with a Canadian company for several years, ABCo decided to go into partnership with this company in 1989, thus establishing its first foreign affiliate. This venture works profitably, and close contact is maintained by monthly visits from ABCo officials. In considering other foreign operations, ABCo decided not to make use of government agencies, consulates, or banks. All contracts were to be joint ventures. Intending mostly to check markets first in order to see their possibilities, ABCo did not want to incur a high monetary risk. The company's policy was chiefly to offer technological assistance to firms abroad through licensing and royalty agreements. One licensee per country seemed ideal to ABCo's executives.

International Developments

ABCo's Canadian affiliate provided the addresses of interested firms it worked with in English-speaking countries. ABCo, in turn, placed a salesman in charge of developing relations with such firms. For two years, this salesman and his two successors, appointed from within and outside the company, had no success. At the end of 1990, another salesman from within, this time with international experience (he had previously worked for Icelandic Oil), was promoted to the new rank of manager of international sales. This promotion from salesman to sales manager included a salary raise to the managerial level, permission to make international telephone calls, and the opportunity to make two trips to Europe. Within six months, he had identified a licensing opportunity with a company in Iceland. The proposed agreement would give the Icelandic firm perpetual rights to market ABCo's bag-in-a-box in Iceland and Scandinavia (Denmark, Norway, and Sweden). ABCo was to supply the production machinery, the technological know-how, and continuous updates on technological progress made in the bag-in-a-box manufacturing process. The Icelandic company was to buy the plastic film from ABCo in Norfolk, Virginia, at the going United States market price. ABCo had three choices: the firm could commit itself to the licensing agreement and allow the Icelandic firm to retain the rights to the Scandinavian market, to ship fluid boxes to the Scandinavian market on its own, or to make a direct investment and produce the product in Scandinavia.

PAPPIRSVORUR

Pappirsvorur, Ltd., located in Reykiavik, Iceland, was the firm being considered for licensing by ABCo. Since the population of Iceland is only 200,000, the firm could effect a sizable operation only by exporting its products from Iceland. Exporting would be facilitated by Iceland's membership in the EFTA (Europe Free Trade Association), of which Austria, Denmark, Great Britain, Norway, Portugal, and Switzerland are also members. EFTA is also affiliated with the European Common Market. This affiliation entitles firms in the members' countries to favorable tariff and trade regulations.

Gilvi Henrickson, owner of Pappirsvorur, has large interests in Icelandic Oil, Icelandic Airlines, and Icelandic Steamship Corporation. He also has very good connections with Scandinavian business executives and politicians. He was able to persuade the Swedish legislature to pass a school-milk law requiring all school milk to be served in the bag-in-a-box.

Pappirsvorur proposed to share the Scandinavian market with two competitors. The firm's expected sales from approximately 14.1 million units of fluid boxes would be roughly $6 million annually. Of this income, ABCo would receive a 5 percent royalty plus its markup on the plastic film exported to Pappirsvorur.

Revenues from the Icelandic Market

The sale price of each unit is $377.81 per thousand fluid boxes of 2½ gallons and $492.61 per thousand of 5-gallon fluid boxes. It is likely that ABCo would be able to absorb 50 percent of the market that Pappirsvorur intends to develop. Its competitors would probably absorb the rest. Roughly half of the mix would be 2½-gallon boxes; the other half, 5-gallon boxes. Pappirsvorur would also buy half of its plastic film from ABCo. The other half would be supplied by Pappirsvorur itself. (See Exhibits 3.5 and 3.6.)

There are many problems for ABCo to consider if it goes into the Icelandic market. ABCo has only a short time in which to decide. Pappirsvorur is already moving into the market, and two competitors are there. The market will soon be divided up.

ABCo might find a partner for a joint venture instead of licensing Pappirsvorur. This would be rather difficult in the time available, since checking out a partner, obtaining information, making an agreement, and starting operations takes time. Or ABCo might set up operations by itself. It still would have to move quickly, which could lead to costly errors in the long run. For example, it might choose the wrong location or lose bargaining power. Also, few managers are available for a Scandinavian operation, and none of ABCo's officers seems willing to head operations there.

Exhibit 3.5

FINANCIAL ANALYSIS OF PAPPIRSVORUR'S PROPOSAL TO ABCo*

Item	Cost of Manufacture† (per 1,000 units)	Sales Price in United States (per 1,000 units)	Sales Price in Iceland (per 1,000 units)
Tube	$ 35.40	$ 43.50	$ 47.01
2½-gallon bag	103.77	138.00	151.80
5-gallon bag	133.75	175.50	193.00
2½-gallon box	112.50	148.00	179.00
5-gallon box	169.25	224.75	251.60

Import and tariff from the United States to Sweden:
2½-gallon unit $57.54
5-gallon unit $70.20

COST BREAKDOWN BASED ON THE U.S. SALES PRICE:

Variable Costs		Fixed Costs	
Revenue	$1.00	Auto-sealer (to put seals on the bag)	$ 42,000
Labor	0.143	Box filler and sealer	59,000
Materials	0.573	Filler only	38,500 (C2B)
Overhead	0.036		63,000 (C2T)
Transportation and duties	0.164	Building for Icelandic venture	110,000–140,000

*One 2½-gallon bag contains approximately 1 square meter of plastic film. A 5-gallon bag contains approximately 1.4 square meters of plastic film.
†The cost of manufacture includes only variable overhead, labor, and material.

Even if all the planning were done carefully, ABCo might enter the market too late and have to fight for a market share from established competitors. Neither their strength nor the strength of Gilvi Henrickson is known, but a man who can induce a foreign legislature to pass a law must have strong ties with the country and could prove to be a strong competitor to ABCo. In addition, ABCo would face legal problems which cannot be fully assessed but might be severe. It could happen that after only a few months of operations, ABCo would be required by a court to stop working and withdraw, incurring heavy losses. But if the 5 percent royalty payment plan to Pappirsvorur were implemented, the legal problem would disappear, but the price of ABCo's products would suffer because of the lost tax advantage.

ABCo is an aggressive company, which in the past years has steadily expanded. Building a plant in Scandinavia could be a financial success. But given the constraints of time, it would probably be better to continue to work with the Icelanders. ABCo could instead keep in mind the possibility of expanding abroad at a later time and start to train its management for foreign operations.

As Smith left for the board meeting, he felt confident that ABCo's executives would make a decision about the Icelandic market that would be compatible with the company's policy of international development.

Exhibit 3.6

ABCo's OPTIONS

1. ABCo ALLOWS PAPPIRSVORUR TO DEVELOP THE MARKET:

Revenue

7 million, 2½ gallon @ $0.37781 per unit	=	$2,644,670
7.1 million, 5 gallon @ 0.4926 per unit	=	$3,497,531
Total		$6,142,201
5 percent royalty		$ 307,110

Plastic needed

7 million bags @ 1 square meter per bag	=	7,000,000 square meters
7.1 million bags @ 1.4 square meters per bag	=	9,940,000 square meters

ABCo will supply half of this material.

Sales price (1 square meter)	0.09550
Transportation	(0.00438)
Costs	(0.07004)
	$0.02108 per meter
	(8.5 million square meters)
Total costs	= $179,180
Profit	$485,290
Less 1—tax rate	0.52
Net profit	$252,350

2. ABCo DECIDES TO MANUFACTURE THE PRODUCT IN THE UNITED STATES AND SHIP IT TO SCANDINAVIA. THE NET CASH FLOW WOULD BE AS FOLLOWS:

Revenue: Figured at half of what Pappirsvorur could sell, because the competition would probably do better against ABCo since it does not have Pappirsvorur's political and economic connections.

Sales	=	$3,071,110

Cost

2½-gallon units, 3.5 million @ $0.25167 per unit	=	$ 880,845
5-gallon units, 3.5 million @ $0.3384 per unit	=	$1,184,400
Duties (0.147 of Scandinavian price)	=	$ 447,825
Manager of foreign operations	=	$ 80,000
Total cost		$2,593,070
Profit before taxes		$ 478,040
Taxes (0.48)		.52
Net income		$ 245,600

Fixed costs

Machine capacity of sealer (250 days per year* @ 7.5 hours per day)

$$* = 840 \text{ units per hour}$$
$$= 1,575,000 \text{ units}$$

7.1 million units at 1.575 units per machine = 5 machines

It will be assumed that the distributors will fill their own boxes, since prices do not include this service.

5 machines @ $42,000	=	$210,000
Building (allocated space)	=	100,000
Initial Investment		$310,000
Payback period ($310,000/$245,600)	=	1.26 years

Exhibit 3.6 (Cont.)

3. ABCo BUILDS A FACTORY IN SCANDINAVIA.

Costs:

All costs would be the same as 2, except that there would be no import duty.	
Profit before taxes, from second choice	$478,040
Plus tariff and transportation costs to Sweden	30,660
	447,825
	956,525
Minus Scandinavian tax rate = 0.53	.47
Net income	$449,600
Payback period ($310,000/$449,600) =	8 months

4

EASTERN DOWNS

In the fall of 1991, Jon Chesterton was facing one of the most challenging assignments of his career.* As the recently appointed director of marketing for Eastern Downs racetrack, he had been asked by Carmen King, general manager of Eastern Downs, for his recommendations regarding marketing strategy and the "general direction" of racing operations for the 1992 season and beyond. Chesterton knew that, because the 1991 racing season had been the worst, from a financial point of view, in the track's history, its owners and management were considering some radical changes in racing operations. They were therefore not looking to him for a "business as usual" marketing plan. Rather, they wanted his ideas, from a marketing standpoint, on new strategies and policies that could help turn around the track's declining fortunes.

THE RACETRACK

Eastern Downs was generally regarded to be one of the finest thoroughbred racecourses in the eastern United States. It was situated on the fringes of two major metropolitan areas and drew patrons to its thoroughbred meeting from both those areas,

*Eastern Downs is a fictionalized case—a composite profile of information drawn from several racetracks in the eastern United States—that represents problems many tracks are currently facing.

from its immediate vicinity, and from several nearby resort communities. The facility consisted of approximately 400 acres of property on which were situated the racing surface and main grandstand building, along with a sprawling backstretch area on which were located stables, practice facilities, dormitories for backstretch employees, and a variety of other support facilities.

Eastern Downs was a closely held company originally established by the late Donald Kimberley, Sr., in 1940 when the track was constructed. Ownership was still largely in the hands of the Kimberley family, and Donald Kimberley, Jr., was the principal owner and primary custodian of the family's interests in the track business. Although he delegated the official responsibilities of track management to others, he was himself a racing enthusiast and could be seen viewing the races from his private box on most racing days. Moreover, he usually accepted management's invitations to attend meetings at which significant policy matters were to be discussed. Indeed, it was the perception of most of the track's employees that Mr. Kimberley could be found somewhere on the grounds every day during the racing season.

The track had been very profitable in its early years of operation, during the heydey of popularity of horseracing in America. As more tracks were built during the 1940s and 1950s, public interest in horseracing appeared to peak, and because of the maturation of the business, only a few additional tracks had been built since that time. The profitability of Eastern Downs had been slipping continuously throughout this period, and, although the Kimberleys were secretive about financial information, it was generally known that in 1991 the track had failed to reach its break-even point.

Horseracing was still one of the most popular professional sports in America as measured by overall paid attendance figures, and thoroughbred racing attendance had actually exhibited some recent growth (see Exhibit 4.1). Eastern Downs had also experienced some attendance growth in recent years. However, modest revenue gains had failed to keep pace with substantial increases in operating costs.

Exhibit 4.1

TOTAL ATTENDANCE AT U.S. THOROUGHBRED RACING, 1940–1989

Year	Attendance
1940	8,500,000
1941	10,000,000
1942	10,693,837
1943	14,000,000
1944	17,914,908
1945	19,422,395
1946	24,859,505
1947	25,704,853
1948	25,257,337
1949	23,811,890
1950	24,121,223
1951	27,017,000
1952	29,177,027

Exhibit 4.1 (Cont.)

1953	31,238,263
1954	31,355,798
1955	31,230,724
1956	32,104,373
1957	32,999,842
1958	32,837,691
1959	33,754,790
1960	34,795,007
1961	35,857,001
1962	37,257,070
1963	38,636,295
1964	40,827,872
1965	40,737,009
1966	40,913,694
1967	40,595,855
1968	41,517,104
1969	42,893,379
1970	44,854,675
1971	46,750,643
1972	45,590,028
1973	47,234,843
1974	48,823,814
1975	51,249,076
1976	51,242,451
1977	50,571,908
1978	50,587,804
1979	49,579,377
1980	50,084,231
1981	51,425,024
1982	51,851,587
1983	50,169,430
1984	50,284,324
1985	50,499,754
1986	47,913,693
1987	52,824,412
1988	54,840,709
1989	56,194,565

Source: 1989 Survey on Sports Attendance (Hightstown, NJ: The Daily Racing Form, 1989).

In common with many other privately held sports enterprises, the operation of Eastern Downs had never truly been directed toward maximization of profits. All the owners had other businesses that were primarily responsible for their wealth, and they appeared to view the track as a vehicle for their own amusement as much as for the amusement of the track's patrons. In addition, the track served as the locale for many activities that supported the owners' other interests, including entertaining of their business associates and clients. There was thus no direct way to measure the actual *implicit* return on their investment. Moreover, economic benefits of vertical integration accrued to those who were also horse owners or breeders. However, the prospect of actually *losing* money from racing operations had created a consensus among the owners that management ought to do what it could to improve the track's business performance.

COMPETITIVE ENVIRONMENT

Understanding a racetrack as a business requires an appreciation of the fact that it is a complex service operation that offers its patrons several levels of potential benefits. At the most general level, it represents an afternoon or evening of entertainment. In addition, it offers an opportunity for spectator involvement in a competitive sporting activity. Unlike many other sporting events, it also offers an opportunity for legally sanctioned wagering. These activities also offer possibilities for social interaction with others of like interests. Finally, many tracks offer dining facilities which, in some cases, become an attraction in their own right. Although each of these benefits can be derived from other activities, in combination they define the unique appeal for horseplayers of a day at the races.

The early history of success at Eastern Downs could be attributed to the fact that it had delivered each of these benefits at a high level of quality and with little or no competition in its immediate vicinity. Many local residents viewed the track as providing a convenient entertainment package that did not require a trip to a metropolitan center. Eastern Downs was the only racetrack in the area, and also the only major sports facility. Even in the absence of direct competition in the area, Eastern Downs had always maintained a reputation for the high caliber of its racing, which also drew many horseplayers from other tracks' geographic markets. For over 30 years, the track also had a local monopoly on legal wagering. As for its dining facilities, Eastern Downs offered both a snack bar and restaurant, and the latter was known to attract many nonhorseplayers from the local area.

In each of these areas of its former strength, Eastern Downs was now extremely vulnerable to competition. To be sure, it was still the only track in the area, and it had maintained the support of its core market of serious racing enthusiasts. However, as a setting for entertainment and dining, it was now only one option in a vastly expanded marketplace. Population growth in the area had resulted in the establishment of many new entertainment and dining facilities over the years, and improvements in transportation now gave local residents easier access to entertainment and sporting events in nearby metropolitan areas.

Even in the relatively strong area of racing operations, there were competitive threats. Although tracks in other markets did not compete directly with Eastern Downs for patrons, they did compete for the limited pool of quality horses and jockeys. Tracks in the larger metropolitan areas attracted large numbers of patrons and could therefore offer larger purses to horse owners. Management had always maintained that this track's reputation (especially for certain traditional, high-visibility races on its schedule), compensated for some competitive disadvantage in this regard, but conversations with knowledgeable horseplayers indicated that they perceived some slippage in the quality of the fields at Eastern Downs in recent years.

It was in the area of wagering, however, that Eastern Downs faced its most serious forms of competition. Illegal wagering had been the only local competition in 1940. Although there was no direct evidence available, most observers felt that there had been growth in illegal gambling over the years, so this was still of competitive concern. However, it was the proliferation of *legal* gambling opportunities that caused management the greatest concern. The establishment of casino gaming in Atlantic City, New Jersey, in 1978 resulted in the attraction of a regular flow of gamblers and a large proportion of discretionary leisure dollars from much of the eastern United States for each of the intervening years. For example, even though Eastern Downs was a considerable distance from Atlantic City, local residents could be seen every morning boarding buses at a stop less than a mile from the track for casino-subsidized day trips to that city.

The emergence of state lotteries was another serious concern. Lotteries were less popular than casinos as measured by gross wagering (see Exhibit 4.2), but they were the largest single source of gambling revenues (see Exhibit 4.3) due to the larger percentage of wagering retained by lottery operators.

Eastern Downs' management had watched with chagrin as legislators in the state's capital (and in most of the neighboring states) had approved lottery-enabling legislation, and as newly formed lottery commissions reinvested a considerable proportion of their revenues toward heavily promoting their product. This was a particular sore point in the racing industry, because state racing commissions had made no concerted effort to promote horseracing in spite of the millions of dollars state governments extracted from the industry each year. There were, however, some promising signs that the racing industry could attract increased support from state governments. Financial troubles in the industry had made legislators with tracks or horse farms in their districts more sensitive to the potential impact of a track's failure upon state revenues and the local economy.

The combined effects of casinos and lotteries were obviously unfavorable insofar as they challenged horseracing for the discretionary wagering dollar. On the other hand, some in the racing industry felt that the publicity and promotion associated with those activities would ultimately help racing by making gambling more socially acceptable and by significantly expanding the gambling-prone segment of the population.

In reviewing this situation, Chesterton agreed that the environment for marketing a gambling operation had improved significantly. However, he felt that the marketing challenge at hand was to attract members of this gambling-prone segment to horseracing in particular and that the difficulty of this challenge should not be underestimated. Barriers to successful marketing could be found in existing public attitudes and perceptions, which in turn limited the feasibility of certain marketing and promotional strategies.

With respect to public attitudes (excluding the opinions of the small segments who were strongly pro- and antigambling), research had shown that the image of horseracing had become encrusted with certain negative stereotypes, particularly among younger people (see Exhibit 4.4). By contrast, casinos were widely viewed as glamorous places in which to part with one's money. Perceptions of lotteries were relatively neutral, but the intensive distribution of lottery tickets had made them the "convenience goods" of the wagering marketplace.

Exhibit 4.2

U.S. GROSS GAMING HANDLE, 1989

Industry	Gross Wagering (handle)
Parimutuels	
Horses	
Track	$ 11,155,011,075
OTB	2,775,058,960
Total	$ 13,930,070,035
Greyhounds	
Track	3,183,112,602
OTB	28,571,564
Total	$ 3,211,684,166
Jai-alai	552,746,477
Total parimutuels	**$ 17,694,500,678**
Lotteries	19,468,330,000
Casinos	
Nevada/New Jersey slot machines	65,790,588,454
Nevada/New Jersey table games	127,774,754,003
Cruise ships	2,073,500,000
Other casinos	22,300,000
Noncasino devices	301,600,000
Total casino	**$195,962,742,457**
Legal bookmaking	
Sportsbooks	1,434,952,978
Horsebooks	403,178,763
Total bookmaking	**$ 1,838,131,741**
Card rooms	3,798,437,500
Bingo	3,772,029,542
Charitable games	3,990,444,149
Indian reservations	400,000,000
Total legal	**$246,924,616,067**
Illegal gambling	
Numbers	5,550,305,120
Horsebooks	8,128,905,535
Sportsbooks	27,387,198,884
Sportscards	2,119,702,209
Total illegal	**$ 43,186,111,748**
Grand total	**$290,110,727,816**

Note: Column may not add to totals due to rounding.

Source: Gaming & Wagering Business, Vol. 11, no. 7, July 15, 1990.

Exhibit 4.3

U.S. GROSS GAMING REVENUES, 1989

Industry	1989 GROSS REVENUES	
	% Retained	Amount
Parimutuels		
Horses		
Track	19.82	$ 2,210,565,678
OTB	22.10	613,149,322
Total	20.27	$ 2,823,715,000
Greyhounds		
Track	19.71	627,243,054
OTB	18.99	5,427,066
Total	19.70	$ 632,670,120
Jai-alai	19.50	107,766,036
Total parimutuels	**20.14**	**$ 3,564,151,156**
Lotteries	**49.44**	**$ 9,625,142,352**
Casinos		
Nevada/New Jersey slot machines	6.61	4,350,125,000
Nevada/New Jersey table games	2.43	3,103,516,000
Cruise ships	9.65	200,000,000
Other casinos	10.14	2,262,000
Noncasino devices	39.22	118,300,335
Total casino	**3.97**	**$ 7,774,203,335**
Legal bookmaking		
Sportsbooks	3.19	45,775,000
Horsebooks	14.88	59,993,000
Total bookmaking	**5.75**	**$ 105,768,000**
Card rooms	**8.00**	**303,876,000**
Bingo	**24.00**	**905,287,000**
Charitable games	**28.00**	**1,117,324,362**
Indian reservations	**30.00**	**120,000,000**
Total legal	**9.52**	**$ 23,515,751,295**
Illegal gambling		
Numbers	51.00	2,830,655,611
Horsebooks	17.00	1,381,913,941
Sportsbooks	4.55	1,246,117,549
Sportscards	60.00	1,271,821,326
Total illegal	**15.58**	**$ 6,730,508,427**
Grand total	**10.43**	**$ 30,246,259,722**

Note: Column may not add to totals due to rounding.

Source: Gaming & Wagering Business, Vol. 11, no. 8, August 15, 1990.

Exhibit 4.4

RESULTS OF A RACE TRACK IMAGE STUDY

Average Rating: Semantic Differential Scale

Left	5.0	4.0	3.0	2.0	1.0	0	Right
Like to go to race track often				●			Seldom, if ever, go to race track
Enjoy racing			●				Don't enjoy racing
I know something about race horses					●		I know nothing about race horses
Most races are rigged	●						Most races are run honestly
I like to bet on horses				●			I don't like to bet on horses
I often win at the track					●		I never win at the track
Going to the races with a group is fun.		●					Going to the races with a group is boring
You can only win if you get a hot tip	●						You need to know horses and jockeys to win
I enjoy seeing the horses themselves				●			I don't care much about horses
Most track customers are seedy characters			●				Most track customers are upright citizens
I like other kinds of gambling		●					Race track gambling is my favorite kind

Source: Hale N. Tongren, "The Sport of Kings," in *Cases in Consumer Behavior* (Englewood Cliffs, NJ: Prentice-Hall, Inc., 1987).

With respect to promotion, both casinos and lotteries made major payoffs to small bettors on a regular basis and publicized these events extensively. Even occasional patrons therefore harbored the hope that the next dollar they wagered might completely change their life-styles. By contrast, racetracks had not yet found ways to turn two-dollar bettors into instant millionaires. Winning at the track was generally perceived to require knowledge of the sport, handicapping skills, and a willingness to become involved in the activity over a long period of time. Many in today's society appeared unwilling to put in this considerable investment of time and effort for an uncertain and relatively modest return.

FACILITY UTILIZATION

As a newcomer to the racing industry, Chesterton had initially been astonished to find that something that would be viewed as a serious problem by most other businesses was essentially taken as a "given" by track management. This "something" was the fact that a track facility responsible for enormous fixed costs year-round was being used to generate significant revenues for only about four months each year.

The racetrack had always been operated on a seasonal basis, from June to September, and was closed to the public at other times, except for the major dining facility, which was occasionally rented out for group functions or catered affairs. Chesterton had observed in manufacturing environments that increases in facility utilization often translated into dramatic increases in profitability. He therefore saw no reason why the racetrack's "excess capacity" could not be utilized to generate additional revenues.

Unfortunately, implementing this concept turned out to be more difficult than Chesterton had anticipated. For example, substantially extending the thoroughbred racing meeting was not feasible. Racing schedules were regulated by the state's Racing Commission, in part so as to minimize direct competition among tracks within the state. Nonoverlapping meetings were ultimately a benefit to all, because some of the best horses in the region could follow a "circuit" in which they were alternately stabled at several tracks during each track's season. Because of this, it would be difficult to attract support from the horsemen for even the few additional racing dates likely to be granted by the Racing Commission.

One alternative under serious consideration, however, was the addition of a harness racing meeting. Harness racing, Chesterton had learned, was in some ways a completely different sport from thoroughbred racing, as horses bred and trained for harness racing were a quite different "product" from thoroughbreds. Many other tracks had been successful with either harness schedules exclusively or with alternating harness and thoroughbred meetings, and harness racing was very popular in certain markets (see Exhibit 4.5).

Exhibit 4.5

RACING ATTENDANCE IN FOUR MAJOR CITIES, 1988

	New York	Los Angeles	Chicago	Detroit
Thoroughbreds	4,759,274	8,227,944	2,484,539	778,516
Harness	1,482,440	307,009	1,576,957	1,132,304
Total	6,241,714	8,227,944	4,061,496	1,910,820

Source: 1988 Survey on Sports Attendance (Hightstown, NJ: The Daily Racing Form, 1988).

The addition of a harness meeting would pose several problems, although most appeared manageable. First, harness racing required a modification of the racing surface. Second, the stable facilities were limited. For these reasons, among others, it was not feasible to run concurrent or overlapping harness and thoroughbred meetings. The Racing Commission would also permit Eastern Downs to add a harness meeting only if schedules could be coordinated with those of other tracks. This would probably require some adjustment of Eastern Downs' thoroughbred schedule. The most workable arrangement, given the track's limited capability for heating patron and backstretch areas during the winter months, was to run one meeting from spring to midsummer and another from midsummer through the fall.

TARGET MARKET SEGMENTS

The primary question regarding the harness alternative was the likely market response. Eastern Downs' expertise in thoroughbred racing wouldn't automatically translate into the establishment of a successful harness program. Even if a high-quality program could be developed, it was uncertain whether sufficient numbers of patrons could be attracted, since many thoroughbred enthusiasts did not patronize harness racing, and vice versa. Also, that portion of the thoroughbred meeting shifted out of the summer season would lose patrons from the area's seasonal and resort communities.

Although Eastern Downs had itself conducted little market research, Chesterton had recently reviewed a variety of studies available from other sources. He realized that marketing of the track's existing or proposed racing programs had to take into account variations in the interests and motivations of potential patrons. First, a fundamental distinction could be made between what could be called regular, occasional, and nonpatrons. Regular patrons were primarily serious horseplayers and those who accompanied them. Occasional patrons visited the track from time to time, but tended to view racing as only one among many forms of available entertainment. Nonpatrons had never been exposed to the sport, had been exposed but showed no interest, or refused to patronize racing because they viewed it as inconsistent with religious or other values.

With reference to the harness alternative, Chesterton felt that occasional patrons would be just as likely to attend a harness as a thoroughbred event, and nonpatrons just as difficult to attract to either. His main concern was with regular horseplayers, and for good reason. In common with customers of many other industries, horseracing patrons reflected the so-called "80–20 principle," whereby a small proportion of customers account for a large proportion of revenues. Although many other sporting and entertainment businesses could rely on attendance figures as a reflection of their marketing success, racetracks relied much more on the amount actually wagered, or parimutuel handle. In this regard, regular patrons were often a minority of those in attendance (particularly on weekends) but, because of higher per capita wagering, usually accounted for a large proportion of the total handle.

Studies at tracks with both thoroughbred and harness schedules showed that many patrons were regular attendees of one or another of these sports but not of both. The implication of this finding was that much of Eastern Downs' loyal thoroughbred following might not visit the track during a harness meeting. However, Chesterton felt that some of this research did not apply to Eastern Downs, which did not face direct thoroughbred competition in its local market, as did many of the other tracks studied. Local horseplayers, he felt, would therefore have nowhere else to go during the proposed harness meeting and would eventually acquire an interest in the sport. Nevertheless, a local pool of harness racing fans would still require some cultivation. Some additional research and modified marketing appeals would be required, because available information suggested demographic and psychographic differences in the profiles of thoroughbred and harness enthusiasts. Many in management also felt that it was important to identify and attract additional patrons beyond those already attending. Some suggested that the funds available for wagering to any given patron were essentially limited. Because of this, a person who attended additional thoroughbred racing events, or attended both thoroughbred and harness events, would be required to lessen the level of wagering per visit. If this were the case, the net result for the track of attracting an existing pool of regulars to the facility more frequently would be increased attendance but without incremental wagering revenue.

OTHER APPROACHES TO FACILITY UTILIZATION

These same difficulties had been noted in objections to another proposed alternative means of improving track utilization, "simulcasting." Modern technologies had made it possible to offer live telecasts to patrons of a given track of races originating at a track in another part of the state, in another state, or even in another country. Wagers can be placed at the receiving track in an arrangement whereby the proceeds are shared by both tracks.

Simulcasting can be used by a receiving track in a variety of ways. Telecasts can be offered during the intervals between live races. Telecasts can be offered as a separate program, either earlier or later in the day, during an existing meeting. Finally, telecasts can be offered as a separate program during the off-season. Supporters of simulcasting among Eastern Downs' management tended to favor the last of these approaches, because they felt it would cause less cannibalization of the wagering dollar than either of the others. However, there were those opposed to simulcasting on other grounds. For example, one member of the Kimberley family was adamantly opposed to any televised racing program because he felt it removed the patron from the actual experience of the sport and was thus a step toward a dramatic industry consolidation in which a small number of remaining tracks would one day be beaming the sport to patrons in theaters and betting parlors. Nevertheless, Chesterton knew that this was a minority position and also that regulatory and contractual obstacles to simulcasting could probably be overcome.

Because of the various difficulties in expanding racing programs, Chesterton had recently begun to think about possible non-horseracing activities that could increase revenues during the off-season. For example, a friend had suggested automobile racing events as a possibility. Unfortunately, although the grandstand could accommodate patrons for such events, a completely different racing surface would have to be created at the end of each horseracing meeting and then dismantled before the beginning of the next. This would be feasible only if a regular auto racing schedule could be developed, and Chesterton's few inquiries to date had resulted in expressions of interest only in individual, one-day events. In any case, Eastern Downs' management had no expertise in auto racing, and might not agree to the kinds of financial and personnel commitments that such a new venture would require.

It appeared to Chesterton that the ideal off-season utilization of the track, given various constraints, would be a continuous round of varied activities, each of which would require minimal modification of the facility and little or no commitment by management. Independently produced activities such as concerts, country fairs, automobile auctions, and the like had already been presented at other tracks, although the results had been mixed. As an example of possible negative consequences, one nearby track had been the scene of a rock concert that attracted an unruly crowd, with attendant security and damage problems. However, by anticipating such contingencies in contracts with reputable promoters, the track could limit its own costs and risks and assure itself of some profit from such events.

Patrons of activities that were so different from horseracing were unlikely to be the same kinds of patrons that the track saw during the racing season. Some in management saw this as a drawback, others as an opportunity. There were those who argued that attracting persons with no interest in horseracing to the track would bring in a few dollars but would offer no long-term benefit to the track's primary business. Some even suggested a negative effect if the track's mission became blurred or if horseplayers began to resent the mixed use and therefore lost their emotional identification with the facility (i.e., as their "turf"). On the other hand, some argued that increasing the awareness, among nonpatrons, of the track as a pleasant place to spend an afternoon or evening, would increase the probability that such persons might revisit the track during the racing season.

MARKET DEVELOPMENT

Chesterton had begun to formulate a set of recommendations to management focusing on improving utilization of the track. However, two recent phone conversations with friends outside the industry were causing him to rethink that approach. Chesterton often turned for business and personal advice to his old college roommate, Bill Sektal, who was now a financial executive for a leading firm. Bill had listened patiently to Chesterton's recitation of the pros and cons of various ideas, but had ultimately concluded that all were exercises in futility. Recent trends in attendance and revenues, he argued, showed that horseracing as an industry was in the mature stage of its life cycle and was probably headed into a period of decline. Even if Eastern Downs survived the inevitable shakeout, it could never achieve the kind of revenue growth needed to compensate for inevitable increases in operating costs. Moreover, Sektal insisted that the track's owners were behaving irrationally from an investment standpoint. He noted that the owners' property had limited revenue-generating potential as a racetrack, but would be worth a fortune if sold to developers in the currently improving real estate market in the area. Given current tax laws, the owners would thus be best advised to close the track and sell the land, putting the proceeds into more promising ventures. Because he believed that they would sooner or later come to this conclusion regardless of whatever was now recommended, Sektal told Chesterton of a marketing opening in his own firm and urged him to apply for it.

The conversation with Bill Sektal resulted in a sleepless night for Chesterton. The following morning he decided to seek out a more constructive opinion and called another old friend. Ziggy Maleski had worked with Chesterton in the marketing department of a consumer products firm and was currently working in an overseas subsidiary of the same firm. Chesterton remembered Maleski not only as a creative marketer but also as an inveterate optimist. He was therefore not surprised when, after listening to the same facts, Ziggy responded with enthusiasm for the challenge. The tack he recommended, however, was not to concentrate on the facility utilization issue, but rather to focus on expanding the market for horseracing. In terms of company politics, he reasoned, the track's owners and managers tended to be racing enthusiasts as well as businessmen, and would therefore be more receptive to visions of more horseplayers flocking to the track than they would be to visions of screeching automobiles or hordes of rock music fans. More important, the large numbers of occasional and nonpatrons in the population were in fact promising targets for market development.

Chesterton was predisposed toward Maleski's market development arguments. For one thing, his conversation with Sektal had made him aware that, if the facility utilization approach was truly nothing more than a holding action for a declining business, Eastern Downs would offer him very little in terms of professional challenge or career opportunity. In addition, his own experience as a recent nonpatron had taught him that people unfamiliar with horseracing *could* find it to be an exciting and attractive sport if properly educated.

Racetracks in general had done little formal marketing until recent years, and much of what was currently being done could best be described as haphazard. Also, they had tended *not* to be "market oriented," with a primary focus on identifying the wants and needs of actual or potential customers. Instead, most were "product oriented" insofar as they assumed that horseplayers would automatically be drawn to the track by certain events and amenities. As a result, most of the "baby boom" generation had come to adulthood without much exposure to the sport. The proportion of the adult population that had *never* attended a horserace was now greater than the proportion that *had* ever attended. The potential market for horseracing was therefore substantially greater than that portion of it that had already been tapped.

It would certainly not be easy to attract large numbers of these persons to the races. Such tactics as special events, subsidized bus service from nearby population centers, and promotions such as free admissions and giveaways, could be expected to bring more of them to the track from time to time. Because of low per capita wagering by occasional patrons, many of these visitors would have to be converted eventually into regulars in order for this approach to be worthwhile. However, this approach *would* address the objective of building a long-term consumer franchise for the industry. Chesterton now believed that he could retain his own personal commitment to the industry only if he remained convinced that horseracing had a promising future. At this point in its history, he told himself, horseracing was suffering not an inevitable decline, but rather one caused by neglect of the marketing function.

An awareness-building and trial-inducing program would be most effective, Chesterton reasoned, in relation to younger people whose entertainment preferences were still developing. Research indicated that most horseplayers had first attended the races at a young age during a visit with a parent, older friend, or relative. This was true for persons attracted to other sports as well. Unfortunately, state regulations often prohibited attendance at racetracks by children below a certain age or for evening racing events. (Chesterton felt this to be unfair, since no similar regulations prevented children from witnessing such things as violent brawls during hockey games or other spectator sports.) Of course, the track did not actually want to attract children to the facility as bettors. However, regulations limiting children's attendance prevented them from being exposed to the sport and had the additional negative effect of removing a visit to the track from the "consideration set" of spectator sports that some families might otherwise attend. As things now stood, racing was not attracting enough of the young adults in such families.

Chesterton had read about a track in another state that dealt with this difficulty by promoting frequent "family days" when the horses were not running. On these days it offered free admission, staged practice races, and provided facilities for picnicking and other family-oriented activities. Although the direct payoff from such promotional activities, in the form of new fans, might not occur in the short term, redefinition of the public image of horseracing as wholesome family entertainment could begin to benefit the industry almost immediately.

Another target group of interest was single adults and young couples, particularly the mythical, free-spending "yuppies." Chesterton thought that the track's restaurant could be positioned in such a way as to attract some of these people, particularly in the evenings. Instead of emphasizing the sporting and entertainment aspects of horseracing (Eastern Downs' usual promotional themes), Chesterton thought he could appeal to this segment by portraying the track as a social center.

Group promotions could be a way for the track to induce "trial" of racing by members of various new markets. Contacts could be expanded with fraternal and ethnic organizations, school groups, and major area employers. Chesterton felt that persons who first experienced racing in the context of social interaction with their peers would find it more satisfying than would persons who visited as solitary individuals.

Chesterton informally discussed these ideas with other track personnel, most of whom were enthusiastic. However, one long-time employee raised a cautionary point. Mixing middle-aged, regular horseplayers together with young singles and families in the same facility, he suggested, ran counter to these groups' natural tendencies to avoid one another. The track was better off, he suggested, focusing its efforts on a single target market, and, given their higher wagering levels, regulars ought to be the track's full-time concern.

Chesterton reflected on this argument for some time, because he knew that marketing efforts often became ineffective when a firm tried to direct too many different appeals to too many market segments. He decided, however, that in this case the track had to build a bridge from its patrons of the past to those of the future, so the fragmented effort was necessary. As for mingling these groups, he noted that the track had always offered different seating and dining areas, which had resulted in a form of informal, patron-determined, demographic segegation.

Unlike marketing managers in other industries, Chesterton felt limited in the degree to which he could manipulate the major marketing variables. His *product* was relatively fixed by tradition and regulation. He could embellish it somewhat to appeal to younger audiences (e.g. provide additional entertainment between races), but that could alienate the more traditional patrons. Changes in wagering policies, such as establishing more high-payoff "exotic" wagers, might be popular with some patrons, but would diminish the current advantage of those who had developed handicapping skills. The *price* charged to patrons was largely self-determined. Aside from nominal admission and parking fees, the cost of a day at the races depended primarily on discretionary wagering. *Distribution* was constrained by the fixed location of the facility, except for such activities as off-track or telephone betting, in which Eastern Downs could not participate. In any event, attempts to "bring racing to the fans" could have the negative effect of discouraging track attendance and thereby reducing revenues from such ancillaries as parking, program sales, and food concessions.

The one marketing area in which some significant changes could probably be made was *promotion*, although here too there were major constraints. Certain forms of advertising, in particular, were difficult to utilize effectively. For example, television time had always been viewed by track management as prohibitively expensive, particularly because ads placed with stations in the two nearest metropolitan areas would result in many wasted impressions on persons outside the track's geographic market. Local radio had been used for spot announcements, but some in the industry felt that radio was inherently unable to convey the *visual* excitement of racing. Local sports fans were also far more likely to listen to radio stations in nearby cities than to local stations. Eastern Downs had primarily used billboards along nearby highways for reminder-type advertising and newspapers for announcements and free-admission couponing. One important role of advertising was to maintain the track in a "top-of-mind" position among occasional patrons, for whom a visit was often the result of an impulse rather than of advance planning.

Chesterton could find no research evidence to support the track's media choices, but concluded that years of experience had probably resulted in a relatively satisfactory mix. However, the recent penetration of *cable* television into the track's market area probably warranted a reexamination of the feasibility of TV advertising. Chesterton thought that the cost-effectiveness of ads placed on cable TV would be favorable because there would be no wasted impressions on people outside the immediate market area, and because cable might reach a relatively upscale segment. He had scheduled an appointment with the local cable company's sales representative to explore this possibility.

Newspapers were particularly important in the promotion mix of Eastern Downs because those in which the track regularly advertised were receptive to the track's press releases, and also periodically had their sportswriters do feature articles about the track or about racing in general. This kind of publicity was probably the best vehicle for consumer education short of actually showing people around the track. Chesterton thought it best to continue these efforts. However, he planned to initiate contacts with writers beyond the sports section. He hoped that publicity pieces might appear in the "entertainment" or "life-style" sections consulted by persons in the new market segments targeted for development.

There also appeared to be several ways for Eastern Downs to stretch or increase its promotional dollars. The track could engage in "cross-promotions" with other local or national advertisers. Some corporations might even be willing to *sponsor* major races, which would be a source of both additional revenues and valuable publicity. However, in order to attract such interest, the track would have to demonstrate to these firms that racing fans were good potential customers for *their* products or services.

It occurred to Chesterton at this point that his different target markets required actions directed toward quite different marketing objectives. Most of his ideas and enthusiasm had been geared to attracting new patrons. However, he also needed to keep the existing pool of regular patrons happy. He had given no thought as yet to their specific needs, although he felt that filling the grandstand with new fans and improving the image of the sport would also reinforce the commitment of the regulars. Another problem was that of converting new or occasional patrons into regulars. Chesterton felt that making the experience of a visit to the track as entertaining as possible for these people would result in repeat business. Gambling-prone persons who developed an interest in horseracing would then convert themselves over time.

There was, of course, a limit to the extent to which the image of horseracing could be influenced by the promotional efforts of any one track. What would ultimately be needed, Chesterton felt, was a concerted, industry-wide promotional campaign aimed at increasing primary demand. Such campaigns were often conducted by trade associations for their members, and were currently conducted by most professional sports leagues. Unfortunately, convincing the various tracks, state commissions, and interest groups involved in horseracing to cooperate in such an endeavor would be a formidable task.

A general meeting had been scheduled for the coming week, at which time Chesterton was expected to present his recommendations to management. (Some of the owners were also likely to be in attendance.) Chesterton had by now learned enough about racetrack operations to know that there were no easy answers to the track's problems. Because of this, he was considering presenting an overview of all the possible directions that could be taken, urging that management begin taking steps in each of them. This approach would offer an opportunity for him to demonstrate his grasp of the range of issues at hand without having actually to commit himself to a particular strategy.

However, he wondered whether it might be better to focus upon a particular strategic direction, with achievable objectives, and to offer a marketing plan consistent with it. This approach would demonstrate his ability to identify and address the track's most important problems. If he took this tack, he would have to decide whether to emphasize operational issues, such as facility utilization, or specific marketing issues, such as target market selection and development.

Finally, Chesterton felt that he would have to develop an inventory of internal data needs that had to be satisfied, and of new research that needed to be conducted, prior to specific marketing planning. He realized that he could not gather much of the actual data prior to the upcoming meeting, but he wanted to be as well prepared as possible.

5

SEARS, ROEBUCK
AND COMPANY (A)

While Richard W. Sears was working as a railroad station agent around 1886, he purchased a shipment of gold-filled watches mistakenly shipped to a jeweler. Sears sold this shipment of watches at a profit to other station agents and ordered more for resale.

In 1886, Sears began the R. W. Sears Watch Company in Minneapolis and the following year moved his business to Chicago where he advertised for a watchmaker. Alvah C. Roebuck answered the ad, Sears hired him, and by 1893, the corporate name of the firm became Sears, Roebuck and Company.

Sears and Roebuck realized that if they offered value at a reasonable cost, the company would prosper. Sears also recognized that mass merchandising to a largely rural population was achievable through a rapidly expanding postal system. Thanks to volume buying, developing railroad and postal systems, and rural free delivery and parcel post, Sears offered farmers a viable alternative to the high-priced rural stores. This alternative became the mail order and catalog business that is the basis for today's Sears, Roebuck Corporation.

Since its inception, Sears has had the foresight and flexibility to change and evolve its manner of doing business and the types of services it provides as social and economic trends have changed.

When chain stores began to blanket the country, cutting into Sears' mail order business, and American cities began expanding while rural populations began dwindling, Sears opened its urban retail stores.

When the automobile gave rise to the mobile shopper, the company anticipated that these shoppers would abandon crowded urban stores for the easy parking convenience of suburban centers, resulting in a great growth of Sears retail outlets. When the populace demanded other services such as easy credit terms and insurance, Sears also provided them to its customers.

Today, more consumers than ever want to shop nights and weekends and are increasingly willing to buy goods by mail and phone. Sears has been at the leading edge of these trends as well as an innovator in the development of in-home electronic shopping systems for the future. Since 90 percent of all adult Americans shop at Sears at least once a year, Sears management is committed to furthering the viability of its special franchise with the American consumer and is dedicated to the proposition that Sears is where America shops.

SEARS CORPORATE STRUCTURE

Today, Sears, Roebuck and Company has business groups in merchandising, insurance, real estate, financial services, and world trade. In order to provide positive reinforcement of names most recognizable to its customers, corporate management recently designated its five major businesses as Sears Merchandise Group, Allstate Insurance Group, Coldwell Banker Real Estate Group, Dean Witter Financial Services Group, and Sears World Trade, Inc.

Sears Merchandise Group[1]

The Sears Merchandise Group is headed by a chairman and chief executive officer and consists of merchandising, credit, and international operations. Currently, all headquarters buying departments are organized under merchandise vice presidents, who report to the senior executive vice president of merchandising and are responsible for developing the merchandising program and buying goods in related lines.

Sears' field organization is divided into eastern, western, northern, and southern territories, each with a territorial headquarters headed by an executive vice president. The vice president monitors the performance of all personnel and operations in that territory, including retail stores and catalog merchandise distribution centers. Territory staff supplements the headquarters' organization in all merchandising and operating activities.

Sears' retail stores and catalog operations are organized into administrative units called retail groups and catalog merchandise distribution groups. A group is made up of several stores in a large metropolitan area such as Boston, Chicago, and Los Angeles or several stores in a larger geographical area outside major metropolitan areas. The responsibility of each group office is to coordinate pricing, advertising, merchandise assortments, customer services, and merchandise delivery in all stores under its supervision.

[1]The writing of this case predates the present-day situation wherein Sears has divested itself of certain subsidiaries. However, this case is designed for the student to examine the earlier 1980s' period at Sears.

The company's catalog distribution centers distribute merchandise to stores and catalog outlets in a specified area of the country, usually servicing Sears' customers in several states. The merchandise group has a policy of responding to consumer demand for high-quality, innovative merchandise without equivalent price increases. The Cheryl Tiegs signature sportswear line, an example of this policy, was a major success for Sears in the early 1980s (Exhibit 5.1). Exhibit 5.2 includes examples of other innovative products such as the Kenmore Sensorsew One Hundred, a computerized sewing machine, and the DieHard-powered rechargeable Reel-1 lawnmower.

Business Systems Centers   In the early 1980s, Sears ventured into specialty stores by opening five Business Systems Centers in Boston, Chicago, and Dallas. These stores carry a broad line of electronic equipment under Sears' and other major brand names including computers, typewriters, copiers, calculators, and dictation equipment aimed at the small-business market. Expansion included the subsequent

Exhibit 5.1

CHERYL TIEGS SIGNATURE SPORTSWEAR AD*

*Designer-inspired separates from the company's popular new line of Cheryl Tiegs signature sportswear.

Exhibit 5.2

KENMORE SENSORSEW ONE HUNDRED AND THE REEL 1 LAWN MOWER

The new Kenmore Sensorsew One Hundred is one of the world's most advanced sewing machines.

An innovative addition to Sears full-line of lawn and garden implements, the new Reel-1 power-propelled electric reel mower cuts an 18-inch path, and includes a 12-volt DieHard battery with recharger.

opening of 45 additional centers with another 40 to open in each of the following two years.

Sears Advertising   To support product development and sales, Sears conducts a unified advertising program to set Sears apart from its competitors. The campaign includes ads to generate day-to-day sales for individual stores and products and corporate ads building on the reputation: "You can count on Sears" (Exhibit 5.3).

This national campaign, concluded in 1982, was developed from research that showed Sears' crucial strengths to be customer satisfaction, credit when needed, service to customers when they move, free replacement of a product if it fails, and an enormous product selection.

Computerized Operating System   Central computerized operating systems are an integral part of Sears' retail, catalog, service and distribution management, and control. A computer network centralized through group offices records purchases at point of sale, aids with a particular store's inventory control and merchandising, and assists with advanced merchandise planning. The network is connected to all phases of operations including accounting, distribution, buying, and credit.

Service   The company's service network covers all geographic areas of the country. Service technicians can repair any appliance purchased at Sears, either by visiting a customer's home or by a customer bringing a small appliance to a store or service center. The company's computerized service records make it possible for most customers to call a center and have the service representative instantly read out a complete list of the customer's appliance purchases, their warranty status, and service history. The system then prints out a service order for each customer request and prepares a route sheet for service technicians.

The company also has innovated "Service While You Wait" to speed customer service on carry-in appliances. The goal of this service is to repair small appliances at the service center while the customer waits. It is currently being offered in most of the company's major service centers. "Service While You Wait" and the computerized service records of the company are integral parts of the company's strong reputation for service.

Sears Catalogs Sears catalogs are big business—big in the sales volume they produce (which runs into the billions of dollars) and big in their costs, which run into millions of dollars.

All catalogs are printed outside the company. The biggest catalogs are the general ones, which are published twice each year—one for the spring–summer selling season, the other for the fall–winter selling season. Each general catalog contains more than 1,300 pages and weighs about 5 pounds.

In addition, Sears issues summer and winter seasonal catalogs of about 200 pages each, and a Christmas Wish Book of more than 500 pages annually. The seasonal catalogs are designed to stimulate sales and to supplement merchandise assortments in the big catalogs. The company also issues "special value" supplements as well as specialized catalogs aimed at specific markets with specific needs.

Exhibit 5.3

EXAMPLE OF A NATIONWIDE AD

Because of the varied tastes of customers and the different climates of the United States, Sears issues each of its five major catalogs in several different editions. Approximately 300 million catalogs and supplements are printed each year.

Catalog merchandise is sold at catalog order desks in retail stores, through catalog sales offices, and through the company's independent sales merchants in all states, Puerto Rico, and APO locations throughout the world. While catalog sales offices are operated by Sears employees, independent merchants sell catalog merchandise to customers in small communities and receive a commission from the company for their sales.

Market Research   Research is critical to centralized buying in a massive retail and catalog operation such as Sears. Each Sears department buyer must know as many facts about the market as possible before making commitments for production and inventory. Sears' research organization—one of the largest in the country—conducts the following types of studies: market profile, segmentation, attitudes, motivation, preference, satisfaction, and end use.

Sears Laboratories   The Sears Merchandise Development and Testing Laboratory occupies approximately 125,000 square feet of space in the Chicago area. There are also several smaller, somewhat specialized laboratories located in the United States and overseas. Each year Sears spends several million dollars to operate the laboratories.

The product evaluation section of the laboratory evaluates engineering prototypes, Sears' and competitors' merchandise, product safety, and product performance and assists in specifications development.

The technical service area of the laboratory works on the aesthetics of a product and works with Sears buyers and manufacturers in setting up quality control procedures and ways of producing the same or better products at lower costs.

Manufacturing Suppliers and Affiliates   Second in importance only to the company's specialized force of buyers is its long-term supplier relationships, many of which go back to the turn of the century.

Part of the company's merchandising goal is to strengthen even further the company's strong supplier structure. Sears' aim is to buy 60 percent or more of the company's needs in a certain product line from a single supplier. With this kind of arrangement, both the supplier and the company can establish a favorable rate of profit and can control costs. It also gives Sears a greater buying advantage, as the supplier will be able to maximize plant use more efficiently. The end result is better prices to the consumer and a better job of supplying services to retail and catalog facilities.

Distribution   After the manufacturing and packaging of Sears merchandise is completed, the merchandise is transported directly to a Sears store or distribution center. Several kinds of distribution centers are used: retail, catalog merchandise, appliance, fashion merchandise, floor covering, and import centers. After merchandise arrives at these locations, it is reshipped directly to a customer or local selling unit.

Planning   Sears' National Facilities Planning Group develops the framework for merchandising, planning, and operating all Sears stores. The Store Planning and

Visual Merchandising divisions of this group are responsible for planning Sears' stores, both inside and out. Planners make precise recommendations about the layout of space, the proximity of divisions and items and lines within divisions, the arrangement of merchandise, and the development of proper fixtures.

Sears sells its broad lines of general merchandise through a variety of selling locations nationwide. Retail stores are the largest and most visible means. The company has four types:

- Full-line department stores, or "A" stores
- Medium-sized department stores, or "B" stores
- Hard-line merchandise stores, or "C" stores
- Surplus stores

Although most of the company's "B" stores have 50,000 to 70,000 square feet of sales area, Sears designed a medium-sized department store for smaller markets in 1978. These stores have 30,000 to 40,000 square feet of sales area. The smaller stores incorporate the company's strongest merchandise assortments of tools, apparel, appliances, and automotive supplies, while making the most efficient use of personnel, equipment, centralized merchandising, inventory control, accounting systems, sales reporting, and service department mechanization—all programs available to the larger stores.

Credit   With approximately 25 million active credit accounts, Sears regards its credit customers as an important asset and has always strived to meet their needs.

The company's entire credit system is completely automated and linked by a computer network called "Credit Information System" (CIS). CIS enables all Sears credit central offices to communicate with each other, transfer accounts, obtain credit authorizations, and provide information on individual accounts. Sears credit centers throughout the country work closely with data, accounting, and processing centers to carry out the company's large credit business. These offices are responsible for credit approvals, credit collection, adjustments, inquiries and complaints, and liaison work with local credit bureaus.

International Operations   The international group conducts retail merchandise and credit operations in Mexico and Canada through its Canadian subsidiary, Simpsons-Sears Ltd.

Growth Strategies   Sears' management feels there are five interrelated strategies which are the key to financial performance:

- A more comprehensive approach to annual planning, addressing each segment of the merchandise business individually and involving management at all levels
- Reductions in cost that systematically examine each level of business in an effort to achieve new efficiencies
- Development of comparable quality goods at lower cost while maintaining gross margins
- Consistent and appealing presentation of merchandise for which Sears has allocated significant resources for the development of new display concepts and contemporization of existing stores
- Development of aggressive selling programs to support buying and presentation efforts

Allstate Group

Allstate is primarily a property-liability and life insurance group of companies serving the insurance needs of millions of individuals. Within its corporate headquarters in Northbrook, Illinois, a Chicago suburb, Allstate operates through regional offices. The company is headed by a chairman and chief executive officer. The Allstate Group is the second largest domestic property-liability insurance writer and the second largest writer of personal automobile and homeowners insurance policies.

Although Allstate uses many systems of distribution, the nucleus of its sales force remains the thousands of employee agents who sell its products in Sears stores or through neighborhood offices. Allstate also has developed an independent agent force to sell the company's products in rural areas where there is no full-time Allstate agent.

Other Businesses   Allstate is involved in other businesses that are diverse and span the globe. Allstate Life Insurance Company was established in 1957 as a major move toward product diversification. Based on direct premiums written, Allstate ranks among the top 15 writers of domestic life insurance. The company began its international operations in 1959. The introduction of property and liability lines to Japan is the latest expansion of the international group.

The insurance needs of business enterprises are served through the company's commercial divisions and subsidiaries:

- The Commercial Insurance Division and Northbrook Property and Casualty Insurance Company meet a broad spectrum of primary business insurance needs.
- Northbrook Excess and Surplus Insurance Company is a major factor in the excess and surplus lines field.
- The Reinsurance Division writes reinsurance nationally and internationally.
- The Group Insurance Division of Allstate Life Insurance Company writes a full line of employee benefit products.

Allstate makes auto, boat, home equity, and personal loans as an adjunct to its insurance business. In addition, approximately 1 million people count on the Allstate Motor Club for travel-related services.

Coldwell Banker Real Estate Group (formerly The Seraco Group)

In 1979 Sears established a task force to assess the profitable and expanding operations of its wholly owned real estate and financial services companies. This led to the 1981 formation of the Coldwell Banker Real Estate Group, the country's largest independent commercial and residential real estate broker.

Out of the task force's recommendations also came the formation of The Seraco Group, a management arm, headed by a chairman and chief executive officer.

Formation of The Seraco Group in February 1980 was brought about by a recognition of the earnings, cash flow, and growth potential in commercial real estate equities and residential real estate finance. It united several ongoing and successful businesses under a new management organization: Homart Development Company, The PMI Group, and Allstate Enterprises Mortgage Corporation.

Homart Development Company, founded by Sears in 1959 as a developer of shopping centers, is today the third largest shopping center developer in the nation, with more than 41 million square feet of retail space to its credit. Since the formation of Seraco, Homart has evolved into a multiline commercial developer, expanding its expertise into the development of office buildings, multiuse projects, and convenience centers.

The PMI Group provides three primary financial services to homeowners. PMI is the nation's fifth largest insurer of first mortgages, offering lender protection in cases where down payments are less than the traditionally required 25 percent, and is a leader in insuring second mortgages and home equity loans. PMI also provides intermediary financial services between mortgage lenders and capital markets, pioneering the issuance of publically offered participation certificates backed by a pool of conventional mortgages purchased from many lenders.

Seraco's mortgage banker, Allstate Enterprises Mortgage Corporation (AEMC), originates mortgage loans primarily backed by the FHA or VA and sells them to investors in the secondary market. AEMC offers loan production facilities in 29 locations and services loans for approximately 46,600 mortgagors and 140 investors nationwide.

The number of Seraco companies increased in the early 1980s with the acquisition of Coldwell Banker & Company. Coldwell Banker's geographic representation, combined with its premier industry position, will facilitate a forceful entry by Sears into the brokerage business and a "rounding out" of the group's residential real estate financial services. In addition, it provides a new depth of services and expertise for Seraco's ongoing commercial real estate development activities.

Coldwell Banker operates 249 residential real estate offices, 54 commercial real estate offices, 24 mortgage banking offices, and 32 real estate management offices. In addition, Coldwell provides referral and relocation services internationally, institutional capital management, escrow, appraisal and consultation, development management, title insurance, and insurance brokerage services.

Coldwell Banker Residential Affiliates, Inc., was formed in the early 1980s to accelerate residential brokerage expansion into middle-sized and smaller markets through franchising. The Group now has the capabilities to relocate families, sell their homes, sell them new homes, help them find financing, insure their mortgages, and build and manage their work spaces and shopping centers. In addition, myriad real estate services are now available to corporations, institutions, and pension funds. These expanded services also have the potential to work with other groups within the Sears, Roebuck and Company family.

Based on the continuing strong demand for real estate products and services nationwide, the Group remains committed to the objective of prominence in this marketplace.

Dean Witter Financial Services Group

The nucleus for this group was formed in late 1981 when Sears acquired Dean Witter Reynolds Organization and joined it with Allstate Savings and Loan Association, now known as Sears Savings Bank.

Dean Witter Reynolds is an international financial services company involved in securities and commodities brokerage, investment banking, insurance, and money management. The only such firm with offices in all 50 states and Washington, D.C., Dean Witter numbers 4,500 professional account executives among its 11,500 employees in some 330 offices in the United States, Canada, the Far East, and Europe and services in excess of 740,000 individual and corporate accounts.

Sears Savings Bank is the 10th largest savings association in California and the 16th largest in the nation. Nearly 100 branch offices throughout the state offer a variety of financial services, including interest-paying checking accounts and telephone bill payment services. A traditional provider of mortgage monies, Sears Savings Bank activities include new mortgage investments and commercial lending.

Sears provides Dean Witter with a broad capital base essential for major financial services, and product synergism that is substantial for Dean Witter customers: real estate packages, tax-advantaged investments, creative insurance packages, investment banking organizations, and mass marketing skills. Dean Witter provides Sears a means of achieving its objective of becoming a leading provider of financial services.

The Dean Witter Financial Services Group provides a broad range of financial services through four Dean Witter Financial Services units:

- DeanWitter Reynolds, Inc., the fourth largest registered broker-dealer in the United States, conducts security trading including individual securities and commodities brokerage, and institutional sales and dealer trading activities.
- Dean Witter Capital Markets provides investment banking services consisting of corporate and public finance and syndicated offerings.
- Dean Witter Reynolds Intercapital, Inc., a registered investment advisor, provides mutual funds and other money management services. Among others, Intercapital manages the Sears U.S. government money market trust. Begun in late 1981, it is a money market trust that invests in U.S. government securities.
- Dean Witter Reynolds International, Inc., and Dean Witter Reynolds, Ltd., handle overseas securities and commodities brokerage, securities dealings, and investment banking activities.

Sears World Trade, Inc.

Sears has established a world trading company to compete in world trade markets, described in the press release shown in Exhibit 5.4.

FINANCIAL PERFORMANCE

During the last half of the 1970s, total operating revenues grew, but in 1980, net income dropped by $194 million due to increases in costs and expenses. Consolidated operating revenues increased by $2.2 billion in 1981, reflecting revenue increases in Sears' major business groups with substantial increases again in 1982 and 1983.

The Sears merchandise group is the dominant revenue producer, providing approximately 73 percent of total operating revenues, followed by Allstate Insurance with 24 percent. The merchandise group reported gains in revenues of 8.3 percent to a record $18.23 billion in 1981, after flat years in 1979 and 1980 due to poor economic conditions.

Exhibit 5.4

SEARS, ROEBUCK AND COMPANY PRESS RELEASE

Sears World Trade, Inc.

In March 1982, Sears, Roebuck and Company announced formation of a new international trading company, Sears World Trade, Inc.

Sears World Trade, Inc., was formed to deal in import, export, countertrade, and third country activities and will provide related management and financial services to American and foreign firms seeking more efficient access to international markets. The company will serve as the focal point for a number of international activities of Sears, Roebuck and Company and its subsidiaries.

The company will establish offices in about 20 countries by the end of 1983. It will deal in consumer merchandise, industrial equipment, agricultural products and equipment, various commodities, advanced technology products, and countertrade.

The company will also provide management expertise and consulting in all phases of merchandise distribution, from product manufacture to the establishment of retail sales and services facilities. Sears currently has management service agreements with retail groups in Australia, Chile, Colombia, and Japan.

In sourcing products and components worldwide, Sears World Trade will draw upon the parent company's established network of overseas buying offices, now responsible for nearly $1 billion of U.S. imports annually. Sears World Trade will utilize the buying power and skills of this network to develop a considerable business in sourcing products and components for other U.S. companies·and "third country" trade—that is, trading between two foreign countries. Research shows that great potential exists for the sale of products made by overseas Sears suppliers to companies in other overseas markets.

Sears is also well positioned to help other companies plan and execute countertrade—the various barter and counterpurchase transactions which have become prevalent in world trade in recent months.

Of greatest interest to American manufacturers are the plans of Sears World Trade to provide a uniquely efficient mechanism for exporting goods and technological know-how from the U.S. Sears currently exports U.S. products to 30 countries. In some cases, these exports are to foreign retailers, but sales also are made to regional distributors and to local trading companies. Sears World Trade plans to build aggressively on this export base.

Allstate Insurance Group's revenues totaled $6.8 billion in 1981, an increase of 10 percent over 1980.

Coldwell Banker Group's revenues of $491.1 million represents an increase of 17.4 percent from 1980. (These do not include Coldwell Banker & Co. acquired December 31, 1981.) The percentage return on equity has increased slightly after dropping in 1980, and the price/earnings ratio for 1981 and 1980 has returned to the 1978 level after a drop in 1979.

The acquisitions of Dean Witter and Coldwell Banker in 1981 had a somewhat dilutive effect on Sears earnings per share in the near term because of the issuance of Sears common stock in connection with the two acquisitions. Exhibit 5.5 provides a five-year summary of consolidated financial data and a three-year summary of business group and segment financial data.

Exhibit 5.5

SELECTED FINANCIAL DATA

Sears, Roebuck and Co.
Five-Year Summary of Consolidated Financial Data

Operating results millions	**1981**	1980*	1979*	1978*	1977**
Operating revenues	**$27,357**	$ 25,161	$ 24,528	$ 24,475	$ 22,878
Costs and expenses	**25,375**	23,401	22,581	22,381	21,095
Interest	**1,520**	1,133	918	741	480
Operating income	**462**	627	1,029	1,353	1,303
Per cent of revenues	**1.7**	2.5	4.2	5.5	5.7
Realized capital gains and other	**184**	62	87	32	(4)
Income taxes	**10**	99	320	509	513
Net income	**650**	610	830	909	829
Per cent return on average equity	**8.2**	8.1	11.4	13.4	13.3
Financial position millions					
Investments	**$13,662**	$ 11,428	$ 10,064	$ 9,079	$ 8,018
Receivables	**10,745**	8,905	8,930	8,612	8,693
Property and equipment, net	**3,312**	3,153	3,061	2,969	2,850
Merchandise inventories	**3,103**	2,715	2,680	2,813	2,709
Total assets	**34,509**	28,319	26,991	25,219	23,341
Short-term borrowings	**3,233**	4,436	4,293	3,990	4,237
Long-term debt	**5,324**	2,965	2,966	2,808	2,327
Total debt	**8,557**	7,401	7,259	6,798	6,564
Per cent of debt to equity	**103**	97	97	96	101
Shareholders' equity	**8,269**	7,665	7,446	7,063	6,468
Shareholders' common stock investment					
Book value per share (year end)	**$23.77**	$24.32	$23.44	$21.84	$20.09
Shareholders (Profit Sharing Fund counted as single shareholder)	**354,050**	349,725	339,459	326,086	286,773
Average shares outstanding (millions)	**316**	316	320	322	320
Net income per share	**$2.06**	$1.93	$2.60	$2.82	$2.59
Dividends per share	**$1.36**	$1.36	$1.28	$1.27	$1.08
Dividend payout per cent	**66.0**	70.5	49.2	45.0	41.7
Market price (high-low)	**20¾–14⅞**	19½–14½	21⅝–17⅞	27⅞–19¾	32¾–24⅛
Closing market price at year end	**16⅛**	15⅜	18	19¾	25¼
Price/earnings ratio (high-low)	**10-7**	10–8	8–7	10–7	13–9

* Restated for change in fiscal year from Jan. 31 to Dec. 31 (see note 1, page 43).

** Financial data for 1977 has not been restated for the change in fiscal year; selected data may not be comparable to data for 1981 through 1978.

Exhibit 5.5 (Cont.)

Sears, Roebuck and Co.
Summary of Business Group and Segment Financial Data

millions		Year Ended December 31	

Operating Revenues	1981	1980*	1979*
Sears Merchandise Group			
Merchandising	$18,229	$16,831	$16,813
Credit	1,040	967	924
International	933	877	786
Sears Merchandise Group total	20,202	18,675	18,523
Allstate Insurance Group			
Property-liability insurance	5,932	5,469	5,083
Life-health insurance	737	602	572
Consumer finance	145	126	129
Allstate Insurance Group total	6,814	6,197	5,784
Coldwell Banker Real Estate Group			
Real estate	108	98	83
Related real estate services, including savings and loan operations	383	320	285
Coldwell Banker Real Estate Group total	491	418	368
Corporate	105	88	11
Inter-group transactions and reclassifications	(255)	(217)	(158)
Total	$27,357	$25,161	$24,528

Group Income			
Sears Merchandise Group			
Merchandising	$352	$219	$362
Credit	(83)	(25)	16
International	16	35	48
Sears Merchandise Group total	285	229	426
Allstate Insurance Group			
Property-liability insurance	333	386	358
Life-health insurance	68	58	57
Consumer finance	5	6	7
Allstate Insurance Group total	406	450	422
Coldwell Banker Real Estate Group			
Real estate	74	11	31
Related real estate services, including savings and loan operations	(12)	16	28
Coldwell Banker Real Estate Group total	62	27	59
Corporate	(103)	(96)	(77)
Total	$650	$610	$830

Assets			
Sears Merchandise Group			
Merchandising	$ 6,507	$ 6,149	$ 6,389
Credit	7,282	7,132	7,276
International	841	824	745
Sears Merchandise Group total	14,630	14,105	14,410
Allstate Insurance Group			
Property-liability insurance	8,999	8,344	7,535
Life-health insurance	1,716	1,463	1,334
Consumer finance	791	726	772
Allstate Insurance Group total	11,506	10,533	9,641
Coldwell Banker Real Estate Group			
Real estate	951	499	450
Related real estate services, including savings and loan operations	3,423	3,089	2,769
Coldwell Banker Real Estate Group total	4,374	3,588	3,219
Dean Witter Financial Services Group	4,123	—	—
Corporate, excluding goodwill	465	536	225
Inter-group reclassifications	(589)	(443)	(504)
Total	$34,509	$28,319	$26,991

See accompanying financial statements.
*Restated for change in fiscal year from Jan. 31 to Dec. 31 (see note 1, page 43).

6

SEARS, ROEBUCK
AND COMPANY (B)

CREATING A GLOBAL TRADE ORGANIZATION*

In early February 1986, Charles Moran, a strategic planning director with Sears, Roebuck and Company, was wrestling with the future direction for Sears World Trade (SWT), the U.S. retail giant's ambitious entry into the complex world of international dealmaking. After shaking up the subsidiary's management, narrowing its mission, and scaling down its operations, he wondered: Had SWT's parent finally charted the right course in unfamiliar territory? Revenue had climbed dramatically since the offshoot was formed in 1982 as part of Sears, Roebuck's diversification strategy, but with 1985 results showing an accumulated loss of $48 million, he questioned whether the changes had gone far enough.

Moran's recommendation to Edward Brennan, Sears, Roebuck's newly in-

*Materials for this case have been gathered by Arthur P. Ismay and J. Alex Murray from public sources, most notably *The Washington Post* and *The Wall Street Journal*. The case is intended for class discussion only and not to demonstrate effective or ineffective decision making.

stalled CEO, was due by the end of March, when he was scheduled to direct his attention to the troubled Dean Witter Financial Services Group. Turning from the summary of SWT's financial results, he reviewed the public account of the trading company's erratic course chronicled in the business press.

SEARS WORLD TRADE MAKES FIRST FOREIGN ACQUISITION[1]

Sears World Trade, Inc., the international trading subsidiary of Sears, Roebuck and Company, has announced the acquisition of Price and Pierce, a 170-year-old group of British timber and pulp brokers.

The purchase price was approximately $6 million in cash, Sears World Trade said.

The deal, signed in London early Saturday, is the first foreign venture for the fledgling arm of the country's largest retailer.

Formed last year, Sears World Trade is the Chicago-based parent company's fifth business group. It has headquarters in Washington and offices in eight foreign countries, as well as domestic offices in New York and Chicago. Earlier this year, Sears World Trade bought its first company, a Boston management consulting firm named Harbridge House.

Price and Pierce operates in more than 25 countries on five continents. It was originally established to help the British penetrate Napoleon's blockades.

Now the largest group of timber and pulp agents and brokers in the world, Price and Pierce had a total trade volume last year of over $500 million.

Price and Pierce was a publicly held company until 1971, when it was bought by Tozer, Kemsley, and Millburn, a British holding company. Sears said the group was "one of Tozer, Kemsley's more profitable subsidiaries." Roderick M. Hills, a former chairman of the Securities and Exchange Commission who now heads Sears World Trade, termed the acquisition a "linchpin" in the firm's plans to enter the field of international agribusiness.

Hills pledged that Price and Pierce will maintain its autonomy as well as its current management while under Sears' aegis.

Sears World Trade's activities (see Exhibit 6.1) are wholly capitalized by the parent company. The subsidiary's senior vice president, Curt Hessler, said that Sears World Trade plans more foreign and domestic acquisitions and joint ventures.

Eventually, he said, its operations should consist in equal parts of general trade, merchant banking, and consulting in high-technology fields.

To give it shipping capabilities, Sears formed a joint venture with the German freight forwarding company, Schenkers International Forwarders Inc., which allows Sears access to a network of 350 offices around the world.

Then there are the less formal arrangements that Sears has made, giving it special access to hard-to-crack markets in countries such as Mexico and the Philippines.

All this shows that Sears World Trade is a company in a hurry. "We're running

[1]Adapted from *The Washington Post*, October 17, 1983.

Exhibit 6.1

SEARS WORLD TRADE CHANNELS OF DISTRIBUTION

Product Segment	Marketing	Sourcing	
Customer.	North America Europe Far East	North America Far East South America Caribbean Basin	
Light Industrial	North America	Far East South America	
Agribusiness	North America	Europe Far East South Asia	
Forest	Europe North America	North America Europe Southeast Asia South America	

like hell" to become the biggest and best American trading company, said Hills. "We just keep looking for these building blocks around the world."

In 1983, its first year of actual operations, Sears recorded $79 million in sales but piled up losses of $12 million—reflecting the heavy start-up costs. (see Exhibits 6.2, 6.3, and 6.4.) It has about 1,000 employees, enough for a company six times as

---

Exhibit 6.2

SEARS WORLD TRADE, INC., STATEMENTS OF INCOME
(Millions), 1983–1985

	YEAR ENDED DECEMBER 31		
	1985	1984	1983
Revenues	$236.4	$189.4	$ 79.1
Costs and expenses			
Cost of sales	181.3	138.7	57.1
Selling, general, and administrative	72.9	93.3	44.1
Interest	2.0	3.5	0.4
Total costs and expenses	256.2	235.5	101.6
Operating loss	(19.8)	(46.1)	(22.5)
Other income	1.5	0.7	0.2
Loss before income taxes and equity in net income (loss) of unconsolidated companies	(18.3)	(45.4)	(22.3)
Income tax benefit	(8.1)	(21.1)	(9.9)
Equity in net income (loss) of unconsolidated companies	(0.3)	(0.5)	0.3
Net loss	$(10.5)	$(24.8)	$(12.1)

large, and is in the process of renovating a twin-towered Washington landmark at Pennsylvania Avenue at Seventh Street NW to be its world headquarters.

Hills said the bulk of Sears' 1983 business—$60 million worth—came in the fourth quarter and could be annualized at $240 million. He predicted 33 percent growth for this year, with "a better than average chance" that sales will reach even higher, to $350 million.

Within five years, however, Hills sees Sears World Trade contributing between 10 and 20 percent of the parent company's $50 billion in sales. That amounts to sales of $5 billion to $10 billion a year, which Hills said is less important than the fat profit margins he expects the trading organization to generate.

Until recently, Sears executives have been reluctant to talk about the trading venture. "We've been trying to avoid publicity," said Hills. "Given the size of Sears, it's so easy to overblow what we are trying to do. I'm going to do my damnedest to understate everything."

There is no hint of understatement, however, in Hills's enthusiasm for the new venture. In public speeches and private conversations, he goes against "those who think this is the worst of all times to go into world trade."

"But to go into it at any other time would be suicidal," he continued. "In a gentle environment it would be insane to compete with the big Japanese companies, who take a lesser return on investment (than we'd ever take), reportedly profit margins as low as one-tenth of a percent of sales."

With trade patterns in flux as they are today, Hills added, a new competitor—such as Sears—has a chance to gain a foothold.

Exhibit 6.3

SEARS WORLD TRADE, INC., FINANCIAL CONDITION, DECEMBER 31, 1984–1985 (Millions)

	DECEMBER 31	
	1985	1984
Assets		
Cash	$ 17.2	$ 13.4
Receivables	85.6	73.6
Inventories	22.7	8.2
Property, equipment and other	20.3	18.7
Total assets	$145.8	$113.9
Liabilities		
Accounts payable and accrued expenses	73.1	58.1
Short-term borrowings	9.9	6.4
Other liabilities	7.4	7.1
Total liabilities	$ 90.4	$ 71.6
Capital	$ 55.4	$ 42.3

Exhibit 6.4

SEARS, ROEBUCK AND CO. FIVE-YEAR SUMMARY OF BUSINESS GROUP AND SEGMENT FINANCIAL DATA, 1981–1985 (Millions)

	1985	1984	1983	1982	1981
Revenues					
Sears Merchandise Group					
Merchandising	$21,549	$21,671	$20,439	$18,779	$18,229
Credit	2,098	1,894	1,404	1,158	1,040
International	2,905	2,943	3,246	730	933
Sears Merchandise Group total	26,552	26,508	25,089	20,667	20,202
Allstate Insurance Group					
Property-liability insurance	8,244	7,551	7,004	6,487	5,970
Life-health insurance	2,089	1,404	1,079	930	737
Non-insurance operations	46	34	41	42	37
Allstate Insurance Group total	10,379	8,989	8,124	7,459	6,744
Dean Witter Financial Services Group					
Securities-related operations	2,031	1,845	1,544	1,110	—
Consumer banking operations	826	651	564	487	451
Dean Witter Financial Services Group total	2,857	2,496	2,108	1,597	451
Coldwell Banker Real Estate Group	949	826	704	470	110
Sears World Trade, Inc.	236	189	79	—	—
Corporate	188	170	117	120	105
Inter-group transactions	(446)	(350)	(338)	(293)	(255)
Total	$40,715	$38,828	$35,883	$30,020	$27,357
Net income					
Sears Merchandise Group					
Merchandising	$ 447	$ 656	$ 654	$ 456	$ 352
Credit	294	243	144	18	(83)
International	25	6	(17)	(42)	16
Sears Merchandise Group total	766	905	781	432	285
Allstate Insurance Group					
Property-liability insurance	490	505	469	399	344
Life-health insurance	114	155	83	74	68
Non-insurance operations	1	1	3	2	2
Allstate Insurance Group total	605	661	555	475	414
Dean Witter Financial Services Group					
Securities-related operations	—	(45)	69	36	—
Consumer banking operations	13	12	31	(9)	(19)
Dean Witter Financial Services Group total	13	(33)	100	27	(19)
Coldwell Banker Real Estate Group	86	76	48	52	73
Sears World Trade, Inc.	(11)	(25)	(12)	—	—
Corporate	(156)	(129)	(130)	(125)	(103)
Total	$ 1,303	$ 1,455	$ 1,342	$ 861	$ 650

Exhibit 6.4 (Cont.)

Assets					
Sears Merchandise Group					
Merchandising	$ 8,240	$ 8,332	$ 6,771	$ 6,687	$ 6,507
Credit	11,887	11,825	10,312	7,889	7,390
International	1,917	1,881	2,064	544	841
Sears Merchandise Group total	22,044	22,038	19,147	15,120	14,738
Allstate Insurance Group					
Property-liability insurance	13,372	11,913	11,140	10,080	9,032
Life-health insurance	3,520	2,591	2,154	1,881	1,716
Non-insurance operations	53	49	61	57	53
Allstate Insurance Group total	16,945	14,553	13,355	12,018	10,801
Dean Witter Financial Services Group					
Securities-related operations	18,720	12,760	7,282	4,129	4,123
Consumer banking operations	7,253	6,408	5,155	4,307	4,013
Dean Witter Financial Services Group total	25,973	19,168	12,437	8,436	8,136
Coldwell Banker Real Estate Group	1,451	1,236	1,045	958	970
Sears World Trade, Inc.	146	114	101	—	—
Corporate	1,835	1,513	1,451	762	465
Inter-group eliminations and reclassifications	(1,977)	(1,549)	(1,360)	(753)	(704)
Total	$66,417	$57,073	$46,176	$36,541	$34,406

"The company's hallmark," Hills said, "will be its ability to add value to the materials it trades in"—therefore 'creating new products' and services instead of merely buying and selling commodities.

In Indonesia, for instance, Sears will help develop Indonesian forest resources and, in exchange, will gain permission to export raw logs to China, South Korea, and Japan. It will, furthermore, help China develop a pulp industry with the logs bought from Indonesia. To accomplish this, Sears will sell China the pulp mill and the logs and then peddle the pulp it produces elsewhere—producing sales and profit for Sears every step of the way.

In Mexico, where Sears is the largest retail chain, the trading arm is helping 10 manufacturers upgrade their consumer goods—first for the domestic market in Sears outlets, and then for world trade. Through Sears, Mexico will create a new group of exports to bring hard currency to its economy, which is heavily in debt.

"When we go to Mexico, the Philippines, Indonesia, Malaysia, China, what we are trying to do is add value to their country and trade off the value we create," said Hills. "We form new industries. That's why Sears, more than any other trading company, is welcomed with open arms."

Helping countries develop their export potential allows Sears World Trade to import goods ordinarily prohibited and to export raw materials, such as Indonesian logs, despite export bans.

Because many Third World countries lack the hard currency to buy goods, Sears is developing a specialty in countertrade—a massive game of barter only a giant corporation can play. It involves, for instance, taking sugar in exchange for breeding hogs, knowing that eventually the sugar can be sold. But it can take many trades before goods are converted to cash. "It lets Americans use their ingenuity," said Hills.

"If you trade throughout the world, you are going to deal with countertrade sooner or later. And that means knowing how to negotiate for the right product at the right time," said Philip Rowberg, the countertrade expert that Sears hired away from General Motors Corp.

Hills thinks the new trading company will be able to capitalize on Sears' global reputation and its network of 1,100 suppliers spread around the world. These suppliers have experience in producing consumer goods for world markets, while the Sears people understand the capabilities of international manufacturers.

Although Sears World Trade intends neither to become the supplier for its parent corporation's retail outlets, nor to restrict itself to trading in products made by its suppliers, this access gives it "an enormous edge on the world in sourcing consumer-related goods," Hills said.

Sears also advises retail chains in Third World nations and industrialized countries on marketing techniques and finding new sources of products. In Indonesia, Sears is helping spruce up stores and set up credit card operations, along with improving local manufactured products until they reach world-class status.

SEARS TRIES NEW ROLE AS WHEELER-DEALER IN WORLD TRADE[2]

From teaching Mexican companies how to make better consumer goods to developing China's capacity to produce plywood from Indonesian logs, Sears, Roebuck and Company, the world's largest retailer, has emerged as a large-scale international deal maker.

Though barely two years old, the retailer's Washington-based Sears World Trade has spread a network of operatives throughout the world in the first American challenge to the giant, well-established Japanese *sogo shosha* (trading companies) in the volatile field of international trade.

Sears is only one of several major American companies that have moved into the field of international trade in the past two years, but its plans are the most ambitious and it has gotten off to the fastest start. Among the other large corporations aiming to become a force in international trade are K mart and General Electric Co. In addition, 20 export trading companies have been formed under a law passed by Congress 18 months ago, and another 50 applications are pending in the Commerce Department.

[2]Adapted from *The Washington Post*, April 9, 1984.

At the helm of the Sears operation are some well-known Washington hands—starting with its chairman, Roderick M. Hills, head of the Securities and Exchange Commission under President Ford, and its president, Frank C. Carlucci, undersecretary of defense until he quit government in late 1982 to join Sears World Trade. Carlucci, who has held high-level positions in every administration since Richard M. Nixon's, also served as deputy director of the Central Intelligence Agency and as the number two man in the Office of Management and Budget and the former Department of Health, Education and Welfare, and was an exceptionally well-regarded ambassador to Portugal.

Hills is acutely aware of speculation that the new Sears venture is top heavy with Washington insiders but lacks the underpinnings necessary to succeed in international business. "People like to make fun of the fact that we hired high government officials," he said. "We didn't do that. What we hired was people with a wide variety of backgrounds. We hired three people, maybe four, who have a long history of success in dealing with foreign governments. That includes myself and Carlucci. That includes Thomas D. Boyatt, who runs South American operations for us."

"We've hired far more people who have experience in international banking than former government officials," Hills added.

Nonetheless, the list of Washington heavy-hitters is impressive. Carlucci's administrative assistant, for instance, is Susan Clough, who was personal secretary to President Carter. Sears World Trade's senior vice president is Curtis A. Hessler, a former assistant secretary of the treasury. Dr. Henry E. Simmons, a former HEW deputy assistant secretary for health, runs the Sears unit designed to sell health technology around the world.

Also on board are ex-IBM executive Jennifer Stockman, wife of President Reagan's budget director David Stockman; Alan Woods, a former deputy secretary of defense; and Linn Williams, former vice president and general consul of the Overseas Private Investment Corp. (OPIC). And though he downplays the role of the big names, Hills knows how important they are for Sears' business.

He spoke, for instance, of chatting with Mexican President Miguel de la Madrid Hurtado and added, "Most of the time we're invited to meet with the head of state, when our competitors can't get in to see them."

"There is not an investment banker or central banker who will not receive us," he said later. "They'll receive us because they received us before and we had something intelligent to say. It doesn't mean they agree with us."

Just in case the door-opening power of its executives isn't enough, Sears World Trade has made a series of joint ventures and corporate purchases designed to speed its growth as a major force in international business.

Sears has established a close working relationship with Japan's third largest *sogo shosha*, C. Itoh & Co., which gives the retailer the benefit of that company's well-established trading network, and formed a trading company with two Italian firms to open opportunities in that country.

In the United States, Sears set up a $35 million joint venture with First Chicago Co., a bank holding corporation that is the parent of First National Bank of Chicago, and has strong ties to businesses in the Midwest. First Chicago's 650 account specialists are being trained to keep their eyes peeled for potential business opportunities for Sears World Trade.

HILLS OUT AS CHAIRMAN OF SEARS WORLD TRADE[3]

Roderick M. Hills resigned today as chairman of Sears World Trade, Inc., just a few hours before he was scheduled to meet with financial analysts and reporters for a major presentation. Hills's remarks for Sears' annual outlook session had already been printed when it was announced he was stepping down as head of Sears' Washington-based trading company. His speech instead was delivered by Richard M. Jones, vice chairman and chief financial officer of the firm, who will assume Hills's duties.

Sears' chairman, Edward R. Telling, disclosed that Hills will return to his old law firm of Latham, Watkins and Hills, where he had been a partner from 1978 to 1982 before joining the new Sears subsidiary.

The announcement of Hills's departure came as a surprise to some analysts at the meeting and provoked speculation that he had been ousted.

Started two years ago, Sears World Trade reported a loss of $4.2 million on revenues of $40.7 million for the first three months of this year. The loss was more than three times that incurred for the same period a year ago, when revenue was $4.3 million and losses were $1.2 million.

Despite the higher losses, Telling told the analysts that the company is still very committed to the subsidiary. "We're prepared to put sizable seed money in for a long period of time to make this venture work."

SEARS WORLD TRADE STARTS BIG CUTBACK[4]

Sears World Trade, Inc., designed to be Sears, Roebuck and Company's challenge to world domination by Japanese traders, has begun a major staff cutback by laying off about 100 to 150 of its employees, company officials confirmed yesterday.

The layoffs—equal to about 10 percent of the company's work force—come just three months after the subsidiary's chairman, Roderick M. Hills, abruptly left and was replaced by Sears Roebuck's vice chairman and chief financial officer, Richard M. Jones. Company officials said the layoffs followed an intensive reevaluation of the company and reflect a desire to cut expenses, which many Sears officials privately felt had grown out of hand when the two-year-old company was starting.

For the first half of this year, the Sears subsidiary lost $10.1 million—more than three times the losses incurred during the same time period of 1983, when it lost

[3]Adapted from *The Washington Post*, April 25, 1984.
[4]Adapted from *The Washington Post*, August 1, 1984.

$3.3 million. Revenue, on the other hand, had quintupled from $12 million for the first half of last year to $73.8 million for the same period this year.

CARLUCCI NAMED CHAIRMAN OF SEARS TRADE UNIT[5]

Sears, Roebuck and Company, reaffirming a directional shift for its international trading subsidiary, yesterday named Frank C. Carlucci to be chairman and chief executive of the Washington-based Sears World Trade, Inc.

Carlucci will take over the post held until recently by Roderick M. Hills.

Sears, Roebuck Chairman Edward R. Telling told *Washington Post* reporters and editors earlier this week that a practice of "posturizing . . . and building expectations beyond all reason" at Sears World Trade led the parent company to shake up management.

Carlucci is expected to bring the subsidiary back in line with the company's original expectations, Sears officials said yesterday.

Telling said it was never his intention to make the Sears unit America's answer to Japanese trading companies, known for their mastery of the intricacies of international world trade. Hills, on the other hand, had said he wanted the subsidiary not only to export and import goods but also to arrange for the development and manufacturing of goods, particularly in the Far East.

However, Telling made it clear that he envisions a more limited role for the two-year-old Sears World Trade.

"We never intended to be a Japanese trading company," Telling said in a lunch with *Post* reporters and editors earlier this week. Rather, Telling said, with Carlucci's appointment, the company will return to "where we started. It's a general trading company" that will be a distributor of consumer goods, including light industrial products such as electric drills and processed food.

"Forget Asia, the Pacific Basin, all these exotic parts of the world," Telling said. "There's a tremendous amount of food imports into this country . . . We don't know anyone who has a better distribution system than we do."

Telling said he hoped Sears would find foreign sources for its suppliers. "We have a source structure at Sears . . . that no one has."

Noting that the largest general trader in the world does only $2 billion of business, Telling said Sears is a long way from that level of business. "If it takes 10 to 15 years to be a meaningful player, then we will be patient."

Without ever mentioning Hills's name, Telling discussed why he believed it was necessary to replace the former chairman of the Securities and Exchange Commission. "For a period of time, for whatever reason, someone was stating goals or possibilities that would make one blink. The phone would ring at Sears headquarters in Chicago the next day, but it had already made *The Washington Post*."

Trade officials who have dealt with both Hills and Carlucci said Carlucci will

[5]Adapted from *The Washington Post*, September 20, 1984.

make a better team player. "Hills was a flamboyant idea man trying to create a new world in trade," one official said. "Carlucci's history and career, on the other hand, make it clear he is an excellent team player."

SEARS NAMES BRENNAN TO NO. 2 POST[6]

Sears, Roebuck and Company yesterday named Edward A. Brennan as its new president and chief operating officer.

The selection of Brennan—who until yesterday was head of the Sears Merchandise Group—ended months of speculation over who would win the company's number two spot and, most likely, take over the top post of chairman late next year when its current chairman, Edward R. Telling, is scheduled to retire.

"This signals a new era for Sears," the nation's largest retailer, said John S. Landschulz, financial analyst with the Chicago firm of Mesirow & Co.

A dynamic merchandiser who nearly has tripled the sagging retail division's profits since he took over the merchandise group in 1980, Brennan had been considered the frontrunner for the presidency. The other two candidates were Donald F. Craib, Jr., chairman of Sears' Allstate Insurance Group, and Richard M. Jones, Sears' vice chairman and chief financial officer.

Financial analysts considered Brennan the most assertive of the candidates and the most inclined to continue the aggressive expansion policy charted by Telling. Under that policy, Sears has transformed itself from the nation's largest retailer into an all-round service company, selling real estate under its Coldwell Banker subsidiary and offering a host of financial packages under Dean Witter Reynolds, Inc., which it purchased in 1982. Additionally, Sears has launched Sears World Trade, Inc., which is designed to be the company's answer to Japanese trading companies.

Even though Dean Witter and the trading subsidiary have incurred substantial losses—so much so that the trading company just trimmed 150 employees from its 1,000 member staff—Telling has said he remains committed to Sears' diversification.

Financial analysts predicted Brennan will continue to support these ventures aggressively. Yet, given Brennan's strong background in retailing—he worked in that division of Sears for 27 years—he probably will place more emphasis on the merchandise group than on the new financial services.

SEARS WORLD TRADE TO ACQUIRE 75 PERCENT OF TRADING FIRM[7]

Sears World Trade, Inc., seeking to acquire a large marketing base in Europe and Asia, announced Friday that it has reached a tentative agreement to buy 75 percent of the European, North American, and East Asian trading operations of Hagemeyer, N.V., a large, general trading company with headquarters in the Netherlands.

Sears World Trade also said it is proposing to acquire a 20 percent stake in the remaining operations of Hagemeyer, including its Southeast Asian trading operations.

[6]Adapted from *The Washington Post*, August 15, 1985.
[7]Adapted from *The Washington Post*, September 9, 1985.

"This will give us the operational capability we need" to become a full-fledged trading company that can distribute consumer products worldwide, said Frank C. Carlucci, chairman and chief executive officer.

"At Sears World Trade, we have good sourcing and product capability and good specialized skills, such as consulting, but we don't have a distribution network on the ground, complete with customer base. This completes the final equation for us," he said.

Sears officials said it would have been difficult for the company to achieve the same distribution network from scratch.

The 80-year-old Hagemeyer company distributes brand-name consumer goods worldwide, including items made by Polaroid, Panasonic, Triumph, Christian Dior and Olympus. Company revenue totaled $840 million last year.

Carlucci noted that the acquisition is a good fit for the money-losing Sears World Trade. The company has been trying to reposition itself from an intricate international trading company—arranging the development and manufacturing of goods as well as selling them—into a general trading company that primarily distributes consumer goods here and abroad.

The company has come a long way in "cutting our losses," Carlucci said. However, he noted the company still has a way to go before being profitable. For the first half of the year, Sears World Trade lost $4.9 million on revenue of $105 million.

The acquisition, which is estimated to cost about $25 million, is expected to be completed over the next several months.

SEARS TRADE TAKES ON A SMALLER CHUNK OF THE WORLD; $25 MILLION ACQUISITION BOOSTS COMPANY'S HOPES[8]

In 1894, on the cover of one of its earliest catalogs, Sears, Roebuck and Company proclaimed: "Our trade reaches around the world."

Today, 91 years later, the nation's largest retailer seems more determined than ever to make the slogan come true through its three-year-old Washington-based subsidiary, Sears World Trade, Inc.

Despite substantial start-up problems and great skepticism in the financial community, the so-far-unprofitable subsidiary appears committed to becoming a serious player in the increasingly competitive and risky international trading market.

The latest sign of that commitment came only a month ago, when the company announced it had agreed to buy an 80-year-old European and East Asian trading company, Hagemeyer, N.V., for $25 million.

Despite the more than $40 million in losses Sears World has incurred in the past three years, "we believe it's a viable concept, and we will continue to pursue it. . . . It's an important part of the family of companies in Sears, Roebuck," Jones said.

"We are quite confident we're on the right course," added Sears World chairman Frank Carlucci last week in a rare interview. Given Sears World's initial troubles—which led to the resignation of its first chairman, Roderick M. Hills, 18 months

[8]Adapted from *The Washington Post*, October 14, 1985.

ago—Carlucci and other top executives have been reluctant to talk about the subsidiary and its future.

But now, confident that the Hagemeyer acquisition has put Sears World on a surer path to success, officials are beginning to speak out.

Grand Plans Scaled Back

Initially, Sears World set out to be the American challenger to world domination by Japanese traders. It drew up intricate plans to become a full-fledged international trading company—one that could arrange the financing, development, manufacturing, and sale of a wide array of goods, often through Sears, Roebuck and its subsidiaries.

But those grandiose plans have been dramatically scaled back. Now Sears World's goal, first and foremost, is to be a trader of the type of consumer goods for which Sears, Roebuck is known. "We were involved in too many activities and built a cost structure that couldn't be supported by revenues in the immediate foreseeable future," Carlucci said. "We needed to focus down on what we could do best."

No longer a part of Sears World's plans are projects to import and export high-technology equipment, such as computers or components for computers. Also dropped was the goal of becoming a major international trader in health care products, such as pharmaceuticals, chemicals and hospital supplies. Under this scenario, Sears World had planned, among other things, to equip foreign hospitals with U.S.-made goods.

Similarly, the company has scaled back its global focus; now it is centering most of its attention on Europe, North America, and Asia.

Today, Carlucci said, "we are a consumer goods company. Once we have done that, we can move into other areas."

Trading on Sears' Strengths

Along with the subsidiary's president, Charles F. Moran—a long-time Sears employee who has been instrumental in developing corporate strategy—and Sears, Roebuck vice chairman Jones, Carlucci has overseen the trading company's restructuring.

The subsidiary should trade on Sears' strengths, Carlucci said. Through contracts with worldwide manufacturers to make products for Sears, the company "has a unique sourcing capability, a very large physical distribution system, and an unparalleled skill in designing and developing a product," he said.

Carlucci bristled at the description of Sears World as a trading company. "It is a bit of a misnomer. It conjures up a bunch of people sitting around a table saying, 'I'll sell you this at $20.' 'No, I'll bid $22.'"

Rather, Carlucci said, "We're in the process of structuring long-term relationships between buyer and seller where we would bring our technical and physical skills to bear. That's very different from a traditional image of a trading company."

Carlucci declined to name the specific companies doing business with Sears World. But he willingly gave examples of the types of projects under way.

For the past three years, for instance, Sears World has been handling all the imports for a U.S. company that sells athletic footwear. Venture capital for the same company was provided by Sears World's sister firms, Allstate Insurance Co. and Dean Witter Financial Services Group. The trading arm then supplied a letter of credit for financing and import services, including cargo management, document handling, custom clearance, and warehousing. Sears says this is now one of the fastest-growing shoe companies in the country.

In another example, a Sears World electronics engineer, observing that Japan would make a good market for computer software, translated some programs into Japanese; the trading company's Tokyo office began distributing the product.

Meanwhile, Sears World has been buying microwave ovens in Japan and distributing them in England through a retailer. Sears World provides the retailer "with the selling expertise accumulated by Sears, who is the number one volume seller of microwave ovens in the United States," a corporate said.

In a countertrade agreement with Brazil, Sears has been exporting home furnishings products from Brazil, earning export credits that it is passing on, in turn, to a separate company that is importing telecommunications equipment into Brazil.

Although Sears World is focusing most of its attention on consumer goods, it also has been looking at other areas.

One of those areas involves trading light industrial goods, such as electrical and plumbing components and electronics. For example, Sears World has bought radio speakers for a large automotive company in the United States.

"We can do it more readily than they can," Carlucci said, noting Sears, Roebuck's already large purchases of radio speakers.

Sears World is also experimenting with importing processed food, such as tomato paste, canned tuna, and pineapple, and selling it to food brokers in the United States under a Sears World label. "There are a lot of small brokers out there," Carlucci said. As more food is purchased from abroad, "there will be a need for someone to provide economies of scale, so we would expect that area to grow."

Despite its reduction in scope, Sears World is not yet profitable, having lost $4.9 million on revenue of $105 million during the first half of 1985. Although this year's loss was less than half the $10.1 million loss incurred during the first six months of 1984, many financial analysts—especially those who follow retailing companies—are still very skeptical of Sears World.

"I think they're klutzes," said Edward Weller of E. F. Hutton Group, Inc. "I don't know why they want to be in the business."

"I hope it's going to go away," said Walter F. Loeb of Morgan Stanley & Co. "It should be an adjunct to the merchandising group, not a separate entity . . . which is fraught with a lot of politics. I'm not sure that politics is what Sears understands."

International trade experts, on the other hand, praise Sears for its ambitious efforts.

"This is one of the first real trading companies this country has," said Ray A. Goldberg, a professor of agriculture and business at Harvard Graduate School of Business. "This is good for Sears and the country as a whole. . . . Despite their losses, it's not too optimistic to expect them to be in the black next year," he predicted.

"Sears is doing something very difficult," said David Fredericks, a principal and

U.S. managing director for Fredericks, Michael & Co., a New York consulting and merchant banking firm for traders.

"I applaud them for trying to enter the toughest business in the world. It is rapidly building a trading organization from scratch so it can be an influential trading company in the international world of trade. It is a bold task. If anybody can succeed, they can. They have the financial muscle and a great sourcing operation—Sears sources probably more than any other operation in the world."

Hagemeyer Deal Is Critical

The Hagemeyer acquisition is critical to the company's future, Fredericks added. "It enables them to learn to distribute outside the United States and learn about commodities trading slowly."

Not only is Hagemeyer a large distributor of consumer goods, it is also the third largest distributor of coffee in the world.

According to Carlucci, that fact is coincidental to the acquisition, which should be completed at the end of the year. "We're not ready yet to get into the commodity business," he said.

Despite his praise for Sears World, Fredericks faults Sears for locating the trading subsidiary in Washington. "No trader of any consequence is in Washington. They are located in New York or Chicago."

Carlucci has heard that criticism before. Nonetheless, he is adamant that the company stay in Washington. "We have a decided advantage here," he said, citing the proximity of embassies, the State Department, and numerous international organizations. And, he adds, "on a nice day, you can get into New York faster than most commuters."

7

CORMARK AND THE ONTARIO PSYCHIATRIC ASSOCIATION (A)

On January 25, 1988, Ms. Terry Green, a research associate with Cormark Communications, Inc., in London, Ontario, agreed to prepare a research proposal for the Ontario Psychiatric Association (OPA).* The OPA was about to launch a province-wide public relations campaign, and initial research was needed to describe the attitudes of the general public toward psychiatry and psychiatrists. Cormark's research proposal was to be reviewed by the OPA in less than three weeks.

THE OPA'S PUBLIC RELATIONS CAMPAIGN

The OPA was founded in 1956, with an initial membership of about 200. By 1988 its membership numbered 801, which constituted just over 75 percent of Ontario's 1,050 psychiatrists. Its activities included developing the association's role in continuing education and advocating for its patients on mental health issues. These activities were governed by an elected council, an executive, and several permanent

---

*This case was prepared by David Large under the supervision of Assistant Professor Julia Bristor. It is intended to serve as a basis for class discussion rather than as an illustration of either effective or ineffective management.
Copyright © 1988. The School of Business Administration, the University of Western Ontario.

committees; ad hoc committees, appointed as required by the executive, augmented the elected bodies.

In the first quarter of 1987, the OPA's Executive Committee decided to launch a province-wide public relations campaign directed at Ontario's 9 million residents. In April the committee circulated a questionnaire to its membership requesting feedback on several suggested strategies for the campaign. Seventy-five percent of the 156 respondents felt that the OPA should employ the services of a communications firm to convey the OPA's objectives.

In October, an OPA ad hoc committee on media issues acted on this endorsement, investigated several communications organizations, and chose to work with Cormark. Cormark was established in 1978, and was one of the city's leading full-service communications agencies. The firm was able to provide a wide range of services, including research, public relations, advertising, and sales promotion. Cormark's staff of 24 included writers, artists, a public relations specialist, a media planner, and an account group. Ms. Green had worked with Cormark as a research associate for the past seven years.

Cormark and the OPA regarded the development, implementation, and monitoring of a public relations program as a seven-step process, involving

1. specification of a target audience, or sequence of target audiences to be addressed over time
2. determination of the *real* attitudes of the target audience toward psychiatry and psychiatrists
3. determination of the *desired* attitudes of the target audience from the point of view of the OPA
4. setting of public relations objectives based on achieving congruence between the real and desired attitudes
5. communication of these objectives and supporting rationale to the OPA membership
6. development and implemention of an appropriate, professionally guided, public relations campaign
7. monitoring, evaluation of, and ongoing adjustment of the program

In terms of the first step, Cormark and the OPA agreed that the target audience—in the short term—should be "the general public," since the OPA's clientele was drawn from the general population of the province. On January 25, Ms. Green was asked to prepare a research proposal that would satisfy the requirements of the second step of the process. The proposal was to be delivered to the OPA on February 12; if it were approved, the deadline for the completion of the actual research would be sometime late in the summer of 1988. The budget was to be approximately $20,000.

RESEARCH DESIGN

The purpose of Cormark's research was to provide the members of the OPA with a descriptive status report on the attitudes of the Ontario public toward psychiatry in general and psychiatrists in particular. Except for this stated purpose, the OPA had not provided any further guidelines regarding particular objectives. These were to be discussed at the presentation of the research proposal. The OPA was new to the concept of preparing for a public relations campaign and was seeking guidance in this respect.

Ms. Green had considerable experience in the design of attitude surveys. For example, she had recently completed a study to determine the attitudes of producers toward a major food processing company; in that project, eight focus groups in four locations throughout Ontario were used. Based on early discussions with the OPA, a Cormark executive felt that such groups might be an appropriate methodology for the current problem. A qualitative technique, however, was by no means the only alternative. Ms. Green had successfully used quantitative techniques in other attitude surveys; a nearly completed attitude survey for a tax preparation firm had involved a survey of 400 people in the firm's target market.

Consequently, in contemplating the research design challenge of the OPA study, Ms. Green was considering both qualitative and quantitative techniques, including the following:

Qualitative Techniques

1. Five-person minifocus groups
2. Ten-person focus groups
3. Personal in-depth interviews

Quantitative Techniques

4. Telephone survey
5. Shopping mall survey
6. House-to-house survey
7. Mail survey
8. Mail panel
9. Mail omnibus
10. Telephone omnibus

The first seven options were normally done in-house, but subcontracts were possible if the work was geographically distant. Between these options, out-of-pocket costs and response rates varied widely. Minigroups and focus groups, which were often used in attitude studies, required about $70 per participant to cover the in-house costs of recruitment, cash incentives, room rental, and refreshments. In-house expenses for personal in-depth interviews were approximately the same. Telephone surveys, with refusal rates typically in the range of 10–40 percent, averaged about $12–15 plus long-distance charges for a 25-minute interview. A shopping mall survey would cost about 30 percent more than a phone survey, a house-to-house survey at least double plus transportation. Finally, because of expected response rates of only 5 percent or so, the effective out-of-pocket cost of a mail survey would be about $25–30 per respondent. For all the options described, subcontract costs would be significantly greater.

The last three options could be done only by subcontract with a few of the larger marketing research corporations, and again costs varied. For about $340 per closed-ended question, a custom-designed mail panel questionnaire could be sent to 1,000 Ontario adults, with tabulations and final reports to be returned to Cormark by July 31. The price per question would rise to $600 for a 2,000-member mailing, and the report date would slip to August 31; open-ended questions commanded a 50 percent premium in either case. Panel response rates for any given mailing were typically 75 percent. Quoted prices for a mail or telephone omnibus were nearly double those of the mail panel for an equivalent sample size, but service was available on a monthly or quarterly basis, and the number of responses was guaranteed.

CONCLUSION

The OPA was expecting a research proposal for step 2 from Cormark on February 12. Research objectives and budget were not the only design considerations. Ms. Green recognized both the sensitive nature of the subject material, and the highly trained and sophisticated nature of the audience of the research (i.e., the psychiatrists themselves). Further, the OPA had suggested that attitudes in the general public might vary with age, background, and prior experience with psychiatry. The complexity of these issues rendered the research design choice a difficult one.

8

CORMARK AND THE ONTARIO PSYCHIATRIC ASSOCIATION (B)

Ms. Terry Green reviewed the marketing research report that she had just completed for the Ontario Psychiatric Association on May 3, 1988.* The Phase 1 report contained the results from 15 in-depth interviews that had been conducted by Ms. Green in March, in London, Ontario. Eight themes had emerged about the public's attitudes toward psychiatry and psychiatrists; these themes would now serve as the framework for designing a Phase 2 questionnaire to be mailed to 1,000 members of an Ontario mail panel. The manager of the panel mailout needed a polished questionnaire within two weeks.

EVOLUTION OF THE RESEARCH PROGRAM

Late in 1987, the Ontario Psychiatric Association (OPA) engaged Cormark Communications, Inc., to begin a provincewide public relations campaign. On January 25, 1988, Ms. Green, a Cormark research associate, was asked to prepare a proposal for

---

*This case was prepared by David Large under the supervision of Assistant Professor Julia Bristor. It is intended to serve as a basis for class discussion rather than as an illustration of either effective or ineffective management.
Copyright © 1988. The School of Business Administration, the University of Western Ontario.

research directed at the discovery of existing attitudes of the Ontario general public toward psychiatry and psychiatrists.

After careful consideration of the purpose of the research, its design constraints, and many design options [see Cormark and the Ontario Psychiatric Association (A)], Ms. Green proposed a two-phase research strategy:

Phase 1: qualitative research, consisting of a minimum of 15 depth interviews, in order to identify issues relevant to the general public's perception of psychiatry and psychiatrists

Phase 2: quantitative research, consisting of the development of a survey questionnaire based on Phase 1 issues and its administration to a mail panel of 2,000 Ontario residents

This proposal was submitted by Cormark to the OPA on February 15 (Exhibit 8.1). It was accepted in its entirety by the OPA, except that the size of the mailing was to be reduced from 2,000 to 1,000. The OPA felt that the slight loss of statistical precision was more than offset by savings in cost and schedule. The research was to be completed no later than August 31, 1988, and total billings were not to exceed $20,000.

Exhibit 8.1

CORMARK AND THE ONTARIO PSYCHIATRIC ASSOCIATION (B)
RESEARCH PROPOSAL

PROPOSAL FOR RESEARCH INTO PUBLIC ATTITUDES
TOWARD PSYCHIATRY

Prepared for: Ontario Psychiatric Association
Prepared by: Cormark Communications, Inc.
Date: February 15, 1988

BACKGROUND AND OBJECTIVES

The Ontario Psychiatric Association (OPA) is interested in undertaking a public relations campaign. As the OPA ad hoc committee on media issues has already determined, development of a successful public relations program will involve the following steps:

1. Choice of a target audience, or sequence of target audiences, to be addressed over time
2. Determination of the target audience's *real* and *desired* (from point of view of OPA) attitudes toward psychiatry and psychiatrists
3. Based on degree of congruence of (1) and (2), setting of *public relations objectives*

Exhibit 8.1 (Cont.)

4. Communication of above objectives and supporting rationale to OPA membership
5. Development and implementation of an appropriate, professionally guided, public relations program
6. Evaluation and consequent adjustment of the program

The OPA has identified a number of relevant target audiences for its public relations efforts; these include the media, legislators, the medical community, and the general public. At this stage, a decision has been made to focus on the general public as a primary target audience. Consequently, the OPA plans to commission research which will

investigate, at a general level, the views and attitudes of the Ontario public with respect to psychiatry and psychiatrists.

At the conclusion of the research, Cormark will be in a position to present the OPA with a clear, objective, and statistically valid asessment of how psychiatry and psychiatrists are perceived by the identified target audience: the public of Ontario. The OPA will then be unified in its perception of the situation and will have a sound basis for development of a communications program.

CONSIDERATIONS

The choice of research methodology was strongly influenced by three factors:

1. For many people, psychiatry will be a sensitive subject. Efforts were made to choose the methodology that would be least subject to interviewer bias and most likely to secure well-considered, honest responses. Moreover, emphasis was placed on developing a research vehicle that would "ask the right questions," that is, questions that would address the relevant issues in a clear and unambiguous manner.
2. There probably will be differences in attitude among respondents; for example, differences might emerge by age group, background, or prior personal experience with psychiatry. The research should capture such differences if, indeed, they do exist.
3. The OPA will be using the research as a basis for developing its public relations program. Therefore, the research must be credible and statistically extensible to the population.

PROPOSED RESEARCH METHODOLOGY

A two-part methodology is proposed. Phase 1 will consist of qualitative research directed toward development of the questionnaire which will be used in Phase 2, the quantitative portion of the study.

Exhibit 8.1 (Cont.)

Phase 1

The primary researcher will conduct a minimum of 15 in-depth interviews, in order to identify the relevant issues relating to the public's impression of psychiatrists and psychiatry. General topic areas for discussion will include (1) understanding of the role and training of psychiatrists (versus other counselors), (2) attitudes toward mental health, (3) views of psychiatrists' capability/ability to help, and (4) perceptions of the types of problems which psychiatrists do/should deal with. A general interviewing guide will be prepared at the outset of Phase 1; input and—subsequently—approval will be sought from the OPA. During Phase 1, OPA will also be asked to provide any relevant past research relating to the public perception of psychiatry; this will be reviewed by Cormark. At the conclusion of Phase 1, Cormark will present a draft questionnaire to be used in the quantitative phase of the study. A relatively short questionnaire, consisting of up to 15 closed-ended questions, has been budgeted for.

Phase 2

A mail panel has been chosen as the most appropriate vehicle for administration of the questionnaire. The sample size of 1,500 (achieved through 75 percent return on a mailing of approximately 2,000) allows for good statistical validity of results. In addition, the mail panel approach offers the following advantages:

- No interviewer bias.
- Confidentiality—and *perception* of confidentiality—of response for the participant.
- Completion of questionnaire within the home at the respondent's leisure.
- Anonymity; it is clearly a research study, with respondents chosen by virtue of their interest in participating in research (there is no possibility of respondents feeling that their names have been released by their doctors, for example).
- Flexibility to include teenagers as well as appropriate representation of age groups as per the demographic patterns of the province.
- Coverage of the entire province, again in keeping with demographics (about a third of respondents for Toronto, for example, and a quarter from areas with less than 5,000 population).

At the conclusion of Phase 2, OPA will be provided with computer tabulations of responses (by demographic variable) as well as a written and verbal interpretive report. Phase 1 will require one month to complete, while Phase 2 will require two months. This timing depends upon OPA's ability to provide input in a timely manner.

Phase 1 Research

On March 21 and 22, Ms. Green conducted 15 in-depth interviews. The respondents, representing a range of ages, social situations, and occupations, had been recruited from a central file of previous focus group participants. Each interview followed the same discussion guide (Exhibit 8.2), but there was some degree of freedom for a person to discuss any topic in more detail. Ms. Green's summary report for Phase 1 was submitted by Cormark to the OPA on May 3 (Exhibit 8.3).

Phase 2 Research

In Phase 2, the eight attitude themes discovered in the Phase 1 research would be explored by a questionnaire mailed to 1,000 members of an Ontario panel. In order to gain opinions from a variety of age groups, families receiving the questionnaire would be instructed to have it completed by the person in the home whose birthday was nearest.

Exhibit 8.2

CORMARK AND THE ONTARIO PSYCHIATRIC ASSOCIATION (B)
QUALITATIVE METHODOLOGY AND DISCUSSION GUIDE

METHODOLOGY FOR QUALITATIVE INVESTIGATION OF PUBLIC ATTITUDES TOWARD PSYCHIATRY

1. Purpose

The primary purpose of the qualitative investigation was to identify the relevant issues relating to the public's perception of psychiatrists and psychiatry.

2. Methodology

Fifteen in-depth interviews were conducted by Terry Green on March 21 and 22. Recruiting was done utilizing our central file of focus group respondents, and an attempt was made to represent a range of ages, social situations, and occupations. Respondents included

- a retired general manager of an insurance company who was 79 years of age
- a middle-aged male teacher
- a young (midtwenties) and an older (midfifties) housewife
- a young man (early twenties) in a minimum wage job
- a male and a female high school student

Exhibit 8.2 (Cont.)

- a female nurse
- a clergyman
- an unemployed woman involved in a part-time retraining course

The respondents were paid $15 for participating in the interviews which lasted approximately 30 minutes (but ranged from 20 minutes to 2 hours). The discussion guide that follows was utilized.

3. Discussion Guide

Introduction: "Our company has been hired to do a large-scale survey to determine the attitudes of the Ontario public toward mental health. Before we design the questionnaire which will be used for that survey, we are talking to some people about mental health. These discussions will help us to decide what sort of questions we should be asking in our larger survey."

Question areas

- Just to start off, how do you define mental health? What do you think of as mental health problems? Do you feel that mental health problems are more prevalent today? Or more "talked about"?
- What are the sources of help for people with mental health problems? Do you feel that people are more willing/more apt to seek professional help for their mental health problems today?
- Probe for differences between psychologists and psychiatrists. Do you have an idea how they differ? Training? Type of problems they deal with? Cost? Effectiveness?
- Thinking of psychiatrists, specifically, what sort of problems do you feel that psychiatrists deal with? What proportion of people receiving psychiatric care do you feel are in hospital? How do you feel that psychiatrists treat people? Drugs? Do you feel that drugs are prescribed too readily? "Talk?" In what way is the psychiatrist's "talking" effective? How have you developed your views of what is involved in psychiatric treatment? Are you quite sure about "what would go on," or is it a bit of a mystery to you?
- Do you feel that psychiatrists really do help people? Are people "cured"? Or do they come back for more treatment? What would happen to these people if they hadn't received help? Are the people who see psychiatrists "ill"?
- What kind of people see psychiatrists? Why? Why do you have this view? How do people know when to see a psychiatrist? Or do they?
- What are the positive aspects of seeing a psychiatrist? And the negatives? Is there a "social stigma" involved with seeing a psychiatrist? Why? Would you change your opinion of a person if you learned that they were seeing a psychiatrist? And do you feel that most people would change their opinion? Would someone be well advised to tell his or her employer that he or she was seeing a psychiatrist? Would this affect the person's career?

Exhibit 8.2 (Cont.)

- How would you, personally, react if your family doctor suggested that you see a psychiatrist?
- Do you feel that people are *afraid* of going to see a psychiatrist? Why? Is there a fear of institutionalization? Forms of treatment that the patient would not want? Any other fears?
- How do psychiatrists compare to other doctors? Why would a doctor choose to specialize in psychiatry? Would psychiatrists be more or less clever than other doctors? Is psychiatry more difficult or demanding?
- What do you feel psychiatrists are like *as people*? What do they look like? Would you trust them? Are they well adjusted, in terms of their own lives? Do they have more or fewer problems, compared to other people?

Exhibit 8.3

CORMARK AND THE ONTARIO PSYCHIATRIC ASSOCIATION (B)
PHASE 1 SUMMARY REPORT

REPORT ON QUALITATIVE INVESTIGATION
INTO THE PUBLIC PERCEPTION OF PSYCHIATRY

Prepared for: Ontario Psychiatric Association
Prepared by: Cormark Communications, Inc.
Date: May 3, 1988

EXECUTIVE SUMMARY

The Ontario Psychiatric Association has commissioned Cormark to conduct a large-scale quantitative study into the attitudes of the Ontario public toward psychiatrists and psychiatry. To provide guidance for the development of the instrument which will be used in this quantitative study, qualitative research was conducted. On the basis of the qualitative investigation, it is recommended that the following issues be addressed in the quantitative phase:

1. A backdrop: public perception of mental health problems in 1988.
2. Psychiatrists versus psychologists: a blurry distinction?
3. *Who* seeks psychiatric help: an upper class luxury?
4. How do psychiatrists treat: does any of it *really* help?
5. The "stigma": does it still exist?
6. Fear of psychiatry: is it internal, external, or a nonissue?
7. Personal acceptance of psychiatry: is it good, but only for other people?
8. Psychiatrists as people: how are they regarded?

Exhibit 8.3 (Cont.)

REPORT ON QUALITATIVE INVESTIGATION INTO THE PUBLIC PERCEPTION OF PSYCHIATRY

1. A Backdrop: Public Perception of Mental Health Problems in 1988

The participants in the qualitative research generally had a broad-based view of mental health problems and frequently related their definition of a person's mental health to that person's ability to function in society. Some of the participants distinguished between physically based and emotionally based mental health problems. For most, emotionally based problems were regarded as illness, just as were the physically based problems. Overall, there was an impression that mental health problems were more prevalent today than in the past, say, 20 years ago. Likewise, there was an impression that the proportion of the population seeking some type of help for mental health problems was higher today than in the past. While most of the participants seemed to find these trends acceptable, or even positive, a minority felt that they reflected "a weakness" in today's society. Proponents of this point of view seemed to feel that most people who sought psychiatric help were not "really" ill and could have overcome their problems on their own by simply exercising some strength of character.

> I've seen people who all they needed was a good kick in the pants. They didn't need a psychiatrist at all. They were just spoiled. Other people spoiled them and they in turn spoiled themselves.

> It's our society. We live in an age where everyone feels they have to turn to someone for help.

At the extreme, this logic was developed to the point of suggesting that psychiatric treatment was being used as a ploy which enabled the patient to avoid resolving his or her problems rather than as a positive step.

> They go [to a psychiatrist] to bail them out of the realities by giving them a crutch to lean on. In other words "I'm under the care of a psychiatrist, so therefore you've got to be nice to me because I'm really not myself."

2. Psychiatrists versus Psychologists: A Blurry Distinction?

When asked to identify sources of help for mental health problems, the respondents gave a wide variety of answers ranging from family and friends to social workers or shelters and, finally, psychologists and/or psychiatrists. The distinction between psychiatrists and psychologists was, indeed, blurry. Some participants had no idea of the differences and appeared to

Exhibit 8.3 (Cont.)

have little knowledge of the training required for either profession. At least one respondent had clearly confused the two:

> Oh, the psychologist: he's the one that's the doctor. I think the psychologists would handle the tougher problems.

Others attempted to draw the line between psychologists and psychiatrists on the basis of *who* they treated, or *how* they treated.

> I don't really know the difference, to tell you the truth. Maybe psychologists are for children and psychiatrists for adults.

> Psychiatrists probably deal more into your past than psychologists.

Interestingly, a few of the participants were well aware of the differences between psychologists and psychiatrists and had developed the opinion that psychologists were generally more effective. This view was articulated by two of its proponents:

> A relationship with a psychiatrist would be based more on talk than activities and actions, and I think activities and actions are probably more important than conversation . . . I think probably the less professional, the more successful. They meet the immediate need.

> Psychologists . . . I think they're closer to the patient.

3. Who Seeks Psychiatric Help: An Upper-Class Luxury?

The majority of the participants seemed to feel that the propensity to see a psychiatrist varied with socioeconomic level:

> I think psychiatrists would more likely end up with people from the higher socioeconomic groups.

In some cases, the participants indicated that the people in the higher socioeconomic classes had "more time to think about themselves" and, consequently, a greater tendency to feel that they had problems:

> Stereotype of a psychiatrist is an image of someone dealing with somebody else who is very intelligent as well but is overstressed for some reason and is trying to get to the bottom of their problem or is self indulgent.

In other cases, the participants suggested that the lower socioeconomic groups had an equal—or even greater—incidence of mental health problems but a tendency to leave them untreated until they became debilitating.

Exhibit 8.3 (Cont.)

> Mental health, a lot of times, is tied in with education and financial ability. You can almost tell where people are, from an income point of view by what help they seek when they are mentally ill. The upper class goes to a psychiatrist—or M.D.—the poor people end up in your Ontario hospitals.

Indeed, the generalization that more upper-class people saw psychiatrists seemed to refer to the population of people who had chosen to seek psychiatric care on a private basis rather than to the population which was hospitalized. There was a large variation in opinion as to the relative proportion of psychiatric patients which was hospitalized.

The participants' definitions of socioeconomic class were tied not only to income, but also to education. There was a tendency to assume that the two factors were correlated, although a couple of the more thoughtful participants suggested that education was, in their opinion, the more significant determinant of whether a person would tend to see a psychiatrist. That is, they felt that a well-educated person in a lower-income range would be apt to seek psychiatric help for a mental health problem, while a less educated person in the same class would not.

> middle and upper income go more, for sure. Lower income wouldn't even think of it. . . . The lesser educated might still think there's a stigma.

Some of the participants indicated that psychiatric care resulted in a high out-of-pocket cost to the patient, while others felt that the cost of such care was covered. Those who felt that psychiatric care was expensive were, not surprisingly, much more likely to describe psychiatric care as a "luxury for the wealthy":

> The upper socioeconomic levels are much more prone to go to a psychiatrist than the lower. You have to be able to afford to say you have a problem.

4. How Do Psychiatrists Treat: Does Any of It Really Help?

The participants all had opinions about the nature of psychiatric treatment and views as to its effectiveness. In a minority of cases, these attitudes were based on direct personal experience, more often, however, they had been acquired indirectly through friends or even Ann Landers, popular magazines, and television!

> I relate a lot of what I think about psychiatrists from what I see on TV.

The overwhelming impression of the nature of psychiatric treatment was that it was "all talk."

Exhibit 8.3 (Cont.)

Their main arsenal is the exposure of one's self to one's self so naturally that is conversation.

They just let them talk, and try to relate what they're saying to something that might have happened in the past, and eliminate or erase whatever happened in the past that's causing the problem.

The majority of the participants could not identify, in any specific sense, why "talking to a psychiatrists about your problems" would be any more beneficial than talking to your friends, family, or anyone else who would make time to listen to you. In other words, there seemed to be little understanding of the techniques and approaches used in treatment, or of the results which were sought (beyond "getting better"). Consequently, some stereotypical criticisms emerged—the view that psychiatrists "don't know the answers":

They're supposed to be perfect. They're supposed to know all the answers. But they don't know any more answers than you or I do.

and the thought that "people with friends don't need professional help":

They say that there's no psychologist in the world as good as a good friend. If you can go to one good friend on whom you can depend for an honest answer and tell him your problems, and listen to what he says, that's 10 times better than all the psychiatrists in the world.

I'm sure it must be a very scientific profession, but what they do escapes me. My friend calls me and I talk to her and I begin to think I should hang out my shingle.

"A good minister, social worker . . . who has time to give you" . . . would probably be a lot better than a psychiatrist or a hospital.

In the qualitative research, quite divergent opinions were expressed with respect to whether psychiatrists were effective in helping people overcome their problems.

I suspect that psychiatry doesn't get that close to solutions.

We've got more people off their rockers today than we ever had, and we've got more psychologists than we've ever had.

They're viewed as quack doctors—couch doctors—but they *do* help. As I am getting older and understanding more I can see they really help people, people I've known.

Before my mom or my girlfriend got sick [and went] I would have looked down on someone who went. But my mom, she's all better now.

Exhibit 8.3 (Cont.)

5. The "Stigma": Does It Still Exist?

Throughout the qualitative research, the social stigma of seeing a psychiatrist repeatedly emerged as a theme. There was a perception that people who had sought help for mental health problems might not want to admit this, in that it would somehow reflect poorly on them.

> People would much rather have a heart attack than to be institutionalized on a psychiatric ward.
>
> It took me a long time to admit to my peers that I was going to see a psychiatrist. It's almost a feeling of failure—that, somehow, you had failed. You aren't in control . . . you can't handle your job . . . something has happened to you and you have failed.
>
> Nobody wants to think that there's something wrong with their head . . . and there's a social stigma with the whole psychiatry business.

The social stigma of seeing a psychiatrist seemed to relate to the view that most people would think less of someone who required this type of help.

> I think that if a friend of mine went to a psychiatrist because he couldn't solve his problem any other way, his friends who knew he had gone would wonder about him.

Indeed, the majority of the participants agreed—sometimes with hesitation—that they, personally, would think less of someone who was seeing a psychiatrist. Others had an opinion that was quite the reverse, suggesting that they would respect someone who sought help:

> I think people tend to feel that going to a psychiatrist . . . is something only sick people do. My own view is that the people who go to psychiatrists are the people who are trying to avoid being sick.

In the limited sample involved in the qualitative research, the more tolerant viewpoint was expressed by younger participants. Even these participants were cognizant of a general social stigma, however, and recognized that their own attitude was not representative of society, as a whole. For this reason, they tended to agree that a person seeing a psychiatrist might be well advised to "be careful" about who they shared this information with. For example, there was a consensus that an employee might inhibit their career development by advising their boss that they were undergoing psychiatric treatment.

Exhibit 8.3 (Cont.)

6. Fear of Psychiatry: Is It Internal, External, or a Nonissue?

Most of the participants agreed that fear was an issue affecting the attitudes toward, and acceptance of, psychiatrists and psychiatric treatment. One of the major fears associated with seeing a psychiatrist was the social stigma which has just been described: the fear that someone "might find out." Other external fears related to "what the psychiatrist might do to them": institutionalization and drug therapy were the main concerns.

> The older people who have heard various horror stories about institutions and what goes on in them tend to be very upset when you recommend a psychiatrist. They think they would be "put away to the funny farm." You read stories about people who have been locked up since childhood.
>
> I know they do use a lot of drugs, but I wish they wouldn't.
>
> [Drugs are] given too freely and too easily. A lot of drugs are used.

7. Personal Acceptance of Psychiatry: Is It Good, But Only for Other People?

The participants seemed to fall into three groups in terms of their attitudes toward psychiatric treatment. At one extreme, some of the participants had no use for psychiatry—not for other people, and not for themselves.

> I wouldn't want myself to go and see a psychiatrist because I know it's a dead-end street.

At the other extreme, one young participant had made the decision to see a psychiatrist of her own initiative, with little apparent hesitation.

> A friend of my mom's at work went and I thought "Well if it helped her, why not me?" I find it really good.

In between these two poles, the majority of participants felt that psychiatry had a place and could serve a useful purpose—usually for other people! In personal terms, these individuals would not generally agree readily to working with a psychiatrist.

8. Psychiatrists as People: How Are They Regarded?

The participants' views of psychiatrists ran from one extreme to the other:

> I would think that they [psychiatrists] are very well educated, and I assume that most well-educated people are very well adjusted and have everything in control.

Exhibit 8.3 (Cont.)

The bulk of them are lazy, slovenly dressed . . . sit there with their cigarette hanging out and their endless coffee cup. They're too lazy to really do anything about a problem.

Maybe they're a bit wacky themselves!

Many of those who felt that psychiatrists had more than their share of mental health problems related this to the nature of their work:

A lot of those psychiatrists—they seem to be slightly off themselves—it almost seems that the mental instability rubs off on them a bit.

If a person deals with all those problems every day, its got to affect you somehow. And my assumption is that it's not always in the positive.

On the other hand, there was limited recognition of the fact that psychiatrists could learn to cope with the stresses of their profession, without it adversely affecting their lives.

They [psychiatrists] are average people. I'm sure they get problems like everybody else. They're just normal people doing their job like most people, they have to separate their job from their life-style.

As compared to other medical specializations, there was a sense that psychiatry was not as "important" as some:

Psychiatrists are at the lower end of the specialization scale.

One respondent aptly pointed out that psychiatry was relatively new, as compared to some other areas of medicine, and—consequently—less well understood. The need for education programs was raised in this context, with many of the participants suggesting that they might benefit from a more clear understanding of the role of psychiatrists and nature of psychiatric treatment.

The original research proposal, submitted to the OPA on February 15, suggested that up to 15 closed-ended multiple-choice mail panel questions were feasible in Phase 2 under the research budget. However, during April, Ms. Green had successfully negotiated a price reduction for each question. As a result, 27 closed-ended multiple-choice questions would now be possible in the forthcoming questionnaire. Complete demographics of the head of household were available at no extra charge.

Upon completion of the fieldwork, the mail panel company would provide Ms. Green with a computer tabulation of the results. At a minimum, this would include a count of the responses to each question, by response category, and, where relevant, basic statistics such as mean, standard deviation, and standard error.

In addition, it was possible to have these responses cross-tabulated against other questions in the survey. The simplest way of doing this—and the way required by the mail panel company—was to select certain questions against which *all other questions* would be cross-tabulated. These selected questions were called *banners*. For example, Ms. Green intended to include a question to determine the sex of the respondent; she felt that it would be useful to cross-tabulate the answers to that question against all others. To accomplish this, she would specify to the mail panel company that she wished to have "Sex" appear as banner in the final tabulation report. The two categories constituting this banner, "male" and "female," would take up two *columns* (Exhibit 8.4). The tabulation report format allowed for a maximum of 36 columns.

Exhibit 8.4

CORMARK AND THE ONTARIO PSYCHIATRIC ASSOCIATION (B)
CROSS-TAB FORMAT

Q9. IN EVERY CLOUD THERE IS A SILVER LINING

Example question

Question response categories	SEX (Banner heading)		Column heading
	MALE	FEMALE	36 columns →
STRONGLY AGREE			
AGREE			
NEUTRAL			
DISAGREE			
STRONGLY DISAGREE			
NO ANSWER, NO OPINION			
TOTAL			
MEAN			
STANDARD DEVIATION			
STANDARD ERROR			

Therefore, when Ms. Green submitted her questionnaire, it would also be necessary to submit a "tab plan" that specified all the banners that she required. These banners could be chosen from among all of the questions, as long as no more than 36 columns were required to display the response categories. If there were more than 36 total response categories in the desired banner questions, it was possible to request that certain response categories be "collapsed together." For example, the questionnaire might ask for the respondent's age by 5-year groupings (are you 20–24, 25–29, 30–34, 35–39, etc.); this could be collapsed into 10-year groupings for the purpose of the banners (20–29, 30–39, etc.).

CONCLUSION

It would be difficult to explore thoroughly the eight attitude themes with a maximum of 27 closed-ended questions, but the manager of the panel mailout needed a polished questionnaire and tab plan in two weeks.

9

CELESTIAL SEASONINGS, INC. (A)

STATEMENT OF PHILOSOPHY

Celestial Seasonings is a consumer packaged goods company committed to marketing internally manufactured, health-oriented, high-quality products to the consumer and sold via health food and mass market outlets. Our job is to serve consumers by filling voids in the marketplace with quality products that consumers want. Our mission is to solve major health problems according to our corporate definition. Our objective: a healthy, nourished, disease-free, exercised public.

Under the name Celestial Seasonings, the product line and style of magic is set for the future. We sell high-quality products with the most beautiful packaging possible. Each package is sprinkled with bits of wisdom and is designed to give consumers an added bonus . . . Lighthearted Philosophy.

For stockholders our objective is a minimum sales growth of 27 percent compounded annually with a minimum of 27 percent growth in earnings. Celestial offers shareholders the opportunity to reap financial reward while getting people healthy.

For our employees, our objective is to build a strong and stable company with dynamic opportunity for upward mobility through loyalty, pursuit of excellence, hard work, and quality. This company is dedicated to mutual reward systems based on the achievement of worthwhile and aggressive goals. We remain loyal to the continual search and practice of advanced management systems that build working bridges between exempt and nonexempt employees, believing that a united, fully utilized work force can accomplish far-reaching objectives with work satisfaction and mutual reward for all. Our philosophy encourages creative, productive, possibility thinking throughout the organization.

In summary, the foundation of Celestial Seasonings is based on serving health needs through good products and expressed in a beautiful form. Our profit will increase 100-fold by dedicating our total efforts to these ends, which in turn will make this world a better place for our children and our children's children.[1]

BOULDER, COLORADO, 1982

Boulder, Colorado, is a sleepy but fashionable town located north of Denver on the Front Range of the Rocky Mountains. During the early 1970s, hippies trudged through its streets lugging worn backpacks and sleeping bags, many of them living from hand to mouth supporting themselves by panhandling or selling "dope" to university students around The Hill area of town. Today, Boulder presents a more affluent face to visitors. The hippies have either left town or have cashed in their patched jeans for snappier, more socially acceptable though casual attire—Chemise La Coste shirts and L. L. Bean chinos, for example. Many have joined the ranks of the young professionals and zip around the town in foreign-made cars, said to be better than domestic models for mountain driving.

Jogging and bicycling are popular Boulder pastimes. Former marathon Olympic star Frank Shorter is now a local businessman selling chic running shorts and shoes in his own shop on the Mall, which marks the center of town. Most of the youthful, health-conscious people in town are glad not to have a ragtag population marring their peaceful local scenes of outdoor cafés and trendy businesses done up in natural cedar or red brick façades. Casualness seems to be a fetish.

CELESTIAL SEASONINGS BACKGROUND

In this idyllic setting Mr. Mo Siegel, president and co-founder of Celestial Seasonings, Inc., reigns over his herb tea kingdom, an empire that includes among its all-natural products such innovative no-caffeine offerings as Red Zinger, Mandarin Orange Spice, and Cinnamon Rose herb teas, graphically tricked out in flamboyant fantasy packaging (see Appendix A). Celestial competes in its own small market, the $75-million-a-year herb tea share of all tea sales, with other counterculturally costumed competitors—Select, San Francisco Herbs, Lipton, and the rest. The purchaser of Siegel's tantalizingly titled teas buys not only a beverage to sustain body but messages from such unlikely and diverse sources as Abraham Lincoln and Sophia Loren to sustain the soul. "Please write, we like to respond. We are interested in your suggestions, ideas, queries, quotations, and short essays for use on the packages," invites a box-top bit of prose. Mo Siegel, himself an inveterate collector of quotations, includes pithy morsels of wit and wisdom in business correspondence. Under the cable and Telex information on a recent Siegel letter, the reader is treated

[1]Corporate files.

to some Goethe: "Whatever liberates our spirit without giving us self-control is disastrous."

Mr. Siegel sits at mission control site between a portrait of Lincoln on one wall and the Iced Delight bear on the other. He has little reason to meditate on disasters these days with his closely held Celestial Seasonings now dominating the domestic herbal tea market with annual earnings of more than $1 million. Sales to foreign markets have leaped to 6 percent of Celestial's total current annual sales. Still a dwarf in the overall $825 million black tea market, Celestial at $23 million a year in sales has stunned the big tea marketers by making steady inroads into major supermarket chains, gourmet, and health stores and into foreign markets during the late 1970s and early 1980s.

Tea giants such as Thomas J. Lipton, until as recently as 1980, tended to discount Celestial's entrepreneurs as amateurs playing flower-child games in a tough marketplace. Now Lipton and others look at Celestial, a company that has experienced a high growth rate, as a feisty wunderkind to emulate and contend with. Lipton in 1982 began marketing herb teas packaged in rainbow colors at prices close to Celestial's—about 5½ cents a bag, although Lipton packaged its herbals in packs of 16, while Celestial preferred the 24-teabag format.

The compelling Mr. Siegel was the subject of wide-ranging publicity.[2] He popped up regularly on television programs such as "Merv Griffin" and "Donahue," and business magazines took turns publishing a colorful sketch of the president who was given to quotable remarks as he ruminated aloud. "We have an obligation to make the shelves astonishing! to keep magic alive," he said when asked about Celestial Seasonings' devotion to creative packaging. "We must continue to create beautiful, outstanding-quality packaging with truthful writings." Later he told the casewriters upon entering the elegant Celestial board room, "We want Louvre quality in our artwork," and "If Walt Disney could do it better, we aren't interested" (Exhibit 9.1).

Some of the press that Siegel received suggested that the success realized for Celestial "just sort of happened." In fact, Mo Siegel is a very ambitious person, addicted to reading management books, Drucker being one of his favorites. "I like big rather than small," he admitted to us with a gleam in his eye. Then he explained how he recruited outside of Celestial to professionalize management, hiring a regional manager from Lipton and a plant manager from General Mills. Along the way he recruited a vice president of PepsiCo for his marketing team and brought in a chief engineer from Pepperidge Farm. Celestial's head tea brand manager was recruited from Quaker Oats, another from Vaseline Intensive Care, and still another from Samsonite. Clearly, Siegel sought marketing expertise for the company from proven training camps. He followed marketing stories of large companies as if they were detective novels: "Tylenol is bright" and "Johnson & Johnson is as good as P & G." And his strategy was pragmatic: "We don't have the time or the money to test in the same way as Quaker."

---

[2]See Eric Morgenthaler, "From Hippies to $16 Million a Year," *The Wall Street Journal*, May 6, 1981; "What's Brewing at Celestial," *Money*, January 1981; Margaret Thoren, "It Wasn't the Bankers' Cup of Tea . . . ," *The Christian Science Monitor*, April 21, 1981; and Barth David Schwartz, "How to Make a Million Doing Your Own Thing," *Fortune*, June 4, 1979, among others.

Exhibit 9.1

CELESTIAL SEASONINGS GRAPHICS

An ancient tea for the tensions of a modern world.

"For 2,000 years my ancestors have sipped ginseng tea when they wanted to relax.

"So I have followed carefully their wise advice, combing the steppes of Siberia and the vast reaches of China to find the rarest and best ginseng. And from it, I've made one of the most relaxing herb teas in the world: Emperor's Choice.

"Of course, an emperor's taste requires a delicious tea, too.

"So I combined the best cinnamon, licorice root, rosehips and other herbs and spices. And created a flavor to please the most discerning royal palate.

"And I made my tea without caffeine. Or anything artificial.

"Try Emperor's Choice. You'll see why my ancestors said: 'A few sips of this delicious tea everyday can help chase the woes of the world away.'"

—The Emperor

Available In your favorite health or natural food store.

Naturally caffeine free. For your good health.

His objectives for the company were specific and hardhitting. In 1981, which was "the first year for our real-live-moving-growing marketing department," Siegel decided that any product line not reaching $10 million in sales in five years should be discontinued. Other objectives included the achievement of a 30 percent increase of tea sales in standard units; a broadening of grocery volume from 35 percent to 55 percent on at least four items; and the expansion of tea section placements from 15 percent to 30 percent on Sleepytime, Mandarin Orange Spice, Cinnamon Rose, Country Apple, Iced Delight, Red Zinger, Almond Sunset, Emperor's Choice, Peppermint, and the variety-pack four flavors.

Siegel believed that Celestial should continue expanding trial tastings among nonusers and increase the frequency of consumption among users from 1 to 2 cups each day. Since Colorado was Celestial's most active market area, Siegel's 1981 goals stated that the company needed "to determine upside volume potential outside of Colorado." Finally, and perhaps most important since Siegel claimed he was not interested in being a "food company" but was interested in preventive health care, Celestial targeted an improvement in its position in health food stores through a carefully orchestrated shelf management program in 1981 and 1982.

Siegel is not particularly modest about what he thinks are Celestial's most successful characteristics. At the top of the list he counts the distinctive and unique aspects of Celestial, including quality, packaging, products, names, and writings. In the "tricky herb industry" because of the adverse publicity about herbs and regulatory difficulties, he believes that he has accomplished no small feat in achieving the "highest quality standards in the herb industry." Because health products, not food, is the area in which he is interested, Siegel believes Celestial's success to be inextricably tied to its provision of a "real alternative to other caffeinated hot beverages." That the company has embraced a "wide variety of flavors and product concepts" he believes is all to the good. The lead products in Celestial have a strong consumer positioning and best of all—from Mo Siegel's perspective of the health-focused "corporateur" as he terms himself—Celestial's products remain all natural and health oriented. Exhibit 9.2 summarizes Celestial's strengths, weaknesses, and strategies for the 1980s as seen by top management.

Not that everything is coming up rosehips, however. Celestial has experienced its share of problems. A brief and abortive romance with a product called Salad Snacks failed to meet quality control standards. Juice products, despite great corporate hopes, could not make a go of it.

Observed Siegel, "The caution is that we deal with limited resources, both people and finances, and we cannot effectively execute against multiple priorities especially when the objectives are not compatible with our central corporate mission. The key is maximum sales effectiveness. An example of the dilution of resources was the introduction of BreakAway during the major drive for Iced Delight—no one's fault—and penetrating a new channel of distribution—placing Salad Snacks in produce departments—without adequate development of our basic business. Launching VITA during the key prewinter sales drive on Herb Tea would have been a similar mistake."

Mo Siegel hardly underestimates the importance of marketing. One of his trump suits has been a strategy of strong and consistent marketing to the health foods

Exhibit 9.2

STRENGTHS, WEAKNESSES, AND STRATEGIES OF CELESTIAL SEASONINGS

Strengths

Growth via health consciousness
Strong consumer loyalty
Financial stability and excellent gross margins
Distinctive packaging
Readily acceptable flavor varieties
Significantly higher brand awareness than the competition
Professional management
Vertical integration: from raw product to finished teabag

Weaknesses

Extensive product line
Premium product line
No line pricing
24-teabag count
Compressed timetables

Strategies for the 1980s. Continue to Take the Leadership Position in

Unique packaging
Inventing blended herb teas
Offering the largest selection of blended teas
Offering special packs
Ability to sample
Offering the best quality herb teas
Marketing solution teas, for example, Sleepytime

market segment. As markets drift away from hot caffeinated products, there Celestial will be. The sweet dream of high coffee prices has always kept spirits high at the tea factory, and the strong growth of health food stores has been a trend that fueled the Celestial team's marketing enthusiasm. With increasing professionalization of the team, however, no one is naïve enough to think that people can rest on their tea leaves and achieve continuing growth. Rather, the annual building of new distribution channels is seen as a perennial strategic topic as are plans to develop a wider product mix (Exhibit 9.3). Always Celestial is striving to improve its professional approach to sales and marketing.

Exhibit 9.3

ADVERTISING FOR A NEW (1982) PRODUCT

Delicious to the core.

Before you decide on your favorite Celestial Seasonings Herb Tea, try this one.

Country Apple Herb Tea is a delicious blend of apples, rosehips and cinnamon enhanced by hibiscus flowers and chamomile, with absolutely no caffeine.

The flavor of Country Apple unfolds with each sip, as the aroma of orchards takes you back to breezy afternoons in the country and all your fondest memories.

Try our new Country Apple Herb Tea. Then pick your Celestial favorite.

MARKETERS AND MARKETING AT CELESTIAL

Keith Brenner, a pleasant, self-assured Canadian—some might say slightly arrogant—became vice president of marketing at Celestial in 1980. Before that, marketing at Celestial had been strictly an in-house, family affair. Brenner, who owned his own beverage manufacturing company in Canada, met Mo Siegel at a food show. He worked with Celestial first as a consultant, assisting the company in its attempt to enter the natural beverage market, an effort that flopped. Although Brenner hoped to work in general management, he was asked by Siegel to head the marketing function of the organization. He has not put aside his preference to get into general management where he could be involved in finance and production as well as marketing.

Besides his stint as a beverage manufacturer, Brenner acquired an impressive set of credentials from his work with Pepsi-Cola in Canada and with General Foods. Like Siegel, he attained success early. At 32 he was a vice president and general manager for Pepsi-Cola, globetrotting for a three-year period to Pepsi operations in South Africa and the Philippines as well as serving in Canada. He cited as his major reason for joining Siegel and Celestial "the opportunity to impact a healthy growing concern instead of attempting to climb the ladder in a vast corporation."

Both Brenner and Siegel believe in the Celestial mystique: "Our goal is to manufacture only healthful, nutritional products—nothing artificial." At Brenner's urging, Celestial planned to abandon its sole caffeine product, Morning Thunder: "Since Celestial Seasonings' customers are a segment based upon their penchant for natural food products, a clean bill of health with customers will be strengthened by severing ties with caffeine."

As for his marketing efforts, Brenner terms Celestial "an alternative kind of company which has achieved success without hammering people with incessant advertising. We tell a simple story in a colorful way, only the truth, not embellished with a lot of hoopla."

Brenner professes a belief that "Celestial's success was a major reason why Lipton decided to enter the herb tea market. Instead of thinking that such competition works to Celestial's detriment, we credit the Lipton move to raising overall public awareness of products such as ours. In fact, the Lipton competition creates a bigger market for everyone." Brenner is sanguine about growth possibilities for Celestial even though teas was a low-growth category, according to the marketing vice president, 1 percent annual growth, the same as the population growth rate. "Any extra we get has to come out of somebody else's business, but there is a trend by large stores to stock more nutritional foods . . . health foods and the like . . . which is good for us. This will help us reach our target of 25 percent annual growth, compounded, but only through 1985, I believe, with our present product line. This means that to continue meeting our objective we must develop new ideas—beyond herbal teas." Brenner's overall strategy for growth in 1982 was succinct: "First, we widen our grocery distribution base with tea section placement. This has been difficult, but it gets easier as we get stronger. Second, we go after consumer awareness and trial through the use of Sunday supplement coupons, trial packages, and displays. Last, we move more strongly into the iced tea market, which is three times larger than that for hot tea."

Regarding trips into the marketplace, Brenner has confessed, "I do get into the field occasionally, but not enough." Like Siegel, he is emphatic that one distribution channel cannot be sacrificed to another. "We had 100 percent distribution in the health food outlets, so we moved into the supermarkets. But we are not neglecting our health food outlets."

LIFE AT THE TEA FACTORY

The music of James Taylor wafted through the tea factory on a typical day in 1982 as Italian-made machinery moved the teas 24 hours a day on a computerized schedule. This new equipment made it possible to pack the major Celestial blends into horizontal boxes, found by market testing to lure the purchaser more effectively than vertical packages. Employees in production appeared to be blissfully engaged in their tasks. The cafeteria awaited them at some point in their shift, with a meal of natural foods— soup, salad, granola cookies, and a selection from the company's herb tea line. Mo Siegel, who frequently dresses in shorts and a sports shirt for the office, and rides his bicycle to work, stresses quality of the workplace.

If it is possible to tell something about a person or an organization by surveying the reading material that is strewn about, perhaps the following survey of books and magazines in the Celestial Seasonings' employee waiting room offers some insights: Pierre Teilhard de Chardin's *Man's Place in Nature*; M. Scott Myer's *Every Employee a Manager: More Meaningful Work Through Job Enrichment*; works by Drucker and Toffler; and copies of the periodicals *New Health, New Age, Prevention, Runner, New West, Runner's World,* and *Processed Prepared Foods.*

In one section of the main plant, Marelynn W. Zipser, Ph.D., a food technologist and the mother of Mandarin Orange Spice, Cinnamon Rose, Iced Delight, and BreakAway, presides over herbs and test tubes in a pristine but cheery testing laboratory. As manager of new product development, Zipser reports directly to Brenner. "I take the concept and turn it into reality," she explained. Among her research and development tasks, Dr. Zipser conducts taste panels—mainly among women's groups and employees—to test the latest reactions to Celestial's expanding product lines. Quality and taste of the tea are as important to Celestial as other major points of difference with their competition: packaging style and graphics, the number of teabags per box, premium pricing, and channels of distribution. Thus, Celestial taste tests against Select, Alvita, Golden Harvest, Health Valley, Traditionals, San Francisco Herbs, Worthington, Horizon, and other regional and local brands in the health food market as well as Bigelow, Lipton, and Magic Mountain in the grocery market.

Systematic product development grew out of Mo Siegel's demands for specific types of products that he and Brenner instructed Zipser and her group to conjure up in the laboratory. "Conservative planning plus optimistic action plus intelligent work equals success" is a favorite Siegel maxim, which seems eminently practicable in the laboratory part of the tea factory.

HISTORY OF CELESTIAL

In the beginning were the herbs. Siegel, his wife Peggy, and sidekick Wyck Hay pioneered the operation by gathering Colorado mountain herbs with other friends "for fun" and selling them to local health food stores. These were the early days of health food awareness of the late 1960s and early 1970s, and Siegel and Hay's philosophy then was to provide a pleasant living for themselves and a congenial group of Boulder comrades by selling a product that was good for people. "One of the things we found in Europe is that people who live to 100 drink a lot of herb tea and eat herbs continually," Siegel states.

The company's appellation, derived from the fanciful nickname of a female friend who participated in the early days of Celestial's movement into what some have termed "cosmic capitalism," suggests the tone and tempo of those early times. Celestial began as a relatively tranquil cottage business in which Siegel, Peggy, and friends patiently stuffed the heady concoctions of orange peel, wild cherry bark, rosehips, hibiscus flowers, lemon grass, and peppermint into hand-sewn, hand-stamped muslin bags with solicitous instructions to buyers as to the particulars of brewing and steeping, along with a reminder to them that a bit of honey would enhance flavor. This early, successful blend, entitled Red Zinger, propelled Celestial out of the cottage and into a corporate setting. In 1982 Celestial required six buildings to house its manufacturing, warehousing of herbs and spices from 35 countries, and other functions.

From the outset, Celestial espoused causes and amplified these from its boxes—reminding customers about a foundation needing support to protect vanishing species of flowers, sometimes warning about world hunger, and promoting save the whales or other conservational causes. Celestial saw itself as having an instructive, positivistic mission, perhaps as important as its more pedestrian, grocery-focused one. "Happiness is the only thing we can give without having" and other messages of its kind became inherent aspects of Celestial's packaging concepts. But such aphorisms were more to Celestial than a way of selling tea. Siegel's enterprise was a mission (see Appendix 9B, a brief biography).

With lots of help from his friends, Siegel organized a corporate structure based on communitarian concerns and centered on quality-of-life issues: concern with providing employees enough time for family and leisure, flexitime, pleasant working conditions, and many more. As the alternative to business that they were, the merry band was not quite able to do away with a hierarchical structure, and they developed a seven-person board of directors, most of them major stockholders, to hold down the fort. Living was easy then with only a few blends in their tea portfolio, and only 50 or so stockholders in the entire corporation.

MOVING INTO THE 1980s

Red Zinger was ultimately joined by some 40 other herbals, including a new tea in 1982, Almond Sunset: "a wonderfully romantic blend of herbs with the soothing natural flavor of almonds. A delicate blend of lovely things like rich roasted carob, barley and chickory root; spiced with cinnamon, sunny orange peel and a hint of anise seed. . . . Almond Sunset will remind you of holiday cookies baking in the oven of a farmhouse kitchen." Introduction of new products was carefully considered; Celestial's marketing and advertising budget was expected to be $5 million in 1982.

Seeking to market Celestial more aggressively, Siegel recognized the "be big or bust" paradigm that has ruled decision making at the larger beverage companies and the expansion imperative that was its corollary. New products, including body care preparations and vitamins, loom large in Siegel's mind as he looks toward product expansion and toward a goal of 27 percent compounded annual growth (Exhibit 9.4) with anticipated sales of $50 million by the mid-1980s.

As time went on Celestial people gave less attention to the fun-and-games enterprises of more carefree years, for instance, the world-famous Red Zinger bicycle races, a promotional activity the company sponsored from 1975 to 1980 because "Mo Siegel is into bikes." The races underscored a long-time Siegel belief that if more people rode bikes as their only transportation, the world would be a better place. "Celestial Seasonings is dedicated to improving the quality of life on this planet, having a major concern in environmental life," he wrote in literature promoting the Red Zinger Bicycle Classic. In 1980, however, it became an issue of bicycle races or teas for Celestial, just as it became an issue of hiring executives with sophisticated managerial expertise versus possible corporate extinction. Case in point: in the summer of 1980 the company came close to being swallowed by General Mills due to one disgruntled, major stockholder's wish to rid himself of $1 million worth of Celestial's stock. Siegel saved the day by borrowing money to purchase the stock himself.

Exhibit 9.4

ANNUAL CHANGES IN DOLLAR SALES, FISCAL 1973–1982
(net sales in thousands of dollars)

FISCAL YEAR	DOLLAR SALES	
	Amount	Increase
1973	$ 70	—
1974	293	+320%
1975	1,316	+350
1976	2,930	+125
1977	5,636	+ 92
1978	8,887	+ 58
1979	10,524	+ 18
1980	11,557	+ 10
1981	16,662	+ 44
1982	23,327	+ 40

Source: Celestial Seasonings records.

In hiring heavyweight marketing types like Keith Brenner to draft a new marketing strategy, the main component being to move the herbal teas out of the less trafficked, speciality sections of grocery stores into the mainline beverage sections, Mo Siegel underscored his ambition to be big rather than small. Siegel and Brenner shared a perception that "the 35- to 50-year-old market remains to be captured if Celestial is to be truly successful." See Exhibit 9.5 for estimated herbal tea market shares from 1978 to 1980.

There were significant changes in Celestial's corporate culture once new management began to join the firm. Several members of the original cadre left the company presumably because of the new style of life at the tea factory. Although Siegel continued promoting quality of work life, his corporateurial mind was on priority markets for Celestial and criteria for selecting such markets. He reread his Drucker and listened to his cassette tape course on strategic planning. And he repeated to himself a six-word formula: "Concentrate on preventive health care foods." If such foods were curative in nature, so much the better.

Exhibit 9.5

MARKET SHARE (in $)
ESTIMATED U.S. HERBAL TEA MARKET, 1978–1980

	1978	1979	1980
Celestial Seasonings	38%	33%	30%
Magic Mountain	5	12	11
Lipton	—	—	8
Bigelow	—	4	8
G.N.C.	4	4	4
Other	53	47	39

Source: Company records.

A LOOK TO THE FUTURE

To keep the team spirit alive, Mo Siegel retreats frequently with his top staff members to discuss possible new directions for Celestial Seasonings. "We must operate in a basically unfriendly environment as retailers become more self-assured as to their position in relation to manufacturers." In the periodic strategic planning sessions in scenic and secluded Colorado resort areas, top managers at Celestial concentrate in 2½-hour segments on such tough-to-analyze questions as, What business are we in? What business should we be in? What is our company philosophy? Is our philosophy changing and if so in what ways? Who are our customers and how are segments changing? What are Celestial's strengths and weaknesses? What threats and opportunities face us over the next several years? Is caffeine compatible with Celestial? What are our criteria for business development?

Underlying the retreats' agendas was Siegel's own ambition for the company: "To be a billion dollars in sales at the turn of the century."

Exhibit 9.6 depicts Celestial Seasonings' organizational structure; Exhibit 9.7 is a photograph of the founder; and Exhibit 9.8, from Celestial's press kit, summarizes some of Mo's reflections for successful living.

Exhibit 9.6

ORGANIZATIONAL STRUCTURE

Board of Directors

Board of Directors	
Mo Siegel, Chairman	Bob Cameron
John Hay	Charles Beiderman
Bernard Jakacki	Monique Koehler

President/CEO

Executive Secretary

Media Relations Director   VP Sales   VP Marketing   VP Operations   VP Finance   Consultant

---

Exhibit 9.7

1982 PHOTOGRAPH OF MO SIEGEL, PRESIDENT/CEO

"I want to help change the course of American business, I want to help make all forms of Art more available to the American people, and I want to get the word out on health and fitness."

Mo Siegel, President
CELESTIAL SEASONINGS, INC.

Exhibit 9.8

DISTILLATION OF MO'S IDEAS FOR SUCCESSFUL LIVING

MO SIEGEL
THE HERB TEA MAN

ON SUCCESSFUL LIVING:

IDEAS: The best ideas are the ones that fill a need. If people want to make money, start with an idea that fills a need for someone else. Do something useful!

GOALS: I'm a believer in goal-setting. If you know what you want, it's pretty hard to lose.

FAILURES: I've had plenty. You've got to learn to accept them. You're going to fail sometimes. Don't be afraid of it.

HARD WORK: Be persistent. Work hard, but use your intelligence.

HIRING: Never hire anyone else unless they're smarter than you are in the area in which they're going to be working for you.

MARKETING: What does the public think of it? Is it good for other people?

BELIEVING: You could do something you don't believe in, but it really takes the fun out of it. I've had some hard times along the way, and if I didn't believe in the product, I would have sold the company a long time ago.

HEALTH: People are tired of paying doctors, and they want to stay healthy. I see people around the country getting more interested in prevention.

INCENTIVES: If we want the labor force to work well, why not let them own part of it?

LABOR: Create a condition in which the work force feels better about their lives. What is good for labor should be good for management and vice versa.

FAITH: There is only one place to have faith and that is in God. The disappointments that are hardest to bear are those that never come. Faith in an active life is a positive attitude.

Source: Company's 1982 press kit.

MO SIEGEL
THE HERB TEA MAN

MO'S STEPS TO SUCCESSFUL LIVING

1. Do something worthwhile for someone else.

2. Have faith, maintain a positive attitude.

3. Learn the art of setting goals, what you want.

4. It isn't enough to work hard, you must work SMART!

5. Do not be afraid to fail.

6. Don't take yourself too seriously.

7. Stay healthy.

8. Believe in and be dedicated to quality.

9. Do not be afraid to take a risk.

10. Family love and support maintain stability and help you keep priorities in perspective.

Appendix 9A

DESCRIPTION OF SELECTED PRODUCTS

CELESTIAL SEASONINGS

AMERICA'S #1 SELLING HERB TEA

SLEEPYTIME®: Our No. 1 Selling Herb Tea — The perfect before bedtime drink. A great non-caffeinated tea with chamomile, spearmint leaves and lemon grass with seven other herbs. Helps you relax and wind down from a hectic day. Designed to round off the day's rough edges. Its sweet flowered flavor can be enjoyed by young and old.

MANDARIN ORANGE SPICE: One of our most popular teas. The delicious flavor of imported natural mandarin oranges makes this tea drinkable any time of day. We captured a tangy citrus flavor with just the right spice bouquet by combining orange peels, hibiscus flowers, rosehips, blackberry leaves and a touch of sweet cloves, a flavor you will also enjoy iced.

CINNAMON ROSE™: A bright, refreshing tea that combines the sweet explosion of imported cinnamon with the naturally round flavors of rosehips, orange peels, blackberry leaves and sweet cloves. A uniquely flavored herbal blend that is excellent both hot or cold.

COUNTRY APPLE™: The luscious apple flavor unfolds with every sip. The aroma of Country Apple Herb Tea will take you back to breezy afternoons in a country orchard. Truly an apple adventure, combining rosehips and hibiscus flowers for a bit of tartness, chamomile and chicory for smoothness and body, plus cinnamon and nutmeg for just the right touch of spice.

ALMOND SUNSET™: Our newest tea, a romantic blend of herbs with the soothing natural flavor of almonds. A delicate blend of rich roasted carob, barley and chicory root; spiced with cinnamon, sunny orange peel and a hint of anise seed. A taste for almond lovers of all ages.

RED ZINGER®: A Celestial tradition, imitated often but never equalled. The deep ruby red color, the tangy citrus flavor, the powerful bolt of flavor. All these combine to make Red Zinger a unique herbal soft drink enjoyed by young and old alike. Red Zinger is an indescribale brew that can only be appreciated by tasting it.

Soothing teas for a nervous world.®

Appendix 9B

MR. SIEGEL'S RÉSUMÉ AND MISSION

1780 55th Street
Boulder, Colorado 80301 U.S.A.
(303) 449-3779

Cable: CELESEAS BLDR
TWX: 910-940-3448

MO SIEGEL
630 Spruce Street
Boulder, Colorado 80302
(303) 447-9599

Business Address: 1780 - 55th Street
            Boulder, Colorado 80301
                (303) 449-3779

EDUCATIONAL HISTORY

1967
and on-going   Attended parochial schools; attended numerous
                      college courses; completed numerous professional
                      CEO and executive seminars and courses.

On-going   Independent Study - I am a devoted and perpetual
                      student of the health sciences, business management,
                      religion, philosophy, and government. I am
                      currently engaged in authoring a series of programs
                      for political reform in the United States which
                      began with the publication of the essay "Fire in
                      the American People".

1979   Travel Study - I sponsored a three-week, 5,000
                      mile study-tour of health and nutrition through
                      the Soviet Union with special focus on "The Garden
                      of the Centenarians" in the Trans-Caucasian
                      Republic of Azerbaijan and Georgia, home of the
                      "long dwellers."

1980   Travel Study - I completed a three week interior
                      study tour of China, involving the study of food
                      production and Chinese herbal science.

                      Other travels include North America, Central
                      America, South America, Europe, Middle East,
                      and Asia.

EMPLOYMENT HISTORY

1968 to
1970   Owner, health food store; first mate, commercial
                      fishing vessel, Key West, Fla.; harmonica playing
                      sandwich board advertiser; carrot juicer salesman.

Appendix 9B (Cont.)

1970 to
present

Founder, President and Chairman of the Board,
Celestial Seasonings Herb Tea Company, Boulder
Colorado.

My responsibilities at Celestial Seasonings
include planning, organizing and directing the
over-all growth and development of the company;
providing executive management to the divisions
of Operations, Marketing, Sales, Human Resources,
and Finance.

My principal goals have been to ensure the
achievement of all corporate objectives and
the fulfillment of all responsibilities to
employees, shareholders, and customers by
directing all executive decisions affecting
the current and long-range operations of the
company.

PERSPECTIVE ON CELESTIAL SEASONINGS

In 1971 Celestial Seasonings sold a grand
total of 10,000 hand-sewn tea bags, containing
hand-picked Rocky Mountain herbs, to a small
group of health food stores.

Celestial now imports herbs from 35 countries
for use in blends which are milled at the
Boulder plant at a rate of over 4 million
pounds per year . . .

In 1982 Celestial will manufacture and serve
700 million tea bags and the fiscal year sales
will exceed twenty-five million dollars . . .

Celestial Seasonings Herb Teas are available
in more than 35,000 retail outlets throughout
the world including 60% of all U.S. supermarkets
and foreign distribution in Canada, Australia,
New Zealand, and Great Britain.

PROFESSIONAL ACCOMPLISHMENTS

Founder of America's finest International Class
stage bicycle race; formerly the Red Zinger Bicycle
Classic, now the Coors Classic.

Podium Speaker at the Democratic National Convention
1980; served on the Rules Committee of the Democratic
National Party, 1980.

Keynote Speaker for numerous professional, religious,
and civic organizational activities.

Appendix 9B (Cont.)

Guest appearances on ABC-TV's "Success, It Can Be Yours, PM Magazine, Donahue, Donahue on Today, HBO's "Money Matters", Merv Griffin, Mike Douglas, Dinah Shore, Sandy Freeman, USam, 700 Club, Cable Health Network.

Featured in People Magazine, Sports Illustrated, Wall Street Journal, Fortune Magazine, Money Magazine, BusinessWeek Magazine, New York Times, Los Angeles Times, San Francisco Chronicle, Boston Globe, Chicago Sun-Times, Christian Science Monitor, Washington Post, Denver Post, Rocky Mountain News, Seattle Times, Minneapolis Tribune, In-Flight Magazines, US Magazine, San Jose Mercury News, Seattle Post Intelligencer.

CHARACTER SKETCHES

Abiding concern...The health and fitness of the American people. Political reform.

Personal Heroes...Jesus, Abraham Lincoln, Walt Disney, Thomas J. Watson (founder of IBM), Dr. Kenneth Cooper (founder of the Aerobics Institute), Eddie Merckx (six-time Tour de France champion).

Quote..."I want Celestial Seasonings to enter the 21st century as one of America's leading corporations."

Favorite tea bag homily..."Angels can fly because they take themselves lightly."

Quote..."Where we go in the hereafter, depends on what we go after here."

Dream...of the day when the typical American employee enjoys the dignity and the equity he has earned and deserves.

Hoped for epitaph..."Mo Siegel was a good father."

Explanation of insatiable appetite for social and business advance...Because I don't believe that when St. Peter asks me, "Mo, what have you done with your life?", that it will be sufficient to reply, "Well, I cornered the herb tea market."

Quote..."I want to help change the course of American business, I want to help make all forms of Art more available to the American People, and I want to get the word out on health and fitness."

10

CELESTIAL SEASONINGS, INC. (B)

BACKGROUND

Celestial Seasonings had its beginnings in 1969, when a young man named Mo Siegel began gathering wild herbs in the forests and canyons of the Rocky Mountains surrounding Aspen, Colorado.* The following year, when Mo and a young friend, Wyck Hay, found a bountiful harvest of wild herbs growing in the Boulder area, they decided to start a small herb tea business, believing that other health-conscious individuals might also appreciate the flavor and benefits of such beverages. "Mo's 36 herb tea," a blend of their favorite flavors, became the first product. Five hundred pounds were sold to one local store. A year later, Wyck's brother, John Hay, became the third partner. In what had then become a family venture, the three owners and their wives designed and produced a special package for their herb tea, "Mo's 24." The first 1,500 Celestial Seasonings tea packages were muslin bags, sewn and stamped entirely by hand for the 1971 harvest.

John and Mo sold their crop of herb tea to stores throughout Colorado, New Mexico, and on the East Coast, importing herbs rather than picking their own raw materials. Thus the dream of a national herb tea company slowly materialized. A new

*The authors are indebted to Mo Siegel, who collaborated closely in preparation of Celestial Seasonings (A) and whose contributions and entrepreneurial spirit informed development of this (B) narrative; to Barney Feinblum, who generously shared his time and financial and marketing insights and reviewed the manuscript; as well as to several Celestial Seasonings staff members who willingly participated and provided various supplementary materials.

herb tea blend, destined to propel Celestial Seasonings to new heights of sales success appeared on store shelves in January 1972—it was "Red Zinger," an overnight sensation and year after year one of the company's best-selling products. In the 1980s, Celestial Seasonings became the largest herb tea marketer in the United States, its products available in health food stores and supermarkets nationwide, and boasting one of the most modern automated manufacturing operations in the industry. [For additional historical material, see Celestial Seasonings, Inc. (A).]

Among many harrowing episodes on the road leading to growth, profits, and good deeds, the following narrative (Exhibit 10.1) which Mo was fond of recounting portrays the determination, intrepidity, and good-natured articulateness of the stellar corporation's young founder. This anecdote reveals how an early effort to buy hibiscus proved not to be Mo's cup of tea.

Exhibit 10.1

MO'S SEARCH FOR THE ELUSIVE HIBISCUS

"Early in 1974 we were running out of hibiscus, the key ingredient in our Red Zinger tea, and our sources had abruptly dried up. I headed for Mexico; it was close and I believed the product would be readily available. I drove alone to the state of Guerrero where I met a man whom I'll call 'Sanchez.' He seemed to be a very important person in the village of Tierra Colorado, which lay near the valley where most of Mexico's crop was grown. I was told that 'Very little hibiscus is moved without his say-so.' My immediate impression, that he was an untrustworthy character, compelled me to try elsewhere.

"After wandering into several dead ends, I arranged with a willing supplier to ship the product to our Boulder doorstep, and within five weeks. I then strapped a few bags to the top of my Datsun for the return trip, pleased with the successful negotiations. At the border, customs officials were more than a little quizzical about those sacks full of suspicious-looking plants, but I was finally waved through.

"No hibiscus arrived as promised. A call to my supposed supplier produced excuses and nothing more. 'The deal fell through,' he said, which meant to me that Sanchez headed off the shipment, forcing me to buy from him. Sanchez cheerfully agreed to send all the hibiscus I requested, but the price had risen to $1.80, almost twice the $1.00 per kilo originally quoted. What could I do? He next insisted that I come down and personally load the shipment. Not supervise the loading, but physically perform the labor. Again, I had little choice but to comply. Eager to get this matter settled, I headed for that out-of-the-way speck on the map, with $5,000 cash in my pocket, resigned to accepting the price-gouging and other toilsome terms of my smiling 'benefactor.' Since there was no

Exhibit 10.1 (Cont.)

place else to stay, he was good-natured enough to put me up at his house.

"Next morning, while wandering about in search of breakfast, I encountered some men who offered to sell me hibiscus at $1.45 a kilo. What a lucky break! With some of my new-found amigos, I hopped into the back of their dilapidated pickup truck. The $5,000 began to burn in my pocket as I concluded after the first two hours of swerving and bumping over the backroads that this might not be such a good idea after all. I began playing my harmonica to relieve the tension, like a kid whistling past the graveyard. Four hours of driving seemed a lifetime, but finally we careened into a tiny settlement where several inquiries provoked only hostility from the inhabitants, who told me to beat it. I agreed, pronto, and quickly urged the driver, my would-be supplier, to drive me back to our starting point. Approaching Sanchez, hat in hand, I confessed rudeness and stupidity, hoping to arouse his paternal instinct, leading to forgiveness and then to delivery of the critical product.

"It worked. I strained to load and stack the herbs, and then secured them onto a truck for the journey to Colorado. Back once again in the safe environs of Celestial, it came as only a fleeting surprise, when the long-awaited shipment arrived, that Sanchez had rigged the scales and shorted me 20 percent in Tierra Colorado. Nor was I particularly amazed to find heavy rocks among the hibiscus leaves in some of the sacks. I resolved, however, not to do business with the likes of Señor Sanchez ever again. We began scouring the globe, finding hibiscus in Sudan and Egypt. Fledgling suppliers were persuaded to enlarge their operations for big-scale export. Our purchasing department then arranged for farmers in China to plant seeds and grow the plants to meet Celestial's requirements. Inadvertently, Celestial stimulated a rapid increase in worldwide hibiscus production, and I derived a certain pleasure from throwing a real zinger at Sanchez, who for a decade thereafter exported little of the product to the United States."

Source: Adapted from document, corporate files, 1983.

1983: RECALL—PRODUCT AND PROSPECTUS

Celestial Seasonings, Inc., withdrew a planned public offering of 910,000 shares of common stock in late 1983, owing to a supply problem with an herb used in one of its products.[1] According to one newspaper report, the "Comfrey" herbal tea product (which accounted for 1 percent of Celestial's total sales) was recalled so ingredients could be tested for the potential presence of an undesirable herb in the blend.[2] Management decided to postpone plans for launching the initial public offering until the matter could be resolved.

[1]"Celestial Seasonings Halts Initial Offering," *The Wall Street Journal*, November 11, 1983, p. 33.
[2]"Company Recalls Herbal Tea," *The Colorado Springs Gazette Telegraph*, November 13, 1983, p. 1.

The narrative and data in Exhibit 10.2 were excerpted from the company's registration statement filed with the Securities and Exchange Commission (in accordance with provisions of the Securities Act of 1933, amended).

Exhibit 10.2

PRELIMINARY PROSPECTUS—SEPTEMBER 23, 1983

THE COMPANY

The Company is the largest manufacturer and marketer of herb teas in the United States. . . . sold primarily in supermarkets and health food stores and, to a lesser degree, through drugstores and mass market retailers. In March 1983 the Company began to market its CamomilD™ line of botanical shampoos and conditioners under the brand name Mountain Herbery, primarily through health food stores. In addition, since 1975 the Company has sold, through mail order, product-related merchandise such as tea canisters, "Tea"-shirts, and posters and, in the fall of 1982, commenced an intensive program of marketing such merchandise through its Celestial Arts division.

The Company has two wholly owned subsidiaries, Celestial Transport, Inc., and Celestial International, a domestic international sales corporation ("DISC").

Currently, the Company estimates its share of the domestic herb tea market to be in excess of 40%. It also estimates that its herb tea products are available in substantially all of the health food stores in the United States and in 75% to 80% of the major supermarkets in the country. Celestial Seasonings' products are sold primarily in the United States and in several other countries, including Canada, Australia, Great Britain, and New Zealand.

Celestial Seasonings was incorporated in Colorado on March 17, 1972, by Mo Siegel, chairman of the board and president of the Company, and John D. Hay, a director of the Company. On August 31, 1983, the Company was reincorporated in Delaware.

USE OF PROCEEDS

. . . The Company expects to use a significant portion of [the proceeds] for expansion of its herb tea business through increased promotional and advertising activities and the purchase of equipment to expand its manufacturing capacity; a portion for development of its health and beauty aids business (now limited to marketing CamomilD shampoos and conditioners manufactured by an unaffiliated company), promotional and advertising activities for Mountain Herbery products, and the purchase of equipment

Exhibit 10.2 (Cont.)

for the manufacture of health and beauty aid products; a portion for research and development for the creation of new products; a portion to purchase 51 acres of land, the site for the proposed construction of a headquarters, manufacturing, and distribution facility; and the balance for the possible acquisition of other businesses, yet to be identified, in the natural, botanical, and health product industries and for working capital purposes.

SELECTED FINANCIAL DATA

The consolidated financial statements for the year ended June 30, 1983 were examined by Peat, Marwick, Mitchell & Co., whose report with respect thereto appears elsewhere in this Prospectus. The financial state-

	YEAR ENDED JUNE 30,				
	1979	1980	1981[a]	1982	1983
	(dollars in thousands, except per share amounts)				
Consolidated Statement of Earnings Data:					
New sales	$ 10,416	$ 11,559	$ 16,310	$ 21,397	$ 27,025
Cost of sales	5,604	6,194	8,305	10,430	12,269
Gross profit	4,812	5,365	8,005	10,967	14,756
Selling, general, and administrative expenses	3,557	3,818	5,744	7,958	11,192
Operating income	1,255	1,547	2,261	3,009	3,564
Interest income (expense) and other, net	(96)	(441)	(129)	(2)	126
Earnings before income taxes	1,159	1,106	2,132	3,007	3,690
Income taxes	450	439	988	1,282	1,497
Net earnings	$ 709	$ 667	$ 1,144	$ 1,725	$ 2,193
Earnings per share	$ 0.19	$ 0.17	$ 0.32	$ 0.49	$ 0.63
Weighted average shares	3,810,044	3,835,216	3,578,848	3,512,446	3,489,612
Cash dividends per share	$ —	$ —	$ —	$ —	$ 0.05357
Consolidated Balance Sheet Data					
Net working capital	$ 1,711	$ 1,825	$ 2,086	$ 3,425	$ 3,274
Total assets	5,293	5,280	6,786	8,323	13,101
Long-term obligations, excluding current maturities	523	283	243	334	1,483
Stockholders' equity	2,378	2,920	3,742	5,388	7,349

[a]In fiscal 1981 the Company adopted the last-in, first-out ("LIFO") method of costing inventory. Previously, the first-in, first-out ("FIFO") method was used. The effect of the change was to reduce net earnings by approximately $123,000 ($0.03 per share) in fiscal 1981 from what would otherwise have been

Exhibit 10.2 (Cont.)

ments for each of the four years ended June 30, 1982 were examined by Fox & Company.

RESULTS OF OPERATIONS

The following table is derived from Celestial Seasonings' Consolidated Statement of Earnings:

| | YEAR ENDED JUNE 30, | | |
	1981	1982	1983
Net sales	100.0%	100.0%	100.0%
Cost of sales	50.9	48.7	45.4
Gross profit	49.1	51.3	54.6
Selling, general, and administrative expenses	35.2	37.2	41.4
Operating income	13.9	14.1	13.2
Interest income (expense) and other, net	(0.8)	—	0.5
Earnings before income taxes	13.1	14.1	13.7
Income taxes	6.1	6.0	5.6
Net earnings	7.0%	8.1%	8.1%

Net Sales   Net sales increased $5,087,000 from fiscal 1981 to fiscal 1982 (a 31.2% increase) and $5,628,000 from fiscal 1982 to fiscal 1983 (a 26.3% increase). Most of this increase resulted from increased sales volume; price increases during this period were substantially below the rate of inflation. During this period, the Company was able to substantially increase the distribution of its herb teas in supermarkets. In fiscal 1983 at least one Celestial Seasonings herb tea product was available in 75% to 80% of the major supermarkets in the United States, up from 50% to 55% in fiscal 1981 and 65% to 70% in fiscal 1982. In addition, Celestial Seasonings has been able to maintain its strong health food store position. The Company believes that it has benefited from increased industry spending on advertising and promotion in recent years, which has resulted in increased consumer acceptance of herb tea. The Company also believes that it has benefited from the increased concern regarding caffeine and the trend toward healthier, more natural products. In fiscal 1983 the Company introduced the Mountain Herbery hair care product line and created its Celestial Arts division to enhance product-related sales.

Cost of Sales   Cost of sales decreased to 45.4% of net sales in fiscal

reported. There was no cumulative effect on prior years since the ending inventory in 1980 is the beginning inventory for LIFO purposes. The report of certified public accountants concurred with the change and was qualified as to consistency.

Exhibit 10.2 (Cont.)

1983 from 48.7% of net sales in fiscal 1982 and from 50.9% of net sales in fiscal 1981. This reduction is primarily the result of increased productivity due to investment in capital equipment and increased volume. Cost of sales as a percentage of net sales also benefited during this period from greater volume discounts from suppliers, the strength of the U.S. dollar against foreign currencies, and a product mix with higher gross margins.

Selling, General, and Administrative Expenses   Selling, general, and administrative expenses in fiscal 1981 were 35.2% of net sales. These expenses increased to 37.2% of net sales in fiscal 1982 and to 41.4% of net sales in fiscal 1983. The component of these expenses represented by general and administrative expenses declined, primarily because it increased at a slower rate than the growth rate of net sales. The selling expense component increased as a percentage of net sales because, as costs in other areas decreased, the Company increased its marketing expenditures in order to improve market share during this period of rapid growth in the herb tea market and to respond to increased competition.

Net Earnings   Earnings after income taxes as a percentage of net sales increased from 7.0% in fiscal 1981 to 8.1% in fiscal 1982, primarily as a result of the decrease in percentage of the cost of sales and other income, which was only partially offset by the increase in selling, general and administrative expenses as a percentage of net sales. In fiscal 1983, the Company maintained its earnings after taxes as a percentage of net sales at the level achieved in fiscal 1982 (8.1%) while at the same time increasing the selling, general and administrative expense percentage. The Company's effective income tax rates were 46.3%, 42.6%, and 40.6% in fiscal years 1981, 1982, and 1983, respectively. The decrease in effective tax rates for fiscal 1982 and 1983 was primarily attributable to investment tax credits and deferred DISC income.

Seasonality   Celestial Seasonings' business currently is seasonal because herb tea sales occur predominantly during cold weather. The Company's sales and earnings peak during the winter (the Company's third fiscal quarter), and it experiences nominal earnings or losses during the summer (the Company's first fiscal quarter). Celestial Seasonings' net sales by quarter for the fiscal years ended June 30, 1982 and 1983, stated in thousands, were as follows:

	NET SALES (UNAUDITED) THREE MONTHS ENDED			
FISCAL YEAR	September 30,	December 31,	March 31,	June 30,
1982	$3,694	$5,495	$6,815	$5,393
1983	$4,514	$7,126	$8,487	$6,898

Celestial Seasonings expects sales of its iced herb teas to increase in proportion to total herb tea sales and expects to develop new products

Exhibit 10.2 (Cont.)

such as health and beauty aids. These factors should reduce the seasonality of its business. Because the Company's earnings are currently seasonal, quarterly results may not be indicative of results for the entire fiscal year.

First Quarter of Fiscal 1984   During the first quarter of fiscal 1983 (the quarter ended September 30, 1982), Celestial Seasonings had net sales of $4,514,000, and, based on preliminary data, the Company expects that net sales for the first quarter of fiscal 1984 (the quarter ending September 30, 1983) will increase approximately 10% over the prior year's quarter. Celestial Seasonings had net earnings of $293,000 ($0.08 per share) for the first quarter of fiscal 1983. The Company currently expects nominal earnings or a nominal loss for the first quarter of fiscal 1984, which is consistent with the Company's historical seasonal pattern. The Company anticipates that selling, general, and administrative expenses as a percentage of net sales will increase in the first quarter of fiscal 1984 over the relatively low levels experienced in the first quarter of fiscal 1983 as a result of increased marketing and advertising expenses, costs of new product introduction and costs related to changes in the Company's method of distribution of herb tea products. Due to the seasonality of herb tea sales, results for the first quarter of the Company's fiscal year may not be indicative of results for the entire fiscal year.

LIQUIDITY AND CAPITAL RESOURCES

In fiscal 1982 and 1983, the Company has emphasized the addition of new products, requiring an increase in working capital. These increases have been financed through current operating income and surplus cash reserves, and long-term borrowings have not been necessary for these purposes.

As of August 31, 1983 the Company had available bank lines of credit, bearing interest at the banks' prime rates, totaling $9,000,000 of which approximately $7,500,000 was unused. Management believes that these lines of credit, combined with cash currently available in short-term investments and the proceeds from this offering, will be adequate to finance the Company's requirements in the near future. In fiscal 1984, cash expenditures for land and equipment, which are anticipated to total approximately $2,000,000, are expected to be financed through the proceeds of this offering and the available bank lines of credit.

BUSINESS

Celestial Seasonings' primary business is the manufacturing and marketing of a variety of blended herb teas in tea bags and loose packages. The

Exhibit 10.2 (Cont.)

Company is the country's largest manufacturer of herb teas. The Company's herb tea sales accounted for approximately 96% of total revenues for the fiscal year ended June 30, 1983. The Celestial Seasonings tea-bag line consists of 20 blends and 7 single-herb teas, listed here by product name.

Blends		Single Herbs
Almond Sunset™	Lemon Mist®	Chamomile Flowers
Cinnamon Rose®	Mandarin Orange Spice™	Comfrey Leaves
Country Apple®	Mellow Mint®	Foenugreek
Diet Partner®	Mo's 24®	Lemon Verbena
Emperor's Choice®	Morning Thunder®	Peppermint
Ginseng Plus®	Pelican Punch®	Rosehips
Grandma's Tummy Mint™	Red Zinger®	Spearmint
Iced Delight Lemon®	Roastaroma®	
Iced Delight Mint®	Sleepytime®	
Iced Delight Orange®	Sunburst C™	

Six of the blends accounted for approximately 50% of revenues for fiscal 1983. Celestial Seasonings obtains trademarks for its product names to the extent possible and has a policy of aggressively defending its trademarks.

The Company also markets a line of CamomilD shampoos and conditioners under the Mountain Herbery label. This line was introduced in March 1983 and accounted for approximately 2% of total revenues for fiscal 1983. The Company also sells product-related merchandise, such as "Tea"-shirts, tea canisters, posters, and herb charts, through its Celestial Arts division. Celestial Arts' sales accounted for approximately 2% of fiscal 1983 revenues.

THE HERB TEA INDUSTRY

Herb tea is a beverage brewed from dried herbs (fruits, flowers, leaves, seeds, bark, roots, or spices) that are blended in combination or presented as a single-herb tea product. Herb teas do not contain black or green tea (which come from the tea plant *Thea sinensis*) and generally do not contain caffeine.

Herbs are grown, dried, cut, sifted, blended, and packaged into herb teas. Herb tea is sold in tea bags (small infusion bags made of filter paper containing herbs and used to prepare individual servings of the beverage) and loose (in containers, but not in tea bags, and used by the consumer to make tea using a tea strainer). Herb tea sold in tea bags is milled to a finer degree than is herb tea sold loose. Although sales of instant tea constitute

Exhibit 10.2 (Cont.)

a significant portion of the market for black tea, there is currently no significant production of instant herb tea.

The major markets for herb tea are supermarkets and health food stores. Herb teas sold in supermarkets generally may be found in the tea section or in the specialty food or nutrition sections. Other markets include institutions (such as restaurants, food service organizations, and schools), specialty food stores (gourmet shops and ethnic food stores), and mail order.

Annual sales at wholesale in the United States herb tea market are currently estimated to be approximately $70,000,000. Of this total, supermarket sales account for approximately 75%, the health food market segment accounts for approximately 20%, and the balance is accounted for by the institutional, specialty food store, and mail order markets.

By way of comparison, annual sales at wholesale of black tea are currently estimated to be approximately $700,000,000. The market for black tea includes plain black tea, flavored black tea (black tea with flavorings added) and instant black tea. Flavored black tea is not considered an herb tea because it is made from the *Thea sinensis* plant, which contains caffeine.

Although herb teas have been consumed for thousands of years in Europe, the Orient, and elsewhere, the U.S. herb tea market is relatively new. Celestial Seasonings was the first to popularize blended herb teas in the United States. The herb tea market began to grow rapidly in the early to mid-1970s, which the Company attributes to a general trend among consumers to be more health conscious and to consume beverages containing less or no caffeine. This trend started among consumers shopping in health food stores and has expanded to include supermarket shoppers.

The herb tea market began to grow at a faster rate in the early 1980s when major tea companies entered the herb tea market and competition for supermarket sales intensified. Such competition, in the Company's opinion, has helped spur growth of the herb tea market by increasing public awareness and acceptance of herb tea. It also helped to open increased shelf space for herb tea in the tea section of supermarkets, which is largely responsible for significantly higher sales of herb teas in 1981, 1982, and 1983. It is expected that the demand for herb tea over the next several years will increase, although not at the same rate that characterized the 1970s and early 1980s.

Markets and Customers for the Company's Herb Teas

Celestial Seasonings estimates that there are approximately 35,000 major supermarkets in the United States, that is, those with annual sales in excess of $1,000,000. Supermarket sales of herb teas are estimated to consti-

Exhibit 10.2 (Cont.)

tute approximately 75% of total herb tea sales. It is estimated that the Company has the largest market share in the supermarket segment, with approximately 40% of that market share and distribution in 75% to 80% of these stores.

The Company estimates that there are approximately 8,000 health food stores in the United States, substantially all of which carry Celestial Seasonings herb tea products. Sales of herb tea through health food stores account for approximately 20% of total herb tea sales. Although there are no reliable independent measures, the Company believes that it is the market leader in the health food segment of the herb tea industry and estimates that it has a market share in the health food segment in excess of 50%.

Celestial Seasonings' herb teas are distributed in the United States through three primary channels: products are made available to health food stores through health food distributors, products are made available to supermarkets through supermarket distributors, and products are sold directly to supermarket chains through brokers. The Company's herb tea products are also distributed in other countries, including Canada, Australia, Great Britain, and New Zealand. The Company also sells to drugstores and mass merchandisers. The Company sells its herb teas to approximately 400 accounts, the largest of which represented approximately 2% of total revenues for fiscal 1983.

The Company anticipates that it will devote effort to maintain its overall market leadership by continuing to solidify its dominant position in the health food segment, by attempting to expand its leadership position in the supermarket segment, by developing such other segments as the institutional market, and by striving to increase its international sales.

The Company's Herb Tea Operations

Suppliers   Celestial Seasonings purchases herbs from numerous foreign and domestic manufacturers, importers, and growers. The Company purchases approximately 80% of its herbs from outside the United States, from South and Central America, Europe, Africa, and China. Herb purchase arrangements with suppliers are generally made annually and in U.S. currency. Purchases are made through purchase orders or contracts and vary with respect to price, delivery terms, and product specifications.

The Company's herb purchasers annually visit major suppliers around the world to procure herbs and to assure quality by observing production methods and providing product specifications. Higher demand for herb tea in the United States is causing a higher domestic demand for herbs, but the Company believes that domestic demand is not a substantial factor in worldwide demand for herbs. The Company's ability to ensure a continuing supply of herbs depends on many factors that are

Exhibit 10.2 (Cont.)

beyond its control, such as unstable political situations in the foreign countries from which herbs are imported, embargoes, changes in national and world economic conditions, currency fluctuations, and unfavorable climatic conditions.

Many herbs are presently grown in countries where inexpensive labor makes labor-intensive cultivation possible and where the Company often must educate the growers about product standards. The Company performs laboratory analysis on incoming herb shipments in order to assure that they meet its quality standards and those of the Food and Drug Administration to the extent applicable.

Celestial Seasonings purchases all of its packaging materials domestically. The Company obtains, on a purchase order basis, all of its tea bag paper from a single domestic supplier, from which it has purchased paper since 1976. That supplier is also the major source of tea bag paper for the black tea industry. The Company has identified one other domestic source and two foreign sources from which it believes it could obtain tea bag paper of comparable quality at a comparable price. The ability of the Company, in common with all tea manufacturers, to assure a continuing supply of bagged tea depends upon the continuing access to tea bag paper.

Of the Company's suppliers, none accounted for more than 10% of total purchases during the last fiscal year.

Production and Equipment   From its inventory of herbs, Celestial Seasonings produces a variety of blended herb teas in tea bags and in loose packages. Approximately 60 herbs go into its blends. The Company cleans, cuts, sifts, blends, and packages herbs into finished products at its facilities in Boulder, Colorado. The Company's major competitors purchase premilled herbs from suppliers.

Celestial Seasonings uses air gravity separation to clean herbs for subsequent milling through its automated milling and sifting equipment, at which stage herbs destined for tea bag and loose-packed products are separated and further milling is conducted on the herbs that will be placed in tea bags. Individual herbs are combined in the Company's blending system, and then the blends are taste tested to ensure flavor consistency. Although the Company is a leader in developing the technology for cleaning, milling, and sifting herbs, that technology is still evolving. The Company conducts extensive quality control testing in its laboratory throughout the manufacturing process for the purpose of ensuring that the herbs and its products comply strictly with the Company's quality specifications and those of the Food and Drug Administration to the extent applicable.

A continuous line of automated equipment deposits the blended herb tea in tea bags and packages them in boxes, and then cases. Celestial Seasonings believes that its tea bagging lines are the most automated in

Exhibit 10.2 (Cont.)

the country. It runs two lines, each line containing two bagging machines. Each machine produces at the rate of approximately 900 tea bags per minute.

Following final packaging and quality control, the packaged herb tea is transported, generally on trucks operated by the Company's subsidiary, Celestial Transport, Inc., which leases a fleet of 7 tractors and 2 trailers and owns 10 trailers. The Company currently ships approximately 85% of all its incoming herbs and outgoing finished products domestically through Celestial Transport, Inc.

Herb Tea Product Development

A majority of the existing Celestial Seasonings herb tea blends were created by Mo Siegel, President of the Company. The Company now employs a Ph.D. food technologist, who develops and revises herb tea products and continuously tests new blends of herbs, using herb experts and volunteer "tea-tasters." Four of the Company's five top-selling herb tea blends were developed and introduced in the last five years. Tea-tasters are also used to test any changes made in currently available blends and to compare Celestial Seasonings herb teas with competing brands.

Packaging and Artwork

Celestial Seasonings herb teas are packaged in lightweight boxes with colorful artwork and light-hearted philosophical phrases and stories. From its inception, the Company has considered artistic packaging to be an integral part of its overall philosophy and marketing program. Packaging and artwork are constantly being reviewed and improved to make the most colorful and interesting presentation. The Company has won several advertising awards for its packaging. The Company's artwork appears on the trucks operated by its subsidiary, Celestial Transport, Inc., which won an award in 1982 for the best-decorated trucks. The Company believes that there is marketing potential for its artwork, through its Celestial Arts merchandise and through licensing. See "Other Products."

Due to the importance of product package design and artwork to the success of its herb tea business, the Company has taken, and will continue to take, vigorous action to protect against the imitation of its products and packages and to protect its trademarks and copyrights.

OTHER PRODUCTS

In March 1983 the Company introduced a line of CamomilD shampoos and conditioners under the Mountain Herbery label, which is manufactured by an unrelated company to the specifications of Celestial Season-

Exhibit 10.2 (Cont.)

ings. The line is sold primarily through health food stores and accounted for 2% of total revenues for the fiscal year ended June 30, 1983. The Company also sells product-related material, such as "Tea"-shirts, tea canisters, posters and herb charts though its Celestial Arts division, which accounted for 2% of fiscal 1983 revenues. The Celestial Arts division sells to customers through direct mail.

Celestial Seasonings believes that its botanical and herbal expertise can be applied to other product areas and that its generally recognized strengths in product quality, creative product names, attractive packaging, and brand-name recognition are transferable to other product areas. The Company anticipates that it will take advantage of its positioning in the natural, botanical, and health product area by expanding in the natural health and beauty aid industry. The Company intends to purchase equipment for the manufacture of health and beauty aid products and to conduct research and development programs for new health and beauty aids and other products. In addition, the Company will consider acquisition of businesses in related industries that fit with the Company's herbal expertise, its distribution channels, and its philosophy of developing and promoting healthful, natural, and botanical products.

COMPETITION

Competitive factors in the herb tea industry include product quality and taste, brand-name awareness among consumers, interesting or unique names for herb tea flavors, product packaging and package design, supermarket shelf space, reputation, price, and advertising and promotion.

Celestial Seasonings is the herb tea industry leader. Its generally recognized competitive strengths include high quality, a reputation for healthy and natural products, attractive packaging, interesting product names, and herbal expertise.

Other major competitors in the herb tea industry include Thomas J. Lipton Company ("Lipton"), R. C. Bigelow, Inc., and the Magic Mountain product line of Iroquois Brands Grocery Products, Inc. There are several other competitors that sell to the health food industry, and there are other regional herb tea companies. Potential entrants to the herb tea industry include manufacturers of black tea and flavored black teas that are not yet in the herb tea market, many of which have substantially greater financial resources than the Company.

Lipton entered the herb tea market on a national basis in the fall of 1981 and rapidly achieved trade leadership in the supermarket segment, thereby quickly attaining the number two position in the herb tea industry as a whole. Throughout this period, the Company held its market share leadership in the herb tea industry as a whole. The Company regained su-

Exhibit 10.2 (Cont.)

permarket trade leadership from Lipton in the summer of 1982 and has since maintained its leadership in that segment as well.

The Company has recently entered the health and beauty aid market by introducing Mountain Herbery shampoos and conditioners and intends to develop and market new health and beauty aid products. The health and beauty aid market is highly competitive, and many products competing with the Company's products are manufactured by companies with substantially greater financial resources than the Company.

EMPLOYEES

Celestial Seasonings has approximately 200 employees, none of whom is affiliated with unions. The Company believes it has very good employee relations.

The Company seeks to enhance productivity through the quality of its work environment. The work environment fostered by the Company includes the encouragement of employee participation in work teams directed at improved productivity, the promotion of confidence and personal growth of employees, the absence of time clocks and reserved parking, periodic Companywide meetings, an employee assistance program, and employee benefit plans.

Employee Benefit Plans

Celestial Seasonings currently maintains two tax-qualified retirement plans, an Employee Stock Ownership Plan (the "ESOP") and an employee thrift plan (the "Thrift Plan"). The Company also maintains a gainsharing program, under which annual cash awards are made, based on performance in excess of management objectives. These plans are available to all employees, subject to certain minimum age and employment requirements.

The purposes of the ESOP are to enable the Company to attract and retain competent management and staff personnel, by giving its employees a direct interest in the financial success of the Company, and to provide retirement benefits for Company employees. Deductible contributions are allocated to the participants annually in accordance with a formula that takes into account both the salary of the employee and the length of service with the Company. The trustee of the plan is required by the terms of the ESOP to invest the assets of the plan primarily in shares of Common Stock. The trustee holds the assets of the ESOP and makes distribution to participants upon retirement, death, disability, and other events specified in the ESOP.

In order to participate in the Company's Thrift Plan, eligible employ-

Exhibit 10.2 (Cont.)

ees must elect to contribute between 1% and 15% of their compensation to the plan. From its profits, the Company matches the first 6% of a participating employee's contributions on a sliding scale based upon the employee's length of service with the Company. Participating employees are permitted to direct the trustee to invest up to one-half of their accounts in the Thrift Plan in shares of the Common Stock of the Company. Any amounts that are not directed to be used to purchase shares of the Company's Common Stock are invested by the trustee at its discretion. Benefits are paid from the Thrift Plan upon retirement, death, disability, or termination of employment. In addition, participants may withdraw Company contributions after specified periods of participation and may withdraw their own contributions upon demonstration of financial hardship.

GOVERNMENT REGULATION

The domestic herb tea industry is subject to the jurisdiction of the Food and Drug Administration (the "FDA"). Because the herb tea industry is relatively new to this country, the agency has not established uniform standards of acceptability for some of the herbs that the Company uses. While approximately 90% of the herbs used by the Company are on the list of substances "generally recognized as safe" by the FDA, some of the Company's major herb ingredients do not have any standards established by the FDA. Adverse action by any governmental regulatory agency, particularly if accompanied by publicity (as is often the case), could have an adverse effect on the Company and public acceptance of its products. Additionally, such action could result in government or court orders forbidding the Company from using certain herbs essential for the manufacture of currently produced tea blends.

MANAGEMENT

Directors and Executive Officers

Information concerning the Company's directors and executive officers is set forth as follows:

The Board of Directors is divided into three classes, with the three-year term of office of one class expiring each year. Officers serve at the pleasure of the Board of Directors.

MO SIEGEL. Mr. Siegel, founder of Celestial Seasonings, has served as its President since its inception over 13 years ago. He is an acknowledged expert in herbs, as well as a leader in the health food industry. Mr. Siegel has received considerable national publicity and attention because of his

Exhibit 10.2 (Cont.)

Name	Age	Positions with Company
Mo Siegel[3]	33	Director, Chairman of the Board, President
John D. Hay[1]	38	Director
Robert D. Cameron[3]	50	Director
Bernard C. Jakacki[2]	49	Director
Charles L. Biederman[2]	49	Director
Monique S. Koehler[1]	39	Director
John G. Mancino	36	Vice President of Operations
Barnet M. Feinblum	35	Vice President of Finance, Secretary, Treasurer
Keith E. Brenner	38	Vice President of Corporate Development
Paul F. Enright	43	Vice President of Marketing and Sales

[1]Term expires in 1984 (Class A).
[2]Term expires in 1985 (Class B).
[3]Term expires in 1986 (Class C).

efforts to improve the health habits of the American people and his willingness to use progressive and innovative management practices. His pursuit of progressive management has contributed to the successful growth of the Company. He has been actively involved in community projects and management organizations and is a member of the Young Presidents Organization. Mr. Siegel created the majority of the Celestial Seasonings blended herb teas.

JOHN D. HAY. Mr. Hay is a co-founder of the Company and holds a bachelor's degree in business administration from Adelphi University in New York. He has been a director since inception of the Company and served as Co-president of the Company from 1974 to 1978 and as Chairman of the Board in 1977 and 1978. Mr. Hay is currently president and chairman of the board of directors of Cell Technology, Inc., a cancer research company, and a director of Natural Horizons, Inc., a natural foods grocery company in Boulder, Colorado. See "Certain Transactions with Management and Others." Mr. Hay is a founder and director of the Boulder School for Religious Studies.

ROBERT D. CAMERON. Mr. Cameron has been a director of the Company since February 1981 and has 30 years' experience in the food industry. Since 1976, Mr. Cameron has been the vice president of sales for Specialty Brands, a major processor of specialty food products, including Spice Island spices, Marie's refrigerated dressings, and Aunt Millie's sauces.

BERNARD C. JAKACKI. Mr. Jakacki received his bachelor's degree from the University of Pennsylvania and his Master of business administration degree from the Wharton Graduate School of Business in 1960. Mr. Jakacki was elected to the Board of Directors in November 1981. During his 25 years in the food industry, Mr. Jakacki was the director of product management for the Thomas J. Lipton Company from 1962 through 1973

Exhibit 10.2 (Cont.)

and a vice president of Continental Grain Company from 1973 through 1977. Since 1977, he has been president and chief executive officer of Quality Bakers of America, a bakery cooperative accounting for approximately 25% of U.S. supermarket bakery product sales.

CHARLES L. BIEDERMAN. Mr. Biederman received his bachelor's degree from Colgate University and his master of architecture degree from Columbia University in 1959. Mr. Biederman was elected to the Board of Directors in November 1981. Mr. Biederman is the former president of Levitt Building Systems, a division of International Telephone & Telegraph Corp. Since 1975, Mr. Biederman has been a senior partner of Robert Rouse and Associates, a firm engaged in the marketing and sale of condominium properties throughout the country. He is also the president of C. L. Biederman, Inc., a real estate investment firm and is an active member of the American Arbitration Association.

MONIQUE S. KOEHLER. Mrs. Koehler has been a director since January 1982. Mrs. Koehler is a former vice president of purchasing and vice president of marketing for Private Formulations, Inc., a division of Revco D.S., Inc., a major manufacturer of private-label vitamins and over-the-counter drugs. She is vice president and secretary of Koehler-Iversen, Inc., a New York–based advertising agency, and since 1978 has been chief executive officer of MSK Associates, a manufacturing representative and consultant to the vitamin and pharmaceutical industries.

JOHN G. MANCINO. Mr. Mancino has held the position of Vice President of Operations since 1973. Mr. Mancino holds a bachelor's degree from Colgate University. Prior to joining the Company, he was employed as a consultant to the city of New York and other municipalities in the field of technical business evaluation. In addition, he was employed as a vice president for Pisces Production, a company engaged in aerial photography and other related services.

BARNET M. FEINBLUM. Mr. Feinblum holds a bachelor's degree in industrial engineering and operations research from Cornell University and a master of business administration degree from the University of Colorado. His work experience includes production management with Samsonite Corp., Levitt Building Systems, a division of International Telephone & Telegraph Corp., and Stanley Structures Co. Mr. Feinblum joined the Company in August 1976 as Production Manager and was appointed Director of Finance in October 1979, Vice President of Finance and Secretary in November 1980, and Treasurer in May 1982.

KEITH E. BRENNER. Mr. Brenner holds a bachelor's degree in economics from the University of Calgary. His background includes sales and marketing experience as a product manager for General Foods Corporation, various assignments with Pepsi-Cola Canada, Ltd., and experience as marketing director of Africa for PepsiCo International. Mr. Brenner joined the Company in September 1978 and was appointed Director of Marketing in

Exhibit 10.2 (Cont.)

January 1980 and Vice President of Marketing in November 1980. He was appointed Vice President of Corporate Development in April 1983.

PAUL F. ENRIGHT. Mr. Enright holds a bachelor's degree in food distribution from Michigan State University. Mr. Enright's previous experience includes his serving as territory sales manager with General Foods Corporation, as division sales manager of Mead Johnson & Co., and, from 1975 until joining the Company as Vice President of Sales in July 1980, as director of sales operations with the Coca-Cola Company Foods Division. He was appointed Vice President of Marketing and Sales in April 1983.

Management Remuneration

The following table sets forth information concerning remuneration paid or accrued by the Company for services in all capacities during the fiscal year ended June 30, 1983 for each of the five highest-paid officers and directors whose aggregate remuneration exceeded $50,000 and for all officers and directors as a group.

	CASH AND CASH-EQUIVALENTS[1]	
Person and Position	Salaries, Fees, Bonuses	Securities, Property, and Other Personal Benefits[2]
Mo Siegel, Chairman of the Board, President	$136,535	$ 289
John G. Mancino, Vice President of Operations	101,546	281
Barnet M. Feinblum, Vice President of Finance, Secretary, Treasurer	91,851	231
Keith E. Brenner, Vice President of Corporate Development	100,199	261
Paul F. Enright, Vice President of Marketing and Sales	98,947	401
All officers and directors as a group (10 persons)	559,078	1,463

[1]The amounts reported in the table do not include amounts expensed by the Company that may have value as personal benefits to such individuals, but that are made in connection with the conduct of the Company's business. All such personal benefits, which include the President's automobile, the use of a Company-owned condominium in Avon, Colorado, and two Company bicycles, are to facilitate job performance and to minimize work-related expenses. Although the amount of such personal benefits and the extent to which they are related to job performance cannot be specifically or precisely ascertained, the Company has concluded that the aggregate amount of such personal benefits does not exceed $5,000 for each person named or included in the table.

[2]Included in this column are the cost of insurance premiums.

Exhibit 10.2 (Cont.)

Directors' Compensation

Members of the Board of Directors of the Company are reimbursed for their out-of-pocket expenses incurred in connection with attendance at meetings of the Board of Directors, including travel and lodging expenses. Each director who is not also an employee of the Company receives a fee of $3,000 per year, plus $500 per day for each meeting attended and for special assignments.

PRINCIPAL AND SELLING STOCKHOLDERS

The following table sets forth information as of August 31, 1983, regarding securities owned by directors, officers, 5% stockholders, and each of the selling stockholders.

Directors, Officers and 5% Stockholders*	SHARES BENEFICIALLY OWNED PRIOR TO OFFERING		Number of Shares Offered	SHARES TO BE BENEFICIALLY OWNED AFTER OFFERING	
	Number	% of Total		Number	% of Total
Mo Siegel	1,022,266	29.4	104,869	917,397	23.3
IntraWest Bank of Boulder As Trustee for Employee Stock Ownership Plan of Celestial Seasonings, Inc.	365,176	10.5	—	365,176	9.3
John D. Hay	309,246	8.9	35,000	274,246	7.0
Lucinda M. Ziesing	173,880	5.0	35,000	138,880	3.5
John G. Mancino	156,100	4.5	35,000	121,100	3.1
Keith E. Brenner	68,558	2.0	11,200	57,358	1.5
Barnet M. Feinblum	53,662	1.5	—	53,662	1.4
Paul F. Enright	52,696	1.5	—	52,696	1.3
Charles L. Biederman	14,000	(4)	—	14,000	
Bernard C. Jakacki	14,000	(4)	12,600	1,400	
Monique S. Koehler	700	(4)	—	700	
Robert D. Cameron	700	(4)	—	700	
Total	2,230,984	64.1	233,669	1,997,315	50.7
All officers and directors as a group	1,691,928	48.6	198,669	1,493,259	37.9

*Other selling stockholders owned 922,740 shares prior to the planned offering

Source: *Preliminary Prospectus dated September 23, 1983, 910,000 shares, Celestial Seasonings, Inc.—common stock ($0.01 par value). The initial public offering price was anticipated to be between $12 and $15 per share.

KRAFT, LIPTON, LEVERAGED BUYOUT

In 1984, Kraft, Inc., acquired Celestial Seasonings, paying approximately $40 million for the company. The foods unit of Dart & Kraft presumably intended to cash in on health trends by acquiring Celestial's dominant brand name and attractive growth potential. The new subsidiary's estimated earnings of just over $3 million in 1983 amounted to slightly more than one-half of 1 percent of the parent's operating profits of $554 million on sales of $6.7 billion for the year. Kraft was not expected to install its own management, at least not soon, with Mo Siegel agreeing to stay on as chairman-president for at least two years. Kraft contributed marketing expertise, expanded Celestial's promotional horizons with a larger advertising budget ($4.0 million in 1986), and helped the company diversify and expand internationally.

Before founder Siegel left the company in January 1986, he was instrumental in selecting Barnet M. Feinblum, the company's treasurer for four years, as new president of Celestial. Barnet Feinblum brought his financial and other management strengths to the position, intent upon holding to the company's established traditions, ethics, and mission. Exhibit 10.3 outlines the corporate philosophy, repeating tenets of the faith from earlier years, modifying some, and adding others.

Exhibit 10.3

CELESTIAL SEASONING BELIEFS

OUR QUEST FOR EXCELLENCE

We believe that in order to make this world a better place in which to live, we must be totally dedicated to the endless quest for excellence in the important tasks which we endeavor to accomplish.

OUR ENVIRONMENT

We believe in fostering a working environment which promotes creativity and encourages possibility thinking throughout the organization. We plan our work to be satisfying, productive, and challenging. As such, we support an atmosphere which encourages intelligent risk taking without the fear of failure.

OUR PRODUCTS

We believe in marketing and selling healthful and naturally oriented products that nurture people's bodies and uplift their souls. Our products must be superior in quality, of good value, beautifully artistic, and philosophically inspiring.

DIGNITY OF THE INDIVIDUAL

We believe in the dignity of the individual, and we are totally committed to the fair, honest, kind, and professional treatment of all individuals and organizations with whom we work.

Exhibit 10.3 (Cont.)

OUR EMPLOYEES

We believe that our employees develop a commitment to excellence when they are directly involved in the management of their areas of responsibility. This team effort maximizes quality results, minimizes costs, and allows our employees the opportunity to have authorship and personal satisfaction in their accomplishments, as well as sharing in the financial rewards of their individual and team efforts.

We believe in hiring above-average people who have a "hands-on" approach to work and quest for excellent results. In exchange, we are committed to the development of our good people by identifying, cultivating, training, rewarding, retaining, and promoting those individuals who are committed to moving our organization forward.

OUR GROWTH

We believe in aggressive, steady, predictable, and well-planned growth in sales and earnings. We are intent on building a large company that will flourish into the next century and thereafter.

OUR CONSUMERS AND CUSTOMERS

We believe that our past, current, and future successes come from a total dedication to excellent service to those who buy our products. Satisfying our customer and consumer needs in a superior way is the only reason we are in business, and we shall proceed with an obsession to give wholeheartedly to those who buy our products. Our customers and consumers are king, and we are here to serve them.

OUR DREAM

Our role at Celestial Seasonings is to play an active part in making this world a better place by unselfishly serving the public. We believe we can have a significant impact on making people's lives happier and healthier through their use of our products. By dedicating our total resources to this dream, everyone profits: our customers, consumers, employees and shareholders. Our actions are building blocks in making this world a better place now and for future generations.

Source: © 1987 by Celestial Seasonings, 1780 55th Street, Boulder, CO 80301-2799

Barnet Feinblum's penchant for in-house entrepreneurship was instrumental in cultivating employee creativity and strengthening Celestial's competitive muscle through participation groups. Feinblum directed Celestial's well-established teamwork methods, designed to stimulate growth and profits through new-product development, toward entrepreneurial ends. To these "adventure teams," launched in the spring of 1984, nontea products were of increasing interest, but the tea lines, foundations of the company's success, occupied center stage. When vice president of finance, Barnet volunteered to lead a group looking at black tea products. His team members, who possessed skills and took assignments paralleling those of key individuals in the company, came from marketing, sales, purchasing, production, data processing, and product testing. Assignments for the groups led to members' stretching beyond their normal job responsibilities.

In examining opportunity areas, the beginning exercise included market assessment. For example, Feinblum, serving as president and team leader of the adventure team "company," began by describing the billion-dollar retail tea market as having four parts: (1) herb tea sales total $100 million; (2) regular black tea (48- and 100-count orange pekoe bags) accounts for $450 million and instant black tea for $350 million; (3) premium specialties—such as traditional English Breakfast or Darjeeling—amount to $35 million; and (4) flavored teas—usually 95 percent black tea plus flavorings like spice or almond—represent sales of $65 million.

Next stage: explore company strengths and weaknesses, its ability to compete. Celestial's 25 flavor varieties were estimated to fill about half the nation's herbal teacups. The adventure team concluded they could ill afford to go after the giant marketers of black tea, and traditional teas seemed to be outside the company's major areas of strength, so this segment was rejected. After a process spanning four months, a conclusion was reached: flavored teas held sufficient potential to merit investment.

As deliberations continued, the team had to go beyond choosing a product focus and speculating about market targets to reasoning through several key issues, such as the likely impact of such new products on existing lines and markets, status of production capacity, requirements for packaging, elements of market-based pricing, distribution channel requirements, and promotion opportunities.

Feinblum's belief in rewarding people for trying, not just for succeeding, stimulated the kind of team interaction that could lead to expanded market penetration and improved corporate performance. Although the report card on flavored black teas was not complete, the 10 new products brought onstream through the adventure team's creative efforts and effective follow-through by their corporate counterparts appeared to be alive and well as the company closed the books on 1989. Exhibit 10.4 lists products available as of October 1987.

Celestial's move into national television advertising during the mid-1980s included hiring Mariette Hartley as a key spokesperson for the company's products, including the new flavor varieties developed by the Feinblum adventure task force. Exhibit 10.5 is an example of the campaign, which continued into 1989.

From 1983 to 1989, a dozen or more upper-level executives resigned their posts at Celestial Seasonings to pursue their own interests, some because they felt the company had outgrown its entrepreneurial roots with the Kraft acquisition and would soon lose the cultural aspects that led to their hiring on in the first place. The intensity of individual commitment to building the herbal tea business was carried into their own ventures where each hoped for personal and corporate success similar to that enjoyed in their Celestial affiliation. Celestial's employee stock ownership program had enabled some of those striking out on their own to amass seed capital that made it possible.

Exhibit 10.4

CELESTIAL SEASONINGS, INC., PRODUCT LIST, OCTOBER 1987

Flavored black tea*

Amaretto Nights®
Apple Spice and Tea
Bavarian Chocolate Orange™
Cinnamon Vienna*
Citrus and Tea
Irish Cream Mist™
Lemons and Tea
Oranges and Tea
Raspberries and Tea
Swiss Mint™

Premium teas*

Classic English Breakfast™
Darjeeling Gardens™
Extraordinary Earl Grey™
Morning Thunder®
Timeless Orange Pekoe®

Caffeine-free tea†

Herbal teas†

Almond Sunset®
Chamomile
Cinnamon Apple Spice™
Cinnamon Rose®
Cranberry Cove®
Emperor's Choice®
Ginseng Plus®
Grandma's Tummy Mint®
Lemon Mist®
Lemon Zinger®
Mandarin Orange Spice®
Mellow Mint®
Mint Magic™
Mo's 24®
Orange Zinger™
Peppermint
Raspberry Patch®
Red Zinger®
Roastaroma®
Sampler I
Sampler II
Sleepytime®
Spearmint
Strawberry Fields™
Sunburst C®
Variety 4 Pack
Wild Forest Blackberry®

*Contains caffeine
†Contains no caffeine
Source: *Corporate document.

Many predicted the Kraft-Celestial marriage would be on the rocks within a year because of differences in operating philosophies. These dire predictions failed to materialize, but indeed, culture clashes presumably led to Kraft's putting Celestial up for sale in late 1987 after helping, during the four years of its ownership, to expand the company's shelf space in supermarkets and boosting its ad budget to a reputed $6 million figure in 1988, as sales revenues climbed to the $40 million mark. President Feinblum's offer to buy the company from Kraft was rejected, and "Relations between Kraft's pin-striped executives and the Levi-clad Feinblum . . . deteriorated."[3] Kraft's agreement to sell the feisty tea company to Lipton, a principal Celestial marketplace adversary, faced delays from an antitrust suit filed by smaller competitor R. C. Bigelow, alleging potential monopoly stemming from the Lipton/Celestial merger, so the parent sold the company to Feinblum and partners in November 1988. Analysts estimated that to service the $45 million debt portion of the $60 million purchase price would require a doubling of revenues to $80 million over five years, along with an improvement in operating margins. Sales revenues continued to rise in 1989 over 1988.[4]

[3]"Why Celestial Seasonings Wasn't Kraft's Cup of Tea," *Business Week*, May 8, 1989, p. 76.
[4]Dennis Morgigno, "For a Nervous World," *American Way*, January, 1990.

Exhibit 10.5

CELESTIAL SEASONINGS®

"Little Friend" :30 TV

(Music under) MARIETTE HARTLEY: OK, you ready?
GIRL: Ready.
MARIETTE: OK.

If you think Celestial Seasonings only makes great herb teas, wait'll you try these.

First, new Fruit & Teas.

All natural tea blends

made with lots of real fruit.

GIRL: Mmm, yum!

MARIETTE: And new After Dinner Teas.

GIRL: Watch your nose.

(SFX: SIPPING)

Ahh, it's practically dessert!

That's new Fruit & Teas for anytime

and new After Dinner Teas...for after dinner.

(SFX: SIPPING)
GIRL: What if you drink it after lunch?

MARIETTE: You turn into a frog.
(SFX: LAUGHTER)

ANNCR (VO): Celestial Seasonings. Teas...more tastefully done.

11

MEASUREMENT RESEARCH AND DEVELOPMENT, INC.

"The question is: Should we develop, manufacture, and sell this transducer to industry?" David Jennison was conducting a meeting of his engineering staff. Jennison was vice president and general manager of the Product Development and Manufacturing Department of Measurement Research and Development, Inc. (MRD), a company formed in the mid-1960s by a group of research scientists who had left their posts at various scientific laboratories in the United States and Europe to become entrepreneurs.

The transducer under consideration could measure the proximity of a metallic plate relative to the face of the device. This feat was accomplished by driving the sensor with a 1-megahertz (MHz) signal that induced eddy currents in the metallic plate. The resulting electrical signal was inversely proportional to the distance between the sensor face and the metallic plate. Movements of 1 micro inch—about 0.01 the amount a copper penny expands when held in one's hand—could be measured accurately and with highly reliable repeatability.

Some measurement applications that MRD engineers thought would be useful to industry were vibrating motion of structures at frequencies up to 40 KHz (kilohertz); eccentricity of rotating shafts; shake table motion; thickness, buckle, and flatness of metal; oil film thickness; and other precision deflection, motion, and position applications. A tested quality control application was that of measuring the thickness of Teflon coatings on parts of telephone assemblies. Measurement accuracy was not lessened by water or oil media between the sensor and the metallic object being sensed, and there was negligible effect from temperature, humidity, moisture, and pressure.

Field tests, in experimental settings, demonstrated the instrument's and associated electronics' reliability as key components in computer-controlled process applications; with robot systems; and as stand-alone sensors, with digital readouts, in automated quality assurance procedures. Engineers in the test companies' production and laboratory facilities were favorably impressed, most reporting performance superior to that achieved with existing equipment.

COMPANY BACKGROUND

MRD, based upon its founders' analytic talents in nucleonics and related scientific fields, quickly developed a reputation for competency and earned a spot as one of the top 100 defense contractors. The organizers wished to provide facilities and a favorable environment for conducting research and development studies, believing that they could eventually design and manufacture measurement and test equipment, initially to fulfill their Department of Defense (DOD) contracts and later to sell to industry as spinoff products. By the mid-1970s, MRD's product capabilities included research, design, testing, production, and on-site evaluation of measurement instrumentation.

Product development comprised activities in electromechanical devices, such as the system that MRD was considering making and selling, nuclear test and neutron instrumentation, and ceramic materials. Diversification was a goal of the manufacturing group.

Corporate officers, both at MRD and at the company that acquired them soon after they started, were proud of the organization's ability to integrate scientific disciplines with applied engineering and of their reputation for providing highly competent, responsive, and uniquely integrated project teams to solve complex problems.

MRD competence included weapons systems analysis (vulnerability, reliability, effectiveness, countermeasures, materials); phenomenology (nuclear radiation effects, meteorology, hydrodynamics, thermodynamics, electromagnetic fields and waves, and high-voltage discharges); and data processing (software and consulting services).

Along with other electronics companies' representatives, MRD's scientists met regularly with top electronic warfare (EW) personnel and Defense Department staff to help decide upon U.S. responses to anticipated increased sophistication of U.S.S.R. target-tracking radar systems in surface-to-air missiles and interceptor aircraft. In 1982, American outlays for EW research and development were predicted to increase by 15 to 20 percent annually over the ensuing 10 years, most of this, according to several experts, slated for equipment purchases, but with the recent turn of events in the Soviet Union and Eastern Europe, this was questionable? MRD was a high-tech defense analysis contractor but did not manufacture EW hardware.

PRODUCT PLANNING MEETING

Besides David Jennison, also present at the meeting were George Benson, electrical engineer, in charge of designing and developing the instrument and its related electronics; Julie Pendegrast, a recent electrical engineering graduate of Rensselaer Polytechnic Institute, hired by Benson a few months earlier; John Hooper, a Ph.D. physicist and one of the company's organizers, previously headed a government research facility in New Mexico; Helen Brezneski, formerly a technician at the company, promoted in 1990 to assistant production manager in the manufacturing group; and Henry Gallagher, primarily experienced in aircraft and radar-site management while a colonel in the Air Force, employed in 1990 as sales manager for MRD's product development and manufacturing group.

Jennison continued: "We must decide whether to go ahead with this effort and, if we proceed, what are the next steps? What uncertainties must be resolved? So, let's share ideas."

"Well," George Benson spoke with conviction and enthusiasm, "we know that our studies in nuclear effects and other hostile environments give us an obvious edge. No competitor is state of the art like us, a point we've proved with the high-temperature pressure gauges. I bet I'm speaking for all of us in saying we ought to go full steam ahead."

"I agree with you, George, up to a point," Julie said, "but most of the company's experience has been with DOD and in other applications for the government. What we're talking about now is a departure. Industrial applications for the sensor are different from what we've dealt with in the past, and MRD isn't as well known as others who are already in the markets we want to sell to."

"True," added Hooper, "we may not be able to go at this the same way we have with DOD customers because what has been successful with our friends in the nuclear testing business probably won't work for industrial buyers—I'm talking primarily about marketing approaches. Speaking for the operating committee, I'm also concerned about other risks that can't be ignored."

"What risks, John?" asked Benson.

"Financial risks," Hooper responded. "We have some development money, but not much to spare unless the payoff potential is fairly high and reasonably certain. Then, too, I'm referring to the risk of damaging MRD's national reputation if the new instrumentation doesn't perform in the industrial setting according to our high standards. We became one of the top 100 prime contractors by delivering top-quality work, on time, to DOD."

Brezneski, who had been listening intently, interjected, "I was afraid you were doubtful of our ability to produce and deliver the system on time. Is that the main point, or is it more a matter of instrument performance?"

"A little of both, Helen," replied Hooper. "We have had some problems recently turning out components that function within specifications. And the EW group has received a few complaints about slipped deadlines on their reports; they blame this on delays in manufacturing delivery of test units to support the study contracts. However, David tells me those problems were mainly in getting units out of the calibration lab and all of that is running smoothly now."

"I can tell you, when it comes to performance," Benson stated, "there is no problem, John. This sensor has absolutely superior specs and will easily get the low-level measurements required for industry's mechanical engineering types. And you know the old saying about pioneers—they're the ones with arrows in their backs. But competitors won't be close behind us on this one because we have the superior technology and a good lead time. Our lab results and reports from government users make me totally optimistic. Further . . ."

Jennison interrupted: "Nevertheless, George, there is a difference between lab testing and field use, which is what Julie was referring to. And the market study last month tells us that the kinds of users we'll have to contact have different needs from present customers. We're still having difficulty getting our MRD pressure systems accepted for field tests by industry, so why should it be any different with this one? Hank tells me that forecasting sales will be a guessing game the first couple of years."

Henry Gallagher expressed a quandary: "I wonder if sales reps will be able to shift gears to call on different kinds of prospects for the new system. The market research study shows we aren't well known to the markets we are interested in; that means a lot of missionary effort. As it is, I'm having trouble motivating the reps to cover R&D labs that send inquiry cards for our proven products. Market coverage is spotty, any way you look at it. And with the company's stated intent to distribute in Japan and Europe, a lot of gearing up will have to be done in advertising and for other kinds of selling. It'll be a new ball game."

Benson's enthusiasm was unchecked: "I was wondering, Hank, if we shouldn't make this a separate effort, maybe even hire a sales manager to run the show, hire new reps, get someone to do the advertising for us, and do sophisticated sales planning."

On this note, the two-hour discussion began to wind down, with a consensus that several tasks remained: additional market analysis, evaluation of alternative strategies for domestic and foreign sales of all products, and consideration of changes in the rep organization and in the advertising program.

"There's one other concept we might reserve for a future agenda," Jennison concluded, "and that's the notion of this department becoming a separate division, or a full-fledged subsidiary, because we actually have a separate business from the other businesses in the company. John and I have discussed it, and if it's reasonably. . . ."

He was stopped by Hooper: "I meant to bring those statements with me tonight, Dave, but I forgot to pick them up from accounting. We're not sure how fairly they represent your group's status, but they ought to be close enough for planning. By the way, I told them to add in that work you just finished for us on the Navy contract; I think it was around $100,000. Tell you what, I'll send those financial statements to you Monday." The summary Hooper referred to is presented in Appendix 11A.

"Thanks, John," said Jennison, and turning to his staff, "Have a nice weekend, gang. See you Monday." As the others filed out, animatedly discussing how close they were to having the new product perfected, Jennison ruminated over MRD's lack of marketing experience, the multitude of tasks that lay ahead, and the limited time in which to get them all done. At 9:30 P.M., after analyzing inventory data, sorting out his calendar for the coming week, and making a note to himself to review the consultant's report before the staff's next meeting on the new product effort, he locked the office and bade goodnight to the security guard.

Appendix 11B presents a condensed version of the consultant's executive summary, along with two diagrams—one a conceptual view of future income sources and the other a model for responding to inquiries, said to be a problem urgently in need of attention—which were to serve as items for discussion at a forthcoming meeting between MRD management and the consulting group.

OTHER PROBLEMS FACED BY JENNISON

While attending various group meetings at MRD, it became apparent to the casewriter that several issues should be addressed along with the ones posed in the product planning session. Some of these were

1. Space available for assembly was crowded.
2. There was lack of standardization in sensors; with the exception of displacement transducers most systems were custom-built.
3. With no stock items, delivery dates were gradually lengthening, and, as assemblers worked longer hours to meet schedules, defects and rejections from the calibration laboratory increased.
4. Parts outages were gradually increasing.
5. Time lags in responding to requests for quotations (RFQs) were increasing, although negative effects, based on customer feedback, seemed negligible.
6. Requests were increasing for calibration lab technicians to shorten time spent on their function; attempts to shortcut calibration procedures were leading to organizational conflicts, defective shipments, increased service costs, and dissatisfied customers.
7. A current large job shop assembly contract, which was producing immediate cash flow, was being given more attention by quality control personnel than the somewhat longer-term transducer operation.

TO: John Hooper

FROM: Accounting/Finance Department

The accompanying exhibits represent the accounting department's best current estimates of what the balance sheet and operating statement figures would be if the product manufacturing group had been separate from the rest of MRD for the year just ended and for the two previous fiscal years.

Please note that we've added the subcontract orders done mainly in the machine shop and temporary production area. That amount brings the revenue estimate to approximately $800,000. The percentages for the last year are comparable to those reported by such companies as Dun & Bradstreet and Robert Morris Associates for electronics companies in the same size range as MRD.

Finally, we have attached ratio calculations, and because we thought you and Mr. Jennison might be interested in some return-on-net-worth calculations, we put together the RONW chart.

RATIOS CALCULATED FROM FINANCIAL STATEMENTS

FACTORS AND RATIOS	CURRENT YEAR	LAST YEAR	TWO YEARS AGO
Profit margin	.06	.03	−.153
Capital turnover	1.6	1.9	1.1
Return on assets	.096	.057	−.168
Leverage	2.00	2.564	13.143
Return on equity	.192	.146	−2.21
Net profit to net worth	.192	.146	−2.23
Net profit to net sales	.06	.03	−.153
Net sales to fixed assets	5.33	8.26	2.27
Net sales to net worth	3.2	4.87	14.57
Current ratio	2.59	2.33	2.47
Acid test	1.44	1.48	1.42
Receivables to working capital	.697	.795	.714
Inventory to working capital	.721	.636	.714
Collection period	68.44 days	67.24 days	71.57 days
Net sales to inventory	5.16	6.79	5.1
Net sales to working capital	3.72	4.32	3.64
Long-term liability to working capital	.535	.636	2.357
Debt to net worth	1.00	1.56	12.14
Current liabilities to net worth	.540	.846	2.71
Fixed assets to net worth	.600	.590	6.43

BALANCE SHEET

	FY JUST ENDED		TWO YEARS AGO		THREE YEARS AGO	
	Amount	% of Total	Amount	% of Total	Amount	% of Total
ASSETS						
Cash	$ 40,000	8%	$ 50,000	10%	$ 15,000	6.5%
Marketable securities	5,000	1	20,000	4	2,500	1.1
Receivables, net	150,000	30	175,000	35	50,000	21.7
Inventory, net	155,000	31	140,000	28	50,000	21.7
Total current assets	$350,000	70%	$385,000	77%	$117,500	51.0%
Plant and equipment, net	$150,000	30%	$115,000	23%	$112,500	49.0%
Total assets	$500,000	100%	$500,000	100%	$230,000	100.0%
CLAIMS ON ASSETS						
Bank loans (short-term notes)	$ 25,000	5%	$ 50,000	10%	$ 5,000	2.2%
Accounts payable (suppliers)	75,000	15	80,000	16	15,000	6.5
Income taxes (provision for)	10,000	2	10,000	2	2,500	1.1
Current maturities (long-term debt)	25,000	5	25,000	5	25,000	10.9
Total current debt	$135,000	27%	$165,000	33%	$ 47,500	20.7%
Long-term debt	115,000	23	140,000	28	165,000	71.7
Total net worth	250,000	50	195,000	39	17,500	7.6
Total claims	$500,000	100%	$500,000	100%	$230,000	100.0%

OPERATING STATEMENT

Net sales	$800,000	100%	$950,000	100%	$255,000	100%
Cost of sales	520,000	65	665,000	70	179,000	70
Gross profit	280,000	35%	285,000	30%	76,000	30%
Selling, delivery expense	96,000	12	114,000	12	30,600	12
Officers' salaries	72,000	9	66,500	7	64,000	25
Other general administrative expenses	64,000	8	76,000	8	20,400	8
Profit (loss) before taxes	$ 48,000	6%	$ 28,500	3%	($ 39,000)	(15%)

Note: The Product Development and Manufacturing Department's sales have been running at about 3 percent of total MRD revenues, increasing from 1 percent 5 years ago. Corporate revenues have risen at a compounded rate of 12 percent annually for the past 10 years.

Figure 1

FLOW DIAGRAM OF RETURN-ON-NET-WORTH CALCULATIONS
(DATA FOR LAST FISCAL YEAR)

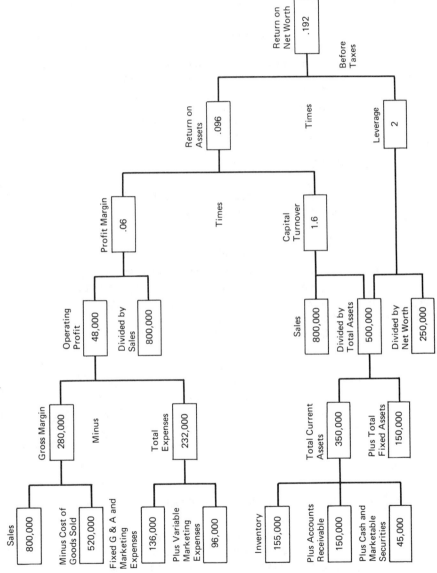

Appendix 11B

CONSULTANT'S REPORT TO MRD: EXECUTIVE SUMMARY

OBJECTIVES OF THE MARKET SURVEY

1. To help evaluate general potential in the industrial (commercial as opposed to government) sector for MRD's displacement transducers.
2. To find out from those respondents who classed themselves as prospective purchasers of transducers which product characteristics they considered to be most important.
3. To discover respondents' opinions of the displacement measuring systems produced by various companies. A related objective here was to find out the extent of awareness of MRD.

CONCLUSIONS

Potential exists in most standard industrial classifications (SICs) surveyed, with major potential in the following:

SIC 3511	Steam engines; steam, gas, and hydraulic turbines; and steam, gas, and hydraulic turbine generator set units
SIC 3522	Farm machinery and equipment
SIC 3531	Constructin machinery and equipment
SIC 3611	Electric measuring instruments and test equipment
SIC 3621	Motors and generators
SIC 3622	Industrial controls
SIC 3711	Motor vehicles
SIC 3712	Passenger car bodies
SIC 3721	Aircraft
SIC 3722	Aircraft engines and engine parts
SIC 3811	Engineering, laboratory, and scientific and research instruments and associated equipment
SIC 3821	Mechanical measuring and controlling instruments, except automatic temperature controls.

RANKING OF IMPORTANCE OF PRODUCT FEATURES

In descending order, output linearity, temperature stability, price of complete system, noncontacting feature, and frequency response (the last two were rated equally). Obviously, their needs differ greatly from current buyers of MRD systems.

Appendix 11B (Cont.)

RESPONDENTS' PERCEPTIONS OF COMPANIES AND PRODUCTS

Two major producers were very well known, and their systems were rated as excellent; four others were known to many, but their measuring systems were considered to be inferior to the top two; MRD was next to last in the group of five least known companies; respondents "guessed" the company's transducers to be high in both quality and price.

SURVEY RESPONSE RATE AND USER CATEGORY

A total of 614 responses were received from a sample of 1,629 (about 38 percent), of whom 320 (about 52 percent) classed themselves as potential buyers of MRD systems. This figure is weighted neither by the number of systems each lab and plant might use nor by the urgency of need.

RESPONSE BY STATES

MRD's coverage appears to be adequate in a few higher-potential states, but inadequate in most. The territory already assigned to one nuclear instrumentation representative accounts for 29 percent of total potential respondents, and that covered by another nuclear rep group equals 16 percent of potential measured by the survey. However, it is unlikely, because they primarily sell nuclear products, that these reps cover more than 20 percent of MRD transducer prospects. We recommend that literature packets be sent immediately to all those indicating any interest at all and that telephone calls be made to the group expressing a high level of interest.

Please note Figure 1, which, although arguable, portrays our schematic of potential revenue sources and their relationships to a yet-to-be-defined revenue target. When we meet to discuss this report, setting sales targets should be on the agenda. Figure 2 gets at what we talked about on the phone—an urgent need to streamline the process of responding to inquiries. This file, currently manual, should be on magnetic tape, purged regularly, and used as a control and planning tool.

Figure 1

A CONCEPTUAL VIEW OF FUTURE INCOME SOURCES

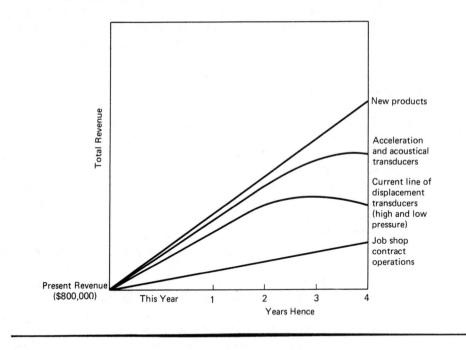

Figure 2

THE MRD INQUIRY CARD KIT

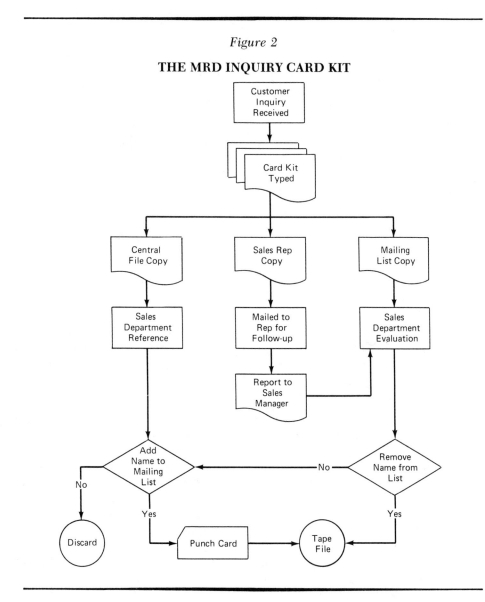

12

DIGITAL PRODUCTS CORPORATION

ro•bot   n. 1. a machine that resembles a man and does mechanical, routine tasks on command as though it were alive. 2. a person who acts and responds in a mechanical, routine manner, usually subject to another's will; automation. 3. any machine or mechanical device that operates automatically, with human-like skill.[1]

The word "robotics" did not appear in the 1981 edition of *The American Heritage Dictionary of the English Language*. The Robot Institute of America had only a handful of members, including 10 manufacturers, as recently as 1978. When thinking of a robot, one's image may well be of the dictionary version—an R2D2, a machine that performs actions similar to those of a person—and not a less spectacular electronic device that, in its own way, also emulates human beings. Digital Products Corporation (DPC), far from a General Electric, Bendix, Unimation, or Hitachi—leaders in robot manufacturing and marketing—is not engaged in producing steel-collar workers or electronic movie stars; rather, this Florida-based company has been responsible for helping a major national retailer, the U.S. Army, morticians, and other institutions and individuals use the telephone more efficiently.

---

[1]Jess Stein, ed., *The Random House Dictionary of the English Language, The Unabridged Edition* (New York: Random House, 1967), p. 1239.

"We call it The TELSOL Electronic System.[2] It sells for $9,450," Marketing Vice President Burton J. Weiss said, "and can do the work of six full-time phone solicitors. We made it to be relatively maintenance free—the only moving parts are in the recording mechanism. All the rest is space-age technology." Exhibit 12.1 presents a list of features and specifications. A national network of distributors sells the automatic phone robot.

TELSOL is a telecomputer/automatic phone robot that can be programmed to call, talk to, and collect responses from people whose telephone numbers are selected by the owner. The manufacturer employs a team of professional scriptwriters

---

Exhibit 12.1

TELSOL FEATURES AND SPECIFICATIONS, 1982

FEATURES	SPECIFICATIONS	
Built-in monitor and lighted display; indicates number called while listening to response.	TELSOL	15½″ wide × 23″ deep × 6″ high; 115/120 volts AC approximately 30 watts; 4-hour battery backup for number storage; phone line connector supplied. FCC Registration No.: AB3985-62472-P-C-E. Ringer Equivalence No.: 0.0A0.0B.
Enter up to 500 phone numbers at a time. It takes just 2 minutes to store them on standard cassette tapes for later use or reload them into the machine.		
Calls both local and long distance.		
Compatible with both touch-tone and dial phone systems.	Timer	Connects to TELSOL with cable supplied; battery powered.
Built-in FCC-registered coupler complies with telephone regulations.	Printer	12½″ wide × 11″ deep × 5″ high. Connects to TELSOL with cable supplied; requires standard AC connection; requires approximately 40 watts.
Use your own announcements or our professionally prepared scripts.		
Patented voice activation waits for human response before beginning message.		
Voice activation provides efficient use of response tape.	SM-1	Single message unit used for notification message or a series of questions and recorded answers.
Stores unanswered calls for later use.		
Battery backup retains numbers in the event of power failure.	MM-1	Similar to SM-1 except may be used for up to seven different messages. While responses are played back, the display shows number contacted to allow correlation of answers to messages.
Easily attaches to direct phone lines.		
Timer permits unattended use during time periods when people are most available.		

Source: Corporate product brochure.

---

[2]Also referred to as TELSOL Phone Robot in DPC's *1982 Annual Report.*

and people who use their voices professionally to develop messages for use on the machine. It has found outlets for its electronic energies in notification, solicitation, collections, and marketing research/polling applications. Some example calling statements appear in Exhibit 12.2 for these various applications. The sales brochure claims

> Using the TELSOL personal communication system to tell your customers of sales, delivery schedules, and investment opportunities relieves your employees of making hundreds of routine calls and makes sure every customer receives the same cheerful message.
>
> It is an efficient means of notifying people and it has several advantages to you: it can improve your cash flow, increase traffic, reduce warehouse space requirements, and reduce dry service calls. These savings can be passed to your customers in the form of better service at lower costs, which, of course, leads to long-term price reductions.

Exhibit 12.2

EXAMPLE STATEMENTS FOR VARIOUS TELSOL APPLICATIONS

Notification

Please pick up the merchandise you ordered from XYZ department store.

Our serviceperson will be at your home between 10 A.M. and noon on Monday.

Our special for this week is _____.

There is a job available that requires your experience. Please call the XYZ employment office.

Mention this call when you visit our store, and you will receive a free _____.

Solicitation

Would you be interested in a no obligation appraisal of your property?

Are you interested in the cost savings of having your carpet cleaned rather than replaced?

Did you know that 1 of 10 Americans will suffer a disabling accident on the job this year?

Would you like to receive a free discount coupon for _____?

Collections

Please call Mr. Jones at the XYZ Bank regarding an important matter.

We are certain you want to keep your credit record in good order.

We are certain that you would not want to lose your benefits after making so many payments.

Market Research/Polling

What radio station do you listen to?

What's your favorite television program?

Are you registered to vote?

Weiss calls his Fort Lauderdale company "the undisputed champion of this market. It's the fifth medium—it goes beyond direct mail, newspapers, radio, and television. It's a moneysaver, but it isn't just efficient, it's also effective. TELSOL generates high response rates, and because it arouses people's curiosity, in many cases, it's better than its human counterparts." Weiss is proud of the company's reputation for customer backup, including a WATS line to Digital's Service Department. Documentation includes an illustrated step-by-step procedural manual, and the company provides what has been claimed to be "the strongest warranty in the industry."

TELSOL uses standard cassette tapes to record responses and holds numbers in memory, which are transferrable to standard cassettes for further use. Its memory stores up to 512 seven-digit numbers, has touch-tone and dial-pulse features, and provides for multiple question-and-answer sequences. Also, it will hold unanswered and busy numbers in abeyance, recalling them automatically. An electronic timer turns the unit on and off.

"That's important," observed Weiss, "and when owners have failed to turn it off, they've gotten some bad press because the system will keep on calling, regardless of the lateness of the hour, unless programmed to stop."

"Let's assume," Weiss expounds on the unit's versatility, "that you're a retailer who wants to promote a special sale to a few hundred customers. The 15-second tape could be used to make the basic announcement. Then, either from the credit files or some other source, consumers' phone numbers would be entered into the unit's memory—and the memory itself can also be used as a file for numbers from previous promotions. While all the clerks and department managers go about their business, TELSOL contacts the households and prints out the numbers that have been reached. We have found that where two-way dialogue is involved, people are intrigued enough to carry on a conversation with the machine. They don't resent it. Still, a bit of humor on the tape also helps to prevent people who might not like it from being upset."

If the person called is not cooperative, the system disconnects after non-responses to the first two questions and then proceeds to dial the next number.

TELSOL is lightweight and portable, making it easy to transport from place to place as needed. TELSOL is being used by a nationwide retailer, which by early 1982 had purchased over 1,000 units, making it the biggest customer to that point to install in its catalog departments to notify customers that their orders are ready to be picked up; a direct-sale home products firm, which prospects for new distributors and salespeople; and Army recruiters, who tell and sell via TELSOL in sparsely settled areas. All sorts of marketing research is conducted by the two-way feature in the device—asking and recording answers. It is also used for cold canvassing by some insurance firms; charity fundraisers find it helpful in boosting contributions; auto dealers call prospects to invite them in for a test drive; and a funeral home uses the device to advertise its preplanned burials.

"Our 1981 sales ran to about $4 million, and I believe we will exceed $6 million in fiscal 1982." Weiss has speculated that this number might double by 1985. "Once buyers find out the machine can be cost-justified in less than a year, we have their attention. I see TELSOL as a prime device to boost productivity, a goal that almost every business has today. We have competitors, but their equipment is not equal to ours."

DIGITAL PRODUCTS BACKGROUND

After sinking $40,000 into DPC stock, Marton Grossman, an ordained rabbi and owner of a housewares import business in New York City, was conversing with a friend and customer, Leopold Cohen, who owned a chain of women's dress shops and household goods stores in New Jersey. With its stock down to 12½ cents a share, DPC was staggering under $250,000 debt and was considering filing for bankruptcy under Chapter 11. Neither investor had an electronics background, but they decided then and there—it was June 1971—to buy the firm.

In 1980, after their company turned its first profit, there was discussion among analysts of its potential for profits of $20 million a year by 1990. The stock, if adjusted for a recent split, would have been selling at about $44 a share in early 1982.

TELSOL Phone Robot sales to distributors approximated $7 million in the year ended March 31, 1982, but certain distributors were depending on reselling the units before paying DPC, so at year-end the company adopted a policy of recording sales to certain distributors on a cash basis. This change, plus the costs associated with rapid expansion of the TELSOL distribution network, resulted in a loss of $94,732 for the year. Exhibit 12.3 provides a review of selected financial data for the years 1977 to 1982.

Grossman and Cohen attribute the survival of their company to sales of TEL-SOL, but other products just beginning to earn their way have been added. One is Dial/Eze, a device that automatically dials and protects a user's satellite network telephone access and authorization code. Another is TW-3, a coin acceptor, promoted as jamproof, that "rejects 92 percent more slugs and foreign coins than other such devices" and that is adaptable for all types of U.S. and foreign coins. In 1982, Bally became the coin device's exclusive distributor for Nevada, and the New Jersey Gaming Commission approved it for use and sale in that state.

Grossman, born in 1931 in Romania, was to survive World War II concentration camps, later arriving penniless in the United States. Cohen, born in 1916, learned business from running a production line in his parents' sewing factory before starting his own retail stores. Setting up two women's dress shops in Florida provided enough cash flow to help keep the electronics company afloat between 1974 and 1978. Then, in 1978, TELSOL was bought from a bankrupt company and refined by Digital's engineers before going on the market later that year. Its first application was a test use by the national retail chain for notifying customers that their catalog orders had arrived. Then, it would call later to tell them the purchase would be delivered, if the customer had chosen not to pick it up.

In June 1981, Digital Products moved to its new 17,500-square-foot facility designed to house administrative functions, manufacturing, engineering, and research and development. Assembly space in the new quarters would enable the company to increase production capacity for estimated needs covering the next five years. The organization was still lean in early 1982, with about 60 employees, including engineer David Bowers, one of the three founders who commented on the pre–Grossman/Cohen days, "Our engineering was fine; we just didn't have much business sense." Concluded Cohen, in remarking that their success stemmed from following business

Exhibit 12.3

SUMMARY OF SELECTED FINANCIAL DATA FOR DPC, MARCH 31, 1977–1982

	1977	1978	1979	1980	1981	1982
Total assets	$384,213	$512,917	$427,048	$1,249,656	$2,432,449	$7,933,199
Long-term debt	761	165	—	—	—	645,000
Net sales	243,815	150,278	71,282	1,591,014	3,904,444	4,026,194
Income (loss) from continuing operations	(178,767)	(159,672)	(256,299)	321,871	833,814	(94,732)
Net income (loss)	(73,798)	(65,441)	(231,699)	479,106	813,670	(94,732)
Per Share Data*						
Income (loss) from continuing operations	$(.05)	$(.05)	$(.08)	$.08	$.21	$(.02)
Net income	(.02)	(.02)	(.07)	.13	.21	(.02)
Cash dividends per common share	—	—	—	—	—	—

*Common shares and equivalents.

instincts and knowing whether or not an electronics product was worth selling, "Those judgments mattered a lot more than knowing how to build the products."

Believing, along with Cohen and Grossman, that "little guys can still do it," Burt Weiss reflected upon their success as he contemplated tentative marketing plans for 1983. "What," he wondered, "lies in store for TELSOL, specifically? Based on the current configuration of our distributor network, what can we do—what should we do—as a company to back them in their various marketplaces? What goals would be reasonable through 1985? And what of the five years after that—is it too early to think seriously about directions for TELSOL from 1986 to 1990? How can our marketing staff coordinate DPC's and distributors' efforts so we can achieve mutually acceptable targets in sales, profits, and growth? Finally, what kinds of competition should we be alert to, given that patent protection in this business is far from absolute?"

13

ROBINSON ASSOCIATES, INC. (A)

Robinson Associates, Inc., is a full-service management consulting and marketing research firm and national clearinghouse for census data services. It has close ties to senior academic personnel at several leading universities. It brings together a professional interdisciplinary team ranging from social psychology to math and physics, from econometrics to engineering and business, from computer scientists to well-rounded generalists with experience in hands-on research in marketing, new product development, corporate strategy, and venture analysis.

This paragraph, from a 1982 Robinson Associates' (RAI) brochure conveys the firm's desired position in the field of management counsulting and marketing research. It all began two decades earlier.

COMPANY BACKGROUND

In the early 1960s, the Marketing Science Institute (MSI) was founded in Philadelphia primarily through the energetic espousal of Thomas B. McCabe, Sr., chairman and chief executive officer of Scott Paper Company. MSI's mission was to advance the science of marketing. Numerous corporations added their names to the banner of sponsorship, and Patrick J. Robinson was appointed to be its director of management studies and, later, research director. Mr. McCabe's advocacy combined with support from Wroe Alderson, marketing theorist and Wharton professor, provided significant impetus for locating the Institute in Philadelphia and promoting an affiliation with the Wharton School and its faculty.

"Great care had been taken to avoid any domination of MSI by Wharton for fear of the Institute's becoming parochial in its interests, thus diluting its universal appeal as a center for advancing the development and applications of management science to supplement marketing art," Patrick Robinson recalled. "After Alderson's death, strong leadership was lacking to bring about a workable agreement, even though several of us thought affiliating with Wharton would be a suitable arrangement. Then an attractive suitor appeared in the person of Dean George Baker of the Harvard Graduate School of Business Administration [HBS] who proposed close ties with the proviso that MSI relocate to Boston. The offer from this respected institution was accepted by Mr. McCabe and MSI's trustees. Although I graduated from HBS, my family's preference was to remain in the Philadelphia area."

Several friends who had been working with Robinson as Marketing Science Institute project consultants encouraged him to form a research consulting firm, a sort of "son of MSI," offering their participation as professional associates. As Patrick Robinson remembered, "It didn't take much of a nudge to move me to make the commitment. Almost exactly 10 years earlier, Wroe Alderson had persuaded me to leave my very satisfying position with Imperial Oil Limited [Esso/Exxon in Toronto, Canada] to join Alderson Associates as his successor. While that transition had not been achieved, I did join Mobil Oil in New York as head of integrated operations planning. Three years later, Wroe was instrumental in having me invited to Philadelphia as the newly formed MSI's research director. I made that transition in June 1963, although the actual title did not pass to me until about four and a half years later."

Asked about how the organization's role was developed, Robinson summed it up as follows: "RAI's mission statement was conceived over a series of discussions about alternative scenarios, but the primary thrust became that of concentrating on applying research and development momentum from work at MSI. It was exciting to contemplate being a catalyst for adopting and exploiting the commercial potential of applied mathematical psychology, experimental design, and systems simulation, based on behavioral measures and sensitivities."

He assumed that several Institute sponsors and member companies would underwrite some pioneering applications of multidimensional scaling and related multivariate statistical analysis projects, which were to become the primary focus of RAI's interdisciplinary team efforts. "Getting underway, however, proved to be a nontrivial challenge in 1969 at a time when money was tight and the timing seemed less than propitious," Robinson said.

Funds suppliers did not have the courtesy to array themselves in parade formation for Mr. Robinson's scrutiny and choice, but luck intervened. At a New Year's Eve dinner dance at his country club, Robinson chanced to be seated with a fellow member who was founder and head of a successful industrial engineering performance evaluation consulting organization. Sufficiently intrigued by the Robinson concept, the dinner companion offered to help secure a credit line from a local bank. Robinson continued: "Armed with this support I went to a valued friend and leading corporation lawyer who set up the incorporation and arranged a lease so we could retain some of MSI's old office facilities at the University City Science Center. He also became corporate secretary. Then, with the help of a former MSI colleague, I established computer operations and engaged a scientific programmer to maintain and operate our program library."

The practical expertise and high technology RAI brought to its prospects and clients consisted of many years of experience in the conduct and teaching of management science and applied research in marketing and related corporate planning, venture analysis, physical distribution logistics, management information and control systems design, new product development, appraisal, and promotional positioning. Hard-cover books and monographs and other publications distilled findings resulting from expenditures of some half million dollars annually at MSI. RAI's strategy was to run on the tracks laid down at MSI. The following goals, according to Robinson, have been paramount:

1. Offer an intimate knowledge of the consumer and industrial goods and services markets and channels of distribution.
2. Provide conceptual guidance for progressive business managers and researchers in considering the implications and demands of taking full account of the marketing management concept in product planning and market development.
3. Make available the sensitive new tools of perceptual and preference mapping, cluster analysis, and systems simulation for definitive measurement and analysis of people's choice behavior, "gap analysis," promotional positioning, and understanding of the competitive dynamics of market structure and semantics.
4. Provide creative and innovative consultation to brand and product managers and others concerned with performance improvements and the impact of change on company operations, organization, and information for decision support systems and adaptive experimentation in the marketplace.
5. Make available enhanced qualitative front-end-focused group interview (FGI) capabilities for understanding people's attitudes, motivations, semantics, occasions of use, and tentative hypotheses for further refinement and quantitative testing. (The modern framework of these FGIs included two-way mirrors, plus video and audio taping of sessions for editing and content analysis. RAI psychologists focused on critical incidents, both favorable and adverse, plus convergence on possible causal relationships in the buying process, apparent barriers to entry, conventional wisdom concerning a given category, and its effective competition, plus any unfulfilled needs or expressed anxieties or frustrations.) Additionally, quantified choice and ranking tasks for subsequent perceptual and preference computer mapping of FGI respondents' mental models was offered as an augmentation to the basic qualitative service.
6. Stress implementation as the driving force of any assignment. RAI insisted, insofar as the bounds of good taste and business etiquette would permit, on asking so-what and what-if questions on the potential value of any anticipated end product of a research or counseling assignment.

Robinson reviewed the early phases of the firm's development: "Our first two years got off to a modest start. We were getting the word out on what could be done with our new technology and learning how we should present and price our differential advantage versus firms using more traditional methods. We traveled to client firms such as Lever Brothers, General Foods, British Petroleum, the American Bankers Association, Air Canada, RCA, Campbell Soup, Sears, Roebuck, Eastman Kodak, and others we were fortunate to attract. A project was often conceived, designed, priced, and sold in the course of a few hours' discussion and a handshake.

"In those early days, our in-house computer support came from a mathematically sophisticated professional who went on to advanced computer architecture consulting. She was followed by a specialist who came to us from a local computer science college. The senior project specialist's background was math, physics, and operations research. RAI's corporate treasurer, financial counselor, and investor was another HBS graduate and close friend who devoted many evening and weekend hours to help our undercapitalized, fledgling business get started and stay on course while operations were grossing scarcely $200,000 annually."

After successfully negotiating a debenture refinancing through its bank, with the funding by an imaginative petroleum transportation company's president, RAI was able to move from the University City Science Center, where it had been for a year, to offices in Bryn Mawr. "Engineering this move meant that none of our principal professionals would be more than 15 minutes from the office. We also wanted to have a more pleasant and congenial setting for client visits. This building is adjacent to the train station, less than 20 minutes from Philadelphia on the so-called 'Paoli Local,' which serves the Main Line. It's also within 10 minutes of the Pennsylvania Turnpike and just 35 minutes from the airport. First-class lodging and restaurants, as well as many historic sights such as Valley Forge, are within a 20-minute driving radius.

"RAI has always stressed the belief that there's nothing more practical than a good theory. For example, when a good mechanic or a physician examines symptoms, and decides what to do, theory is the framework for that judgment, and implementation is the means to obtaining results.

"During those early years, we hated to lose for the wrong reason; all right, if we were seen as too technical or even beyond a budgetary limit, but let us not lose because of our failure to communicate convincingly. Perhaps a prime example of falling on our collective faces occurred when we were invited to address Scott Paper's marketing research and brand management people. We pulled out all the stops.

"We had prepared elaborate slide materials and a presentation of market measurement and analysis tools and examples of end product visualizations of what we might do for Scott Paper. We even had custom built for us a cubic-foot Lucite model of a three-dimensional perceptual-and-preference joint-space map of competing brand imagery and segmented ideal points to use in explaining how such a graphic picture could indeed be worth a thousand words. We also brought a 25-inch video monitor and videotape deck with excerpts from focused group interviews edited for the presentation, to be held in a conference room at Scott headquarters.

"There we were, six in number. The meeting room was fully prepared at the appointed early starting time, with an anticipated half-day presentation ahead of us. It was all downhill from there. First, the audience was slow to assemble, apparently owing to unexpected demands on people's time. Then we got the word to proceed without waiting. We were also informed that certain key people present had to take part in a senior executive meeting and could only remain for 30 or 40 minutes. The rest of the morning we tried to cope with a shifting agenda for late arrivals and early departures—on top of the inherent challenge of being 'separated by our common language.' The best we ever got from this entire costly exercise was a report that an internal memorandum at Scott had sized RAI up as 'the best qualified marketing research firm in the country.' The memo went on to state that Scott would consider RAI favorably if its current suppliers didn't work out satisfactorily on some very large ongoing and pending assignments, including at least one reportedly in the six figures. What a disappointment!"

Researchers affiliated with MSI, and then with RAI, produced myriad articles and books stemming from their work. Publications were considered to be very important for a firm such as RAI, carrying much more influence, if published in appropriate journals, than advertisements and other promotion. This notoriety helped the firm to compete against large and aggressive competitors. Robinson mentioned a project conducted for International Air Transport Association (IATA):

"At the beginning of our second five-year period, RAI embarked on some particularly challenging major projects involving its full range of trademarked 'Behaviormetrics' mathematical psychology tools. The most ambitious of these assignments was a six-country, cross-cultural, trade-off segmentation analysis of transatlantic air fares for IATA, headquartered in Geneva. The process of winning this contract involved our first major confrontation with a wide array of leading domestic and European research firms. We had to compete with many experienced firms nominated by IATA headquarters and by some 30 participating transatlantic air carriers. A few screening committee members favored dividing the project among several research firms. We argued strongly in favor of a single firm conducting all the research to have a common basis for cross-comparisons, market structure modeling, and forecasting the cross-elasticity of demand between scheduled carriers and charter flights—under a wide range of optional slates of competing air fare configurations. The final 40-page RAI proposal won the entire contract of approximately \$300,000."

EXAMPLES OF PROJECTS

In discussing RAI's starting lineup of clients, Robinson described some early projects:

Lever Brothers

"Among our first clients was Lever Brothers in New York. We worked as a general sounding board consultant for some very receptive executives and researchers, including Alden Clayton, currently MSI's research director.

"One of the most fascinating Lever projects at that time involved a category-wide study of the use of fabric softeners in the wash. This ambitious challenge was commissioned directly by an imaginative senior vice president who felt that traditional research had not provided satisfactory insights into why roughly half the households in the United States used fabric softeners, while the other half did not.

"As often happens with our research, some of the results appear perfectly obvious *after* the fact, just like $E = mc^2$, not mb^2, I suppose. In this instance one 'obvious' finding was that fabric softeners soften clothes does indeed go without saying. Herein lies an example of its being sometimes just as important to know what *not* to do. On the other hand, we discovered that the key discriminating factors separating users from nonusers were task-related associations. We discovered the mental imagery of mainly female users associated with the activity 'using a fabric softener in your wash' as related to pleasurable or family-oriented activities such as airing out a room or bringing in fresh flowers or powdering a baby or wearing perfume. All these had a refreshing scent and rewarding or caring qualities. In contrast, the nonuser associated using a fabric softener with chorelike activities such as peeling potatoes or cleaning out a closet.

"The implications seemed clear: develop product features and positionings, and supporting thematic and copy point appeals, designed to emphasize freshness and less chorelike effort in use, plus being a concerned parent giving pleasure to other family members. Passage of time has demonstrated a successful industrywide move in this direction."

DuPont/Canada

"The findings of the Lever project were somewhat reminiscent of an early MSI development project with DuPont of Canada in 1966 in connection with justification of a new plant for synthetic fibers for women's panties. Some members thought the way to achieve sufficient demand would be by dropping the price; others thought not. We were invited to try to help determine the relevant policy.

"In this prototype project, we used female respondents and a sample of various types, makes, and prices of panties as the stimulus set for gathering nonverbal similarities, judgments, and preference rankings. What emerged were six or seven distinctly different behavioral market segments, homogeneous within segment as revealed by the congruence of their perceptual and preference maps.

"In none of these segment maps was there any evidence of the classic economic unidimensional sensitivity to price. The simplest case partitioned all briefs into one cluster with another cluster of bikinis and a lone pettipant by itself. We called this simplistically oriented segment—rather uncharitably in retrospect—'Miss Plain Jane.' A much more challenging segment exhibited three clusters of panties—plus the outlying pettipant. Everyone from DuPont and MSI was completely baffled as to how to interpret this important segment's characteristic map. Only when I suggested that we let a typical respondent see the 'mirror of her mind' did the solution to the puzzle become 'obvious.' In fact, she instantly pointed out that one cluster contained 'dress-up panties,' one contained 'everyday panties,' and the remaining cluster, plus the lone pettipant, were 'unacceptable panties.'

"Aside from this categorical breakout, which accounted for one dimension in the two-dimensional map, the other dimension was immediately apparent to this respondent as quality. So each cluster had better and not-as-good panties. Furthermore, the highest-quality item in the entire stimulus set turned out to be the lone pettipant—over in the unacceptable category, yet highest in perceived quality of workmanship. We called this segment 'Miss Sophisticate.'

"The policy implications of this benchmark study seemed clear. Don't cut price to create new demand. Reinforce the tendency that many women are conditioned to accept having a wardrobe for dress-up, from underwear to outerwear. Even if no one else sees you, you know yourself—besides you might faint and be taken to the hospital or who knows what! Furthermore, manufacturing matching panty and bra sets to resemble beachwear should have great appeal and might also influence the plainer dressers to be more socially aware and concerned about their total appearance, at least for dress up occasions.

"We had also mapped words as a separate task to determine something of the imagery of the relevant semantics of fabric and style such as comfortable, sexy, durable, attractive, and the like. These maps were useful in providing timely input to the creative wordsmiths."

British Petroleum

One of RAI's initial clients was British Petroleum, when it came to the United States in search of a successful market entry to complement its anticipated North Slope petroleum production bonanza in the Arctic. BP had purchased 10,000 Sinclair service stations and wanted the research consulting firm to help[1]

1. Identify the primary attitudes of representative groups of motorists toward service stations and their supplying petroleum companies.
2. Assess the perceived variability of service station purchasing environments, key buying influences, and dealer attitudes to identify significant marketing problems.
3. Suggest alternative advertising themes and related marketing policies and formulates to facilitate initial rebranding and future development of BP's retail sales in the United States.
4. Design potentially profitable supplemental analyses, fieldwork, and hypotheses for testing as inputs to the advertising creative process and to marketing planning.

Robinson related that, "In May of 1969, we conducted 21 focused group interviews throughout the eastern region from New England to Florida, among motorists and dealers. All interviews were both audio and videotaped and later content analyzed and indexed for critical incidents. These indexed incidents were then dubbed onto summary tapes of selected topics of concern to management. Specifically, the subject categories included multigrade gasoline; product quality; self-service; TBA and other products; facilities; credit cards; promotions, games, and stamps; international/British; car care; price; trust; gettng out of car; station personnel; and Sinclair's present image.

"Psychological and marketing policy interpretations of these highlights were then prepared topic by topic for strategic planning and policy interpretations in the context of the project objectives. A 20-minute final report presentation was summarized on videotape to supplement overhead projector slides and discussion. Additionally, perceptual and preference maps were employed to facilitate these interpretations and competitive and BP image-related questions.

"This intensive qualitative project was completed on schedule in only three

[1]Adapted from corporate files.

months for a fee of approximately $50,000. It was instrumental in guiding management at a critical time while selecting an advertising agency, in deciding 'how British' to be, in burying Sinclair's dinosaur logo, and in introducing BP as a major retail gasoline brand. Only the prolonged delays in bringing the North Slope developments to fruition held up the orderly pursuit of market development goals that were carefully planned years earlier," Robinson concluded.

American Bankers Association

Another example of an early project, for the American Bankers Association, was a DELPHMAPP futures project focusing on the anticipated impact of computers and high-speed communications on the monetary and payment system—the so-called "checkless" or "less check" society. "At that time I was also serving as marketing and management science consultant to the ABA," Robinson recalled. Robinson and a partner met for a two-and-a-half-day executive retreat with senior bankers to consider the alternative future scenarios to the year 2000 for the commercial banking industry, combining traditional Rand Corporation Delphi procedures with RAI's multidimensional scaling and related procedures.

The result of this project for ABA executive staff and senior bank committee colleagues was a definitive action plan for research and development at ABA—including input to its decision to move its headquarters from New York to Washington, D.C. The likely impact of single-statement banking, preauthorized payments, overdraft banking, automated tellers, electronic funds transfer, and competitive demand deposit instruments were all foreseen and screened to reveal policy implications to suggest prudent allocation of Association resources and setting priorities to serve members.

Campbell Soup Company

One of RAI's first comprehensive perceptual and preference mapping projects was conducted for Campbell Soup. "The resulting study proved to be a very stimulating challenge that brought high praise from the major advertising agency concerned—specifically from BBD&O's research vice president and the Campbell Soup account group. The agency, and Campbell's 'red and white' label management, vigorously acted upon the findings, which had significant policy implications for product positioning, store promotions, thematic and copy point appeals, portion size packaging, and the complementary and substitutable roles of soup in the family menu," Robinson said.

"The completed report was first presented in 1971. Over the ensuing decade, this report has periodically provided sources of working hypotheses, innovations, and a benchmark for identifying significant trends and shifts in people's perceptions, preferences, and the mental associations of soup and serving occasions. Oddly enough, the study seemed to disappear in the mid-1970s and then to reemerge, quite by chance. In 1981, RAI was asked to present the findings once again and to provide fresh copies of the report.

"One of these presentation occasions involved an old friend, Horace Schwerin, who had achieved recognition for his syndicated commercial testing services. He had retired from his entrepreneurial career, becoming a stimulating maverick member of Campbell's management team. Among the ideas we surfaced together, in reviewing the 1971 'golden oldie,' were a number of surprisingly fresh insights with policy implications for the 1980s, respecting single-portion servings, the clustering of soup types in people's minds, the nourishing image of soup, and its suitability and role in various menu and serving occasions.

"While we conducted subsequent studies for Campbell," Robinson concluded, "none, it seems to me, came close to the scope and excitement of this early baseline investigation."

RCA

An example of a Robinson Associates' industrial marketing research project came when RCA was still committed to computers and to a new feature called "virtual memory." This ambitious crash project was commissioned by the office of the president when considerable belt-tightening was under way throughout the RCA Computer Company.

Robinson reviewed a few particulars of the RCA effort: "For the client, a great deal was at stake, so we were given free rein to conduct the investigation in an effort to obtain strategic policy guidance at a most critical time. Consequently, we spent considerable time trying to obtain every possible insight of potential value to management. One aspect that I was particularly keen on was an *objective* performance-space taxonomy, based on published engineering features, performance data, and costs for a wide array of competing hardware to contrast where different people 'were coming from' by using our *subjective* clustering routines. We had nine major customer categories, plus RCA sales representatives, some in-house product designers, market planners, and headquarter's respondents. This variety of respondents was designed to permit congruence analysis among the groups' perceptual clusters as well as against the objective clusters.

"Results were fascinating and revealing. We had understood that members of RCA management consciously planned their past strategy to go head on against IBM. However, to disguise the sponsorship of the project, we prepared our questionnaires so that IBM, RCA, and Univac were equally featured, and a number of other makes were also covered explicitly, but less prominently. In the final analysis, we concentrated on the RCA versus IBM perceptual and preference comparisons and statistically discriminating background characteristics as a basis for drawing our most important inferences. The policy implications seemed clear, and we hastened to put our presentation of findings before the chief executive officer and others.

"Trying to deliver our message to its intended audience at RCA's headquarters near Boston proved to be one of the most frustrating problems I've ever faced. The president's executive aide tried desperately to get the executive group together but was thwarted at the eleventh hour and fifty-ninth minute by news that RCA worldwide headquarters had just discharged the computer company president and planned to sell off the entire division. We were too late! We felt that we had thrown our best Sunday punch but had missed the target in a way that really hurt. When we work for a client, we think the results should be a win-win outcome. Here, we faced a lose-lose proposition if there ever was one.

"The loss for RAI almost became literally true when we sought our final payment for a completed assignment that no one knew anything about! It had indeed been a secret project—no recorded agreement, no purchase order, no verbal arrangements with accounts payable—nothing. I made several trips to RCA's Cherry Hill, New Jersey, procurement offices to plead our case. To make matters even worse, other suppliers with more conventional arrangements were apparently facing partial payments as settlements in full on the assumption of an insolvent situation. Eventually, we were paid, but only after other members of management read the hastily assembled final report, really just a hard copy of our overhead transparencies, because we hadn't planned on anything other than an oral report before a small, top-level audience.

"Two footnotes to this case came to light later: When Univac bought RCA's System 70 and other assets and its established customer base, Univac was able to utilize our findings to some extent—although the 'not-invented-here' resistance was noticeable among some of the entrenched sales management.

"Within the past several years, it was reported in the media that an internal 'bookkeeping error' of over $20 million came to light respecting how RCA's computer division had been doing prior to its dissolution. This discrepancy might have spelled the difference in top management's untimely decision to sell out; we can never know."

Ford Motor Company

"Another fascinating project was conducted for the Ford Motor Company, in collaboration with Rogers National Research, and involved gathering information to help design a new compact car, the Fairmont. This study slightly preceded the first major energy crisis in 1974 and focused on people who were already interested in a downsized or economy vehicle. This full-profile multiple trade-off analysis research provided a significant lead in Ford's product planning once the energy crisis occurred and began to affect an even larger cross section of new car buyers. Subsequently, over 1 million Fairmonts were sold. A contributing factor to this success was the fact that, when the energy crisis struck, Ford was relatively well situated with its new car designed for compact car buyers." Robinson seemed pleased with these results.

SUMMARY OF RAI SERVICES

RAI's diversity was represented in its 1982 and 1983 brochures:

1982's Focus

Robinson ruminated, "In three decades computer technology has moved an incredible distance forward in helping to plot today's marketing decisions. Yet many companies use yesterday's methods. Yesterday's navigation method was to follow the compass, and yesterday's question was, 'Am I going in the right direction?' With to-day's sophisticated navigational systems the question could be, 'How do I steer through the rings of Saturn?'" In that year's brochure an impressive listing of computer software tools was begun with the assertion that "we created the word 'Behaviormetrics' for our own use. . . ." Some of the methods and models listed are given in Exhibit 13.1.

1983's Focus

In addition to its customary emphasis on applied science in marketing, RAI turned the spotlight on other dimensions of its consulting expertise in the 1983 brochure: strategic planning, management consulting, business and opportunity audits, acquisitions and divestitures, trends assessment, expert testimony, and decision support systems design and software development. The apparent goal was to promote a broader array of services, responding, as Patrick Robinson put it, "to all of the important questions asked by management and to help make more manageable the complex environment of the 1980s, to sharpen skills, to enhance decisions, to make implementation more effective and efficient, and to improve performance in our client organizations." It was obvious in listening to Robinson describe his vision for RAI

Exhibit 13.1

METHODS AND MODELS USED BY ROBINSON ASSOCIATES, INC.*

DELPHMAPP. Quantitative extension of Delphi futures techniques for technological and social forecasting.

CONSCREEN. Perceptual and preference mapping, clustering and associated multivariate techniques.

SPEEDMARK. Nationally distributed test market simulation modeling for predicting brand switching and market shares.

MULTIPLE TRADEOFF ANALYSIS (MTA). RAI's unique version of conjoint measurement and related techniques for new product development and appraisal.

PRODUCT DEFICIENCY ANALYSIS (PDA). The definitive system for studying established products and their competitors in the search for relative weaknesses and potential improvements and repositionings.

MICROSTRUCTURED STUDY. Projectable qualitative/quantitative small-group research based on experimental design.

BENEMAX. A totally new set of five computer-based research procedures for aiding in the optimal design of advertising and promotional materials and the prediction of market impact.

POSSE. An integrated suite of 28 comprehensive programs with unmatched capabilities in quantitative policy optimization, potential market assessment, market segmentation, product positioning, and new product design or improvement.

*All methods and models are registered properties of RAI.

---

that the firm would continue to expand its presence as a consulting force in the fields
of consumer durables and nondurables, industrial products, agricultural products,
energy industries, information and electronics, finance and insurance, medical and
pharmaceutical, communications, transportation, and other fields of endeavor.

PEERING INTO THE FUTURE

Three quotations from RAI's 1983 datebook stood out as the casewriter browsed
through this expensive promotional item distributed to the firm's numerous blue-
chip clients:

> It requires a very unusual mind to undertake the analysis of the obvious.
> —Alfred North Whitehead
>
> A distinction that does not further understanding is no distinction.
> —Goethe
>
> Analysis kills spontaneity. The grain once ground into flour springs and germinates no
> more.
> —Frederic Amiel

To these pithy axioms, Patrick J. Robinson might respond that the obvious never is,
that the distinction that furthers understanding is usually attainable by astute analysts
working hand-in-glove with enlightened managers, and that analysis need not mean
paralysis.

A visit with Patrick Robinson, whose unfailing enthusiasm often approaches
evangelical fervor, reveals the optimism of one who has observed marketing managers becoming increasingly involved in upper management and who has helped
marketing research to grow as a strategic planning tool, particularly in larger corporations. Clearly, he views his craft as an integral part of "the art of the possible" in an
intensifying search by many companies for new marketing opportunities and new
product niches. More than ever before, upper-level managers concerned about improving performance are turning to investigative and analytic models with origins
dating back to the advent of electronic computers. However, a credible claim to excellence in the consulting field is hard to come by; recognition such as that earned by
RAI is exceptional, even though the firm, in terms of revenue, is far from ranking
among the top 50 suppliers of research.

Robinson is tenacious: "Despite a few setbacks that have cropped up unexpectedly, we have adhered to the original set of precepts that guided our formation. That
early philosophy remains unchanged as we continue diligently to improve service to
RAI clients by enhancing research designs and demonstrating innovativeness in
computer software. Our 25 full-time staff members are never satisfied with previous
achievements—their attitude is 'onward and upward.'"

14

ROBINSON ASSOCIATES, INC. (B)

BACKGROUND

Incorporated in 1969, Robinson Associates, Inc. (RAI), soon acquired international recognition as an innovative marketing research, management science, and computer applications consulting company.* Results-oriented abilities in applying advanced computer modeling, multivariate statistical, and related analytic methods—many of them proprietary—held considerable appeal for operating and staff managers at dozens of client companies as they sought to identify profitable new product opportunities and to solve numerous complex business and institutional problems.

ORIGINS

RAI's roots lay in the Marketing Science Institute (MSI), a non-profit organization founded by 29 of the nation's largest corporations in Philadelphia in 1962. Patrick J. Robinson—previously manager of marketing and operations research at Imperial Oil Limited in Canada and director of integrated operations planning and new acquisi-

*The authors are grateful to Patrick Robinson for granting access to his company's strategic business plan, July 1987–June 1992, from which much of the content for this case study was adapted. Mr. Robinson deserves, at a minimum, co-authorship credit for Robinson Associates, Inc. (B).

tions negotiator at Mobil Oil—joined MSI in 1963 as research director and director of management studies, a post he held for five years until the Institute relocated to Harvard University in 1968. MSI's mission was to supplement marketing art with science through developing pragmatic, commercial applications of the multidisciplined, advanced research coming out of leading universities and innovative corporations. This interdisciplinary philosophy embraced the fields of statistics, mathematics, psychology, social psychology, mathematical psychology, cultural anthropology, economics, operations research, finance, risk-and-venture analysis, experimental design, computer science, and related fields.

Robinson's collaborators in the earlier years at MSI and, subsequently, at RAI, included, among others, Paul E. Green and Yoram Wind of the University of Pennsylvania's Wharton School, Charles Hinkle of the University of Colorado at Colorado Springs, and Jay Minas of the University of Waterloo, Canada, all of whom served variously as strategists, research designers, analysts, and project managers at MSI and whose names appeared on the letterhead printed at RAI's genesis in 1969.

During the first 10 years, RAI projects conducted for a wide variety of clients usually ranged in price from $40,000 to $200,000, intermingled with smaller- and larger-scope assignments. The consulting process typically involved market measurement and analysis, followed by development and application of dynamic mathematical and econometric forecasting models, computer-based tools to help clients determine optimal pricing and product delivery strategies, to allocate scarce corporate resources to achieve profitable market development and improved product positioning, and to assist in new concept generation and screening, competitive market segmentation, demand forecasting, and brand-switching evaluation and projection.

Robinson's fledgling company continued to operate out of MSI's University City Science Center (USCS) facility in Philadelphia until 1970, when it moved headquarters to Bryn Mawr, although maintaining its computer operations at USCS for its ready mainframe access.

Precepts and practices guiding RAI were summarized by its CEO in the 1987 five-year strategic plan as a set of goals and tasks:

- Provide clients with the highest-quality service possible at reasonable cost.
- Maintain leadership in the forefront of applied marketing research methodology and related management science and computer applications.
- Develop industry-specific expertise providing clients with substantive knowledge, combined with an appropriate mix of interdisciplinary capabilities.
- Emphasize implementation potentials for achieving practical results by exploiting RAI's advanced methodological capabilities and hands-on experience.
- Design and develop simple-to-use interactive decision support software to facilitate clients' comprehensive analyses of their data and market intelligence.
- Develop a creative "think tank" environment for RAI personnel that fosters the full contribution of individual talents and personalities, benefiting by positive synergism among all participants.
- Maintain high standards of professional ethics and responsible public relations in the business and professional communities.

RAI'S PRIMARY PRODUCTS FOR RESEARCH AND ANALYSIS

Exhibit 14.1, an RAI advertisement, provides a brief overview and chronology of the company's contributions to the advancement of marketing science and strategic corporate planning.

Reviewing selected RAI product milestones over the company's 20-year history, Robinson commented on several.

1969   "We extended traditional Delphi futures research and conducted studies of industrial buyer behavior, evaluating determinants of vendor selection employing various nonverbal, multidimensional scaling techniques and cluster analysis. Our psychologists pioneered the augmented focused group interview (AFGI™), in which videotaped groups were content-analyzed and the clinical results cross-compared with output from nonverbal perceptual and preference mapping and trade-off tasks— all at the individual participant level. These workshops provided powerful new ways of conducting exploratory, first-stage research for strategic policy projects."

1970   "Known commercially as MULTIPLE TRADEOFF ANALYSIS®, this important new price-sensitivity and attribute trade-off measurement procedure supplemented RAI's perceptual and preference mapping and clustering of benefit-seeking segments."

1971   "SPEEDMARK®, an accelerated substitute for the usual test markets, was designed to employ empirical data from in-home or in-store product placements to obtain market performance measures. It is useful in predicting demand using alternative marketing mixes, including advertising appeals, couponing, packaging, pricing, product design variations, and alternative channels of distribution."

1973   "PRODUCT DEFICIENCY ANALYSIS® enables marketers to examine one's own and competitive products for potential 'Achilles heels.' Procedures of experimental design, CONSCREEN®, and MULTIPLE TRADEOFF ANALYSIS® were combined to focus on relative competitive strengths and weaknesses as well as cross-elasticity of demand brandswitching."

1974   "BEHAVIORMETRICS® product development system was launched, combining AFGIs™, DELPHMAPP®, CONSCREEN®, SPEEDMARK®, and MULTIPLE TRADEOFF ANALYSIS®, to produce holistic guidelines for generating and screening concepts, appraising new products, and modeling competitive market structures. Multinational trade-off segmentation for cross-cultural analysis in six countries was applied and presented at the American Marketing Association's annual Attitude Research Conference."

1975   "Borrowing from experiments conducted by leading agricultural colleges and government statisticians, we introduced MICROSTRUCTURED STUDIES®, a procedure that projects results from relatively small samples, employing highly efficient fractional-factorial experimental designs."

Exhibit 14.1

AN RAI ADVERTISEMENT

1976–1977 "Increasingly sophisticated and efficient demand forecasting models, tailored to specific client needs, and dynamic 'what-if' sensitivity testing simulation capabilities were developed."

1982–83 "We introduced hybrid conjoint measurement as part of POSSE™ technology and our proprietary benefit maximization, or 'BENEMAX'™ system, for thematic and copy-point appeal, reach, and intensity measurements. Both of these comprehensive optimization systems were developed by Dr. Paul Green, purchased from him by RAI.

"POSSE™ was applied to a challenging multimarket project duirng 1983–84. This research assignment, which included residential, commercial, industrial, and agricultural respondents, and priced in the $600,000 range, was an extraordinary morale booster for us. This client had searched the United States for several months visiting 10 prospective suppliers before requesting proposals, which were systematically screened and reduced to two contenders. When the final decision was made, the letter of acceptance began, 'As a result of our proposal review meeting yesterday, your firm was selected to conduct the . . . study. A copy of the average rating of our nine-person review committee is attached for your information. RAI is identified as Company B. [See Exhibit 14.2.] Welcome aboard!'

"This was a startling numerical comparison of their screening panel's idealized supplier point score profile for us and the other finalist. Of course, it was tremendously gratifying and reinforcing for us, a high point for everyone at RAI."

By Patrick Robinson's assessment, "The COMPASS POINTS™ image management system represents RAI's most sophisticated PC-based new product in the late 1980s. Others that can function in conjunction with it include a generalized market share simulator and BENEMAX™ (benefit maximization product positioning and ad-

Exhibit 14.2

SUMMARY OF PROPOSAL RATINGS

		AVERAGE ASSIGNED POINTS	
Rating Category	Maximum Points	Company A	Company B
1. Understanding of the problem	20	11.6	18.9
2. Technical approach	20	11.3	17.7
3. Analysis plan	20	10.1	17.7
4. Project schedule	5	5.0	5.0
5. Project organization	5	3.0	5.0
6. Project staffing	15	4.7	14.4
7. Firm qualifications	5	3.1	5.0
8. Cost	10	6.9	5.8
9. Rate discretionary points	10	1.0	7.3
Total available points	110	56.7	96.8

vertising system). These and related decision support programs combine advanced marketing research, market intelligence and business information in a user-friendly, interactive, menu-driven format. Available for analysis promptly following data collection, this system results in significant cost savings over more conventional data management and analysis methods.

"Ready accessibility of sophisticated business research and strategic planning procedures in these new RAI tools greatly expands their appeal and application among marketing research, corporate planning, consulting, and product management personnel. These and related RAI products are expected to become part of the 'tools of the trade' over the period covered in our business plan (1987–1992)."

In describing his company's interactive system for modeling markets, Robinson judged that "These visually attractive and intuitively appealing, decision support systems enable noncomputer people to conceptualize and evaluate feasible-alternative situations based on the realities of the marketplace—as modeled in a realistic computer microcosm. Providing these PC computer deliverables substantially enhances the revenues produced by RAI's customary survey research. They also provide RAI, for the first time, with a basis for a potentially more predictable stream of revenues owing to the ongoing nature of some of the installed PC systems data entry and systems support."

Exhibit 14.3 portrays the integrated nature of RAI's series of proprietary computer programs. "Behaviormetrics" is the umbrella term for the various modules that measure, analyze, model, and forecast buyer and specifier behavior. Each one can also stand alone as a research tool.

Exhibit 14.4, a 1990 advertisement, illustrates different applications of RAI technology for five clients, 1969–1989, and Appendix 14A contains a listing of Robinson Associates' clients.

In 1987, as the indefatigable and charismatic Pat Robinson pondered RAI's progress from a nascent and somewhat unsteady entrepreneurial consulting firm to that of acknowledged leader in marrying the art of marketing with innovative marketing research, management science, and computer applications, he weighed, against financial constraints, the need to forge ahead with developing PC-based interactive systems: "The combination of knowing both how to collect data efficiently and to analyze marketing research information and also how to implement effectively PC-based programs gives RAI a unique advantage over other single-function marketing research, general consulting, or computer systems companies. Unfortunately, current financial constraints tend to limit the generic development of interactive systems, except as by-products of funded assignments in the form of current projects. With sufficient funding, a vigorous research and development effort for these high-profit-potential products can be instituted. The development of these and other PC systems and software-based products can be accelerated and, even more importantly, currently available programs can be more successfully marketed."

CORPORATE OBJECTIVES AND PLANS

With an inadequate capital base, and the costs of the desirable move to its new Bryn Mawr Research Center in Radnor Township during June 1986, RAI's enhanced sur-

Exhibit 14.3

BEHAVIORMETRICS® MODULES INTEGRATION

I. EXPLORATORY RESEARCH:

DELPHMAPP®	AFGI™	MICROSTRUCTURED STUDY®
Creative Workshops, using classic Mathematical Psychology Methods, to Achieve Experts' Consensus on new Business Opportunities	Mathematically-Augmented Focused Group Interviews for both Clinical and Quantitative Analysis of Subjective Experiences, Motivations and Semantics	Small Samples, structured by Experimental Design, for Stratified Random Sampling and Incidence-rate Projections back to Populations

II. MARKET STRUCTURE ANALYSIS:

CONSCREEN®	MULTIPLE TRADEOFF ANALYSIS®	PRODUCT DEFICIENCY ANALYSIS®	SPEEDMARK®
Systematic Concept Screening and Testing, Employing Multi-variate Statistical Tests, Perceptual and Preference Mapping, Clustering and Tradeoffs	Full Profile Conjoint Analysis of Alternative Products and Cross-cultural Choice Modeling of Behavioral Market Segmentation and Switching	Perceived Performance Measurement and Brand Switching Analysis to Test Relative Competitive Strengths, Weaknesses and Market Potentials	Nationally-Distributed Placements of Products and Promotions for Simulated Test Marketing and Predictive Modeling of Realistic Market Potentials

III. PRODUCT DESIGN OPTIMIZATION AND PRICING

PRODUCT OPTIMIZATION AND SELECTED SEGMENT EVALUATION (POSSE™) (Suite of 28 Related Programs)	ELASTIMAX™
• Experimental Design and Stimulus Preparation • Categorical Variable Optimization • Utility Function Estimation • Continuous Variable Optimization • Choice Simulators • Continuous Variable Sensitivity Analysis • Response Surface and Objective Function Estimates • Time Path Forecasting	Estimation of self-and Cross-elasticities of Demand and Indifference Curves, using a First-order Markov Process for Steady-state Market Projections of Price-Induced Brand Switching (and other Comparable Elasticities)

IV. OPTIMUM PROMOTIONAL POSITIONING & BENEFIT SEGMANTATION:

BENEFIT MAXIMIZATION (BENEMAX™)	
• Optimum Benefit/Feature Bundles • Homogeneous Benefit-Seeking Segmentation	• Perceived Image Associations and Benefit Delivery • New Benefit-Bundle Testing and Unique Positioning

V. PROMOTIONAL IMPACT MEASUREMENT:

COPYMETRICS™
• Pre-exposure Perceptual and Preference Imagery and Evaluative Features/Benefits • Realistic exposure to alternative promotional Thematic and Copy Point appeals in common competitive contexts (sample partitioned for test commercial variations) • Post-exposure impact measurement of communication efficacy, revealing immediate shifts in Brand/Corporate Imagery, Purchase Intentions and Evaluative Tradeoffs

VI. MARKET INTELLIGENCE DECISION-SUPPORT

COMPASS POINTS™
• Complete Disaggregated, Highly Compacted and Optimized Customer Records/Respondent Surveys/Panelists' Data, maintained in PC, for Immediate access using Interactive, Menu-driven, Inquiry Refinement Systems (Executive Work Stations) • Personally-defined, a prior and post hoc Segmentation "Cuts" of data - - available in Tabular, Graphic and Mapping color presentation formats • Comprehensive Facilities to Analyze Image Data and draw Statistical Inferences

Exhibit 14.4

SOLUTIONS FOR FIVE RAI CLIENTS, 1969–1989

vey research and decision support systems advanced at the expense of promoting growth in more established marketing research approaches and general consulting activities. Available funds, management time, and market cultivation efforts were severely taxed in support of these new systems. Occasionally, the company's attention was diverted from concentration on central objectives. Robinson commented on such disturbances in 1985–1986: "During this vexing transition period RAI's internal product mix temporarily took on a computer-oriented emphasis that shifted attention away from RAI's unique cutting-edge strength of tackling challenging client projects. True, advanced computer technology was always a mainstay, a great RAI strength, but this deflection was primarily mainframe based and only occasionally resulted in delivering systems for a client's in-house use. The reverse is now the case. Many projects are currently delivered as both a static written report and a dynamic PC computer model."

RAI's corporate growth objectives,[1] including personnel, facilities, organization, financial controls, and capital required to attain these objectives, are intended to

1. Increase revenues from the existing survey research systems and software development and general consulting activities from approximately $1.5 million to over $5 million.
2. Begin exploiting the company's ability to do profitable and ongoing multiple-client projects. These projects can include ad hoc studies and periodic surveys for the hospital and health care, pharmaceutical, electric utility, airline, automotive, banking, and other client industries. Combined clients may be groups of interested corporations that would pool information requests and share core results plus having tailored sections for individual proprietary use.
3. Initiate new market development and new product development programs. These will exploit fully the considerable interdisciplinary research and development capabilities in marketing science systems and PC-based software that have already been implemented and are expected to evolve over the next five years. These modern products will take advantage of the new wave of IBM and similar enhanced PC hardware and software systems. RAI believes that, with well-designed and effectively implemented marketing efforts, decision support systems revenues can approach $4 million within five years.
4. Continue developing the interdisciplinary professional teamwork and integrated support staff required to achieve the targeted revenue projections. This growth will entail selective hiring of key client-contact people, additional scientific computer programmers, and seasoned survey research project managers. In parallel with this evolutionary growth, appropriate upgrading-of-skills training and development will continue at all levels. Also, the addition of incentive programs designed to attract and retain key people will be implemented. These personnel policies are expected to provide for stock option plans, discretionary bonuses, and other suitable incentives.
5. Achieve optimum utilization of existing facilities and expand these facilities as cost justifies. Concurrently, plans are in place to upgrade existing computer, word processing, facsimile transmission, and production equipment. These facilities are being integrated using local area networking and desktop publishing capabilities. Flexible communication will be achieved both internally and with clients' equipment.
6. Implement well-planned organizational guidelines and procedural policies that will retain small company, innovative flexibility, while establishing orderly operational and financial controls to keep projects on schedule and to ensure financial integrity and profitability.

[1]The indented material in this section is adapted or quoted from RAI's 1987–1992 strategic plan.

7. Expand capacity in a sequential cost-justified fashion, based on available financial resources. While this objective may be attained through reinvestment of internally generated earnings, an adequate line of credit is required to facilitate operational flexibility. Additional capital may be obtained to accelerate achieving these objectives in more timely fashion for the creation and distribution of new product lines.

EXISTING BUSINESS GROWTH

Revenues from existing business are conservatively estimated to grow to the $5 million area over the next five years. In relative terms, this means increasing RAI's present level of activity by some combination such as 3 large assignments or 12 small ones per year. The basic staff to accomplish this growth objective is already in place and fully operational. The only additional costs involve selective addition of survey research project people and computer programmers as and when fully cost justified. A continuing program of hardware and software updating and replacement is required to support adequately the computer programming and systems development effort.

A significant increase in the level of market development, through appropriate print media advertising, sales promotion (e.g., mailing demonstration diskettes and videotapes to selected prospects), and follow-up personal contact activities will also be required. Because of the high degree of leverage built into this situation, the forecasted increases in revenues can have a dramatic impact on profitability. Clearly, if the growth rate can be accelerated, the "bottom line" impact can be exceedingly attractive in terms of discounted cash flow rates of return.

Even though the company's current capital base is relatively thin, and since the rate of growth is necessarily governed by available capital, the projected growth can be largely financed by retained earnings. Because of the inevitable unevenness of substantial cash receipts, an initial credit line of $150,000 is required to provide much needed operating flexibility. This fluctuating accommodation will enable the company to operate more efficiently by reducing financial and other cost penalties. Even the facilitating of more timely payments to suppliers can result in improved credit terms and a strengthened bargaining position and improved margins. These operating improvements can also produce other benefits, including more effective cash management and a measure of overall stability.

PERSONNEL REQUIREMENTS

As a consequence of operating on a limited budget, RAI's marketing efforts, both for a promotional media budget and direct sales effort, have not been sufficiently intensive to exploit RAI's considerable potentials for growth. To obtain the forecasted sales and support levels under this strategic business plan, RAI needs to hire several key people at a professional level during the period. One such qualified new professional, with an MBA from University of Chicago, has joined RAI as of June 1987 as market development coordinator, bringing special skills and connections in the hospital and health care fields.

In support of market development, the existing business forecast reflects planned increases in various promotional activities. These increases complement the addition of an experienced and proven marketing research/market development professional to supplement RAI's present capabilities. Such additions will be followed, as cost justified, by augmenting RAI's project management staff and other resource people during the planning period. Similarly, RAI's computer and systems capabilities will require several programmers to handle the increased assignments anticipated over the projected period. Additional support personnel will also be hired as cost justified.

The anticipated multiclient survey research business is essentially a spinoff of RAI's existing custom business. The major requirement for exploiting this area is a more concentrated market development effort to recruit and sustain a minimum client base required for large syndicated projects. This growth will require market development activities in the field, including on-site client office sales presentations. These activities are expected to cost-justify a corresponding increase in survey research and computer personnel to handle the added business volume. Once started, the multiclient business will feed on itself. Each new project will not only be continuing, but can be expected to attract more new clients.

Since RAI is already experienced in designing and using computer-assisted telephone interviewing facilities, these efforts will be expanded using part-time interviewers on site as required to bring more data collection, data reduction, and tabulation capacity in-house, a form of vertical integration. In addition, key individuals and collaborating firms will be sought for joint venture interests. Related administrative tasks can be readily absorbed into the corporate framework.

Sales of systems and software require seasoned, high quality, and relatively aggressive personnel. A professional approach is essential for the total systems selling of easy-to-use, yet sophisticated, approaches to providing timely access to vital market intelligence and competitive image tracking. RAI intends to obtain access to key buying influences through commission-based representation to develop this activity profitably in conjunction with advertising and direct response mailings, including distribution of demonstration diskettes and supporting promotional literature.

To attract and retain the experienced professionals needed, suitable incentives are also contemplated, such as discretionary bonuses, a stock option plan, and appropriate fringe benefits. Ideally, RAI will create a compensation package that can lower fixed overhead, yet make possible substantial employee gains for superior performance. The company presently has employee health, life and disability insurance programs comparable to most large companies. Within the next two years, RAI expects to develop a contributory employee savings plan consistent with RAI's insurance representative's evaluation of advantageous long-term tax and personal growth potentials.

The combination of well-trained and highly motivated employees, a traditional RAI strong point, will allow RAI to compete effectively with much larger firms. Such companies can become "muscle bound" by layers of administration and reduced internal communication that stifle the creative initiative and complete involvement of their employees. As RAI grows, the esprit de corps that has characterized the firm since its inception will be sustained. This will be accomplished by avoiding administrative excesses while retaining an informal, yet professional working environment.

By providing RAI's team of interdisciplinary employees the best tools of the trade, in a very suitable working environment, creativity can be fostered and access to current developments in relevant professional areas can be maintained. All of this is consistent with maintaining RAI's image with corporate clients as being a premier think tank with can-do capabilities.

ORGANIZATIONAL AND FINANCIAL CONTROLS

At present, RAI has an informal process for monitoring project progress, a moderately sophisticated double-entry accounting system, and internal financial controls appropriate for a small company. Cash flow projections, project bidding, and various reports and analyses are handled by an IBM PC computer. A program for measuring project costs against budget has been developed and is used on an ad hoc basis. Company policies and procedures, while applied consistently, are not completely formalized.

As the company grows in numbers of people, dollars handled, equipment, and physical facilities required, changes in corporate structure (e.g., divisions or subsidiaries created or acquired), additional internal controls will be put into place. This orderly growth must be managed carefully to retain as much small-company flexibility as possible, consistent with ensuring fiscal integrity.

NEW CAPITAL REQUIREMENTS

Orderly growth in RAI's existing business can be funded out of retained earnings with the assistance and operating flexibility of an adequate credit line. Retained earnings will be plowed back into the business, used to eliminate long-term obligations, and applied to a well-designed discretionary, results-oriented incentive program to reward and encourage key employees.

RAI's present facilities can accommodate approximately five more people without major refurbishing expense. During 1988 and 1989, refurbishing of unused portions of the building can provide the additional offices and work areas required to accomplish the orderly expansion and balance of facilities. This expansion is estimated to require $50,000 to $100,000 leasehold improvements and will provide the flexibility to house additional personnel appropriate to accomplish our five-year objectives.

The multiclient programs are essentially natural outgrowths of existing business. New capital is required primarily to fund accelerated market development and related promotional efforts, as well as funding additional computer and other support personnel. Also, some new equipment is required to complete RAI's integrated computer, word processing, and desktop publishing systems. It is estimated that additional investment capital of at least $100,000 should be sought to accelerate these developments beyond a basic boot-strap evolution. Even though the planned business potentials are based on the existing systems and software technology within the company, these targets will require orderly steps, as previously described, in the sales and promotional areas due to the specialized nature of these markets.

To fully exploit near-term market opportunities on a "maximum-effort" basis could justify a significantly higher level of capital support—estimated at $860,000 over the five-year period. While this major input may not be essential, it is certain to increase the likelihood of fully achieving and exceeding the targeted growth in a much shorter time period. Even within the stated five-year planning horizon, availability of additional working funds can yield greater efficiencies and productivity improvements beyond those projected: probably by as much as a 20 to 30 percent higher bottom line for all years affected.

As to the timing of outside financing, RAI could be in position by the fall of 1987 to attract $500,000 in new funding. Efforts will be made to raise this capital privately. We will also consider other avenues, including possibly a public offering if growth continues to improve with current momentum.

EPILOGUE—BY PATRICK J. ROBINSON

"Between 1987 and 1990 a number of significant events shaped RAI's course—some auspicious, some adverse. The most unfavorable occurrence was loss of a major decision support systems client. Continuing work with this client began in late 1982 and resulted in the following note to RAI, accompanying the reworked version of our 1983 baseline study for the client: "FYI. This is the final result after (Mr. _____) and I had our way with your presentation. Mr. _____'s supervisor called the job 'very professional,' which is an unusual comment for him—so, three cheers for a job well done!" Also, the following paragraph appeared in the preface to this GM Image Management System Baseline Study:

> "The technical and analytical expertise of Robinson Associates, Inc., made this report feasible at an early date. Were it not for the eagerness of this organization to apply the latest marketing science techniques to practical corporate problem-solving, this project would probably have taken a much more ordinary, and mundane, form. Because of this firm's high level of creative excitement, the GM Image Management System is truly 'on the cutting-edge of technology' in management information systems.

"Over the succeeding four years this tracking study of some 150 domestic and foreign cars, station wagons, vans, and trucks grew from a semiannual consumer survey sample of 2,000 to some 10,000 respondents in each wave. RAI worked with General Motors headquarters and divisional personnel to design the survey instruments and to supervise the conduct of the nationally distributed fieldwork.

"In addition to designing and conducting this marketing research, RAI also developed a comprehensive interactive decision support system to utilize accumulated data in disaggregated form on IBM PCs. This menu-driven system maintained the complete respondent records (on hard disk storage) and employed attractive color graphics with so-called windows, pull-down menu screens, and many flexible output options, including simple tabulations; pie, bar, and line charts; and multidimensional scaling procedures. The last generated presentation-quality perceptual and preference maps for all conceivable segments of market niches, as defined interactively by system users.

"From 1983's baseline study beginning, the GM Image Management System evolved until by 1988 it had been adopted by all the car divisions (including Saturn), the truck division, the European divisions, and the authorized advertising agencies of all these users. Because of the escalating size of the desired waves of panel data, many challenges arose for compacting data bases and optimizing programs (written initially in FORTRAN and subsequently in the powerful and technically more appropriate language of C). The initial design and implementation stages were seriously plagued by the fact that RAI was one of the very first users of various Microsoft, and then later Ryan-McFarland FORTRAN, compilers—the former particularly were found to contain many hidden "bugs." These took considerable time to discover, and many routines could not even be corrected in time to be useful. This pioneering work was a difficult and costly hurdle confronting PC-based, decision support systems development. Eventually, RAI's professionals switched from FORTRAN to C. This transition became inevitable in order to overcome the many vexing technical obstacles in the development of the generic COMPASS POINTS™ system and the specific GM applications version. RAI published an illustration of the generic system structure as follows (Exhibit 14.5):

Exhibit 14.5

COMPASS POINTS: A MODERN ROSETTA STONE FOR DISAGGREGATED MARKET INTELLIGENCE DATA

Marketing researchers and product managers often review field surveys, customer records, and consumer tracking studies in search of valuable market intelligence and meaningful segmentations. The required data bases can become voluminous when maintained in completely disaggregated form. A common dilemma arises when such data are transformed through totaling or averaging. Data storage is reduced, but useful information can be lost or masked in these aggregation processes. Knowing what details to keep and which to discard presupposes knowing what is potentially relevant—or alternatively making (often heroic) assumptions to simplify records. Today's high-speed, large-storage-capacity PCs can, by quickly focusing attention on salient facts and essential clues, minimize the risk of discarding essential fine structures and potentially profitable insights. Storage alone is *not* the solution. Economical and easy access is.

Cutting through and interpreting the "paper mountain" requires an efficient "Swiss Army knife." COMPASS POINT™ is such a tool. Illustrated in the following flow diagram is this comprehensive, menu-driven, "hub-and-spoke" design information system. It is capable of permitting users to

Exhibit 14.5 (Cont.)

INTERACTIVE (COMPASS POINTS™) IMAGE MANAGEMENT SYSTEM

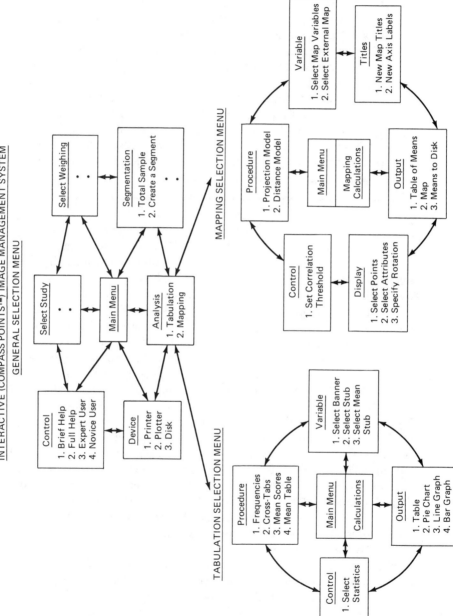

Exhibit 14.5 (Cont.)

screen and analyze very large files in real time, without requiring keyboard skills or methodological sophistication.

    This comprehensive and flexible PC-based system is a *productivity
tool*. It provides fresh answers and new directions, using cross-tabulations,
color graphics, and precise multidimensional scaling methods for perceptual and preference mapping. COMPASS POINTS™ accommodates up to
32,000 detailed survey records in completely disaggregated data bases.
Another unique feature is the incorporation of a technically superior, multidimensional scaling algorithm. This new "D-Scale" procedure was developed in collaboration with RAI's senior academic consultant, Dr. Wayne
DeSarbo. D-Scale provides a number of very desirable spatial display and
diagnostic properties. These facilitate the rigorous interpretation of perceptual and preference relationships.

    "Paralleling RAI's proprietary image management system development work
(currently embodied in RAI's COMPASS POINTS™ system) was a specialized internal records and secondary data manipulation system, designed to handle production,
sales, and inventory data in a time series analysis system. (See Exhibit 14.6.) This
powerful, short-interval data updating system was first developed for GM, with
budgetary support from Electronic Data Systems (EDS). The system employed a
unique hub-and-spoke design which permitted very efficient and flexible access to
various computational paths for the large data bases maintained on hard disk storage
devices; with provisions for up- and downloading from host archival-storage mainframe computers. RAI also began developing an optical disk storage option for updating and disseminating revised supply, demand, and inventory data.

    "As these GM-related, PC-based projects evolved from 1983 through 1988,
RAI found its systems development activity evolving through creeping commitment.
De facto, RAI fell into the role of a monopsony supplier, with basically only one large
customer, GM/EDS. As net annual revenues from these activities rose above half a
million dollars, RAI's systems design and programming staff grew to five full-time
professionals, plus several skilled contract programmers. The pressures to deliver,
despite various obstacles, became somewhat intense. In retrospect, RAI had discovered just how difficult it is to produce new operational systems and PC software,
while pushing the evolving hardware envelope.

    "Then came a most unfortunate large-company perturbation. GM had acquired
EDS and appeared to proceed over a several-year period through a sequence of
culture-shock transformations. These culminated in the stormy departure of the EDS
founder and former CEO, Ross Perot, in the face of profound disagreements with
Roger Smith, CEO of GM. Not long after this, EDS began to enforce its "master
agreement" with all GM Divisions, insisting that everyone discontinue PC-based systems in favor of strictly mainframe systems.

    "Despite this turbulence, RAI remained as a seemingly secure supplier of
unique marketing support PC systems design and maintenance. During this period,

Exhibit 14.6

SALES RETRIEVAL, PRODUCTION, AND INVENTORY
INTELLIGENCE SYSTEM

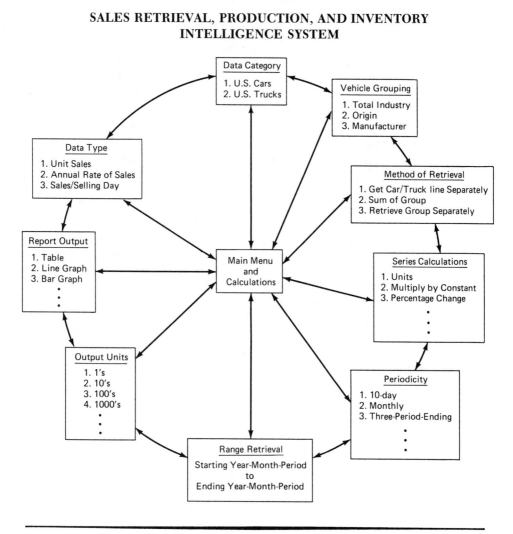

RAI was promoting distributed processing, with combined PC and mainframe systems capabilities. Since RAI had a credible history of mainframe computer science and management science applications, this line of reasoning seemed to be gaining acceptance. Steps were also taken to install RAI's mainframe program suites of POSSE™ and BENEMAX™ on the GM Engineering Center mainframe as a start toward achieving this potentially valuable distributed processing linkage.

"Then came the crunch, in late 1988. The word went out that *all* PC applications were to be dropped. Immediately. This occurred between the end of the GM budget year (September) and the EDS budget year (December). Unfortunately, for RAI, the initial assumption that this drastic order 'would not apply to RAI' turned out to be a false hope—despite attempts by certain user groups to fend off the inevitable. What followed was unpleasant and costly and a blow from which RAI is still recovering some two years later. Although RAI had been led to expect that there would be at least a year to effect a transition, if such an event ever occurred, this was not to be.

"In the year following this costly lesson in how not to have too many of one's eggs in one basket, an orderly process of attrition and 'outplacements' was administered at RAI. This expensive process was essentially consistent with a strong humanitarian philosophy which the company has held to for over 20 years. Since then, RAI has regrouped and reemphasized its roots and its interdisciplinary approach to problem definition, market measurement, analysis, modeling, and forecasting. As part of the plan in 1987, RAI began 'networking' with several leading business research and consulting firms to conduct joint projects, to explore positive synergism potentials, and to achieve 'critical mass' through appropriate joint venture operations or other forms of collaboration.

"While continuing to move in the direction of new approaches (including knowledge-based and interactive management systems), RAI management came to recognize that continuing to seek to be innovative and among the best entails certain risks. The old Marketing Science Institute was planned as a pioneering, nonprofit organization. RAI has continued, as the descendant of MSI, to carry on some of this innovative momentum. But there are practical limits. Clearly, maintaining an innovative leadership position cannot be the most immediately profitable path, nor the line of least resistance. However, being 'creatively different' is an important ingredient in attracting and holding imaginative professionals and progressive clients. In the long run, this offers the potential of reasonable 'fun and profit' for both RAI and its clients."

Appendix 14A

Clients of RAI:

CONSUMER DURABLES
Bissell, Inc.
Ford Motor Company
General Electric Company
General Motors Corporation
   Buick Division
   Cadillac Division
   Chevrolet Division
   Oldsmobile Division
   Pontiac Division
   Saturn Division
Isuzu
Polaroid Corporation
Sears, Roebuck and Company
Subaru of America
Tappan Appliances
Toro Company

CONSUMER NON-DURABLES
Campbell Soup Company
Carl's Hamburgers
Cigarrera LaModerna
Clairol, Inc.
CPC International, Inc.
General Foods Corporation
Genesee Brewing Company, Inc.
Green Giant Corporation
Hallmark Cards
Heineken International Beheer B.V.
L'eggs Products, Inc.
L'erin Cosmetics
Lever Brothers Company
Mobil Chemical Company
Pizza Hut
Stroh Brewery Company
Tasty Baking Company
Wendy's
Whataburger

INDUSTRIAL PRODUCTS
CertainTeed Corporation
E.I. DuPont de Nemours & Company
Eastman Kodak Company
Graphic Arts Marketing
  Information Services (GAMIS)
ICI Americas, Inc.
McJunkin Corporation
Microdot Corporation
Millikin & Company
National Printing and Equipment
  Supply Association (NPES)
Parker Hannifin Corporation
Phillips & Jacobs, Inc.
The PQ Corporation
Rockwell International
St. Joes Mineral Corporation
Standard Pressed Steel
Tour & Anderson Inc.

AGRICULTURAL PRODUCTS
Amchem Products, Inc.
American Cyanamid Company
Dow Chemical Company
International Harvester Credit Corp
Monsanto Agricultural Products Company
PPG Industries
Sperry New Holland
3M Company

ENERGY INDUSTRIES
Applied Management Sciences, Inc.
Atlantic Richfield Company
British Petroleum Company
Central Hudson Gas & Electric Corporation
Empire State Electric Energy
  Research Corporation (ESEERCO)
Electric Power Research Institute (EPRI)
Imperial Oil Limited
New York State Energy Research
  Development Association (NYSERDA)
Southern California Edison Company
STP Corporation
Sun Oil Corporation

INFORMATION & ELECTRONICS
American Telephone & Telegraph (AT&T)
Bell Telephone Company of Pennsylvania
CISI network Corporation
Electronic Data Systems (EDS)
GTE/Sylvania
IBM Corporation
Litton Industries
Power Thinking Tools
RCA Corporation
Sperry Univac
Texas Instruments, Inc.
Xerox Corporation
Xerox Systems

FINANCE & INSURANCE
American Bankers Association
American Express Company
Atlantic Financial
Bankers Trust
Citibank, N.A.
Colonial Penn Insurance Company
Connecticut Bank & Trust Company
First National Bank of Denver
First Pennsylvania Bank, N.A.
First Tennessee Bank
Industrial National Bank
Insurance Company of North America
Meridian Bancorp, Inc.
Provident National Bank
Visa International

PHARMACEUTICAL & HEALTH CARE
Beaumont Hospital
Food and Drug Administration
Johnson & Johnson
Magee Rehabilitation Hospital
McNeil Pharmaceuticals
Merck, Sharp & Dohme
Mercy Catholic Medical Center
Modern Medicine
Philadelphia Health Plan
Schering-Plough Corporation
SmithKline Beecham
Thomas Jefferson University Hospital
Warner-Lambert Company

COMMUNICATIONS
CBS, Inc.
COVIDEA
Cox Enterprises
Della Femina McNamee WCRS
Department of Commerce
Downe Publishing
Hoffman/Miller Advertising, Inc.
Levine Huntley Schmidt & Beaver, Inc.
Lewis & Gilman, Inc.
Metromarket Newspapers, Ltd.
National Geographic Society
Newspaper Advertising Bureau (NAB)
SSC&B Inc.
Young & Rubicam

TRANSPORTATION
Air Canada
Amtrak
Canadian Ministry of Transport
Canadian National Railways
Continental Airlines
International Air Transport Association (IATA)
Interstate and Ocean Transport Company
National Car Rental Systems, Inc.
New York Air
Pan American Airlines
TWA

OTHER
American Airlines Decision Technologies
Greenfield & Chimicles
Harcum Junior College
INTERACT
Laventhol & Horwath
Law Enforcement Assistance Agency
National YMCA
Philadelphia 76ers
QUESTAR
Synergic Resources Corporation
The New York Yankees

ROBINSON ASSOCIATES, INC.

500 SOUTH ROBERTS ROAD · BRYN MAWR, PA 19010-1137 · (215) 527-3100 · 24-HR FAX: (215) 527-2421 · CABLE: SYNERGISTIC

NEW DIRECTIONS IN CREATIVE RESEARCH . . . . PROJECT PLANNING . . . . IMAGINATIVE CONSULTING

15

A. POE DESIGNS, INC.

My involvement with A. Poe Designs began at a cocktail party for past and present members of the governor's staff. I was a past staff member who had left public service to return to the business arena. While listening to a number of "political" conversations, I heard someone talking about profits, margins, and a new business venture, and I gravitated to that side of the room to find the source of this interesting conversation. I was surprised to find a past working associate, Ann Poe, who had left political life a few years before I had, was married, had a child, and was trying to begin a business in her home, combining career and family responsibilities. An artist and fine seamstress, Ann was designing and manufacturing women's fabric purses and fabric-lined picnic baskets, with accessories. As she put it, "I've been working on this project, off and on, for about two years now, and I still don't have a clear idea of how to get these items on the market. I don't have any business background and am not the selling type, so I'm really at a standstill."

The project sounded interesting, so after more discussion I volunteered my assistance. I was teaching at a local college and thought I could spare some time to lend a hand. Little did I realize what lay ahead of us. Our experience together might be best termed a "quest for focus."

BACKGROUND OF THE PRODUCT

The line of A. Poe Designs included three sizes of women's handbags, a briefcase for women, and accessories in the three purse colors of blue, salmon, and green. The accessories were seen primarily as loss leaders used to stimulate the purchase of the handbags, not necessarily to generate profit. These accessories, made in the same fabric as the purse to match the item chosen, included a matching glasses case and a zippered makeup case. The purse sizes combined functionality with fashion to create a purse size for virtually any use. The smaller purse might be used for day or evening, while the medium-sized purse would be perfect for "the woman who has everything" and carries it with her. The larger tote was an ideal bag for an exercise/aerobics class or as a diaper bag. All items were machine washable ensuring ease of care and unlimited use in or out of doors. With the accessories designed to complement the item selected and purchased, each creation offered an additional incentive for purchase.

I had asked Ann about the care of the fabric since shrinkage or fading could ruin the product's reputation and her business as well. "Oh, I get the fabric from a domestic manufacturer," she continued. "He seems reliable but won't quilt the fabric; so I use a local quilter to do each ream for me. The small floral prints are basically a French pattern and are very similar to the Pierre Dioux designs; however, my fabric is at least half the price of theirs. I've washed all the purses that I've made so far and they come out just fine, no shrinkage or bleeding, but as for fading, I'm not sure what they'll do. I did make one for my mother-in-law a few years ago and she uses it all the time. She's never said anything about fading, so I assume fading isn't a problem— this is really fine fabric."

I was also curious about her picnic baskets and how she saw those items fitting into the purse line; one normally doesn't see purses and picnic baskets in the same line. "Well, I had a lot of excess fabric that didn't have the contrasting trim, so I used it to line some picnic baskets and make table cloths with matching napkins," she continued. "It used up most of my excess fabric and people were selling them on consignment; so I decided to keep making them until I found some other use for my excess fabric that didn't have the contrasting design." She explained further: "You see, the body of the purse is made with the floral fabric. When I purchase the floral fabric, it has a contrasting design along two borders. Of course, I have more floral fabric than contrast, so I use the excess floral fabric for the accessories and the picnic baskets."

MARKET EVALUATION

I proposed that Ann do some market testing to determine what items and colors in the line appealed to potential customers. We tested a group of 200 women on the campus where I taught. Since research funds were limited, we segmented our market group to younger women. We felt that this group would give us a reliable measure of the product's acceptance. The results demonstrated that blue was the favored color with salmon coming in as a very close second. The most popular size was more difficult to determine since the smaller and medium-sizes were almost equal in demand preference. The larger tote was well received but not as a purse. The picnic baskets were well liked but not at our suggested price levels. The following data summarize results of the research:

Question 1: If purchasing this product, which size would you choose?

SIZE PREFERENCE

	Number	Percentage
Small purse	85	42.5%
Medium purse	83	41.5
Large tote	32	16.0

Question 2: If purchasing this product, which color would you choose?

COLOR PREFERENCE

	Number	Percentage
Azure blue	81	40.5%
Salmon red	77	38.5
Medium green	42	21.0

Question 3: What price range do you apply to each size/item?

PRICE PREFERENCE

	Range	Percentage
Small purse	$40– $ 70	80%
Medium purse	60– 80	75
Large tote	80– 100	65
Briefcase	80– 100	40

Although the purses were favorably received, only 80 percent of those tested would purchase at the suggested prices. The briefcase suffered the most with only 40 percent of those tested willing to spend that much for a fabric briefcase.

Question 4: Of what is your current purse made?

CURRENT PURSE MATERIAL

	Number	Percentage
Leather	70	35%
Fabric	80	40
Other	50	25

This test was completed during the spring and summer, which can explain the high number of fabric purses recorded.

Question 5: Where do you purchase your purses, totes, or related items?

PURCHASE POINT

	Number	Percentage
Department store	107	53.5%
Women's store/boutique	62	31.0
Specialty store	23	11.5
Mail order/catalog	8	4.0

This group showed a high percentage of purchases in department stores over specialty stores. It should be noted as well that many specialty stores are in the area of this college campus.

Question 6: What is the average price of your purses?

AVERAGE PRICE OF PURCHASE

	Number	Percentage
Between $30 and $36	7	3.5%
Between $37 and $44	20	10.0
Between $45 and $52	23	11.5
Between $53 and $59	53	26.5
Over $60	97	48.5

Question 7: Would you purchase this purse/briefcase?

PURCHASE RATE

	Number	Percentage
Yes	184	92%
No	16	8

The overwhelming majority of persons tested would purchase the product; and they normally spent over $60 for their purse purchases.

Question 8: Would you purchase this purse/briefcase for these prices?

PRICE/PURCHASE RATE

		Yes	No	Yes Percentage
Small purse	$50	196	4	98.0%
Medium purse	70	156	44	78.0
Large tote	80	102	98	51.0
Briefcase	80	80	120	40.0

The demand for each product dropped off drastically when high price levels were reached. Value added was not perceived sufficient to justify the higher prices.

Question 9: What do you see as the quality measure of these products?

QUALITY RATING

	Number	Percentage
Excellent	172	86%
Good/Fair	26	13
Poor	2	1

Question 10: What would cause you *not* to purchase these products?

PRODUCT LIMITATIONS

	Percentage
Fabric does not last	62%
Fabric could fade or shrink	45
Needs care instructions	47
Questioned guarantee if any	53

The area of most concern was that of the construction and its ability to withstand use and proper routine care.

Question 11: What is your opinion of the picnic basket?

PICNIC BASKET PERCEPTIONS

	Number	Percentage
More than favorable	185	92.5%
Favorable	15	7.5
Unfavorable	0	—

All those tested liked the picnic basket both in terms of overall construction and contents.

Question 12: Would you purchase these baskets if you felt the price correct?

PURCHASE RATE

	Number	Percentage
Yes	195	97.5%
No	5	2.5

The vast majority saw a personal use for the picnic baskets and would use them as well as purchase them if they found the price acceptable.

Question 13: Would you purchase the picnic basket for these prices?

PRICE/PURCHASE RATE

		Yes	No	Yes Percentage
Small	$150	55	145	27.5%
Large	225	20	180	10.0

Clearly, the price was too high.

DISTRIBUTION

We discussed several methods of distribution, ranging from mail order to consignment distribution and even personal selling, which Ann had basically used for the past year. I asked her who was currently buying her purses and how purchasers found out about them. "Most of the orders come from my mother-in-law's friends. She travels a great deal. People see her tote and ask her where she got it, and that leads to my getting a few orders. Normally, people will ask for a tote with the matching little purse. There's a lot of demand for that among the cruise ship set."

We decided to try the women's boutiques to see how they might feel about distributing our handbags. The area we chose was characterized by households with incomes ranging between $70,000 and $100,000. We started by personally contacting each boutique. After 10 contacts and 2 sales, we decided that this technique was far too expensive.

I asked Ann, "Do you know of anyone who could put together a photo layout/ mailer for us? How about your friend who works as a printer downtown?" That weekend we took several photos of the line in use and in traditional display pose, and Ann's printer friend mounted the shots that we selected and printed selling copy.

Armed with 10 sets of the photo layout, we compiled a list of the most likely and largest customers of women's clothing and accessories. The next step was to compose a sales letter and enclose the layouts to send to prospects. Each "packet" also contained a "fact sheet" to explain the product, its prices and options, in the case of the picnic basket, and an order sheet. We had reduced our costs from $27.00 for a personal call to $7.00 for the direct-mail technique.

The choice of selective distribution rather than intensive or exclusive was based upon the assumption that our demographic segment was not quite priced at the exclusive end of the market, which would require more value added on the part of the product and increased promotional coverage to communicate this exclusivity of ownership, therefore increasing our costs. Our costs prevented pricing at a level low enough to merit distribution through larger department stores, which would require us to sell to them for less and would create demand that we could not meet at the current level of production. Until production increased considerably, selective distribution seemed well-fitted to our capabilities and suited the image of the product.

Choosing the selective mode of distribution was also based on our need for relative control of the line and its development as well as the need for increased compatibility within the line. By distributing in only fine women's shops, the perceived quality of the product benefited as did the reputation of the store in distributing only selective items. The knowledge that only other fine women's shops would be carrying this line increased the owner's desire to carry the line as well. This then ensured compatibility among the distributors and harmony within the channel.

COSTS AND PRICING

After approaching several potential distributors, we found a major problem—keystoning. A typical dialogue between Ann and a store owner will illustrate:

Ann: We're asking $40 for the small purse, $50 for the medium, and $60 for the la-
dies' tote. (Ann had arrived at these prices by keystoning her price relative to
her cost, that is, if it cost her $16 to make the small purse, she sold it for $32.)

Owner: Oh. That's a bit high for me. You see I keystone my prices. If you sell the
small to me for $40, I sell it for $80. So the tote would run $120, and I don't
think I can get that for the tote, not even if I threw in the matching makeup
case for free!

Ann: Well, what do you think might be a reasonable price that would give you an
equitable margin?

Owner: I'd say about $24 for the small, $28 for the medium, and $38 for the large
tote.

Ann: I couldn't sell them that cheap, I'd only make about $8 per purse.

Owner: Well what are you selling the picnic baskets for?

Ann: $150 for the picnic basket for two and $235 for the basket for four.

Owner: You're way out of my range there. I'm afraid I can't take any of the line.

It was plain to see that the prices must be adjusted and the line expanded to include another "enticer." Since many people who purchased the tote got the small
purse to match, we decided to make a briefcase to stimulate demand for the smaller
purse as well. We then analyzed our costs (itemized in Exhibit 15.1) and reduced
them to lower our price. The new prices ranged from $22 for the small purse, $40 for
the medium, $60 for the tote, and $60 for the briefcase. We priced the glasses case at
$6 and the makeup bag at $8. We marked the large picnic basket down to $150 and
the picnic basket for two to $120. Since we felt that the $32 matching purse would
stimulate their sale, we priced the tote and briefcase around $60 (see Exhibits 15.2
and 15.3).

Exhibit 15.1

PRODUCTION COSTS AND WHOLESALE PRICES

Item	Labor*	Materials	Total	Wholesale Price
Small purse	$ 6.00	$10.00	$ 16.00	$ 32.00
Medium purse	6.00	14.00	20.00	40.00
Large tote	10.00	20.00	30.00	60.00
Ladies' briefcase	10.00	20.00	30.00	60.00
Glasses case	1.00	2.00	3.00	6.00
Makeup case	1.50	2.50	4.00	8.00
Picnic basket for 2	20.00	60.00	80.00	125.00
Picnic basket for 4	20.00	80.00	100.00	150.00

*Computed at $3.50 per hour.

Exhibit 15.2

THE COLLECTION

Bags of uncommon quality. Made of the finest domestic cotton, treated with DuPont Teflon. Machine washable in cold water. Line dry. A variety of sizes to meet your every need. Available in three delightful colors: salmon red, loden green, and azure blue. Bags are fully lined, with a zipper closure and reinforced bottom. Accessories are also available.

The briefcase is fully lined with a large inside pouch and a zipper pocket.

Price List		Accessories	

Ladies' briefcase
    10″ × 16″
	$60.00	Glasses case
		    Fully lined with a
		    velcro closure
			$6.00

Ladies' tote
    Size: Approx. 9″ high ×
    18″ long
	$60.00	Makeup bag
		    6″ × 9″, fully lined
		    with a zipper closure
			$8.00

Ladies' medium bag
    Size: Approx. 7″ high ×
    14″ long
	$40.00		

Ladies' small bag
    Size: Approx. 5″ high ×
    10″ long
	$32.00		

Exhibit 15.3

PICNIC BASKET DESCRIPTION

Baskets are made of Hong Kong rattancore and peel. They are fully lined with quilted, reinforced weaver's cloth (50 percent cotton, 50 percent polyester). The lining can be easily removed for washing. Napkins and tablecloth are made of cotton and are also machine washable. Plates, mugs, and storage containers are made of durable plastic and are dishwasher safe on the top rack. Also included is a waiter's corkscrew, cheese knife/spreader, and chopsticks. Matching flatware and handmade cutting board are available at additional cost.

Prices	Options

Picnic basket for four, $150 each
    Basket size: 20″ × 14″ × 8½″
Picnic basket for two, $120 each
    Basket size: 18″ × 12½″ × 7″
	Cutting board, $10
	Flatware, $6 per place setting

PROMOTION

The next pressing issue was promotion. Because of limited funding, promotion was restricted to personal calling and mailing. (The purse is a small purchase, relative to other wardrobe expenses, and advertising seemed an unaffordable luxury.) As I told Ann, "This market segment is relatively homogeneous in terms of needs and demography. The only purpose for advertising, therefore, would be to differentiate this purse among other handbags or to cultivate a 'fad' of some sort. Since the achievement of either of these objectives might push demand beyond what we can supply, I'd suggest that we test the market first to see if there is a need for advertising and what type would be the most effective."

Our promotion strategy, then, relied heavily on direct mail to generate demand from store owners. Direct mail was chosen based upon some secondary research by my students. Their research uncovered some interesting facts concerning direct mail:

1. Seventy-five percent of the people who receive direct mail feel favorable about it.
2. Eighty times more leads result from direct mail than from ads placed in newspapers or magazines.
3. Mail's total share of all advertising budgets has increased 46 percent in the past five years.
4. The cost of direct-mail advertising is .0073 times the total cost of a personal call, on the average.
5. The Direct Mail Marketing Association (DMMA) ran ads for nine years to offer a mailing list Name Removal Service. Some 163,000 people accepted the offer to have their names removed from mailing lists for a $5 fee. Yet 200,000 people responded by asking to be put on **more** lists.

It appeared that mail marketing promised great growth in the future both as a channel of advertising for A. Poe Designs and as a sales medium to potential ultimate purchasers. We considered also exploring this avenue to determine if mail-order houses such as Lands' End or L. L. Bean might be interested in distributing the A. Poe Design Line.

CONCLUSION

My job was done—providing focus and direction to help Ann make a go of her idea. We had tested the market, adjusted costs and prices, developed the product fact sheets and order forms, and created direct-mail selling packets. My final recommendation was that she lower her prices even further to ensure greater success. Basically, I wanted to see the wholesale prices come down about 30 percent, but Ann was reluctant. So the prices remained as shown in Exhibits 15.2 and 15.3.

Ann's final comment: "I never knew there was so much to do to begin a simple, small business. It's amazing how much preparation time you spend before you even begin to make a sale. If most people knew how much time and money it takes, I doubt they would begin their own businesses. But at least the hard part is over; now all I have to do is sell."

16

DELOREAN MOTOR COMPANY: TEN YEARS LATER

"The reasonable man adapts himself to the world; the unreasonable one persists in trying to adapt the world to himself. Therefore all progress depends upon the unreasonable man." Thus wrote eccentric British playwright George Bernard Shaw in *Man and Superman*. John Zachary DeLorean (JZD) was called by detractors unreasonable, visionary, rebellious, and even eccentric. Some thought him outrageous, starting an automobile manufacturing company from scratch after leaving one of the highest-paying and most prestigious jobs in the auto industry only two years previously, concluding a phase in his career during which he had often tried to recast the world of giant business to his own specifications, determining eventually that the system was intractable. Many likened him to a Horatio Alger zealot, possessed of an indomitable pioneering spirit and supreme self-confidence.

ENGINEER, MANAGER, MAVERICK, ENTREPRENEUR

John Z. DeLorean (Exhibit 16.1) was widely lionized, in industry and in society as well. Some of this deference extended into such realms as liquor advertisements, one of which, for a well-known brand of Scotch, began with the headline: "One Out of Every 100 New Businesses Succeeds. Here's to Those Who Take the Odds."

DeLorean startled the business world in 1973 when, at age 48, he resigned his position as group vice president of North American Car and Truck Operations at General Motors. At the time of leaving the auto giant, he was considered, both within and outside corporate walls, to be a leading candidate for the presidency of General Motors, understandable speculation, for his rise in the automotive industry had been meteoric. After receiving a bachelor's degree from Lawrence Institute of Technology and a master's degree from the Chrysler Institute, he joined Packard in 1952 as a member of that company's engineering team, and in 1956, at age 31, he was named head of research and development. Later that year he left the ailing automaker to take a position as director of advanced engineering with GM's Pontiac Division, subsequently contributing the wide track concept and the Grand Prix, a new "personal luxury car" based on GM's intermediate chassis. The Grand Prix spawned other GM derivatives, the Chevrolet Monte Carlo and Oldsmobile Cutlass. These "A Specials," so-termed because they shared the same special version of GM's "A" body, were the company's largest selling body style until redesigned for the 1978 model year. During his tenure at GM, DeLorean was awarded some 44 patents for technological innovations such as the recessed windshield wiper and the hidden radio antenna.

Exhibit 16.1

PHOTOGRAPH OF JOHN Z. DELOREAN 1982

Source: DMC corporate public relations photograph.

In 1965 JZD was named general manager of Pontiac and a vice president of General Motors, the youngest man ever to head a GM Division. By the time he was tapped for larger responsibilities as head of Chevrolet in 1969, Pontiac's U.S. market share had climbed from its 1958 level of almost 5 percent to more than 9 percent.

DeLorean was given the helm of Chevrolet—at age 44, the youngest man to hold that position—with the mission to reverse a seven-year trend of declining profits. He reorganized the division's unwieldy management structure, increased manufacturing efficiency, improved car quality, and revitalized advertising. By 1971 dealer profits had increased over 400 percent, the corporation's earnings were up even more, and Chevrolet became the first nameplate in the world to sell more than 3 million cars and trucks in a single year. The outstanding sales records set at both Pontiac and Chevrolet are still standing.

In 1972 DeLorean was appointed group vice president in charge of GM's American car and truck operations. With the presidency in sight, just six months later he left the auto colossus. Always the "unreasonable man," an individualist in both his private and professional life, DeLorean had become progressively disenchanted with the way America's automotive industry functioned and, most significantly, with the kind of product the industry was offering the public. "Simply put," DeLorean said, "I wanted to build cars the way I wanted to build them, and the system at General Motors just didn't allow for that. I was primarily concerned with two problems endemic in the auto industry in this country: the annual model change that made a purchaser's car obsolete long before it was worn out and the fact that cars wore out too soon." DeLorean's solution was what he called the "ethical" car, a vehicle that would spit in the eye of traditional annual model restyling and that would not rust, corrode, and collapse around its owner in two or three years.

With the concept of such a car in mind, DeLorean took his leave from the General Motors hierarchy in April 1973, allowing his auto idea to gestate for a year while serving as president of the National Alliance of Businessmen, an organization devoted to finding jobs for disadvantaged Americans, a cause JZD had championed during his GM days.

BIRTH OF DELOREAN MOTOR COMPANY

The first steps toward bringing his dream to fruition were taken when he formed the John Z. DeLorean Company in 1974, certainly not the most propitious time to bring a new car to market. The first OPEC oil embargo created an upheaval in Detroit as the major makers scrambled to bring their products into line with the demands of a radically changing world. Moreover, there had not been a successful car company start-up in the United States since Walter P. Chrysler formed the Chrysler Car Co. in 1926.

DeLorean's strategy, however, was not to confront established producers head on. GM, Ford, Chrysler, American Motors, and imports had the products, production capability, organization, and money to adapt to the market's demands. DeLorean chose to aim his car at a segment of the automotive market that has historically been relatively immune to both economic cycles and petroleum supply and cost— the higher-priced specialty market. Specifically, he intended to produce a limited-production sports car that, although expensive, would adhere to his definition of the ethical car.

To obtain funds for the early development, DeLorean formed the DeLorean Sports Car Partnership; additional capital was obtained through forming the De-Lorean Research Limited Partnership. Finally, the DeLorean Motor Company was established as the basic operational entity in the enterprise. As his automobile took shape on the drawing board, he began canvassing the United States for well-established auto dealers interested in becoming part of the organization. Each joining dealer bought a minimum of $25,000 of DeLorean stock and agreed to purchase be-tween 50 and 150 cars in the first two years of production, to stock $6,000 worth of spare parts, to erect a $3,000 sign, and to invest $1,000 in special tools. Over 340 deal-ers were sufficiently impressed with JZD's concept and track record to ante up the necessary capital outlays.

Initially, DeLorean approached various states as well as the federal government to secure the additional financial backing needed to get the program off the ground. When these attempts proved unsuccessful, he turned his attention to opportunities offered overseas, finally settling on Northern Ireland as a site for the manufacturing subsidiary.

The British government proved to be an agreeable partner, advancing nearly $200 million to the project.

THE DELOREAN MOTOR CAR

In January 1981, the Dunmurry plant came onstream, its first output destined to re-ceive favorable attention from auto experts and enthusiasts. Some called it an honest-to-goodness sports/GT car; others predicted that the DeLorean would become a cult car, a status symbol of individualists; most agreed it was handsomely styled and fun to drive.

With a body styled by Giorgio Giugiaro and an overhead-cam V-6 sourced from the manufacturing consortium of Peugeot-Renault-Volvo, the DeLorean did have a strong GT pedigree. But it was said by corporate marketing to be "a car that offers more than exotic styling and sports car performance." It also offered outstanding economy for a car in its class. The stainless steel exterior was immune to corrosion, and, echoing DeLorean's concern when he left GM, styling changes would not be an annual event. The introductory announcement was made by DeLorean: "The De-Lorean offers a long list of standard features typically extra cost on other cars: air con-ditioning, leather seats, tilt and telescoping steering wheel, stereo sound system, complete instrumentation, electric windows, power brakes, etc. And something not available anywhere else: gullwing doors. When it comes to exterior color, however, the DeLorean is like a precious metal version of Henry Ford's black Model T: "any color you like, as long as it's the silvery hue of stainless steel."

Some thought DeLorean fastidious and a perfectionist, citing his dissatisfaction with the problem of smudgy fingerprints lingering grubbily on the stainless steel skin. A polymer chemical treatment was devised to solve that imperfection. Another anecdote: in late 1981 JZD sent 30 of his Irish workers from Belfast to the company's

California quality-assurance center for indoctrination in the kind of precision body fitting the boss expected to see.

PRODUCT DESCRIPTION

The DMC is pictured in Exhibit 16.2. Exhibit 16.3 outlines the vehicle's product characteristics for the 1981–1982 production runs.

GOVERNMENT REGULATIONS

Government standards for safety, fuel economy, emissions, and product warranty are applicable to all autos sold in the United States and additional, more stringent standards for emissions prevail in California. The DeLorean met all currently applicable standards into mid-1982. Regulations specified that passenger automobiles must boost average fuel economy from 22.0 miles per gallon in the 1981 model year to 27.5 miles per gallon for 1985 and thereafter. Both Congress and the Department of Trans-

---

Exhibit 16.2

THE DELOREAN MOTOR CAR

Source: DMC corporate public relations photograph.

---

portation had considered standards after 1985, but none had been established by mid-1982. Failure to meet the standard for a given year results in imposition of a fine for each vehicle of $5 for each tenth of a mile per gallon by which the fleet falls short of the standard.

MARKET REACTIONS AND BUYER PROFILES

Car and Driver comparison tested the DeLorean against higher-priced Porsche 911SC and Ferrari 308 GTSi and lower-priced Datsun 280-ZX Turbo and Chevrolet Corvette.[1] The newcomer received good marks. Also, DeLorean's car was being compared by some auto buffs with the Mercedes-Benz 300SL gullwing coupe produced in 1955, selling at $6,800 new, which in 1982 was cited as worth over $100,000. Clearly, some early buyers of the DMC reportedly were thinking not just about the thrills of being the first in their communities to drive it, but also were contemplating its value as a longer-term investment that would appreciate in value.

A DeLorean marketing official expressed a desire for better understanding of purchasers with a statement and a question, followed by a tentative answer: "The car

---

Exhibit 16.3

THE DELOREAN SPORTS CAR NEWS RELEASE—1981

BELFAST—From the moment of its first public appearance the De-Lorean has been a design success. Its carefully crafted lines, from the pen of Ital Design's Giugiaro, broke new styling ground in the world of high-performance automobiles. But there's more to the DeLorean than sleek Italian styling, sweeping expanses of glass, and lustrous stainless steel.

The heart of the DeLorean is the 2.85 liter (174 cid) overhead-cam V-6 engine that nestles within the rear wishbone of the chassis. The engine faces the rear with the five-speed manual or three-speed automatic transaxle extending toward the front of the car. The engine's heads and block are cast in aluminum alloy.

The engine is fed by a Bosch K Jetronic mechanical fuel injection system that produces 130 SAE net horsepower at 5,500 rpm and 162 foot pounds of torque at 2,750 rpm. That's good enough for 0–60 clockings in the 9–10 second range and a top speed of approximately 125 mph.

But straight-line performance isn't the total DeLorean story. The Renault five-speed manual has a top gear ratio of 0.821:1, which at cruise has the V-6 loafing along well down in the rpm range, and that in turn means some very impressive fuel economy figures: 19 mpg, city; 29.4 mpg, highway.

Handling, of course, is a vital part of any high-performance sports

[1]*Car and Driver*, December 1981, pp. 39–47.

Exhibit 16.3 (Cont.)

car, and DeLorean's engineers, in concert with Lotus, have developed a suspension system that has given the DeLorean excellent handling characteristics. The independent front suspension has parallel unequal-length upper and lower control arms, coil springs, shock absorbers, and an anti-roll bar. The independent rear suspension has trailing arms with uppper and lower unequal-length parallel, transverse control arms; coil springs; and shock absorbers. All this is connected to the driver by a sensitive and quick-responding rack-and-pinion steering system.

The best suspension bits and pieces in the world, however, are just so much metal until they're hooked to the wheels and tires that make it all work. At the front, the DeLorean has 6″ × 14″ alloy wheels wearing 195/60HR-14 Goodyear NCT steel radial tires. The rear wheels are larger, 8″ × 15″ and carry 235/60/HR-15 rubber. The Goodyear NCTs (neutral contour tires) represent the latest high-performance tire technology from Goodyear and have been specially designed for the DeLorean. The distinctive tread pattern was derived directly from Goodyear Formula 1 racing tires.

Four-wheel disc brakes, manufactured by Lucas-Girling, provide the stopping power. They're located outboard with 10″ front and 10.5″ rear discs. The braking force has been carefully biased front-to-rear to ensure maximum control in emergency situations.

The work force at DeLorean Motor Cars Limited, the manufacturing arm of the DeLorean Motor Company, now numbers almost 3,000. In October 1978 the plant site in the small town of Dunmurry, just outside of Belfast in Northern Ireland, was nothing more than an undeveloped green field. In less than two-and-a-half years that green field was turned into the most modern car manufacturing facility in the world with nearly 700,000 square feet under roof. The plant can produce 30,000 cars a year without expansion. In 1982, based on planned production of 25,000 cars, DeLorean will export some $500,000,000 worth of products, making it the largest exporter in Northern Ireland.

The first shipment of DeLoreans landed at the port of Long Beach in California in mid-May, and distribution to dealerships began shortly thereafter. The new DeLorean is also arriving through a port of entry in Wilmington, Delaware.

The company has established quality-assurance centers at three locations: Bridgewater, New Jersey; Troy, Michigan; and Santa Ana, California. At the QACs each car undergoes a thorough inspection to ensure it meets the company's high standards before it is shipped on to a dealership.

Although U.S. sales have always been the top priority, the company is thinking of establishing distributorships in other countries.

Source: DMC corporate public relations.

is designed to appeal to a multitude of buyers, from owners of Cadillac Sevilles to Porsche 924 turbos. The question still remains—what kind of person would spend $26,000 and up for this car? We have partially answered that question by examining profiles of early customers. Specifically, DeLorean buyers are well-educated males, have incomes in the range of $50,000 and up, are successful in business—typically company presidents or owners of their own firms—and are risk-takers."

Earlier in the process of product design, while serious structural changes could still be made, the prototype DeLorean was shown to selected samples of shopping center customers. Mostly, reactions were favorable, and a majority thought the car would be more expensive than the company's targeted price of $20,000 to $25,000. A mail survey also revealed a great deal about the potential DeLorean customer who had already made a deposit on the promise of near-term delivery. These, and matched samples of respondents with comparable demographic characteristics, reacted favorably to the prospect of owning a DeLorean automobile. Most who were favorably disposed wanted (1) value for the money, (2) a car useful for daily driving, not just weekend jaunts, and (3) a car that was unique and attention getting.

EXPANDING DISTRIBUTION

Management considered expanding sales efforts to Canada, Europe (Austria, Belgium, France, Germany, Italy, Luxembourg, the Netherlands, Switzerland, and the United Kingdom), and the Middle East (Bahrain, Kuwait, Lebanon, Qatar, Saudi Arabia, and the United Arab Emirates) in 1982. The distribution structure would be a single distributor in each country, with a dealer network strategically located throughout each country selected. DeLorean Limited planned to provide related services, such as processing vehicles through customs, providing technical training, and maintaining parts inventories. It was anticipated that the distributors appointed by DeLorean Limited would also be handling a complementary line of automobiles, with dealerships and support facilities in place.

PRODUCT LINE EXPANSION PLANS AND THE U.S. MARKET

The two-seat DeLorean was to be only the beginning. DeLorean's dream—and the future of his company—depended on further incursions into the upper-priced automotive market. That future included the planned introduction of a twin-turbo, twin-intercooler version of the car. DeLorean also planned to introduce a sedan to compete in the Mercedes and BMW market. Some features would be derived from the sedan's sports car progenitor—stainless steel skin, rear engine, gullwing doors, and perhaps the lowest coefficient of drag of any car ever manufactured in volume.

The most important concentration for U.S. automakers had traditionally been the standard sedan, the family automobile, although it was rapidly becoming less standard, giving way to downsizing and other styling and technical changes. Still, sheer market volume placed it at the top of the heap of Detroit's revenue producers. The 1960s and 1970s brought sweeping changes in American consumers' purchasing behavior. A car with its chief claim that of occupying the "ugly" position came into being, along with an array of other economy cars and an assortment of high-priced upscale vehicles from Europe. Market segmentation became an auto industry watchword in the mid-1970s, and thinking smaller in the United States was dictated by fuel crises and destructive competition of foreign imports, notably those from Japan. U.S. Goliaths were succumbing to the foreign Davids' attacks.

Downsizing and weight-shaving technology, sleeker aerodynamics in body contours, and engineering innovations in suspension systems, engines, and other underneath parts of the vehicle became part of U.S. automakers' efforts to recapture a position as Americans' preferred modes of transportation. Such was the competitive direction to serve the majority of car buyers who were looking for four- to five-passenger cars. Customers for the most part were turning to some combination of price, comfort, safety, and economy. The penchant for economy, however, began to diminish as gasoline prices held steady in late 1981 and 1982, supplies appearing to be plentiful. And fuel efficiency in many big cars was steadily improving.

ADVERTISING AND PUBLICITY—1981

Publicity for JZD's newcomer was provided quickly and plentifully by America's media, particularly in newspapers and periodicals; television news programs highlighted the first boatload of DMCs arriving at Long Beach and the arrival of the first cars at various dealerships. For its advertising agency, DeLorean selected Avrett, Free and Fischer, the agency that created campaigns for, among others, Contac's "tiny time pills" and Meow Mix cat food commercials with the fleet-footed "dancing" feline. Agreement was reached to launch paid mass media promotion for the new car using "The DeLorean. Live the Dream" as headline. One of the print ads is shown in Exhibit 16.4. The first television campaign was launched during the U.S. Open Tennis Championship in the fall of 1981, 30-second spots in a seashore setting, gulls flying overhead, DMC doors swinging up by themselves and a driverless car racing along the wet sand.

PRODUCTION NOTES—1981

Some of the money advanced to the company as loans would become outright grants— not required to be paid back—if certain numbers of employees were hired within a specified period of time. The total of 2,000 employees, scheduled to be met after five years of production, was realized in the fall of 1981. Although it was not mandated by the British government, the DeLorean facility at Dunmurry maintained a policy of 50:50 hiring ratio between Protestants and Catholics.

Some Ulster businesses were willing to join forces with the new auto venture; some were not.

"Those who did take a chance on DeLorean are on the pig's back now." That's the verdict of one Ulster businessman who is enjoying the snowball effect of supplying the controversial car plant which is now getting into top gear. . . . How have Ulster manufac-

Exhibit 16.4

"LIVE THE DREAM" ADVERTISEMENT

Your eyes skim the sleek, sensuous stainless steel body, and all your senses tell you, "I've got to have it!"

The counterbalanced gull-wing doors rise effortlessly, beckoning you inside.

The soft leather seat in the cockpit fits you like it was made for your body.

You turn the key. The light alloy V-6 comes to life instantly.

The De Lorean. Surely one of the most awaited automobiles in automotive history.

It all began with one man's vision of the perfect personal luxury car. Built for long life, it employs the latest space-age materials.

Of course, everyone stares as you drive by. Sure, they're a little envious. That's expected. After all, you're the one Living The Dream.

Start living it today at a dealer near you.

<u>A dealer commitment as unique as the car itself</u>. There are 345 De Lorean dealers located throughout the United States. Each one is a stockholder in the De Lorean Motor Company. This commitment results in a unique relationship which will provide De Lorean owners with a superb standard of service.

For the dealer nearest you, call toll free 800-447-4700, in Ill., 800-322-4400. **⊐MC** DE LOREAN MOTOR COMPANY

THE DE LOREAN. LIVE THE DREAM.

turers responded to this challenge on their own doorstep? Their reaction has been mixed apparently, perhaps reflecting the divided opinions on the project's long-term prospects of success. And the fainthearted do not have the makings of true entrepreneurs. . . . The challenge to local industry is still open to takers. For those prepared to work at them, there are still some opportunities at the end of the DeLorean rainbow.[2]

MARKETING AND FINANCIAL SITUATION IN 1982

In the last half of 1981, some 4,600 DMC cars were sold, with net profit of $3.7 million reported for the quarter ending August 31. "And we expect a lot of black ink in 1982," said DeLorean. By the end of 1981, the firm had spent $217 million, including $137 million in loans and investments provided by government agencies of Northern Ireland, $52 million borrowed from banks, and approximately $8 million from dealers and others, and it was seeking further funding.

Break-even for the Belfast facility was estimated to be 10,000 cars annually, and Northern Ireland officials were working to reduce the break-even point to 7,000 vehicles by introducing efficiencies in manufacturing costs and creating overhead savings. At the start of 1982, the company was producing 80 cars a day—a yearly rate of 20,000—with plans to increase production up to 120 units daily.

Quests for additional funding were unsuccessful in early 1982, following postponement of plans to offer the public 2,250,000 shares of a new company, DeLorean Motors Holding Company, at $12.50 a share, to raise equity capital. This offering was scheduled for late summer 1981, when total new car sales in the United States had declined from the previous dismal levels of sales in 1979 and 1980. The four major U.S. automakers reported 1980 aggregate losses totaling over $4 billion, with the slide continuing albeit at a decreased rate in 1981. Aggressiveness of the multinationals—for example, BMW, Fuji Heavy Industries (Subaru), Honda, Datsun, Toyota, and Volkswagen—added to the fiercely competitive environment.

Britain's Conservative government refused to add to the grants, loans, and guarantees advanced to the Belfast company over the period 1977 to 1981 and, along with the U.S. staff, was looking for investors willing to put up some $75 million. DeLorean, who remained in control of the New York companies, which continued buying and distributing cars made in Belfast, reportedly intended to invest $5 million of personal assets as a supplement to other sources.

One economy measure was in progress when the casewriter revisited DeLorean's New York headquarters in May 1982—employees were completing the move from DMC's 43rd floor, 280 Park Avenue offices, to the less expensive 35th floor, accompanied by a staff reduction from 30 to 15 people in the executive offices. Such cost controls at corporate level were seen by the staff as evidence of intent to cut back on some of the frills, although there was no indication that John DeLorean had changed his view that to sell a quality product one should be in classy surroundings.

Appendix 16A provides a summary of selected passages from management's discussion and analysis of financial conditions and operating results.

[2]*Belfast Telegraph*, November 26, 1981, np.

Appendix 16A

MANAGEMENT'S DISCUSSION AND ANALYSIS OF FINANCIAL CONDITION AND RESULTS OF OPERATIONS

From commencement of the DeLorean enterprise through the end of fiscal 1980, the Company obtained approximately $178.6 million of financing. These funds were used for research and development for the DeLorean, the construction of Limited's manufacturing facility in Northern Ireland, the establishment of a distribution network, and working capital. Approximately $150 million was supplied by agencies of the Government of Northern Ireland in the form of grants, long-term loans, and equity investments. Of this amount, approximately $15.5 million was expended by DRLP, and approximately $3.4 million was expended by a research and development limited partnership (DeLorean Sports Car Partnership), which interests therein were exchanged for the Company's preferred stock, and approximately $8.2 million and $1.3 million was realized from the proceeds of the sale of the Company's common stock to DeLorean automobile dealers and other investors, respectively.

Due primarily to delays in production experienced in May 1981 as a result of political unrest in Northern Ireland, Limited required additional working capital loans, and in May requested, and in June and July received, from DOC an additional guaranty facility for up to 7 million pounds ($13.02 million) in additional working capital loans.

In May 1981, the Company completed a financing agreement with the Bank of America, whereby the Bank is providing transit financing covering shipment of automobiles and parts from Northern Ireland to the United States. The agreement provided for up to $33 million of credit facilities payable at various dates not later than October 31, 1981 for vehicles and December 31, 1981 for parts. While Motor hopes to extend the Agreement, it has no commitments for an extension, and if the Agreement is not extended or replaced and the Bank of America elects to discontinue financing on a shipment by shipment basis, Motor would not have sufficient funds to finance its inventory.

In addition, Limited's agreement with a major supplier of components permits Limited to purchase components on extended payment terms, subject to the continuing availability of export financing and approval from French Government export authorities, thereby providing Limited with significant amounts of working capital. There can be no assurance that such French export financing will continue, and if it does not continue, the Company would have need for significant working capital.

Based on present production and shipping schedules and existing dealer purchase commitments, the Company does not anticipate that it will require additional working capital financing arrangements in the short term, assuming that the DOC guaranteed working capital loans (referred to above) which are due December 31, 1981 and transit financing (re-

Appendix 16A (Cont.)

ferred to above) are extended or replaced. There can be no assurance that present production and shipping schedules will be met or that the working loans and transit financing will be extended or replaced.

During the quarter ended August 31, 1981, the Company determined that additional grants for capital expenditures were available from the Government of Northern Ireland in excess of those already received. Such grants are at a rate of 30 percent of qualified expenditures and relate to capital expenditures which are in excess of those covered by 50 percent grants.

The Company estimates that its capital expenditures through the end of fiscal 1982 for the Sedan and homologation programs plus the cost of an engine development program will be approximately $41 million.

The development of the Sedan, from design through initial commercial production, is at present estimated to cost approximately $80 million in 1981 dollars, of which the Company plans to expend approximately $19 million by the end of fiscal 1982. As of the date hereof, the Company has no funds available, or commitments therefore from outside sources, for the Sedan program, although the Company intends to negotiate for financing of the Sedan project with NIDA and DOC. There can be no assurance that the Company will be able to obtain the required funds.

The total cost of the homologation program is currently projected to be approximately $4 million, of which approximately $2 million is estimated to be expended by the end of fiscal 1982. The Company expects to expend on engine development for fuel economy, emissions, and performance improvements approximately $20 million through the end of fiscal year 1982. As of the date hereof, the Company has no funds available or commitments therefore from outside sources for the homologation and engine development programs. The costs of the engine development program after fiscal 1982 cannot now be predicted with accuracy because they will depend on the future regulatory and competitive environments for the DeLorean, as well as on whether any product changes are made by the manufacturer in the engines supplied for the DeLorean. The Company believes, however, that such future costs are likely to continue to be substantial.

RESULTS OF OPERATIONS—1980 AND 1981

In June the Company began to sell vehicles to dealers and accordingly is no longer considered a development stage enterprise. Since June the Company has recorded revenues from the sale of vehicles and parts of $25,656,612 and gross profit of $5,228,172. Sales to dealers totalled 1,084 vehicles as follows: June, 320; July, 256; and August, 508.

The Company has established three Quality Assurance Centers in the United States which perform vehicle inspection and preparation prior

Appendix 16A (Cont.)

to delivery to dealers. The cost of these centers is part of cost of sales and totalled $2,442,965 for the three months ended August 31, 1981 and was comprised of $696,945 in June, $745,865 in July, and $1,000,155 in August, with costs per vehicle sold $2,178 in June, $2,914 in July, and $1,969 in August. The Company believes the cost per vehicle will decline from the levels experienced during the start-up of distribution operations.

The increase in research and development expense of $4,065,227 for the nine-month period ended August 31, 1981 compared to August 31, 1980 is a result of higher preproduction costs, final staging, and testing of facilities and equipment during the phase immediately preceding commercial production. The decrease of $5,389,995 for the quarter ended August 31, 1981 compared to August 31, 1980 reflects a reduction in the need for research and development activities during commercial production.

Selling, general, and administrative expenses increased for both the three months and the nine months ended August 31, 1981 compared to the same periods in 1980 due to the finalization of the parts and automobile distribution networks and dealer training together with the marketing of the car.

During February and August of 1981, Limited reached the 1,000 and 1,500 employee levels, respectively, which resulted in the conversion for financial statement purposes of long-term loans of £6,500,000 ($14,332,500) and £3,250,000 ($6,045,000) to deferred grants. These grants are being amortized as related employment costs are expensed.

Capital grants for the construction of the manufacturing facility and production equipment also are amortized into income in 1981 as related capital assets are depreciated. The amortization of all grants for the three months and nine months of fiscal 1981 was $3,061,250 and $6,138,650, respectively.

Source: Company Form 10-K, 1982.

17

ECLIPSE FILMS

Eclipse Films was an independent film production company long on talent, but short on funds. The principals in Eclipse all had significant experience in making motion pictures from *E.T.* to *Where the River Runs Black*. However, they had always worked for others, usually the major companies such as 20th Century Fox and Paramount. Now they were attempting to fund and produce their own feature films. With the help of a consultant, they developed and began to circulate a prospectus to potential investors.

Twenty of the prospectuses were given to an agent who felt he had good access to foreign investors in Korea and Taiwan and was about to leave on a trip to Asia. The prospectuses were accompanied by a cover letter which read as follows:

Dear (Agent's Name):

Attached are prospectuses for the feature film projects that we have been developing. Both stories have appeal across the board and should do well domestically and in foreign markets. They are small films that fill a definite market niche and provide what we feel is a very appealing entry point for investors looking to come into the entertainment industry for the first time.

We have tried to keep this prospectus as simple and understandable as possible; however, should you have any questions, or need any more information, please call.

We wish you a safe and successful journey.

Best regards,

John Doe and
Sue Smith

ECLIPSE FILMS

PROSPECTUS INTRODUCTION

The worldwide marketplace for commercial feature films has grown significantly over the past 10 years and shows every sign of continuing strength. There are currently about 4,000 feature-length films produced in the world each year. Many of these are for local consumption only, particularly in countries like India and China. About 1,500 titles per year have potential for commercial exploitation in the international marketplace. A little less than one-third of these by volume, though almost 60 percent by value, are produced in the United States or are financed, distributed, and controlled by American owners. Due to major changes that have recently shifted ownerships in the American film industry, things are rapidly changing in the world market.

In *The Wall Street Journal* (May 1990), an article written by staff reporter Kathleen Hughes on the movie industry made the following observation: "Right now, there is a very receptive market for films. Last year was a record one at the domestic box office, with revenues topping $5 billion. Seven movies brought in more than $100 million each in theaters, meeting Hollywood's definition of blockbuster." The growth of other revenue outlets has made producing movies more lucrative and less risky. Money from foreign distribution, videocassettes and network and cable television sales can help make even a box-office flop profitable a few years down the road.

For example, MGM/UA Communications Co.'s 1988 film *Willow* appeared early on to be a flop. It cost about $55.5 million to make and took in only $27.8 million in the studio's share of box office revenues. But Paul Kagan Associates estimates that foreign theatrical rentals added another $41.8 million, domestic video another $18.2 million, domestic television $15.3 million, and foreign video and television $21.7 million, bringing total revenues to $124.7 million, making the film ultimately profitable.

Such growing markets helped total feature film revenue hit the $10 billion mark for last year, four times the level of a decade ago, says Art Murphy an analyst for the daily *Variety*.

The article goes on to attack the giant waste of box office revenues in a game of "can-you-top-this" spending that has driven the major studios into a bidding war for top movie scripts and blockbuster hits. However, Ms. Hughes's statement is valid; movies are less risky than they used to be. Which is not to say that they aren't a gamble, because they are. But, like all gambles the risks must be weighed against the potential gains. Eclipse Films has two relatively low-budget film projects ready to be made. (See Exhibits 17.1 and 17.2.) Scripts have been finalized, shooting budgets completed, directors tentatively set, and commitments offered for foreign distribution rights. What remains is the primary financing to underwrite the cost of production.

Exhibit 17.1

SCRIPT 1 SYNOPSIS

PRESS ENTER

We are immersed within a computer microchip; energy particles fly in all directions as strange, digitized sounds reverberate within a sea of silicon. Suddenly the clacking of computer keys begins, and the title "PRESS EN-TER" appears, letter by letter. The darkened background is energized with light pulses, there is more clacking of keys, and we pull back slowly from the chip's interior to reveal the internal circuit boards of the computer, surging with colors and patterns of energy. As we pull back through the computer screen, we see the digitized image of a man's bearded face, his eyes fixed and glowing with an unnatural intensity. The face grows larger, and we enter one of the man's eyes, revealing a digitized BRAIN. We whirl along the brain's outer surface, past glowing brain cells and complex networks of dendrite tentacles glistening with colors. We hear a man's VOICE whispering hoarsely, as sparks flare up in widening patterns, creating a hypnotizing effect. Suddenly a GUNSHOT rings out, and a man's head falls onto the keyboard, the same man seen before. There is silence, darkness—and then a ringing telephone: it is the dead man's computer, calling Victor Apfel.

Victor is a recluse, a Vietnam vet who has decided that he prefers the 1950s to the 1990s, and he receives a telephone call from a dead man that will change his life forever. Victor finds his neighbor, Charles Kluge, is dead, a suicide surrounded by a houseful of sophisticated computers. As Lieutenant Osborne investigates, it becomes evident that Kluge was collecting information on everyone in his neighborhood, information about falsified tax returns, illicit affairs, and other juicy items, apparently as a prelude to blackmail.

The mystery deepens as the police call in Lisa Foo, a sexy Asian computer expert from Cal Tech, to unravel the tangled web of computer files and databases that Kluge left behind. It appears that, for some reason, Kluge has left all his worldly possessions to Victor, and the Lieutenant finds it remarkable that Victor says he hardly knew the man. Lisa continues to explore and probe the computer network, hoping to unlock its

Exhibit 17.1 (Cont.)

secrets, while Victor tries to fill her in on what little he knows about Kluge. Later, Lisa is still at the keyboard when she discovers a file headed "NATIONAL SECURITY AGENCY—TOP SECRET RAMPART." Kluge was into more than just neighborhood gossip.

Back at home, Victor tries to forget this intrusion from the outside world, but he is dragged back into it, literally, when he is kidnapped by two henchmen who rough him up and demand answers about Kluge and the computers. Victor resists, is beaten, and is left unconscious in a field.

Meanwhile, Lisa continues exploring Kluge's computer programs when she is visited by her boss, Bert Stryker, who works not for Cal Tech but in fact for the National Security Agency (NSA), a supersecret communications agency of the federal government. Stryker threatens to expose Lisa's shady past in North Vietnam if she doesn't crack the secrets of Kluge's computer, and as he leaves with his two henchmen, Victor spots them. Victor argues with Lisa and demands to know who Stryker is, and what is her real involvement with him. Lisa finally admits her NSA status and reveals that Kluge had access to all the most important government computer systems in existence, and apparently was collecting intelligence in a number of highly sensitive areas, all for his own purposes.

Later, Lisa invites herself to Victor's for dinner, and Victor begins to find himself coming out of his shell as they talk. The next day Lisa does more work with Kluge's computer and advises her boss Stryker and another NSA computer type, Peter, about her progress: she seems to be close to entering the heart of the system. Victor starts to pick up on the fact that Kluge's computer, somehow, is activating programs that are harassing and wreaking revenge on people in the neighborhood. When he tells Lisa, at his place, they speculate on Kluge's motives and eventually start to make love, for the first time. After the lovemaking, Victor has another flashback to Vietnam and a seizure, and Lisa helps him get through it.

When Victor goes to the VA hospital for his seizures, he and the doctor discuss a theory that sound and light waves can activate certain brain states in human beings. Later Victor and Lisa talk about a computer activating certain states in the human brain. Lisa then visits Stryker in his office and confronts him with her suspicion that he and Kluge were in fact working together. Stryker threatens her with exposure or worse if she doesn't keep her mouth shut. Lisa and Victor meet again at Kluge's house the next day, and they find out that Stryker is dead, possibly killed by a computer program that activates certain destructive brain states.

It is then that Lisa and Victor begin to realize the enormity of Kluge's plan: to design a computer brain to plunder all of the nation's top secret computer systems, sell the data to the highest bidder, and kill all those who stand in the computer's way. More major military computer systems fail, and Victor and Lisa race to track down the computer links and stop Kluge, who they have discovered is still alive and controlling his machines.

Exhibit 17.1 (Cont.)

Lisa faces death at the hands of Kluge, and Victor is forced to choose between Lisa's certain destruction or his own death at the hands of Kluge's most diabolical creation: his own brain imprinted on an invincible machine. In the end, the tension builds to an incredible climax as Victor and Lisa fight for their survival against almost insurmountable odds.

PRESS ENTER Production Budget Summary

Description	Total
Story and script	$ 352,000
Producer and staff	383,220
Director and staff	411,240
Cast	3,010,800
Fringes	88,432
Total above the line	$4,245,692
Production staff	522,040
Extra talent	83,600
Art design/set construction	463,880
Grip and set operation	215,480
Special effects	326,000
Property	137,160
Wardrobe	75,000
Makeup and hair	56,960
Lighting/electrical	222,240
Camera	229,800
Production sound	95,600
Locations	393,418
Transportation	236,260
Film and lab	153,600
Fringes	217,004
Total production period	$3,427,882
Editing and projection	229,668
Post production	256,000
Delivery items	86,000
Music	120,000
Total Postproduction	$ 691,668
General expenses	141,000
Total below the line	$4,260,550
Total above and below the line	$8,506,242
Insurance (3%)	255,186
Contingency (10%)	850,624
Completion bond (4.5%)	382,780
Grand Total	$9,993,848

Eclipse Films is seeking financing of one or two motion pictures for worldwide distribution. This package includes synopses of both scripts and production budgets (Exhibits 17.1 and 17.2), the investment offering and brief biographies of the producers (Exhibit 17.3). We have already started securing written offers for the foreign distribution on both features and the budgets presented.

The following is one possible financing structure for your review. This structure follows the general pattern that Morgan Creek Productions has used with such films as *Young Guns, Dead Ringers, Major League, Skin Deep,* and *Enemies, A Love Story.*

1. Eclipse would initially look to contract with an organization such as Sovereign Pictures, or J&M Film Sales, or August Entertainment (from whom we already have an offer) to handle all theatrical (cinema) and home video distribution of the film outside the United States and Canada. (For our own purposes, here we may wish to withhold the rights to whichever country financing is obtained from.) Normally we could expect to receive, in return, a commitment equal to 30 to 35 percent of the budget of the film. This percentage seems to stay relatively consistent regardless of director and cast. In other words, if we sign a bigger-name director or a more important (and expensive) cast, these companies are generally still willing to put up as much as 50 percent of what would be a larger budget.

2. We would then seek to make a deal for domestic U.S. home video rights to this/these film(s). Depending on budget and cast, we could strike a deal where someone like Media Home Entertainment or HBO Home Video would offer an amount equal to between 30 and 40 percent of the budget in return for these rights. When we get an offer equal to 30 percent of the budget together with "foreign rights" from (1) above, we have now covered 70 percent of the cost of the film.

3. At this point, we have the following rights to the film which are still free to be dealt with:

- all rights within the investor's country
- U.S. theatrical and pay-TV rights
- worldwide free-TV rights

4. It is at this point that we need a major investor who would be prepared to cover the remaining 40 percent of the budget *plus* the releasing costs (primarily prints and advertising) of opening the film in the U.S. markets. These costs will generally run, for a *major studio* film, about 25 to 40 percent of the film's production budget (over and above the budget).

5. If such an investor were available to us, we would be able to begin active production on this film and at the same time make a "gross releasing" deal with one of the mini-major film studios, for example, New Line Cinema, Miramax, or Hemdale Releasing Corporation. This kind of a deal would involve having one of these minimajors distribute the film in the U.S. theatrical market using our investors' funds (up to an agreed amount) to pay the print and advertising (P&A) costs. The studio would collect the "gross rentals" from the theaters, subtract a 20 to 25 percent "distribution fee," and remit the balance to us.

There is very little risk in this type of deal of losing anything on U.S. theatrical rights. After the first weekend the film will establish its marketplace and will adjust the P&A spending accordingly. The *worst* that could be expected is to recover the releasing costs of the film.

6. Given the mini-major release, the pay-TV rights in the United States can be sold for an amount equal to between 15 and 30 percent of the film's original budget, depending upon cast and how well the film does in theatrical release.

7. The remaining rights—primarily free-TV rights around the world—can be licensed out to a syndicator such as Viacom or ITC, and it would be fair to expect that a minimum guarantee of a sum equal to 10 percent of the original budget would be available.

These rights, however, are where the recurring sales lie and can go on producing a stream of income for many, many years.

According to the foregoing formula, with a total film budget of $5 million, we would seek to cover the cost of production as follows:

Non-U.S. theatrical and home video (excluding investor's country)	$2,000,000	(40%)
U.S. home video	$1,500,000	(30%)
Investment funds	$1,500,000	(30%)
	$5,000,000	(100%)
Prints and advertising	$2,500,000	
Investment contribution	$4,000,000	
U.S. theatrical gross rentals (if the film is a relative failure)	$1,500,000	
Less: 25% distribution fee	(375,000)	
Net proceeds	$1,125,000	
U.S. pay-TV sale (15% of budget)	$ 750,000	
Worldwide free-TV	500,000	
Total net proceeds	$2,375,000	

Remember, however, that the investor also holds all rights to the film in his or her own country.

Exhibit 17.2

SCRIPT 2 SYNOPSIS

FACE

Helio is a pretty boy who lives in the barrio in Rio de Janeiro but has expensive tastes, and he knows for a fact that his fortune is in his face, at least as far as rich women are concerned. His pal Zico, a petty gangster and confirmed family man, laughs at Helio's dependence on women while Helio defends himself by saying that he has a gift from God: to make women smile, in pleasure and in pain. Helio glides among the back alleys

Exhibit 17.2 (Cont.)

of his Third World metropolis, servicing his women clients and trying to keep peace with his jealous girlfriend Lula, until that one moment when—in a nightmarish accident—both his face and his future are ruined in one horrific split second. After the accident, Helio recovers in the hospital and slowly discovers that his face is now a papier-mâché caricature, a pulpy and scabrous mass, requiring him to wear a mask in public in order not to offend. Lula, his girlfriend, tries to be kind, but she now sees Helio only as a freak, not as her lover. Since no other woman will look at him either, Helio's expensive life-style collapses, and with no money, he forces himself to apply for government aid, encountering a long and frustrating tangle of forms and bureaucratic rebuffs. One night, after more rejection, Helio returns to his apartment, hungry for Lula. She resists him, and in a rage, he slaps and rapes her.

The next day, still hurting with anger and shame, Helio hears of a clinic that may do the facial surgery that he so desperately wants. There he meets Dr. Godoy, a surgeon who is intrigued with Helio's descent from grace and says there may be a chance for him. The doctor also describes in detail the proposed surgical reconstruction of Helio's face, phase by phase, and loans him a surgical textbook to study.

Helio returns to Lula, buoyed by the good news, only to discover that she has taken her clothes and left. Helio is thrown into despair, and now with no money at all, he scavenges for food and is finally forced to go to Zico for help. There he learns the trade of the lowly pickpocket and begins to discover the depths of his resentment and anger.

At his next medical appointment, Dr. Godoy sadly tells Helio that there are no government funds available for his operation. Helio now has no hope, and decides to leave for his mother's old hometown, a place where he can be alone. There, he stays in a cottage belonging to a family friend and begins to devise a bizarre plan to save himself: self-surgery on his own face. He buys scissors, medication, and razorblades and, over a period of months, undertakes the painstaking realignment of skin and muscle tissue necessary to restore humanity to his shattered face. It is a gruesome process, clumps of flesh being razored back, layered, and reshaped. Time passes, Helio's face improves, and he at last resolves to return to Rio. On the return trip, no longer wearing a mask, Helio is amazed to find that no one looks twice at his surgical handiwork. In a final sequence, Helio meets with Dr. Godoy again, who is impressed with Helio's skill as an amateur, and says that he will break all the rules to see that Helio gets a final operation that will improve his face even more, and finally offers Helio a job in the hospital as a surgical orderly. As they go to lunch, Helio and the Doctor pass right by Lula, Helio's old girlfriend. She looks at Helio but does not recognize him, as he bumps into her and murmurs "Forgive me" on the crowded street. As he walks away we know that, at last, he has found his new life.

Exhibit 17.2 (Cont.)

FACE Production Budget Summary

Description	Total
Story and script	$ 163,000
Producer and staff	188,347
Director and staff	195,030
Cast	1,326,000
Fringes	38,934
Total above-the-line	$1,911,311
Production staff	161,810
Extra talent	21,608
Art design/set construction	174,600
Grip and set operation	77,370
Special effects	109,800
Property	27,850
Wardrobe	32,000
Makeup and hair	64,700
Lighting/electrical	153,200
Camera	137,406
Production sound	42,000
Locations	173,900
Transportation	188,000
Film and lab	68,500
Fringes	102,612
Total production period	$1,535,356
Editing and projection	98,000
Postproduction	118,500
Delivery items	26,000
Music	45,000
Total postproduction	$ 288,500
General expenses	60,000
Total below the line	$1,883,856
Total above and below the line	$3,795,167
Insurance (4%)	151,806
Contingency (10%)	379,517
Completion bond (5.5%)	208,734
Grand total	$4,535,217

Exhibit 17.3

THE INVESTMENT OFFERING

The business of Eclipse Films is to produce, finance, and exploit one or more quality theatrical motion pictures (the "Pictures").

A financial agreement is to be arranged between the Investors and Eclipse Films with Eclipse Films as Manager.

The investor will fund 100 percent of the production cost(s) of the picture(s).

Eclipse Films will arrange for distribution for the Pictures in all media worldwide.

FUNDING OF FINANCING PARTNERSHIP BETWEEN INVESTORS AND ECLIPSE FILMS

The financing Partnership will be funded with a minimum of $5 million from the proceeds of a private offering of limited partnership ("the Offering"). Eclipse Films may obtain additional funds from borrowing secured by guarantees in foreign distribution contracts, provided that (1) the amount of borrowing secured by any single Picture does not exceed 70 percent of such Picture's Negative Cost and (2) the amount of borrowing in aggregate does not exceed 50 percent of the proceeds of the Offering.

USE OF INVESTORS' FUNDS

Negative Cost

The Investor is obligated to fund all costs incurred in connection with the development, preparation, production, completion, and delivery of the Pictures ("Negative Cost"), provided that (1) the budgeted Negative Cost, as approved by the completion guarantor, does not exceed $10 million and (2) the average Negative Cost of all Pictures funded does not at any time exceed $7.5 million. However, the Investor will have the option to commit funds in excess of these limits either in the full amount of the budgeted Negative Cost or any lesser amount agreed to by the parties. If the Investor elects to limit its investment, the Producers or the Distributor may fund the balance of the Negative Cost.

Any balance so funded shall be recouped only after the Investor has fully recovered its investment in such Picture.

Theatrical Distribution Costs

Eclipse Films will arrange to fund all costs and expenses incurred by the Distributor in connection with the theatrical release of the Picture in the

Exhibit 17.3 (Cont.)

United States and Canada ("Prints and Advertising"), up to a maximum of 50 percent of the amount of the Negative Cost. Eclipse Films will have the option to fund Prints and Advertising in excess of this maximum, if additional funds are required for any Picture. If Eclipse Films elects to limit its investment, the Distributor may fund the additional Prints and Advertising required.

"Investment" by the Investor, Producers, or Distributors shall mean the sum of any investment by each in Negative Cost and Prints and Advertising.

DISTRIBUTION OF ECLIPSE FILMS

Domestic Theatrical   Companies such as New Line Cinema, Mira-Max, and Hemdale Releasing Corporation will be approached to provide theatrical distribution for the Picture(s) in the United States and Canada.

Domestic Home Video   It is expected that Home Box Office ("HBO"), a subsidiary of Time Warner, Inc., will distribute the Picture(s) to the videocassette and videodisk markets in the United States and Canada. It is expected that an agreement between HBO and Eclipse Films would provide that HBO advance all costs of advertising and cassette manufacturing.

From the home video revenues, HBO deducts a distribution fee and, after recouping advertising and manufacturing costs, remits the balance to Eclipse Films.

Domestic Pay TV   In addition to home video, HBO's agreement with Eclipse Films would provide for distribution by HBO to the pay television markets.

Domestic Free TV   At the present time, Eclipse Films would approach Viacom International and/or Media Home Entertainment to distribute the Picture(s) to the free television markets, which include the major commercial networks, ad hoc barter networks, basic cable, and syndicated sales to independent broadcast stations.

Foreign   Eclipse Films has received an offer from Gregory Casante, president of August Entertainment, to handle foreign distribution of the Picture(s), based on the budgets and proposed directors. Distribution contracts will be assigned to Eclipse Films, to be used as collateral for loans to augment funds.

Other   Other markets, including merchandising, music and book publishing, soundtracks, and nontheatrical sales, will be sublicensed to companies which specialize in these markets.

Exhibit 17.3 (Cont.)

Distribution Fees

Eclipse Films, negotiating with a U.S. distributor, under current market conditions, can expect to have distribution fee deductions calculated as a percentage of gross receipts, as follows:

Domestic Theatrical	Theatrical Gross Receipts
5 percent	$0– 2 million
10 percent	$2– 5 million
15 percent	$5–10 million

Domestic Home Video	Home Video Gross Receipts
5 percent	$0– 5 million
10 percent	$5–10 million
15 percent	In excess of $10 million

Domestic Pay TV	Pay TV Gross Receipts
0 percent	$0–.5 million
10 percent	$.5–1 million
15 percent	In excess of $1 million

Domestic Free TV	Direct Distribution	Subdistribution
Network	30 percent	+5 percent
Basic cable	30 percent	+5 percent
Syndication	30 percent	+5 percent

DIVISION OF REVENUES

All Gross Receipts shall be paid to Eclipse Films. After deduction of distribution fees paid and residuals paid to guilds and unions, the balance will be distributed as follows.

1. One hundred percent to the Investor until such time as it has received an amount equal to its Investment.
2. Thereafter, 100 percent to Eclipse Films and/or Distributor(s) if either has an Investment in the Picture, until such time as each has received any amount equal to its Investment in the Picture.

In the event that both Eclipse Films and the Distributor(s) have an Investment in any Picture, then proceeds shall be shared pro rata, pari passu, between Eclipse Films and Distributor.

3. Thereafter, 90 percent to Investors and 10 percent to Eclipse Films until such time as Investor shall have received an amount equal to 125 percent of its Investment in the Picture.
4. Thereafter, 80 percent to Investors and 20 percent to Eclipse Films until

Exhibit 17.3 (Cont.)

such time as Investor shall have received an amount equal to *150* percent of its Investment in the Pictures.

5. Thereafter, 70 percent to Investors and 30 to Eclipse Films until such time as Investor shall have received an amount equal to *200* percent of its Investment in the Picture.

6. Thereafter, 20 percent to Investors and 80 to Eclipse Films.

RISK FACTORS

The risk factors should be carefully examined by potential investors, since, like any other business, an investor could lose all or some of his money. Through no fault of Eclipse Films, a poor distribution decision could affect the marketability of a film. Public tastes are changeable, and a negative critical review could impact the film's success. Unforeseen circumstances could cause delays in income revenues. Eclipse Films cannot guarantee full recovery of investment funds.

PROFIT POTENTIAL

Below is profit information on a few of the films in which Eclipse Films' principal partners have been involved. These figures do not include revenues generated from cable TV, network TV, foreign TV, merchandising, foreign theatrical, or U.S. home video and foreign video, which guarantee an even *higher* gross sale and profit margin.

Figures below indicate approximate box office draw only:

Title	Budget (millions)	Box Office (millions)
E.T., the Extraterrestrial	$35	$700
Close Encounters	24	153
War Games	14	73
Cocoon	21	85
Ghostbusters	33	230
Splash	7	71

THE PRODUCERS[1]

JOHN DOE. Mr. Doe's working history in motion pictures and special effects traces a megahit path to *The Abyss, E.T., Cocoon, Splash, Close Encounters of the Third Kind, The Right Stuff, Ghostbusters, Star Trek, 2010,*

[1]The experience of each of the producers is real; however, their names have been disguised to provide them the privacy normally extended to celebrities of the motion picture industry.

Exhibit 17.3 (Cont.)

War Games, European Vacation, Dune, Harry and the Hendersons, and this summer's release, *Flight of the Intruder.* Mr. Doe's expertise is multi-faceted. He contributes technical inside knowledge of film making, from conceptualization to final realization. His supervisory skills and managerial abilities add to his solid reputation in the business.

SUE SMITH. Ms. Smith has a 10-year background in the entertainment industry. She has served as programming manager for cable and pay-TV and has produced for TV as well as motion pictures. In addition, she promoted and produced live pay-per-view concerts and championship fights. Rounding out her accomplishments, she also handled TV advertising and public relations and has been involved in all phases of TV and film production, most recently serving as production coordinator on *Flight of the Intruder* for Paramount.

TOM BROWN. Mr. Brown's extensive production and finance experience in the motion picture industry began at the London branch of First Chicago Bank, where he was responsible for the Film & Entertainment Finance Unit. After receiving an MBA from the London School of Economics, Mr. Brown supervised the financial packaging of such films as *The Mountain Men, Final Countdown,* and *A Change of Seasons.* Moving into production, he was associate producer on *The Stone Boy,* starring Robert Duvall and Glenn Close for 20th Century Fox, and produced *Where the River Runs Black* for MGM.

GEORGE WHITE. Mr. White, a Canadian citizen who presently resides in Los Angeles while he completes *Bright Angel* for an August opening through Hemdale Releasing Corporation, produced *Criminal Law* with Gary Oldman and Kevin Bacon last year. He begins production on *Troubled Waters* with Max Von Sydow and Isabel Rosselini this summer.

18

OMNI AUTOMATED SYSTEMS

Bob Waters, a field sales engineer for the Custom Systems Division of Omni Automated Systems, had just learned from his friend Steve Anderson, the purchasing agent for Gentech Office Equipment Company, that Gentech had decided to purchase a robotic test cell from one of Omni's competitors. (See Appendix 18A.) The test cell was for Gentech's new printed circuit board (PCB) soldering line. The Gentech account was the third robotic work cell sale that Waters had lost over the past two months and the eighth overall. Waters had felt confident that Omni had the inside track on this bid due to Omni's past business relations with Gentech, Waters good personal relations with Gentech's personnel, and Omni's superior product offering. He had been working on this sale for over a year and knew that the loss of this sale would severely impact his chances of future robotic work cell sales to Gentech, as that firm continued to automate its PCB manufacturing operations.

Waters's boss, Doug Barnum (Omni regional sales manager), was concerned about Waters's lack of success at selling this new product line. Since its introduction, accounts that Waters worked on have yielded only two sales, a 20 percent success ratio. Other Omni salespeople, however were experiencing at least a 50 percent success ratio on their major accounts. During this period, Waters continued to have good success at selling Omni's other product lines. Because both Waters and his boss were certain that Gentech personnel were fair in their decision, they decided to conduct a review of his call reports to see if a flaw in his sales presentation may have led to the loss of the Gentech sale.

BACKGROUND INFORMATION

Omni has provided state of the art electronic assembly equipment to electronics manufacturers for more than 20 years. It maintained a competitive advantage over its competitors by continually bringing innovative products and technologies to the marketplace. It was one of the first firms to apply robotics to electronics assembly and was also one of the first firms to offer assembly machines for surface-mount device application. In addition to its acknowledged technological strengths, the firm was also well known for its product quality and reliability. It manufactured a broad line of assembly equipment, from simple component insertion machines to complex robotic work cells. Omni captured a 30 percent market share in 1984 on more than $500 million in sales. Its corporate headquarters were located in San Jose, California, and it had regional sales offices throughout the United States, Europe, and Japan.

The application of robotics to electronics assembly was first introduced in 1983. Prior to this time, robotics was primarily applied to heavy industrial and automobile assembly applications. Omni built upon the research and development of robotics like Adept and Unimation and system houses such as Chad Industries and Robotic Automation to introduce its first robotic work cells. Although Omni did not conduct research in the development of robots, it did devote considerable resources toward finding new applications for this emerging technology.

Bob Waters joined Omni in 1979, after an eight-year career at one of Omni's primary competitors, Universal Assembly (UA) Corporation. Waters normally achieved sales in the top 10 percent of Omni's sales force. He was personable, energetic, and well liked and respected by his colleagues and management. Upon arriving at Omni, he was assigned the highly competitive but very lucrative Silicon Valley sales territory and was quickly successful in landing several major contracts.

Gentech Office Equipment Company manufactured a variety of office equipment, from copier/duplicators and facsimile machines, to personal computers and word processors. Gentech was a recognized world leader in the office equipment industry, with sales in 1984 in excess of $2.8 billion. Gentech had manufacturing operations in several locations around the world, but its San Jose plant was its primary PCB assembly facility.

In recent years, Gentech had experienced significant market share and profit margin erosion due to intense foreign competition. Benchmarks revealed that Gentech had fallen behind the industry in utilizing advanced electronics design and manufacturing techniques. As a result, Gentech initiated a major program to modernize and automate its manufacturing facilities. This program would cost between $30 and $40 million and would be conducted over a five-year period.

The new soldering line recently ordered by Gentech from Ace Electronics would completely automate its soldering process and would cost approximately $2 million. Gentech's current soldering line requires the boards to go through four separate stages before the soldering is complete. At each of these stages the boards must be manually loaded and unloaded. This results in a high number of damaged boards due to improper handling and inconsistent solder joint quality due to variations in the solution temperature and chemical balances. The new soldering line would virtually eliminate material handling and would add a computerized process control system which would monitor each stage of the process. The robotic test cell would be placed at the end of the soldering line to move boards from the soldering line to the Bitmico PCB testers and to drive the test machines. This would be Gentech's first attempt at robot automation. Gentech had contracted with Moore & Associates, a consulting firm to help draw up plans on how the new soldering line and robotic test cell would be integrated into its existing assembly line. The robotic test cell would cost approximately $500,000.

Bob Waters and Steve Anderson had become fairly close friends over the past several years. Their children went to the same school, and they lived only a few blocks apart. Their families occasionally got together for social outings, and once or twice a month they would play a round of golf together. Although they were personal friends, Anderson made it a rule to keep business and pleasure strictly separate. Rarely did they talk about business except when Waters made calls on Gentech.

Waters considered Gentech to be an extremely important account and attempted to contact the firm at least once a month. Gentech was one of Waters's first major sales when he joined Omni. Its annual purchases occasionally totaled as much as $80,000. Furthermore, due to the size of its manufacturing operations, it was a prime candidate for future major purchases from Omni.

WATERS'S CALL REPORTS

Waters reconstructed his activities for the period he had been working on the Gentech sale by reviewing his call reports.

February 4, 1991

Received a call from Anderson. He said that Gentech was about to initiate a bidding process to procure a robot system that was to be a part of Gentech's new soldering line. Anderson asked if Omni had a product that would satisfy Gentech's needs. Told Anderson that Omni could custom build any robotic work cell that he might need. Arranged to visit him the following day.

February 5, 1991

Called on Anderson. Discussed with him the overall requirements of the work cell and the bidding process to be used. The robotic test cell was to be part of Gentech's new soldering line that was purchased from Ace Electronics. The line was to be installed in February of 1985. The test cell had to be delivered and operational within one week of the installation of the soldering line. An operational mockup of the test cell had to be demonstrable at the vendor site 30 days before delivery for initial acceptance testing.

Anderson said that a new bidding process was being instituted this year. Unlike previous capital acquisitions, where vendors were heavily involved in negotiating equipment specifications and cost, product requirements would be drawn up by Gentech personnel, and the supplier would provide a sealed bid at a final presentation. Preliminary bids and product proposals would be used to narrow the number of vendors submitting final bids down to four or five. The final selection would be made jointly by the Purchasing, Manufacturing, and Test Engineering organizations. Anderson would represent Purchasing; Jim Thompson, manager of manufacturing operations would represent Manufacturing; and Carl Jefferson, a senior engineer, would represent Test Engineering. Kevin Reilly, vice president of northern California operations, would also participate in the decision.

Anderson furthermore said that detailed specification for the test cell would not be made available for the preliminary bid phase; these specs would be given only to those vendors selected to submit final bids. Proposals and preliminary bids were to be generated based on preliminary specs available through the Moore consultant. Anderson gave me the name of the Moore consultant and also gave me the name of an Ace engineer for details on the soldering line and a Bitmico engineer for details on the testers.

Returned to the office and reviewed the situation with the boss (Doug Barnum). Discussed the importance of getting this initial sale in order to have the best shot at Gentech's future robotic automation needs. Surmised that Gentech had instituted this new bidding process in an attempt to get more aggressive pricing from the vendors. Concluded that pricing would therefore be the primary factor in selecting a vendor. Discussed the pricing strategies that we might use and those that might be used by our competition. The boss told me to keep him apprised of the situation and let him know if there was any way he could help. Took home a competitive analysis of the robot industry that was prepared by our marketing group.

February 6, 1991

Called Kevin Reilly at Gentech to try to set up an appointment to meet him. Was told by his secretary that "Mr. Reilly does not interact directly with salespeople" and that Anderson should be contacted for all sales-related issues. Tried to explain to her that I needed only a few minutes of his time, but she said that there were no exceptions to the rule.

Wrote the Moore consultant in Los Angeles for the test cell spec. Reviewed specification on the robots that we use in our work cells and specifications on work cells that we had done in the past. Forwarded a recommendation letter from Albany Computers for the robotic insertion cell I sold the company last year for its assembly line.

March 4, 1991

Received specs from Moore (see Appendix 18A). Looked them over with Paul Johnson (Omni's systems design engineer) and discussed possible hardware configurations that could be used in the test cell. Asked him to put together a tentative system for Gentech. Gave him the names of the Ace and Bitmico contacts in case he needed additional information on the soldering line of the testers. Called Thompson at Gentech and made an appointment to meet him for lunch next week.

March 8, 1991

Visited Anderson before meeting with Thompson. Found out that eight other firms would be making proposals along with Omni. Asked him how Omni's chances looked for getting invited for the final bidding stage. He said that as long as our bid wasn't way out of line we should have no problem getting past the preliminary bid stage. Showed him Johnson's preliminary proposal for test cell. He was impressed by the technology and sophistication of the system. Went over the features of the robots that we use in our work cells, stressing the accuracy and speed of the robot and the direct-drive technology used which allows high torque to be generated at relatively low motor speeds. Left him a stack of literature, a copy of Johnson's proposal, and the Albany Computer's testimonial letter.

Met with Thompson and his assistant, Roberts, for lunch. Discussed their situation in the factory and the acquisition of the soldering line and test sell. Thompson and Roberts seemed to be somewhat skeptical about the robotic test cell and the technology upon which it was based. They said that they had read about robots in various trade journals and seen some of them on television, but had never had a chance to see one in person. Told them about all the robotic work cells that Omni had built and offered to show them one of the robots at our facility. Tentatively scheduled their visit for next week.

After lunch I reviewed Johnson's proposal with Thompson and Roberts. They both seemed concerned about reliability and system downtime. I pointed out some of the backups and redundancies built into the system which increase system reliability, and our past track record for high reliability. I also pointed out that due to the proximity of Omni relative to our competitors, Omni was clearly in the best position to provide prompt emergency service in the unlikely event that they had a system failure. They agreed. Left them with copies of the same literature I had left with Anderson.

March 19, 1991

Picked up Thompson and Roberts for our plant visit. Dropped by Anderson's office to see if he wanted to come along. He said he had a meeting later on that day and couldn't. On the way over to the plant we talked about a variety of things, including how well the Warriors basketball team was doing this year. Thompson seemed to have a real interest in basketball so I invited him out to tomorrow night's game. Asked Roberts if he wanted to come along but he said he had plans for tomorrow night. Made arrangements to pick up Thompson at his house.

Once we got to the plant, I showed Thompson and Roberts a robot that was similar to the one that Johnson had proposed for their test cell. Ran a demonstration program which made the robot insert various sized components into a PCB and transfer it to different workstations. Thompson and Roberts were very impressed. Showed them how to use the teach pendant and how easy it was to program the robot. Ended our visit by showing them around the facility.

March 20, 1991

Picked up Thompson at his place. Took him out to a nice restaurant on the wharf before the game. During dinner, I reemphasized the servicing advantages of going with Omni. Asked him what he thought Omni's chances were in landing the deal. He said that he really didn't know yet and that choosing a vendor was the least of his worries. He was taking a lot of heat from the union because the new soldering line and the robotic test cell was going to displace 12 employees. I told him how other companies were dealing with the problem and assured him that things would work out. The Warriors won the game 110 to 109.

March 27, 1991

Visited Anderson. Found out that there were problems with the specs. He wasn't sure what the nature of the problems were but he knew that completion of the spec was behind schedule. Arranged a meeting with him, Thompson, Jefferson, and my boss, Doug Barnum, for early next month. Suggested that Reilly be invited also, but Anderson thought he wouldn't attend.

Went to see Thompson. Asked him about the problem with the specs. He said that there was some controversy over who should be responsible for generating the specs, Manufacturing or Test Engineering. He said that no matter which way it went, "Manufacturing would get its needs addressed." Suggested to him that clearly Manufacturing should control the specs since it will be responsible for operating the equipment. He smiled and left to attend to other business.

Ran into the foreman on the assembly floor. He seemed to be pretty unhappy about all the changes that were being made to the assembly line. He complained about the fact that he "had just spent six months getting things running smoothly and now they were going to change things all over again." I sympathized with his position but reminded him how much more efficiently his operations were going to run after the new soldering line and test cell were installed. He agreed that in the long run his operations would probably be better off.

Asked him how the Omni component insertion machines were performing. He told me that one of the machines was down and had been waiting for parts for two days now. Called the people at the service center to find out what was taking so long to service his machine. Was told that the parts were on back order and that they wouldn't be available for at least another day. Apprised them of the situation and suggested that they borrow the parts from another machine that was down in the field. Was assured by them that his machine would be repaired before the end of the day. Relayed the information to the foreman who was grateful for the favor.

April 3, 1991

Barnum made an excellent presentation to Jefferson, Thompson, Roberts, and Anderson on the company and the product line. He reviewed the company's financial status, its position in the market place, our major account customers, and our reputation for quality and service. He also went into quite a bit of detail on the product line, and in particular the robotic work cells. Few questions were asked during the presentation, although Roberts did raise a concern about spares availability for the robot system. Assured him that Gentech's problem with the insertion machine was an isolated case and that spares were always readily available for the robot systems. Distributed to everyone a leather folder with the Omni logo on it and an Omni pen and pencil set. Introduced myself to Jefferson, who, according to Anderson, was probably still upset about having to share responsibility for generating the specs with Thompson. Thompson was supposed to develop Manufacturing's requirements while Jefferson was supposed to define the detailed technical requirements for the system.

April 22, 1991

Checked in with Anderson to see how things were going. He said that both Engineering and Manufacturing had stopped working on the specs until after the preliminary bids were in. This would give them time to understand what their real requirements were and give them an opportunity to look over the preliminary bids.

Spent the afternoon with Thompson discussing the trade-offs between payload requirements and the impact that it has on cycle times and the maximum velocity that can be achieved by the robot arm. Carefully reviewed with him the impact this decision could have on the throughput of the assembly line and the types of boards that the line could handle. Left him with some additional literature describing the latest developments in robot controllers.

Visited the foreman on the assembly floor. Found him watching an operator load components in the insertion machine for another assembly pass on the boards. He complained that the machines should be more flexible and support any size component in each of the feeds instead of restricting each one to only certain sizes of components. I told him that upgrades to provide that capability were available for the newer machines but weren't available for that particular machine. Explained to him that upgrade kits were usually developed only for the more recent model year machines.

May 28, 1991

Worked with Johnson in developing our tentative bid. Suggested to him that price, reliability, and throughput, in that order, should be the key factors in developing this proposal. After several hours of discussions, we finally agreed on a system. I included variable-speed conveyors, 20-board capacity buffer/loader, 5-axis direct-drive Adept robot, and a 68020-based robot controller with teach pendant. The controller would include 80 MB of hard disk, 4 MB of memory, five external ports, and the standard software development environment. It would also include a one-year warranty and an optional service contract which would entitle Gentech to hardware maintenance and all software upgrades. I felt that based on the preliminary specs from Moore, the robot we selected gave Gentech a perfect compromise between payload capacity and minimum cycle time. Discussed pricing of the system with Barnum and decided to offer only a moderate discount for the preliminary bid state and then a much more aggressive discount for the final bid. The bid would go in at $479,000. The service contract would be offered at 10 percent of list price, or $50,000 per year.

June 25, 1991

Checked with Anderson to see how our bid looked. He smiled and told me that all the bids weren't in yet and that a decision would be made sometime in early August. Arranged to play a round of golf with him next weekend.

August 5, 1991

Received a letter from Gentech inviting Omni to bid on the final specifications. Visited Anderson later that day to see if I could gather more information on the bid. Found out that the other firms invited to bid were IAS, Robotic Automation, and UA Corporation. When questioned about our preliminary bid, Anderson suggested that our bid appeared high. Assured him that once we had the final specs we would give them the best price-performance combination available. Asked about the other aspects of our bid, and he told me that the best person to talk to would be Jefferson. Went to look for Jefferson, but he had already left for the day.

That evening I reviewed the specs and the price lists of our competitors. IAS is a small entrepreneurial company with approximately 15 installations nationwide. Felt that IAS probably could offer Gentech a better price but lacked the experience and stability that Gentech would want from a vendor. Robotic Automation has more experience in robotic applications but it has no other products in the electronic assembly market and its experience in these applications is limited. Although UA offers the same types of robots in its work cells, it doesn't manufacture its own conveyors and board loaders. It could therefore not offer the same level of customization in its work cells nor be as price competitive as Omni could. UA could offer more capabilities in its robot controller than any of the other companies, but these additional capabilities would come at a considerable additional cost to Gentech. Gentech would need these additional capabilities only if it found itself in the unlikely situation of needing to reprogram the robot to perform significantly more complex functions than are currently planned for the test cell.

August 6, 1991

Spent the afternoon with Jefferson. Noticed that copies of the literature that I had left with Anderson and Thompson were sitting on Jefferson's desk. Asked him how our proposal looked. He said the proposal looked fine at this point but reminded me that the final specs were still under development. Reviewed with him various features of the robot and robot controller that were proposed for the test cell. He didn't seem as concerned about the controller's capabilities as much as Omni's commitment toward continuing to upgrade and improve the product once it was purchased. He said that the Manufacturing people were concerned about the product becoming obsolete once new technologies were introduced. I assured him that Omni was committed toward continuing to improve and enhance its products and cited numerous examples of how the products in the field were continuing to be improved. Also reminded that software upgrades and enhancements for the controller would be "free" under the maintenance contract. Took note of some technical documentation that he wanted and told him I'd drop it off later than evening.

September 2, 1991

Met with Anderson. Found out that responsibility for developing the specifications had been given to Jefferson. Jefferson would now be responsible for incorporating both Manufacturing's requirements and Engineering's requirements into the final specs. He said the change was made in the hopes that giving responsibility for the specs to one organization would help resolve some of the problems they had in coordinating the task. Anderson also confessed that neither group had been able to make much progress on the specs due to a lack of criteria upon which the specs could be developed. This problem became apparent when they tried to merge Manufacturing's and Engineering's requirements and found that many of the requirements conflicted. Upon further investigation, it was discovered that the two organizations had developed their requirements based upon different criteria. Furthermore, after reviewing the preliminary bids, it became obvious that each vendor had also made different assumptions about the criteria in developing their specifications. Jefferson therefore had contacted the Moore consultant and requested assistance in developing appropriate criteria. Jefferson was due back at the end of the week.

I knew that this would give me an opportunity to influence the specs and ensure that they contained certain features standard in our robots and conveyors. Having these features in the specs would give Omni a clear advantage in the bidding. Made a note to see Jefferson early next week.

September 16, 1991

Spent the morning with Jefferson discussing the benefits of the Omni system. Made sure to place special emphasis on features standard in our robots and conveyors that increase the mean time between failure and reduce the likelihood of component failure. Felt confident that he recognized the Omni advantages. Left him with some highly technical literature which described these features.

Went to visit the foreman on the assembly floor and found him talking to one of the software engineers that Gentech had recently hired to work on its process control system. Asked him if he thought he might also be doing some work on robotic test cell and he said that that was a possibility. Told him about the extensive programming environment that came with our controllers and the fact that the system could be programmed off-line without disrupting production. He mentioned that he had heard from a friend last year about all of the bugs in the Omni programming environment and wondered if they had been fixed yet. I smiled and assured him that those problems were long since past and that we now had an extensive quality assurance program in place. Also told him about the many horror stories I had heard about the programming environments in the UA and IAS systems and that my understanding was that some of those problems were still not fixed.

September 30, 1991

Met with Jefferson at his request. He said he had been reading a trade journal about the state of the art in robot systems and had noticed that Omni was rarely mentioned in the article as a leader in the field. He said that he was concerned about selecting a vendor that would maintain a state-of-the-art product since future robotic installations would most likely involve the same vendor. I told him about some of our pending product announcements and the types of advanced research that we were involved in. I also reminded him that although we might not lead the robotics industry as a whole, we did lead the industry in the field of robotics applied to electronics assembly, the field that Gentech should be most concerned about. He agreed and seemed satisfied that Omni could meet all of its future requirements.

October 15, 1991

Had lunch with Anderson. Found out that Thompson had been transferred to another organization within Gentech and that Roberts had been promoted to plant superintendent. Anderson wouldn't discuss the circumstances surrounding Thompson's transfer and encouraged me not to bring it up with Jefferson or Roberts. Also discovered that Reilly had formed a new group called Computer Integrated Manufacturing to be responsible for the various computer systems that manufacturing had acquired. Asked Anderson if he thought this new group would have any say in the selection of the test cell. He said that Jefferson would be representing their interests and that no changes to the selection committee were anticipated. Invited Anderson, Roberts, and Jefferson to the Robots 8 conference that was to be held in Santa Clara at the end of the month. Left exhibit passes and the location of Omni's hospitality suite with Anderson.

October 29, 1991

Met Anderson, Roberts, and Jefferson at our hospitality suite. Introduced them to our vice president of marketing, Dan White, and several other Omni executives. Took them on a tour of our exhibit booth and showed them our work cell demonstrations. Gave them each a ticket to tonight's conference gala dinner and encouraged them to stay for the festivities. Learned from Anderson that the specs would be ready by November 15. Told him that I would come by to pick them up and then excused myself to meet another client.

November 15, 1991

Picked up the final specs from Anderson. He said that the bid presentation for all four suppliers would be held on January 20. We would be given two hours to make our presentation, at the end of which we were to hand in our final bid. Our assigned time slot was from 1 to 3 P.M.

Went back to the office to review the specs. The specs contained some unexpected requirements. Gentech had gone along with our robot and conveyor specifications but is also specifying additional board loading capacity and a significant number of additional capabilities in the robot controller. The board loader would be no problem, since we custom build our own; the robot controller however, could be a problem. Asked Johnson to start putting together our final proposal and arranged for him and Barnum to participate in the formal presentation. Called Jefferson and arranged to meet with him after the holidays.

November 29, 1991

Spent the afternoon going over the final specs with Jefferson. Found out that the additional capability in the robot controller was required for a bar coding system that Gentech planned on installing in the future. Discussed various alternatives for providing that capability and sold him on one that could be satisfied by our current controller. Reviewed all other aspects of the specs with him, pointing out Omni benefits and features along the way. He seemed satisfied that Omni could deliver as promised. Stopped by to see Roberts and Anderson, but both were tied up in a meeting for the rest of the day.

December 18, 1991

Sent Anderson, Roberts, and Jefferson each a bottle of Scotch for Christmas.

January 10, 1992

Reviewed our final proposal with Johnson and Barnum. The proposed system contained only minor modifications from the one submitted for the preliminary bid. Decided to include more memory and a larger disk in the controller and modify the board loader specs to conform to those called for in the final specifications. After several hours of discussion, we decided to go in with a bid of $458,000.

January 21, 1992

The presentation went extremely well. Barnum started with a brief corporate overview, stressing Omni's reputation for innovation, reliability, and service. Johnson followed with a discussion of the technical aspects of our proposed test cell, making sure to point out how each of the requirements in the Gentech specs was satisfied. I summed up the presentation and handed the bid to Reilly. Anderson thanked us for a "superb" presentation and said that we would hear from them by late February.

February 26, 1992

Received a call from Anderson notifying me that Omni had lost the bid. He said that the committee had narrowed the field down to Omni and UA and that UA had just edged us out. He couldn't pinpoint any one particular reason for the selection, but did say that cost did not play a large factor in the decision since both companies came in at about the same price. He added that each member of the committee had a different reason for preferring UA, but that all were unanimous in the feeling that UA would better satisfy the company's needs. When asked about the possibility of having a meeting to discuss the issue, he replied that his orders were to tell all vendors that the committee's decision was final and that the matter wasn't open for discussion. He congratulated me on the job I had done representing Omni and said that he hoped this decision wouldn't affect our friendship.

Appendix 18A

SPECIFICATIONS FOR ROBOTIC TEST CELL

GENERAL DESCRIPTION

Figure 1 shows the general layout of the robotic test cell. The test cell consists of one incoming conveyor and two outgoing conveyors, a robot, and three Bitmico 8000 testers. The input conveyor receives the board from the solder wash station of the solder line and regulates the throughput to the robot cell. The robot should be outfitted with a double-sided end effector so that board loading and unloading can be accomplished within a minimum cycle time. The robot moves the board from the board loading station to one of the available testers. The robot removes the tested board from the tester with the side of the end effector not holding the board to

Figure 1

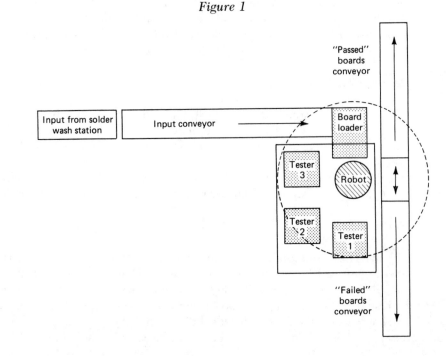

Appendix 18A (Cont.)

be tested. After placing the untested board onto the tester, testing of that board is initiated. The tested board is moved to a bidirectional belt for feeding onto one of the two outgoing conveyors. Based on the results of the board test, the board is placed on either the "passed" or "failed" conveyor.

BOARD SPECIFICATIONS

Boards will range in height from a minimum of 5 inches to a maximum of 24 inches and will range in width from a minimum of 7 inches to a maximum of 30 inches. Maximum warp and twist of the board will be 0.01 inches per inch of board. A fully assembled board will range between 0.5 and 5 pounds in weight. The maximum height of any component on the board will be 0.75 inches. Component bodies will not extend into an area 0.2 inches wide along each edge of the board. A tooling hole is located in the upper left, lower left, and lower right corners of the board. These holes will be 0.15 inches in from each of these corners and will be 0.09 inches in diameter. These holes are used to mount the board into the test fixture.

TESTER SPECIFICATIONS

The testers are Bitmico 8000 in-circuit testers. They are equipped with an RS-232C port which allows communication with the tester. Testing can be initiated and test status (e.g., test in progress, board failed, board passed, tester idle, test fault) can be polled through this interface. An interrupt signal is generated by the tester when testing is complete. The period of time required to test a board varies depending on board complexity, but typically takes 15 to 20 seconds. There is a 10-foot vertical clearance envelope around the test bed. Pins for the test fixture are 0.085 inches in diameter and 1 inch in height. For more details on the tester contact Bitmico customer support.

CONVEYOR REQUIREMENTS

The output conveyor from the solder wash station is 4 feet in height and 2 feet in width and moves at the rate of 15 feet per minute. Boards will be spaced a minimum of 5 feet apart on the conveyor and will be oriented such that the tooling holes are located in the upper left, lower left, and lower right corners of the board. The input conveyor for the test cell should be 30 feet in length and be capable of buffering a minimum of 15 boards.

The output conveyor for the failed boards should be 4 feet in height, 2 feet in width, and 50 feet in length. The conveyor should be capable of

Appendix 18A (Cont.)

speeds ranging from 10 to 30 feet per minute. The conveyor will feed a re-work area where failed board will be processed.

The output conveyor for the passed boards should be 4 feet in height, 2 feet in width, and 55 feet in length. The conveyor should be capable of speeds ranging from 10 to 35 feet per minute. The conveyor will feed a packaging area where boards will be packaged for shipment.

ROBOT CONTROLLER REQUIREMENT

The controller is required to coordinate the actions of the robot, the three testers, the input conveyor, the bidirectional belt, and the two output conveyors. In addition to the normal operation of the test cell, the conditions shown in Table 1 should be handled with the specified remedial actions.

Table 1

Condition	Action
One or more of the testers is inoperative.	Continue testing with the operating testers.
Input buffer is almost full.	Continue testing and issue a warning to the operator.
Input buffer is full.	Stop the robot and signal for the operator.
A tester is not responding.	Continue testing with the other testers and issue a warning to the operator.
N consecutive failed boards have been encountered.	Stop the robot and signal for the operator.
Either of the output conveyors have been shut down.	Stop the robot and wait for conveyor(s) to be restarted.

The robot should be programmable either through a teach pendant or off-line through the controller's software environment. Adequate flexibility and functionality should be provided in the system to allow modification or customization of the system in the future.

SYSTEM REQUIREMENTS

The overall test cell must have a minimum 2,000-hour mean time between failure and a 96 percent uptime. The work cell noise level should not exceed continuous 80 dB.

A safety shield should be included in the design of the test cell. The robot work envelope must not be accessible by the operator without emergency stopping the robot.

Note: This document provides a preliminary description of the robotic test cell for Gentech Office Equipment Company. These specifications are based upon information provided by Gentech, Ace Electronics, and Bitmico Tester Corporation. All specifications are subject to change.

19

THE CHINOOK BOOKSHOP

This is a happy tale about two young people who fell in love with each other and later with an idea, and a dream that came true.[1]

On Tejon Street in downtown Colorado Springs, across from Acacia Park, stands "one of America's finest bookstores," The Chinook. It is a friendly oasis for book lovers and browsers, but it never could be described as a "shoppe." Although its handsome carved wood doors afford two entries from the street side and it goes back hundreds of feet deep inside, in spirit it is far more than just a large bookstore.

Here, let's back up a bit—to 1958 when the bookstore was only in the springtime of its promise, coming to life as the spiritual brainchild of an ambitious young couple. From Dick Noyes, who was hearing a different beat from that marched to by his successful midwestern forefathers, came drive and creativity and experience with the technicalities of the book trade; from his wife Judy came a charm and different kind of creativity that earlier had expressed itself in journalism and broadcasting. The two shared equally a love for literature and books and the world of ideas.

Richard Hall Noyes, born in 1930, was the child of solid citizens of that solid satellite of Chicago—Evanston, Illinois. Dick had an older sister and was the middle of three brothers. As he competed within the family, he grew up aggressive, rebellious, and determined to be a free spirit. His family thought of him as impractical and

[1]Adapted from "CHINOOK: Promise of Spring—Twenty-nine Years of Bookselling on Tejon Street 1959–1979," a promotional booklet by Marshall Sprague.

artistic. At Wesleyan University, he was an average student until his senior year when courses in philosophy and religion motivated him to hard work and high marks. But his ideas for his own future were hazy; he thought of becoming a painter or writer or of pursuing his childhood fantasy and going West to be a cowboy or a forest ranger.

During his junior year at Wesleyan, Dick accepted a blind date, arranged by one of his fraternity brothers, with a sophomore from Vassar. Judy Mitchell was from a New Haven, Connecticut, family that had moved to Jacksonville Beach, Florida, where she went through school. She was a bookish child who learned to read before kindergarten and from then on read everything she could get her hands on—from *Honeybunch* to the Brontës. All during her high school years, Judy worked as a columnist and feature writer for the *Ocean Beach Reporter* and as writer and broadcaster for radio station WJVB. At graduation, her senior class voted her "most likely to succeed," and she entered Vassar, class of 1953. Then came the blind date: on a January morning she stepped bravely off the bus in her 1950s uniform of tweed skirt, white sweater with pearls, and Capezio flats. She was met by a blue-eyed fellow, slender and wiry in white bucks, button-down shirt, and pressed khakis.

Judy and Dick became engaged while she was a senior at Vassar. Dick was drafted soon after his graduation in 1952 and sent off for Army service in the Far East. After her own graduation, Judy became an Army civilian employee and, with the help of her roommate's father, a strategically placed colonel, had herself assigned to Tokyo, where Dick just happened to be teaching in the Army Intelligence School. They were married there in October 1953. They loved life in Japan, but when their tours and Army paychecks ended in the fall of 1954, they moved to the Noyes's family home in Evanston where Dick began job hunting. He had a clear idea only of what he did *not* want to do.

Then, by chance, Dick heard of a year-long, one-at-a-time training program at Rand McNally, the Chicago book publishers. The starting pay was a modest $250 a month. The training program was thorough—offset, letterpress, bindery, makeup, editing, promotion—and Dick went at it for all he was worth. After his training, Rand McNally offered him a textbook, maps, and globes sales territory out West. They chose headquarters in Denver, which Dick had known from his boyhood summers at Cheley Camp in Estes Park and the Ferrington Carpenter ranch at Hayden.

Dick was away sellng books most of the time, roaming by car over the mountain reaches of Idaho, Colorado, Wyoming, and Utah, and Judy played the patient mother of their two daughters, missing the stimulation of her academic and newspaper/radio years. But Dick was getting raises, offers of a prime sales territory in California, and hints of an executive future in Chicago. He was "top salesman of the year" in the Education Division.

Late one Friday afternoon in Dick's hotel room in Salt Lake City the phone rang. It was Judy. She was sick of being alone with the two babies—they'd gotten married to be together, not apart. Dick paused, thinking—for half a minute. Then he said, "There's a Denver plane leaving here in an hour. I'll fly home for the weekend. Get a sitter and we'll have dinner tonight at the Ship's Tavern." They reached a decision that left them elated. Dick had learned plenty about the book trade during his time with Rand McNally and proved he knew how to sell books. They would open their own bookstore. And he knew just the place—Colorado Springs.

SELECTING A LOCATION

They picked the name of the shop from the text of a book they'd just read, A. B. Guthrie's *Three Thousand Hills*, in which Guthrie described those warm winds that melt the snow in minutes and end the gray bleakness of winters in the western high country—"Chinook . . . Promise of Spring." (See Appendix 19A for the Chinook bookmark.)

With the advice of a lawyer, Morton McGinley, their first friend in Colorado Springs, and the help of a realtor, Roy Hackathorn, they got an FHA loan and bought a house on Arcturus Drive in Skyway Park. More help came from Harold Dillon, the Random House "rep" in Denver, although Dillon tended to regard all bookstores as dubious ventures and asked Dick why he didn't take up something sound like trash collecting.

Through that fall of 1958, Dick and Judy toiled among the packing crates, writing publishers, and pumping bookseller friends for guidance—friends Dick had met on his Rand McNally trips. Judy wrote to Bennett Cerf, the *Saturday Review* punster and columnist, who responded kindly with tips about joining the American Booksellers and how to apply for trade information.

Dick and Judy tramped the downtown for weeks to find a proper place for their bookstore. They decided finally on the soon-to-be-vacated Lee's Boys Store space at 208½ North Tejon Street. (Lee's was moving next door to the south.) Dillon was not sold on the location, particularly the fractional number, 208½, an address that he found demeaning. "Sounds like a popcorn stand," he said. But it fronted on Acacia Park with its elderly shuffleboard players and its benches where, Dick reasoned, people relaxing in the sun might wander over to the shop. There also was a lot of walk-by traffic, with downtown business-people, lawyers, and bankers walking from their offices for lunch at Ruth's Oven or the El Paso Club.

Dick was admiring and polite when he called on the city's two long-established bookstores—his main competition. Both of them impressed him in their way. Edith Farnsworth's on Kiowa Street and Their Book Shop on South Tejon had been around since 1924. Dick introduced himself to Edith Farnsworth, a stately lady born in Colorado Springs and held in high regard by the community. Marshall and Anne Cross had bought Their Book Shop in 1949 from Carol Truax, an exuberant personality who spent her time directing the city's cultural affairs. Dick found the Cross's shop attractive but judged it to be poorly placed, too far from the downtown area. Both bookstores, he was told, had a stranglehold on what was called "the carriage trade." In addition, Bob's Books on Pikes Peak Avenue and the old Levine's, downstairs in Wilbur's (where Bryan and Scott Jewelers is now), claimed the rest of the new book market, with the knowledgeable veteran rare books dealer, Henry Clausen, then as now taking care of the demand for used and out-of-print books.

At the same time, Dick was studying the biggest problem—where to find the $25,000 that he felt he needed to get the store started. He was reluctant to ask his family for money, but there seemed no alternative since bookstores historically were the worst of risks. Dick's mistaken notion that the family might have reservations about his future was useful. When he finally approached them for the loan, he had spent most of his free time preparing an elaborate 32-page prospectus designed to overcome any hesitations. It covered the plans in detail, and it turned the trick.

"This prospectus," Dick had written, "is the outcome of almost a year's serious thought, a careful study of material recommended by many hours with booksellers, the American Booksellers Association, and the U.S. Department of Commerce. . . . I believe that several of our ideas are new and noteworthy and that in time the shop will be unique among bookstores in the west."

He went on to explain their choice of Colorado Springs for its prosperity and rapid growth brought on by its military installations and the resplendent and just-opened Air Force Academy (September 1958), its high education level, its existing bookstores, its cultural and transportation facilities, the cost of a three-bedroom house, and its many other demographics in detail.

Dick discussed what he deemed to be the proper size of their store, 2,000 square feet. He stressed plans for "an extensive collection of *good* children's books" with Judy setting it up (eventually becoming nationally known in this subject area). They would begin by stocking all the ABA's "basic book list," Western Americana, in particular, and maps, globes, and greeting cards. Sidelines would include ceramics, jewelry, art objects, egg cups, "and a few imported toys in excellent taste." Most of these sidelines—especially the egg cups—were dropped without regret later on.

Dick estimated first-year sales of $40,000, based on the study. The first-year opening inventory of books would cost $15,000 with other expenses of $13,000. For his salary, Dick would draw $300 a month. Judy, working four hours a day, would receive $80 a month. His Rand McNally–earned bonus would cover the secondhand car and other initial expenses.

Plans for setting up the store moved along through the late winter months of 1959. The February 9 issue of *Publisher's Weekly*, the "Bible of the booksellers," carried the first announcement that the Chinook Bookshop was a-borning, bringing a flock of publishers' reps to the Noyes home. Walt Wilson, teacher of art at the Fountain Valley School, and by now a friend, took on the job of designing the interior. When the old Skyway Cut-a-Corner market closed, Dick picked up discarded counters and cases and adapted them for use at 208½ North Tejon.

As Judy remembered later, "Ours was pretty much a do-it-yourself operation. Dick was good at carpentry and enjoyed it. I did a bit of everything, especially planning the big central counter, the paperwork, the inventory system, and such. We were like children with their Tinkertoys. We had to learn by trial and error how the pieces went together to get the effect we wanted, but learning was marvelous fun."

Early in the spring, Jane Emery, then working at Edith Farnsworth's, turned up at a party at Patty and Walt Wilson's home. Jane, an Easterner with an academic background in social sciences, had just returned to the Springs with her writer-teacher husband Charles Emery, Jr., after several years in New York. The Noyes-Emery rapport was immediate. For some time Dick had been keeping his eye on the progress of a new kind of book, paperbacks. He had a talk with Jane about this in the Wilson's kitchen, and she agreed with him that a paperback boom seemed at the threshold.

They asked Jane to consider becoming the Chinook's first full-time employee. Jane went to work organizing a paperback department and helping in the selection of hardbacks for the planned opening of the store in June. Soon the Noyes garage was jammed with some of the $15,000 worth of books that would comprise the Chinook's initial inventory.

And so the great day of the opening, Monday, June 15, 1959, came at last. The first Chinook ad appeared in the *Colorado Springs Gazette-Telegraph* on Sunday, June 14. It was Judy's effort, displaying even then her characteristic lightness of touch. "Chinook?" the ad inquired. "What is it? An Indian tribe? A kind of salmon? A warm welcome wind?" She continued. "At the Chinook Bookshop you will find the finest selection of maps and globes from Chicago to the Coast . . . and a few surprises." On that same Sunday, Stanton Peckham, the distinguished book reviewer for *The Denver Post*, noted in his book column: "Here's a chinook we hope has a long and glorious future."

Judy and Dick and Jane can remember very little about what happened at that hectic opening. Invitations had been sent to friends, Colorado College people, and other likely customers. "We were so dazed and worn out getting everything ready," Jane says, "yes, and apprehensive. Suppose nobody showed up?" But the turn-out was good, and Jane recalls selling her first book, Irma Rombauer's *Joy of Cooking*. She hurried in triumph to the inventory control file, got the Rombauer card, crossed out the figure "1" and wrote "0," initiating the first reorder.

GROWING PAINS AND PROMOTION

The going was rough for Noyes & Company through The Chinook's first two years. There never seemed to be enough money coming in, and there was a lot going out. Even the free coffee for the browsing customers was a drain. Dick, Judy, and Jane Emery were all things to the store—janitors, gift-wrappers, unpackers of incoming and outgoing books, bank runners with the day's receipts. Many hours were spent discussing new books with the publishers' reps. During the first summer, Dick had supper alone from 4:30 to 5:30 at Ruth's Oven nearby, and then he would return to keep the store open until 9 P.M. hoping to catch a sale from some tourist wandering along North Tejon. He reminisces now, "It's neat to open a bookstore when you're in your late twenties; you can work 15-hour days and still have energy left for the kids."

Each day brought its lessons. To guard against suspected shoplifters, Dick would call out "Dust those books up front, Judy, please." Theft never was much of a problem, in spite of the store's meandering layout, but Jane learned about confidence games when a smartly dressed woman ordered $500 worth of books to be sent to a college library in Kansas and then "borrowed" $10 for lunch—"How silly of me, left my purse at the hotel." She never returned, of course, and there was no such Kansas college.

Rough going or not, Dick was more than a little pleased at the end of the first year to be able to report to his father total sales of $65,000 as against $40,000 he had predicted in his prospectus. And 1959 was not just a lucky year. Thereafter, year after year, sales at The Chinook would increase from 20 to 25 percent annually with a proportionate increase in the size of the staff as it edged toward an eventual 20 people with the annual average inventory of books rising from the first year's $15,000 to over $20,000 at cost, with approximately 40,000 book titles and annual sales well in excess of $1,000,000.

How to explain such progress?

In Judy's words, "A key element was the hard work and devotion of the staff, their love of what they were doing, their pride in The Chinook, and their ability to work in harmony as a team. All of them were ardent readers who could pass their knowledge along to a customer wanting to know something about what he was buying. None of them objected—not much, anyhow—to Dick's attention to the tedious details of the trade that he had learned when he was with Rand McNally: the ins and outs of publishers' policies, tight systems and controls, and fast reordering and follow-up."

The shop's brief statement of policy begins: "The Chinook is intentionally an informal place, dedicated to the belief that its staff is the cream of the crop. For this reason extensively spelled-out do's and don'ts are unnecessary." Dick and Judy flinch at the title "clerk"; there are professional booksellers, not "clerks," at The Chinook. Over the years staff members have come and gone, but the turnover has been modest. As of now the average is over 10 years on the job for the floor sales staffers.

Among Dick's ideas was his stress on proper display. Publishers hired artists and printers to produce book jackets that would catch the eye. So he made it a rule that as many books as possible be placed face-out, in full view.

Walter Wilson contributed an idea for the store's Tejon Street window that followed the jacket display idea. He suggested a piquant character later referred to as "The Invisible Man" (or woman), a figure in the front window suggested by bits of dress, spectacles, a hat, shoes, and a book—all suspended by wire, with a slogan on a poster, usually with some sort of pun. Dick created the figures, and Judy was responsible for the puns.

One window showed the invisible man sitting on a log, "Stumped for a book to read." Another depicted a Cripple Creek miner and the slogan, "A gold mine of a book—it's loded." The sign accompanying the figure of a hiker: "To Thoreau-ly enjoy the fall, pack in mountains of good reading." A cowboy: "Quit horsing around! Wither it rains or snows, it's a cinch for all good chaps to hitch up to the wide range of brand-new reading in The Chinook stable." During the 1960s, a springtime theme had an invisible lady in a flutter of butterflies and the slogan, "It's a breeze to get high on books." Sue Ormes suggested one of the most popular windows, used every January, which has "The Invisible Man" with a broom, with discarded gift wrappings piled high, "Sweeping into the New Year." Friends and neighbors of the Noyeses contribute garbage bags filled with their Christmas wrap after the holiday every year. Hundreds of pedestrians make it a habit to walk by the bookshop to see if there is a new window with a horrible pun. In passing, they stop, of course, to look over the many new books piled around the invisible figure. Dick finally decided to pass along the responsibility for the physical creation of the window display to multitalented Karen Engel, who has been in charge of the shop displays since 1974.

Some things happened by accident. Dick built for $50 a playhouse at home for daughters Catherine and Stephanie. They and the neighbor kids were so entranced by it that he built another, also for $50, in a corner of the bookstore. A pair of large Steiff chimpanzees lived in the two-story house, and children customers were soon asking their parents to "take me to the store with the monkey house." Young parents who once played themselves in the house are now bringing in another generation, parking them with the monkeys while they take their time finding books to buy.

Another factor in The Chinook's growth was the closing of its two major competitors, Edith Farnsworth's and Their Book Shop. Most of the customers of those two established stores then switched their business to The Chinook.

In 1961, the third Noyes child, Matthew, was born. By now, The Chinook and its coffee corner had become a hangout for kindred book-loving spirits. Among them was a small young woman in very high heels and a big droopy hat named Nancy Wood who had a wild desire to be a writer. Nancy was editing an FM radio station weekly filled with local chitchat. One day she asked Judy to write a column on current books. The response to the column was surprisingly good. When Nancy's publication folded, Judy decided to keep on with the column as a promotional giveaway under the title "Currents from The Chinook."

The first "Currents" was a single page mailed out to regular customers at Christmas time. The time arrived when it had grown to six pages and thousands of words of copy. The demand for it grew until the Noyes found themselves mailing it to 6,000 people, some of whom wrote in from all over the world asking for copies and ordering books. The publication gave Judy a chance to develop the talent she had shown in Florida as a teenaged journalist. "Currents" is fast-paced, brightly written, informative, and amusing. It lists the bestsellers but gives considerable space to the books of regional interest and those by local authors.

All these activities advanced The Chinook upward, but paramount was the creativity of the Noyes themselves and their total fascination with the art of selling books. From the start Dick had believed that a bookstore's success derived from promoting books to the nonaddicted reader. He did not mind purveying the obvious bestsellers, of course. But what pleased him most was to see hard-hats or mechanics or any other sort of "unbookish" person wander into the store to buy hunting and fishing maps and then stop to look at books in the do-it-yourself section or to examine the rows of books on cooking or gardening or auto mechanics.

It was to lure such people who may never have read a book for fun to discover the joy of reading that Dick and Judy had decided to stock all kinds of books. There would be books on rock n'roll, veterinary medicine, judo, ancient Greek, taxidermy, science fiction, and the occult—the list is endless. They did not care how exotic a book might be, or that it might take a while to sell. Sooner or later somebody would come across *Finding Your Way with Clay* or *Be Bold with Bananas*, clutch it in triumph, march up to the sales counter, and leave to spread the word that The Chinook was just what Dick and Judy had hoped it would be, "the one place you can find everything."[2]

Dick and Judy marked The Chinook's tenth year in 1969 when annual sales were nearing half a million dollars by leasing the store next door to the north, which had been occupied by John Eastham's Whickerbill Gift Shop, which itself moved up

---

[2]See Jeff Blyskal, "Dalton, Walden, and the Amazing Money Machine," *Forbes*, January 18, 1982, an article about the "democratization" of book buying. "To be blunt about it, books are no longer bought just to be read but, like any other consumer item, to be owned, to be looked at, to be given as presents. Not surprisingly, picture books, sex books and cookbooks are major products. In an age of cable television and video cassettes, people may not necessarily be spending more time reading books, but they are spending more money buying books." (p. 47).

one space. With architect Clifford Nakata (who a year later designed the Noyes's new home) in charge, they tore out a wall, moved a sales counter to its present central position, installed elaborately carved Spanish doors at the two entrances, and surrounded The Invisible Man with a decade of best bestsellers, including the two best in 1959, *Dr. Zhivago* and *Exodus*.

The expansion increased The Chinook's space from 2,500 to 5,300 square feet. Reporting their ten ; birthday in *Publisher's Weekly*, Judy wrote: "Drippity-drop-drop was the sound of the very un-Colorado-like weather. Puh-*wop* was the promising refrain of champagne corks being popped inside The Chinook for the several hundred people dropping in for the festivities."

Dick was a bit irritable that day having just given up smoking, but he did manage a smile when Harold Dillon, the dean of Rocky Mountain publishers' reps, congratulated him on the enlargement with its change of address from the demeaning 208½ to 210 North Tejon. "Never thought you'd make it," Dillon said, "but I couldn't be happier to have been wrong."

NATIONAL PROFESSIONAL INVOLVEMENT

Soon after joining the American Booksellers Association (ABA) the Noyeses supported the regional book scene by attending the first meeting in Denver of the Colorado Booksellers Association where they met Pyke Johnson, Jr., managing editor of Doubleday & Company and others of the larger book world, many of whom would become personal as well as professional friends.

The ABA has a membership of 4,500 bookstores from every state and of some 1,500 publishers who supply bookstores with the 450,000 books in print and the 40,000 or so new books published each year. Its board of directors conducts a maze of projects: the *American Bookseller* magazine, the massive and often revised *Manual of Bookselling*, a Booksellers School with annual workshops, an ABA newswire, and the selection and donation every four years of 500 books to the White House family library. Its 5 standing and 10 special committees address every conceivable aspect of moving books from the nation's stores to the reader.

This swirl of activity comes into sharp focus at the ABA's annual convention headquarters in a hotel in Washington, D.C., or New York or Boston or Los Angeles or Chicago. Thousands of booksellers attend the exhibits, the ABA program of work sessions, banquets, and parties. Reporters, camera operators, and radio and TV people frequent the scene along with the publishers, the bestselling and most flamboyant of authors (James Michener, perhaps, or Irving Wallace), or celebrity authors such as Vincent Price and Lauren Bacall.

It can be suspected that back in 1959, Dick began to think that he, the unknown owner of an embryo bookstore far out in the unregarded West, might some day become active on the board of the ABA. At any rate, Dick and Judy were present at the ABA conventions of the 1960s, giving trade talks and discussing the problems of booksellers far from the eastern scene.

The Chinook's name was gradually getting to be known in ABA circles through Judy's informative articles for *Publisher's Weekly*. Jane Emery and Dick also wrote about the store. One of Judy's most popular articles explained how to put humor into bookstore ads to make sure that they are read.

Her use of puns with "The Invisible Man" was helpful in writing these ads; some were inspired by regular repartee with Dick's father, a veteran punster. One Chinook ad for a local theater group showed an actor ducking rotten eggs and the line "Sure we're egging you on. We want you to make Chinook part of your scene." Another had a parent eating a wormy apple and the line "The best way to worm your way into Dad's affections: choose an a-peeling new book from Chinook for Father's Day." The picture of an angry editor had the line "If the editor finds your work odeious, remember things could be verse. Come to The Chinook and be a-mused. Inspiration like you never metaphor."

In the spring of 1965, Dick and Judy had a pleasant surprise—a phone call from Joseph Duffy, then executive director of the ABA, in Denver at a regional booksellers' meeting with Igor Kropotkin, then president of the ABA and head of Scribner's Bookstore in New York City. Duffy asked casually if the two of them could come down to Colorado Springs to see The Chinook about which they had heard so much. Duffy spoke of his special interest in The Chinook's inventory control.

Soon after the important visitors arrived, as Dick stood with them at the big main sales counter explaining his systems, a stressed sales staffer came waltzing up to the inventory control file remarking loudly and irritably, "Damn it, I can't find a *thing* in these stupid files."

Even so the two ABA big guns must have been impressed by what they saw at Chinook. A few months later Dick received word of his nomination as a director of ABA. From that time on, Dick delegated more and more of the store's operation to the staff as he advanced steadily in the ABA hierarchy, from third to second to first vice president and chairman of standing committees and as a member of the faculty of the national Booksellers School.

Dick came to the ABA board with a strong conviction of the need to restructure the whole operation to reduce the traditional emphasis on the concerns of Eastern booksellers, to broaden the geographical representation, and to develop the abilities of the younger segment of the membership. One of Dick's major contributions as a director was his rewriting of the ABA bylaws in the early 1970s. The excellence of his work in this difficult matter seems to have been rewarded in April 1974 by his election as president of the ABA, one of the youngest and the first of the booksellers from the Rocky Mountain region to hold that office.

By coincidence, Dick's term of office involved greater responsibilities than more recent presidents had faced. One of his two years in office coincided with celebration of the ABA's Diamond Jubilee, its seventy-fifty year. The convention took place in New York with a then record attendance of over 8,000 booksellers and book publishers and authors from all over the world.

AN EXPANDING REPUTATION

With a pleasant exhaustion, the Noyeses survived those four May days of that Diamond Jubilee of Dick's presidency: the entertaining, speaking assignments, press interviews, and attending autographing sessions with celebrities. Less wearing were the more intimate parties in New York's finest restaurants and enjoying the awe inspired by their two-story penthouse suite atop the Hilton assigned to them by the ABA.

One effect of Dick's presidency was to bathe The Chinook in a tide of admiring comment, which became by repetition almost a cliché in book circles. An article in the ABA's *American Bookseller* concluded "and today The Chinook's owners are among the best-known booksellers in the country." In a *Publisher's Weekly* article, "An Interview with Richard Noyes," Lila Freilicher wrote "ABA's president is a perfectionist who, not surprisingly, runs one of the best bookshops in the country." In August 1975, *Town and Country* published an article about Colorado Springs by Patricia Linden who wrote of Dick, "He is the owner of Colorado Springs' far-famed Chinook Bookshop which sells a staggering $700,000 worth of hard- and soft-covered literature on every conceivable subject and has been called 'the best bookshop in the U.S.A.'"

Recently, Pyke Johnson, Jr., a senior editor of Doubleday, who was born in Denver, commenting on the store's twentieth anniversary, wrote, "I have always said that The Chinook was the best bookstore in the United States. At the beginning I might have been bragging a little in the way of a native son. But now I know that, by any standard, or for any reason, this statement is correct. I honor all the people at Chinook who have made it so; I am proud to consider them my friends."

In November 1977, Dick received the Intellectual Freedom Award given by the eight-state Mountain Plains Library Association. He had appeared many times in defense of the freedom-to-read in public hearings both in Colorado Springs and Denver. A co-founder of the Colorado Media Coalition, his impact in censorship matters derived from years as an ardent supporter of First Amendment rights.

In March 1978 Dick was one of two Booksellers members of a delegation sponsored by the U.S. State Department sent to Nigeria to acquaint the booksellers there with American distribution and marketing methods. In October he was chosen as part of a delegation requested by the British government to conduct seminars in London and Oxford on American bookselling and publishing procedures. In March 1979 Dick was one of two booksellers appointed by the Center of the Book of the Library of Congress to a committee of 100 authors, publishers, librarians, and others of the book world wishing to promote more widespread reading in the United States. Judy and Dick Noyes have taught the bookselling section of the Denver University Publishing Institute each summer since its inception in 1976.

Judy, meantime, was becoming known for her enthusiasm and expertise in selling children's books. Her reviews of new children's books appeared in *The New York Times* and *Publisher's Weekly*, and she was a founder of the liaison committee formed between the American Booksellers Association and the Children's Book Council to get better communications established between children's booksellers and editor/publishers.

THE CHINOOK STAFF'S ASSIGNMENTS

Dick and Judy enjoy their staff, now numbering 20, all of whom share their fascination with books and delight in a camaraderie rare in any business. Customers often comment on this atmosphere of fun and good nature in the midst of obvious busyness. Jane Emery recalls that Edith Farnsworth had told her "the most fun you'll have is the initial setting up of the store." But that's not how it turned out at all, says Jane. "It's been fun right along."

Francie Armstrong, who has assisted in the management of the paperback department for 15 years, agrees that the lighthearted atmosphere has been a major appeal for customers and staff, too. And Francie has a theory as to why such competent people come and remain at Chinook: "We are part of a team, but there is also a great feeling of individual respect and freedom." She also stresses the dedication and quality of the service. "The people on this staff will knock themselves out to get books for customers." That this service is appreciated is reflected in the many thank-you letters The Chinook special-order department receives from grateful customers.

Phyllis Zell's skill as head of special orders and out-of-print book finder has brought her queries and customers from all over the world. With the help of Mark Burski, she processes at least 200 special orders a week for Colorado Springs customers, not to mention the out-of-town and institutional business. Anne Cross, a Coloradoan who knows the town inside and out and was co-owner of Their Book Shop, is another longtimer (over 11 years). Carol Williams has been Chinook's prized keeper of the books for over a decade and is now assisted by Glenda Olderag, Wanda Jeavons, and Kim Mersman. Claudia Castle, who *insisted* upon working at The Chinook following her graduation from Mount Holyoke in 1970, now serves as the shop's "memory bank" for authors and titles.

Dick has always had a particular feeling for the kids who started as janitors after school and then worked up to better things their junior or senior year in high school. Lance Selkirk was the first, followed among others by the Koller and Garner Brothers, Jim Dunn, and recently Dave Kosley and Scott Chambers. The shipping room group, long the only male bastion at the Chinook was integrated finally and happily by three stalwarts, Sharon Sprague, Karen Engel, and Kathryn Redman.

So, what of the future? "We'll see," says Dick. "There has been pressure from many advisor-friends to expand—to branch The Chinook into a regional minichain. Dick and Judy see that as an option, but not a very agreeable one. The three Noyes children—Catherine N. Boddington, now 26 and a graduate of Bennington College; Stephanie, 25, a graduate of St. Lawrence University; and Matthew, 17, an undergraduate at Wesleyan University—have worked at the bookshop, and there is always the possibility of a second generation to carry on.

One thing is certain: Dick and Judy and the staff are fiercely independent booksellers who are dedicated to excellence and are determined that the present-day Chinook will never change its style, personality, and its belief in complete, personal service. They believe that The Chinook is a unique, personal place, selling "a commodity created to meet the needs of people seeking knowledge, wisdom, and pleasure."

Appendix 19A presents additional information related to the case study.

Appendix 19A

RICHARD NOYES'S PHILOSOPHY OF SELLING

These three statements come from Dick's notes on selling, used in teaching courses mentioned in the narrative:

1. The average book on successful selling actually assumes that the customer does not want or need the product, is basically pretty ignorant, and must be coerced into buying. This is their premise, and the specific advice they give obviously is based on it. Almost always these sales technique manuals imply a basic lack of integrity (a hucksterism) that may be appropriate for the life insurance salesman but certainly has no place in retail bookselling. The good bookstore should work for long-range, repeat business—there's no room for the hard sell, the one-night-stand sort of thing.

2. Never make a casual recommendation—if it's way off base, your store has probably lost that customer. Highly personal recommendations can be difficult, especially if the customer doesn't give you much to go on. If there's quite a void of information, attack from the flanks. What has the person read recently and enjoyed? If the book is a gift, find out the profession of the recipient, or his or her age, hobbies, attitudes, etc.—it's amazing how much you can piece together once you get the hang of it. . . . You sincerely want that person to like that book; it's your recommendation, and if correct it's awfully good for business.

3. Your ad in the telephone directory is your least expensive, most effective advertising. Surely your store's telephone salesmanship deserves prime consideration.

FROM AMERICAN BOOKSELLERS ASSOCIATION

Permission has been granted by American Booksellers Association (the casewriters are especially grateful to Allan Marshall for his cooperation) to reprint in this portion of the appendix parts of "ABA Bookstore Financial Profile," the results of an ABA study, published in 1981 by American Booksellers Association. The key findings presented here are very similar to the conclusions reached in a similar ABA study of booksellers, published in 1977.

1. **Overview.** The key findings of this report, in other words, confirm what everyone has been saying. The erosion of profitability in bookstores over the past four years has been measured and found to be alarming. Relief has come from some publishers through improved terms. Whether it came early enough or is adequate enough to help booksellers pull themselves out of the red will be the key finding of the next survey.[1]

2. **Reducing Costs and Improving Profits.** Meanwhile, we asked respondents to this survey to share with other booksellers the methods they have found practical in reducing costs and improving profits. All but 20 stores replied to this question, which indicates that the vast majority are trying to control their own destiny. Of the 300 respondents,

[1]"ABA Bookstore Financial Profile," p. 1.

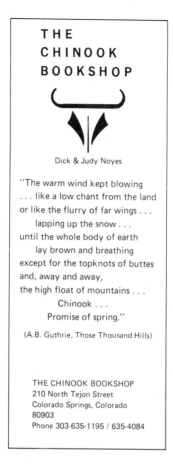

THE CHINOOK BOOKSHOP

Dick & Judy Noyes

"The warm wind kept blowing
. . . like a low chant from the land
or like the flurry of far wings . . .
lapping up the snow . . .
until the whole body of earth
lay brown and breathing
except for the topknots of buttes
and, away and away,
the high float of mountains . . .
Chinook . . .
Promise of spring."

(A.B. Guthrie, Those Thousand Hills)

THE CHINOOK BOOKSHOP
210 North Tejon Street
Colorado Springs, Colorado
80903
Phone 303-635-1195 / 635-4084

158 have eliminated nonproductive categories of books

149 are ordering more from wholesalers to cut transportation costs

148 have made greater use of delayed dating plans on invoices

122 have cut back on the amount of advertising

121 are ordering more from publishers to increase discounts

116 are ordering less frequently to cut transportation costs and increase discounts

96 have eliminated special services or have instituted a charge for those formerly offered for free

90 have reduced staff

78 have added sidelines

55 responded to the "Other" category (explained below)

50 have increased emphasis on an area of specialization

44 have added used books to the merchandise mix

33 have reduced the number of hours the store is open

28 have added nonbook services

24 have reduced or eliminated owners' or employee benefits

14 have reduced the size of the store to cut back on overhead

Appendix 19A (Cont.)

Of the 55 stores who responded to the "Other" category, 22 offered the following specifics:

> 5 stores are ordering more carefully
>
> 9 stores are improving their inventory control and stock-turn performance
>
> 2 stores have relocated to reduce rent
>
> 2 stores are tightening up on budgets
>
> 4 stores have increased their co-op advertising

3. **Average Years of Operation and Average Hours Open.** If any single table confirms preconceived notions about bookstores, it is the one that follows, which shows that the larger stores have been in operation for more years than the smaller ones. The larger a store becomes, the more hours it is open per week as well. Neither years of operation nor hours open, however, have any apparent effect on profitability. Indeed, it appears that the most profitable stores have been in operation the shortest time, which may confirm the theory that management becomes lax after the eighth year of operation. The fact that the least profitable stores have been in business for nearly 10 years might also confirm the theory that some stores are run as a hobby rather than as a means of supporting the owner.[2]

	NUMBER OF STORES	AVERAGE YEARS OPEN	AVERAGE HOURS OPEN (per week)
Single store respondents			
Less than $50,000	20	3.5	49.7
$50,000 to $100,000	36	8.1	48.4
$100,000 to $150,000	29	9.2	54.0
$150,000 to $300,000	44	10.6	58.8
$300,000 to $500,000	16	22.5	59.0
Over $500,000	13	31.6	64.0
Multiple-store respondents	39	16.4	64.0
All stores	197	12.1	55.5
Stores in the top 25% profit range	36	7.6	54.1
Stores in the middle 50% profit range	102	14.4	56.6
Stores in the bottom 25% profit range	31	9.8	53.3

4. **Sales per Square Foot of Occupied Space.** The highest sales per square foot, as the following bar graph demonstrates, does not necessarily yield the highest gross profit, which is dictated by the overall factors affecting profitability. But the bar graph does demonstrate dramatically that the relationship between nonselling and selling space has a direct relationship to profitability among the responding stores.[3]

5. **Sales per Full-Time Employee.** The ratio of sales per employee to total sales measures employee productivity and is generally considered a good

[2]Ibid., p. 6; as reported by 169 stores with annual sales totaling $51,645,316.
[3]Ibid., p. 8.

Appendix 19A (Cont.)

SALES PER SQUARE FOOT OF OCCUPIED SPACE

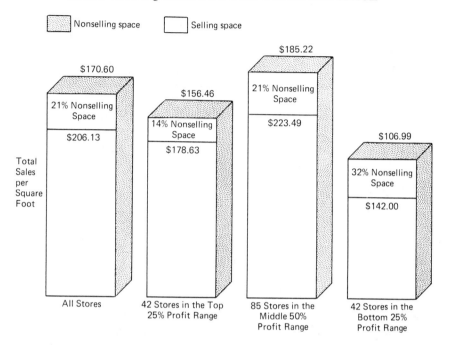

guide to the efficiency of a retail business. There is almost no correlation between the figures given by respondents in 1977 and 1981 due to a marked difference in method of reporting. Sales per employee increase as sales volume increases, but this is not necessarily because each employee in a larger store employs better sales techniques: larger inventories attract more browsing and create more impulse buying.

	Average	Mid Range
33 stores in the top 25% profit range	$45,516	$34,656–56,277
119 stores in the middle 50% profit range	61,855	39,090–66,523
32 stores in the bottom 25% profit range	45,233	27,447–54,266

The highest sales per employee does not necessarily result in the highest profitability, however, as the table demonstrates. The most profitable and least profitable stores in this sample reported virtually identical sales per employee.[4]

6. **Financial Profile, 1981.**[5] The following table shows both the average and the median profit and loss statements for 179 stores with annual sales totaling $48,185,364. All data in this section of the survey are based on the identical store sample.

In the table an "adjusted net profit" entry appears as the bottom line.

[4]Ibid., p. 9; as reported by 184 stores with annual sales totaling $48,364,614.
[5]Ibid., p. 17.

	33 STORES IN TOP 25% PROFIT RANGE WITH ANNUAL SALES TOTALING $4,546,963: Percent of Sales		116 STORES IN MIDDLE 50% PROFIT RANGE WITH ANNUAL SALES TOTALING $38,855,035: Percent of Sales		30 STORES IN BOTTOM 25% PROFIT RANGE WITH ANNUAL SALES TOTALING $4,783,366: Percent of Sales		ALL STORES (179 STORES WITH ANNUAL SALES TOTALING $48,185,364): Percent of Sales	
	Average	Median	Average	Median	Average	Median	Average	Median
Total sales	100.0%	100.0%	100.0%	100.0%	100.0%	100.0%	100.0%	100.0%
Less: Cost of goods sold	61.4	60.5	65.1	65.3	66.7	69.4	64.9	65.7
Gross margin	38.6	39.2	34.9	34.9	33.3	30.5	35.1	34.6
Less expenses:								
Payroll expense (total)	12.7	9.8	16.2	14.4	19.3	19.8	16.2	16.3
Owners' compensation	3.9	5.4	2.5	7.2	2.4	—	2.4	7.5
Wages: employees	8.4	5.0	13.3	10.1	15.6	15.4	13.2	10.0
Employee benefits	.4	.8	.4	.7	1.2	.8	.6	1.0
Data processing payroll	—	—	—	—	.1	—	.1	—
Occupancy expense (total)	7.7	7.6	6.6	6.5	6.3	10.0	6.6	7.8
Rent, mortgage, or building depreciation	5.4	5.1	5.0	4.7	4.5	7.5	4.4	5.4
Real estate taxes and insurance	.6	.6	.5	1.0	.4	1.1	.5	1.3
Utilities	1.0	1.0	.7	1.4	.8	1.8	.7	1.6
Repair, maintenance, cleaning	.7	.7	.4	.7	.5	.6	1.1	1.0
Advertising	1.7	1.8	1.8	1.7	1.8	2.8	1.8	2.2
Telephone/communications	.4	.6	.3	.7	.6	.9	.4	.9
Professional services	.3	.5	.3	.7	.7	1.2	.4	1.2
Stationery and supplies	—	—	.3	.5	.4	—	.3	.7
Data processing exclusive of payroll	—	—	.3	.5	.4	—	.3	.7
Depreciation	.9	1.0	.7	1.4	1.5	1.9	.9	1.7
Travel and entertainment	.4	.9	.2	.8	.8	1.3	.3	1.2
Insurance	.5	.8	.2	.6	.8	1.2	.3	1.1
Credit card service charges	.3	.3	.3	.5	.3	.5	.3	.5
Dues and subscriptions	.3	—	.2	.6	.2	.5	.2	.7
Miscellaneous office expense and postage	.4	.7	.3	.9	.6	.7	.3	1.0
Taxes	.4	.8	.2	.6	.1	.6	.2	1.8
All other operating expense	1.1	1.4	1.2	1.8	2.3	2.3	1.3	2.4
Total operating expenses	27.1%	27.6%	29.2%	32.0%	36.1%	37.0%	29.8%	32.0%
Operating income (loss)	11.5	12.9	5.7	3.1	(2.8)	(7.8)	5.3	2.4
Other income	.4	.4	.4	.7	.5	—	.2	1.8
Other expense	.7	.7	.6	1.2	.5	—	.6	1.4
Net income (loss) before taxes	11.2	12.2	5.5	2.6	(2.8)	(8.6)	4.9	2.3
Less: Allowance for unreported owners' earnings	(3.6)		(3.8)		(3.3)		(4.0)	
Adjusted net profit	7.6		1.7				.9	

Appendix 19A (Cont.)

The adjusted profit results from the inclusion after "net income before taxes" of an allowance for owners' earnings in instances where stores did not report such earnings under the "owners' compensation" entry in the Payroll Expense section of the questionnaire. The rate used in making these adjustments is a composite derived from actual owners' compensation in each size of profitability group.

The resulting adjusted net profit more truly reflects the profitability (or lack thereof) of the reporting stores. For further confirmation of this point, see the table illustrating "Total dollars available to owner" later in the survey.

7. **Summary**[6]

Once again, the financial survey has proven that controlling expenses rather than simply increasing gross margin is the key to profitable bookselling. But it has also shown the difficulty of controlling expenses under recent economic conditions, even in the most profitable stores.

The survey was completed before the effects of publishers' changing terms could have an impact in the bookstores. It is hoped that the next survey will show a better economic future for independent booksellers. If it does, it will be not only because terms have improved, but because booksellers have continued vigilantly to control expenses as well.

Booksellers in the lower sales groups should find some encouragement in the fact that size alone does not guarantee a reasonable profit. A reasonable profit on a small operation, however, is not necessarily a living wage.

[6]Ibid., p. 25.

20

YMCA/USO OF THE PIKES PEAK REGION (A)

In 1869 the first YMCA in the country opened its gymnasium, with old cannonballs, weighing from 18 to 80 pounds, serving as exercise weights. These gyms were called "halls of health." Several decades later, the Colorado Springs YMCA opened its doors, commencing a history that by 1980 amounted to some 60 years of service to civilian and military sectors of the city. The entity comprised the YMCA, YWCA, and the USO, and after functioning for many years in a general-purpose building, it moved into new quarters in 1973. The city's population was 281,000.

Throughout the 1970s, Colorado Springs grew rapidly in population and geographic area, so that the 1973 building was pressing capacity soon after opening. Area population had grown to 350,000 by 1979. Membership in the Y organization increased rapidly, and programs, services, and staff also greatly expanded. USO usage remained level, however.

Because the Y was feeling the pinch of overutilization, and hearing an increasing volume of complaints from its members about these problems, its board of directors agreed to gather data to decide an issue it had discussed for a number of years: whether it was time to plan seriously for construction of a second facility. The board instructed the executive director to contract with a professional consulting firm to gather data on whether and under what conditions the Y should open a second facility.

BACKGROUND

With its founding in 1871, the city became known for scenic topography, healthful climate, cultural and learning activities, and tourist attractions; around these its early economy developed. Semiarid and remote from metropolitan centers, there was little agriculture and industry in the earlier decades. In the 1880s and 1890s a series of important developments—rich mineral strikes, railroad construction, new hotels— accelerated mining and tourist activities, and, consequently, population growth. Some local industry producing brick, tile, lumber, and pottery began. By World War I mining declined as general economic and population growth diminished.

World War II brought a turn toward large-scale military activity and the establishment of several installations over a 20-year period, including the U.S. Air Force Academy, which opened in 1958. While government employment dominated the city in the late 1970s, indications were that the industrial sector, principally electronics and related businesses, would flourish in the next two decades. The city's accelerating population growth fell back to a level of 2 to 3 percent annually between 1975 and 1981, appearing to stabilize at about 2.5 percent, with most new construction activity—single-family and multifamily dwellings and shopping centers—occurring in the northeast suburbs.

The city's sports consciousness was heightened when the U.S. Olympic Committee decided to locate there and to construct its training center on property formerly occupied by a U.S. Air Force headquarters group. Also located in Colorado Springs were the Amateur Basketball Association, U.S. Field Hockey Association, National Archery Association, Professional Rodeo Cowboys Association, U.S. Cycling Federation, U.S. International Skating Association, U.S. Modern Pentathlon and Biathlon Association, U.S. Volleyball Association, and U.S. Athletic Association. Other such groups were investigating the area as a location for their headquarters.

ORGANIZATIONAL STRUCTURE

Although the Y is a worldwide organization, each local unit is autonomous in programs, administration, and finances. The Y belongs to a federation of 1,800 Ys divided into six regional districts, with a national council that meets biannually. The local Y/USO pays 3 percent of certain portions of its income to support the national and regional staff. As general director, appointed in 1979, James Klever devotes full time to local operations and employs professional staff needed to run the institution's programs and nonprofessional staff who provide support functions. The Y's board carries out its functions through a number of committees, subcommittees, and task groups. Exhibit 20.1 portrays the 265-person organization—65 full-time salaried, including 14 professional staff, and 200 part-time hourly workers.

Exhibit 20.1

PIKES PEAK Y/USO PROFESSIONAL STAFF ORGANIZATION CHART

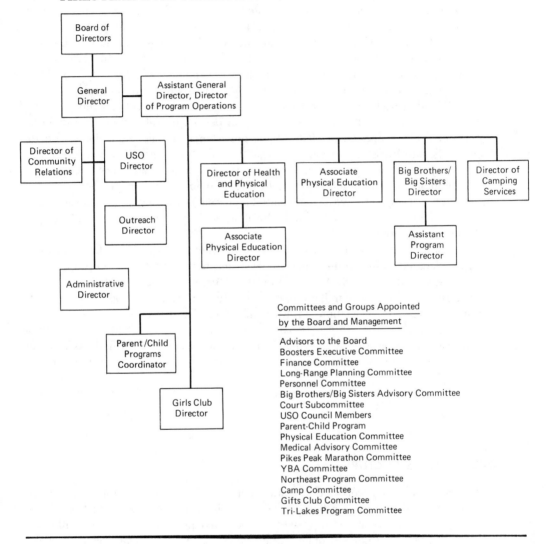

Committees and Groups Appointed
by the Board and Management

Advisors to the Board
Boosters Executive Committee
Finance Committee
Long-Range Planning Committee
Personnel Committee
Big Brothers/Big Sisters Advisory Committee
Court Subcommittee
USO Council Members
Parent-Child Program
Physical Education Committee
Medical Advisory Committee
Pikes Peak Marathon Committee
YBA Committee
Northeast Program Committee
Camp Committee
Gifts Club Committee
Tri-Lakes Program Committee

FINANCIAL PROFILE

Exhibit 20.2 compares selected financial highlights for 1977 through 1981. Although the Y usually came through each year with a balanced budget, a principal goal of board and management was to improve the financial picture in the 1980s, to ensure the future growth and stability of the Y, and to gear up for the capital contributions campaign that would have to be mounted if expansion appeared to be necessary and feasible. Exhibit 20.3 draws some financial comparisons between the Pikes Peak Y and other YMCAs in the United States with a budget size of $700,000 to $2,200,000. The board was pleased with the local Y's relative performance.

Exhibit 20.2

Y/USO SELECTED SOURCES AND USES OF FUNDS, 1977–1981
(in thousands)

	1977	1978	1979*	1980	1981
Sources					
Fees from programs	$ 243.6	$ 256.9	$ 329.3	$ 372.9	$ 445.7
Memberships	436.1	544.5	600.6	726.4	784.3
United Way	—	—	—	224.7	251.7
Contributions	242.1†	291.7†	317.2†	86.0	99.4
Sales of products and services	31.2	31.6	40.3	44.0	37.9
Investments and rentals	72.2	81.0	85.4	65.7	66.0
Miscellaneous	0.8	0.8	0.8	21.0	57.2
	$1,026.0	$1,206.5	$1,373.6	$1,540.7	$1,742.2
Uses					
Salaries	$ 508.7	$ 570.1	$ 673.4	$ 815.9	$ 846.6
Benefits and taxes	58.0	63.1	77.8	95.9	99.4
Occupancy/equipment	228.3	274.4	313.4	366.9	386.8
Building and equipment	—	—	—	46.0	34.3
Program costs	94.8	127.7	113.8	191.7	223.2
Supplies and cost of sales	109.4	137.5	159.9	75.7	67.9
Legal insurance and dues	26.7	33.7	35.2	26.8	40.3
Miscellaneous and dues	—	—	—	17.6	43.6
	$1,025.9	$1,206.5	$1,373.5	$1,540.6	$1,742.1

*Reconstructed estimates in some categories.
†Including United Way allocation for USO and other programs.

Exhibit 20.3

Y/USO BUDGET RATIOS COMPARED WITH OTHER Ys', 1980

	Y/USO	OTHER Ys*
Total payroll as % of total expenses	53%	56%
Benefits and taxes as % of total expenses	6	7
Program income as % of total revenues	24	31
Membership dues as % of total revenues	47	27
Contributions as % of total revenues	20†	20

*Percentages estimated from National Council data.
†Recombining United Way and other contributions.

PROGRAM SMORGASBORD

"Monday Morning Memo" is a weekly Y newsletter mailed to members notifying them of special programs, appealing for volunteers, and providing news of recent events.

Besides the weekly mailer, seasonal catalogs also are mailed to members and to various organizations in the city. These pieces usually included 16 to 20 pages of 100 or so listings of programs and classes, "something for everyone." For example, the spring 1982 mailer, in addition to schedules of facility hours and availability by age and activity categories, announced the Y's corporate goals and the 1982 annual membership fees and described over 100 programs and activities, such as diving instruction, youth ballet, Mexican folk dancing for youth, diapergym, fitness classes for youth and adults, gymnastics, racquetball lessons, ski clinics, theater class, weight training, special parties and celebrations, drawing, ceramics, Christian fellowship hour, and cooking classes.

Anticipating an expanded role in the city's northeast area, brochure mailers heralded an assortment of programs, activities, and classes in several neighborhoods scheduled for 1982. New offerings targeted to the younger families residing in those sections included, for example, Lamaze childbirth sessions, roller skating, and an Easter egg hunt. Discount coupons printed on the mailers offered get-acquainted fees for new customers.

PROPOSED GOALS FOR 1980–1985

In 1979, management and the board of directors were drafting the institution's planning targets for the next five years, an activity in which James Klever, then serving as assistant general director, had participated from the beginning. Exhibit 20.4 contains selected passages from the planning document published that summer.

Planners distinguished goals—somewhat general statements forming a "planning umbrella" for the organization, and ordinarily with a time span of from two to five years—from objectives, which were defined as "specifically measurable statements of attainable outcomes within the framework of operational goals, with a time span of one year or less." Fiscal responsibility and future developments were two of the primary planning topics.

In 1981, spokespersons enunciated a set of 13 goals for the decade (Exhibit 20.5). Some planning guidelines set forth in 1978–1979 were reaffirmed, while marketing (item 6) and program expansion (item 7) were new additions, and financial administration/development (item 11) was modified to recognize unmet needs for physical fitness facilities and programs through the community. During the period in which these goals were being articulated, a creeping commitment to expansion into the northeast portion of the city similarly evolved. "All the signals," Klever reported at a midyear board meeting, "appear to be highly positive for this long-considered expansion."

Exhibit 20.4

SELECTED PASSAGES FROM 1979 PLANNING DOCUMENT

STATEMENT OF PURPOSE

The purpose of the Pikes Peak Y/USO is that of establishing and maintaining a fellowship of individuals and families of all faiths and helping its members develop Christian character and build a Christian society through activities and services that contribute to spiritual, intellectual, physical, and social growth.

INTERPRETATIVE STATEMENT

The Y seeks to help its members:

Develop self-confidence and self-respect and an appreciation of their own worth as individuals

Develop a faith for daily living based upon the teachings of Jesus, that they may all achieve their highest potential as children of God

Grow as responsible members of their families and as citizens of their communities

Appreciate that health of mind and body is a sacred gift and that physical fitness and mental well-being are conditions to be achieved and maintained

Recognize the worth of all persons and work for interracial and intergroup understanding

Develop a sense of world-mindedness and work for world understanding

Develop their capabilities for leadership and use them responsibly in their own groups and community life

Source: Pikes Peak Y/USO. "Proposed Corporate Goals for 1980–1985 and Objectives for 1980," Summer 1979.

PRESENT AND FUTURE: COMPETITION AND PRICING

For two reasons—one, to examine the parameters of a price increase being considered for the downtown facility, and, two, to assess potential pricing strategies for the proposed new facility—management analyzed 1979 membership rates for competing firms in the for-profit sector. Exhibit 20.6 reviews pricing for competitors, and Exhibit 20.7 reports results of 1979 membership rates from Ys in other cities; Exhibit 20.8 shows Pikes Peak Y's fees for 1982. Three Nautilus Fitness Centers, the Lynmar Racquet Club, the Point Athletic Club, and several health spas were located in the northeast/north sector of the community in 1982.

Exhibit 20.5

Y/USO CORPORATE GOALS FOR 1980–1990

1. **Youth.** To develop the foundation for adulthood through youth programs stressing values education.
2. **Family.** To develop and conduct programs that strengthen the traditional family structure as well as deal with the unique needs of all family units, both traditional and untraditional.
3. **Physical Fitness.** To provide a holistic approach to wellness for all ages and populations of the community.
4. **Physical Education and Recreation.** To provide opportunities for all ages to learn new skills, improve skill levels, enjoy healthful physical activities, and provide for worthy use of leisure time.
5. **Program Evaluation.** To structure an ongoing evaluation system to ensure optimum facility usage, program participation, and program validity.
6. **Marketing.** To keep the community continually apprised of Y/USO programs, membership benefits, and volunteer opportunities through a well-structured, cost-effective public relations program.
7. **Program Expansion.** To answer the demands of the community by providing services on a year-round basis that are accessible to different population centers.
8. **Facilities.** To ensure that all existing Y/USO facilities adhere to a total use concept to achieve maximum utilization by all members and expand as necessary to meet growing needs.
9. **Personnel, Lay.** To maintain a strong lay structure of dedicated, involved volunteers, committee people, and board members who actively support the Y/USO organization and its goals.
10. **Personnel, Staff.** To recruit and maintain well-qualified staff members who are dedicated to a high level of quality in Y/USO programs and facilities.
11. **Financial Administration/Development.** To pursue sound fiscal administration and a comprehensive financial development program to expand to meet the needs of a growing community.
12. **Relationships to National Organizations.** To participate actively and meet all qualifications necessary to maintain membership in the National YMCA, Big Brothers/Big Sisters, and USO.
13. **International Understanding.** To develop and conduct programs to increase international awareness, and understanding and to promote world peace.

Exhibit 20.6

COMPETITIVE RATE COMPARISON

NAUTILUS FITNESS CENTER

Memberships for persons over 12 years old. Open 24 hours a day, 7 days a week. Coed sauna, steam with eucalyptus, whirlpool and swimming

Exhibit 20.6 (Cont.)

pool 20' × 40', massage $7 for 30 minutes. Free nursery, free ballet, jazz, exercise, and beginning karate classes. Separate weight rooms for men and women.

Fee structure:

One-year membership	$210 one individual $120 for each additional family member Ex.: family of 4, $570.00
Two-year membership	$300 one individual $200 for the second family member and $180 for each additional family member Ex.: family of 4, $860 or $430 a year
VIP two-year membership	$400 one individual (renewable for $70 a year thereafter) $250 for the second family member $200 for any other family member Ex.: family of 4, $1,050 or $525 a year After two years renewable at $70 a year for one individual and additional family member fees Ex.: family of 4, $395 a year

EUROPEAN HEALTH SPA

Memberships for men/women 18 and over. Great number of weight machines (similar to Nautilus); sauna, steam, inhalation room with eucalyptus, whirlpool, ice pool, swimming pool 20' × 46', sun lamp rooms. Nursery is 50 cents an hour; massage is $7 for 30 minutes.

> Ladies day: Monday, Wednesday.
> Men's day: Tuesday, Thursday, Saturday until 2 P.M.
> Coed day: Friday, Saturday after 2 P.M., Sunday 10–6

Fee structure:

Matinee	6 months, $119 12 months, $250
Bronze	12 months, $340
Silver	18 months, $435 ($290 a year)
Gold	18 months, $595 ($396 a year)

Additional family members over 18, 50% reduction
At end of 18 months, renewable for $200 a year
$100-a-year renewal fee if you join on first visit

EXECUTIVE PARK ATHLETIC CLUB

Recreation facility specializing in handball/racquetball and gymnastics. Hours are 6 A.M. to 10 P.M. Monday through Friday and 9 A.M. to 6 P.M.

Exhibit 20.6 (Cont.)

Saturday and Sunday. Separate men's and women's carpeted locker rooms with sauna and whirlpool. Ten handball/racquetball courts, elevated carpeted running track, pro shop and weight room. A restaurant is located off the main lobby.

Fee structure:

Annual Fitness Membership with No Monthly Dues

Single	$150 annual fee
Couple	$275 annual fee
Child (under 18 years or with a parent)	$ 60
Junior/student (without a parent membership)	$125

The fitness memberships pay hourly court fees of $2.50 per hour regular time and $3.50 per hour prime time (6–8 A.M., 11–1 P.M., 4–8 P.M.)

Regular Full Facility Membership with No Court Fees

	One-Time Initiation Fee	Monthly Dues
Single	$150	$38
Couple	200	55
Junior/student	50	23 (no 4 to 8 P.M. M-F courts)

Gymnastics programs are available at an extra cost.

Fee schedule:

1 class, 1 day per week: $15.00
1 class, 2 days per week: $20.00
1 class, 3 days per week: $24.00
1 class, 4 days per week: $29.00

EPAC members, $2.00 off; additional children, $2.00 off.

GLORIA STEVENS FIGURE SALON

Women over 18 years, $25 introductory fee for 6 weeks' membership plan.

6 months, $152
12 months, $305

Exercise classes conducted every hour. Open 8 A.M. to 8 P.M. Monday through Friday, 8 A.M. to 2 P.M., Saturday. No sauna, whirlpool, or showers. Exercise machines, slant boards, dumbbells.

Exhibit 20.6 (Cont.)

LYNMAR RACQUET CLUB

Membership is currently 900 persons; cut off will be at 1,200. Deluxe facilities including lounge with fireplace, covered swimming pool, eight indoor tennis courts, four outdoor tennis courts, three racquetball courts, separate sauna, whirlpool for men and women, nursery (75¢ an hour), pro shop, weight room.

Plans include 11 Nautilus weight machines to be installed within four months and four new racquetball courts to be built by fall of 1980.

Fee structure:

Type	One-Time Initiation Fee	Monthly Dues
Family	$250	$30
Husband/wife	200	24
Individual	150	18
Junior (under 18)	100	11

Extra charge for tennis and racquetball courts.

Tennis	Racquetball
Prime time, $9 per hour, 5 to 10 P.M.	Prime time, $4 per hour, 5 to 8 P.M.
Regular time, $7 per hour	Regular time, $3 per hour

FOREST EDGE RACQUETBALL CLUB, LTD.

Breaking ground October 1979. Plans call for two racquetball/handball courts. Fitness center will have exercise machines and weights, whirlpool, towel service and lockers, lounge with T.V.

Fee Schedule:

Full Facility Membership (No Court Fees—Unlimited Use)

	Initiation Fee	Monthly Dues
Junior (13 to 18 years)	$ 40.00	$15.00
Individual (19 and over)	75.00	25.00
Couple	100.00	35.00
Family (3 to 4)	125.00	45.00
Family (5 or more)	150.00	55.00

Fee Schedule:

Fitness Membership
(Court Fees Extra: Prime, $4 per Hour, Regular, $3 per Hour)

Junior (13 to 18 years)	$ 26.00	$10.00
Individual	50.00	17.00

Exhibit 20.6 (Cont.)

Couple	66.00	23.00
Family (3 to 4)	83.00	30.00
Family (5 or more)	100.00	36.00

Dependents 19 and over may not be included in a family membership.

Court fees for general public use are regular time, $4 per hour; prime time, $5 per hour.

A MARKET STUDY IN 1978

During the summer term, 1978, three students in a local university's marketing research class conducted a study of 150 households in the city's northeast area, using personal interviews with respondents who were chosen using a random cluster sampling technique. Impetus for this project came from the Y's executive director, who wished to explore potential for a Y program and facility to serve that sector's rapidly increasing population. Selected key conclusions, excerpted from the team's report, are presented in Exhibit 20.9. The students concluded that theirs was an "extremely small sample of the total northeast area" and that "further research in the area must be done before intelligent management decisions can be made." Their "gut feeling" supported locating a facility in the survey area, and they all agreed that the "present location of the Y is a detrimental factor affecting use by the northeast residents."

MEETINGS BETWEEN Y MANAGEMENT AND PROSPECTIVE CONSULTANTS

On May 15, 1979, the executive director and Assistant Director James Klever met with local market research consultants, and, after reviewing the board's deliberations and desires, the director said intuition told him a second facility surely was needed. But what he and the board wanted were concrete data, not only to confirm or to reject their own judgment but also to present to outsiders, especially prospective donors and fundraisers, to generate public support for the new venture should such an effort be undertaken.

"We need to know whether the public, including Y members, really wants us to build a second major facility," he said. "But much more information is needed as well, such as where it should be located and what specific programs, activities, and facilities should be offered." Then he explained how the Y had significantly expanded its variety of activities, programs, and services in recent years, and how the majority of the non-Y public did not recognize the broadened role of the Y in the community. He pointed out that the Y tried to serve not ony a full range of the public's sports and recreational needs but that it also offered extensive educational, cultural, crafts, personal development, health, and other programs—everything from prenatal classes to senior citizens' programs. Looking at the current alphabetical list of Y program offerings, Klever smiled and said, "Everything, if not from A to Z, at least from aquatics and adult handicap classes to yoga and youth theaterworks."

Klever stated there was a whole other set of questions regarding financial matters that he would like answered. There were two types of financial questions. The first included issues such as what would be the construction and operating costs of the new facility, what fees should be charged, and what would be the break-even points.

The other set of financial questions related to alternatives for funding construction. Both Y executives wondered how responsive the community might be to a formal fundraising solicitation by a professional organization and what might be the other alternatives for financing the large capital construction project.

The day after their first meeting with Y management, the consultants drafted a proposed outline of what they understood the Y needed and what they thought their team could do. This outline provided a discussion agenda for the next meeting of managers and researchers.

A week later, the four met again. The researchers began by noting again the tentative nature of their proposal, the need to refine the topics and the process before a firm schedule and consulting fee could be established, and the issue of recognizing and trying to resolve the "everything depends on everything else" problem. An example of the complex and reverse cause-and-effect relationship, they pointed out, was that reliable costs and prices necessary for a valid break-even analysis could not be available until the size and cost of the facility were known. Yet the size of the facility depended on probable user demand, which could not be known until completion of the market survey, which, in turn, required some assumptions about prices.

Klever reminded the consultants that a major point to keep in mind was the Y's limited budget. He said that as a nonprofit community service organization with limited funds, the Y knew that it had to be content with a research study that might not be the most scientifically perfect or the best that money could buy. In reviewing the long list of topics in the consulting group's tentative proposal, he concluded that the cost of doing them all would exceed what the Y could afford to spend.

It became apparent that first and primary research contribution should focus on researching market demand and that financial analysis and fundraising matters ought to be postponed. The rest of the meeting was spent refining market research aspects of the proposal.

Klever said he would like to see two other issues addressed by the research study. First was whether the Y should begin "outreach programming" in the near future, and well before a new facility might be constructed. By this he meant the Y could take some of its programs and staff out to areas of the city far away from its downtown building. This would require renting or borrowing outlying facilities. "This is usually the first step in a Y expansion to a second location," he explained.

Exhibit 20.7

1979 MEMBERSHIP RATE SURVEY

MEMBERSHIP CLASSIFICATION	DENVER CENTRAL	OMAHA CENTRAL*	LINCOLN CENTRAL	OKLAHOMA CITY CENTRAL	WICHITA CENTRAL	PIKES PEAK Y/USO
Youth	$15 (0 to 12) $30 (3 to 17)	—	$60 (6 to 17)	$15 (6 to 14) very limited program	—	$45 (7 to 17)
Student	$90 (18 to 22) (full-time students)	—	—	$40 (15 to 17) $90 (18 to 29) (student)	$68 (18 up) (full-time students)	$75 (full-time students)
Young adult, male and female	—	$80 (15 to 22)	—	—	—	$102 (18 to 24)
Adult male	$155 (over 18)	$145 (over 18)	$120 (over 18)	$175 towel service	$110 (over 18)	$117 (over 25)
Adult female	$150 (over 18)	$145	$120	$175 towel service	$110	$117
Basic	—	$70 ($1.50–$2.00 extra each visit)	$12 (6 to 17) $18 (18 up) $24 family plus daily-use fee of 50 cents under 18 and $2 over 18	—	$15 (plus $3 a day, 18 and over)	—

Family	$235	$195	$198	$330 (husband/wife) $360 (2 children)	$175	$195 regular $126 special
Senior citizen	$85	$75	—	—	—	$75
Businessmen's and women's (not fitness centers)	$255 (men only, sauna and steam)	—	—	—	—	—
Men's fitness center	$335	$295	$246	$295	$325 or $530 (deluxe including 110 massages)	$285
Women's fitness center	—	$240	$189	—	—	$261
Men's fitness and family	—	$340	$300	$450, plus youth or student fee	—	$369
Women's fitness and family	—	$290	$267	—	—	$345
Family fitness center	—	$490	$369	—	—	$462
Nonmember day pass	$3.50	$4 regular, $8 fitness center	$4 regular, $5 fitness center	$4 regular, $10 fitness center	$5 regular	$3 regular, $6 fitness center
Military pass	—	—	—	—	—	$1 and $3
Military family	—	—	—	—	—	$141

*Building fund included in fee ranging from $5 to $25 per year.

Exhibit 20.8

PIKES PEAK Y/USO 1982 ANNUAL MEMBERSHIP FEES

MEMBERSHIP CATEGORY/AGES	RATES	ACW* DOWN	ACW MONTHLY
Youth	$ 48	$ 9.00	$ 4.50
Young adult, 18 to 24	117	20.50	10.25
Adult, 25 and up	144	25.00	12.50
Student, military, rank of E5 and below	84	15.00	7.50
Senior citizen, 65 and up	81	14.50	7.25
Family, parents and all children under 18	240	41.00	20.50
Military family, rank of E5 and below	156	27.00	13.50
Single-parent family	153	26.50	13.25
Men's fitness center, 18 and up	366	62.00	31.00
Women's fitness center, 18 and up	336	57.00	28.50
Family fitness center	594	100.00	50.00
Men's fitness center and family	474	80.00	40.00
Women's fitness center and family	444	75.00	37.50

*Automatic check withdrawal. Increases over the 1980 rates averaged close to 10%, ranging from 4% for a military family membership to an 18% increase for the men's fitness center.

Exhibit 20.9

SELECTED CONCLUSIONS, ADAPTED FROM THE 1978 STUDY

. . . there is a significant demand for a facility such as the YMCA in the northeast area.

. . . 69% indicated they would be willing to support a facility on a membership basis if it offered activities they would use.

. . . many of the activities children were involved in were more inclined toward the types of programs that the YMCA offers or could offer.

. . . their ideal facility would be one within 15 minutes of their homes.

. . . a significant number of people would . . . support a facility if fees were similar to the YMCA's current rates.

. . . 75% planned to remain in the northeast area for at least the next five years.

. . . top 10 preferred activities of respondents (108 answering this question) were swimming (52% expressed this as one of their preferences), tennis (23%), skating (9%), hiking and camping (9%), dance (7%), running (6%), basketball (5%), racquetball (4%), skiing (4%), and arts and crafts (4%).

Source: Marketing research study in conjunction with the Pikes Peak Y/USO, summer 1978.

What he would like to know was (1) whether the public would want and use outreach programming and (2) which specific types of programs and activities would be desired. For example, would the Y have to rent a large facility like a high school gymnasium or swimming pool, or would people out in mostly residential areas want family-type activities such as father-son "Indian Guides," cooking classes, and so on?

The second thing he wanted in the study was feedback on the Y's service and image in the community. "We never have had such an extensive survey of both Y members and nonmembers as this study promises," he observed, "and it would be a shame not to use the opportunity to find out how we are doing, how we are perceived." Admitting that an image analysis was not part of the original and primary purpose of the market study, he wondered if it could be incorporated.

Extensive discussion then ensued about the relevant geographic market. If a new facility were built, in what general area of the city should it be located—northeast, northwest, southeast, southwest?

The Y administration had talked with a number of the city's leading developers, some of whom were members of the board of directors, and they all confirmed the intuition that the major locus of new development should be northeasterly.

The research group, which had consulted with the economic development department of the Colorado Springs chamber of commerce, studying the city's growth patterns, agreed that the major growth forces converged toward the northeast. Private developers and the city's planning officials confirmed this judgment. Klever said that money and time would be saved if the research effort assumed that any new facility would be located in the northeast, so it was agreed to proceed on that assumption.

The 90-minute meeting ended with the plan to put in writing a refined proposal incorporating the issues discussed.

CONSULTANTS' PROPOSAL

A few days later, the consulting team met to consider and draft the proposal to the Y. They quickly agreed that the project was feasible and worth bidding on. Two had served on the Y board; one had been on the design committee for the 1973 building. All knew a large number of local business and community leaders, including those most knowledgeable about and supportive of the Y. One member of the team, a young woman academic, was interested in seeing that the questionnaire and focus groups addressed the special needs of working women. And while all viewed this project as a professional business agreement, they also were personally interested in helping "their" Y as a community service. Therefore, they agreed to do the study for $7,000, about one-third their usual fee for such studies.

Y BRANCH FACILITY FEASIBILITY STUDY, 1980

Presented in August 1980, the consultants' report, some 300 pages in length, including computer printout appendices, came up with three major conclusions:

1. There is strong demand from Y and non-Y members for a second, full-scale facility in northeast Colorado Springs.
2. There is strong demand also for immediate outreach programming even before a new facilty might be built.
3. Because of its facility, staff, and programs, the Y enjoys an outstanding image and reputation in our community.

The report followed with these recommendations:

1. Begin immediate communitywide programming, especially in the northeast area, following the specific program requests enumerated in this report.
2. Begin immediate planning for the construction of a second building in the northeast section, carefully considering the specifics as to facilities and location described in this report.
3. Improve the Y's service by building on strengths that are apparent and responding to the dissatisfactions enumerated in this report.

Appendix 20A contains selected narrative and key figures from the consultants' report.

DECISION POINT, 1980

As he and the board considered results and recommendations of the study, Klever offered several observations: "It isn't unusual for a community to have more than one Y facility in operation, and most cities this size probably have two or three buildings. If we decide to build another unit, I expect it will include a swimming pool, a gymnasium, racquetball courts, and office space."

When queried about facility size and utilization, he speculated: "It will be at least half the size of the current one, which was built 10 years ago, and hopefully will have an outdoor area or be located near a park. Here (downtown) we are packed to overflowing and, when we think of expanding, we want to look at an area where we can serve the family most. That's what made us look to the residential area to the northeast. About 17 percent of present membership is made up of those residents, but the highest population density of young families is in that area, and, if we really want to have an impact on the families, we need to go there."

Y programs in the northeast were held in churches, schools, a bowling alley, a skating rink, and other rented accommodations. "We know the people want us out there. The question is, how much will it cost to build another facility and can we raise that much money? Those are the two issues to be analyzed. Soon we'll have a representative of the national YMCA visit here to help us evaluate those critical questions. We'll tell him what sorts of programs we plan to offer in the northeast area, and he'll tell us how much space we need and how much it will cost."

Given that circumstances favored taking the next steps of deciding whether to build and what programs were most desirable, resolving the capital funding barrier loomed as a significant undertaking. "We've invited a professional fundraising organization to visit us in the spring [1981] to see how much money can be raised for construction. Then, we anticipate a final decision to be made in June by the Y's board of directors."

IMPLEMENTING THE DECISION, 1981–1982

During the fall of 1981 an agreement was reached between the Y and Junior Achievement (JA) to undetake jointly the capital funding campaign for a building to be shared by the two entities. After deciding to commence a program to raise $2 million in donations in January 1982, the Y/USO board president reported in the local press, "The money will be combined with a recent $1.75 million foundation (a local, philanthropic institution) gift to build a 47,000-square-foot structure to house both organizations." The press conference buzzed with comments about the current recession, or as some called it, "depression," and many questions were asked about probabilities of success in such an environment. "We are very optimistic that the city's residents will rally to this cause," the JA president said, "because we have here two organizations that have served this city well and will continue to serve the needs of youth and families in the future."

The Y/USO president talked of plans to include a large gymnasium, a swimming pool of a size similar to that in the downtown facility, four locker rooms, and handball/racquetball courts. The Y/USO would occupy 39,000 square feet with the remaining 8,000 square feet for JA, which would have five meeting rooms, a shop, a materials area, and office space.

"More than 30,000 persons are using the downtown Y/USO annually," the Y/USO president continued, "while JA provides economic and career education to 3,500 youngsters each year. And 60 percent of our client populations, for the Y and JA combined, live in the northeastern section of the city." Two well-known local leaders, one from the civilian and one from the military, were appointed to head the six-month capital campaign.

Fundraising handout materials were prepared to explain in question-and-answer format the nature of the Y and JA, and reasons for the solicitation. "The purpose of Junior Achievement," read one paragraph, "and its five major programs is: To provide practical and realistic education and experience in the private enterprise economic system." And the handout contained endorsements by James H. Rosenfield, president of the CBS Television Network; Frank Cary, chairman of IBM Corporation; and David T. Kearns, president of Xerox Corporation. JA's activities were programmed to serve high school students. Efforts were targeted toward large corporate and foundation gifts as well as toward smaller givers: "A Sack of Nails = $1.00; A Stack of Bricks = $5.00; Some Building Boards = $10.00; and Concrete for a Foundation = $25.00," proclaimed the outside of the contribution envelope. Signifying the joining together of these two service organizations was the logo shown in Exhibit 20.10.

Exhibit 20.10

JOINT LOGO FOR CAPITAL DEVELOPMENT CAMPAIGN

Y/JA Development Campaign

ADDING NAUTILUS EQUIPMENT AT THE DOWNTOWN Y

In 1982, three Nautilus Fitness Centers were operating—in the north/northeast residential sections—and one was scheduled for a fall opening downtown. Lynmar Racquet Club and Point Athletic Club were enjoying growth in total number of members, and numerous women's spas, while not flourishing, continued to attract new customers through special promotional campaigns. Plans were made by Y management to add Nautilus equipment, a decision based upon members' favorable reactions to a December 1981 survey.

Appendix 20A

EXCERPTS FROM CONSULTANTS' REPORT

RESEARCH METHODOLOGY

Questionnaire Design

Choosing the precise questions, phrases, and words must be done with an eye on not only what the fundamental objectives are, but also on how the interviews will be conducted and by whom and on how the answers will be tabulated, arrayed, and compared, whether by machine processing or manually.

Two focus groups of 8 to 10 persons each were formed. Participants were chosen from a cross section of northeast residents who were interested in and knowledgeable about the Y, either as active Y members or as experts aware of our community's development and the Y's role therein. The purposes of meeting with the focus groups were to get their outsider's views of (1) the study's ultimate objectives that had been developed up to that point, (2) what issues might have been overlooked, (3) what impact the study might make on the community, and (4) what and how communitywide developments should influence the study—all for

Appendix 20A (Cont.)

the general purpose of learning how the Y, through this study, could improve its service to the community. Many specific research idea improvements resulted, with the overwhelming general conclusion that time and circumstances mandated serious consideration of constructing a second Y facility. Almost four hours of audio tapes were made of the two meetings, and these were given to Mr. Klever.

The next step was drafting the first questionnaire and discussing it with Mr. Klever and his staff. A second version and yet a third followed; then, there was another evaluation meeting with Y management. After the fourth version was completed, it was given as a pretest interview to a dozen people. The fourth draft was also evaluated by another professional market research specialist from the local college. Then, the fifth and final draft of the in-person questionnaire was completed.

The next three steps included (1) redoing the questionnaire for mail and telephone surveys, (2) choosing the sample interviewees, and (3) hiring and training interviewers. All three steps were undertaken simultaneously.

The Sample

Three sample groups were chosen:

1. 248 households for personal interviews
2. 65 Y members for mail questionnaires
3. 56 Y members for telephone interviews

Concentration of interview households was in city ZIP codes 17 and 18; other ZIPs included were 07, 08, 09, 15, and 19.

Statistical reliability is based upon the sample of 248, even though these were not entirely randomly chosen. To illustrate, if 80 percent of these heads of household respond "yes" to a certain question, then the standard error of that 80 percent figure is plus or minus 2.5 percent, or one standard error; thus, one can say that we would be 67 percent certain that the "true" percentage lies within plus or minus 2.5 points of 80 percent, that is, between 77.5 percent and 82.5 percent. Using the two standard error bound, or 5 percent, one could say that the odds are 20 to 1 that the true percentage is between 75 percent and 85 percent. Strict randomness was not observed because replacement households were sometimes chosen for not-at-homes and refusals.

Collecting the Data

Difficulty, time, and expense of conducting interviews decline in order from personal, to telephone, to mail interviews.

Appendix 20A (Cont.)

Twenty-six door-to-door interviews were first conducted by us personally to understand and interpret both the process and the responses encountered by the hired interviewers. We also handled all the mail questionnaires.

Three interviewers were hired and trained to conduct the bulk of personal and telephone interviews. Each had either prior professional interview experience or substantial academic background. Their special preparation for this project consisted of touring the Y building with a staff member, studying the questionnaire, giving test interviews, and participating in training sessions with us. They were provided with a set of written instructions and a packet of nine materials.

The interviewers, supervised on a daily basis, were directed to contact a random sample of five households in about a five-square-block area carefuly selected by judgmental sampling. They were coached to seek a balance of factors such as sex, single-family versus multifamily residences, day versus night, and weekday versus weekend interviews.

For every interview completed, it was necessary, on the average, to approach about four different residences. On the assumption that the reasons people gave for declining interviews might provide further community comment on the Y, the interviewers filled out a worksheet documenting the households contacted but refusing interviews.

The average personal and telephone interview lasted about 30 minutes.

The 369 families surveyed resided on approximately 300 different streets throughout the northeast quadrant of the city.

Data Analysis

Some parts of the study, particularly those relating to near-term Y programming, were manually tabulated and reported to management as the data were collected, because of the immediate need to begin outreach programming. All the final numerical data were computer-tabulated using the Statistical Package for the Social Sciences, a group of programs developed over the past 10 years by social science researchers, computer scientists, and statisticians. The availability of this data modification, file handling, data description tool simplified considerably the analytic work.

ANALYSIS OF RESPONSES

Introduction

The Y's management will find the lengthy appendix detail behind the summary findings in this section helpful for various purposes beyond this

Appendix 20A (Cont.)

study's focus and extending over a long time. The Y can best judge, in light of its needs and purposes, how best to summarize and organize this secondary material. The lode of raw data is deep and rich—and it is all in the appendices. We will keep the computer program and input deck, and if the Y should want future assistance in processing data, we will be glad to accommodate.

This section summarizes and analyzes the major interview results. It follows in sequence the questions on the forms. The responses reported here come primarily from the computer printouts, but also occasionally from the open-ended questions. Major findings are stressed, with some of the less relevant background material grouped together and summarized briefly.

Personal Interviews Analysis—Community at Large

Zip Code Distribution. Residences of people interviewed in person were distributed throughout the northeast quadrant of the city, with major concentration within a strip along but mostly north and east of Academy Boulevard.

Interviewee Gender. Female interviewees accounted for 69 percent of the sample, males 28 percent, and couples 3 percent. Although we did sample at various times of the day and evening, weekdays and weekends, interviewers found that females most often answered the door and gave the interview information on behalf of the family.

Demographic Data Concerning Children in Household. Of the households interviewed, 56 percent of the families reported one or more boys under age 18 living at home, while 49 percent reported one or more girls. Less than half of the sample population indicated that no children lived at home. Many of the childless households were those of retired persons.

Only 10 to 15 percent of the households reported having children who attended year-round schools. We assume, therefore, that demands for children's programming center on after-school and summer programming for the greater majority of households.

Family Recreation Activities. Families were asked to report their present recreational activities, so that the Y might know more about the recreational profile of people it seeks to serve. The five most frequently mentioned activities were swimming, fishing, camping, skiing and tennis (tied), and hiking, in that order. A ranking of 23 activities is in Table 1.

Membership and Y Use in Personal Interview Sample. Under 9 percent of the 248 households included in the personal interview sample claimed to have a Y member; over half these members used the downtown Y three or more times each week.

Of the group with Y memberships, most maintained either single or

Appendix 20A (Cont.)

Table 1

FAMILY RECREATIONAL ACTIVITIES
($n = 248$)

ACTIVITIES	NUMBER OF MENTIONS	RANK ORDER
Arts and crafts	84	(6)
Baseball/softball	57	(12)
Basketball	56	(13)
Bowling	80	(7)
Camping	103	(3)
Climbing	19	(18)
Dance	43	(16)
Fishing	114	(2)
Football	40	(17)
Golfing	78	(8)
Handball	11	(19)
Hiking	88	(5)
Hunting	54	(15)
Ice hockey	5	(20)
Physical conditioning	71	(10)
Racquetball	58	(11)
Running	73	(9)
Skating	71	(10)
Skiing	94	(4)
Soccer	55	(14)
Swimming	161	(1)
Tennis	94	(4)
Volleyball	24	(19)

family memberships, not fitness center memberships. Interestingly, half the total random sample indicated that a fitness center would be a desirable feature of a new Y facility. Approximately 74 percent of all respondents were unfamiliar with the downtown Y facility, citing their newness to Colorado Springs, the inconvenient distance of the Y from their homes, the expense of using the Y, and lack of time as reasons for their unfamiliarity. Slightly over a quarter of the interviewees had had experience with the Y during the last three years, mainly through their children's involvement in such Y programming as basketball, camp, or swimming.

Interviewees were also queried about other club memberships; one-third responded in the affirmative that they maintained other club memberships, chief among them the Peterson Field facility, an indication of the heavy military population of the northeast area of the city. Nautilus came in as the second most heavily used additional club with many interviewees praising the Nautilus equipment and the relatively low annual fee.

Prefacility Y Programming in Northeast. Y management and

Appendix 20A (Cont.)

board members expressed interest in gauging response to Y prefacility programming in advance of possible Y construction in northeast Colorado Springs, that is, the feasibility of offering swimming lessons, fitness classes, or any of a host of program possibilities under the auspices of the Y, housed in a northeast educational or recreational facility. Interviewees expressed overwhelming approval of such programming, with 83 percent responding affirmatively to the idea. Individual open exercise and organized group exercise and sports programs surfaced as the major program preferences. These were followed closely by learn-to-swim programs and weight-loss classes (Table 2).

It is not surprising that individual preferences for programming clustered around physical fitness types of activities because this general category of programming emerged as an important choice for 66 percent of those interviewed, followed by adult programs (62 percent), individual programs (55 percent), family programs (50 percent), children's programs (48 percent), arts and crafts (45 percent), and educational programs (36 percent). A significant comment from many families: "Our family is in-

Table 2

PREFACILITY PROGRAMMING PREFERENCES
($n = 248$)

PROGRAMMING PREFERENCES	NUMBER OF MENTIONS	RANK ORDER
Dance	72	(9)
Day care	43	(15)
Elderly, special programs	29	(18)
Exercise (group) and sports programs	113	(2)
Exercise (individual) and sports programs	142	(1)
Gymnastics	88	(7)
Parent-child togetherness programs (including singles)	75	(8)
Physical fitness programs, specialized (e.g., cardiovascular)	92	(5)
Preschool educational	32	(17)
Self-defense/martial arts	67	(10)
Single parent-child programs	21	(19)
Smoking clinics	46	(14)
Sports conditioning programs	41	(16)
Stress management	59	(11)
Swim programs (adults and children)	112	(3)
Swim and gym (preschool)	58	(12)
Weight-loss classes	102	(4)
Year-round student programs (break periods)	56	(13)
Youth sports leagues	89	(6)

Appendix 20A (Cont.)

volved in so many activities now, we hardly need more ways of organizing our lives."

Reaction to Projected Y Facility. With 238 interviewees, or 96 percent of the random sample, applauding the idea of constructing a new Y, the personal interview segment indicates strong support of a new facility. Most significant, not 1 person out of 248 disapproved of the idea. The numerous expressions of excitement in the "comments" section of this question reinforce the community's enthusiasm for the prospect of a new facility.

Significant differences of opinion occurred only when people were asked to indicate those features and amenities of a new Y that might be important to **their** families.

Predictably, a large swimming pool, gymnasium, weight room, tennis courts, arts and crafts area, racquetball courts, and an indoor track were mentioned by a large number of those interviewed. A surprising number of individuals mentioned sauna and whirlpool followed closely by a youth game room as desirable amenities for their families. Most of the people we talked to were familiar with the fitness center concept. About 58 percent favored a fitness center component in the new Y, and 109 of

Table 3

FACILITIES PREFERRED IN PROJECTED NORTHEAST Y
$(n = 248)$

FACILITY	NUMBER EXPRESSING PREFERENCE	% OF TOTAL SAMPLE	RANK ORDER
Arts and crafts area	117	47%	(6)
Child care center	77	31	(13)
Fitness center	143	58	(3)
Gymnasium	164	66	(2)
Health food/snack area	75	30	(14)
Racquetball/handball courts	115	46	(7)
Running path (outdoor)	87	35	(11)
Sauna	107	43	(9)
Steamroom	62	25	(15)
Swimming pool (large)	224	90	(1)
Swimming pool (warm, small)	80	32	(12)
Tennis courts (outdoor)	123	50	(5)
Track (indoor)	107	43	(9)
Track (paved, outdoor)	47	19	(16)
Weight room	138	56	(4)
Whirlpool	108	44	(8)
Youth game room	94	38	(10)

Appendix 20A (Cont.)

the 143 who mentioned a fitness center believed that such a center should be restricted to adult use (Table 3).

Location and Transportation Preferences. Possibly because issues of energy and automobile use have been a major national issue during 1979 and 1980, the people who consented to the personal interview were most eager to share their perceptions of where a projected Y should be located and what sorts of transportation issues loomed large in their individual family situations. The location and transportation preference section of the interview is one segment in which the verbatim answers proved more telling than the tabular data (Tables 4 and 5).

Table 4

LOCATION

$(n = 248)$

Location Description	IMPORTANT		UNIMPORTANT	
	Number	% of Total	Number	% of Total
Near a park	150	61%	98	39%
Near Academy Boulevard	92	37	56	63
Near College Parkway	51	21	197	79
Near major shopping center	36	15	212	85

Table 5

TRANSPORTATION

Type of Transportation	YES		NO	
	Number	% of Total	Number	% of Total
Need bicycle access	198	80%	50	20%
Bus	198	80	50	20

Mention of Colorado Springs' busiest thoroughfare, Academy Boulevard, produced extremely negative responses among the interviewees, even those who registered responses of "unimportant" at the suggestion of an Academy Boulevard location for the projected Y. Many of these people seemed to take the existence of the street as an unpleasant but inevitable fact of life. However, almost every person who mentioned Academy as a potentially acceptable location stipulated that a new Y must be located on his or her side of this busy thoroughfare because of safety factors. "Academy is a death trap" was not an untypical comment.

A majority of people commented on access for bicyclists and pedes-

Appendix 20A (Cont.)

trians. Because many women not employed outside the home were interviewed, we received myriad comments about the difficulty of chaufferring children to and from a distant facility. Although 80 percent of the sample indicated a need for public transportation access, most complained that bus service was inadequate in the northeast section of town.

Supervised Children's Programs. In this category 28 percent of the households favored summer day camps, 27 percent after-school programs, 22 percent year-round school vacation activities, and 20 percent day care for young children. Approximately one out of every five households interviewed was open to a more desirable child care or youth supervision program than was currently available. Those who spoke of the need for supervised children's programs were working parents, many of these working mothers, and often single parents. However, fees and transportation arrangements both ranked high on the list of these families' concerns.

Pricing and Membership. After interviewees were given an opportunity to peruse a partial list of current monthly fees at the Y, 209 persons—84 percent of the total random sample—endorsed the present fee structure. Eleven percent judged the structure too high, and 5 percent said it was low for what one gets in the present Y membership package.

Although the pricing and membership question proved to be one of the more sensitive interview areas, with many individuals pausing to comment on the state of the economy and their personal financial situations, 53 percent of the total sample said they would join, 32 percent were undecided, and 15 percent said they would not join if a new Y were constructed in the northeast part of town. Many of the undecided interviewees, while endorsing the idea of a new Y, expressed concern about their personal budgets. A majority of those who responded negatively suggested that their family's recreational needs were well served by either military or existing park and recreation facilities.

The 21 Y members included in the random sample were questioned about continued use of the downtown Y should a northeastern Y materialize; 5 said they would discontinue using the present facility, 2 said they would continue using the downtown facility only, 9 said they would join both, and 3 said they would want different types of memberships. Proximity of the downtown Y to the workplace was cited as the chief reason for maintaining their downtown Y membership even if a new Y were built in their part of town.

Demographic Profile of Personal Interviewees. The random sample reflects a relatively mobile population; 53 percent reported living in Colorado Springs more than five years but only 31 percent at their present residence. In this relatively new and rapidly growing section of the city, 29 percent had resided in their present dwelling for less than one year. When asked whether they expected to be in Colorado Springs for

Appendix 20A (Cont.)

the next five years, 84 percent of the sample answered affirmatively.

Our random sample appears consistent for U.S. Census Bureau data for the Colorado Springs Standard Metropolitan Statistical Area. The age group occurring most frequently (the mode) was in the 26- to 35-year-old segment.

Although very few of those interviewed represented what sociologists term the "professions"—law, medicine, engineering, and the like—53 percent of the families reported a total annual household income of $25,000 or above. Of families interviewed in the random sample, 20 percent reported a military retiree member of the household. A majority of retirees in the sample, all military, were currently working in civilian occupations, several in a self-employed capacity.

Eight and a half percent of respondents were military, and 21 percent of their spouses were military. Twelve percent were single and 88 percent married.

Community Image of the Y. Over 200 people responded when asked what was the first thought that comes to their mind about the Y. Even though many people had limited firsthand knowledge of the Y—its location, programs, personnel, history, or projected plans—impressions of the institution were uniformly positive. "A great place to get in shape!" "Keeps the kids out of trouble!" "Fantastic program!" suggest repeated variations of positive comments.

The Y is viewed as a good place to exercise, with a fine facility, serving children especially well. The Y is seen as responsive to community needs; it has generated predominantly positive feelings, even in those persons who have not had direct contact with it.

The few negative comments about the Y's image centered upon its downtown location, its crowded conditions, and the presence of "undesirable elements" in the Y.

Respondents frequently used this opportunity to urge the construction of a second facility.

Mail/Telephone Interviews Analysis—Y Members

Family Recreation Activities. The five most frequently mentioned recreational activities of Y family members are, in order, swimming, racquetball, running, camping, and hiking (Table 6). The recreational profile of Y members differs somewhat from that of the community-at-large, as can be seen by comparing the ranking of 23 family activities in Tables 6 and 1.

Profile of Y Member Activity. Consistent with our community's high mobility, about 46 percent of respondents have belonged to the Y less than two years and more than 84 percent for five years or less.

By far, the largest percentage of respondents—53 percent—held

Appendix 20A (Cont.)

Table 6

FAMILY RECREATIONAL ACTIVITIES OF Y MEMBERS
(n = 121)

ACTIVITIES	NUMBER OF MENTIONS	RANK ORDER
Arts and crafts	15	(15)
Baseball/softball	16	(14)
Basketball	27	(10)
Bowling	31	(9)
Camping	49	(4)
Climbing	3	(21)
Dance	10	(18)
Fishing	37	(8)
Football	9	(19)
Golfing	19	(13)
Handball	6	(20)
Hiking	47	(5)
Hunting	13	(17)
Ice hockey	1	(22)
Physical conditioning	44	(6)
Racquetball	61	(2)
Running	57	(3)
Skating	26	(11)
Skiing	49	(4)
Soccer	24	(12)
Swimming	78	(1)
Tennis	43	(7)
Volleyball	14	(16)

family memberships, and the next largest was single memberships—27 percent. Surprisingly, while only 8 percent held fitness center memberships, 56 percent said they wanted a fitness center in the new facility.

Seventy-one percent had attended Y programs in the last three years. The most frequently attended classes have been swimming lessons, swimming, lifeline, and arts and crafts.

Twenty-two percent of respondents belonged to other clubs, less than the 34 percent of the community-at-large interviewees who belonged to other clubs. The most used other clubs were, in order, Nautilus, Air Force Academy, Racquet Club, Lynmar, and Executive Park.

Prefacility Programming in Northeast. Interestingly, a somewhat smaller percentage of Y members than the community-at-large approve community outreach programming before a new facility is built—75 percent and 83 percent, respectively. Still only 7 percent disapprove.

The great majority of comments solicited for this question said favorable things like "Great idea," "Get going," and "The community really needs it."

Appendix 20A (Cont.)

Asked to choose among six general types of prefacility programming they desired, respondents selected, in order, physical fitness, adult programs, children's programs, family programs, educational programs, and art and crafts.

To gain more detailed programming suggestions, interviewees were asked to choose among 19 specific programs. The first five choices were, in order, individual exercise and sports programs, group exercise and sports programs, adult and children swim programs, specialized physical fitness programs, and gymnastics.

Reaction to Projected Y Facility in Northeast Colorado Springs. An overwhelming majority of respondents approve the building of a second facility in northeast Colorado Springs—90 percent. Only 3 percent disapprove.

The five facilities most desired in a new facility are, in order, large swimming pool, gymnasium, indoor track, racquetball/handball courts, and weight room. The ranking of respondents' desires for 17 facilities is in Table 7. Some differences in preferences between Y members and the community-at-large show up, with the former preferring more than the latter an outdoor running path and indoor track. But the community-at-large desires, more than Y members, arts and crafts and a fitness center.

Table 7

FACILITIES PREFERRED IN PROJECTED NORTHEAST Y
($n = 121$)

FACILITY	NUMBER EXPRESSING PREFERENCE	RANK ORDER
Arts and crafts area	47	(14)
Child care center	35	(15)
Fitness center	68	(8)
Gymnasium	91	(2)
Health food/snack area	52	(12)
Racquetball/handball courts	86	(4)
Running path (outdoor)	71	(6)
Sauna	58	(10)
Steamroom	47	(14)
Swimming pool (large)	103	(1)
Swimming pool (warm, small)	55	(11)
Tenis courts (outdoor)	63	(9)
Track (indoor)	87	(3)
Track (paved, outdoor)	47	(14)
Weight room	72	(5)
Whirlpool	70	(7)
Youth game room	49	(13)

Appendix 20A (Cont.)

The appropriateness of a fitness center in a new neighborhood Y is an important consideration, for which the study's findings can be summarized this way: 58 percent of the community-at-large favors a fitness center and ranks it third among 17 types of facilities; fifty-six percent of Y-member respondents favor it and rank it eighth. However, it should be noted that only 8 percent of the same Y respondents now have a fitness center membership, and 9 percent have combination memberships, some of which surely include the fitness center. Seventy-six percent of the personal interviewees who want a fitness center think it should be for adults only, while 66 percent of Y member respondents think so.

Pricing and Membership. About current Y fees, 83 percent said they were about right, 9 percent said high, and 8 percent said low. A number of margin comments were made to the effect that most fees were reasonable except for the high price for fitness centers.

To the question whether they would join the new Y, 71 percent said yes, 14 percent said no, and 15 percent said maybe. The majority of comments was that the decision to join would most depend on the new facility's proximity to their home.

Asked how they would alter their membership and what kind of joint membership policy would be desirable, if a new facility were built, 52 percent would want full membership in both facilities and 23 percent would discontinue using the downtown Y. The great majority of comments was that one parent, working downtown, would want a single membership downtown, but the family, especially for children, would want a family or children's membership in the new branch.

Overall Impressions/Evaluation of Y. The first thought about the Y that comes to members' minds is extremely favorable. Typical phrases were "excellent facility," "good place," "a positive feeling." Out of 112 responses to this question, only two were definitely negative.

About a dozen members said their overall favorable impression was marred only by overcrowded conditions.

The three things members like most, and they were chosen about equally, are facilities, staff, and programs. More specifically, the following were most frequently cited: friendliness of staff, pool, racquetball courts, cleanliness, and variety of programs.

The three things members dislike most are overcrowding (especially racquetball courts), location, and inadequate parking, in that order. Also frequently mentioned were inadequately supervised children running too freely, unhelpful staff especially at front desk during busy times, excessive privileges given nonmembers, and thefts.

Overwhelmingly, members urged that the best single improvement the Y could make would be to build the second new facility.

21

YMCA/USO OF THE PIKES PEAK REGION (B)

Since its founding in 1878, the Pikes Peak Y enjoyed steady membership growth by serving the health and fitness needs of Colorado Springs and surrounding communities [see YMCA/USO of the Pikes Peak Region (A)] and emphasizing many special programs designed to provide recreation for the youth of the region. To help meet rising demand for Y services in the populous northeast part of the city, the Garden Ranch facility was built in the early 1980s. In October 1986, expansion including an instructional pool and a second gymnasium was completed at the Garden Ranch Center, at a cost of approximately $850,000, funded by a grant from a local foundation and contributions from two other Colorado foundations. Exhibit 21.1 summarizes selected principles guiding the Y's planning and program development.

Exhibit 21.1

PRECEPTS FOR PROGRAM DEVELOPMENT

Corporate Goal   to provide quality programs and services that make a significant difference in the human condition of people of all ages and backgrounds in the Pikes Peak region.

. . .

Conceptual Statements   Young people should be able to develop the foundation for adulthood through programs designed for family mem-

Exhibit 21.1 (Cont.)

bers to participate in wholesome activities which teach values and human relationships, as well as serve recreational needs.... Children and young adults from low-income families should have the opportunity to enjoy programs at little or no cost to them, which will prepare them to become responsible, caring, and healthy adults, both mentally and physically.

Source: Corporate goals, 1985–1990, internal document.

ENLARGING MARKETING'S ROLE

After the person who had been handling a combination of public relations and marketing responsibilities resigned, Y president Jim Klever moved to enlarge the scope of the organization's marketing position, enlisting Y board members' assistance in writing a job description and seeking qualified individuals for the post. Exhibit 21.2 presents selected portions of the position description. From a field of several applicants, Judith Lakin (bachelor of arts degree in fine arts, University of San Diego, and MBA, University of Colorado, Colorado Springs, with emphases in marketing and finance) was appointed in September 1985. Her job experience included almost five years—recently as marketing director/media director—at PRACO, Ltd., a Colorado Springs advertising agency, production coordinator at Gazo Family Clock Factory in California, and a brief stint as acting registrar at San Diego Museum of Art following graduation from college in 1978.

"When I came aboard," Judi said, "my task was to develop and implement a marketing process for the entire organization, not just publicity, public relations,

Exhibit 21.2

JOB DESCRIPTION, DIRECTOR OF MARKETING, PIKES PEAK Y/USO

...

Reports to   **President.**

Supervises   **Publicity coordinator and any contract support services.**

Function ... responsible for directing the communications and marketing functions of the YMCA/USO for the Pikes Peak region. This includes public relations, media relations, promotional efforts, and internal communications.... also responsible for membership sales to corporations and providing service to corporate membership accounts.

... for marketing and actions necessary for the recruitment of new members and retention of existing members....

Source: Internal document.

and advertising, but also member and employee communication, product and service evaluation, pricing strategies, distribution systems, and systematic, ongoing research." YMCA research projects often included examination of competitive factors and always embraced consideration of how well the Y was serving its clientele.

A SURVEY OF PUBLIC PERCEPTIONS

In the Y's service area, health club activities were very popular, and competition was intense among the numerous athletic facilities. Also, Colorado Springs' mild climate was conducive to year-round outdoor activities for a fitness-minded public. Since the recent bankruptcy of one high-profile health club in the city had increased public wariness in joining such organizations, Judi Lakin worked out an arrangement with a University of Colorado marketing class to conduct research into public awareness of and attitudes toward the Pikes Peak Y, particularly to examine respondents' and YMCA staff's perceptions of various service characteristics. Exhibit 21.3 contains excerpts from the students' report.

Exhibit 21.3

SELECTED PASSAGES FROM YMCA SURVEY

... Management is aware ... that it would be very easy to become complacent in light of the Y's relative success as compared with other fitness organizations ... management is committed to its ongoing effort to identify and meet the changing recreation and fitness needs of the society. The management team also realizes that there may exist a significant gap between employee impressions about member priorities and satisfaction and feelings of members themselves. ... it is important that the management and employees of the YMCA see significant differences, if any, in the areas of service importance and performance so they can work effectively to close these gaps. This survey was designed to identify gaps and provide data for use in designing programs. ...

RESEARCH DESIGN/METHODOLOGY

In order to measure customer image of YMCA services versus the perceived image by Y employees, 22 bipolar semantic differential scale questions were used. The first 10 questions asked the respondent to rate various service characteristics according to level of importance. Throughout the survey, the employees were asked to respond based on how *they felt* the customer would answer. Service characteristics were rated from 1 (not very important) to 5 (very important) and included

- Responsiveness to your needs
- Reliable service
- Quality of facilities

Exhibit 21.3 (Cont.)

- Accessibility of services
- Customized, individualized attention
- Information about available services
- Price of service or fees
- An appropriately skilled staff
- Courteous service
- Prompt service

Part II of the survey asked the respondents to *evaluate* the same service characteristics in order to compare the importance levels with the service evaluations. The same rating scale of 1 (unfavorable rating) to 5 (favorable rating) was provided. The last two semantic differential questions gave the respondent an opportunity to assign an overall rating of how well the Y meets his or her fitness needs and generally how satisfied the respondent is with the services provided by the Pikes Peak YMCA. An open-ended question was provided to allow the respondent freedom to describe the services provided in his or her own words.

The remaining five questions provided a customer profile which indicated facilities used and demographic information, such as sex, age, household income, and member versus nonmember classification.

Customers were selected at random by YMCA staff members. Users of the Y were asked upon entry or exit to spend a few minutes completing the surveys so that the Y could identify its weaknesses. Employee surveys were distributed by the branch managers at each location (downtown and Garden Ranch) at their respective staff meetings. Employees were advised in the instructions to the survey to answer the questions from the customer's standpoint rather than their own. This procedure allowed for the comparison of "how *we* think we are doing" to "how the *customer* thinks we are doing" at providing quality service.

FINDINGS

There were 146 valid user responses, 81 percent at the downtown YMCA, the balance at the Garden Ranch YMCA.

In the YMCA staff or service provider sample, there were 73 valid responses.

IMPORTANCE SCALE

A point important to mention here is the inherent bias that may be present on scales that rate importance. Respondents have a tendency to rate all attributes highly (as important) because the attributes all represent posi-

Exhibit 21.3 (Cont.)

tive qualities which, ideally, should be optimized. This high bias is evident in our survey as only two customer response means and one staff response mean fall below 4 (on a 5-point scale, where 5 is high). This finding indicates the YMCA staff and its customers view the importance of these attributes similarly; the staff has a good idea of what its customers think is important.

EVALUATION SCALE

The importance ratings were higher in all cases, for both populations, than were the evaluations of each characteristic. On this scale, customers were asked to rate how well the YMCA performs in each area, and the staff was asked to rate how they perceived the customers' satisfaction of the services they provide. The staff evaluations were generally all slightly higher than the customer evaluations, but not significantly. They are remarkably similar, again indicating that the staff has a very good idea of how well they are serving their customers.

A more detailed analysis of the evaluation of selected attributes was conducted and may serve to help pinpoint some areas requiring improvement. In the area of a skilled staff, although both customers and staff thought this was an important attribute, both populations rated it lower on their evaluations. A closer look reveals that proportionately more members who use the downtown YMCA rated the skilled staff attribute lower. There were no distinctions in the lower rating by sex, age or income level. The reliability of service was another area rated high in importance, but lower on evaluation by each population. As with the skilled staff, there were no distinctions by sex, age, or YMCA location, but members with more income rated this attribute lower. On the attribute of courteous service, more females, more lower-income customers, and more customers at the Garden Ranch YMCA rated this attribute lower. There were no distinctions in the other categories. Some frequent comments made on the surveys about the courteousness of service were "lack of attentiveness," "aloof," and "not smiling."

Another area rated as important by members and staff, but evaluated lower, was the facilities. The customers who rated the facilities the lowest tended to be users of the downtown YMCA and female. There were several comments on the surveys that indicated the cleanliness of many areas could be improved and that maintenance and upkeep needed attention.

CONCLUSION

Last, the survey contained two overall evaluation questions to gain a perspective on how well the YMCA is generally serving its customers. These

Exhibit 21.3 (Cont.)

comments mirrored the conclusions on the Importance and Evaluation scales. The customers and staff feel that the YMCA is meeting nearly all customer needs. Customers also feel very satisfied with the service the YMCA provides. Comments such as "Couldn't be better," "I enjoy my membership," and "Keep up the good work" were seen frequently on the surveys. Although, as mentioned earlier, slight improvements could be made in some areas, this "report card" indicates the quality of service is high and customers are extremely satisfied. As one customer said "Very good . . . the best thing going in the city!"

Source: "YMCA Survey," May 1987, conducted by students in a University of Colorado, Colorado Springs, marketing class.

Follow-up focus group interviews, conducted by a volunteer member of the Y's marketing committee, shed more light on the specifics of how the Y could enhance quality of service and acceptability of facilities to members, especially in the men's and women's fitness centers in the downtown Y. The Garden Ranch Center, open throughout to the general membership, had no special fitness center.

CHALLENGES TO TAX-EXEMPT STATUS

Challenges to the Y's tax-exempt status increased from several quarters in the mid-1980s. Media, local and state taxing authorities, and the private sector intensified their questioning of the YMCA's charitable character. Critics complained that, in many communities, the YMCA was shifting emphasis from its charitable mission to courting the upscale user of athletic facilities. Health clubs in several U.S. cities announced intent to bring litigation as YMCAs opened fitness centers in office complexes, shopping malls, and other high-use locations. The litigation focused upon the Y's charity tax exemption, alleging unfair competition with tax-paying organizations. Factors contributing to the escalating number and intensity of such challenges were several, including a search by government entities for new sources of revenue, increasing private investment in health clubs, and pressures from government on non-profit service providers to expand services while the government role diminishes as funder and supplier of such services.

Klever distributed to Y board members a summary containing several related points:[1]

The issue is complicated by people's confusion over charity. Perceptions are

- Nonprofits exist only to relieve misery and to serve the poor.
- Nonprofits should not compete with for-profits by serving the same constituents and charging the same prices.
- Nonprofits should be supported primarily by contributions and not fees for services.

[1]YMCA internal document.

Finally, the issue is exacerbated by program, pricing, and promotion practices of some YMCAs. These include

- Exclusive membership rates
- Price comparisons in promotion
- Promotion of fitness programs only
- Program mix limited to physical fitness
- Lack of community service programs
- Lack of educational component in programs
- Lack of community accessibility

Current Challenges

An example of what can happen when these factors converge is in Portland, Oregon, where the Multnomah County tax assessor decided on December 9, 1985 to place all YMCA properties on the tax rolls. That decision, if sustained, will mean that the YMCA will pay back taxes and annual taxes. The challenge to the Y's tax-exempt status began after the Columbia-Willamette Metropolitan YMCA was selected by the Portland Transit Authority to build a facility at a site on the east side of the county. The site is considered prime property. It will be the hub of local bus and rail transportation, and the east side is the county's fastest-growing area.

Private health club owners, angry that the Y had been selected, charged "unfair competition." . . .

"In a unanimous decision, the Oregon Supreme Court on December 29 (1989) upheld an earlier decision by the Oregon Tax Court to tax 2 of the 10 facilities of the Portland YMCA (including) its downtown Metro Fitness Center and a small branch facility in a downtown office building. Both are primarily adult fitness facilities. Even as it upheld the taxability of the YMCA as a whole, stating that 'No doubts need be raised about the generally charitable nature of the YMCA nationally, in Oregon, or in metropolitan Portland.' "[2]

In 1984 the Internal Revenue Service had defined, in the context of an audit of the Springfield, Massachusetts, YMCA, a measure for determining whether YMCA fitness centers would be treated as unrelated business activity subject to income tax. The measure, whether a fitness center membership was affordable to a significant segment of the community, was applied only to the service area of the YMCA being evaluated.

SURVEY OF HEALTH CENTER MEMBERS

As explained in the summary of the IRS decision in the Springfield, Massachusetts case, the favorable outcome was based in large part on the Springfield YMCA's ability to demonstrate, through a survey of its health center members, that health center membership was generally accessible to the community as a whole. The Springfield

[2]Excerpt from "Capital Briefs Special Report," YMCA of the USA, document provided by James Klever for board members.

YMCA collected data on the income and occupational composition of its health center membership using a simple survey form like that shown in Exhibit 21.4. The survey form was mailed to each health center member with an addressed return envelope.

Since the Springfield decision criterion was established, audits of YMCAs with fitness centers have illustrated "affordability" to IRS's satisfaction. However, this test resolved none of the issues raised in the Oregon case and elsewhere as to how "charity" was defined and whether fees for services were consistent with charity tax-exempt status.

Exhibit 21.4

SAMPLE SURVEY FORM

Retaining the tax-exempt status of our YMCA health center depends in part on showing the IRS that the health center membership includes persons from various income levels and occupational categories. To provide us with that information, please indicate your family income and occupational category below. *Please do not give your name.*

Family Income		Occupation	
0–14,999	_____	Clerical	_____
$15,000–24,999	_____	Managerial	_____
$25,000–34,999	_____	Professional and technical	_____
$35,000–49,000	_____	Sales	_____
$50,000–	_____	Other (please specify)	_____

Return the completed form to the YMCA in the enclosed preaddressed envelope—and thanks for your help!

Source: Pikes Peak Y, internal document.

How could the Pikes Peak Y form a strategy to meet these challenges? In Jim Klever's words, "We must be acutely aware of any potential challenges from government or business owners throughout the region. And we—staff and board members—must understand the concepts of charity, charitable purpose, nonprofit status, and tax-exempt status as defined by local, state and federal laws. Then, we must seek opportunities to educate key leaders in government, business, and the media on these matters, joining with other nonprofits to address the issues. This matter is of major concern to us."

To reinforce the public education process, Judi Lakin suggested that advertising and publicity pay heed to expressing clearly the Y's mission and program objectives in promotional materials and advertisements; show how the institution is meeting health and social service needs of Colorado Springs and surrounding communities; and promote flexibility in fees for those unable to pay, offering a variety of options based on ability to pay. "Internally," she said, "we must make sure that performance measures are tied to the Y's mission and objectives, and we should keep current demographic data on our various publics, both member and nonmembers."

The tax-exempt debate appeared to be moving toward legislative closure at the turn of the decade. In a letter to YMCA board members and other key leaders, Jim Klever wrote in the first paragraph:[3]

> For the past three years, congressional debate on the unrelated business income tax (UBIT)—*including the tax rules governing YMCA fitness programs*—has been confined to the House Ways and Means Committee. However, the Ways and Means Committee leadership has said that they will make every effort to complete work on a package of recommended UBIT changes and include this package in the major tax bill expected to move through Congress later this year. If this occurs, it will force the Senate Finance Committee to consider UBIT, and YMCAs will need strong support in the Finance Committee to guard against adverse changes in the fitness center rules.

The letter's thrust was to request help in garnering support in the Senate Finance Committee, of which William L. Armstrong, Republican of Colorado, was a member. Exhibit 21.5 provides an overview of the UBIT issue's status.

Exhibit 21.5

CURRENT STATUS OF THE UBIT ISSUE

The Oversight Subcommittee of the House Ways and Means Committee has been working since early 1987 on a set of proposed changes in the unrelated business income tax rules governing tax exempt organizations like YMCAs. The subcommittee's review of the UBIT rules was initiated in response to aggressive lobbying by various business groups complaining about "unfair competition" by exempt organizations. The subcommittee's draft proposals include more than two dozen recommended changes in the UBIT rules.

The UBIT issue of most direct importance to YMCAs is the tax treatment of fitness programs. Under current IRS rules (the so-called "community affordability" test), a YMCA adult fitness program is not subject to UBIT as long as the YMCA can demonstrate that the members of the fitness center reflect something approximating a cross section of income levels in the community served. As the enclosed paper indicates, the International Racquet Sports Association is lobbying for a significantly tighter rule under which a YMCA fitness program would be taxed unless it primarily serves members of a "charitable class," for example, individuals who are poor, handicapped, or otherwise disadvantaged.

As a result of effective lobbying by YMCAs in districts of Oversight

[3]Internal document.

Exhibit 21.5 (Cont.)

Subcommittee members, the current subcommittee draft proposal would simply "codify" this community affordability test, that is, make the test a part of the Internal Revenue Code itself, and not just an IRS ruling. *Our objective is to ensure that any UBIT legislation passed by Congress takes this approach, rather than adopting the more restrictive rule advocated by the IRS.*

Source: Internal document.

Not only taxation, but also fee assessments by taxing bodies was of concern to the Pikes Peak Y, as reflected in Exhibit 21.6, copy of a letter from Klever to the El Paso County commissioners.

Exhibit 21.6

KLEVER LETTER TO COUNTY COMMISSIONERS

June 16, 1988

[Individual Commissioners]
El Paso County Commissioners
27 E. Vermijo
Colorado Springs, CO 80903

Dear [Commissioner]

Please accept this letter as an expression of opposition to the proposal to impose a fee against day care groups making use of "grassy" areas in county parks. The opposition to the imposition of this charge extends to applying it against for-profit providers as well as nonprofit providers of day care services.

A variety of arguments have been raised in the pro and con discussion of this proposal. The basic issue is not whether day care is a valuable service, whether for-profit groups are enhancing their "profit" by using parks, or whether this amounts to a double tax on the parents of the children involved in these programs. The essence of the issue is that the parks exist to serve the people of the Pikes Peak region, to enhance the quality of their lives, to teach them, to nurture them, and to bring them joy. There is something basically irrational in a proposal aimed at reducing, restricting, and eliminating the use of those parks by children of the Pikes Peak region

Exhibit 21.6 (Cont.)

simply because they use them so much! It seems to me that the persons responsible for the county parks ought to be encouraging park use, especially use that benefits children, rather than discouraging park use and essentially erecting "Keep Off the Grass" signs in our county parks. No enterprise operates well these days without attention to customer service, and when it comes to park use, the children involved in these programs are the customers and they deserve service.

I do not believe that the proposal before you is philosophically sound or in the best interests of the people of the Pikes Peak region and I urge you to defeat it.

Sincerely,

James R. Klever
President

> *Source:* Internal document.

ADVERTISING AND TAX EXEMPTION

Advertising and the tax-exempt question were of concern to the Y's marketing committee members, but all believed that the basic objective remained: sell the product. In the words of Steven Kendall, president of Kendall & Company, an advertising and public relations agency with YMCAs as clients, "marketing is one of the . . . powerful weapons you have in keeping the tax man from your doorstep. If people are questioning your tax-exempt status, they need to understand why you're not a yuppie fitness factory."[4] Marketing, according to this spokesperson, is the only way to communicate these points.

Exhibit 21.7 presents guidelines to assist the Y marketing team in thinking about themes and specific points for advertising copy.

Exhibit 21.7

YMCA ADVERTISING GUIDELINES

Advertising is a legitimate means by which to inform the public on the YMCA's programs and services. The Y should continue to advertise and promote aggressively.

[4]Steven A. Kendall, "The Mission of Marketing: Raise Awareness, Not Tax Questions," *Perspective*, April 1988, p. 12.

Exhibit 21.7 (Cont.)

Furthermore the Pikes Peak Y should develop message strategies for advertising that state benefits to the user, not just features such as equipment, facilities, and price. Price should be stated in terms of affordability to the person, not in comparison with competitors. (Comparative pricing is a strategy usually used in the marketplace when the product is a commodity and the only way to compete is on price.) To be effective, ads should be presented in a manner that motivates the audience to take action.

In its advertising, the Y needs to promote different programs to specific publics at various times throughout the year. By taking a balanced approach to advertising (one that includes health enhancement, youth sports, child care, aquatics and summer camp, for example) the YMCA will be viewed as a multipurpose organization, one that does not offer just fitness center equipment and facilities.

Source: Internal YMCA document.

These guidelines were endorsed by the Pikes Peak Y marketing committee as fundamental principles to be regarded in designing the Y's promotional campaigns.

Exhibit 21.8 contains portions of newspaper advertising copy accompanying a montage picture showing a child swimming, a man lifting free weights, joggers in a group run, and a coed aerobics class.

Exhibit 21.8

PORTIONS OF A 1987 NEWSPAPER ADVERTISEMENT

Headline NOW YOU CAN JOIN THE YMCA FOR 20% LESS

Body Copy When you join the YMCA of the Pikes Peak region, you're investing in over 100 years of excellence. Providing you with quality programs and facilities and a well-educated, caring staff is our goal. Whether there's one in your family or a dozen, the Y has something for all of you . . . for the mind, body, and spirit. Your Y membership gives you convenient downtown and Garden Ranch facilities to use and hundreds of free programs each year. Now, you get the best of the YMCA for less when you buy a new annual membership at a 20 percent discount. Look around, then try the Y (for FREE) between September 2 to 13. We think you'll want to join us and be part of the YMCA family!

- Free Aerobics
- Free Swim Lessons
- Y Nautilus Training
- Universal Machines
- Free Weights
- Adult Fitness Centers

- Indoor Running
- 3 Large Pools
- Certified Instructors
- Family Programs
- 10 Racquetball Courts
- And Much More!

Exhibit 21.8 (Cont.)

Concluding Line   ANNUAL MEMBERSHIPS NOW ON SALE!

Source: Internal document.

Television copy for this 1987 membership sale campaign is presented in Exhibit 21.9.

Exhibit 21.9

YMCA TELEVISION COMMERCIAL COPY   :30 (seconds)

Now you can save 20 percent on new yearly memberships at the YMCA. Plus you'll get use of Ys across Colorado, too. For over a century the Y has been the trusted leader teaching people to swim, providing spacious pools for fitness for the whole family. Weight training—the Y has the best: Nautilus, Olympic, free weights, Universal machines, too. Free aerobics from sunup to sundown. Weatherproof indoor running, racquetball courts galore. Try the Y for free; you'll want to stay for a lifetime. The YMCA: for you, for your family.

Source: Internal document.

SUSTAINING MEMBERSHIP CAMPAIGN

The Pikes Peak YMCA conducted an annual sustaining membership campaign to support programs for underprivileged children in the community. Approximately 2,500 children were served each year with memberships, camperships, program services for Big Brothers/Big Sisters, the Kid's Club, the USO, and a week of camp for deaf and blind children. Wrote campaign chairperson Lea Roads, "We want to continue to serve these children in the same ways in 1988. To do that, we must raise $160,000 in this campaign."[5] Ms. Roads, whose regular job was business development director at United Bank of Colorado Springs, typified hundreds of volunteers, as she served her second year leading a team of 374 Y supporters to achieve the ambitious objective.

PIKES PEAK Y RETENTION EFFORTS

In reviewing the need to enhance retention efforts, Judi Lakin observed that "It costs about five times as much to acquire a member as it does to service an existing mem-

[5]1988 campaign chairperson letter to volunteers and prospective contributors.

ber. Therefore, it makes sense that we make a commitment to existing members and retain their patronage." Exhibit 21.10 presents selected portions of a memo from Judi to management, marketing committee, and board of directors, concerning this issue, ways of capitalizing on retention opportunities at the Pikes Peak YMCA, and her goal to develop a formal retention program for the YMCA/USO of the Pikes Peak region.

Exhibit 21.10

MEMORANDUM TO MANAGEMENT

Background   Twenty urban YMCAs, the largest in the country, recently participated in a study of retention. Prior to developing the study, key staff from each YMCA met to discuss retention problems, identified as follows:

1. It was the feeling of the Urban Ys that "à la carte" memberships chipped away at the YMCA "Association" and "Fellowship" concept because these people were not making a commitment to the organization . . . not buying into the mission.
2. Price positioning devalues our memberships . . . this leads to a price-for-service relationship that breeds less loyalty, involvement or tenure. This moves the individual away from the mission and to individual gain.
3. The Urban Ys felt that YMCAs have moved away from our mission, and our goal of promoting healthy life-styles cannot be achieved in a short-term relationship. Therefore, YMCA programs need to promote the Y's mission.

Our Task   To evaluate the attached methods, suggest other potential methods, and recommend possible research or data needed to develop a formal program.

Pricing

1. Add a joining fee.
2. Portray membership as continuous with no expiration date.
3. Make bank draft the primary system of payment.
4. Increase the difference between member and nonmember fees.
5. Create incentive for joining by increasing member benefits.
6. Interpret increases on a monthly basis rather than annual.
7. Construct profile of members: keep renewal records by category and expiration date.

Membership Services

1. Smile, wave, and acknowledge members; use name whenever possible.
2. Identify staff and volunteers with name tags.
3. Identify staff for backup at service desks if there is a wait longer than 3 minutes.

Exhibit 21.10 (Cont.)

4. For class signups and special events, locate signup away from service desks and customer desk.
5. Recruit volunteers as "greeters" during peak times.
6. Answer phone after three rings, no hold longer than 30 seconds, return unanswered calls to a message center.
7. Train all staff on courtesy and service counter procedure.

Orientation

1. Send letter of welcome within first week of membership.
2. Interview new members to plan greater service for them.
3. Call new members within two weeks and again in four to six weeks.
4. Fitness evaluation on each new member within 30 days, then continuous every six months.
5. See that new members are introduced to others participating in their classes and activities.
6. Connect member with a buddy to call if not in class.
7. Sponsor special member events on a quarterly basis.
8. Provide recognition of achievement whenever possible.
9. Provide exercise buddies with phone numbers.
10. Provide items with members' names on them for ready identification.
11. Have executive director host a reception on a quarterly basis for feedback and new ideas.
12. Conduct frequent surveys with short, issue-oriented cards.
13. Provide a suggestion box with bulletin board for posting responses; Could be a feature in member newsletter: "You Asked for It—You Got It!"
14. Conduct a member satisfaction survey after second quarter of membership.
15. Place a rack with brochures and flyers nearby.
16. Feature a theme of welcome and mission throughout the building.
17. Complete routine facility repair within 24 hours and have accompanying signage.
18. Accomplish major repair within one year and have accompanying signage.
19. Mail quarterly wellness newsletter to members.
20. Focus on face-to-face relationship with members.
21. Communicate the "membership concept" with staff and in all printed materials.
22. Have executive director write a monthly column in staff newsletter on the importance of member relations.

IT'S THE STAFF'S JOB TO MAKE SURE THE MEMBER COMES BACK!!!

Source: Internal YMCA document.

FINANCIAL RESULTS, 1985–1989

Selected financial statistics are presented in Exhibit 21.11.

Exhibit 21.11

SELECTED FINANCIAL STATISTICS, Y/USO PIKES PEAK REGION 1985–1989

	1989	1988	1987	1986	1985
Operating revenues	$ 2,733,783	$2,612,824	$2,463,172	$2,293,663	$2,141,488
Public support					
United Way	393,036	283,947	273,027	160,000	159,994
Contributions	164,564	149,282	149,479	85,571	75,905
Restricted contributions	46,162	25,843	588,486	38,667	—
	$ 3,337,545	$3,071,896	$3,474,164	$2,577,901	$2,377,387
Expenses	$ 3,453,766	$3,070,899	$2,964,352	$2,552,067	$2,366,075
Revenues and public support over (under)					
expenses	$(116,221)*	$ 997	$ 509,812	$ 25,834	$ 11,312

Source: YMCA audit documents.

*Loss on land sale and depreciation are included in this total deficit.

Exhibit 21.12 contains board meeting excerpts of comments on finance and membership.

Although trends appeared to indicate plateauing of membership, usage at the downtown center and the Garden Ranch branch continued to strain capacity limits of both facilities. The board strongly believed a third Y facility in the northeast sector of Colorado Springs was clearly warranted. In 1985, representatives of the strategic planning committee, anticipating probable future expansion, had begun examining likely sites and exploring arrangements for acquiring property in northeast Colorado Springs. A plan was announced in December 1989:

> An agreement has been reached between the YMCA, Vintage Communities, and the Colorado Springs Parks and Recreation Department to transfer ownership of a five-acre parcel in Briargate to the YMCA. . . . Tentative plans call for fundraising to begin in the early 1990s, with the building to be completed by 1995. Now, as the city continues its northerly expansion, the Y will be well positioned to serve residents of those communities.[6]

November 1989 marked the tenth anniversary of James Klever's appointment to the CEO post at the YMCA/USO of the Pikes Peak region. In that time, the Garden Ranch facility was constructed, the staff and budget doubled, the organization was restructured to become a metropolitan association, and plans were laid for further expansion to serve the health and fitness needs of Pikes Peak region residents.

[6]"Y UPDATE," December 1989, p. 2.

Exhibit 21.12

NOTES FROM BOARD MEETINGS

Financial   The year 1989 ended with a surplus of $1,388. The 1990 budget is projected to have a surplus of $5,251.*

Membership/retention   Total membership continues to show the effect of not having a September sale. January is off to an excellent start. The automatic bank withdrawal system is extremely strong. Fitness centers are holding strong. Weakness continues in the general membership segment. Although we are doing a good job encouraging new members to attend an orientation, we need to improve efforts to get them to sign up for free fitness testing. Special attention will be given to training reception desk personnel in this program.*

Total membership is down from 1988 reflecting the lack of a membership sale and a change in removing nonrenewing members from our rosters 30 days following expiration rather than 60 days as was done in 1988. ABW usage continues to grow. Membership usage is extremely high which has caused concern at the downtown center regarding availability of lockers during evening rush.†

*January 25, 1990.
†December 7, 1989.

Source: Internal YMCA document.

22

SEMESTER AT SEA

In October 1877 the Woodruff Scientific Expedition departed New York City on an around-the-world voyage on the steamship *Ontario*.[1] Composed of 400 students and a faculty of experienced teachers, the expedition was to travel as a floating college that would land at interesting points en route for short excursions. "It will afford a rare opportunity for young students to see the world and at the same time pursue their studies in science under the most pleasant and favorable auspices," according to the written purposes set forth by its sponsors. This was the first on-record floating university.

The 1920s saw another effort in the floating university concept of providing "an adventure in education" and "a quest for knowledge about our world" as well as "a preparation for active life." In this endeavor, with New York University as the sponsoring institution, faculty and students were to carry out their studies and social life "with mutual sympathy in an eager investigation of the meaning of ideas and the importance of varied civilizations today." The idea was that participants through world travel would forge lasting friendships with people of other cultures. The 1928 voyage, which took approximately nine months, drew mainly women students. Similar attempts in the 1930s, however, were generally unsuccessful.

The University of Seven Seas aboard Holland-America Lines vessels had its embryonic beginnings and was operated as a private venture in the early 1960s. In-

[1]"Around the World," *Harper's Weekly*, September 1, 1877, pp. 689–690.

terest was lively enough for the operators to begin looking around for a way in which the floating university concept could be practically implemented. A few alumni of previous voyages as well as a group of businessmen from Whittier, California, were among the interested people who saw potential in this type of contained international experience during the 1960s. They approached Chapman College, a church-related liberal arts institution, in an attempt to get the school to take on the shipboard education program, such as it was, and to develop it into a nationally recognized project. After debating at length the pros and cons of such a program, Chapman College decided in the mid-1960s to undertake the project.

Chapman College first developed a University of Seven Seas division—named after the vessel that carried the students—headed up by a staff employed by the school. In these early days, the voyages were comparatively long, including 19 or 20 ports and a variety of itineraries—Mediterranean, Latin American, European, and around the world via several routes. The major problem with the Seven Seas program was that it was not generating a sufficient number of applications to ensure a qualified and motivated student body. When *S.S. Seven Seas* was no longer the ship for the program, the *S.S. Ryndam* was provided and the name of the program was changed to "World Campus Afloat," still under the auspices of Chapman College in its Division of International Studies. Several people at Chapman had been assuming responsibility for the program. The vice president for academic affairs of Chapman, M. A. Griffiths, needed a more permanent staff to provide continuity for planning and to manage the shipboard operation. Lloyd Lewan served on the administrative side in the late 1960s and early 1970s. Mr. Lewan, the only executive from those days remaining with the program, served as a senior academic advisor.

Holland-America Lines offered the program a ship on a contractual basis for two academic semesters each year and in 1969 chose to discontinue the arrangement. Lewan and others were dispatched by Griffiths to evaluate other ships to find a new home for the World Campus Afloat program. Just when options seemed to be running out, Orient Overseas Line, one of many companies owned by shipping magnate C. Y. Tung of Hong Kong, called the World Campus Afloat office and invited key administrators to Long Beach where the *S.S. Orient Esmeralda* was docked. C. Y. Tung was present at the first meeting and expressed great interest in a United Nations university concept and shipboard education in general. Several months after the meeting, a representative of Orient Overseas Line called unexpectedly to announce, "We have a ship for you." The people at World Campus Afloat were surprised to learn that Mr. Tung had purchased *R.M.S. Queen Elizabeth I,* one of the largest passenger ships ever built. Mr. Tung had the *QE I* moved from its moorings in Ft. Lauderdale and taken back to Hong Kong for extensive repairs and refurbishing. After considerable investment and effort, she was redesignated *Seawise University,* after C. Y. Tung, and was about to be used as the principal World Campus Afloat ship when a fire destroyed the vessel in Hong Kong harbor.

Because Mr. Tung had committed himself to providing a vessel for shipboard education, he continued to look for a ship and eventually purchased the *S.S. Atlantic,* renaming it *S.S. Universe Campus.* The ship, refurbished in Baltimore and ready for students in the fall of 1971, was offered to Chapman College on a special contractual basis, with academic control remaining with Chapman College. This relationship continued until 1975 when Chapman discontinued the program. In the midst of campus politics, the World Campus Afloat program was forced to depart from Chapman.

With the program went Griffiths, Lewan, and John Tymitz who had been with the program since 1973. With C. Y. Tung's encouragement, the nonprofit, tax-exempt Institute for Shipboard Education (ISE) was formed, and in 1976 an educational affiliation was formed with the University of Colorado. Semester at Sea (SAS), the new name of the endeavor, had found a new academic home. The University of Colorado agreed to provide academic sponsorship for the program. The Seawise Foundation provided a ship, the *S.S. Universe Campus*. The three-way structure embraced the university, the private foundation, and the corporation. The legal and financial responsibility fell to the Institute for Shipboard Education, the academic responsibility to the university, and the responsibility of providing the ship to the Seawise Foundation.

The agreement between the ISE and the University of Colorado ended with the conclusion of the fall 1980 semester voyage, whereupon the University of Pittsburgh assumed academic sponsorship.

The SAS program presently has a long-term contract with the University of Pittsburgh. Interestingly, Dean Amos from the University of Pittsburgh, a supporter of SAS moving to Pitt, was among the participants of the 1928 around-the-world voyage that developed the original concept of the floating university. So there seemed to be a sense of arriving full circle as SAS settled in at the University of Pittsburgh.

A few states typically contribute many names to the Semester at Sea roster. However the student body is extremely diverse. Students on any one voyage come from approximately 150 universities and colleges throughout the country.

THE ORGANIZATION

The executive director of the Institute for Shipboard Education oversees the direction of the Institute and has specific responsibility for marketing, recruiting, development, and institutional relationships. Any educational institution can participate in ISE programs. The role of the board is essentially advisory and supportive. The director of academic affairs serves as the institutional representative and planning officer of ISE. Both directors are based at the University of Pittsburgh.

Field recruiters, strategically located, travel extensively on behalf of Semester at Sea. Smail offices are maintained in Cambridge, Massachusetts; Boulder, Colorado; and Irvine, California. Each has a representative/recruiter who is available during the regular academic year. From these offices emanate the major recruiting efforts.

The SAS program pays Pittsburgh per unit hour for academic credit generated. The University of Pittsburgh, for its part, provides an academic dean (appointed at least a year in advance) who works with ISE to prepare for the voyage—the overall program, field activities, faculty selection, and core courses. Dr. Lewan credits planning and quality of personnel with "the substantial improvement in the academic quality of the program" that has occurred at Pittsburgh since 1981. Student demographics have changed somewhat with the SAS move East, although upper-middle-class students remain the nucleus of the program because of the cost, ranging from $10,575 to $12,375 for a single semester's room, board, tuition, and passage.

BUDGETING

The university incurs no financial obligation. ISE assumes all financial and legal responsibilities. The shipping line quotes a per diem rate per student to ISE; 40 free positions are allotted for faculty and staff in addition to 25 work/study positions at half fare. Adult passengers who make arrangements through ISE also fall under the per diem rate. ISE pays about 75 percent of the fees received to the shipping line, leaving 25 percent to cover ISE expenses of operation at headquarters and on voyages, and to pay credit hour fees to the university. The in-port trips are practically a break-even proposition for SAS.

To use the ship in a cost-efficient manner, the early 1980s schedules included two 100-day SAS cruises each year. Five or six two-week cruises to Alaska in the summer were chartered to another agency. Now, however, summer sailings are teacher and adult education voyages. These voyages are operated in cooperation with a number of institutions and organizations such as the American Association of Colleges for Teacher Education and the National Education Association. Off-season use of the ship has a direct bearing on the financial situation of the Institute and the SAS program.

The administrators of Semester at Sea had envisioned the S.S. *Universe* serving the program well into the 1990s. Yet the long-term planning of the ISE must include acquiring another ship to serve the program's expanding needs. Mr. C. Y. Tung's death in April 1982 was a tragic loss to Semester at Sea, for it was largely through his good offices that the program has been able to endure. See Exhibit 22.1 for a story that appeared in the SAS newsletter shortly after his death.

Semester at Sea, by virtue of its focus upon "the general improvement of international education and overseas study within higher education" has established networks with a number of other organizations interested in the concept: the American Universities International Field Staff, general shipboard conferences, and the organizational contacts of the University of Pittsburgh and its Center for International Studies, which houses SAS. Another major source of contacts occurs through the vast logistical apparatus of travel agents, suppliers, international contacts, and other connections that are part of every SAS voyage. The Institute has helped develop written planning criteria to achieve SAS goals, an example of which is found in Exhibit 22.2.

STUDENTS AND CURRICULUM

Semester at Sea, a unique program in global education, is designed to provide one special international semester in a student's college career. Credits earned on Semes-

Exhibit 22.1

MR. C. Y. TUNG AND SEMESTER AT SEA

SHIPMATES
A Newsletter for Alumni of Shipboard Education

Spring, 1982, No. 13

SAS Mourns the Passing of A Friend

Mr. C.Y. Tung Dies at 71 in Hong Kong

Mr. C.Y. TUNG
1910–1982

Mr. C.Y. Tung, Chairman of the Board of Directors of the Institute for Shipboard Education, died suddenly in Hong Kong on April 14. Mr. Tung was 71.

Mr. Tung has been associated with shipboard education since 1971, when he purchased the *Queen Elizabeth I* to become a floating world university. When the *Q.E.I* burned in Hong Kong harbor, Mr. Tung purchased the *S.S. Universe*, which has served as the home of Semester at Sea since that time.

C.Y., as he was known to his many friends, was one of the largest shipowners, with a world-wide shipping empire of tankers and container ships. But he found the time to devote to shipboard education, which was his favorite enterprise. In an interview some time ago, he stated, "I have learned that there is a link between ships and education. Ships not only can carry oil to meet energy needs, but also can be used as a center of learning to implement improved understanding among nations."

Mr. Tung visited the Semester at Sea many times, and each time made a hit with the students. His enthusiasm for the educational process seemed to be sensed by the students, and each time he appeared he was given an overwhelming student reception.

The Semester at Sea program, which has become firmly established at the University of Pittsburgh, is expected to continue without interruption. Plans are already under way to utilize the ship year around for educational purposes.

Memorial Scholarship Fund Established

Shipmates is setting up a special scholarship fund, in memory of C.Y. Tung's great contribution to shipboard education. Mr. Tung not only provided the ship which we use, he often underwrote it, and additionally provided scholarships for students from Asia and South America. We invite your contributions to this fund, which will be utilized for funding deserving students who could not otherwise afford to participate in Semester at Sea. Use the enclosed reply envelope.

Exhibit 22.1 (Cont.)

Executive Staff of the Institute for Shipboard Education with Captain Yen and Mr. C.Y. Tung aboard the S.S. Universe in March, 1982, during the annual shipboard conference.

Vision of a Shipowner: "Ships Carry Ideas"

Shipboard education is a very delicate undertaking and requires the bringing together of three important elements. At the hub is a great university, which provides the academic foundation which will guarantee that the program is sound, and which makes it acceptable among other academic institutions. This responsibility has been assumed by the University of Pittsburgh. Second, it requires a solid administrative structure which can bring together twice a year all of the resources necessary to make such a complicated project viable. This is the role of the Institute for Shipboard Education.

But paramount to the concept is a shipowner of vision who can see the vital role which international education can play in the world today, and who is willing to make a ship available for that purpose. C.Y. Tung was this kind of enlightened individual, and more. Not content with providing a ship, he became actively involved with the concept as an active participant. He served as Chairman of the Board of the Institute. He regularly became involved with the annual shipboard conferences, at which he acted as host. C.Y. enjoyed these conferences immensely. He worked to keep up the in-

terest of the United Nations in the concept, and personally provided scholarships to Asian and Latin American students through the Seawise Foundation. In the midst of all of his other projects and responsibilities, he always had time for the concept.

Why should a busy shipowner devote such time to a project which, at best, just paid for itself, and many times required a subsidy? Part of the explanation lies in the Chinese respect for learning and scholarship. But mostly it came from a recognition that all things are related, and in the constant quest for understanding among nations, all available means must be used. His special contribution to this quest was a ship. Ships, he would say, not only carry cargo, they carry ideas. He understood the great role which ships had played in history, as transmitters of new ideas, of cultural diffusion, and as a means of fostering mutual understanding among nations. As a shipowner, he felt that he should bring his special knowledge of shipping in the service of global education, and this became his mission. It was this sense of mission which motivated him to buy the *Queen Elizabeth I* and convert it into a world-circling university.

And it was this sense of mission which prompted him to buy the *Atlantic* for Semester at Sea, converting it into the *S.S. Universe* when the *Queen Elizabeth I* met its untimely death by fire.

C.Y., in spite of his many other accomplishments, liked to describe himself as an educator. And those of us in education were proud to have him as a colleague. He had a nimble mind, a mastery of fine detail, and a broad grasp of concepts. He was interested in all areas of education. In addition to I.S.E., he was a Trustee of the International Council on Education for Teaching, and served on the Board of the Hoover Institution.

C.Y. made an unparalleled contribution to world understanding through ships. The thousands of students who participated in Semester at Sea and those who will participate in the future owe him a great debt of gratitude.

C.Y. Tung was truly a rare individual, and those of us who knew him shall miss him.

— Staff of the
Institute for Shipboard Education

---

ter at Sea meet the usual standards for transfer back to a student's home institution. Typically, more than 50 courses are offered in the disciplines of anthropology, biological sciences, business, economics, fine arts, geography, geology, history, literature, music, philosophy, political science, psychology, religious studies, sociology, and theater arts. Both lower-division and upper-division courses are offered. A "core course" is required of all students. It is designed to develop a heightened sensitivity and awareness of and respect for the global environment in which we live. SAS also offers many courses to enhance experiences in the various ports visited by the students. Exhibit 22.3 provides a cross section of representative courses adapted from the 1990 catalog.

Classes meet daily, except Sunday, while at sea and provide the number of contact hours students would find at their home campuses.

Exhibit 22.2

THE CURRICULAR GOALS OF THE SEMESTER AT SEA PROGRAM

1. Build the insight and background necessary for perceiving and interpreting international problems and differences.
2. Permit students to interact with cultures and peoples of both developed and emerging nations of the world.
3. Increase awareness of the student's own culture through comparison and contrast with other cultures.
4. Extend liberal arts education through firsthand observation and understanding of world issues.
5. Provide a special focus on the international dimension of major liberal arts disciplines: anthropology, sociology, history, geography, political science, philosophy, art, and others.
6. Develop the student's awareness of the interdependence of the world today.
7. Encourage a closer study of the relations between the United States and other nations of the world.

Exhibit 22.3

SAMPLE OF COURSE DESCRIPTIONS 1990–1991

Anthropology 82: Introduction to Anthropology   Digging, the distinctive data gathering technique of archaeology, recovers traces of past societies' activities from the soil. This course will examine archaeology from the anthropological perspective: How to collect these remains scientifically and how to interpret them both in light of anthropological knowledge of behavior in general and specific cases from different parts of the world.

Economics 52: Comparative Economic Systems   A comparative analysis of the way several different types of contemporary economic systems work. Systems covered include some or all of the following: the United States, U.S.S.R., People's Republic of China, Taiwan, Hong Kong, and South Korea. Topics will include comparisons among systems as well as study of individual systems.

Exhibit 22.3 (Cont.)

History 183: *Modern China*   This course will introduce students to Chinese history from the Ch'ing Dynasty (1644–1911) to the present. Lectures will look at traditional China and the intrusions of the Europeans, then concentrate on the nature of political revolution and economic change in the nineteenth and twentieth centuries.

Political Science 164: *Marxism*   Marxism, although it has been exposed to serious challenges in countries where it seemed until recently to be well established, remains one of the major political outlooks of the modern world. This course considers Marxism on three levels: as a prescriptive (or "utopian") political theory; as an empirical or explanatory theory of history, economics, and the state; and (to a lesser extent) as an established system of governance and economic organization.

Theater Arts 82: *Survey of World Theater*   A survey of the elements of theatrical performance in each country or region visited during the voyage. Theater space, history, cultural context, and performance conventions are examined, but emphasis is placed on comparing the theaters of East and West through audiovisual records and live performances.

See Exhibit 22.4 for the schedule adapted from the 1990 catalog. Faculty are drawn from major universities in the United States, augmented by selected experts who serve as in-port lecturers. A recent voyage drew faculty from Stanford University, Colorado State University, Columbia University, the University of Hawaii, the University of Pittsburgh, and others. Typically, 20 faculty and 20 support staff are hired for each voyage, which serves 400 to 500 students and approximately 50 adult passengers.

Exhibit 22.4

CLASS SCHEDULE

Breakfast	0700–0800
1st class period	0800–0915
2nd class period	0920–1035
Core course	1040–1200
Lunch	1200–1330
3rd class period	1245–1400
4th class period	1405–1520
5th class period	1525–1640
6th class period	1645–1800
Dinner	1800–1930
Makeup class period	1845–2000
Community College	2000–2100

The in-country field experiences, both formal and informal, are an essential part of the academic program. Included in the formal program are a number of standard activities—for example, a visit to a university, a U.S. embassy briefing, an ethnic music program, a visit to a factory or an art museum. Many of these are related to specific courses and are faculty led. In addition, a number of optional programs are offered in each port. These programs, which often take the student away from the port city to sites of historical and cultural interest, are not included in the tuition and must be paid for separately. These might include visits to mainland China or to central India, for example. Exhibit 22.5 provides some examples of field program activities. Many students choose to engage in individual projects, independent travel within the country, or special programs such as the home stays, which are encouraged in some host countries.

Semester at Sea must consider economies of scale—a voyage that carries 500 students clearly is more cost effective than is a voyage with only 350. However students who wish to apply for admission to Semester at Sea must be in good standing at their home institutions; a cumulative grade-point average above 2.75 is also required.

Past participants in SAS voyages frequently speak of the experience in the language of those who have been through a religious experience. "It has changed my life," stated Michelle Tschudy, a University of Colorado student majoring in international relations. Alums keep in touch through *Shipmates,* a newsletter for alumni of shipboard education (see Exhibit 22.1). In it Michelle R. Barnwell described her fall 1988 voyage, "I left the ship with a new understanding of who I am. The places I'd visited and the differences I'd seen gave me a deeper understanding of the uniqueness of my own land, greater respect for others around the world, and an increased understanding of my responsibility as a citizen of that world."[2]

Through the newsletter, members of the alumni group keep in touch with each other about personal news, which often has an international cast. One student writes that he is living in Taipei, Taiwan, where he is associated with a magazine, another that he has accepted a teaching position in the Republic of China. A woman employed by International Field Studies invites shipmates to visit her in the Bahamas. Many alumni write in about their international careers. Diane Martin Livingston, a 1968 alumna, writes, "it was my voyage halfway around the world on the *S.S. Ryndam,* 1968–69, that helped me synthesize and focus my ideas. I think that the students who are drawn to this program are self-reliant, adventurous, truth-seeking wanderers from all walks of life and many diverse cultures." A student who hopes to return to India as a missionary writes in about her future plans. Peggy Shull, who went on two voyages, tells about her employment as a travel agent specializing in student travel, "The ship experience made travel a true necessity for me. It also gave me a unique and diversified experience that I put to use in the travel field. I try to pass on to my clients the excitement I first felt on the ship." Often students accept, even seek out, public-speaking assignments to recount their experiences on Semester at Sea. Students seem to feel a heightened sense of responsibility for spaceship Earth as a result of the SAS experience.

[2]From *Essence* Magazine, Vol. 20. no. 4 (August 1989), p. 23.

MARKETING

The Institute develops brochures for recruiting purposes, one of the three direct advertising expenditures. This publication is its major informational and image piece, complete with an attractive photograph of the ship and an itinerary (see Exhibit 22.5). Those who inquire about the SAS program are sent that brochure. What money is available for marketing is primarily spent on brochures and the expenses incurred by recruiters. Over 20,000 brochures are requested and over 1,700 applications are received annually. Semester at Sea recognizes that students, faculty, and staff perform a major recruiting and promotional service because of the importance of the experience. Lewan commented, "The personal selling effort of a past SAS participant is one of the most effective selling strategies available to the program; indeed the personal contact is essential." During the final week of the 100-day voyage, the administration makes it a practice to share information about plans for future voyages with students, faculty, and staff. "The quality and the future of the program are largely determined by the alumni of this organization," Lewan remarked. Certainly the frequent reunions scheduled to bring together "S.A.S. Alums," "Shippies," and "Friends of S.A.S." underscore the faith that the Institute places in its alumni. Their perceptions emphasize key selling points in SAS promotional literature.

Exhibit 22.5

PLANNED SEMESTER AT SEA ITINERARIES, 1990–1991

FALL 1990 (SEPTEMBER 14–DECEMBER 23)	SPRING 1991 (JANUARY 27–MAY 7)
Vancouver, B.C.	Nassau, Bahamas
Kobe, Japan	Casablanca, Morocco
Keelung, Taiwan	Dubrovnik, Yugoslavia
Hong Kong (optional trip to China)	Odessa, Soviet Union
Penang, Malaysia	Istanbul, Turkey
Madras, India	Port Said (optional trip to Cairo)
Port Said (optional trip to Cairo)	Madras, India
Odessa, Soviet Union	Penang, Malaysia
Istanbul, Turkey	Hong Kong (optional trip to China)
Dubrovnik, Yugoslavia	Keelung, Taiwan
Casablanca, Morocco	Kobe, Japan
Port Everglades, Florida	

The recruiting effort is concentrated on campuses that have generated SAS students in the past. The international market, however, looms as a challenge for the future. Currently, the international students who sail with the ship are mostly on C. Y. Tung

scholarships—three to nine each voyage—while the U.S. student profile of the typical SAS voyager, because of the high per student cost, is dominated by percentages
of students from affluent families who attend the so-called "play" universities.

Advertisements for Semester at Sea are placed in the student newspapers of
schools whose students have enrolled in SAS previously. The Institute credits its success in recruiting students to carefully targeted publicity. One example of this publicity is a press release from May 1987 that described the Semester at Sea Program and
listed all the students in the Seattle area who were departing from the spring 1987
voyage.

MANAGEMENT AT SEMESTER AT SEA

The first step in the planning process of an SAS voyage is the selection of an itinerary, a process that begins two years in advance. Next comes the appointment of the
academic dean by the University of Pittsburgh who will work with the director of
academic planning to develop the voyage. Identifying and hiring a core program coordinator is central to the curricular planning for fully orchestrated series of lectures,
reading, and discussions on pivotal global issues. The 1990 course catalog includes a
course entitled "The Politics of Global Economic Relations" in which attention is devoted to the discussion of the multinational enterprise and the opportunities it provides the less developed countries for economic development as well as the threats it
poses in terms of exploitation and diminution of sovereignty. Next an assistant to the
academic dean is hired who will be responsible for registration and field programs related to the faculty.

The development of curriculum precedes the search for faculty, and concentrates on four major areas: the social sciences, the humanities, international business,
and the marine sciences and other sciences with field components. The curricular
pattern is approved by the University of Pittsburgh. The idea is to assemble a hetero-
geneous faculty of people whose experiences and teaching backgrounds complement
each other's and mesh harmoniously with the particular itinerary of the voyage. The
College of Arts and Sciences at the University of Pittsburgh has final approval on all
faculty appointments as well as assuring the academic integrity and standards.

The faculty members are responsible for developing their own syllabi and the
field programs that they are asked to lead in relation to their own courses; however,
the approval of the department chairman is required. The Institute, as resource office, is prepared to offer advice and comment on programs and syllabi generated by
new faculty. Other practica are developed through the Institute office with guidance
from the director of field planning.

Video tapes, library books, supplies, visas, telex traffic, interport lecturers, the
ordering of buses—all this is handled through the ISE office. In recruiting interport
lecturers, the central concern is to book people who are knowledgeable both politi-
cally and geographically about a given area and who will be available in an informal
way to talk to students and faculty on a one-to-one basis in the common areas of the
ship as well as in the classroom situation.

Staff members serve as resident directors, audiovisual personnel, secretaries,
and administrative personnel, as differentiated from faculty members whose respon-

sibilities are restricted to teaching and interacting. "Maintaining peace and order and tranquility—dwelling on the positive rather than the negative are extremely important in a living situation in which 500 people are on a 500-foot-long ship," according to Lewan who considers staff support crucial to the success of the voyage.

The executive dean functions as the "mayor of the city," while the academic dean is roughly equivalent to the chancellor of the university in this temporary community. Theoretically, the executive dean takes care of the safety, the personnel, the atmosphere, and the logistics of shipboard life, while the academic dean attends to academic issues and to the support of faculty. Legally, the ship's captain is in command; however, he defers to the administration on university matters. A good working relationship between the academic and executive deans is of paramount importance in this city of primarily college-age individuals.

Faculty are often presenting new material and teaching with an itinerary in mind rather than a syllabus—a situation that requires very different teaching skills from those demanded on a land campus. "This is one of the toughest teaching assignments in higher education," in Dean Lewan's analysis, "but can be a good professional experience if teachers are willing to grow and be open." Perhaps most difficult of all for many teachers is that they are not only teaching students but are also living with them. It is almost impossible to separate one's personal life from the professional tasks.

The role of the deans is to provide an environment conducive to academic work and to healthy social life. The dexterity with which students handle their assignments has a substantial ripple effect upon the spirit of each individual voyage and the perceptions the students take away with them of shipboard education. Establishing credibility can be a significantly more precarious undertaking for faculty and administrators than in traditional institutional settings. ISE administrators are very familiar with the delicate organizational balance; it has been their task to communicate this through the years to the constantly changing personnel of the program who are unfamiliar with the shipboard experience. Other elements contributing to the uniqueness of the organization aboard ship are the Chinese crew, often unfamiliar with American ways, and the various, frequently conflicting, constituencies on board (e.g., faculty, students, and adult passengers) and the instant-campus aspect of the community. Of paramount concern to ISE, however, is that every person who leaves the ship at the end of the voyage becomes an alumnus or alumna who will speak of his or her experience. Moreover, the Institute bears legal and financial responsibility. One example is that of the spring 1983 voyage when the *Universe* ran aground in Egypt. Through the work of the ISE, the semester continued using the Diplomat Hotel in Jerusalem as a temporary campus. Sometimes, a trip is not without disastrous moments and tragedies, such as when a female student fell to her death while descending a pyramid during the fall 1980 voyage.

FUTURE OF SEMESTER AT SEA

SAS is often compared erroneously with a study abroad program that gives students a long-term experience in one cultural setting. However, Semester at Sea is clear about its goals, among them to introduce students, in a comparative, introductory way, to several cultures, to extend their liberal arts curriculum through firsthand observation, and to enrich their understanding of and concern about world issues.

ISE believes that the fortunes of SAS depend upon the health of the U.S. economy, and the Institute's outlook remains optimistic. The Institute officials feel confident about the commitment of the University of Pittsburgh to the program and about its location in the East, which provides access to a different and expanded market of students. Increasingly, students are being drawn from a wider variety of colleges and universities, including the more prestigious institutions.

The Institute itself, headed by four academic administrators who have worked together over a period of years, is characterized by rapport and interchangeability of roles. This is important since one of these four is on board during each voyage, serving as executive dean. With the death of C. Y. Tung, his successor and oldest son, Mr. C. H. Tung, has pledged his full support to the concept of shipboard education in the "hope that as time goes by, the program will achieve new heights."

ISE has expended considerable effort to improve the SAS image by presenting the shipboard learning experience as a respectable academic program. Because of increased emphasis on academic content since the program moved to Pittsburgh, Semester at Sea hopes to find increased acceptance of the SAS concept and to bolster the intellectual integrity of the program. The major objective is to realize greater success in recruiting good students for the voyages.

The Institute is also interested in involving students in data collection for projects initiated by numerous agencies. Concluded Dr. Lewan, "The whole educational spectrum is available to us, particularly since we have a fixed itinerary and a relatively stable curriculum." With a twinkle in his eyes, Lewan suggested that the ultimate dream is an institute modeled on ISE in several countries, both developed and developing, so that "Shipping can become a viable university concept for the interaction of students who must solve the issues facing their generation, recognizing the reality of interdependence of all nations."

While acknowledging the imperfections and problems of Semester at Sea, Lewan believes that the ISE program plays a vital role in preparing its students, some 900 of them each year, to face the realities ahead in the twenty-first century.

23

COMPASSION
INTERNATIONAL

VISIT TO COMBASE

It was early morning in the sprawling Bolivian city of Cochabamba, and already families were lined up in front of the entrance to COMBASE (Commission for Evangelical Social Action in Bolivia) headquarters. As I walked through the compound with Compassion staff workers, we passed mothers holding crying babies and children chasing one another. Another activity-filled workday was about to begin.

Like so many Third World countries, Bolivia has tremendous needs, even though the government has made great strides in recent years. In some areas, as many as 50 percent of the children die before age 5. Malnutrition and diseases are common among the survivors. Many school children are so weakened and nauseated from lack of good nutrition that they cannot study.

COMBASE is made up of about 60 Bolivian churches that cooperate with Compassion to meet the physical and spiritual needs of more than 2,000 Compassion-sponsored children as well as other Bolivians in need.[1]

BACKGROUND

Compassion International's mission, as proclaimed on the stone-and-brass sign in front of the headquarters building is "Caring for Children and Families in the Name

[1]Stephen Sorenson, "A Busy Day at COMBASE," *Compassion*, January–February 1982, p. 3.

of Jesus." Compassion began in 1952 during the Korean Conflict when Everett Swanson, Compassion's founder, visited Korea and was moved by the plight of thousands of homeless orphan children roaming the streets, struggling to survive. Upon returning to the United States, he initiated the program that was to become the present-day Compassion International. For 16 years, all efforts were concentrated in Korea, helping to support orphans and abandoned children in institutions. Then, in 1968, the organization expanded into India and Indonesia, working primarily with children of widows and poverty-stricken families.

COMPASSION'S WORK[2]

> When asked which was the greatest commandment, Jesus replied: "Love the Lord your God with all your heart and with all your soul and with all your mind." This is the first and greatest commandment. And the second is like it: "Love your neighbor as yourself."

The central purpose of Compassion is to help channel practical assistance and personal caring to children of poverty living in the neediest areas of the world. Who are these children of poverty? They are children

Who are hungry and malnourished

Who live in unspeakable conditions, who have no bed of their own, who are victims of insect and rodent bites

Who do not have shoes or decent clothes to wear, a sweater or coat to keep them warm, a blanket to cover them

Who remain illiterate because there are no teachers, no books, and no money for school fees and supplies

Who have no doctor or health care worker, little medicine, and few adequate treatment centers within reach

Who have no playgrounds, no safe place to play, few toys; who have to work, and who are often robbed of their childhood

Worldwide, 1.2 billion children suffer serious deprivation. In many areas, as many as 50 percent actually die before their fifth birthday.

Compassion ministers to children, families, and communities who find themselves in desperate need.

CONTINUING SORENSON'S COMBASE VISIT

Stephen Sorenson's narrative of a visit to Bolivia afforded the starting point for this case study. To provide a snapshot of Compassion's philosophy and service, his observations are continued here:

"As I entered the building, Paul Stubbs, regional director for Compassion, introduced me to Linda Erickson, a nurse in charge of the pediatrics section who would show me around.

"'Here on the first floor,' Linda said, 'we treat sponsored children ages 15 and up—and their parents—in a general medical clinic on an outpatient basis. Complete

[2]Based on annual report, June 30, 1980, p. 3.

records of vaccinations, dental work, and appointments for each patient are kept in a statistics room.'

"She then led me through a fully stocked pharmacy where prescriptions given out by COMBASE's four doctors are filled and through a first-aid room where immediate treatment is available.

"Linda introduced me to Dr. Hernan Quiroz, who cares for Compassion-sponsored children 15 years of age or older.

" 'I've been here 10 years,' the doctor stated. 'I've had opportunities to work in other places, but I feel called to help poor children, and I want to be where the Lord wants me.'

" 'How do you feel about Compassion's program?' I asked.

" 'The best way to help these children' he quickly responded, 'is to give them medical care, food staples, clothing, and school supplies. Since children represent our country's future, health is very important. These children will be future leaders.'

"Dr. Quiroz then explained how he directly helps children. 'I routinely examine normal Compassion children every six months. If they have problems, then I may see them every two or three months. Anytime they are sick they can come and be examined for free; we charge low fees for medicine. My staff and I also work with COMBASE social workers to assist malnourished children. If we see such physical signs as hair loss, skin changes, or sores in their mouths, we send a note to their social workers and place the children in COMBASE's Meals Program. As a result, we've seen positive growth in Compassion children.'

"On the second floor we visited the social work department. A pretty Spanish girl in her twenties named Christina explained, 'There are six social workers and one supervisor. Each of us is responsible for between 300 and 400 sponsored children in our designated zones. We maintain our own records and visit homes to answer questions that come from Compassion headquarters or to solve problems the families are having. If a mother or child misses a monthly meeting, we check that out, too.'

" 'Why are you working at COMBASE?' Linda asked.

" 'My main purpose is to teach the Word of God to the children so they really learn it,' Christina answered. 'I also like to teach mothers how to care better for their families.'

"A short while later, we joined the other Compassion staff and entered a large room where a monthly meeting for children and adults was starting.

" 'We hold 40 meetings like this a month,' Linda whispered to me.

"After singing a chorus, the mothers and children sat down, and a mother prayed for God's blessing on the meeting. A boy and a girl sang a song in the Ketchua language for us, and a young boy played a song on a homemade charango.

"After Paul Stubbs said a few words, a social worker taught a Bible lesson based on John 20.

" 'Themes and verses for the meetings are set up a year in advance,' Linda told me, 'and every meeting has a Bible lesson in it. Each social worker holds about seven meetings a month, and about 50 children attend each meeting. The mothers and children are required to attend regularly.'

"After the Bible lesson, the mothers and children memorized Bible verses and watched a puppet show put on by the social workers. 'You need more protein than just what's in bread,' the puppets emphasized. 'You need meat and milk, not just chocolate and ice cream. Eat proteins so you'll be handsome like us.' After the laughter subsided, the final business began.

"The first mother and son were called up to the front, where a clerk behind a table looked at the child's identification card, checked his name off an attendance list, and looked at the letter the boy had written to his sponsor. At this time, the child also received a letter from his sponsor. Each child must write to his sponsor at least every three months.

"A second clerk then examined the boy's Sunday school attendance card and medical record card to ensure the child was regularly attending Sunday school and maintaining his medical appointment schedules. After verifying that everything was in order, the clerk gave him a special ticket entitling him to pick up his support money in the form of material goods at the COMBASE store.

"After lunch, Linda and I walked up to the third floor, where a modern laboratory, dental clinic, and pediatric clinic are located. A continual stream of people passed us, and others waited patiently on benches placed against the walls.

" 'Six dentists work here,' Linda said as we entered the dental clinic. A young girl seated in one of the two dental chairs squirmed as a dentist examined her teeth.

"Linda continued, 'The dentists work different shifts and usually see 20 patients a day. They clean teeth, remove teeth, fix cavities, and take X rays just like most dentists do. Compassion-related children only pay half what other patients do.'

"After walking down another hallway, we entered the laboratory. 'This,' Linda said proudly, 'serves all COMBASE patients. The lab staff does blood tests, stool tests to see if patients have parasites, urine tests, and so on for the various departments and clinics.'

"Suddenly a handsome man walked up to me and shook my hand. 'This is Dr. Delphin Carvenas,' Linda told me. 'He's our full-time biochemist who works in hematology, biochemistry, and microbiology.'

"I then asked her to ask the doctor why he is working at COMBASE and helping Compassion-sponsored children

" 'My own professional ethic is to help the poor people,' he commented, 'and it is the poor people who come to COMBASE.'

" 'What's left?' I asked, as Linda and I started down another corridor.

" 'Now we're going to pediatrics,' she said, 'which I coordinate. We have divided the clinic into two parts: sick child and well child.'

" 'What's the difference between them?' I asked.

" 'The term "well child" is a stumbler,' Linda said seriously, lowering her voice, 'because we don't have many completely well children. To us, a well child is one who doesn't have a contagious disease, an infection or fever, or serious malnutrition. We treat about 40 well children a day here, and many other sick children.'

"Stretched out on a table was a young child whose stomach was enlarged. I couldn't help remembering the medical care I had always received while growing up. 'What are the common illnesses?' I asked.

" 'They vary with the seasons,' Linda said, sitting down in her small office. 'Right now we're going into winter, so we see many upper respiratory infections, bronchitis, and pneumonia. In the summer, we see typhoid fever, diarrhea, and intestinal disease. All year long we treat parasite-related problems and chagas—little organisms that multiply in the bloodstream and cause premature heart attacks.'

" 'Do you give vaccinations to every child?'

" 'We vaccinate children up to age 3 for polio, diphtheria, whooping cough, tetanus, and tuberculosis,' Linda continued, 'and the children's parents pay 2 pesos per vaccination. That's less than 10 cents. In the clinic, we also perform regular physical examinations, send children to the lab for lab work or to the dentist, give health talks to mothers who attend monthly meetings, and give growth and development examinations to children up to age 5 to make sure they're developing normal physical and mental skills. We treat quite a few children, considering there are more than 2,000 sponsored children and also their brothers and sisters.'

"As I stood up to leave, I asked Linda what the most rewarding part of her work was.

" 'When I see a mother doing what we teach her to do,' she replied. 'The mothers are learning to help themselves and to care for their children. For example, more children are drinking boiled water instead of the polluted water stored in barrels outside their homes.'

"After we parted, I went downstairs to visit the COMBASE store, where sponsored children purchase essential food, clothing, and school supplies with the tickets Compassion workers give them during the monthly meetings. No money changes hands.

"As I watched, a girl presented her identification card and ticket, and a man behind the counter checked the support list. He then automatically gave her such essentials as shoes, food, and school supplies and a receipt showing how much each item cost. Because she had credit left over after the essentials were purchased, the girl was allowed to choose two notebooks, and she signed a receipt showing she had received the supplies. She and her mother then walked away, and another child stepped up to the window.

"Tired, having experienced COMBASE's schedule for a day, I walked outside and watched families come and go. I saw hope on the mothers' faces as they brought their children out.

" 'What a priceless privilege for them,' I thought. 'Their children can be examined by doctors for free, and the medicines from the pharmacy are affordable. And through the store, children receive essentials they never would receive otherwise if it weren't for sponsorship support.

"Now I'm back in the United States and have easy access to qualified doctors and medicine. But I haven't forgotten the sponsored children who receive regular Bible teaching and important care through COMBASE. Although the needs are great, COMBASE is able to communicate effectively God's love in action to children and families because Compassion sponsors are reaching out in practical ways in the name of Jesus Christ," wrote Sorenson.

CHILD SPONSORSHIP

More than 56,000 children were receiving monthly assistance through the one-to-one sponsorship program. Each needy child was linked with his or her own sponsor, who sends $18 a month to provide for such basic needs as food, clothing, school fees, books and supplies, and biblical training.[3] A sponsor may correspond with his or her sponsored child, provide special gifts, and is encouraged to pray for the child. Many sponsor more than one child; one woman was sponsoring 100 boys and girls in 1981. Sponsors can discontinue sponsorship at any time.

Exhibit 23.1 is a count of sponsored children from 1952 to 1981. Exhibit 23.2 lists totals by countries of residence.

Exhibit 23.1

COMPASSION-SPONSORED CHILDREN, 1952–1981

YEAR	NUMBER OF SPONSORED CHILDREN
1952	35
1953	105
1954	140
1955	210
1956	360
1957	480
1958	720
1959	2,000
1960	3,500
1961	6,200
1962	10,000
1963	12,700
1964	13,800
1965	14,600
1966	15,400
1967	16,700
1968	17,400
1969	16,800
1970	16,355
1971	15,938
1972	15,658
1973	18,970
1974	23,348
1975	26,360
1976	30,993
1977	34,284
1978	40,645
1979	46,517
1980	55,108
1981	56,562

[3]In May 1982, this sponsorship figure was increased to $21.

Exhibit 23.2

WHERE SPONSORED CHILDREN LIVE*

COUNTRY	SPONSORED CHILDREN	PERCENTAGE†
Belize	173	.31%
Bolivia	2,310	4.19
Brazil	37	.07
Burma	2,349	4.26
Colombia	2,150	3.90
Dominican Republic	3,381	6.14
Ecuador	61	.11
El Salvador	1,653	3.00
Fiji	250	.45
Guatemala	588	1.06
Haiti	14,173	25.72
Honduras	26	.04
Hong Kong	650	1.17
India	6,411	11.63
Indonesia	8,247	14.97
Jamaica	42	.08
Korea	5,481	9.95
Liberia	45	.08
Malaysia	257	.47
Mexico	25	.05
Nicaragua	175	.32
Paraguay	43	.08
Peru	11	.02
Philippines	3,129	5.68
Rwanda	1,842	3.34
Singapore	76	.14
Thailand	1,023	1.86
Uganda	315	.57
United States	160	.29
Venezuela	13	.02
	55,096	

*As of January 31, 1981.
†Rounded figures.

Compassion's work was managed by 74 staff people in the U.S. headquarters; overseas staff included 17 expatriates and 93 national workers, in addition to many national pastors, church leaders, and Western missionaries who assisted in supervising individual projects. Exhibit 23.3 shows Compassion's 1981 organizational structure.

As an indication of growth, Sorenson reviewed these figures: "At the end of 1978, Compassion had 867 projects: then we added 195 new ones from October 1979 to October 1980, bringing the total to 1,062 around the world. The number in each country changes constantly due to such factors as political changes, combining projects, and so on."

Exhibit 23.3

COMPASSION'S 1981 FORMAL ORGANIZATIONAL STRUCTURE

Overseas Program Director — Edward Kimball

Administrative Assistant — Mary Wilson

North Asia Regional Office Bruce Dart	Central Asia Assistant Regional Director Paul Mitchell	South Asia Regional Director Laurence McCowan	North and South America Regional Director Paul Stubbs	
Korea Office Kim Yung Ju (Hong Kong, the Philippines)	Burma Office John Thetgyi (India, Thailand)	Indonesia Office Jus Kalempouw (Malaysia, New Guinea, Singapore)	Bolivia Office Jean Johnson	Kenya Office Lynette Walters (Liberia, Uganda, Rwanda)
			Dominican Republic Bill Kent	
			Haiti Office Ronald Gregory	
			(Belize, Brazil, Columbia, Equador, El Salvador, Guatemala, Honduras, Jamaica, Mexico, Nicaraugua, Paraguay, United States, Venezuela)	

MEALS SPONSORSHIP

Compassion was also involved in a meals sponsorship program, in which a sponsor paid $5.00 a month to provide one hungry child with at least 20 nourishing meals a month. This type of sponsorship was not emphasized heavily. It resembled child sponsorship in certain respects. A meals sponsor received a packet describing the specific project where his or her monthly support check was sent and also received photographs and updated quarterly reports. Like child sponsors, meals sponsors received Compassion's bimonthly magazine free, and the following groups regularly received brochures describing the meals sponsorship program: sponsors who canceled their child sponsorship, people who asked for a "no money" packet to see if they wanted to sponsor a child, people who asked for information about Compassion, and small donors who could not afford to sponsor a child. As of June 30, 1981, 2,600 children were receiving meals each school day.

Compassion receives many contributions from friends who are not assigned to a specific project. These funds are used by field staff in areas where the need is greatest.

TYPES OF PROJECTS[4]

Compassion's projects are classified into four major groups: Family Helper Projects, School and Hostel Projects, Children's Homes, and Special Care Centers. See Exhibit 23.4 for percentages of sponsored children by group, for selected years.

Exhibit 23.4

PERCENTAGES OF SPONSORED CHILDREN BY GROUPS, SELECTED YEARS 1976–1981

	1976	1978	1980	1981
Homes	23.2%	37.3%	5.9%	5.2%
Family helper plans	51.0	50.3	42.2	41.5
Schools and hostels	24.0	10.8	50.9	52.4
Special care centers	1.8	1.4	1.0	.9

Family Helper

In this type of project, Compassion staff members and cooperating groups and individuals help children whose families are too poor to care for the children's basic needs and education. This helps prevent abandonment by keeping the children within the family unit. In many cases, the children's mothers are widows or their fathers have abandoned the families or suffered crippling injuries. The sponsorship funds help the children pay for such essentials as food, clothing, school fees and supplies, and medical care. The funds are channeled through the projects' center—in many cases, a local church or mission group.

School and Hostel

With more than 400 primary schools involved in school projects, Compassion clearly emphasizes the importance of education and Bible teaching. Many poverty-stricken children who live in areas where primary education is either unavailable or unaffordable benefit from child sponsorship. They have the opportunity to attend school reg-

[4]Adapted from Compassion's literature, 1981.

ularly because the tuition and related school fees are paid. All the children in schools and hostels—as in all other projects—receive Bible training, school supplies, and clothing. Many of them also receive school uniforms and hot lunches according to their needs. In some countries, children attend government schools. In other countries, children attend church- or mission-operated schools.

Hostels provide bilingual instruction for tribal children who, because they cannot speak the national language, are ineligible to enter public schools and also provide room and board for children who live too far from school to go home after school.

Children's Homes

Although the emphasis on this type of project has diminished, some children who are abandoned or orphaned are cared for in homes where they receive food, clothing, shelter, and other elements of daily care.

Special Care Centers

These centers provide specialized treatment, education, and care for physically and mentally handicapped children. Sponsorship support meets their needs while they are in mission hospitals, clinics, and/or special training schools.

SPECIAL FUNDS[5]

Compassion programs are designed to help children, families, and communities develop their potential in the way God intended. The following programs are helping to remove some of the barriers that prevent this development.

Education Assistance

Deserving youngsters receive the necessary fees for middle school, high school, Bible school, or vocational schools. Additionally, funds are available to provide desks, books, blackboards, teacher training, and so on for schools in needy areas.

Medical Assistance

Support is provided for destitute children who need surgery, hospital care, braces, or other costly medical treatment they otherwise would be unable to obtain.

Community Development

Compassion works with local governments and national Christian leaders to help deprived communities improve living conditions and develop their own resources and skills; it also supports programs to improve health and nutrition, to help provide

[5]Adapted from *1980 Annual Report*, p. 7.

clean water, and to encourage vocational training. Compassion carefully works through Christian leaders within the community who recognize the importance of spiritual needs as well as the physical ones. Compassion's programs help deprived communities improve living conditions and develop their own resources and skills.

Emergency Relief

Special care is provided for victims of famine, floods, hurricanes, war, or other extreme circumstances who are involved in the child sponsorship program.

COOPERATING GROUPS AND INSTITUTIONS

Compassion's field staff cooperates with missionaries, national pastors and church associations, and indigenous Christian leaders associated with numerous missions (Exhibit 23.5).

Exhibit 23.5

COOPERATING MISSIONS, AGENCIES, AND NATIONAL CHURCHES

FOREIGN MISSIONS	NATIONAL CHURCH ORGANIZATIONS
Action International Ministries	Andhra Evangelical Lutheran Church
American Baptist Churches of U.S.A.	Bangkok Evangelical Fellowship of Thailand
Anglican Mission of Great Britian	Burma Anglican Church
Assemblies of God	Burma Baptist Convention
Australian Baptist	Burma Methodist Church
Bible and Medical Missionary Fellowship, U.S.A.	Burma Presbyterian Church
Bibles for the World	Christian Medical College Hospital, Vellore
Christian and Missionary Alliance	Church of South India
Christian Brethren	COMBASE (Bolivia Commission of Evangelicals for Social Action)
Christian Deaf Fellowship	Convention of Baptist Churches of Northern Circars
Christian Missions in Many Lands	Episcopal Church of Brazil
Church of God (Cleveland)	Evangelical Church of India
Church of God of Prophecy	Evangelical Free Church of Burma
Church of the Nazarene	Evangelical Pentecostals
Conservative Baptist	Evangelical Western Center for Children
Evangelical Mennonite Church	Full Gospel Church (Bangkok)
Free Methodist Church	Galilea Baptist Church (Nicaragua)
Latin American Mission	Guatemala Evangelical Ministries
Missionary Church	India Pentecostal Church
OMS International, Inc.	Interamerican Church (Ecuador)
Plymouth Brethren	Interamerican Evangelical Church (Colombia)
Protestant Episcopal Church of U.S.A.	
Salvation Army	
Scheiffelin Leprosy Research and Training Center	
Sepik Christian Akademies	

Exhibit 23.5 (Cont.)

Spanish Evangelical Literature
  Fellowship
Sudan Interior Mission
The Evangelical Alliance Mission
Unevangelized Fields Mission
United Brethren
Wesleyan Church
World Gospel Mission
Worldteam
Worldwide Evangelization Crusade

Liberian Christian Assemblies
Metropolitan Church Association
  (India)
Pentecostal Church of Indonesia
Philippine Assemblies of God
Philippine Baptist Church
Prince of Peace Church
Thailand Baptist Missionary
  Fellowship
The Gospel Church (Fiji)
United Methodist Church of Malaysia

Compassion, U.S.A., cooperates closely with three agencies in its family: Compassion of Australia, Compassion of Canada, and TEAR Fund/Great Britain. Each of these evangelical agencies is autonomous, with its own board of directors and executive staff. Compassion, U.S.A., administers child care projects overseas for these agencies, although each is responsible for its own fund raising and home office administration. Exhibit 23.6 provides a financial summary for the U.S. agency.

Exhibit 23.6

FINANCIAL SUMMARY FOR THE U.S. AGENCY, JUNE 30, 1980*

Expended for program ministries		
Direct grants for children and projects	$5,852,319	
Field and project supervision	561,122	
Sponsor services	179,306	
Total program	$6,592,747	75.4%
Funds for future ministries	383,948	4.4
Expended for supporting services		
Administration	938,735	10.7
Fund-raising	828,138	9.5
Total supporting	$1,766,873	20.2%
Total U.S.	$8,743,568	100.0%

*These figures reflect U.S. income and expense only.

COMPASSION'S FUTURE

Stephen Sorenson offered several observations concerning Compassion's present status and future directions: "We have a reputation for responsible, Bible-based child care and needy-family assistance, and because of Compassion's responsible use of funds, the Better Business Bureau's Philanthropic Advisory Service has given the institution a very high rating. This is not an endorsement of our work but an appraisal of funds use. Compassion also is a member of the Evangelical Council for Financial Accountability. We have excellent relations with evangelical missions, national church organizations, foreign governments and their agencies, and organizations similar to ours. (See Appendix 23A for a summary of some organizations similar to Compassion.)

"Nevertheless, we are not well known among the general public. Also, we have done little promotion through the press to improve visibility with various target publics. This is my feeling. We must take steps to overcome a number of deficiencies in presenting our story to sponsors and prospects. These are our objectives, as I view them." (See Exhibit 23.7.)

Appendix 23B summarizes Compassion's strengths and weaknesses as viewed by Sorenson.

Exhibit 23.7

COMPASSION'S KEY OBJECTIVES FOR THE 1980s

1. To continue to develop effective child development programs that will meet the needs of needy children and their families. This involves helping each child learn
    a. What it means to be a Christian in word and deed
    b. How to maintain a healthy body
    c. How to develop as a responsible member of his family, church, and community
    d. How to be self-supporting and in turn to share with others in need
2. To expand existing child development programs creatively
3. To increase the number of sponsors, thereby increasing revenue and the overall ministry
4. To even more effectively manage the organization's operations as they dramatically expand while continuing to treat sponsors, donors, and the like, on a personalized basis
5. To maintain its strong evangelical emphasis at a time when many similar child development programs are not
6. To keep overhead costs as low as possible so that Compassion can continue to direct the highest percentages of the sponsorship dollar into programs directly benefiting needy children and families
7. To continue to attract high caliber employees who are dedicated to Compassion's goals while at the same time being committed to family, God, and personal relationships
8. To increase its visibility and credibility in the eyes of its various publics
9. To put into practice daily Biblical principles and look to God for direction
10. To continue to maintain excellent relations with its cooperating agencies, missions, national churches, and so on. This means designing into every program a sense of cooperation and an opportunity for national church leaders to participate.

PROMOTIONAL FACTORS

Sorenson's reflections on Compassion's promotion covered mass media and direct mail. He noted that Compassion's advertising program has done very well in recent years. Procurement cost per sponsor was $57.52—an increase of $8.44 per sponsor over the 1978–1979 cost—due to inflation that has particularly affected the magazine advertisements and direct-mail efforts. (See Exhibit 23.8, a summary of new sponsors, based on February 1981 figures.)

Exhibit 23.8

SUMMARY OF NEW SPONSORS, 1978–1979 to 1980–1981

SOURCE	1978-1979	1979-1980	1980-1981*
Television	2,600	2,555	4,490
Magazines	1,190	1,519	1,437
Concerts	108	327	472
Compassion magazine	216	353	273
Direct mail	1,255	654	413
Referrals	303	261	512
Current sponsors	166	152	239
Miscellaneous	338	347	437
Subtotal	6,176	6,168	8,273
Great Britain	869	2,024	1,278
Canada	843	1,440	365
Australia	279	495	564
Total	8,167	10,127	10,480

*Eight months of 1980–1981 fiscal year.

"Compassion has effectively used TV to gain sponsors for many years, and it is important to understand our use of television," emphasized Sorenson. Starting with a Dale Evans special, Compassion developed several others, including "Pat Boone Presents Compassion Children," "Pat Boone and the Little Ones," "Faces of Compassion," "Faces with Pat Boone," "Children of the Third World," and the new television show titled "Children: The World's Most Valuable Resource," which was developed and released in 1981.

An agency in California, in cooperation with Compassion's director of communications, purchased television time. After time was purchased, the communications department was sent a schedule of stations, times, and costs, so an administrative assistant could keep track of telephone response to each viewing.

Sorenson outlined to the case writer the method of handling responses. When an interested individual calls the toll-free number in response to a show, a contract service answers the telephone, asks specific questions, and records the information. The call is then keyed into the CRT unit. Later, Compassion receives important data, such as name, address, and source; the ZIP codes reveal which stations generated the calls. Since Compassion's show is aired at many different times across the country and hundreds of calls may come in within a half-hour period, the answering service is required. Sorenson feels that presently there is no effective way to set up an in-house telephone answering system.

The Assignments Department sends out "no money" packets to the potential sponsors, with instructions to return the packets within 10 days if they do not wish to sponsor a child. When a person sends in a check and requests to sponsor a child, this "money sponsor" will then be assigned a child.

"Direct mail," Sorenson explained, "is an important medium for us." On a regular basis, the Communications Department sends out direct-mail appeals, for such funds as the education fund and the medical fund. New lists must be developed and promotion pieces designed to attract people who have never heard about Compassion. Much emphasis has been placed on sponsors, who could resent high-pressure tactics. Although the mailings are carefully evaluated as to their tone and content in relation to the whole mailing program, Compassion exercises care to ensure that sponsors already sacrificing should not feel pressured to sacrifice more.

Compassion continues to advertise regularly in magazines, but increasing costs are proving to be a detriment. The average cost to gain one magazine-related sponsor in the 18 months ended in June 1980 was $42.22, and those costs have continued to climb. (See Exhibit 23.9.)

Content and appeal of advertisements are represented in Exhibits 23.10 and

---

Exhibit 23.9

1979–1980 MAGAZINE ADVERTISING
(18 months ending June 1980)

MAGAZINE	SPONSORS	COST TO DATE	COST PER SPONSOR
Campus Life	451	$10,481.44	$23.24
Christian Herald	32	1,986.70	62.08
Christian Life	172	10,673.23	62.05
Christian Reader	136	7,119.68	52.35
Charisma	32	2,253.25	70.41
Christianity Today	162	5,581.08	34.45
Evangelizing Today's Child	1	277.10	277.10
Logos Journal	51	4,703.95	29.04
Moody Monthly	645	18,499.33	28.68
Saturday Evening	47	3,069.57	65.31
Today's Christian Woman	45	645.57	14.35
TV Guide	256	20,408.59	79.72
Total	2,030	$85,699.48	$42.22

Exhibit 23.10

COMPASSION MAGAZINE ADVERTISEMENT

C H I L D R E N   I N   N E E D

Amilcar Alvarez Sierra
Guatemala (Age—5)

Malenga Ombeni
Zaire (Age—11)

Wilfrid Genece
Haiti (Age—8)

Tanya Lisa Hoare
Belize (Age—9)

Remedios Limachi
Bolivia (Age—10)

Miguel Castellanos
Colombia (Age—11)

Samson Kabenjera
Uganda (Age—6)

Petra Vargas Tellez
Mexico (Age—10)

Budi Utomo
Indonesia (Age—12)

Pak Yung Sun
Korea (Age—9)

Please Sponsor Me

Each of these children needs a sponsor. You can choose one of them to help, or let us select a needy child for you.

Your support of $21 each month will help provide your child with decent clothing, school fees, books, supplies, and in many cases supplementary food. Also, each sponsored child learns about Jesus Christ through regular involvement with a Christian mission or Sunday school.

You may share your love more personally by exchanging letters, photos, and cards. Your sponsorship may be discontinued whenever you wish.

To begin, complete the sponsor application and mail it with your first monthly check. We'll send you your child's photo, biography folder, and full information. If your choice has already been selected, we'll carefully choose another needy child for your consideration
Please write today . . . a child is waiting for you! ☐

SPONSOR APPLICATION

☐ Yes, I want to sponsor a needy child at $21 a month. My preference is:
☐ Any child who needs me most.

☐ _____ from the pictures shown above. (If already selected when we hear from you, we will carefully choose a similar child.) Indicate second choice here:

_____

My first support check is enclosed for:
☐ $21 (one month), ☐ $63 (3 months), ☐ $252 (one year).

Name ☐ Mr. ☐ Miss
      ☐ Mrs. ☐ Ms. _____

Address_____

City_____ State_____ Zip_____

Gifts are tax-deductible. Please make checks payable to:
COMPASSION INTERNATIONAL, 3955 Cragwood Drive,
P.O. Box 7000, Colorado Springs, Colorado 80933.
Phone (303) 594-9900   CM0982

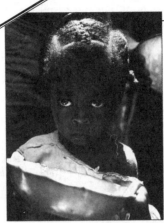

23.11, which appeared in *Compassion* (September–October 1982), a special thirtieth anniversary issue.

Compassion magazine is published bimonthly and, according to Sorenson, has proved an effective means of informing existing sponsors. But in spite of the fact that the magazine's circulation has increased from about 49,000 in the fall of 1980 to a 1981 figure of some 67,000, he stated, that Compassion needs to evaluate critically its entire format. "In my opinion, other similar organizations are publishing nicer magazines that contain more information and interesting articles for sponsors. Now might be a good time to conduct this review, since we will be seeking a replacement for the present editor who retires later this year."[6]

THE SPONSOR PUBLIC

To the general populace, Compassion may not be viewed as being very different from similar organizations, and Sorenson speculated that his organization's sponsors prob-

---

Exhibit 23.12

PROFILE OF COMPASSION SPONSORS, 1981

Age of sponsors	Approximately two-thirds of new sponsors are under 41 years of age.
Income of sponsors	More than two-thirds of all sponsors have incomes under $25,000.
Educational background	One-third of all sponsors have a college degree.
Religious preference	One-third of all sponsors are Baptist or Methodist. Thirteen percent said they were "nondenominational; 7 percent were Roman Catholic.
Motivation	More than one-third of all sponsors first heard of Compassion through a television special. More than one-third learned about Compassion through advertisements.
Christian emphasis	Eighty percent of every age group sampled believe that every child should learn about Jesus Christ and attend Sunday school regularly.
Compassion program	Approximately one-third feel they get too much mail from Compassion office; 87 percent believe Compassion is efficient in providing assistance for their children.
Correspondence/child	In spite of the fact that we have many questions about child's correspondence, 80 percent of current sponsors say they would sponsor if they did not receive letters from the child; only 56 percent of former sponsors agreed to this. Forty-seven percent feel they *do* hear often enough from their children, 86 percent of sponsors say letters are meaningful and satisfying, and 83 percent appreciate the opportunity to write to the child.

---

[6]Sorenson assumed editorship of the magazine effective with the September–October 1982 issue.

ably differ little, if at all, from those contributing to other such organizations. Exhibit 23.12 is a profile of Compassion's sponsors, based on a study conducted by an outside marketing research firm.

Although the sponsor survey was completed in 1981, Sorenson believes that his organization should do another in 1982 so the Compassion staff members can spot trends among the types of people who are becoming sponsors.

Commenting on cancellations and delinquencies, Sorenson indicated a need to monitor these rising trends carefully, a problem faced by similar organizations. Actually, Compassion's percentage of cancellations is lower than that for many similar organizations. But with faltering economic conditions in the United States, he expects there may be an acceleration of delinquencies and cancellations. "I believe we must look at the quality of service—and the contact with sponsors—we are providing and figure out ways they can be improved. For example, we recently revised the letters sent to delinquent supporters so ultimate cancellations will be reduced. We believe regular child letters are also a key factor in reducing sponsor dissatisfaction." Sorenson hopes that data processing printouts, once the new computer system is fully operational, will help to identify overdue child correspondence early enough to correct the problem quickly. Cancellations have ranged from 15 to 20 percent monthly and the delinquency rate from 5 to 10 percent.

Referring to response by telephone, Sorenson commented on his idea to hire someone for that responsibility: "The telephone can be an effective approach for the Correspondence Department to use in communicating with sponsors. I believe we need a full-time person to do this and to help with written correspondence. This will supplement our traditional methods of follow-up. With a little experimenting we can decide how effective the approach might be and how best to use it."

Appendix 23C summarizes Sorenson's proposal for a telephone specialist, indicating qualifications, training, a suggested approach for testing the position, and a list of principal responsibilities for the person hired.

Sorenson explained that Compassion had conducted a telephone calling campaign to see if the approach would help retain delinquent sponsors. The caller was given a list of 150 names, drawn at random by data processing, who would otherwise receive a final reminder. A script was developed, and the caller spent nine hours telephoning 150 individuals.

The final results indicated that 18 had already sent checks; 27 wanted to continue sponsorship; 2 indicated intent to cancel; 3 were uncertain about sponsorship; 50 could not be located; 12 numbers were unpublished; 15 people could not be reached because they were absent when called; 13 were not reached at all after three attempts; and 10 had already made up their minds to cancel. "Keeping in mind the small sample used, we concluded this approach was not feasible," finished Sorenson. Telephone numbers for sponsors are not asked for currently because the computer system does not have room to store them, but the new system will have the capacity.

THE FUTURE

"Thinking further about our approach to promoting what Compassion does," Sorenson summarized, "most of us are convinced that we must employ better ways to relate to various publics—church, college, missions, donors, deferred giving, the press—and the general public that will, of course, be influenced by how we deal with the other publics."

Appendix 23A

OVERVIEW OF COMPETITIVE ORGANIZATIONS SIMILAR TO COMPASSION

SAVE THE CHILDREN

Founded in 1932. Primary emphasis on hot-lunch program for children in Appalachia. Sponsorship program developed later to help feed, clothe, and provide school supplies for needy youngsters. Began overseas operations in 1939 to aid war refugees. Recently began self-help development projects to encourage people in entire communities to improve their own living standards and futures of their children. Member of American Council of Voluntary Agencies for Foreign Service, Private Agencies Collaborating Together, and International Council of Voluntary Agencies. Registered with consulting status with United National Economic and Social Council.

FOSTER PARENTS PLAN

Founded in 1937 to aid children caught up in the Spanish Civil War. Present approaches have evolved into programs comparable in many ways to those of Compassion International.

CHRISTIAN CHILDREN'S FUND

Begun in 1938 to help needy children in China. Program similar to Compassion's in some respects, but does not highly stress biblical teaching in its projects.

WORLD RELIEF CORPORATION

The international relief and development arm of the National Association of Evangelicals, designed to help in refugee relief and development, disaster relief, and self-help development. Active in 43 countries. Has no child sponsorship program.

Appendix 23A (Cont.)

CHRISTIAN NATIONALS EVANGELISM COMMISSION, INC.

Started by two Indian doctors to aid villagers in their home area. No child sponsorship program.

WORLD CONCERN

Provides emergency relief aid for needy individuals, participates in long-term development, but has no sponsorship program. Does collaborate with a number of overseas agencies.

FOOD FOR THE HUNGRY

Does have a sponsorship program, but primary emphasis is on relief and a student volunteer "Hunger Corps" that assists in relief and development efforts.

WORLD VISION INTERNATIONAL

Well-known organization reportedly sponsoring some 300,000 children in 50 countries. Also emphasizes emergency aid and a self-reliance program.

Appendix 23B

SUMMARY OF COMPASSION'S STRENGTHS AND WEAKNESSES*

Strengths

Sound financial management.

Experienced senior staff members at headquarters and in the field who are highly skilled in technical, human, and conceptual aspects of the work; who are highly motivated; who work well as a team and/or individually; who meet regularly to discuss important policies, progress, problems, and so on; and who are committed to the organization's goals and objectives.

Vision for the future that allows the organization to take advantage of opportunities and anticipate problems.

Appendix 23B (Cont.)

A proven track record in the eyes of important individuals, groups, agencies, and organizations cooperating with Compassion in various ways.

Effective relations with key individuals, groups, agencies, and organizations that benefit all aspects of Compassion's work.

The desire to continually improve, to learn, to reach out in new areas.

The recognition that God's blessing is important to the organization's work.

A new headquarters that will allow the organization to manage new programs and absorb tremendous growth in future years.

Loyal sponsors and donors who believe in Compassion's work/ministry and will sacrifice to further its goals and objectives.

Weaknesses

A system of management that, although it is working well now, will need to be adapted so that other management techniques can be used. For example, executive leadership will need to begin choosing middle managers who can take charge of certain areas and report to executive staff.

An inadequate computer system (that will be replaced in the fall of 1982).

Not enough thought concerning all the ramifications of tremendous sponsorship growth and the dramatic need for volunteer assistance.

Overdependence on the use of television to attract new sponsors. Currently, this is not a problem.

Lack of a written, cohesive promotional plan in the Communication Department that will be able effectively to guide future decisions regarding approaches, new personnel, new target publics, and the overall emphases of the department and its current staff.

Lack of regular, in-depth meetings by communications staff members to plan new directions, discuss issues and problems, and in general grow together as a more effective team.

Too little contact with certain publics, such as deferred givers, churches, and college students. More traveling needs to be done to reach certain publics.

*From Stephen Sorenson's perspective.

Appendix 23C

PROPOSAL FOR TELEPHONE SPECIALIST

Position	Compassion Telephone Specialist, Correspondence Department.
Objective	To use the telephone in those areas where we believe it would be the most effective tool to allow us to more effectively communicate with and meet the needs of our sponsors so as to reduce the number of cancellations we receive each month. The telephone would be one of the approaches used by the Correspondence Department to meet its objective.

Appendix 23C (Cont.)

Personnel	To hire one full-time person to do the majority of the telephoning for the Correspondence Department and to help with the written correspondence work.
Hours	To have person work part of the time during the day and part of the time in the evening. We would work toward a W/Th/F 7:00–3:30 and M/Tu 12:00–8:30 schedule.
Qualifications	To hire a person who has the qualifications and experience necessary to minister effectively to the needs of our sponsors. Person should have a good telephone voice and a warm personality. Should enjoy using the telephone. Should be able to pick up facts quickly and to handle negative responses from sponsors in a positive way. Have ability to communicate effectively verbally and in writing. Must be able to keep accurate records and to be able to issue follow-up reports. (Personnel from the Communications Department will use a telephone role-playing exercise with applicants as part of the screening process.)
Training	To have this person report to the Correspondence Department supervisor and to handle the regular dictation work of the department. This is done to prepare the new employee for the role of telephone specialist. New employee will receive the necessary orientation to the work of the other departments to gain a background to enable this person to answer questions of sponsors intelligently. Training period would be 4 to 6 weeks.
Equipment	New employee will need a phone and dictation equipment to record conversations or to dictate follow-up letters. Dictation equipment will be used by person to help with other work in the department.
Scope of project	When trained, new employee will spend 6 hours a day handling telephone needs. The rest of person's time will be used in doing the other work in the department. The success of the telephoning will be the determining factor as to how much of the employee's time will be used in the telephone specialist role. If very successful, this will become a full-time job. (Personnel from the Communications Department will help evaluate trainee's performance by critiquing how well the person actually handled various sponsor problems over the telephone.)
Test areas	For several categories test samples will be set up. Half the people will be called and half will only receive a letter with the results monitored. After three months, our phone calling will be reviewed. Categories that are successful will be expanded. Those not successful will be deleted from the program. New categories can be added at this time.
Initial telephone responsibilities	1. Incoming calls not directed to another employee in the Correspondence Department 2. Angry sponsors 3. Special problems that require dialogue 4. Follow-up or those replies from sponsors we are still waiting on

Appendix 23C (Cont.)

5. Sponsors showing any confusion or irritation about the substitute child offered to them
6. Follow-up on no money requests that have not been responded to
7. Certain categories of departures
8. Cancellations and subrejects because person is angry or those with no reason or a vague reason
9. New sponsor follow-up (see how sponsorship is going after 2 to 4 months)

JULIE RESEARCH
LABORATORIES

The Department of Defense needs to become a more demanding customer with regard to quality, performance, and price. . . . contractors . . . do not automatically provide quality goods and services at the lowest possible cost.[1]

As one who has attempted, and unsuccessfully thus far, to become a supplier of electronic technology to the U.S. Army Missile Command, Loebe Julie agrees with Admiral Rickover's assessment. The drama that began for Julie Research Laboratories (JRL) in 1974 had continued, without any promise of denouement, in 1982.

The seven-year dispute between the Army and Loebe Julie, the small businessman going out of business because of the battle, again has reached an impasse.[2]

Julie Research Laboratories has been spotlighted in numerous media—*Electronic Engineering Times, Federal Times, The New York Times, Daily News, Washington Post, Electronic News,* and others—and was featured on *60 Minutes* in December 1981, all this attention mostly a result of tireless effort by the beleaguered

---

[1]This excerpt from Admiral Rickover's address to the congressional Joint Economic Committee is reprinted from Hyman G. Rickover, "The Moral Responsibility of Business," *Technology Review*, (May–June 1982), pp.12–15, at p. 15. Copyright 1982.

[2]Eric Yoder, "Dying Firm Won't Bet on Army 'Horse Race,' " *Federal Times*, March 1, 1982.

electronics engineer who once believed that benefits in cost and performance of superior equipment would be quickly recognized and such a system purchased by those needing its capabilities. How he discovered the error of this assumption is detailed in two "comic books" commissioned by the inventor, the first published in 1980, the second in 1981 (Exhibit 24.1). Each back cover provides JRL's telephone number and a plea for help, concluding with the statement, "By working together, we may be able to strengthen our country."

THE ESSENCE OF BOOK ONE

Prefacing Book One with "what you are about to read is true," the 44-page publication, plus four information-filled cover pages, was mailed to many, including such notables as Jimmy Carter, then president of the United States; Ronald Reagan, then Republican candidate for the presidency; James T. McIntyre, director, Office of Management and Budget; Congressman Ted Weiss, New York City; Lt. General Donald Keith, Army chief of staff for research, development, and acquisition; A. Vernon Weaver, Jr., Small Business Administration; Senators Jacob Javits and Patrick Moynihan of New York; the Senate Armed Services Committee; Senator William Proxmire of Wisconsin; and a large selection of newspapers, magazines, and television news organizations. What follows are excerpts from Book One.

> This story is about Julie Research Labs, one of a dwindling group of inventor-led high-technology research companies.

> What is a calibrator? . . . All types of instruments must be checked and adjusted—calibrated—precisely, or they won't work properly. Many test instruments are used to adjust these devices. But, what if the *test* instruments are not accurate?

The dangers of inadequate calibration can be illustrated in a missile's guidance system: if the calibration device is not quite accurate, and if the test instrument is somewhat off, its error is added to that of the calibrator. Finally, if the guidance system of the missile is also in error, this factor compounds both the test and calibration errors. The consequences could be disastrous.

> In 1974, the Army decided that they needed better calibration equipment and issued an R.F.P. (Request for Proposals).

> What Julie Labs offered is what the Army asked for: upgraded capability of 2,750 calibrations per year by each technician (up from 800); fully automated; savings of 22,000 hours per year at each installation; identical service, regardless of the location or skill level of the technician; substantially improved turnaround and data.

The booklet narrates how the Army "rejected our bid without even opening it," claiming that the bid allegedly arrived 4 hours and 57 minutes after the hour of closing. JRL protested, illustrating that the Labs' bid was telegraphed in before the deadline, but even with documentation, Loebe Julie said, "The Army refused to reconsider, even though the Western Union supervisor recorded the time our bid was

Exhibit 24.1

JRL CARTOON/NARRATIVE BOOKLETS, 1980 AND 1981*

*Front cover. The artist is Dick Hafer, who calls himself "The Comics Commando," Lanham, Maryland.

TWX-d. All we got was the typical bureaucratic runaround." The booklet narrative reflects Mr. Julie's reaction that a sense of humor is his only escape, for the bid had arrived on time, although not at its final destination within the Pentagon. He pressed the case.

> At last, the problems were over. The Army decided to reinstate our bid. A very strong proposal, comparing the Julie Labs' equipment with the competition, showing many advantages, was presented at a special meeting held with each bidder.

"The response we got," a frustrated Loebe Julie remembered, "was that they just couldn't understand how our equipment could possibly work and still be so superior to the others. We had a portable unit set up just outside the door, in the next office, and told them that in a few minutes we could prove that JRL's equipment could do all that we claimed it could. Besides, the final bids were dramatically different: PRD Electronics came in at about $1.12 million; RCA was $1.94 million; John Fluke bid $1.49 million; Hewlett-Packard's bid was $2.19 million; and Julie Research Labs offered to do what was required for $0.91 million. It's interesting that with such high-powered contestants, all contestants except the John Fluke Company were declared technically unacceptable. Fluke was declared the winner."

"Actually," Loebe Julie continued, "there were three different stories coming out of the Missile Command simultaneously. One report had it that the Army calibration program needed 5 automated calibration systems. The Missile Command decided that any of the five bidders could get the contract by submitting an acceptable proposal. Yet, before evaluating the first bid, word came down that they needed 95 automated calibration systems, but that only one U.S. bidder was qualified to supply these needs, meaning that the contract would be noncompetitive, sole-source purchase, and from the John Fluke Company. And believe it or not, at the same time it was stated by the Missile Command that 95 systems were needed and could be supplied by only one firm—Hewlett-Packard. So we went to the General Accounting Office with a formal protest. We got nowhere. GAO bowed to what they obviously thought was the superior technical judgment of the Army."

By that time, Julie suspected that attempting to operate within the system might not work for a small company with limited resources. Nevertheless, he decided to put the past aside and to prepare a new, unsolicited proposal for the U.S. Army Missile Command to illustrate JRL's superiority over its competition for the calibration needs outlined in the first R.F.P.

"We even added new features, such as graphics display that would allow less highly-trained personnel to operate the system. The Army sent back our proposal, saying in essence, 'No, thank you.' So we went to General Malley who was in charge of R&D at the Pentagon, who was very interested in our claim that we could do a calibration job normally taking 10 hours with other equipment in 25 minutes. The labs confirmed our claims, and further testing at other Army sites provided further proof that our LOCOST system was up to the tasks required. But listen to this: the office that prepared the report for General Malley gave inaccurate summaries of what happened, although the writer did admit our system worked as we said it would, and it cast doubts on JRL's cost benefits. We lost another round. Worse, all this took two months of valuable time."

Julie Labs pointed out 168 errors in the summary report, including Army logic that because it had been unable to solve the technical issues JRL claimed to have solved, it was not likely that the JRL claims were justified. Rejected again, Julie attempted another tack (Exhibit 24.2), and an expression of interest in JRL's work came from the Soviet Union (Exhibit 24.3).

Exhibit 24.2

BOOK ONE, JULIE RESEARCH LABORATORIES*

REJECTED AGAIN.

ABOUT THAT TIME, WE LEARNED THAT WHITE SANDS MISSILE RANGE HAD BEEN USING FOUR DIFFERENT AUTOMATED CALIBRATION SYSTEMS.* THEY WERE NOT PAYING FOR THEMSELVES, SO WE INVITED THEIR PEOPLE TO COME TO GRUMMAN & G.E. SPACE CENTER TO SEE OUR CALIBRATORS IN ACTION.

PLEASE, LET'S GO SEE THE EQUIPMENT, MAYBE THEY'LL HAVE A TREE THAT I CAN SUE.

U.S. ARMY WHITE SANDS MISSILE RANGE

BOB REIB, THE MILITARY COORDINATOR FOR "TECOM" (WHICH OVERSEES WHITE SANDS), IN HIS REPORT OF THE VISITS, STATED: "IT WAS OBVIOUS THAT THE JULIE RESEARCH LABS SYSTEM DID REPRESENT A SIGNIFICANT IMPROVEMENT OVER THE HEWLETT PACKARD 9213C AND JOHN FLUKE 7505/7510 SYSTEMS".*

* THESE WERE THE SYSTEMS BOUGHT BY "SOLE SOURCE" EARLIER.

Exhibit 24.2 (Cont.)

"To no avail," Julie lamented, "and it was all absolutely inconsistent. General Guthrie met with us, and I began to think at that point that patriotism might be at least recognized if not rewarded, but a budget flunky said the Army had no money to buy calibration systems. Precisely at the time when they were advertising to buy 95 manual calibrators for $12 million. Unbelievable! Further, we contended that manually the Army would need not 95 but 150 pieces of equipment to do the job correctly.

"Meanwhile, using interviews and data gained through the Freedom of Information Act, we proved that the cost per calibration was $243 for the John Fluke Systems that were now in use by the Missile Center. This compared to $24 per calibration for the JRL LOCOST systems already in use and $21 for our proposed units.

Exhibit 24.3

BOOK ONE, JULIE RESEARCH LABORATORIES*

Exhibit 24.3 (Cont.)

UPON ARRIVING HOME, THE ORDER WAS TORN UP.

EVEN THOUGH OUR COMPETITORS **DO** SELL THEIR CALIBRATION EQUIPMENT TO THE RUSSIANS, WE DECIDED THAT **WE DIDN'T WANT TO.**

AFTER AN ATLANTA CONFERENCE, IN WHICH GENERALS SAMET, D'AMBROSIO AND HUNT SPOKE OF OUR POOR STATE OF READINESS, COMPARED TO THE RUSSIANS, AND ON OUR LAGGING TECHNOLOGY IN CRITICAL AREAS, WE WROTE TO GENERAL GUTHRIE, THE COMMANDER OF THE ARMY MATERIEL DEVELOPMENT & READINESS COMMAND.

*Pp. 28–29.

The best that in-use manual systems could do was $65 for each calibration. I maintain that these savings are indisputable! So the Army bought the 95 manual systems.

"In October 1979, we made one last attempt, making a proposal, using detailed, documented computer studies, to the assistant secretary of the Army, in which we showed savings of $200 million over the next 10 years. Again, the Army's response was negative, and again they used erroneous data and absolutely faulty logic to reject us. We can only hope that their missile work is less sloppy than their accounting work which was shot through with glaring mistakes."

These mistakes and a subsequent purchase were caricatured on page 37 of Book One (Exhibit 24.4).

And Exhibit 24.5 portrays the saga to June 18, 1980.

Exhibit 24.4

BOOK ONE, JULIE RESEARCH LABORATORIES*

WHILE SEVERAL MAJOR **ERRORS.** AND **FLAT-OUT UNTRUTHS** WERE POINTED OUT DURING THE MEETING, THE ARMY PERSONNEL **REFUSED** TO CORRECT ANYTHING!

WE CHALLENGED THEM TO SHOW THEIR PROOF TO US AND THEY WERE **UNABLE.**

NOW ooo

BACK WHEN GEN. GUTHRIE BOUGHT THE 95 SYSTEMS, WE TOLD HIM AND HIS QUALITY SUPERVISOR, THAT 150 WOULD BE NEEDED, RIGHT?

WELL, GUESS WHAT THEY ORDERED IN MAY OF 1980?

OH, NO!

RIGHT 97 <u>MORE</u> MANUAL CALIBRATION SYSTEMS!

*P. 37.   37

Exhibit 24.5

BOOK ONE, JULIE RESEARCH LABORATORIES*

ON JUNE 5, WE WROTE TO GEN. GUTHRIE, AND EXPLAINED
OUR FEELINGS ABOUT THIS TURN OF EVENTS:

*"Please meet with us to review the facts.... you can still stop the continuing
30-50¢ waste, out of every Army calibration dollar.... The is still time
for you to stop this latest procurement, which will lock the Army into
a wasteful $2,000 million calibration support system, from the year 1980 to
the year 2000..., The obsolete and inefficient manual equipment now
being procured, will again fail to provide the quality calibration
support urgently needed by the Army's
sophisticated weapons systems."*

On June 18, 1980, Gen. Guthrie
rejected our request, stating that
the issues were carefully reviewed,
but that the Army must purchase
"mobile" calibration equipment,
which, he assured us, is all
"modern".

IN JULY, SEVERAL ITEMS OF THIS
"MODERN" EQUIPMENT HAD TO BE
DROPPED FROM THE PROCUREMENT,
BECAUSE, AFTER 20 YEARS, THE
MANUFACTURER WASN'T ABLE
TO SUPPLY THEM.

Exhibit 24.5 (Cont.)

WHERE ARE WE NOW?

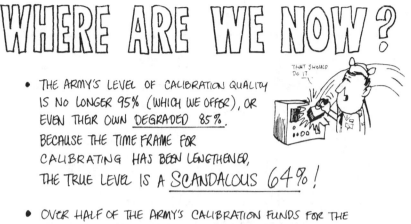

- THE ARMY'S LEVEL OF CALIBRATION QUALITY IS NO LONGER 95% (WHICH WE OFFER), OR EVEN THEIR OWN DEGRADED 85%. BECAUSE THE TIME FRAME FOR CALIBRATING HAS BEEN LENGTHENED, THE TRUE LEVEL IS A SCANDALOUS 64%!

- OVER HALF OF THE ARMY'S CALIBRATION FUNDS FOR THE REST OF THIS CENTURY IS BEING BLOWN ON SLOW, LOW-QUALITY, EXPENSIVE-TO-OPERATE, 1960-STYLE CALIBRATORS.

- STANDARDS ARE BEING FUDGED EVEN MORE. THE OFFICIAL "CALIBRATED" STICKER HAS BEEN SUPPLEMENTED BY ANOTHER STICKER THAT STATES THAT CALIBRATION IS NOT NECESSARY. 50% OF THE ARMY'S EQUIPMENT IS NOW OFFICIALLY NEGLECTED!

- IT HAS BEEN ESTIMATED THAT OUT OF EVERY 66 PIECES OF ARMY EQUIPMENT, ONLY 20 WILL BE WORKING IN TOLERANCE! WORST OF ALL: WHICH 20 ARE THE GOOD ONES?

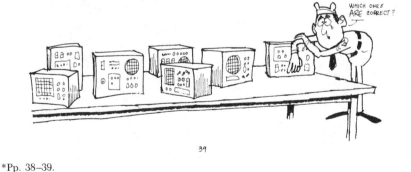

39

*Pp. 38–39.

Mr. Julie posts an admonition near the conclusion of Book One: "Don't be misled by the humor in this booklet" (Exhibit 24.6).

Exhibit 24.6

BOOK ONE, JULIE RESEARCH LABORATORIES*

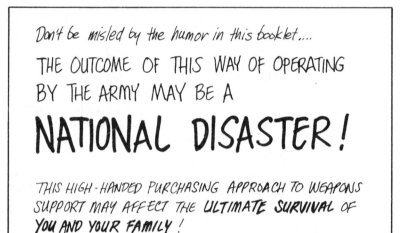

Don't be misled by the humor in this booklet....

THE OUTCOME OF THIS WAY OF OPERATING BY THE ARMY MAY BE A

NATIONAL DISASTER!

THIS HIGH-HANDED PURCHASING APPROACH TO WEAPONS SUPPORT MAY AFFECT THE **ULTIMATE SURVIVAL** OF **YOU AND YOUR FAMILY**!

ARE YOU OUTRAGED?

WE ARE OFFERING THE U.S. ARMY — (YOUR ARMY - SPENDING YOUR TAX DOLLARS) THE FOLLOWING THINGS....

1. SAVINGS OF 25 TO 40% (400-600 MEN) ON SCARCE SKILLED MANPOWER NEEDS!

2. SAVINGS OF 31% (62 VANS) ON SPECIAL EXPENDABLE VAN REQUIREMENT!

3. SAVINGS OF 50% ($60 MILLION) ON START-UP EQUIPMENT & PERSONNEL COSTS!

4. SAVINGS OF 30% ($200 MILLION) ON LIFE-CYCLE (10-YEAR) TOTAL COST!

plus... BADLY NEEDED

QUALITY... WHICH PRESENT WEAPONS SUPPORT CALIBRATION SYSTEMS DO NOT HAVE.

Exhibit 24.6 (Cont.)

IN SUMMARY:

HERE IS WHAT IS BEING SAID ABOUT OUR EQUIPMENT...

- "... the JRL system did represent a significant improvement over the Hewlett Packard 9213C and John Fluke 7505/7510 systems".... "easier to program" .... "more economical for automated support of meters."

  From report by Bob Reib, U.S. Army, Aberdeen, TECOM, dated 22 MAR 78

- "One of the nicest systems I've ever used. If I had to do without it, it would cost me an additional four men."

  Roger Innes, Newport News Naval Shipyard

- "... the LOCOST system can adequately calibrate a large variety of TMDE in periods of less than 30 minutes each."

  From report by Elmer Rogers of the U.S. Army Harry Diamond Laboratory, to Commander, DARCOM, 22 Feb 77

- "LOCOST is the most valuable equipment I've seen in all my years in the calibration industry."

  Charles Weber, Grumman Aerospace Corp.

- "The best investment I ever made."

  Alex McCarovich, General Electric

- "The Julie system with one operator is doing the work previously done by two to three people manually." "Mr. Weber stated that the JULIE system has greater accuracy than other competing systems." "The claim of $12 per calibration is valid." "Downtime has been approximately 1% of on-line time." "G.E. anticipates a real reduction in personnel as a result of buying the system."

  Excerpted from report of JRL users interviewed by John Stolarick for DARCOM

41

*Pp. 40–41

THE EPIC CONTINUES IN BOOK TWO

During the casewriter's visit to JRL in the summer of 1982, Loebe Julie, administrative assistant and technician Pamela Spencer, and other employees were occupied in a variety of activities involved in supplying its automated test systems, calibration systems, and other equipment to some of the country's leading high-technology firms. That the company was keeping its head above water, given the expenses incurred by its leader in fighting the military monolith seemed a minor miracle, but Mr. Julie and his co-workers were a tenacious lot. Appendix 24A shows a financial summary presented by a CPA in June 1981. Already in circulation was Book Two, from which selected quotations and pages are presented. Exhibit 24.7 reflects occurrences according to Loebe Julie after a story in the *Washington Post* recounting Julie's jousting with the powers of the Pentagon.

"Now the word had begun to spread rapidly," Julie recounted, "with over 300 newspapers running some version of our story. Hundreds of stations broadcast it as well, and I was on talk shows in many areas. General Guthrie even announced that he was organizing his own task force to look into the charges we had leveled."

According to JRL's president, "Subsequently, the Army awarded further contracts for millions of dollars worth of additional obsolete equipment. Finally, on July 22, 1980, three GAO Procurement Division investigators showed up here for a 2½-day visit. Skeptical upon arrival, they apparently left convinced that JRL could substantiate its claims. At a point almost a year later, the GAO audit investigators issued a summary report that clearly favored Julie (see Exhibit 24.8). Some observers began calling it "Julie-gate" and others talked of "stonewalling" between Army and White House. Loebe Julie, thought by some to be a latter-day Don Quixote tilting at windmills and by others to be the iconoclast needed for these times, but a man generally admired by all except his military detractors, continued what many feared was a hopeless battle to gain recognition for his firm and acceptance of its equipment by the U.S. Army.

Julie did reach several highly placed public figures. Senator William V. Roth, Jr., chairman of the Committee on Governmental Affairs, U.S. Senate, issued a statement, observing:

> The Army's Inspector General makes three key findings:
>
> > Mr. Julie was not afforded a full and fair opportunity to compete on an equal footing with other suppliers of calibration equipment.
> >
> > The principal reason for this was that Mr. Julie was too aggressive in his marketing techniques to suit the taste of Army procurement officials.
> >
> > Some Army officials made statements in this case which were inaccurate, unproven, inconsistent, or open to misinterpretation.
>
> In short, this is one of the most blatant cases I have seen of the "old-boy network" operating to freeze out a legitimate, innovative small businessman from competition for government contracts. In essence, what happened was that Mr. Julie tried to sell the Army a better mousetrap, but instead it was Mr. Julie who got it in the neck.[3]

As Senator Roth put it, the battle was "not yet over," but it was clear that this son of a Polish immigrant family, and a native of the Bronx, was bruised and less than

[3]Statement of Senator William V. Roth, Jr., chairman, Senate Committee on Governmental Affairs, November 5, 1981, p. 2.

Exhibit 24.7

BOOK TWO, JULIE RESEARCH LABORATORIES*

AFTER 3 MONTHS AND MANY
REQUESTS, THE ARMY SENT
ITS OFFICIAL TASK FORCE RESPONSE...

THEY HAD EARLIER GIVEN GAO THEIR OFFICIAL RESPONSE
TO OUR PROTEST.

THAT'S NICE.... BUT THERE WAS ONE SMALL PROBLEM...,

THE ARMY GOT TRAPPED IN ITS OWN LIES, BY TELLING GAO & CONGRESS CONFLICTING STORIES!

16

Exhibit 24.7 (Cont.)

THE ARMY/GAO STORY	THE ARMY/CONGRESS STORY
1. THE MANUAL EQUIPMENT IN THE VAN CANNOT BE TOUCHED. IT'S ALL STANDARD. IF ANYTHING IS CHANGED, IT WOULD CAUSE TREMENDOUS LOGISTICS PROBLEMS.	1. THE JULIE BOOK SAYS THAT WE'RE STANDARDIZING ON OBSOLETE MANUAL EQUIPMENT *ABSOLUTELY NOT!!!* WE'RE ALWAYS UPDATING THE CONTENTS OF THE VAN, WHEN EVER ANYTHING BETTER COMES ALONG.
2. JULIE DOESN'T MAKE MANUAL EQUIPMENT.* EVERYONE UP TO THE ARMY SECRETARY HAS TOLD THEM THAT AMCC HAS NO REQUIREMENT FOR AUTOMATED EQUIPMENT WHATEVER!!!	2. WHY, WE'RE SO UP TO DATE THAT AMCC JUST RUSHED OUT AND BOUGHT 9 AUTOMATED SYSTEMS .... FROM JOHN FLUKE, OF COURSE.

17

*Pp. 16–17.

Exhibit 24.8

BOOK TWO, JULIE RESEARCH LABORATORIES*

 ON APRIL 3, THE GAO ISSUED THEIR FORMAL, WRITTEN REPORT

(DON'T CONFUSE THIS WITH THE GAO PROTEST DIVISION DECISION ON OUR FORMAL PROTEST — STILL TO BE ISSUED.)

① "THE ARMY, CONTRARY TO WHAT IT HAS TOLD JRL, HAS BOTH LABORATORY AND FIELD REQUIREMENTS FOR AUTOMATED CALIBRATION EQUIPMENT."

② "THE ARMY'S TECHNICAL EVALUATIONS OR JRL'S EQUIPMENT APPEAR TO BE BASED ON SOME QUESTIONABLE CONCLUSIONS, AND ASSUMPTIONS AND LARGELY IGNORE FAVORABLE IMPRESSIONS BY ARMY REPRESENTATIVES WHO SAW THE EQUIPMENT IN OPERATION."

③ "....OUR WORK HAS DISCLOSED THAT THE DEPARTMENTS OF DEFENSE AND THE ARMY NEED TO REEXAMINE THE FIELD ARMY REQUIREMENTS FOR CALIBRATION EQUIPMENT —— TESTS SHOULD ESTABLISH THE MOST COST-EFFECTIVE EQUIPMENT THAT WILL SATISFY VALID ARMY REQUIREMENTS."

④ "THE ARMY ELECTED TO DELETE FROM JRL'S PROPOSAL, COST SAVINGS ATTRIBUTED TO AN OSCILLOSCOPE AND A SIGNAL GENERATOR THAT JRL HAD NOT PRODUCED, BUT IT DID NOT REDUCE THE ASSOCIATED LEASE PRICE FOR THESE DELETED ITEMS FROM WHAT JRL HAD ORIGINALLY PROPOSED."

⑤ "THE ARMY USED ONE WORKLOAD LEVEL TO DETERMINE THE NUMBER OF LOCOST SYSTEMS NEEDED AND A DIFFERENT WORKLOAD LEVEL TO DETERMINE THE MANUAL EQUIPMENT NEEDED."

Exhibit 24.8 (Cont.)

(6) "ARMY TECHNICAL AND COST EVALUATIONS OF JRL EQUIPMENT WERE INCONSISTENT ---- DARCOM MAY HAVE UNDERSTATED PERFORMANCE CAPABILITIES OF THE "LOCOST" SYSTEM AND OVER STATED PERFORMANCE CAPABILITIES OF COMPETING SYSTEMS."

(7) "THE [ARMY METROLOGY & CALIBRATION] CENTER DID NOT CONTACT JRL TO ---- ENSURE THAT IT UNDERSTOOD WHAT JRL HAS TO OFFER."

(8) "THE ARMY'S ASSERTION THAT JRL'S LOCOST SYSTEM IS NOT UNIQUE OR NEW TO THE INDUSTRY NOR STATE OF THE ART IS INCONSISTENT WITH REPORTS FROM LOCOST SYSTEM OWNERS. THE REPORTS SUGGEST THAT THE LOCOST SYSTEM MAY INDEED OFFER ADVANTAGES BECAUSE OF SHORTER PROGRAMING TIME AND SIMPLER OPERATION. FOR EXAMPLE, WHITE SANDS MISSILE RANGE OFFICIALS REPORT THAT 100 PROGRAMS WERE DEVELOPED IN ABOUT 75 HOURS AND THAT AVERAGE PROGRAMER TRAINING TIME WAS 24 HOURS. ANOTHER LOCOST SYSTEM OWNER, AN AEROSPACE COMPANY, TOLD US THAT PROGRAMING PREPARATION TIME ON THE LOCOST SYSTEM RANGED FROM 15 MINUTES TO 1 HOUR WITH MOST PROGRAMS TAKING 30 MINUTES OR LESS. THIS COMPANY ALSO TOLD US THAT IT KNOWS OF NO OTHER COMMERCIAL OFF-THE-SHELF CALIBRATOR THAT WILL PERFORM AS WELL AS THE LOCOST SYSTEM."

I'D LIKE YOU TO TARGET A MISSILE.

ARMY MISSILE COMMAND

HEY, HARRY... WHAT'S THE COORDINATES ON THE GAO HEADQUARTERS?

Exhibit 24.8 (Cont.)

(9) "DARCOM WAS SKEPTICAL OF JRL's CLAIM THAT EQUIPMENT COULD BE PROGRAMED IN ABOUT 15 MINUTES BECAUSE THE ARMY'S EXPERIENCE WITH COMPETING SYSTEMS SHOWED AN AVERAGE REQUIREMENT OF 120 HOURS. REPRESENTATIVES OF HARRY DIAMOND LABORATORIES AND THE ARMY METROLOGY AND CALIBRATION CENTER, HOWEVER, HAD REPORTED OBSERVING PROGRAM PREPARATION FOR A SIMPLE TEST INSTRUMENT IN LESS THAN 3 MINUTES AND THE INSTRUMENT'S CALIBRATION IN ANOTHER 3 MINUTES. THE HARRY DIAMOND REPRESENTATIVES ALSO REPORTED THAT (1) THE LOCOST SYSTEM COULD CALIBRATE A VARIETY OF INSTRUMENTATION IN LESS THAN 30 MINUTES, AS JRL CLAIMED, (2) THE SIMPLICITY OF PROGRAMING AND USING THE SYSTEM WAS EVIDENT, AND (3) THE SYSTEM COULD PRODUCE SIGNIFICANT SAVINGS IN THEIR LABORATORY. "

(10) "IN ADDITION, WE RECOMMEND THAT THE SECRETARY OF DEFENSE REQUIRE THAT AN INDEPENDENT HARDWARE DEMONSTRATION BE CONDUCTED TO ESTABLISH THE COST EFFECTIVENESS AND PRODUCTIVITY INCREASES THAT MAY BE ATTRIBUTED TO AUTOMATING THE FIELD ARMY CALIBRATION FUNCTIONS . "

(11) "DURING OUR REVIEW, WE SAW SEVERAL ASPECTS OF THE ARMY METROLOGY AND CALIBRATION CENTER ACTIVITIES WHICH APPEAR TO WARRANT OUR FURTHER EXAMINATION. ACCORDINGLY, WE PLAN TO PURSUE THESE MATTERS IN A SEPARATE REVIEW TO BEGIN SHORTLY. "

THE ABOVE QUOTES WERE ALL DRAWN FROM THE OFFICIAL GAO REPORT, SIGNED BY THE ACTING COMPTROLLER GENERAL OF THE U.S.

32

*Pp. 30–32.

ebullient about prospects of negotiating the military maze. At the same hearing, Senator Alfonse D'Amato of New York argued,

> We must protect and encourage our innovative, high-technology small businesses. In order to have a strong national defense, we must have a strong defense industrial base. People like Loebe Julie are the foundation upon which this nation's economic and military future are built. His roar of outrage must be heard and heeded, or our future may be bleak indeed.[4]

In a cover letter dated April 8, 1982, the Army's Office of Legislative Liaison sent the latest Army report to Senator Roth. The 14-page summary included these comments:

> Mr. Julie's allegations are addressed in detail, but the key issues he has raised can be summarized in three questions: (1) Has the Army handled this matter in a fair and objective manner? The answer to that question is yes. (2) Have all prospective participants in this test and the procurements associated with it been given a full and impartial opportunity to compete? The answer to that question is yes. (3) Has anyone in the Army and specifically anyone in the U.S. Army Missile Command rigged this test or the procurements associated with it to bias the result, restrict participation, favor the products of any prospective competitor or "get" Julie Research Labs? The answer to that question is no.[5]

"Yet the Army's own impartial Inspector General report came to exactly the opposite conclusions on November 4, 1981," Julie commented. "And nothing has improved. I've circled some of the key passages and phrases of the new report—all of them clearly contradicting that the Army is now 'open and above-board, and making extraordinary efforts to ensure objectivity throughout the evaluation process.' From the Army's newest report, it is patently obvious they are not."

Not seeing himself as an heroic crusader, soft-spoken Loebe Julie did admit that being at war with the U.S. Army was not his first foray into matters of ethics in his profession and into waste and abuse in government. Appendix 24B outlines six of the activities in which he has been engaged since 1962.

Appendix 24C provides a biographical overview of this man who claimed to have invented the better mousetrap, but who could not seem to crack the network leading to contracts with the Army. Not only did the prospective customers refuse to recognize the equipment as a valid answer to their needs, but they seemed to be intent on ignoring inventor Julie and, according to some observers, mousetrapping him in the process. Appendix 24D comprises a response to the published case study from the U.S. Army Material Command and related correspondence.

Returning for a moment to Admiral Rickover,

> . . . we need to create, by actions rather than words, an environment in which those in the Defense Department can operate efficiently and obtain from industry needed goods and services at minimum cost to the taxpayer.[6]

---

[4]"Introductory Statement by Senator Alfonse D'Amato Regarding Mr. Loebe Julie," November 5, 1981.

[5]JRL corporate files.

[6]Rickover, "The Moral Responsibility of Business," p. 13.

To which businessman/scientist Loebe Julie responded wearily, "Amen. Easier said than done, certainly, but something else is certain," according to JRL's president, "getting rid of arrogance and foolishness in the procurement echelons is a step in the right direction."

Appendix 24A

JRL FINANCIAL STATEMENTS, DECEMBER 31, 1980

BALANCE SHEET (UNAUDITED)

ASSETS

Current Assets	
Cash	$110,474
Cash, Dreyfus Liquid Assets	152,762
Accounts receivable:	
Trade, net of $22,178 allowance for uncollectible accounts	192,929
Prepaid expenses	4,575
Inventories	76,542
Total current assets	537,282
Property, Plant, and Equipment, at cost	
Machinery and equipment	96,261
Furniture and fixtures	15,869
Leasehold improvements	5,371
	117,501
Less: Accumulated depreciation and amortization	97,544
Property, plant, and equipment, net	19,957
Total assets	$557,239

LIABILITIES AND STOCKHOLDERS' EQUITY

Current Liabilities	
Accounts payable	$ 25,670
Accrued taxes and expenses	170,261
Loan payable, officer	41,534
Total current liabilities	237,465
Other Liabilities	
Reserve for retirement bonus	9,000
Total other liabilities	246,465
Stockholders' Equity	
Common Stock:	
Par value $1.00 per share; authorized 600,000 shares, issued 442,497 shares	442,497
Capital surplus	154,582
Retained earnings (deficit)	(153,382)
	443,697
Less: Treasury Stock, at cost (24,983 shares)	132,923
Total stockholders' equity	310,774
Total liabilities and stockholders' equity	$557,239

STATEMENT OF INCOME (UNAUDITED)

Sales	$1,410,352
Cost of goods sold	926,735
Gross profit	483,617
Selling and administrative expense	404,400
Net income	$ 79,217
Average number of shares outstanding	417,514
Net income per share	$0.19

SCHEDULE OF COST OF GOODS SOLD

Inventory, beginning	$ 262,972
Purchases	355,635
Labor, production	264,899
	883,506
Less: Inventory, Ending	76,542
Prime cost	806,964
Manufacturing overhead	
Engineering fees	31,778
Rent and utilities	56,156
Factory supplies	19,201
Maintenance and repairs	2,668
Plant protection	3,708
Depreciation, machinery and equipment	1,744
Outside services	4,516
Total manufacturing overhead	119,771
Cost of goods sold	$ 926,735

SCHEDULE OF SELLING AND ADMINISTRATIVE EXPENSE

Sales salaries	$ 22,010
Commissions	3,010
Advertising	13,529
Auto expense	892
Travel and entertaining	11,924
Officers' salaries	63,693
Office salaries	42,476
Telephone and telegraph	19,721
Office expense	4,595
Insurance	18,673
Interest	110,198
Legal and accounting	13,261
Dues and subscriptions	11,227
Supplies and general expense	15,153
Hospitalization insurance	2,449
Postage	3,560
Payroll and miscellaneous taxes	34,238
Stock registration	2,170
Shipping and freight out	8,781
Depreciation and amortization	1,094
New York State and City corporation taxes	1,746
Total	$ 404,400

Source: Company records.

Appendix 24B

SUMMARY OF JULIE PRO BONO ACTIVITIES
(For current activities, see V and VI)

I. Special study on Industrial Utilization of Gifted Engineering Graduates (1962)—
There is evidence that new, creative engineering talent underachieves in American large business. The intent of this study was to improve the fit between corporate management and unrecognized engineering "geniuses."

II. Special Award Program for Gifted Engineering Undergraduates (1964–1967)—
The special study disclosed that several identifiable engineering school mechanisms transform bright, enthusiastic, young Edisons into grey flannel engineering administrators. The Julie program rewarded concentrated, creative, engineering work instead of social-political activities as an encouragement to fledgling engineering innovators.

III. Committee on Ethical Practices in Precision Measurement (1965)—
Science, technology, and industry are critically dependent on accurate observations and measurements. The validity of these measurements depends on the integrity of the measurement practices (procedures) and of the measurement practitioners. Standards of ethical practice and a code of ethics are nonexistent in this critically important field and should be established.

IV. Tier 2 Committee on DOD Procurement (1975–1978)—
The U.S. government's neglect, waste, and abuse of American inventive talent (Goddard et al.) is destroying new innovator/producers and will destroy U.S. world leadership in science, technology, and industry. Improvements in the system can readily be made and are most urgently required.

V. Committee Against Waste and Abuse in Government Procurement (1981)—
Outgrowth of IV. The government's continuing failure to act to correct its own procurement abuses is not only wasteful but is a major cause of the decline of U.S. leadership in science, technology, and industry. This new committee is result (rather than study) oriented and has already singled out the likeliest targets of opportunity in the government for reform and improvement. The specific reform projects are practical, long overdue and if properly selected and pursued can produce major results in a short time span. The committee is admittedly undertaking an extremely arduous task. Nevertheless, with this high challenge comes an extraordinary opportunity to benefit the whole of the United States and its citizens.

VI. American Calibration Association (1981)—
Outgrowth of III. The continued absence of uniform, ethical standards of practice in measurement and calibration,* and the continued lack of official accreditation of U.S. calibration laboratories has caused serious quality problems in the U.S. national measurement system. In a close parallel to the earlier days of medical practice, careless and invalid (quack) practice can easily outadvertise and undercut careful and legitimate practice. There is an urgent need for a national calibration organization, analogous to the American Medical Association, to monitor and maintain legitimate standards of practice for U.S. measurement and calibration.

*Calibration consists of measurements accompanied by an official label or certificate, implying that the measurements were valid.

Source: Company files.

Appendix 24C

BIOGRAPHY—LOEBE JULIE

Loebe Julie is president and chief engineer of Julie Research Laboratories, Inc., which he founded in 1954 to do development work on computerized fire control systems. He received a bachelor's degree in electrical engineering in 1941 from the City College of New York and a Master's degree in mathematics in 1948 from New York University.

Mr. Julie is best known for his pioneering work in the development of ultraprecision components, instruments, and systems designed to increase the accuracy and speed of DC and low-frequency test and measurement for the standards and calibration laboratory. He has received 40 patents for his work in this field and is recognized as the originator of a large number of innovative 1 ppm standards, instruments, and systems. These include the Evanohm resistance standard (1955), the air bath EMF standard (1957), and the Kelvin-Varley divider standard (1957) as well as a number of resistance bridge and potentiometer standards (1955–1965), voltage current and gyrocalibrator standards (1958–1963), and highly sophisticated manual and automated calibration systems (1958–1978). The Julie-ratio bridge is included in the IEEE Standard Code for Resistance Measurements.

Since 1975, Mr. Julie has been campaigning for recognition by the D.O.D. of the importance of small, high-technology companies in advancing U.S. technological strength and reducing wasteful government procurements of obsolete, labor-intensive, manual calibration systems.

Mr. Julie is an active member of PMA and NCSL and has served as a member of the Advisory Committee of the IEEE. He has also served as president of the New York section and as publications chairman of PMA and has taught, lectured, and written extensively, in the United States and abroad, on new developments and methodology in precision measurement.

Source: Company files.

Appendix 24D

DEPARTMENT OF THE ARMY
HEADQUARTERS US ARMY MATERIEL DEVELOPMENT AND READINESS COMMAND
5001 EISENHOWER AVENUE, ALEXANDRIA, VA. 22333

September 7, 1984

Mr. Charles K. Hinkle
University of Colorado
Department of Marketing
1200 University Avenue
Boulder, Colorado 80309

Dear Mr. Hinkle:

Your new coauthored book, <u>Cases in Marketing Management,
Issues for the 1980's</u>, is an interesting publication; and it
appears to be an excellent management academic text.

There is however one case study, "Julie Research
Laboratories," which deserves comment. As the Army's Deputy
Executive Director for Test, Measurement and Diagnostic
Equipment (TMDE), I am intimately familar with the facts
regarding Mr. Julie's dealings with the Army over the past 10-15
years; and in both of his comic books he has misrepresented the
facts, thusly misleading the readers and the students using your
text.

The Army's position on several points in Mr. Julie's comic
books should be made known to you and to the academic community
which employs your publication. I have inclosed a set of
comments from Army records. Each comment is keyed to the
respective page of your text.

Unfortunately, the case study is not balanced. By accepting
Mr. Julie's material uncritically, a distorted and at times
confusing picture is presented. Should you desire additional
information or material, please contact me at (202) 274-8084. I
have also sent a similar letter to your coauthor,
Ms. Ester F. Stineman of Yale University.

Sincerely,

Michael C. Sandusky
Deputy Executive Director
for Test, Measurement, and
Diagnostic Equipment

Appendix 24D (Cont.)

COMMENT ON CASE 24
"JULIE RESEARCH LABORATORIES"

1. *Page 356:* The following is paraphrased from page 7 of Mr. Julie's first comic book:

> In 1974, the Army decided that they needed better calibration equipment and issued an R.F.P. (Request for Proposals). What Julie Labs offered is what the Army asked for: upgraded capability of 2,750 calibrations per year by each technician (up from 800); fully automated; savings of 22,000 hours per year at each installation; identical service, regardless of the location or skill level of the technician; substantially improved turnaround and data.

This is not an accurate statement of the 1974 Request for Proposal (DAAHO1-74-R-0877). This document did not address the total manhours to be saved, nor did it project the number of calibrations. The numbers 2,750 calibrations per year, 800 calibrations per year, and 22,000 hours per year were not part of the Request for Proposal. Furthermore, these numbers bear no reasonable relation to achievable calibration actions or manhour savings. Mr. Julie may have taken information contained in the Request for Proposal and applied his own estimates, but it is inaccurate to say this is what the Army asked for.

2. *Pages 356–358:* Two paragraphs describe the submission of Mr. Julie's initial offer. When the JRL proposal was received at Redstone Arsenal, Alabama (not within the Pentagon as stated on page 358), it was time stamped in Greenwich Mean Time (otherwise known as ZULU Time). However, the letter "Z" which denotes ZULU time was not shown, and it was mistakenly thought to be local time. This particular episode was examined by the General Accounting Office, and Comptroller General Decision B-183288, dated October 14, 1975 states that, "The reported facts indicate the probability of reasonable misunderstanding by responsible Army officials which fortunately was corrected."

3. *Page 358:* The second paragraph describes Mr. Julie's interpretation of how his proposal was received; and inaccurate information is provided concerning the final offers. On page 358, Mr. Julie is quoted as saying: "The response we got . . . was that they just couldn't understand how our equipment could possibly work and still be so superior to the others. We had a portable unit set up just outside the door, in the next office, and told them that in a few minutes we could prove that JRL's equipment could do all that we claimed it could." The Army understood exactly what Mr. Julie had to offer, and the fact was that his proposal was not responsive to the requirements of the Request for Proposal. After protracted discussions and clarifications with Mr. Julie, his proposal was determined to be deficient because of the lack of usable computer memory and the lack of software interface data. The General Accounting Office also addressed this area, and the Comptroller General's decision ruled in favor of the Army and found no basis for the JRL protest.

   With regard to the final offers described on page 358, there are serious misstatements of fact. First, there is no record of an Army official saying that he could not understand how Mr. Julie's equipment could possibly work and still be so superior to the others. Second, the portable unit that Mr. Julie had with him was a direct current and voltage stimulus and measurement system. It had only a fraction of what was being asked for in the Request for Proposal. Contrary to what this paragraph states, Army meterology engineers did see the equipment—and they observed it in operation. As to the final offers, Mr. Julie's best and final offer was

Appendix 24D (Cont.)

not $0.91 million as stated in this paragraph. It was in excess of one million dollars, and in dollar amount it was not the lowest offer. Furthermore, his proposal was rejected because it did not comply with the Army's stated requirements. To be specific, his usable computer memory was very limited. Mr. Julie proposed augmenting a Hewlett-Packard calculator with read only memory chips which did not increase the usable memory as did the microprocessors of the other offerors. Mr. Julie protested the rejection of his offer to the General Accounting Office; and the General Accounting Office denied his protest and upheld the Army's position that its requirements were valid and Mr. Julie's proposal did not meet the requirements.

4. *Page 358:* The third to last paragraph on this page recounts material from page 16 of Mr. Julie's first comic book. This paragraph asserts that,"there were three different stories coming out of the Missile Command simultaneously." The first number mentioned was for five automated calibration systems. This was to satisfy internal laboratory requirements, for use at locations where high densities of calibration workload existed. The same paragraph goes on to proport that the Army needed an additional ninety-five automated calibration systems from the John Fluke Company and that yet another ninety-five systems were needed from Hewlett-Packard. This is not at all correct. Prior to the procurement action described above, the Army made sole source procurements of one John Fluke System and one Hewlett-Packard System. A total of two systems were purchased, not 190 as supposed by Mr. Julie. These two systems were bought to facilitate feasibility tests, and they were not bought for production. These two systems were specifically configured for the evaluation of automated calibration systems in a van-mounted, mobile environment. The purpose of this evaluation was to determine the feasibility of using automated calibration systems in support of field Army requirements. The Army's actions were logical and straight forward. However, this paragraph presents a confused picture that is not accurate.

5. *Page 358:* The last full paragraph on this page contains a serious error. The statement is made that Mr. Julie's equipment "could do a calibration job normally taking 10 hours with other equipment in 25 minutes." This is simply not true, and a simple example can illustrate the magnitude of this error. Take a common digital multimeter, like the John Fluke 8000A, as a test case. This is a durable and widely used 3½-digit multimeter with LED readout. Under carefully timed and controlled conditions, it takes on the average 32.5 minutes to calibrate this digital multimeter with manual equipment. With Mr. Julie's equipment—of the type being described in your text—the average calibration time is about 17 minutes. Two other automated calibration systems that are commercially available can do the same job in 14 minutes with one system, and just under 12 minutes with the other system. Then the paragraph goes on to suggest that, "the labs confirmed our claims, and further testing at other Army sites provided further proof that our LOCOST System was up to the tasks required."

No such confirmations or tests existed in that timeframe. In fact, the equipment that Mr. Julie was demonstrating in that timeframe did not even possess a full set of electrical stimuli. The fact is that Mr. Julie's equipment saves approximately 15.5 minutes per calibration on the typical multimeter. Other systems available on the market produce similar savings—some less and others more. But it is not realistic to characterize the savings in the magnitude suggested in this paragraph. It would be a strange calibration procedure indeed that would take 10 hours, especially for the class of equipment for which Mr. Julie's equipment was being offered. To suggest that this time could be reduced to 25 minutes by the use of his equipment is at variance with the facts, and it is at odds with the fundamental technologies involved.

Appendix 24D (Cont.)

6. *Page 359:* In the only full paragraph, the statement is made that "Julie Labs pointed out 168 errors in the [Army] summary report. . . ." This may be Mr. Julie's assessment, but the Army correctly concluded that his system was not new or unique to the industry; the software preparation time stated by Mr. Julie was optimistic; the system cost was higher than other comparable automated systems; and the throughput performance claims were very optimistic. After years of subsequent experience, these assessments remain valid.

7. *Page 360:* At the bottom of the page, an assertion is made that the Army was inconsistent because it was purchasing 95 manual calibration sets. At that time, Mr. Julie was advised that the Army's evaluation found that no firm requirement existed from large automated systems in a mobile field Army environment: because they were not cost effective or otherwise justifiable at that time. Mr. Julie was invited to submit his proposal in response to the calibration set procurement, and he was assured that he would be given the same consideration as all respondents. Also, he was advised that if he felt that his system offered substantial improvements over the equipment listed in the Request for Proposal, then he should submit a single, unsolicited proposal addressing the specific conditions in the Request for Proposal that his equipment would satisfy. Mr. Julie did not submit an offer on the Request for Proposal.

8. *Page 361:* This paragraph suggests that the cost per calibration was $243 for the John Fluke Systems "that were now in use by the Missile Center." There has never been a John Fluke automated system in productive use at the Missile Center. On the other hand, there had been an older Fluke System at White Sands Missile Range. However, the cost per calibration using this older automated Fluke System was $13.31 per calibration. On the average, it took 0.7 hours (or 42 minutes) to perform a total calibration action. This included administrative paperwork, setup, calibration, teardown, and administrative logging. The direct labor component of this average cost consisted of $16.18 per hour. Even if installation overhead was added in the amount of 55 percent (to $25.08), the resulting average cost per calibration was $19.54. With a newer model of a Fluke System, estimates have shown that when applied to the workload at another site, the cost per calibration is roughly $14.96 during the period the initial investment cost is being amortized. Using the same type of estimating techniques and the same workload site, a comparable cost per manual calibration is $28.97. However, costs per calibration can vary widely, depending on the geographical location, size of workload serviced, and the types of technicians used. Nevertheless, ample evidence exists to show that the numbers cited in this paragraph are exaggerated.

9. *Pages 362–363:* These paragraphs refer to a proposal made by Mr. Julie which claimed a ten-year savings of $200 million. The statement is made that "[a]gain, the Army's response was negative, and again they used erroneous data and absolutely faulty logic to reject us." The fact is that his proposal was given careful consideration. His proposal was based on a concept of centralized support, and it was unsuited for the support structure needed to support the Army. In a meeting with Mr. Julie on this subject, it was made clear to him that the Army requirement was to deliver calibration and repair support to the lowest practical level in the field. Mr. Julie was told that the Army could not function under a concept where combat and support commanders were required to deliver instruments to central locations where the high throughput required for effective utilization of automated systems could be realized.

10. *Page 363:* This page is a reproduction of page 37 of the first comic book. The upper portion of the page asserts that mistakes were made in the Army's analysis. Mr. Julie's version of the meeting in the office of Mr. Douglas is not accurate. It was

Appendix 24D (Cont.)

made clear to Mr. Julie at this meeting that the Army evaluations were considered valid and none of the allegations that he presented had sufficient substance to alter the previous evaluations.

11. *Pages 363–366:* From the bottom half of page 363 through page 366, the suggestion is made that Mr. Julie was somehow correct in saying that the Army would need to purchase additional calibration sets.

    At the time this comic book appeared there were 87 complete calibration sets under procurement. It must be understood that these calibration sets consisted of capabilities that went far beyond the limited interests of Mr. Julie. Generally, his calibration equipment is limited to a certain class of electrical parameters within the area of direct current and low frequency calibration. The 87 sets under procurement covered physical parameters, DC-low frequency, microwave, and even some radiac equipment. Furthermore, the 87 sets were part of a three-year, multi-year contract; and the fiscal year 1980 quantity was for 18 sets. Two of the items in the procurement were no longer manufactured; however, several other manufacturers (including Mr. Julie) produced similar items. Then, pages 369 and 370 show plates where Mr. Julie alleges that: the Army's true level of calibration quality is 64 percent; over half of the Army's calibration funds for the rest of this century are being used to buy slow, low quality, expensive-to-operate, 1960 style calibrators; 50 percent of the Army's equipment is now officially neglected; and only 20 out of every 66 pieces of Army equipment will be working in-tolerance.

    The Army's calibration quality level has been maintained at a constant level of 81–85 percent (that is, 85 percent of all TMDE presented for calibration will be in-tolerance, 15 percent out-of-tolerance). The 64 percent level referred to is attributable to a paper presented by an Army employee. This 64 percent applies to the combined calibration and repair requirements for one particular installation. When repair requirements are extracted, the level approaches 80 percent, even for this particular installation.

    The Army equipment requiring calibration support is not being neglected. Mr. Julie misunderstands the Army calibration system, including the Army's labeling system for identifying or qualifying calibration requirements for specific instruments. Like all other services and activities that have calibration programs, the Army has a labeling system that identifies test equipment requiring calibration and test equipment that does not require calibration.

    Those items that are in a "calibration not required" category are not ignored, but receive normal maintenance at prescribed intervals.

    The statement that only 20 out of 66 pieces will be working in-tolerance is not true. With the Army quality level of 85 percent the number of items in-tolerance at the end of a calibration interval will be 85 out of 100.

12. *Pages 368–375:* The letter dated April 8, 1982 to Senator Roth related to an entirely different topic than previously discussed and was subsequent to the November 1981 Inspector General report and Mr. Julie's conclusion on page 374. The letter documents the extraordinary efforts that the Army made to conduct a fair side-by-side evaluation of available commercial automated calibration equipment. Mr. Julie elected not to offer on the solicitation; three other firms did elect to offer. A fair test was conducted and a small business firm in Massachusetts was competitively selected as the best to meet the Army's requirement. Mr. Julie protested to the GAO the award of seven systems to the small business firm. The GAO denied Mr. Julie's protest and ruled in favor of the Army. Mr. Julie provided various reasons to the GAO why he did not offer; the last being that he would not be competitive from a price standpoint. Please note that there are numerous firms which produce equipment similar to that of Mr. Julie's at substan-

tially lower cost. Some of these systems have less capabilities and others have more. Prices vary from $24,000 each for low quantity purchases to $85,000 for one system versus Mr. Julie's price of $140,000 each paid by the Army on a sole source for six LOCOST 106 systems. Mr. Julie's sytem has been found to be faster than some and slower than others. In summary, Mr. Julie was given a fair opportunity to compete in a side-by-side test and elected for his own reasons to avoid such competition.

13. *Page 369:* This is page 16 from the second comic book and states that, "The Army got trapped in its own lies, by telling GAO and Congress conflicting stories." The Army did not submit conflicting information. An Army response was provided to the Chief of Public Affairs, to be used in responding to media queries; and it was also provided as part of the response to various congressional queries. A copy of this response was provided to the General Accounting Office. All copies of the Army response contained the same information.

14. *Page 370:* This page attempts to show conflicting information. The first set of comments are not mutually exclusive. The equipment is kept in a standard configuration to the extent possible because the calibration sets are proliferated throughout the Army's force structure. But this does not mean that modernization does not occur. It does, and often the result is an upgrade of all sets; so that a new standard configuration is achieved. Regarding comment 2, it is not correct to say that the Army "has *no* requirement for automated equipment whatever!!!"

15. *Pages 371–373:* These pages list selected excerpts from the General Accounting Office Report. The comprehensive Department of Defense response is on file, and if you would care to read it, I will be glad to send you a copy.

University of Colorado at Colorado Springs

College of Business and Administration and
Graduate School of Business Administration

1420 Austin Bluffs Parkway
P.O. Box 7150
Colorado Springs, Colorado 80933-7150
(719) 593-3400

September 20, 1984

Michael C. Sandusky
Deputy Executive Director
Test, Measurement, and Diagnostic Equipment
Headquarters, U.S. Army Materiel Command
5001 Eisenhower Avenue
Alexandria, Virginia 22333

Dear Mr. Sandusky:

Thank you for commenting on Loebe Julie's comic books and his interaction with military and defense groups mentioned in the Hinkle/Stineman

Appendix 24D (Cont.)

case study. With few exceptions, such a case represents a less than exhaustive exploration of all sides of an issue; rather, it is nothing more or less than a company's view of its world interpreted by the casewriters who are collecting data and conducting interviews to write the paper.

A usual disclaimer; "the case study is not intended to represent either appropriate or inappropriate managerial policies and practices," accompanies the case. Rather, its purpose is to stimulate discussion about the company, its management, the marketplace, and relevant macro- and microeconomic environments. Instructors encourage students to examine strengths and weaknesses of the company, and to explore its opportunities and external threats. Students are asked what might Mr. Julie have done differently and what now? These are all rather neutral foci for "disinterested" third parties in the classroom, even if Mr. Julie's comments and attitudes clearly stem from his and his company's vested interests.

One important aspect of this case is the promotional approach employed—the comic book. I suspect students will tend to analyze this from the standpoint of message, medium, objectives (which may be inferred), and target audiences, and how the technique fits with Mr. Julie's overall approach to business development.

With permission, Mr. Sandusky, I would like to include your thoughtful and thorough responses in the next edition, and, meanwhile, possibly send photocopies to current adopters.

Again, thanks for your critique.

Sincerely,

Dr. Charles L. Hinkle
Professor of Business Strategy

Appendix 24D (Cont.)

DEPARTMENT OF THE ARMY
HEADQUARTERS, U. S. ARMY MATERIEL COMMAND
5001 EISENHOWER AVENUE, ALEXANDRIA, VA 22333-0001

November 28, 1984

Mr. Charles Hinkle
University of Colorado
College of Business and Administration
Department of Marketing
P.O. Box 7150
Colorado Springs, Colorado 80933-7150

Dear Mr. Hinkle:

Thank you for your letter of September 20, 1984 in which you outlined the use of your text, Cases in Marketing Management, Issues for the 1980's.

My prior letter and the keyed responses were prepared in conjunction with official U.S. Government duties; therefore, copyright protection is not available and permission to publish is not needed.

We would, however, ask that you footnote the source as the U.S. Army Materiel Command.

Sincerely,

Michael C. Sandusky
Deputy Executive Director
of Test, Measurement, and
Diagnostic Equipment

25

THE MONSTER
THAT EATS BUSINESS

Joseph Sugarman had a problem with the Federal Trade Commission and was not exactly sure how to solve it. He turned to what he knew best, direct marketing, to try to take the heat off. With the help of Dick Hafer, the Washington political cartoonist, a.k.a. the "comics commando," Joseph Sugarman developed a book that he used in a direct-mail campaign to gain support to fight what he saw as "The Monster That Eats Business." The following represents the essence of that book and the plight of Joseph Sugarman.

The Monster That Eats Business

BUREAUCRACY

In which the most dangerous monster in America tries to eat one small business and gets indigestion.

OUR STORY BEGINS IN 1971, IN NORTHBROOK, ILL.

JOE....PLEASE!

JOE SUGARMAN, A YOUNG MARKETING SPECIALIST, STARTED A NEW MAIL-ORDER BUSINESS IN HIS HOME. HE SOLD POCKET CALCULATORS.

SO WHAT? EVERYBODY SELLS POCKET CALCULATORS!

JS&A (THE NAME OF JOE'S COMPANY) WAS THE FIRST COMPANY IN THE U.S. TO NATIONALLY MARKET THE NEW POCKET CALCULATOR.

IN FACT, AT ONE TIME THEY SOLD MORE POCKET CALCULATORS THAN SEARS & ROEBUCK!

SOMEBODY WORKING OUT OF HIS BASEMENT SOLD MORE THAN US?

HE MUST HAVE ONE HECK OF A BASEMENT!

SEARS

3

THE FOLLOWING IS NOT JUST ANOTHER "SCARY STORY". IT HAPPENS TO BE TRUE. THIS MONSTER IS LOOSE TODAY. ALL INDUSTRIES ARE THREATENED BY IT. THE DIFFERENCE IN THIS STORY IS THAT YOU CAN HELP TO LEASH THE MONSTER.

WHEN YOU'VE READ THIS BOOK, YOU'VE DONE HALF THE JOB. THE OTHER HALF WILL TAKE PLACE WHEN YOU TAKE ONE SMALL ACTION WHICH WE WILL DESCRIBE NEAR THE END OF THIS BOOK.

2

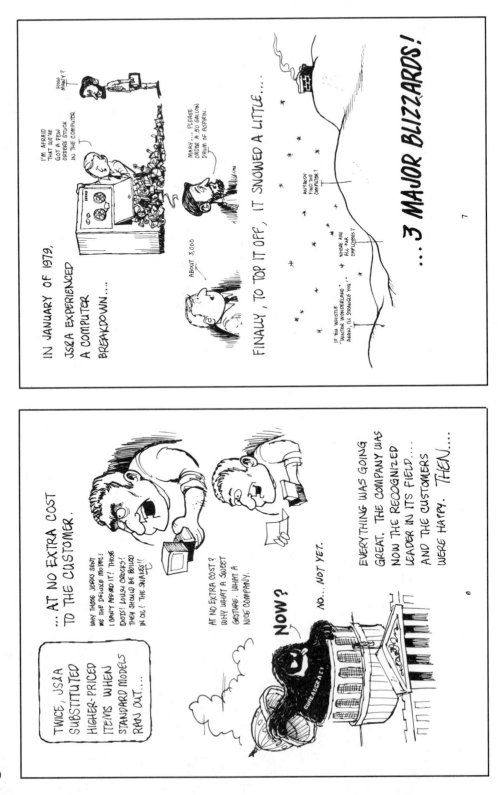

WITHIN A FEW WEEKS, THE COMPUTER WAS UP, THE ORDERS WERE PROCESSED AND EVERYTHING WAS ONCE AGAIN IN OPERATION.

HERE'S THE LAST ONE... MR. P CALCULATOR WANTS ONE R. SMITH.

ONE MONTH LATER, A FEDERAL TRADE COMMISSION INVESTIGATOR DROPPED BY....

YES SIR... CAN I HELP YOU?

YES, I JUST HAVE A FEW TEENY WEENY QUESTIONS.

HE TOLD JS&A THAT THERE HAD BEEN A FEW COMPLAINTS DURING THE PROBLEM PERIOD. ALL HE WANTED WAS JS&A's PROCEDURES, THEIR DELAY NOTICES, THEIR WARRANTIES..... NOTHING MUCH.

NOW!!

BUREAUCRACY

OH BOY!!

THE MONSTER WAS UNLEASHED!

9

8

MR. SUGARMAN, EVERYTHING YOU SAID IS FINE... BUT YOU VIOLATED OUR **RULE** AND YOU MUST PAY THE PENALTY.

DO YOU THINK WE JUST DREAM UP THESE **RULES** TO FEEL IMPORTANT?

WE COULD CHECK YOUR WARRANTIES.

WE COULD ACCEPT YOUR FIRST-BORN CHILD.

SO, JOE SAT DOWN WITH MEMBERS OF THE FTC TO DISCUSS THE CASE....

WE COULD SUBPOENA EVERYTHING IN YOUR FILES

HEH, HEH!

BUT, THE FTC HAD PLANS...

JOE AGREED TO PAY THEIR CUSTOMERS UP TO $90,000 FOR ANY DAMAGES AS A RESULT OF THEIR LATE SHIPMENTS. (HE KNEW, OF COURSE, THAT THERE WERE NO DAMAGES.)

A SUBPOENA WAS DELIVERED...

11

A FEW DAYS LATER, A MESSAGE CAME TO JS&A FROM THE FTC...

OUR PEOPLE HEARD ABOUT THE SNOW AND THE SPOILING OF THE PLANS....

WE DON'T CARE... YOU'RE BEING FINED A HUNDRED THOUSAND CLAIMS.

THE FTC CLAIMED THAT JS&A VIOLATED THEIR RULE WHICH SAYS THAT CUSTOMERS PAYING BY CHECK MUST BE NOTIFIED OF ANY DELAY WITHIN 30 DAYS.

THEY INVITED THE INVESTIGATOR BACK TO DISCUSS IT.

$100,000 MAKES US LOOK LIKE CROOKS. WE'RE REALLY AN HONEST COMPANY!

JOE TOLD HIM ABOUT THEIR EXCELLENT RECORD AND JS&A'S DEDICATION TO THE CUSTOMER'S SATISFACTION.

10

HOW TO HANDLE LATE SHIPMENTS

FTC RULE	JS&A PROCEDURE
CUSTOMERS MUST BE NOTIFIED IN 30 DAYS IF PRODUCT CAN NOT BE SHIPPED BY THEN.	CUSTOMER IS NOTIFIED IMMEDIATELY UPON FINDING THAT DELIVERY WILL BE MORE THAN 30 DAYS. CUSTOMER HAS OPTION OF CANCELLING IMMEDIATELY.
GO AHEAD AND DEPOSIT CUSTOMER'S CHECKS WHEN RECEIVED.	DEPOSIT CHECKS WHEN SHIPMENT IS ASSURED.
ENCLOSED SELF-ADDRESSED BUSINESS-REPLY ENVELOPE FOR CUSTOMERS USE WHEN CANCELLING AT END OF 30-DAY PERIOD.	CUSTOMER CAN EASILY CANCEL AT ANY TIME BY USING OUR TOLL-FREE TELEPHONE NUMBER.

NOTE: FTC RULES APPLY TO CHECK CUSTOMERS ONLY. CREDIT CARD CUSTOMERS ARE NOT PROTECTED BY THE FTC RULE.

JS&A RULES APPLY TO BOTH CHECK & CREDIT CARD CUSTOMERS.

13

12

75 COMPLAINTS, OVER 8 YEARS! 75 COMPLAINTS, OUT OF 800,000 ORDERS!

THE POST OFFICE OFFICIAL IN CHARGE OF COMPLAINTS SAID THE LEVEL OF COMPLAINTS WAS QUITE LOW FOR A COMPANY OF JS&A'S VOLUME - EVEN DURING THE COMPUTER PROBLEM.

(AT FIRST, HE DIDN'T EVEN KNOW OF THE COMPANY.)

YOU SEEM LIKE A NICE BUNCH OF BOYS.

U.S.P.S.

NOW HOW DID THE FTC GET THE 75 COMPLAINTS (PLUS THE 225 FROM JS&A'S PROBLEM PERIOD)?

LET'S SEE.... HAVE WE WRITTEN TO THE BETTER BUSINESS BUREAU IN QUITO, ECUADOR?

PAUL TURLEY HIS BULLSHIP

Simple.... BY SENDING LETTERS ALL OVER THE COUNTRY, SOLICITING COMPLAINTS FROM CONSUMER ORGANIZATIONS AND LEGAL OFFICES.

17

JS&A WAS THREATENED WITH IMMEDIATE FILING OF THE RECOMMENDATION FOR A $100,000 FINE IF THEY DIDN'T NEGOTIATE.

TURLEY SAID THAT IF JOE AGREED TO A MINIMUM OF $10,000, HE WOULD AGREE TO A MAXIMUM OF $100,000. THE FTC WOULD THEN EXAMINE ANY EVIDENCE JS&A WANTED TO OFFER, PLUS THE OTHER COMPLAINTS THE FTC HAD, TO DETERMINE THE SEVERITY OF THE PENALTY.

LATER AN FTC INVESTIGATOR SHOWED UP AT JS&A'S OFFICE WITH A LIST OF COMPLAINTS HE WANTED TO CHECK.

LOOK, LET'S BE FRIENDS AND SIGN AN AGREEMENT... OR I'LL HAVE TO BEAT YOUR HEAD RIGHT DOWN TO YOUR BELT, LITTLE BUDDY.

FINE

HOW MANY COMPLAINTS DID YOU RECEIVE PRIOR TO OUR COMPUTER PROBLEM?

75

16

THE FTC INVESTIGATOR WAS EXTREMELY HOSTILE AND SARCASTIC DURING HIS VISIT. THE PROOF THAT JS&A WAS AN HONEST, RESPONSIBLE COMPANY FELL ON DEAF EARS. HIS MIND WAS ALREADY SET.

IT PAINS US TO ADMIT THAT JOE'S HOSPITALITY REACHED A DREADFUL LOW AT THAT POINT.

UPON REFLECTION, JS&A'S ATTORNEY PHONED THE FTC AND SAID THAT THE INVESTIGATOR COULD RETURN IF HE WISHED.

19

COULD ANY PRIVATE ORGANIZATION SEND OUT SLANDEROUS LETTERS ALL OVER THE COUNTRY WITHOUT LEGAL RECOURSE?

IN THE MEANTIME...

JOE DISCOVERED THAT MANY OF THE COMPLAINTS SENT TO THE FTC SAT THERE FOR UP TO FOUR MONTHS BEFORE THEY ANSWERED THEM ...... WHILE JS&A ANSWERED THEM IN FOUR DAYS!

EVERY ONE OF THE COMPLAINTS WAS CHECKED IN JS&A'S RECORDS. EVERY ONE HAD ALREADY BEEN RESOLVED.

18

HE WENT TO HIS LAWYER AND TOLD HIM THAT HE WAS GOING TO ATTACK THE FTC!

JOE... YOU CAN'T TAKE OUT FULL PAGE ADS IN THE WASHINGTON POST AND THE WALL ST. JOURNAL!! THE GOVERNMENT WILL RUIN YOU.!! THEY'LL SMEAR YA.!! THEY'LL RIP YOUR LIMBS OFF AND GOUGE YOUR EYES OUT!!!

SO, THE ADS RAN.

THE INVESTIGATOR RETURNED, AND JS&A CONTINUED TO LOOK OVER HIS LIST OF COMPLAINTS.

ONCE AGAIN, THEY ALL HAD BEEN RESOLVED. SOME CASES THERE WAS HUMAN ERROR. SOME CASES WERE CUSTOMER ERROR. ALL WERE ISOLATED INSTANCES AND ALL HAD BEEN RESOLVED.

BUT TURLEY WAS NOT CONVINCED THAT JS&A WAS A GOOD COMPANY AND INSISTED THAT THEY AGREE TO PAY THE $100,000.

JOE REFUSED.

RIGHT HERE, THE ENTIRE STORY TURNS IN A NEW DIRECTION..... JOE HAD AN IDEA!

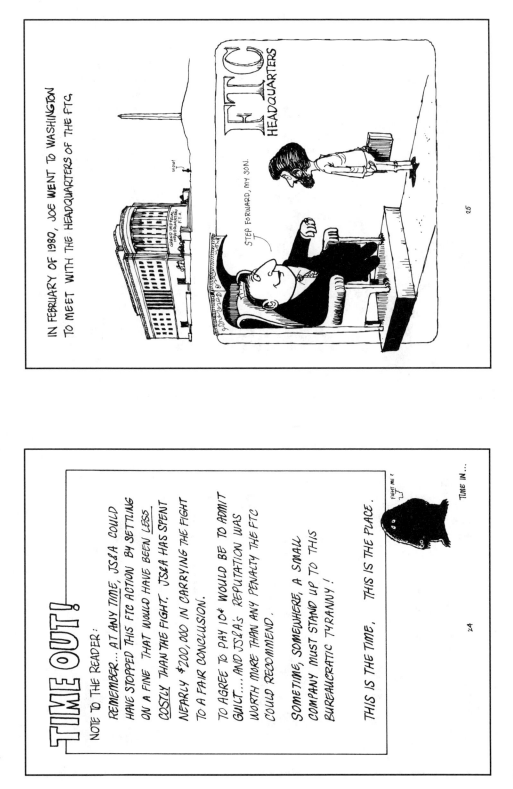

WHY ARE YOU PICKING ON US?

WHEN THE MAIL-ORDER COMPANY, "AMERICAN CONSUMER," WAS IN BUSINESS AND ACCUSED OF BEING DISREPUTABLE, YOUR SAME CHICAGO OFFICE DIDN'T TRY TO FINE THEM EVEN $1.00!

AH, BUT THERE'S GOOD REASON, MY SON.

YOU SEE, WE'RE NOT SET UP TO GO AFTER FRAUDULENT COMPANIES.

YOU'RE NOT SET UP TO GO AFTER "FRAUDULENT" COMPANIES?

OF COURSE NOT...

THEN YOU MEAN THAT YOU REALLY GO AFTER THE...THE...

THAT'S RIGHT! THE.....

26

LEGITIMATE COMPANIES......

JS&A WENT TO COURT—

OUR ONE ATTORNEY

vs.

THEIR SEVEN ATTORNEYS (TWO FLOWN IN FROM WASHINGTON, AT GOVERNMENT EXPENSE.)

YOU WANT MY CLIENT'S BIRTH CERTIFICATE AND KINDERGARTEN REPORT CARD?

THE JUDGE STRONGLY AGREED WITH THE FTC. THE MICROFILM FILES OF ALL OF THE BUSINESS JS&A EVER DID WERE TURNED OVER TO THE FTC.

FOR ALMOST A YEAR, THE FTC HAS SAID ALMOST NOTHING ABOUT JS&A's CASE. THEY'VE SPENT MONTHS LOOKING THRU THEIR RECORDS—FINDING NOTHING NEW THAT HADN'T ALREADY BEEN TOLD THEM.

NOW IN EARLY 1981,

THE FTC HAS DROPPED THE OTHER SHOE!

27

WITHIN THE NEXT FEW DAYS, THE FTC INTENDS TO RECOMMEND TO THE COMMISSION

THAT JS&A BE FINED..... NOT THE $10,000 SPOKEN OF.... NOT THE OUTRAGEOUS $100,000... BUT AN ABSOLUTELY ABSURD

$275,000

NOW ASK YOURSELF...

DO YOU BELIEVE OUR FRIENDS AT THE FTC ARE BEING JUST A TEENSY VINDICTIVE?

28

WHY NOW? YOU MIGHT ASK.

COULD THE CHICAGO OFFICE'S TOP MAN BE ELIGIBLE FOR REPLACEMENT UNDER THE NEW NATIONAL ADMINISTRATION?...HMMM. ONE LAST CHANCE TO MAKE A NAME?

OR, COULD THE ENTIRE FTC BE CONDUCTING A VENDETTA AGAINST JOE?

NOTE

DURING THE PAST TWO YEARS, THE LOCAL BETTER BUSINESS BUREAU HAS RECEIVED ONLY TWO COMPLAINTS AGAINST JS&A.... BOTH QUICKLY RESOLVED.

SO HERE WE ARE .....

THE BUREAUCRATS HAVE HAD THEIR DAY.

THEY'VE SCARED AWAY MANY OF JS&A'S CUSTOMERS. THEY'VE SLANDERED JS&A'S GOOD NAME.

THEY'VE PROTECTED THEIR PRECIOUS RULE.

AND NOW, THEY STAND PREPARED TO DELIVER THE DEATH BLOW.

IF PRESIDENT REAGAN CALLS, I'M NOT IN.

TURKEY

BUREAUCRACY

JS&A

29

THAT BRINGS YOU UP TO DATE

THE BUREAUCRACY HAS DONE ITS BEST TO DESTROY ONE OF AMERICA'S MOST INNOVATIVE COMPANIES — AN HONEST COMPANY THAT HAS PROVIDED OUTSTANDING SERVICE TO ITS CUSTOMERS AND DARED TO STAND UP TO AN UNFAIR ATTACK BY THE FTC.

WHAT CAN YOU DO?

JS&A DESPERATELY NEEDS CONGRESS TO INVESTIGATE THIS CASE!

AT THE END OF THIS BOOKLET, JS&A WILL GIVE YOU THE NAMES OF THOSE INVOLVED IN OVERSEEING THE FTC. WRITE THESE CONGRESSMEN.

WE NEED YOUR HELP. THE SYSTEM NEEDS YOUR HELP.

WHAT CAN I DO?!!

SHUT THEM UP THEY'RE MAKING SENSE!

31

BUT JOE WILL NOT GIVE UP. HIS SMALL COMPANY HAS ONLY BEGUN TO FIGHT!

THE FREE ENTERPRISE SYSTEM IS BLEEDING AND LIMPING.... BUT IT IS NOT DEAD!

JS&A HAS HOPE THAT THE NEW ADMINISTRATION WILL TAME THE BLOATED BUREAUCRACY.

JS&A SUBMITS THIS CASE HISTORY TO PRES. REAGAN AND HIS TEAM - AND ASKS FOR THEIR HELP.

30

NOW

ARE YOU READY FOR THIS?

THE ONLY REALLY VALID ARGUMENT PRESENTED BY THE FTC WAS THAT JS&A DIDN'T USE THE CORRECT WORDING ON THEIR DELAY NOTICES.

THE FTC RECENTLY ADVISED JS&A THAT THEIR DELAY NOTICE - USED SINCE THE PROBLEM PERIOD - WAS NOT PROPER.

THE WORDING BROKE THE RULE AND JS&A WAS STILL VIOLATING IT.

AND WHERE DID JS&A GET THE WORDING?

THIS IS NOT A LEGAL NOTICE!

THAT'S ODD. THIS IS THE FORM THAT WAS APPROVED BY YOUR OFFICE AFTER OUR PROBLEM.

'NUF SAID?

32

CONGRESS MUST INVESTIGATE THE CONDUCT OF THE FTC IN THIS CASE... AND ARGUE ALL, THEY MUST DO IT PROMPTLY, BEFORE JS&A IS LED THROUGH A LENGTHY COURT BATTLE.

PLEASE HELP WRITE THE PEOPLE BELOW & SEND A COPY TO JOE.

LET'S JOIN TOGETHER TO FIGHT THE MONSTER THAT'S TRYING TO DEVOUR JS&A!

Please write:

THE HON. JOHN D. DINGELL, CHAIRMAN, HOUSE SUBCOMMITTEE ON OVERSIGHT AND INVESTIGATIONS, UNITED STATES HOUSE OF REPRESENTATIVES, WASHINGTON, D.C. 20515

and

THE HON. GEORGE BUSH, VICE PRESIDENT OF THE UNITED STATES THE WHITE HOUSE WASHINGTON, D.C. 20500

33

I'LL TAKE A LIE DETECTOR TEST TO PROVE THAT EVERY STATEMENT I'VE MADE ON THIS CASE AND IN THIS BOOKLET IS THE ABSOLUTE TRUTH.

. . . about this battle

By Joseph Sugarman

I would like to thank Dick Hafer, the Washington political cartoonist, for taking the time to both investigate and write about my case in this booklet.

I am the target of an FTC vendetta. The story you have just read is true. My battle now is to take my case out of the hands of a group of vindictive FTC officials who must smear me or lose their credibility and give it to an independent committee of Congress to examine my evidence. Then I can prove that the FTC is indeed conducting a vendetta against me.

I have transcripts, documents, tape recordings and, of course, our own records which prove that the FTC has misled Congress and the public on my case.

In addition, I have other examples of FTC abuse that I am investigating. My case isn't unique. I've just been fortunate enough to have the resources and the guts to stand up against their tyranny.

My battle goes beyond the issues in my case. If a federal agency can conduct vendettas against any citizen, then all citizens are in danger. This illegal activity must stop and your help can make a difference.

If you could write Vice President Bush, Congressman Dingell, and your own con-gressmen requesting an investigation of my case, your efforts can help start a chain of events that may eventually lead to steps which would prevent what happened to me from happening to others. But you must act now.

I have not accepted any contributions in this battle nor do I want any. But many of you have asked to be kept closely informed on the progress of my case—an effort that has become quite costly. To keep everybody informed, I have published a newsletter called the "JS&A/FTC Battle Report" to which you can subscribe. The cost is $10, and the report will be mailed to you as new developments take place in my case. Upon receipt of your subscription, you will also receive an updated detailed report on the entire case.

The FTC needs help. I am prepared to work with Congress to help straighten out the FTC and limit their capacity to go after legitimate companies while leaving the fraudulent companies alone.

After I win, I plan to help the many others who have the will to fight but who are not as fortunate as I am. If you know of other businessmen who have been unfairly attacked by a federal agency, I want to hear about them too. You can also assist by helping me get national distribution for this booklet. Note the cost on the order form. Please act to help me, today.

Joseph Sugarman, 43, is President and Creative Director of JS&A Group, Inc., the company now under attack by the FTC. His background includes three years with the armed forces, a small stint as a CIA agent and the former president of an advertising agency. He was selected in 1979 as the Direct Marketing Man of the Year and is a director of the Center for Entrepreneurial Management. Mr. Sugarman is also a member of several national trade associations. He is married, has two young daughters, and resides in Northbrook, Illinois, a suburb of Chicago. He is a lecturer, speaker, inventor, author, commercial instrument-rated pilot, amateur radio licensee and both an award-winning photographer and advertising copywriter.

26

MARY KAY COSMETICS, INC. (A)

BACKGROUND OF THE COMPANY

A proliferation of products and a change of partners that might dazzle a square dance caller have characterized the cosmetics industry in the late 1970s and the 1980s. Witness Eli Lilly's purchase of Elizabeth Arden, Squibb's acquisition of Lanvin-Charles of Ritz, Pfizer's takeover of Coty, Norton Simon's of Max Factor, Colgate-Palmolive's of Helena Rubenstein, not to mention British-American Tobacco's gobbling up Germaine Monteil.

Accompanying the change of corporate identities there has been a distinct shift in management styles as practiced in cosmetics concerns. The "flair and flamboyance" of the old school cosmetics moguls—the Revsons, Rubensteins, and Ardens of the industry—has been replaced by a new breed of management types. Charisma has given way to pragmatism. The new styles are diverse, however—as urbane, cool, and international as ITT-trained Revlon's chief executive, the Frenchman Michel Bergerac, or as fundamentalist, *nouveaux riches*, and Texas-grown as Mary Kay Ash, founder and driving force behind Mary Kay Cosmetics, Inc., whose pink Cadillac incentive plan for sales agents and skyrocketing corporate profits have made Mary Kay a legend in the highly competitive American cosmetics business.

In 1963 Mary Kay Ash, a much decorated veteran of in-home sales (Child Psychology Bookshelf, Stanley Home Products, World Gift) founded Mary Kay Cosmetics, Inc., on $5,000 for product formulas, containers, and secondhand office equipment and on the belief that women could be sold on using a proven skin care regimen through an educational approach. Mary Kay Ash's expertise in the area of human motivation and in direct sales combined with son Richard Roger's wizardry in finance and marketing catapulted the company from its humble Dallas beginnings to a major national cosmetics corporation. Exhibit 26.1 charts this growth pattern. By August 1976 Mary Kay Cosmetics was listed on the New York Stock Exchange.

Mary Kay Cosmetics consists of "a scientifically formulated line of skin products" that is presented to the user programmatically during home beauty shows with emphasis on Mary Kay's Five Steps to Beauty (Exhibit 26.2). Over 50 percent of the company's sales are derived from the basic skin care line. Skin, body, and hair care products in addition to cosmetics, toiletries, and fragrances compose the remainder of the relatively small Mary Kay line (Exhibit 26.3).

The company uses self-employed women billed as beauty consultants to introduce the products to customers in the home where customers sample the products and are instructed in their use. This deceptively simple format has resulted in dramatic growth in the company's sales and sales force since the beginning, when Mary Kay Cosmetics had only 9 consultants. By 1981 net sales were $235.3 million, and about 150,000 consultants were selling the products (and one presumes faithfully using them). Exhibit 26.4 analyzes the productivity of the Mary Kay salespeople. Major distribution centers in the United States assure rapid delivery of the products to the consultants who are able to provide the customers with their products without delay at the beauty show. Thus, there should never be a gap between ordering and receiving the product as there is in Avon's distribution method.

An oft-quoted management truism in the cosmetics industry is Michel Bergerac's conclusion that "every management mistake ends up in inventory." Mary Kay has addressed this concern and has avoided the pitfall through its unique distribution and operations systems. Charged with the task of instantaneously providing each consultant with the inventory she requires at the moment she requires it, Mary Kay has developed five domestic regional distribution centers, located in Atlanta; Chicago; Los Angeles; Piscataway, New Jersey; and the corporate warehouse in Dallas. Dallas is mission control for the company, where the products are manufactured and the orders received. The Marketing Department has instant access via computer to individual and unit sales. Manufacturing uses the data bank at Dallas to control inventory by forecasting and planning products' runs. On the microlevel, directors of sales units are only a toll-free call away from comprehensive information about the performance of their unit or of specific individuals.

In 1978 Mary Kay Cosmetics formed a sister company in Toronto that has evolved into one of Canada's largest cosmetic enterprises. As of 1971 and 1980, respectively, separate operations were launched in Australia and Argentina. The Argentine Mary Kay undertaking has run into difficulties because of international problems. During May 1982, in the midst of the dispute between Argentina and Britain over the Falkland Islands with sky-high inflation in Argentina, Mary Kay was forced to write off $1.5 million there in a reassessment of the value of the company's marketing unit in Argentina.

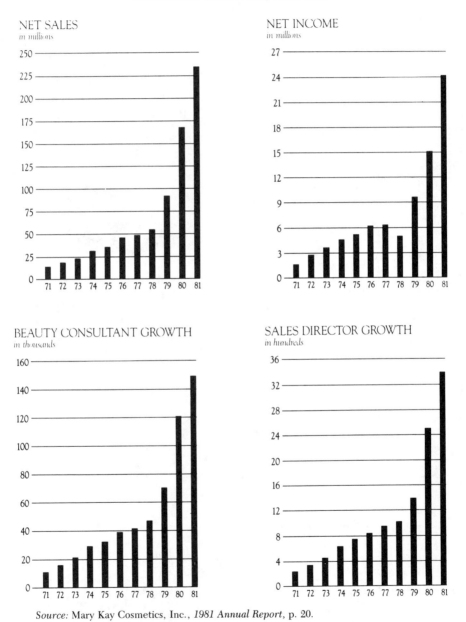

Exhibit 26.1

MARY KAY GROWTH, 1971–1981

NET SALES
in millions

NET INCOME
in millions

BEAUTY CONSULTANT GROWTH
in thousands

SALES DIRECTOR GROWTH
in hundreds

Source: Mary Kay Cosmetics, Inc., *1981 Annual Report*, p. 20.

Exhibit 26.2

THE FIVE STEPS TO BEAUTY

THE FIVE STEPS TO BEAUTY

MOVEMENT OF APPLICATION

Follow this movement of application when applying Cleansing Cream, Cleanser, Magic Masque, Skin Freshener, Night Cream or Moisturizer:

Always apply with the tips of the fingers. Beginning with the neckline, apply with upward and outward motion. Be sure to use the ring finger when working around the delicate tissue near the eyes. Remember to stroke delicately — don't massage.

1 CLEANSE

All of the Mary Kay cleansing products cleanse the skin deeply, thoroughly and gently, penetrating and loosening impurities and softening the skin.

Cleansing Cream Formula 1 and Formula 2 — Smooth on face and throat. Follow movement of application. Remove with warm, wet facial cloth.

Cleanser Formula 3 — Shake well. Apply thoroughly to face and throat. Lightly pat water on top of cleanser and follow movement of application, working cleanser into a foam. Splash skin with warm water and remove remainder with warm, wet facial cloth.

2 STIMULATE

Mary Kay Magic Masque® stimulates circulation, removes impurities and dead surface cells. Also brightens, refines and freshens the skin.

Magic Masque Formula 1 and Formula 2 — After cleansing, smooth on face and throat, avoiding eyes and mouth. Let dry for approximately 10 minutes. Soften and gently remove with warm, wet facial cloth. Apply Skin Freshener and allow to dry naturally. Use Magic Masque twice a week.

3 FRESHEN

Mary Kay Skin Freshener further stimulates circulation, makes pores appear smaller and removes any residue of previous products.

Skin Freshener Formula 1 and Formula 2 — Apply a few drops to clean cotton pad and gently smooth on face and throat. Avoid use in the immediate area of the eye. Allow to dry naturally. Always use Skin Freshener after Magic Masque.

4 LUBRICATE/MOISTURIZE

All of the Mary Kay moisturizing products help to smooth and condition the skin, working as a preventive measure against dryness.

Night Cream Formula 1—After cleansing and freshening, moisten face and throat with warm water and gently apply a very small amount of Night Cream. Leave overnight.

Night Cream Formula 2—After cleansing and freshening, gently smooth a small amount of Night Cream over face and throat. Leave overnight.

Moisturizer—After cleansing and freshening, gently smooth a thin film on the dry areas of the face.

5 PROTECT

Mary Kay's Day Radiance® provides daytime protection for the skin with a subtle tint of color that covers minor imperfections and gives a smooth, even-toned finish to your complexion. Day Radiance is available in perfectly blended shades, ranging in color from the lightest to the darkest skin tones, including white and yellow shades for highlighting and correcting.

Day Radiance Formula 1— Provides an emollient moisture base and luminous powder finish. Using fingertips, apply a thin film to a moistened face. When using Moisturizer under Day Radiance, do not moisten face.

Day Radiance Formula 2— Water based product that provides a fresh sheen without shine. Shake well. Using fingertips, blend over a dry face with outward sweeping strokes.

Each morning, cleanse, freshen and protect.
Each evening, cleanse, freshen and lubricate/moisturize.
Twice a week, stimulate.

Source: Mary Kay, Inc., promotional literature.

Exhibit 26.3

ANALYSIS OF SALES BY PRODUCTS, 1977–1981

	1977	1978	1979	1980	1981
Skin care products for women	48%	50%	49%	52%	49%
Skin care products for men	2	1	1	2	1
Makeup items	21	21	26	22	26
Toiletry items for women	13	12	10	10	10
Toiletry items for men	2	3	2	2	2
Hair care	4	3	2	2	2
Accessories	10	10	10	10	10
Total	100%	100%	100%	100%	100%

Source: Mary Kay, Inc., *1981 Annual Report*, p. 21.

Exhibit 26.4

MARY KAY COSMETICS SALES ANALYSIS, 1970–1982E

YEAR	SALES (000)	NUMBER OF BEAUTY CONSULTANTS AND SALES DIRECTORS AT YEAR END	AVG. NO. OF BEAUTY CONSULTANTS AND SALES DIRECTORS	SALES BEAUTY CONSULTANT AND SALES DIRECTOR (Productivity)	YEAR-TO-YEAR INCREASES IN PRODUCTIVITY
1982E	$346,000	190,000	175,000	$1,980.0	3.4%
1981E	242,000	150,000	140,072	1,915.0	9.0
1980	166,938	120,145	94,982	1,757.6	11.5
1979	91,400	69,820	57,989	1,576.2	26.9
1978	53,746	46,158	43,282	1,241.7	0.7
1977	47,856	40,407	38,818	1,232.8	−3.4
1976	44,871	37,229	35,176	1,275.6	13.3
1975	34,947	33,123	31,042	1,125.8	−6.0
1974	30,215	28,961	25,234	1,197.4	1.4
1973	22,199	21,508	18,805	1,180.5	−3.1
1972	17,232	16,103	14,142	1,218.5	1.5
1971	12,367	12,181	10,299	1,200.7	7.2
1970	8,091	8,418	7,224	1,120.0	−6.3
Average annual growth					
1975–1980	36.7%	29.4%	25.1%	9.3%	
1970–1975	34.0	31.5	33.9	0.1	

Source: Mary Kay, Inc., data.

MARY KAY ASH'S PERSONAL STORY

Mary Kay Ash's personal story is a rags-to-riches success saga in the great American tradition, and it mirrors the stories of many of the company's beauty consultants. In her autobiography, the best-selling *Mary Kay*, "the success story of America's most dynamic businesswoman," published by Harper & Row in 1981, Mary Kay tells of her life. In the company literature, this simple story is told and retold, and the lesson of self-discipline is underscored (Exhibit 26.5). Mary Kay Ash received the Horatio Alger Award from Dr. Norman Vincent Peale in 1978, and the company refers to Mrs. Ash's story as "a Horatio Alger Story."

Exhibit 26.5

MARY KAY—A HORATIO ALGER STORY

A CHILDHOOD FILLED WITH CHALLENGE

From a small Texas town to national prominence was not an easy journey. Mary Kay's success can largely be attributed to the discipline and independence she learned in her childhood.

The youngest of four children, she was born in the small town of Hot Wells, Texas, where her parents owned a hotel. When her father's health deteriorated and he became an invalid, the family moved to Houston so Mary Kay's mother could find work.

While her mother worked 14-hour days managing a restaurant, seven-year-old Mary Kay stayed home cleaning, cooking, and caring for her father.

Throughout those early years, Mary Kay's mother strongly influenced her daughter by encouraging her to excel in everything she did and told her over and over again, "You can do it." Whether in school or at home, Mary Kay wanted to be the best. Another lasting influence on her life has been her Christian faith. Her sincere convictions enabled her to express her love and affection toward those around her, and her faith has also been the cornerstone of her business success. Her basic philosophies are "God first, family second, career third," and the Golden Rule.

YOUNG ADULTHOOD

After finishing high school, Mary Kay married and had three children. Her husband was soon called away for World War II active duty, leaving Mary Kay with mounting financial problems. She worked as a secretary at a Baptist Church to help support the overwhelming cost of raising three children.

Exhibit 26.5 (Cont.)

A postwar divorce left Mary Kay the lone support of her young family. With the same determination that brought her through her earlier years, Mary Kay became a dealer for Stanley Home Products, a direct sales party plan company. This job enabled her to earn a living and still spend time with her children.

After three weeks of work and average sales of only $7 worth of products per party, Mary Kay attended a sales convention. She sat in the back row and decided that she would one day be crowned "Queen of Sales." Upon sharing her goal with the president of the company, Frank Stanley Beveredge, he replied, "Somehow, I think you will."

Mary Kay triumphantly won the crown the following year and eventually moved to Dallas where she continued her 13-year career with Stanley Home Products. But this was only the beginning of Mary Kay's rise to success.

Later, upon joining World Gift, a company that sold decorative accessories, she quickly became National Training Director. In 1962, though, she experienced a personal ordeal that threatened her health and her career. She suffered from a rare form of paralysis on one side of her face, but after surgery and several months of hospitalization, she recovered completely.

THE COMPANY BEGINS

Upon her recovery and after her retirement from World Gift, Mary Kay remarried and began to think about starting her own direct sales company. She planned to run the sales divison, while her husband acted as administrator. One month prior to the launching of the company, her husband had a heart attack and died. Mary Kay's three children joined their mother in the early days of the new venture. Today, Richard Rogers, her youngest son, is the president of Mary Kay Cosmetics, Inc.

Source: Mary Kay, Inc., promotional literature, 1981.

THE BEAUTY CONSULTANT AND THE BEAUTY SHOW

The lifeblood of the Mary Kay organization is the beauty consultant and director force who have generated Mary Kay's phenomenal sales and following. Independent beauty consultants, who buy their own sample case and products, are organized into sales units led by a sales director. Mary Kay Ash believes the cash system has assured the health of the company. "At Mary Kay, our consultants and directors pay in advance for their merchandise with a cashier's check or money order—no personal checks."

It's impossible for a Consultant to run up a debt with the company. Therefore, we have few accounts receivable. We don't have the expense of collecting bad debts, and we pass the savings on in the form of higher commissions. This way, everyone benefits. Most financial people just marvel at it—it's unheard of for a company of our size.[1]

Richard Rogers sums up the distribution plan this way: "Each Mary Kay consultant is an independent contractor. They are not employees of the company. Mary Kay serves as a wholesale house—freight in, freight out. The consultant buys directly from the company at wholesale prices and sells at retail prices. The difference is her profit."

Although the beauty consultant is in business for herself, the point is stressed in the corporate literature that "she is not by herself." The director is available as a consultant and teacher to the beauty consultant to help her successfully present the all-important beauty show. An effective director, according to the company, can handle in embryo the problems of poor consultant performance and thus control turnover in the ranks.

Because the beauty consultant is not a cosmetologist, federal and state laws prohibit her from applying cosmetics to the faces of the five or six participants at each show. Rather, her task is to assist each woman who attends the session, usually held at the home of a voluntary hostess, to determine her skin type and to answer questions about the five-step Mary Kay beauty process. "This is an effective teaching method. We don't sell—we teach!" emphasizes Mary Kay. "Polite persuasion" is the Mary Kay euphemism for selling. The hard sell is avoided, according to the literature.

In its *1981 Annual Report*, Mary Kay Cosmetics, Inc., shared with readers the philosophy of the beauty show.

> The Beauty Show *is* our primary marketplace. Its importance cannot be overstated. Here the Consultant has undivided attention as she presents the entire line. She has ample time to give each guest personal attention. The customer learns valuable tips on skin care and grooming and, because she receives her order at the Show, puts the lessons into practice immediately.

During the course of the two-hour beauty show, the consultant demonstrates, presents, persuades, collects, and delivers. (Exhibit 26.6 is the price list for Mary Kay products demonstrated in the beauty show). In addition to the sales activities implicit in the show, a consultant may recruit other consultants and arrange bookings for future shows at the demonstration. The person who agrees to host a show at her home "earns" Mary Kay products. Often if the consultant notes a potential customer's reluctance to purchase because of the cost, she may suggest that the woman earn products by hosting.

To become a consultant a woman submits a signed beauty consultant agreement with a cashier's check or money order to Mary Kay Cosmetics. The pink beauty showcase is then shipped immediately to her from Dallas. Before she is a full-fledged consultant, a recruit must attend three beauty shows with an experienced consultant, book five beauty shows for her first week's activity, and attend training classes con-

[1]Mary Kay Ash, *Mary Kay* (New York: Harper & Row, 1981), p. 29.

ducted by a director in her area. Because each Mary Kay show provides yet another opportunity to recruit beauty consultants into the company, to book future shows, and to establish reorder business, Mary Kay puts a premium on running a smooth and professional show. Mary Kay consultants are expected to present a well-groomed, Mary Kay–cosmeticized image and to dress in a manner consistent with Mary Kay Ash's personal philosophy of feminine attractiveness.

Mary Kay annual reports feature attractive models representing the consultants on their appointed rounds, dressed in tailored suits, tastefully manicured, coiffured, and made up, usually wearing soft, pastel blouses and Mary Kay jewelry (golden bumblebees and Mary Kay pins are sought-after prizes in the company). The ideal image of the consultant is that of the "dressed-for-success" career woman.

A career woman should dress in a businesslike manner. Personally, I'm opposed to wearing pants on the job. In fact, that's a company policy at Mary Kay (except in the manufacturing area). After all, we are in the business of helping women look more feminine and beautiful, so we feel very strongly that our Beauty Consultants should dress accordingly. We suggest they always wear dresses to Shows, rather than pants, and we emphasize well-groomed hair and nails. After all, can you imagine a woman with her hair up in curlers, wearing jeans, calling herself a Beauty Consultant—and trying to tell other women what they should be doing to look good? We're really selling femininity, so our dress code has to be ultra-feminine.[2]

Exhibit 26.6

1982 MARY KAY PRICE LIST

ITEM	PRICE	✔
Complete Collection (as shown)	$71.00	
Basic Skin Care	39.00	
CLEANSE		
Cleansing Cream Formula 1, 4 oz.	6.50	
Cleansing Cream Formula 2, 4 oz.	6.50	
Cleanser Formula 3, 3.75 oz.	6.50	
STIMULATE		
Magic Masque Formula 1, 3 oz.	7.50	
Magic Masque Formula 2, 3 oz.	7.50	
FRESHEN		
Skin Freshener Formula 1, 5.75 oz.	7.50	
Skin Freshener Formula 2, 5.75 oz.	7.50	
LUBRICATE/MOISTURIZE		
Night Cream Formula 1, 4 oz.	12.00	
Night Cream Formula 2, 4 oz.	12.00	
Moisturizer, 2.8 oz.	12.00	
PROTECT		
Day Radiance Formula 1, .5 oz.	5.50	
Day Radiance Formula 2, 1 oz.	5.50	
☐ Ivory Beige ☐ Toasted Tan ☐ Light Beige ☐ Cinnamon ☐ Medium Beige ☐ Chestnut ☐ Warm Beige ☐ Coffee ☐ Suntan Beige ☐ White ☐ Suntan ☐ Yellow ☐ Honey Tan		
GLAMOUR COLLECTION		
Blush Rouge	4.00	
Eyeliner ☐ Black ☐ Brown	5.00	

ITEM	PRICE	✔
Eyebrow Pencil ☐ Black ☐ Brown ☐ Auburn ☐ Charcoal ☐ Light Brown ☐ Blonde	$ 3.00	
Mascara ☐ Black ☐ Brown	5.50	
Lip and Eye Palette (Complete with 2 brushes)	14.50	
Lip Palette (Complete with lip brush)	12.50	
Eye Palette (Complete with eye brush)	12.50	
Retractable Lip or Eye Brush	2.00	
Lip or Eye Palette Refill Great Fashion Lip Color Shade Selections: ☐ Pinks ☐ Plums ☐ Russets ☐ Reds ☐ Corals ☐ Spices Great Fashion Eye Shadow Shade Selections: ☐ Blues ☐ Greens ☐ Browns ☐ Plums	4.00	
Blusher ☐ Soft Pink/Soft Peach ☐ Tawny Rose/Tawny Amber ☐ Cinnamon/Mahogany	8.50	
Lip Liner Pencils ☐ Raisin/Ripe Cherry	6.50	
Lip Gloss	4.50	
SPECIALIZED SKIN CARE		
Moisturizer, 2.8 oz.	12.00	
Facial/Under Makeup Sun Screen, 2.7 oz.	7.00	
Hand Cream, 2.8 oz.	5.50	

ITEM	PRICE	✔
BODY CARE		
Cleansing Gel, 8 oz.	$ 7.00	
Buffing Cream, 6 oz.	7.50	
Moisturizing Lotion, 8 oz.	6.50	
Sun Screening Lotion, 6 oz.	8.50	
BASIC HAIR CARE		
Shampoo for Normal/Dry Hair, 8 oz.	4.50	
Shampoo for Oily Hair, 8 oz.	4.50	
Protein Conditioner, 8 oz.	6.00	
Intense Conditioner, 3 oz.	7.00	
Non-Aerosol Hair Spray, 8 oz.	4.50	
FRAGRANCE BOUTIQUE		
Avenir Spray Cologne, 2 oz.	15.00	
Intrigue Spray Cologne, 1.75 oz.	10.00	
Facets Spray Cologne, 2 oz.	11.00	
Facets Cologne, 1 oz.	6.50	
Angelfire Spray Cologne, 1.75 oz.	12.00	
Exquisite Body Lotion, 8 oz.	6.50	
MEN'S PRODUCTS		
Mr. K Skin Care System	34.50	
Cleanser, 2.7 oz.	4.50	
Mask, 2.6 oz.	6.50	
Toner, 2.6 oz.	4.50	
Moisture Balm, 2.5 oz.	12.00	
Sun Screen, 2.7 oz.	7.00	
Mr. K Cologne, 3.75 oz.	9.50	
Mr. K Lotion, 3.4 oz.	4.50	
ReVeur After Shave Cologne, 3.75 oz.	10.00	

Source: Mary Kay, Inc., price list for beauty consultants.

[2]Ibid., p. 10.

MOTIVATION—MARY KAY STYLE

Within the honeycomb of the sales unit—the basic organizational entity in Mary Kay, though it is not included in the company organization chart—the consultant receives weekly sales training and encouragement, sings Mary Kay booster songs, and applauds the successes of others. Personal vignettes are as legitimate in this revival-style gathering as is instruction in specific sales techniques. The professionalization program at Mary Kay also includes regional workshops, Jamborees (conducted by national sales directors), leader's conferences, and seminars. "The Seminar" is the "multimillion-dollar extravaganza" staged each year at the Dallas Convention Center where thousands of Mary Kay consultants and directors converge for inspiration, entertainment, and education—Mary Kay style. It is in this immense convention forum that Mary Kay leaders are recognized publicly, where they share their own sagas of success with the audience. Here the Cadillacs, mink coats, diamond bumblebees, and other coveted Mary Kay status symbols are meted out to the deserving ones, and here women aspire to these material rewards by goal-setting activities for the coming year. Seminar classes, conducted by successful Mary Kay directors, teach the intricacies of sales technique, bookkeeping, leadership, customer service, and other skills necessary for Mary Kay entrepreneurship. In 1980 the special effects staff for the seminar arranged for the pink Buicks and Cadillacs to "float" phantomlike through mist onstage via a remote control process much to the delight of the assembled. Seminar showmanship has proven effective in creating the Mary Kay myths.

The company believes that tangible symbols of success motivate the Mary Kay women and serve to fuel the belief "that if they work hard enough—if they give of themselves—that they will be successful, personally and professionally." Vacation trips, prizes, contests, photographs of Mary Kay with members of the sales force, and constant praise are among the motivators the company has used with great success. In 1980, 311 sales directors earned more than $30,000; 98 earned more than $50,000. Almost 500 are designated as "Cadillac-status" directors. The highest-paid Mary Kay saleswomen are the national sales directors, a group of more than 39 women who began as consultants. They average more than $150,000 annually. Mary Kay Cosmetics gives a great deal of publicity to these star earners, for example, Helen McVoy who started back in the humbler days of the company and now earns $300,000 a year.

EARNINGS

A consultant is in business for herself and therefore her earnings are determined by her sales at retail. She purchases products from the company at a discount (up to 50 percent) from retail and her gross profit is the difference between her purchase price and the retail selling price that she herself determines.

In 1981 Mary Kay Cosmetics raised prices 16 percent and simultaneously upped the commission thresholds to increase productivity on a sustained basis. If the consultant wants to qualify for a 50 percent discount, she must order $1,000 of products at the suggested retail price. Previously an $800 order qualified her for a 50 percent discount. Selling $800 of merchandise currently entitles her to $360. Price hikes and the revised commission thresholds allow the consultant to increase her earnings if she manages to maintain her customer base. But there is no time to rest on her laurels, because the Mary Kay system is geared toward the saleswoman who aggressively builds her business.

While it is relatively easy to become a Mary Kay consultant, the company demands considerably more of those women who wish to qualify as sales directors. The labor of the sales director is sweetened by the possibility of substantially increased financial rewards over the consultant status, however. Like the consultant, the sales director is self-employed. As the resident advisor for her unit, she supplies her people with inspiration, positive suggestions for improving sales performance, and business advice of all kinds. A carefully orchestrated program for the directors and a rigorous screening process that admits only those women who have met stringent performance standards in terms of volume sales and number of recruits assures that the directors will be an experienced, aggressive sales group. In 1982 the company numbered 3,500 directors. The director-in-qualification travels to Dallas (at her own expense, as is the case of travel arrangements for the entire Mary Kay sales force) to receive training in management of a sales unit.

The directors' commissions were revised upward in 1981 along with the consultants'. To receive the pink Cadillac ("those little pink jars mean little pink cars"), the director must maintain a wholesale volume of $12,000 per month. Under the previous commission scheme, the director earned 12 percent if her unit volume topped $6,000. After the revision, her unit needed to "politely persuade" customers to buy from $8,000 to $12,000 to receive 12 percent. Although the director currently gets only 11 percent on unit volume between $5,000 and $8,000, a 13 percent commission is now possible for the director on volume over $12,000. The director must maintain the momentum of her unit if she is to succeed. Simply put, success for consultants spells success for directors, and vice versa.

GROWTH OF THE COMPANY

Inside and outside of Mary Kay, declining recruitment of consultants was expected in the early 1980s, and the 50 percent growth rate experienced up until 1980 was considered unsustainable. Anxiety that the company might reach an early saturation point due to its rapid growth has proved to be groundless, however, with 180,000 consultants projected by December 1982.

Cosmetics, along with beer and cigarettes, have generally been earmarked "recessionproof." Yet cosmetics unit sales in late 1981 and 1982 for Mary Kay and other companies did falter as disposable incomes declined in a recessionary environment. During this period Mary Kay Ash's autobiography went on sale. Her promotional tour to major U.S. cities to discuss her life, career, and company on television and radio provided unprecedented visibility for the Mary Kay message and gave recruitment a shot in the arm. The company spent an estimated $450,000 in television and other advertisements during this period (Exhibit 26.7).

Exhibit 26.7

ADVERTISING FOR THE MARY KAY AUTOBIOGRAPHY IN *PEOPLE MAGAZINE*

"YOU'VE GONE PRETTY FAR FOR A WOMAN." THEY SHOULDN'T HAVE TOLD ME THAT.

"I had been a success in my field for more than 25 years. A promotion to a top executive position was long overdue. Instead, I was passed over again and again. Has that happened to you?

"Well, my response was to create an opportunity that would reward women for what they were really worth!

"My dream was to offer women not only a wonderful new Skin Care Program, but also an opportunity to prove how far we can go."

Today Mary Kay Cosmetics has more than 120,000 Beauty Consultants on three continents and our sales are in the hundreds of millions of dollars!

Now the Mary Kay story is available in a book.

It is a personal business history of a dream that happened when all the skeptics said it would fail.

"If you have ever been told you can't do something,

Yes, there really is a Mary Kay. Portrait by Francesco Scavullo, June 1981.

my story will prove you can. I urge you to read it right away, and I hope it will open some closed doors and closed minds in your life."

It's available at your local bookstore. Or ask your Beauty Consultant how you can get a copy. If you don't have a Consultant, look in the Yellow Pages under Cosmetics/Retail. Or call toll-free (800) 527-6270.

THE MARY KAY PHILOSOPHY

At Mary Kay, attention to the family unit is central to company ideology. Mary Kay Ash often states the formula, "God first, family second, career third." Since most Mary Kay consultants have families, the organization realizes that enlisting family cooperation makes for happier, more successful Mary Kay salespersons. A husband who is unfavorably disposed to his wife's Mary Kay career, "who gets upset when she comes home an hour late from an evening beauty show" may be "disastrous" to the business. So Mary Kay consultants are urged early on to enlist the cooperaton of husbands with tact and caring. At the seminar in Dallas each year, husbands participate in workshops led by experienced Mary Kay husbands designed to imbue them with "that Mary Kay enthusiasm" at best or at least to help them handle issues that sometimes arise in a Mary Kay household: ego crises that occur when a wife brings in more income than her spouse, household crises when a woman may not be on hand to perform all the "wifely" functions to which the family has become accustomed, readjustment problems for the family when the wife and mother may be away from home attending Mary Kay functions. To cheer those husbands left at home when wives are in Dallas, training to be directors, letters are dispatched to them from Mary Kay headquarters thanking them for the support they are giving to their wives' careers.

> If you are a working woman, getting your husband involved is so important! It's always been my observation that *people will support that which they help to create*. When a woman goes to work, she must not only sell her husband on her career, but if she's wise, she'll find ways to get him involved. Once he's involved, she'll get his support. One area where many of our Beauty Consultants have gotten their husbands involved is in the bookkeeping and record-keeping that goes with any business. Many sales-oriented women don't especially like record keeping, so they welcome their husband's help in this area, and it's been our experience that most husbands enjoy keeping their wives' records.[3]

To assist the woman in rendering the family the time that is theirs, and to Mary Kay Cosmetics its fair share, Mary Kay Ash advocates good time management. Since she has found that getting up at five in the morning gives her an additional workday each week, she urges consultants and directors to join her Five O'Clock Club: a routine of rising early each morning, using the early hours to dress, apply makeup, do household chores, and prepare to begin Mary Kay business-related activities by 8:30 A.M. The ideal consultant will stop for a half-hour lunch and stay with business until five in the evening. In the best of all possible Mary Kay worlds, a woman will earn enough to allow her to delegate many household duties to a housekeeper, the better to perform her sales duties. Getting organized, however, is key to the success of the woman who cannot afford a housekeeper:

> I know many women do manage to wear all those hats, but it can certainly take its toll. In order to be effective in their careers and still be good wives and mothers, they must be organized. As a general rule, I have found that getting organized is one of the biggest problems working women have. And if a woman is trying to wear a great many hats and she isn't organized, she's operating under a tremendous handicap.[4]

A unique feature of the company is the flexibility built in for working mothers. Inherent in the company philosophy is the notion that women working as a team can cover for each other in case of family emergency. The beauty show will go on, but perhaps another consultant will carry on when a woman needs to care for a sick child or spouse, a procedure called "the dovetail system."

The Mary Kay organization becomes an extended family for its sales force, a bountiful maternal figure dispensing prizes of minks, diamonds, and Cadillacs to dutiful daughters. The nonhierarchical family atmosphere of the company promotes high morale, according to Mary Kay and upper-level staffers.

[3]Ibid., p. 72.
[4]Ibid., pp. 169–170.

The personal touch—be it serving cookies mixed up by Mary Kay Ash with her own hands at company functions or sending Christmas, birthday, anniversary cards, and condolence messages—underscores the familial concept of the organization and builds company loyalty. The allegiance of the sales force to the company, personified in Mary Kay Ash, surfaces in every aspect of the consultant's training. In problem solving, consultants are asked to think what Mary Kay herself "would do in your situation," much as if Mary Kay Ash were an exemplary, albeit absent, mother. Adopting Mary Kay Ash's personal routine as their own in many cases, consultants and directors are attached to Mary Kay by an umbilical cord of personal habit and life-style. Many of the sales force display photographs of Mary Kay in their workspaces at home.

SKIN CARE PRODUCTS AND MARY KAY

Mary Kay Cosmetics in 1963 had hit upon an idea whose time had come with its introduction of skin care products, now the staple of almost every major cosmetics house. The basic five-step skin care process includes cleansing, stimulating, freshening, moisturizing, and protecting the skin. The company suggests that the basic set not be broken as it is the centerpiece of the Mary Kay concept, that is, to teach people how to care for their skin.

> The best reason to start a new company is that *there is a need for what you have to offer,* or that you're better than what is being offered. When we began, no cosmetic company was actually teaching skin care. All of them were just selling rouge or lipstick or new eye colors. No company was teaching women how to care for their skin. So we came into a market where there was a real need—and we filled it. Oddly enough, it's still true today that women are not knowledgeable about skin care, despite all the information on television, in magazines, and in newspapers. They buy a product here, there, and everywhere, but they don't have a coordinated program. We fill a void by helping women understand how to take care of their skin. So, if you want to start a successful business, you must offer something different or something better than what is available.[5]

In what is being called a "cosmetic revolution" by some, major cosmetics firms in the 1980s are taking scientific approaches to beauty. While the promise of cosmetics before the 1980s was one of glamor, the present appeal is made to the customer's consciousness that the scientific result of good skin care is healthy, younger-looking, cleaner skin. Advertising stresses the chemical properties of collagen, linoleic acid, and many more. Consumers are presumed, in such high-tech ads, to be conscientious about skin care and conversant with its sophisticated vocabulary replete with such terms as "cell renewal," "exfoliation," and "hydration."

This scientific approach began in the 1960s when Dr. Erno Lazlo introduced his pathbreaking line of skin care products to an enthusiastic public. Worship at the altars of Revlon's Eterna 27 and Clinique also began in the 1960s and has continued into the 1980s.

Scientific research in the 1950s set the stage for the cosmetic revolution, al-

[5]Ibid., p. 120.

though Mary Kay Cosmetics maintains that the original recipe for its skin preparations emanated from a hide tanner in Texas.

From the 1950s to the 1970s, soluble collagen became available to cosmetic chemists at that time seeking a protein to be used in products to treat dry, flaking, aging skin.[6] Marketing research had demonstrated (and continues to reveal) that approximately 90 percent of American women perceive their most serious skin problem to be dry skin.

Accordng to scientist Bernard Idson of Hoffman-La Roche, when it was understood that it is not oil but water that causes skin to be soft and flexible, cosmetic marketing shifted emphasis from total emolliency to the moisturizing qualities of various products. Idson and other researchers found that a water level of less than 10 percent in an individual's skin results in dried keratin, which causes lowered skin elasticity, a characteristic of sun-damaged, chapped, and aged skin.[7]

With over half its sales in the skin care area, Mary Kay finds itself in the 1980s heavily invested in the fastest-growing product category in cosmetics. Industry analysts project continued growth for skin care products, estimating in optimistic moments the general moisturizer market to number 100 million persons.

PSYCHOGRAPHICS, DEMOGRAPHICS, AND MARY KAY

Psychographic market segmentation stretches beyond the more traditional demographic and socioeconomic descriptors used to predict consumer behavior. Product psychographics are bound up with product promises, price-value perception, and the overall image of the product. Because of this relational posture, psychographic market segmentation is particularly applicable to the behavior of the cosmetics purchaser, who according to an old aphorism, is buying not only a product but hope. In a way, however, proponents of the scientific approach to marketing skin care are placing bets on a consumer's responding to demonstrations of empirical results and moving away from purchasing merely out of *hopes* that the product will deliver.

The last decade has seen a tremendous consumer responsiveness to computerized and education-oriented beauty programs (Clinique) and carefully orchestrated, scientific-based programs to control "age zones" (Charles of Ritz). According to those in the testing area at Ritz, their test methodology for the product Age-Zone Controller used 100 subjects and, according to Eileen Kregan, director of consumer education for Charles of Ritz (1982), "consisted of making silicone skin replicas of the subject's outer eye area on the first, seventh, and fourteenth days of the test. To measure line reduction, light was passed through the positive skin replicas and a transparency was made. Direct measurements were then made of the transparencies to determine what changes occurred in the length and number of age lines over a 14-day period." Advertising for the product will reflect the scientific findings.

Mary Kay relies much more heavily on the educational than on the high-tech

[6]See R. D. Todd and L. I. Biol, "Soluble Collagen: New Protein for Cosmetics," *Drug and Cosmetic Industry*, Vol. 117 (October 1975), pp. 50–52.

[7]See Bernard Idson, "Dry Skin Moisturizing and Emolliency," *Drug and Cosmetic Industry*, Vol. 117 (October 1975), pp. 43–45.

approach with its customers. Quality control is a term that surfaces more often at Mary Kay than specific scientific terminology and vocabulary. The company envisions customers as interested more in the process of using the product than its specific theoretical underpinnings.

The demographic trends as projected by U.S. Census figures indicate that Mary Kay will continue to find an increasing number of women customers in the 25- to 44-year age group, a group Mary Kay has already targeted as one vitally interested in skin care. Projections call for the 63 million persons in the 25- to 44-year age group in 1980 to increase to 80 million in 1990. Although the teenage and early-twenties market is dwindling, this should not be problematic for Mary Kay since its products presently do not get high visibility among this group due to the beauty show method of sales.

Mary Kay Cosmetics sees many positive signals in the 1980 Census data (Exhibit 26.8). Constructing "the woman of the '80s," the company profiled a woman "in her mid-30s" (Exhibit 26.9).

Exhibit 26.8

U.S. POPULATION PROJECTIONS BY AGE GROUP (BOTH SEXES)
(in millions)

Age Group	1970	1975	1980	1985	1990	COMPOUND % INCREASE (DECREASE)			
						1975 vs. 1970	1980 vs. 1975	1985 vs. 1980	1990 vs. 1985
15–19	19.3	21.0	20.6	18.0	16.8	1.7%	(0.4)%	(2.7)%	(1.4)%
20–24	17.2	19.2	20.9	20.5	18.0	2.3	1.7	(0.5)	(2.6)
25–29	13.7	16.9	18.9	20.6	20.2	4.3	2.3	1.7	(0.4)
30–34	11.6	14.0	17.2	19.3	20.9	3.8	4.2	2.3	1.6
35–39	11.2	11.6	14.0	17.3	19.3	0.6	3.8	4.9	2.2
40–44	12.0	11.2	11.7	14.1	17.3	(1.3)	0.9	3.8	4.1
45–49	12.1	11.8	11.0	11.5	13.9	(0.7)	(1.4)	0.9	3.8
50–54	11.2	12.0	11.7	10.9	11.4	1.4	1.4	(1.4)	0.9
55–59	10.0	10.5	11.4	11.1	10.4	1.0	1.7	(0.5)	(1.3)
60–64	8.7	9.2	9.8	10.6	10.4	1.1	1.3	1.6	(0.4)

Source: U.S. Department of Commerce, Bureau of Census, 1970, 1980, Series P-25, *Population Estimates and Projections.*

As Mary Kay Cosmetics looks to the 1990s, it sees a population in which 60 percent of all women will be working. Women working outside the home have clearly demonstrated that they spend more on cosmetics than do their counterparts in the home. One-third of all households will be composed of single persons, people who have discretionary income to spend on their own needs. Mary Kay sees great opportunities to convert a "middle-aged" population to skin care products. On another level, there will be a large middle-aged working female population from which to recruit the corps of Mary Kay consultants. That the number of women entering the labor force is tapering off (in 1980, 50 percent of the female population between ages 18 and 65 were working) does not appear to be of major concern to the company.

MARY KAY AND THE FOOD AND DRUG ADMINISTRATION

Inquiries made to the Food and Drug Administration (FDA) regarding the claims made by cosmetics companies for their products is a major escalating problem at the

---

Exhibit 26.9

THE WOMAN OF THE '80s

Her husband has a good job, but they could use extra income. They have one child.

She has completed some college and would like to return, part-time, for more. She is highly inclined to a job or career—both from economic necessity and from a desire to experience something new and to test her abilities.

The woman of the '80s has a new awareness of political affairs but, at the same time, is keenly aware of improving herself, physically, intellectually and professionally.

She wants to live life on **her** terms. She is interested in acquiring things and achieving goals, but above these she places **experience**. She is not content to be a spectator. While she may admire the looks and figure of a fashion model, she would rather **be** one.

Even though she enjoys her homelife, she seeks to expand her world by finding a part-time job or full-time career. This new world makes her more aware of her appearance. She works hard to stay fit; she is nutrition-conscious; she cares deeply about how she looks—her wardrobe, her skin and her grooming.

To the ends of feeling and looking good, she has educated herself in the accoutrements of fitness and appearance. She is more conscious than her mother's generation about matters of sophistication, taste in clothing and cosmetic fashions.

She eagerly searches for products and services that satisfy her powerful sense of self and her need for self-improvement. She is a customer in the market for what Mary Kay has always offered. And now, more than ever, she is willing to try both our products and our career opportunity.

The inevitable meeting of Mary Kay and the woman of the '80s usually takes place at a Mary Kay beauty show.[8]

[8]*1980 Annual Report*, p. 5.

---

agency, which is receiving less funding than it says it needs to investigate. The FDA sustains the burden of proof in establishing that the claims made by cosmetics companies are misleading to the consumer. Although cosmetics companies, including Mary Kay, express concern about a climate of increased regulation, the FDA complains that "we are not in any position to challenge the cosmetics industry. It is a $12 billion industry being regulated by a handful of people at the FDA."

Until the 1970s, the government took a strong stance with regard to the regulation of cosmetics formulations. Consumer activism across the board in the 1970s resulted in more stringent regulation of the industry. The use of dyes, hexachlorophene, and mercury in cosmetics and toiletries sparked debates and engendered legislation on the appropriate labeling of cosmetics. Major regulatory requirements imposed on manufacturers included

Responsibility for the safety of the cosmetic being marketed

Responsibility for required testing to determine toxicity, irritation, and/or sensitivity to the product

Compliance should the FDA insist on further discretionary testing by an FDA-appointed, independent organization to verify the safety of ingredients

Mandatory labeling of cosmetic packages or containers with specific ingredients in order of predominance, although flavor and fragrance need only be indicated by the words "flavor" and "fragrance"

A waiting period of 20 days before the release of the new product after notification of the FDA

Reports of increased regulation hover over the industry, but the fact is, according to the *1982 U.S. Industrial Outlook,* that less than 1 percent of the FDA's budget goes toward regulation of the cosmetics industry. The FDA depends on voluntary programs for the reporting of product formulas and adverse effects, for example, the Cosmetic Ingredient Review (CIR), a screening and warning process to alert the industry to possible harmful effects of cosmetic ingredients.

Mary Kay's reaction to regulation has resulted in expansion of its laboratories, acquisition of capital equipment to support skin science, and development of contacts in the scientific fields of dermatology and skin science. "Regulatory agencies are responding to increased scientific information, ensuring a more complex environment in the '80s for our entire industry," the company reported to stockholders in 1981.

OF TOILETRIES AND COSMETICS

Increasingly the distinction drawn between toiletries and cosmetics is becoming a matter of semantics. Because they are higher priced, cosmetics theoretically are geared to the individual whereas toiletries at a lower unit price are targeted to the mass market. The mode of distribution of cosmetics—through department stores and drugstores on a franchise or semifranchise basis or through direct sales—differs from that of toiletries, which are found in mass marketing outlets. This distinction is beginning to blur as cosmetic houses begin limitedly to place lower-priced lines in grocery stores and discount houses, although it is doubtful that toothpaste will appear in department stores. More utilitarian in nature, toiletries, including shampoos, toothpastes, and deodorants because of their proletarian nature, occupy a more competitive marketing niche, one in which higher promotional advertising expenditures are the rule. Lipsticks, fragrance products, eye makeup, face makeup, and the treatment lines—the mainstays of cosmetics—tend to engender a strong brandname loyalty if the product delivers, even though it may be less advertised than a toiletry. A satisfied Mary Kay customer, for instance, often will use no other brand of cosmetic, although she may use several brands of toothpaste. May Kay and other cosmetic companies are making strong bids to sell toiletries as cosmetics, especially in the hair care line, by marketing a cluster of such products as a hair care program with much the same educational approach found successful for the skin care line (Exhibit 26.10).

A common property to both cosmetics and toiletries is their appeal to the psyche of the user. No one would argue with the idea that people buy these products with the expectation that they will look and feel better after using them.

Analysts have concluded that one problem in capturing the potentially vast market for men's cosmetics is in breaking down the image that it is normal for a man to buy toiletries but somehow "abnormal" for him to purchase cosmetics. In recent years men appear to have been convinced that colognes are acceptable masculine cosmetic items. Mary Kay and other firms believe that growth in the men's cosmetic market will be slow and will probably begin with a skin care line accompanied by an educational process of some sort.

MARY KAY COSMETICS AND THE FUTURE

Returning to the familial theme at the end of her autobiography, Mary Kay reflects on the possibility of her retirement—if and when she can no longer present the glamorous, ageless public persona that people recognize through photographs such as the one taken by celebrity photographer Francesco Scavullo for the cover of her book. In passing she remarks that her mother's skin, even at age 87 "looked wonderful."

Looking toward the long term, Mary Kay Cosmetics purchased 176 acres of land in Dallas in June 1981 to pursue a major four-year expansion program to encompass production, distribution, and administrative facilities. Construction was set to start in October 1982 on the first of several manufacturing and distribution facilities.

> We're also so fortunate to have as president my son, Richard, who has filled in for me on many occasions and won the hearts of our people. He, one day, will not only fill his job as chief executive but mine as well, as motivator of our people.[9]

Exhibit 26.11 portrays the management team at Mary Kay Cosmetics.

The development strategy to see the company through a lengthier expansion period will call for construction as needed to support sales, to be financed from retained earnings. The leased 300,000-square-foot manufacturing facility allows Mary Kay Cosmetics to support $400 million in sales volume. The $12 million site development project, underway in 1982, was capitalized and also financed by internal cash

[9]Ash, *Mary Kay*, p. 205.

Exhibit 26.10

TOTAL U.S. COSMETIC AND TOILETRY TRENDS IN MARY KAY'S RELEVANT MARKETS, 1970–1980*

YEAR	SALES MANUFACTURING (millions) PRICES	PRICE INCREASE (Decrease)	REAL SALES (Increase)	U.S. FEMALE POPULATION (millions)	COSMETIC AND TOILETRY SALES PER WOMAN† (Mfg. Prices)	REAL COSMETIC USE INDEX‡ (Per Capita)
1980	$3,950			113.6	$29.55	1.33
1979	3,653			112.7	27.55	1.36
1978	3,317			111.8	25.18	1.32
1977	3,040	$	$	110.9	23.29	1.20
1976	2,816			110.1	21.71	1.25
1975	2,476			109.2	19.27	1.19
1974	2,275			108.5	17.84	1.16
1973	2,110			107.7	16.62	1.15
1972	1,980			106.9	15.74	1.10
1971	1,875			106.0	15.06	1.04
1970	1,735			104.9	14.08	1.00

% Increase (decrease)

1980–1979	8.1%	10.1%	(2.1)%	0.8%	7.3%	(2.8)%
1979–1978	10.1	6.0	4.1	0.8	9.4	3.4
1978–1977	9.1	4.0	5.1	0.8	8.1	4.1
1977–1976	8.0	4.0	4.0	0.7	7.3	3.3
1976–1975	13.7	7.2	6.5	0.8	12.7	5.5
1975–1974	8.8	4.6	4.2	0.6	8.0	3.4
1974–1973	7.8	6.4	1.4	0.7	7.3	0.9
1973–1972	6.7	0.0	6.7	0.8	5.6	5.6
1972–1971	5.4	(0.8)	6.2	0.9	4.5	5.1
1971–1970	8.1	2.5	5.6	1.0	6.9	4.4

Compound growth

1980 vs. 1970	9%			1%	8%	3%
1980 vs. 1975	10			1	9	3
1975 vs. 1970	7			1	6	3

*From sources believed reliable. Excludes toothpaste and other categories in which Mary Kay does not compete.
†Assumes 85% of US. cosmetics and toiletry industry sales of products Mary Kay sells are used by women.
‡Cosmetic and toiletry sales per woman minus price increases, indexed to 1970.
§Not available.

flow and limited bank borrowing—a conservative fiscal strategy consistent with Mary Kay Ash's personal philosophy of paying cash rather than incurring heavy, long-term debts.

Exhibit 26.11

MARY KAY MANAGEMENT TEAM, 1982

MARY KAY ASH, Chairman of the Board.

RICHARD ROGERS, President. Co-founder of Mary Kay Cosmetics, Inc. Served as General Manager, Vice President. 1968 "Marketing Man of the Year" Award from North Texas Chapter of the American Marketing Association.

GERALD M. ALLEN, Vice President, Administration. Responsible for planning, organizing, and directing the delivery of administrative services to the beauty consultant and supervising a staff of sales promotion directors. Supervises company security, communications and word processing, sales administration and compensation programs. B.B.A., Arlington State College.

J. EUGENE (GENE) STUBBS, Vice President, Finance, and Treasurer. Responsible for financial planning and accountable for company's financial assets and profitability objectives. Directs the treasury, controllership, and internal audit functions. Also responsible for all financial reporting. M.B.A., University of Texas; C.P.A.; B.B.A., Texas A & M University.

RICHARD C. BARTLETT, Vice President, Marketing. Responsible for planning and implementing marketing strategy including incentive programs, education and development of consultants, special events and meetings, public relations, and market-related research. B.S., University of Florida.

MONTY C. BARBER, Vice President, Secretary, and General Counsel. Responsible for supervising activities prescribed by law and the company regulations, establishing legal policies, advising and rendering opinions, supervises the public affairs program. As corporate secretary, attends to administrative matters for the board, shareholder relations, consumer relations, and coordinates all contribution requests. J.D., University of Texas; B.B.A., University of Texas.

JOHN BEASLEY, Group Vice President, Manufacturing. Responsible for planning, organizing, and evaluating all manufacturing decisions. Directs the development of the product line and ensures the quality of the products. B.A., Georgia Tech, Industrial Engineering National Merit Scholarship.

Exhibit 26.11 (Cont.)

PHIL BOSTLEY, Vice President, Operations. Responsible for planning, directing, and coordinating the distribution of all Mary Kay cosmetics and sales aids through regional distribution centers. Also responsible for directing the forecasting of product mix, the maintenance of inventory levels and coordinating the company's data processing group. B.A., Penn State University, math and science.

MYRA O. BARKER, PH.D., Vice President, Research and Product Development. Responsible for planning and directing skin technology, process technology, and product development. Directs regulatory and medical affairs and ensures product safety. Ph.D., Tulane University, biochemistry; B.S., University of Texas, chemistry.

BRUCE C. RUDY, PH.D., Vice President, Quality Assurance. Responsible for the procedures that assure the quality of raw materials in the product line. Controls the finished products certifying that they meet cosmetic, FDA and company standards. Plans and directs quality audits of all phases of product development, research, manufacture, and distribution. B.S., E. Stroudsburg State College; M.S., Clemson University; M.B.A., Columbia University; Ph.D., University of Georgia.

PAT HOWARD, Vice President, Manufacturing Operations. Responsible for manufacturing material control including purchasing, warehousing, production, planning, and international manufacturing. B.S., St. Mary's University; M.S., Texas A & M University.

JACK DINGLER, Vice President, Controller. Responsible for all operating financial functions of the company, including expenditure review, to ensure the continuation of the company's sound financial position. B.B.A., University of Texas at Arlington, accounting; C.P.A.

WILLIAM H. RANDALL, Director, Marketing Services. Responsible for marketing research, incentive program, visual communications, marketing publications, communications, and creative efforts. M.B.A., Harvard; B.A., Rutgers, economics.

DEAN MEADORS, Director, Public Relations. Responsible for all public relations activity. M.S., University of Illinois, advertising; B.S., University of Illinois, journalism.

NETTA JACKSON, Director, Product Service. Responsible for the marketing rationale for product development. Ensures that the company remains competitive in price and positioning. Active in sales force training. B.S.B.A., University of Arkansas, marketing.

Exhibit 26.11 (Cont.)

MICHAEL C. LUNCEFORD, Director, Public Affairs. Responsible for monitoring of local, state, and federal laws and regulations; community liaison with emphasis on corporate philanthropy. Master's program, Southern Methodist University, business administration; M.S., Southern Methodist University, public administration; B.B.A., East Texas State University, business administration, finance/economics.

Richard Rogers has publicly set the goal of $500 million in annual sales by 1990, emphasizing that 35 percent of the Mary Kay business is repeat sales to faithful customers. "As we grow, we're bringing our customer base forward," he states. His plan for growth reflects the guarded optimism of industry analysts. They predict that beauty products will rebound in the 1980s as the economy limps toward recovery. Most companies are placing their chips on moisturizing products, although many will continue diversification strategies, for example, Chesebrough-Ponds, a leader in the moisturizing business with Vaseline Intensive Care Lotion, but also a leader in spaghetti sauce, children's clothing, and casual footwear with the Ragu, Health-tex, and G. H. Bass brands. Meanwhile, Avon, Mary Kay's most look-alike competitor, continues to diversify. In 1982 Avon began peddling magazine subscriptions along with its vast cosmetic and costume jewelry lines. In a surprising 1979 move, Avon picked up Tiffany and Company, the preeminent jewelry concern.

Mary Kay intends to ride the moisturizing and skin care wave. Its Basic Skin Care Program will remain the staple product line. While other cosmetic companies (Avon and Bonne Bell, to name just two) are sponsoring women's running, bowling, and tennis competitions, Mary Kay Cosmetics will channel its energies into support of women working—for Mary Kay. An Avon piece of advertising copy reads, "At Avon, sports, health and beauty go naturally together." Mary Kay, however will continue to endorse a work and beauty ethic.

Introduced in 1982, the four-step Body Care Program seemed the next logical step for Mary Kay Cosmetics, a continuation of the company's appeal to the 25- to 44-year-old segment. Other major product constellations for the 1980s include Specialized Skin Care products (sun screen and hand cream), the Glamour Collection (cosmetics), and the Beauty Boutique, an array of bath and after-bath products. In keeping with the programmatic presentation pioneered in the Skin Care System, the company has developed a Basic Hair Care System, including shampoos, conditioner, and hair spray. Mary Kay Cosmetics hopes to nurture the presently minuscule market for the Mr. K. line of men's skin care products.

> I've talked about how important it is for women to look good, but I think men care just as much about their appearance. However, unfortunately, often you'll see a man dressed in beautiful clothes, with good-looking shoes, an expensive briefcase, well-groomed hair, and manicured nails—but whose face could look so much better with a little help! A woman wouldn't look complete without her face made up. So why shouldn't a man do the same thing?[10]

[10]Ibid., pp. 130–131.

As the company feels its way through the 1980s, it will accentuate quality control aspects ensured by a vigilant R&D policy. John Beasley, vice president of manufacturing, addressed this major concern in an interview, which appears as Appendix 26A. Also, see Appendix 26B, an excerpt from *U.S. Industrial Outlook.*

Because of the style of life that Mary Kay is selling along with the product—that of the independent, well-compensated, career woman beauty consultant—the company has not been altogether successful in translating the Mary Kay concept into other, non–English-speaking, more patriarchal cultures. Mary Kay Cosmetics internally appears sanguine that "the philosophy of Mary Kay Cosmetics has proven well suited for women everywhere," but this remains a debatable area in places like Japan.

May Kay Ash has stated on many occasions that Mary Kay Cosmetics is "in the business of helping women create better self-images so that they will feel better about themselves." Whether she is invoking Ralph Waldo Emerson's "Nothing great was ever achieved without enthusiasm" or leading her devoted consultants and directors in a chorus of "That Mary Kay Enthusiasm," Mary Kay Ash, genius of direct sales motivation, thinks and dreams enthusiasm: "My own dream," she states in her autobiography, "is that Mary Kay Cosmetics will someday become the largest and best skin care company in the world."

Appendix 26A

JOHN BEASLEY ON QUALITY CONTROL AND RELATED TOPICS*

Q: How does the quality of Mary Kay products compare with others on the market?
A: We direct our research and development and all our efforts toward producing the finest products we can produce. We know what other companies are producing. We understand all major competitive concepts, formulas, and approaches. But our focus is on producing the best product for the Mary Kay system. You see, we have a different orientation from most cosmetic companies. We can't just produce a product for a particular market segment. Our skin care products are used in a teaching system, so we are systems oriented. Our products work together, they're modular, and there's a synergism between them.
Q: Wasn't Mary Kay a pioneer in teaching skin care?
A: Mary Kay, as a specialist in skin care, has set trends for the only product segment of the market that's really growing. In 1963, we began marketing a five-step program of skin care. In 1976, we started teaching the scientific basis of skin care to and through our beauty consultants who today number over 150,000. Now every major cosmetic company in the country is talking about the scientific basis of skin care.
Q: How did the new Body Care System happen?
A: We've always had products aimed at body skin. The idea evolved from what we had learned about facial skin care. Body skin is different from facial skin, yet there

*The following is an interview with John Beasley, vice president, Manufacturing Group for Mary Kay Cosmetics, Inc. Mr. Beasley has been with Mary Kay since September 1975 and is currently responsible for planning, organizing, and evaluating all U.S. and international manufacturing decisions. A major portion of his responsibility is quality assurance. The interview was conducted in May 1982 at Mary Kay's corporate headquarters in Dallas.

Appendix 26A (Cont.)

are functional needs that need to be addressed in a complementary way. Body care was a natural extension from the Mary Kay tradition of scientific skin care.

Our Body Care products have been formulated according to the same high standards we use in skin care. We've tested them and used them ourselves. We've come up with a very, very high-quality system for an economical price.

Q: What standards do you use internally for making product decisions?

A: We came up with four factors that have to be included in every decision that is made from every level. Since we are a participative management organization, everybody has to know what the rules are, exactly what is important. The first thing that has to be considered in every decision is quality . . . the impact on product quality. The second is service. Service to the beauty consultant and consumer.

The third thing that everybody has to take into account is the flexibility of the decision. What range does it work in? The fourth is the actual cost of the decision: total cost of capital investment, impact on cost of goods, and cash flow.

We teach all management and some hourly people to use the four criteria. I will not look at any proposal that doesn't address these four things—and the first thing I see has to be quality. Richard Rogers [president of Mary Kay] uses the saying "If it's worth doing, do it right." That is the kind of quality statement that underlines everything we do all day long. That's the way the company was founded.

Q: You mentioned you are a "participative management organization." How does this work at Mary Kay?

A: You cannot get quality by having only one part of your company responsible for quality. The assumption that the better traditional organizations have made is that if you want to get something accomplished, you have to focus on it through a special part of your organization.

Our assumption here is much different. Everybody is in charge of quality. The Research and Development Department is in charge of quality. The Marketing Department is in charge of quality. The Material Control Department is in charge of quality.

The actual "Quality Assurance" function serves as a measuring device. The quality audit measures how well we are matching our stated quality standards. These specifications are set in a type of committee process that starts in research and development and get approved right up through the CEO in final form. From there our job is to expand them *backward*, through all the maze of processing, all the way back to vendor level. It's very much like the idea behind the Japanese quality circles when you get everybody involved in focusing on quality. For example, in 1976 we gave everybody in the hourly (nonexempt) group an across-the-board pay increase, explaining that we were adding the quality inspection responsibility to their job. We said, "Part of your job is to make sure we always produce Mary Kay quality."

Q: How did they respond to this?

A: Many of them consider quality to be the predominant part of their job. The people in the plant don't simply report a problem; they are actually the ones doing the rejecting. And most of them are very tough. They see things that you and I won't see because they have developed a whole different set of skills out there. We normally produce on only one shift, we hire special people, we evaluate them and reward them. Mary Kay was always, from the very beginning, attracted to people who are quality conscious. If you look around, you see a very consistent type of

Appendix 26A (Cont.)

person in dress and quality standards. When new people come in from other companies, and we've had to do a good bit of recruiting because we've grown so fast, they usually come from companies that were more interested in cost as the first factor. Even top executives don't understand that quality is the first criterion. So we create a whole culture that reinforces our standards.

Q: How many of the products Mary Kay sells are made in your own facilities?

A: We manufacture probably 99 percent of the products in house; and 100 percent is quality inspected here. The same quality standards apply internationally. In general, if they don't pass the same quality standards that we use here in the United States, they don't go to the consumer.

Q: How does your sales force respond to this?

A: The sales force is very, very conscious of the quality aspect. Sometimes there has been some disappointment when we've said, "We're sorry, we can't sell this product because it's not Mary Kay quality." But it's very important to the sales force that they be very proud of the products and systems they teach . . . and sell.

Q: What are your long-term goals for Mary Kay?

A: We want to be the finest teaching-oriented skin care company in the world with sales of $500 million by 1990. That's our corporate objective. It has been stated in our annual report, and everybody around here can quote it.

Q: How do you begin to meet that goal?

A: Research and development is the leading edge. Since 1975, Research and Development has grown from 1 Ph.D. and a technician to a staff of 47. We recruited Dr. Myra Barker to be our vice president of research and development. We go after the top 10 percent of the people in the country who have the skills that we're looking for and personal integrity. They don't come necessarily from the cosmetic industry. Many have come from the drug industry because we see cosmetics, especially skin care products, more like drugs than traditional glamor products.

In addition, the Research and Development Department is in the forefront in developing new technology. We have a group that has been formed to do nothing but research how the skin relates to the rest of the body and how it relates to its environment. A very large part of the research and development budget, for example, is aimed at research all over the world. We're funding a research dermatologist in Wales who is doing research into skin attribute measurement. We have grants in England. When you came in, I was signing a purchase order that goes for a research grant to Southwestern Medical School.

Q: What types of tests are you doing?

A: There are many levels of testing and two major issues: one is safety, one is efficacy. We don't take risks with the consumer. Our products must meet acceptable levels in terms of oral toxicity . . . sensitization . . . irritation. We are having to stretch current technology in establishing some new standards in the industry in the area of comedogenicity, the interaction of the new product, the environment, and the skin-causing comedones (acne).

We screen raw materials at the vendor level. If you get something that's 99 percent pure, it means it's 1 percent impure. In our business we're interested in the 1 percent impure. We made substantial investments in computerized instrumentation so that we can screen raw materials routinely for impurities.

Efficacy testing is also something that is fairly new. Cosmetic products used to be a coverup, but now we're producing skin care products that are functional.

Appendix 26A (Cont.)

We need to measure how a product actually performs, but we're having to develop the technology.

Q: As vice president in charge of manufacturing, how do you challenge your departments?

A: We have no negatives in terms of product quality, number one. We can't afford any big savings in quality. We have to be consistently above the line in terms of the impact on the consumer. Consistently positive! Then what we try to do is to raise that line to the top of the industry. We establish a consistent quality level, and then we figure out how to make that better. That's our drive, our constant challenge. The quality standard has never, ever been stagnant. We always strive to be the best we can be.

Appendix 26B

SUMMARY OF COSMETICS PROSPECTS FOR 1982 AND THE LONG TERM

Moderately priced products are expected to sell best, especially hair, skin, nail, and eye care products.

Fragrances will become more popular, especially among men, in the 1980s.

Ethnic cosmetic sales are expected to pick up.

Up to 45 percent of males in the population will use cosmetics by 1986.

Sun-screen agents that reportedly protect skin from damaging ultraviolet rays will be added to many skin care products to prevent premature aging, wrinkling, or cancer of the skin.

An estimated 65 percent of all cosmetics are purchased on impulse, although during recessionary periods consumers are most cost conscious.

The industry's principal target group of teenagers and young women is shrinking, although the "baby boom" generation is aging and is likely to spend money for beauty aids.

Among the present 20- to 35-year-old age group, there is a much larger lower-income sector.

Rising costs of raw materials and the high cost of research are the scourge of the cosmetics industry.

New products are essential for greater sales, yet new product introductions lag because of the decrease in research and development.

The skin care market, including moisturizers, sun-care creams, lotions, scrubs and cleansers, collagen and elastin protein rejuvenating agents, is growing and reached $2.5 billion in 1981 because of increased concern among consumers over aging skin, personal cleanliness, and the damaging effects of ultraviolet rays.

Hypoallergenic and fragrance-free products have been demonstrated to be most successful in the skin care market.

Appendix 26B (Cont.)

The hair preparations market increased to $2.2 billion in 1981 due to consumer interest in healthy looking hair and frequent shampoos by both men and women. Women frequently use cream rinse and hair conditioning products, although an untapped male market exists for such products. Hair spray remains popular with older women.

Industry shipments of cosmetics, toiletries, and fragrances were valued at $9.9 billion in 1981, only a 0.6 percent increase from 1980, as opposed to a 2.6 percent average annual increase from 1972 through 1981.

Source: 1982 U.S. Industrial Outlook.

27

MARY KAY COSMETICS, INC. (B)

BACKGROUND

Mary Kay Cosmetics, Inc. (MKCI), incorporated in 1963 in Texas, is engaged in producing and distributing cosmetics, toiletries, and related products under the Mary Kay trademark.* Products manufactured by or for MKCI are distributed primarily in the United States, which in 1989 accounted for 90.3 percent of sales. Canada produced 5.5 percent, and the remainder came from operations in Australia, Argentina, West Germany, and Mexico. (Selected facts on Mary Kay International are listed in Appendix 27A.)

All outstanding common voting stock of Mary Kay Corporation (the company organized in 1985 for accomplishing the leveraged buyout of MKCI) is held by Mary Kay Ash, founder and chairman emeritus of MKCI; Richard R. Rogers, son of Mrs. Ash, chairman of the board and chief executive officer of MKCI; Janice L. Rogers, former wife of Richard R. Rogers; and certain other family members and trusts.[1]

MKCI's products are sold through independent salespersons, called beauty consultants, to consumers in their own homes. Five regional distribution centers lo-

*The authors express appreciation to the numerous MKCI officers and managers who contributed interviews, materials and guidance in developing this case study. Contributors included, among others, Mary Kay Ash, chairman emeritus; Richard R. Rogers, chairman and chief executive officer; Lawrence Cox, executive vice president and treasurer; and Richard C. Bartlett, president and chief operating officer.

[1]See Appendix 27B for a listing of executive officers and directors of MKCI.

cated in California, Georgia, New Jersey, Illinois, and Texas and one each in Australia, Canada, Argentina, West Germany, and Mexico supply beauty consultants with MKCI products.

Company revenues and operating profits have been principally determined by the number of beauty consultants and sales directors, and MKCI's recruitment of salespersons has been largely a function of its commission structures and incentive programs, introduction of new products and marketing programs, general economic conditions, and competition from other cosmetics companies.

BEAUTY CONSULTANTS

By the mid-1980s, the proportion of U.S. women holding primary jobs outside the home approached 60 percent, so Mary Kay management altered its recruiting focus, concentrating on working women, shifting some selling opportunities to the workplace. An estimated two-thirds of the company's sales consultants hold primary jobs, and selling to fellow employees outside working hours provides opportunities to earn extra money. Further, consultant recruitment rates respond contracyclically to economic indicators—in recession, the recruiting fields are greener, but in a flourishing economy, pickings can be slim.

In 1986, management stemmed the termination rate by lowering the minimum order required for consultants to remain active. Additionally, a credit card program (at a cost to the company of 1.35 percent on credit card purchases) was inaugurated to assist salespeople over the rough spots and to encourage new recruits to sign on. Shortly after the program was installed, credit card sales accounted for 30 percent of the company's total, and order sizes were bigger than when cash was paid, a phenomenon with which direct-mail companies have long been familiar. MKCI termination rates promptly declined to 1983 levels.

Sales of merchandise to beauty consultants are final, although it is MKCI's policy to replace defective merchandise or merchandise on which a beauty consultant has made an exchange or refund to a customer. In addition, MKCI agrees with each beauty consultant that, upon termination of her relationship with MKCI (whether voluntary or involuntary), MKCI will repurchase from her all unused, currently stocked MKCI products that she has on hand at a price equal to 90 percent of her cost of such products if returned within one year of purchase. MKCI maintains a policy of destroying such returned products.

While some of Mary Kay's competitors and peers within direct selling appeared to be moving away from traditional selling methods, Mary Kay believed that busy consumers appreciated the personal attention and convenience of being served in their homes and offices. "Mary Kay understands the value of our beauty consultants as a customer service force," Bartlett observed. "We have an unswerving commitment to helping consultants succeed and thereby providing our customers with the highest level of service and product quality."

Curran Dandurand, senior vice president, Marketing Group, said Mary Kay consultants are in an ideal position to meet the needs of today's working women. "Today's consumers are realizing that retail stores are not providing the personalized service they expect. Our knowledgeable consultants are able to meet the growing need for personalized service." The company's market research indicated that cosmetics consumers felt Mary Kay beauty consultants were knowledgeable about skin care, as well as a variety of current cosmetic fashions and could help them achieve the right look for their life-styles.

Bartlett mentioned that "We have intensified programs to increase the professionalism of beauty consultants, boosting their customer service capabilities. Industry sources tell us that, out of all cosmetics companies, Mary Kay continues to have the highest brand loyalty for our skin care product line."

SALES REVENUES

Net sales for 1987 increased to $325.6 million from $255.0 million in 1986, an increase of 27.7 percent. This increase is attributable to a 4.9 percent increase in the average number of beauty consultants selling MKCI's products and a 21.7 percent increase in the average sales productivity per beauty consultant as compared to 1986. Management thought the increase in the average number of beauty consultants and their sales productivity was the result of several changes implemented by MKCI during 1987 and 1986.

In January 1987, MCKI announced changes to its beauty consultants' compensation programs. These changes included increased bonus amounts for increased monthly sales production, increased commissions to senior-level members of the sales force, and revisions to the incentive automobile programs. In February 1987 MKCI introduced new glamour products and packaging, including eye shadows, refillable glamour compacts, new formulas for lip colors, translucent pressed powder, and a new loose face powder. In May 1987, MKCI introduced new products for men's skin care, including a shave cream, and in July 1987, new items were also added to MKCI's specialized skin care product line. Also in July, MKCI announced a year-long anniversary contest to celebrate MKCI's 25th anniversary. The contest was designed to enhance sales productivity and recruiting.

"Customer acceptance of new and reformulated Mary Kay products and a significant increase in the productivity of its independent beauty consultants, who sell the company's products, resulted in a 24.6 percent increase in sales for 1988 over 1987 for Mary Kay Cosmetics, Inc." In reporting the annual results at the company's 1989 annual Dallas seminars, Richard C. Bartlett, Mary Kay's president and chief operating officer, said the growth trend, though moderated, has continued into the first two quarters of 1989.

"Sales for Mary Kay in 1988 were $405.7 million compared with $325.6 million in 1987. During 1988, Mary Kay added a nail care system, tube lipstick, and a line of skin blemish treatment products. We have also developed new marketing strategies to attract more career women as customers and as consultants," Bartlett said. "At the same time, improved incentive programs have contributed to an increase in the sales productivity of the individual beauty consultants."

For the quarter ended March 31, 1989, new sales reached a record high of $105.5 million, up 14.5 percent compared to 1988 first quarter sales of $92.1 million.

The increase was again paced by the continued success of the new products introduced in 1988 and the introduction and promotion of new formulations of the company's hair care product line during the quarter.

Net sales for the quarter ended June 30, 1989 were expected to total approximately $116 million, up 10.8 percent compared to 1988 second quarter sales of $104.7 million. Bartlett attributed the second quarter growth to introduction of the company's Sun Essentials line of sunscreen products and new packaging for Mary Kay's skin care products. "Sales for the six months ended June 30, 1989," he said "are estimated at approximately $222 million compared with sales of $196.8 million for the same period a year ago, an increase of 12.8 percent."

Exhibit 27.1 summarizes selected statistics for Mary Kay Cosmetics, Inc., 1982–1989.

"During 1988, Mary Kay enhanced its lead as the most efficient manufacturer of cosmetics in the U.S. in terms of annual sales dollars per employee ($275,000)," President Richard Bartlett said. The company produced 138,000,000 units with 475 manufacturing employees yielding a record 290,000 units each. "We're also very proud of the error-free service levels in our five strategically located distribution centers; from these centers, millions of Mary Kay products quickly make their way to virtually every city and community in the U.S."

COMPETITION

On the basis of information available from industry sources, management believes there are approximately 13,000 companies (including both direct-sale and manufacturing companies) with products that compete. One such competitor, Avon Products, Inc., is substantially larger than MKCI in terms of total independent salespeople, sales volume, and resources. In addition, MKCI's products compete with cosmetics and toiletry items manufactured by cosmetic companies that sell their products in retail or department stores. Several such competitors, including Revlon, Inc., are much larger than MKCI in sales and hold substantially more resources. MKCI is also subject to competition in recruiting independent salespersons from other direct-selling organizations.

THE AVON GAMBIT

Avon Products, Inc., seemed attractive to would-be acquirers in 1989, with a hostile $2.1 billion bid by Amway Corporation, which was dropped, much to the relief of at least one of the 1.4 million Avon ladies around the world, according to the article, who feared being pressed into adding the vast array of Amway products to an already substantial line of cosmetics, gift items, and jewelry.[2] Then followed a rejected expression of interest from John Rochon, MKCI vice chairman and chief financial officer (former vice chairman of Mary Kay Corporation, MKCI's holding company), who reportedly wished to buy part or all of Avon Products, Inc.[3] Mr. Rochon was quoted

[2]"Sallie Cook Is One of a Million Reasons Amway Liked Avon," *The Wall Street Journal*, May 19, 1989, p. 1.

[3]"Avon Rebuffed Mary Kay Aide in Talks Recently, Sources Say; Fight Is Possible," *The Wall Street Journal*, May 22, 1989, p. A3.

Exhibit 27.1

MARY KAY COSMETICS, INC., SELECTED STATISTICS, 1982–1989

	1989	1988	1987	1986	1985*	1984	1983	1982
Net sales ($000)	450,493	405,730	325,647	255,016	248,970	277,500	323,758	304,275
Interest expense ($000)	43,606	37,248	40,391	40,694	4,242	5,273	2,886	1,284
Net income (loss) ($000)	6,770	(8,998)	(20,888)	(55,502)	18,624	33,781†	36,654	35,372
Total assets ($000)	351,948	289,043	261,568	284,180	272,166	217,554	180,683	152,457
Long-term debt ($000)	335,886	278,524	254,996	289,956	295,532	3,826	3,915	4,669
Average number of consultants and sales directors	192,804	170,316	148,080	141,113	145,393	173,101	195,671	173,137
Average annual productivity	$ 2,337	$ 2,382	$ 2,199	$ 1,807	$ 1,711	$ 1,603	$ 1,655	$ 1,757

*In December 1985 the company went private in a leveraged buyout.
†Includes gain on sale of land, $15,047,000.

Data sources: For 1984: *1984 Annual Report* and Form 10-K, December 31, 1988. For 1989: Numerous MKCI officers and managers, including Mary Kay Ash, Richard R. Rogers, Lawrence Cox, and Richard C. Bartlett.

Note: Pursuant to the LBO, operations were restructured through successive disposals of excess real estate, consolidation of manufacturing and distribution, reformulation of product lines, and changes in incentives affecting recruitment and termination of sales consultants. The LBO's viability seemed virtually assured even at relatively low rates of growth in revenues, and Mary Kay's debt securities were generally viewed as attractive by the investment community.

Borrowings in 1989 were used to finance acquisition of Avon stock. MKCI's operating performance during 1989 was below the level that will be required in 1990 and 1991 to meet all of its debt covenants and to satisfy cash requirements of debenture obligations.

as affirming his investor group's continuing interest in acquiring Avon, with the intention, if successful, of maintaining Mary Kay's and Avon's separate independent sales forces.[4] Some analysts observed that although MKCI's leveraged buyout was successful, the company remained highly leveraged and, with $406 million in sales compared with Avon's approximately $3 billion, was much smaller. (In LBOs, the debt incurred to buy publicly held shares is repaid through operating profit or proceeds from selling assets.) In November, a group comprising oil heir Gordon Getty, Argonaut Partners I, L. P. (an investment arm of Mary Kay Cosmetics, Inc.), and the Fisher real estate family of New York acquired approximately 9.6 percent of Avon's common stock, which presumably came as a surprise to Avon officials. The intent of the investment was not explained publicly.

MISSION STATEMENT

In conjunction with the kickoff of Mary Kay's annual seminar in July 1989 at the Dallas Convention Center, President Richard Bartlett reported a "remarkable period of innovation spanning 1988 and 1989. The company introduced new products, declared a moratorium on animal testing, and launched a national public education program designed to help detect and prevent skin cancer. . . . even Mary Kay 'pink' and the company's logo are new." As the wellspring of change for the company, in a subsequent interview, Bartlett pointed to Mary Kay's mission statement as uniting the goals of the company's manufacturing, distribution, and marketing staff and independent beauty consultants worldwide:

> To be preeminent in the manufacturing, distribution, and marketing of personal care products through our independent sales force. To achieve total customer satisfaction by focusing on quality, value, convenience, innovation, and personal service.

"We equate preeminence with total customer satisfaction," he concluded, "and we celebrate quality—that is our company's new credo." Promoting the celebration of quality internally was intended to keep the goal of total customer satisfaction uppermost in the minds of 1,500 corporate employees and, in the first quarter 1990, some 200,000 beauty consultants.

PRODUCTS AND PACKAGING

MKCI's product lines comprise skin care products for women and for men, glamour items, toiletry items for women and for men, accessories, and hair care products. Skin care products in various formulas related to skin types include cleansers, skin fresheners, facial masks, moisturizers, and foundation makeup and are sold in sets as a five-step beauty program. Each item may be reordered separately.

Glamour items include lipstick, nail care products, lip and eye colors, mascaras, blushers and blush rouge, automatic eye liner, eye-defining pencils, lip-defining

[4]"Mary Kay Vice Chairman Says His Group Remains Interested in Avon Products, Inc.," *The Wall Street Journal*, May 26, 1989, p. A7.

pencils, eyebrow pencils, loose face powder, translucent pressed powder, and lip gloss.

Toiletry items include a body care regimen (primarily hand and body lotions), bath products, and colognes. MKCI also manufactures hair care products, consisting of shampoo, hair conditioner, styling gel, and nonaerosol hair spray.

The men's product line consists of a cleansing bar, toner, facial conditioners and oil absorber, sunscreen, moisturizer, and shave cream.

In recent years, emphasis has been placed on glamour items as well as skin care. The Mary Kay Color Logic^{SM} Glamour System promises "No more guesswork. No more mistakes," calling it "The personalized way to choose your most flattering makeup shades." The approach harmonizes personal coloring, wardrobe choices, and life-style in helping the user decide which colors are most suitable. The beauty consultant recommends specific Mary Kay shades to help the customer achieve the desired look, from dramatic to natural, or in between. Basic guidelines permit experimentation, offering a variety of options. ColorLogic's two key principles are color harmony and contrast, which provide a basis for selecting cheek, lip, and nail colors that take into account choice of clothing, one's personal coloring, and level of contrast between skin tone and hair color.

Accessory items—samples, makeup mirrors, cosmetics bags and travel kits, packaging, and literature—are sold to beauty consultants and sales directors who use them as hostess gifts, business supplies, and sales aids.

Exhibit 27.2 shows sales percentages by product groups, 1986–1989.

In a continuing program of developing new products, the company introduced several during 1988–1989:

- Sun Essentials, a new line of 100 percent fragrance-free and PABA-free sun protection products, as well as a special lip protector, was introduced in April 1989. These products for the face and body contained sun protection factors ranging from 8 to 30.

Exhibit 27.2

SALES PERCENTAGES BY PRODUCT GROUPS, 1986–1989

	YEARS ENDED DECEMBER 31,			
	1989	1988	1987	1986
Skin care products for women	38%	38%	40%	46%
Skin care products for men	1	1	2	1
Glamour items	27	28	32	24
Nail care products	7	7	—	—
Toiletry items for women	10	13	13	15
Toiletry items for men	3	3	3	3
Hair care products	2	1	1	2
Sun care products	2	—	—	—
Accessories	10	9	9	9
total	100%	100%	100%	100%

- A new line of foundation shades for dark complexions was introduced in June 1989. These bronze foundations, in five shades and three formulations, marked Mary Kay's commitment to serving the special cosmetics needs of black and Hispanic women.
- A new nail care system, one of the company's most successful product introductions, achieved a 5 percent share of the nail care market in five months of sales in 1988.
- A personalized hair care line, formulated to meet the needs of all hair types, was introduced in January 1989.
- Packaging unveiled in June 1989 displayed a new logo on gold-accented white containers and features a softer, more delicate shade of pink on the caps of bottles.

"We are proud of our new packaging," said Curran Dandurand. "It is carefully designed to be beautiful, yet functional, and to convey a sophisticated, feminine look that will maintain its appeal for years to come. In addition to style and beauty, the new packaging features improvements such as softer-sided bottles and tubes and informational inserts detailing product benefits and use. Inner liners are now in jars to reduce evaporation during storage and shipping and to provide a seal to maintain the product's purity and freshness. Polyvinyl chloride containers were changed to high-density polyethylene plastic to achieve a higher moisture barrier that also reduces evaporation. This allows for tubes that are easier to squeeze and containers that are more readily recyclable.

"Product cartons are also improved, featuring the Westvaco high-gloss plastic coating for a harder, shinier, and more durable finish, one that stays in better condition longer. Mary Kay is one of the first companies to use Westvaco coating in a large-scale product launch. Folding cartons also feature unique thumb notches to permit easier, more convenient opening.

"We spent two years designing, developing, and perfecting the new product packaging," concluded Dandurand. "We viewed over 200 different designs before selecting the packaging we felt would place our products a cut above those of the competition."

In the summer of 1989, Mary Kay became one of the first cosmetics companies (as well as a leader in Texas) to place the Society of the Plastics Industry's (SPI) recycling code on its plastic containers. The company has also been a leader in the legislative arena by supporting the enactment of legislation requiring the SPI code system currently adopted by 16 states. The code identifies primary resins in plastic containers and speeds retrieval for recycling into such useful products as stuffing for pillows, carpet backing, and "plastic" lumber. Also, Mary Kay announced in 1990 its aim to become the first major cosmetics company to use recycled paperboard for all product cartons.

ETHICS, ANIMAL TESTING, AND PRODUCT SAFETY

U.S. public interest in ethics grew dramatically in the 1980s, and standards applied to corporate behavior appeared to undergo significant modification. Ethics in dealing with employees, sales consultants and directors, customers, and the public generally has always been of manifest concern with MKCI management, a domain in which vigilance has been exercised and leadership provided by senior officers as well as others. Richard Bartlett observed that

... leaders can create an ethical corporate culture that brings out the ethical in people. ... we must consider the impact [of decisions] on the larger society ... beauty consultants, employees, communities in which we are located, business partners such as suppliers, science, medicine, the cosmetics industry, the pharmaceutical industry, and the direct selling industry.

I called a meeting ... to come to a decision about one ethical issue, product safety.

... our beauty consultants ... were being unfairly attacked and their work disrupted by radical animal activists who demanded that we stop testing our products using mice, rats, and rabbits.

... other voices in the decision included our lawyers, our chief scientific officer, public affairs and public relations people, medical researchers, and other leaders of the cosmetics industry. Animal activists ... were clamoring for no testing; Congressman Wyden of Oregon held some hearings and wants more testing. ...

My decision was that the safety of the people who use our products must come first, even if it meant continued disruption and added cost.

... to minimize the disruption, in May we announced a moratorium on animal testing while we develop new testing technology. Mary Kay Cosmetics was the first company to take such a step. Our goal was to take the high ground.

The decision may mean putting a hold on new products for a while which could mean lost sales. And it does mean additional investment in evaluating alternative tests and developing new ones.[5]

MKCI management assumed a leadership role encouraging the cosmetics industry to explore alternative, nonanimal testing methods and to share the results for the benefit of all. "Since 1981," Bartlett said, "we have participated in the development of alternative testing methods." In 1989 he recommended formation of a "blue ribbon" panel of industry and academic scientists as well as public policy specialists and regulators to address the issues. Thomas J. Stephens, Ph.D., director of product safety at Mary Kay Cosmetics, announced at a workshop conducted at the Johns Hopkins Center for Alternatives to Animal Testing that MKCI sought such collaboration. "During the moratorium," Dr. Stephens said, "Mary Kay Cosmetics plans to evaluate in vitro alternative test methods using cell culture technology in place of traditional procedures utilizing laboratory animals." Many in vitro methods had been developed in recent years at Johns Hopkins' CAAT laboratories in Baltimore.

THE SKIN WELLNESS PROGRAM

As the company unveiled its Skin Wellness[SM] program in 1989, Mary Kay Ash envisioned that the company's beauty consultants worldwide would join the fight against malignant melanoma and other types of skin cancer, teaching consumers prevention measures and detection methods. The founder and chairman emeritus observed, as the public service program was introduced at Mary Kay career conferences in 22 metropolitan areas throughout the country, that skin cancer would claim the lives of

[5]From "Quickly Take the High Ground," commencement address at the University of Dallas Graduate School of Business, August 4, 1989.

nearly 8,000 of the more than 50,000 Americans diagnosed with the disease in 1989. These statistics from the American Cancer Society reflected skin cancer as the most common form of cancer, with incidence increasing.

MKCI's public service program consisted of an instructional video and brochure picturing and describing the disease's early warning signs, explaining how to perform monthly skin examinations recommended by ACS. In addition to preventive information, materials included an exclusive easy-to-use body map for consumers to record changes in skin conditions, consulting a dermatologist when necessary. A percentage of sales of selected sunblock products was slated for donation to ACS. According to Myra Barker, Ph.D., chief scientific officer of MKCI, "The overall goal of the Skin Wellness program is to help minimize the occurrence of skin cancer by teaching preventive measure and to encourage early detection through regular skin self-examination."

Mary Kay was also one of the founding sponsors of the Cosmetics, Toiletries and Fragrance Association's (CTFA) "Look Good Feel Better" program. Designed to aid cancer patients, the program offered cosmetic assistance to women undergoing chemotherapy and radiation therapy. CTFA, the American Cancer Society, and the National Cosmetology Association were also sponsors.

Mary Kay published a 25-page booklet, "Consumer Guide to Cosmetic Ingredients," which not only listed ingredients in each of its products but also cross-referenced and described the function of each ingredient used. This consumer education tool was one of the most extensive in the cosmetics industry.

FESTIVAL OF FRIENDS

As related in Mary Kay Cosmetics (A), dreams continued to become reality for thousands of MKCI consultants and directors at the company's 26th anniversary "Festival of Friends" seminar held in July 1989. Seminar participants watched enthusiastically as Mary Kay Ash entered the Dallas Convention Center aboard a 12-foot-high, multicolored satin and crepe paper float, the symbolic highlight of opening ceremonies. In her welcoming address, Mrs. Ash noted, "How appropriate that we should gather together at Seminar '89 as a Festival of Friends, for that is exactly what we are. Now our friendship even extends around the world, from Canada to Australia, West Germany, Argentina, Singapore, Malaysia, Thailand, New Zealand, Uruguay, and, most recently, Mexico and Chile—with more to come. When I started Mary Kay Cosmetics 26 years ago, I never thought I'd get past Waxahachie. . . . We are all friends, united in the Mary Kay spirit." To the company's beauty consultants, Mrs. Ash is not just an abstract corporate symbol, a figurehead; rather, she is their inspiration, a living symbol of what they hope to achieve. That beauty consultants identify with her is continually reinforced with the Mary Kay Ash message, "If I can do it, so can you."

Appearing before a standing-room-only crowd, Mary Kay, her son and chairman of the board, Richard Rogers, and the president, Richard Bartlett, welcomed consultants in lavishly staged opening ceremonies recognizing national sales directors, new directors, "go-give" winners, teachers, and "galaxy of stars" winners. Adding sparkle was a cast of singers, dancers, jugglers, unicycle riders, and drill team, all carrying colorful banners and parasols. Festival of Friends was laced through with education, inspiration, motivation, and special messages from the senior management trio during four consecutive three-day sessions attended by over 23,000 consultants and directors and some 2,000 husbands who also participated in special seminar sessions designed for them. (For a listing of selected facts about the 1989 seminars, see Appendix 27C.)

MKA's MANAGEMENT PHILOSOPHY

May Kay Ash's "golden rule" management treats everyone at every level and in every position with fairness and consideration, a philosophy embodying principles set forth in her second major book[6] and epitomized in unrelenting zeal to help others realize their potential, a persistent emphasis on others, both employees and customers.

> When you enter our Dallas home-office building, you'll be greeted by larger-than-life photographs of our National Sales Directors. While some companies use paintings or sculptures or perhaps images of their product to make a statement, we want our message to be: "We're a people company."[7]

She takes pride in the open-door policy of the executive suite, reinforcing a people focus:

> We are a "people-to-people" company, not an "office-to-title" company. . . .
>
> And so you won't find any titles on the doors of our corporate offices. . . .
>
> We also facilitate a friendly, relaxed atmosphere by addressing each other by our first names. . . . it's still Mary Kay and Richard to everyone.[8]

Plaudits on the dust jacket have *Megatrends'* author John Naisbitt lauding the volume as "a common sense guide to the new people-centered management . . . a wonderful high-touch antidote to all those boring business school books" and Tom Peters, *In Search of Excellence* and other books: ". . . terrific!" concluding with the admonition, "every manager ought to read it." A favorable review also appeared in *The Wall Street Journal*, October 15, 1984.

The volume's fundamentals may be summarized in nine precepts and principles listed on its dust jacket (Exhibit 27.3).

In a portion of the book, a passage titled "It's a Grand Old Flag," Mary Kay states, "The pride we feel for our work and our company is similar to that which we feel for our country. We are proud to be Americans—and we are proud to let everyone know it." She cites Richard Rogers's closing remarks at one of the company's seminars: " 'I feel our free enterprise system is important because without it you would not be here. I would not be speaking. Mary Kay Cosmetics would not exist. And the Mary Kay dream would never have become a reality.' "[9] The golden rule and

---

[6]Mary Kay Ash, *Mary Kay on People Management* (New York: Warner Books, 1984), 184 pages. Her first volume, cited in Mary Kay Cosmetics, Inc. (A), is *Mary Kay*, published by Harper & Row, 1981.

[7]Ibid., p. 11.

[8]Ibid., pp. 83–84.

[9]Ibid., p. 110.

Exhibit 27.3

A GUIDE TO "GOLDEN RULE MANAGEMENT"

This is the management philosophy that turned Mary Kay Ash's storefront cosmetics business into a multimillion dollar corporation in just 20 years. Based on the age-old golden rule, it encourages managers to treat staff, customers, suppliers—everyone—with the same care, consideration, and concern they would like to receive themselves. It brought spectacular success to Mary Kay. Here's how it can work for you.

- **Recognize the Value of People.**   People are your company's number one asset. When you treat them as you would like to be treated yourself, everyone benefits.
- **Praise Your People to Success.**   Recognition is the most powerful of all motivators. Even criticism can build confidence when it's "sandwiched" between layers of praise.
- **Tear Down That Ivory Tower.**   Keep all doors open. Be accessible to everyone. Remember that every good manager is also a good listener.
- **Be a Risk Taker.**   Don't be afraid. Encourage your people to take risks, too—and allow room for error.
- **Be Sales Oriented.**   Nothing happens in business until somebody sells something. Be especially sensitive to your customers' needs and desires.
- **Be a Problem Solver.**   An effective manager knows how to recognize real problems and how to take action to solve them.
- **Create a Stress-Free Workplace.**   By eliminating stress factors—fear of the boss, unreasonable deadlines, and others—you can increase and inspire productivity.
- **Develop and Promote People from Within.**   Upward mobility for employees in your company builds loyalty. People give you their best when they know they'll be rewarded.
- **Keep Business in Its Proper Place.**   At Mary Kay Cosmetics the order of priorities is faith, family, and career. The real key to success is creating an environment where people are encouraged to balance the many aspects of their lives.

patriotism are quite compatible ingredients in the company's management mix, and while others share the faith and practice its tenets, clearly Mary Kay continues to be principal exemplar of the doctrine.

FOCUS ON THE FUTURE

As standard bearer and chief cheerleader for the employees and independent sales consultants and directors at the 1989 seminar, Richard Bartlett pointed optimistically to 1990 and the decade ahead, "exciting . . . for Mary Kay." He predicted and outlined a quintet of tasks uppermost on his to-do list:

- To maintain its competitive edge in the marketplace, the company will continue to evaluate and update its product lines as technology and trends change.
- The company is expanding its selection of shades and formulations to better meet the needs of Hispanic and black women, estimated to be the fastest growth market in the cosmetics industry. In addition, it will emphasize service and products for mature women and for youth.
- The company will continue to encourage professionalism and career opportunities for its international network of beauty consultants, through business training and support services, such as market research and advertising.
- It will expand manufacturing capabilities at the Regal Row complex (in Dallas).
- The company will enhance the success of its beauty consultants through already well-established direct support programs, which are helping to cement the loyalties of millions of customers to Mary Kay products and people.

"We look to 1990 as our greatest year ever," Bartlett concluded.

Appendix 27A

MARY KAY INTERNATIONAL MISCELLANEOUS FACTS*

Mary Kay Cosmetics, Inc., has five wholly owned subsidiaries in

- **Melbourne, Australia**
  opened 1971
  Ian Ross, president
- **Mississauga, Ontario, Canada**
  opened 1978
  Ray Patrick, president
- **Buenos Aires, Argentina**
  opened 1980
  Dr. Gerardo Segura, president
- **Munich, West Germany**
  opened 1986
  Oswald Hofmeister, president
- **Monterrey, Mexico**
  opened 1988
  Jorge Moeller, president

Mary Kay Australia has a wholly owned subsidiary in **New Zealand,** which opened in January 1989. It operates out of the Melbourne office.

The Company also has a **joint venture** operation in **Bangkok, Thailand** (Somsak Panswat, managing director)
    opened in November 1988
    manufactures product in Thailand

Mary Kay independent distributorships exist in

Appendix 27A (Cont.)

- **Singapore** (Benjamin Tan, managing director)
  buys product from Australia
  opened November 1988
- **Panama City, Panama**
  buys product from United States
  opened March 1986
- **Uruguay**
  buys product from Argentina
  operates from Buenos Aires office
- **Santiago, Chile** (Alfonso and Josephina Bariolhet)
  buys product from Argentina
  opened May 1989

Each international operation sells the Mary Kay basic skin care and glamour products plus selected items from the rest of the complete product line, including fragrances, men's products, hair care, body care, sun care, and so on.

Mary Kay Cosmetics, Inc., has a worldwide sales force of 192,804 independent beauty consultants.

Independent Distributorship

An individual in a foreign country is licensed to manage (under the supervision of the Company) the Mary Kay sales and marketing plan and use the Mary Kay trade name. Product is purchased in large quantities by the distributor from the Company and sold to consumers through authorized Mary Kay beauty consultants.

Joint Venture

In a business partnership between May Kay Cosmetics and another corporation, the Mary Kay marketing plan is jointly managed, and products are distributed through authorized independent beauty consultants.

Wholly Owned Subsidiary

A wholly owned subsidiary is a corporation whose parent company is Mary Kay Cosmetics, Inc., and the only shareholder is Mary Kay Cosmetics, Inc. (U.S.). Wholly owned subsidiaries are operated by a locally recruited Mary Kay staff.

About Each Country

Argentina   Population: 31.03 million; capital, Buenos Aires, population 2.9 million; dominant language, Spanish, followed by English, Italian, German. Currency: australs.

Appendix 27A (Cont.)

Australia   Population 15.97 million; capital, Canberra, population 251,000; dominant language, English. Currency: Australian dollars.

Canada   Population: 25.61 million; capital Ottawa, population 819,000 (including neighboring suburb of Hull); dominant language, English, followed by French. Currency: Canadian dollars.

Mexico   Population: 79.56 million; capital, Mexico City, population 9 million; dominant language, Spanish, followed by English. Currency: Mexican pesos.

West Germany   Population: 61.05 million; capital, Bonn, population 292,200; dominant language, German. Currency: Deutsche marks.

Thailand   Population: 52.65 million; capital, Bangkok, population, 5.5 million; dominant language, Thai, followed by English and Chinese. Currency: Thai bhats.

Singapore   Population: 2.59 million; dominant language, English, followed by Chinese, Malay, and Tamil. Currency: Singapore dollars.

Malaysia   Population: 16.11 million; capital, Kuala Lumpur, population 1 million; dominant language, Malay, followed by English, Chinese, Tamil, tribal dialects. Currency: Malaysian ringgits.

Panama   Population: 2.23 million; capital, Panama City, 830,700 population; dominant language, Spanish, followed by English and Indian languages. Currency: Panamanian balboa.

Uruguay   Population: 2.98 million, capital, Greater Montevideo, population 1.36 million; dominant language, Spanish. Currency: Uruguayan new pesos.

Chile   Population: 12.33 million; capital, Santiago, population, 4.13 million, dominant language, Spanish. Currency: Chilean peso.

New Zealand   Population: 3.25 million; capital, Wellington, population, 343,200; dominant language English. Currency: New Zealand dollars.

*December 31, 1989.

Appendix 27B

MKCI EXECUTIVE OFFICERS AND DIRECTORS AND COMPENSATION

The company's board of directors is composed of Richard R. Rogers, John P. Rochon, and Monty C. Barber. Each director has served as such since 1985. The executive officers of the company are as follows:

Appendix 27B (Cont.)

NAME	OFFICES HELD
Richard R. Rogers	Chairman of the board, president, and chief executive officer (November 1987–present)
	President (October 1985–November 1987)
John P. Rochon	Vice chairman of the board (February 1990–present)
	Vice chairman of the board and chief financial officer (November 1987–February 1990)
	Vice president and chief financial officer (October 1985–November 1987)
Monty C. Barber	Executive vice president, secretary, and general counsel (November 1987–present)
	Vice president and secretary (March 1986–November 1987)
Lawrence G. Cox	Vice president, treasurer, and chief financial officer (February 1990–present)
	Vice president and treasurer (November 1987–February 1990)
	Treasurer (October 1985–November 1987)

All directors and executive officers of the company are elected annually to serve until their successors have been elected and qualified. Each director and executive officer of the company, except John P. Rochon, is also an executive officer of MKCI. Mr. Rochon is 38 years old, and until February 1990 he also served as a director and executive vice president and chief financial officer of MKCI.

The executive officers and directors of MKCI, their ages, offices, and, in the case of directors, the year they were first elected as a director, are as follows:

NAME (AGE)	OFFICES HELD	DIRECTOR SINCE
Mary Kay Ash (71)	Chairman Emeritus of the Board (November 1987–present)	1963
	Chairman of the Board (August 1963–November 1987)	
Richard R. Rogers (46)	Chairman of the Board and Chief Executive Officer (November 1987–present)	1964
	President and Chief Executive Officer (January 1968–November 1987)	
Richard C. Bartlett (54)	President and Chief Operating Officer (November 1987–present)	1977*
	Executive Vice President, Marketing (January 1986–November 1987)	
	Vice President, Marketing (January 1977–January 1986)	
Gerald M. Allen (48)	President, International Division (November 1987–present)	1968*
	Executive Vice President, Sales and International (January 1986–November 1987)	
	Vice President, Administration (January 1968–January 1986)	
Monty C. Barber (58)	Executive Vice President, Secretary, and General Counsel (January 1986–present)	1968*
	Vice President, Secretary, and General Counsel (January 1968–January 1986)	

Appendix 27B (Cont.)

Lawrence G. Cox (39)	Executive Vice President, Treasurer, and Chief Financial Officer (February 1990–present)	1985
	Executive Vice President and Treasurer (November 1987–February 1990)	
	Senior Vice President and Treasurer (January 1986–November 1987)	
	Treasurer (February 1984–January 1986)	
	Director of Risk Management and Assistant Treasurer (July 1983–February 1984)	
Patrick E. Howard (41)	Executive Vice President, Manufacturing Group (January 1986–present)	1986
	Vice President, Manufacturing Group (October 1984–January 1986)	
	Vice President, Manufacturing Operations (October 1981–October 1984)	
	Director, Material Control (January 1977–October 1981)	
Larry Harley (49)	Executive Vice President, Distribution Group (July 1989–present)	
	Senior Vice President, Distribution Operations (January 1986–July 1989)	
	National Director of Distribution (February 1985–January 1986)	
	Director of Marketing (June 1984–February 1985)	
	Director of North Central Distribution & Training Center (January 1982–June 1984)	
	Branch Manager, North Central (December 1974–January 1982)	
Barbara Beasley (34)	Executive Vice President, Sales Group (January 1990–present)	
	Senior Vice President, Marketing (November 1987–January 1990)	
	Vice President, Marketing Communications (January 1986–November 1987)	
	Director, Communication Resources (May 1984–January 1986)	
	Director, Visual Communications (August 1982–May 1984)	
	Manager, Visual Communications (June 1980–August 1982)	
Myra O. Barker, Ph.D. (44)	Senior Vice President and Chief Scientific Officer (February 1989–present)	1986
	Senior Vice President, Research and Development/ Quality Assurance (January 1986–February 1989)	
	Vice President, Research and Product Development (February 1979–January 1986)	
Bart Bartolacci (52)	Senior Vice President, Sales (January 1986–present)	
	Director of Sales Development (September 1980–January 1986)	
Curran Dandurand (31)	Senior Vice President, Marketing Group (January 1990–present)	
	Vice President, Product Marketing (November 1987–January 1990)	

Appendix 27B (Cont.)

	Director, Product Marketing (August 1986–November 1987)
	Product Manager, Product Marketing (September 1984–August 1986)
	Marketing Research Analyst (November 1982–September 1984)
	Product Planning Analyst (December 1980–November 1982)
Lowrance Hodge (55)	Senior Vice President, Manufacturing Operations/Engineering (November 1987–present)
	Vice President, Manufacturing Operations/Engineering (January 1986–November 1987)
	Vice President, Manufacturing Operations (November 1984–January 1986)
	Director, Staff Development (January 1983–November 1984)
Bruce Wilke (40)	Senior Vice President, Distribution Operations (July 1989–present)
	Vice President, Southwest Regional Distribution (January 1986–July 1989)
	Director of Southwest Distribution and Training Center (January 1978–January 1986)
	Southwest Branch Manager (September 1974–January 1978)
	Manager of Consultant Records (October 1971–September 1974)
Betty Bessler (57)	Vice President, Human Resources (January 1986–present)
	Director of Personnel (May 1979–January 1986)

*Except for the period from December 4, 1985 to January 8, 1986, during the LBO process.

All directors and executive officers of MKCI are elected annually and serve as such until their successors have been elected and qualified. All executive officers of MKCI have been employed by it for at least five years.

Richard R. Rogers is the son of Mary Kay Ash.

The following table sets forth all cash compensation paid for services rendered in all capacities to the company and its subsidiaries (including MKCI) for the year ended December 31, 1989 to each of the five most highly compensated executive officers and to all executive officers as a group:

NAME OF INDIVIDUAL OR NUMBER OF PERSONS IN GROUP	CAPACITIES IN WHICH SERVED IN 1989	CASH COMPENSATION
Mary Kay Ash	Chairman Emeritus of the Company; Chairman Emeritus of MKCI	$ 300,000
Richard R. Rogers	Chairman of the Board, President, and Chief Executive Officer of the Company; Chairman of the Board and Chief Executive Officer of MKCI	750,000

Appendix 27B (Cont.)

John P. Rochon	Vice Chairman of the Board and Chief Financial Officer of the Company; Executive Vice President and Chief Financial Officer of MKCI	238,500
Richard C. Bartlett	President and Chief Operating Officer of MKCI	265,000
Gerald M. Allen	President, International Division of MKCI	212,000
All executive officers as a group (15 persons)		$2,689,974

The foregoing table includes information with respect to each person who was an executive officer at any time during 1989, but only with respect to the periods during1989 that he or she served as such. Certain executive officers received compensation during 1989 in the form of various noncash personal benefits. Such compensation did not exceed the lesser of $25,000 or 10 percent of the compensation reported in the foregoing table for any of the above-named individuals, nor did the aggregate amount of such compensation for all executive officers as a group exceed 10 percent of the compensation reported in the table for the group.

Source: Form 10-K, December 31, 1989.

Appendix 27C

MARY KAY COSMETICS, INC., 1989 SEMINAR FACT SHEET

- More than 23,000 consultants and directors are expected to attend the four consecutive three-day seminar sessions held at the Dallas Convention Center.
- More than 2,000 husbands will join their wives and a large percentage will attend special seminar sessions designed just for them.
- The Mary Kay Seminar ranks as the largest continuously held convention in Dallas. The first seminar was in 1964.
- Ten local hotels are booked ten years in advance to accommodate the seminar participants.
- The stage measures 60×120 feet and takes 150 workers eight days to build.
- TV and audio presentations will require 500 pages of script per seminar.
- More than $6 million worth of prizes will be awarded.
- The list of top prizes to be awarded to seminar participants include

180	all-expense-paid trips to Australia
30	all-expense-paid trips to New Zealand
1,564	diamond rings
16	husband rings
6	fantasy gifts (valued at $5,000 each)
350	diamond bumble bee pins

Appendix 27C (Cont.)

- 2,791 Mary Kay consultants and directors were awarded the free use of automobiles this year as a result of their team or unit performance.
- This year 280 cars have been awarded to Texas consultants:
  - 25   Cadillac winners
  - 229   Grand Am winners
  - 26   Buick Regal winners
- To date there are 5,552 Mary Kay cars on the road nationwide.

28

TIME INC./SEAGRAM

The case for advertising frequency—and its effect on people's buying habits—receives a major boost in an exhaustive and groundbreaking study just completed by Jos. E. Seagram & Sons and Time Inc.[1]

Released to advertisers, agencies, and media in late 1982, "A Study of the Effectiveness of Advertising Frequency in Magazines" presented the results of an extensive study into the relationship of magazine advertising frequency and brand awareness, advertising recall, favorable brand rating, willingness to buy, and product use and purchase. Selected passages from the report have been extracted for this narrative.

BACKGROUND

Because of the complexity of the problem and the high costs involved, studies attempting to answer the question "How much frequency is enough?" have generally shied away from large-scale projects involving participating consumers. Ordinarily they have drawn on the results of experiments in behavior and learning conducted by pioneer psychologists, have sought answers through manipulating mathematical

[1]"Major Study Details Ad Effect on Sales," *Advertising Age*, June 21, 1982, p. 1.

models, or have taken other approaches that were financially and methodologically feasible and showed promise of providing operational findings. "Even fewer have examined the effect of frequency as it relates specifically to advertising in the print medium."[2]

Four characteristics set this study apart from previous ones:

1. **Scope.** This study extended over a 48-week period and generated findings from a base of 16,500 respondents and 132,000 data points.
2. **Design.** The design permitted control of all insertion frequency variables, without forced exposure, in a natural environment.
3. **Range of information.** This included both changes in attitudes and changes in behavior that resulted from changes in the frequency of "opportunities to see" advertising.
4. **Focus.** This was the first study ever to deal with the effects of frequency of advertising in magazines.[3]

HIGHLIGHTS OF THE STUDY[4]

Objective   To examine the relationship between "opportunities to see" advertising in print and advertising effectiveness, at predetermined levels of advertising frequency, and in a controlled "real-world environment."

Advertising Effectiveness Measures Evaluated   Brand awareness, advertising awareness, brand rating, willingness to buy, recent product use, and recent product purchase.

Advertising Frequency Levels Evaluated   Control group—no insertions; light frequency—one advertising insertion every four weeks of the study; moderate frequency—two advertising insertions every four weeks of the study; and heavy frequency—one advertising insertion each week of the study.

Design Criteria   Magazine advertisements studied were inserted in standard copies of *Sports Illustrated* and *Time.* These copies were then mailed in the usual fashion to known subscribers of these magazines.

Markets chosen were the state of Missouri and the city of Milwaukee.

Products studied were eight Seagram brands that had low usage in these markets. There was reasonable distribution of the test brands in the markets studied, assuring that should a consumer want to buy the brands, they would be available.

Another criterion was that no other advertising would be scheduled for these brands in the test markets during the course of the study. This assured that the only advertising that could affect respondent attitudes and behavior toward the test brands was the advertising programmed in the study.

[2]Time Inc., "A Study of the Effectiveness of Advertising Frequency in Magazines," 1982.
[3]Ibid., p. 10.
[4]This section is adapted from ibid., pp. 15–17.

Experimental Design The experimental design was balanced both to ensure that each group of respondents was involved in some way in every brand and to permit matched comparisons for all test measures at all levels of frequency. To achieve these objectives, the respondent sample was divided into four groups, with each group receiving magazines containing ads for each brand at different controlled levels of frequency. As Exhibit 28.1 demonstrates, over the course of study, for example, group 1 received magazines with no ads for brands A and E, 12 ads for brands B and F, 24 ads for brands C and G, and 48 ads for brands D and H. Similarly, each of the other groups received magazines with ads at different levels of frequency for each brand.

In analyzing the data, responses were pooled for each level of frequency. For example, to study the effects of every-week frequency (48 insertions), responses were pooled from group 1 for brands D and H, from group 2 for brands C and G, from group 3 for brands B and F, and from group 4 for brands A and E.

Sample and Response Subscriber lists were "cleansed" to ensure that no respondent received ads in both *Time* and *Sports Illustrated* even if subscribing to both. The duration was 48 weeks, with fieldwork completed between November 1979 and September 1980. The sample base was just over 21,000 with a 77 percent completion rate; 80 percent of the respondent base of approximately 16,500 were liquor users. Questionnaires were mailed weekly to subsamples of subscriber respondents, with no participant receiving more than one (see Appendix 28A for related questionnaire). Data were analyzed only for liquor users, and brands were weighted equally, so that results from larger brands did not distort the results from small brands for any measure. Ads were chosen by Joseph E. Seagram & Sons, Inc., and then were arranged in printing and binding so that, over the course of the project, each appeared an equal number of times in the front and the back of each magazine and an equal number of times facing right and facing left. Fieldwork data collection, tabulation, and editing were carried out by Lieberman Associates; curve fitting was

Exhibit 28.1

EXPERIMENTAL RESEARCH DESIGN MATRIX

Group	DESIGN							
1	0X	12X	24X	48X	0X	12X	24X	48X
2	12X	24X	48X	0X	12X	24X	48X	0X
3	24X	48X	0X	12X	24X	48X	0X	12X
4	48X	0X	12X	24X	48X	0X	12X	24X
	A	B	C	D	E	F	G	H
				BRAND				

prepared by Marketmath, Inc. (In this case study, we include only narrative, not graphs.)

MAJOR FINDINGS[5]

1. *Significant changes in consumer attitudes were apparent beginning with the first insertion.* It has been postulated that at least three ad exposures are required to make a significant impact on consumer attitudes.

   Contrary to this assumption, the data show that, while reported levels of awareness of advertising built slowly, reported levels for such measures of attitude as brand awareness, favorable brand rating, and willingness to buy jumped sharply following the first "opportunity to see" advertising.

2. *Gains in reported levels of brand awareness and in favorable attitudes toward advertised brands were still being achieved at the end of the campaign.* Contrary to previously held theories, favorable effects resulting from "opportunity to see" advertising did not level off or drop in the later weeks of the study.

   For some measures of attitude, reported increases did diminish briefly in the early weeks of the campaign following the initial jump. This may have occurred because these early ad exposures served to bring back to mind previously held attitudes based on experience.

   For all attitude measures, the decline was temporary, and, in later weeks, a stable pattern of increase was established. This pattern of increase then remained constant for the duration of the campaign.

   By contrast, the rate of increase in levels of awareness of advertising tended to flatten in the later weeks of the campaign.

3. *More frequent "opportunities to see" advertising resulted in higher average weekly gains in measures of attitude.* Study findings confirmed the assumption that greater advertised frequency (more opportunities to see advertising) produces greater advertising effect.

   For all measurements, increased levels of exposure resulted in more favorable attitudes toward advertised brands.

4. *Changes in behavior as a result of frequent advertising were greater than changes in attitude.* For all brands, opportunities to see advertising resulted in greater increases in product use and purchase than in measures of awareness, favorable brand rating, and willingness to buy.

   For example, at the heaviest frequency level, in an average week, brand awareness increased 36 percent, favorable brand rating gained 45 percent, willingness to buy increased 59 percent, recent reported product use rose 72 percent, and recent reported product purchase jumped 170 percent.

5. *It was more difficult to change attitudes toward "high-awareness" brands than it was to change attitudes toward "low-awareness" brands for the low-usage brands studied.* Although study findings showed that frequent advertising resulted in substantial gains in both awareness and favorable attitudes for all brands studied, they also revealed a distinct difference in the pattern and magnitude of increase between high- and low-awareness brands.

   Increases were substantially greater for low-awareness brands than for high-awareness brands. The size of the increase reported for low-awareness brands also proved to be more sensitive to increases in advertising frequency. For both high- and low-awareness brands, gains were still being achieved at the end of the campaign. Also for both, the magnitude of change was greater for measures of behavior than for measures of attitude.

[5]This section is adapted from ibid., pp. 17–19.

6. *Awareness of advertising may understate the effects of advertising.* Although awareness of advertising increased during the test, these increases did not consistently reflect changes in attitudes that resulted from the advertising.

For example, in an average week, 14 percent of respondents in the control group reported seeing advertising for high-awareness brands in the past four weeks. However, they were not exposed to any advertising for these brands in that period. At the same time, 75 percent of respondents in the high-frequency group reported seeing no advertising for these brands. This was despite the fact that they had opportunities to see 48 ads in the period.

More significant, changes reported for such measures of advertising effectiveness as brand awareness rose more rapidly than did awareness of advertising. This indicates that people are affected by advertising even when they claim they cannot recall having seen it.

In sum, the findings suggest that while awareness of advertising can provide some indication of consumer response to advertising, it is, at the same time, limited in its ability to reflect accurately the effectiveness of advertising.

CONCLUSIONS[6]

The study was designed specifically to explore the effects of frequent magazine advertising on attitudes and purchasing behavior.

The findings, however, also offer insights into the dynamics of advertising itself and provide clues that could have practical application in planning media strategies.

1. *Magazine advertising works.* At its most basic level, the study reaffirms the effectiveness of magazines as an advertising medium.

   As the data demonstrate, "opportunities to see" advertising in magazines dramatically increase brand awareness. To an even greater degree, it produces favorable attitudes toward advertised brands and stimulates product purchase. This is true even when the people affected cannot recall having seen the advertising.

   More important, gains in reported brand purchase are greater than gains in favorable brand rating. This seems to suggest that advertising in general and magazine advertising in particular may trigger changes in behavior without corresponding changes in attitude.

   Several conclusions are also clear about the effects of increasing the frequency of opportunities to see advertising.

2. *More is better.* Although reported gains in the levels of response to study measurements are not always proportional to increases in opportunities to see advertising, the data show that greater frequency does result in greater advertising effect.

   The relationship between increased frequency and increased advertising effect is particularly apparent for low-awareness brands.

3. *There are no fixed rules for effective frequency.* The data also indicate that no fixed, specific number of ads is necessary to change attitudes effectively. No minimum number appears to be required. The first ad produced a significant effect.

   There is no maximum frequency level after which ads seem to lose effectiveness. Awareness and favorable attitude levels were still on the rise at the end of the 48-week study.

[6]This section is adapted from ibid., pp. 19–21.

4. *"Low-awareness" brands benefit the most from heavy, sustained frequency.* Data seem to indicate that new brands or low-awareness brands might have the most to gain from frequent advertising.

   This is perhaps true because consumers have no preconceived opinions of these brands and therefore have no deeply entrenched attitudes to overcome. Whatever the explanation, there appears to be a direct relationship between increasing frequency and increasing effectiveness. For low-awareness brands, more seems almost always to be better.

5. *For "high-awareness" brands studied, campaign duration appears to be important.* For high-awareness brands, the first ad produces a substantial increase in awareness and favorable attitude. This, in turn, is followed by a temporary fall back and a subsequent return to rising levels of awareness and favorable brand rating. This seems to suggest that a campaign of extended duration may be required to overcome entrenched attitudes toward these brands.

6. *Other observations.* In assessing the results of the study, it should be emphasized that all products studied were low-usage brands that had not been advertised in the test markets for some time. The study did not examine the effect of frequency on heavily advertised, high-awareness, high-usage brands.

   Therefore, no firm conclusions about the effect of frequency on established brands of this nature can be drawn from the findings. A cessation or reduction in advertising might harm such brands, however. If a leading brand were to lose acceptance as a result of a reduction in advertising, it would have difficulty regaining its position in the marketplace, the data suggest.

   It should also be noted that the study findings represent only the minimal effects of advertising. First, a repeat purchase or a first purchase made by a respondent after the 48-week study period would not have shown up in the data. Second, liquor advertising, in general, is severely limited in its creative approach. Due to governmental and industry restrictions, benefits cannot be claimed, and it is forbidden to depict liquor consumption.

   It is likely, therefore, that reported gains would have been greater had the ads studied been fewer. It is probable also that a study of longer duration would have revealed greater long-term changes in respondent attitudes and purchase patterns.

   In addition, the insertion of as many as six liquor advertisements per issue also created a magazine environment with greater clutter than is usual. If, as some theorize, advertising effectiveness is diminished by clutter, then the effectiveness of the advertisements studied, particularly at the highest levels of frequency, was probably understated.

Director of research for Time Inc.'s magazine group, Robert Schreiber summed it up: "This study shows that advertising really works. Intuitively we have always believed this; now here is the evidence to back it up." Should advertisers and agencies be skeptical of the results because Time Inc., was a sponsor? "Absolutely not," rejoined Schreiber, "because the other partner in the pioneering venture was Seagram, which had no vested interest whatsoever in promoting the value of increased advertising. Further, the outside research agencies involved are noted for their integrity."

Appendix 28A

QUESTIONNAIRE

This is an edited version of the questionnaire used in the Time Inc./ Seagram research. Response categories for products have been omitted to avoid identifying brands under study.

1. Which of the following beverages have you had in the past 4 weeks? (Check as many as apply.)
    ☐ Coffee   ☐ Soft drinks   ☐ Wine
    ☐ Tea   ☐ Beer   ☐ Liquor

2. Please check the brands of beer listed below you have ever heard of.

3. Please check the brands of wine listed below you have ever heard of. As an aid to help you answer the next few questions, we have enclosed pictures of the bottles of the next group of brands, about which we would like your opinion. When answering the following questions, please refer to these pictures.

4. Please check the brands of liquor listed below you have ever heard of.

5. Now, we would like you to give your overall impression of each brand listed below, based on any experience you have had or anything you have heard or read about each brand.
    To do this, please rate each brand by using the 0 to 10 scale shown here. The more favorable you feel about a brand, the higher you should rate it. The less favorable you feel about a brand, the lower you should rate it. A "0" rating means you feel the brand is one of the worst of its type and a "10" rating means you think it is one of the best of its type.
    For each brand, please circle how you yourself rate the brand, feeling free to use any number on the scale that best describes how you feel.

6. In column 1 below, please check the brands of liquor you yourself have ever used, at home or in a bar, cocktail lounge, or restaurant.

7. In column 2 below, check the brands of liquor you yourself have used in the past 3 months, at home or in a bar, cocktail lounge, or restaurant.

8. In column 3 below, please check the brands of liquor you yourself have used in the past 4 weeks, at home or in a bar, cocktail lounge, or restaurant.

9. Now, in column 1 below, please check the brands of liquor you bought a bottle(s) of in the past 3 months, for your own use, to serve to guests, or as a gift.

10. In column 2 below, please check the brands of liquor you bought a bottle(s) of in the past 4 weeks, for your own use, to serve to guests, or as a gift.

11. In the past 4 weeks, did you happen to go to a store to buy a bottle(s) of liquor, ask for one of the brands listed below (under Q. 12), and find that the store did not have that brand in stock?
    ☐ Yes   ☐ No
    If yes in Q. 11, answer Q. 12.

12. Please check which, if any, of the following brands you asked for but found that the store did not have.

13. Suppose you were going out to buy some bottles of liquor today, for your own use, to serve to guests, or as a gift. For each brand listed below, please check how likely you would be to consider buying it. (For each brand listed, check one box on each line.)

Appendix 28A (Cont.)

14. Some people only have a cocktail or a drink of liquor at social gatherings or on special occasions, while other people find it relaxing to have a cocktail or liquor drink before meals or in the evening after work. Generally speaking, please check the statement below that comes closest to how often you yourself have a cocktail or liquor drink. (Check only one answer.)

☐ More than once a day
☐ Once a day
☐ Two or three times a week
☐ Once a week
☐ Two or three times a month
☐ Once a month
☐ Once every two months
☐ Two or three times a year or less often
☐ Never have a liquor drink

15. Please check how often you or someone else in your household serve cocktails or liquor drinks to guests in your home. (Check only one answer.)

☐ More than once a week
☐ Once a week
☐ Two or three times a month
☐ Once a month
☐ Once every two months
☐ Two or three times a year or less often
☐ Never serve a liquor drink

16. For each type of liquor listed below, please check whether or not you yourself happened to drink that type of liquor, either straight or in a mixed drink, in the past 6 months. (Please be sure to answer for each type of liquor.)

For each type of liquor you have had in the past 6 months, answer Q. 17.

17. For each type of liquor you happened to drink in the past 6 months, please check the statement which comes closest to describing how often you had it. (Please give one answer for each type of liquor you drank in the past 6 months.)

18. For each type of liquor listed below, please check whether or not you or someone else in your household served it to guests in your home anytime in the past 6 months. (Please be sure to answer for each type of liquor.)

For each type of liquor served to guests in past 6 months, answer Q. 19.

19. For each type of liquor served to guests in the past 6 months, please check the statement which best describes how often you served it. (Please give one answer for each type of liquor you served to guests in the past 6 months.)

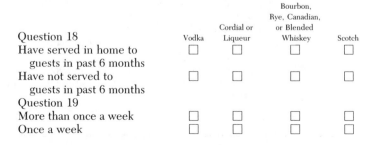

Question 18	Vodka	Cordial or Liqueur	Bourbon, Rye, Canadian, or Blended Whiskey	Scotch
Have served in home to guests in past 6 months	☐	☐	☐	☐
Have not served to guests in past 6 months	☐	☐	☐	☐
Question 19				
More than once a week	☐	☐	☐	☐
Once a week	☐	☐	☐	☐

Appendix 28A (Cont.)

Two or three times a month	☐	☐	☐	☐
Once a month	☐	☐	☐	☐
Once every two months	☐	☐	☐	☐
Two or three times a year or less often	☐	☐	☐	☐
Never serve this type of liquor drink	☐	☐	☐	☐

20. In column 1 below, check the brands you recall noticing any advertising for in the past 3 months.

21. In column 2 below, check the brands you recall noticing any advertising for in the past 4 weeks.

Now, just a few questions for classification purposes:

22. What is your sex?
    ☐ Male   ☐ Female

23. What is your age?
    ☐ Under 25   ☐ 35–49   ☐ 65 or older
    ☐ 25–34   ☐ 50–64

24. What is the highest level of schooling attained?
    ☐ Grade school   ☐ Some high school
    ☐ Completed high school   ☐ Some postgraduate school
    ☐ Some college   ☐ Postgraduate degree
    ☐ Graduated college

25. Is the head of your household
    ☐ Employed full-time?   ☐ Not employed?
    ☐ Employed part-time?

26. Please check the category of employment
    ☐ Professional
       (such as doctor, attorney, teacher)
    ☐ Management/executive
    ☐ Own a small business
    ☐ Salesman
    ☐ Clerical (such as secretary, typist, clerk)
    ☐ Skilled trade/technician (such as farmer, truck driver, construction, machinist)
    ☐ General/labor
       (such as janitor, domestic, laborer)
    ☐ Uniformed services
       (such as police officer, firefighter, armed services)
    ☐ Retired
    ☐ Student

27. What do you estimate your total family income was in the past 12 months? (Please include income from all family members and all sources, such as wages, profits, dividends, rentals, etc.)

    ☐ Under $10,000   ☐ $35,000–49,999
    ☐ $10,000–14,999   ☐ $50,000–74,999
    ☐ $15,000–19,999   ☐ $75,000–99,999
    ☐ $20,000–24,999   ☐ $100,000 and over
    ☐ $25,000–34,999

Source: "Major Study Details Ad Effect on Sales," pp. 52–54.

29

COKE TRIES TO COUNTER THE PEPSI CHALLENGE

INTRODUCTION

The Coca-Cola Company was ranked as the 46th largest industrial corporation on the basis of sales in 1984. With 36.4 percent of domestic soft drink sales volume, Coca-Cola was still ahead of its nearest rival, Pepsi Company, Inc., which had 25.6 percent of the domestic sales volume. Still, Coca-Cola needed to address several issues to ensure its leadership and growth in the soft drink industry. One issue was how best to deal with increased competition in a maturing soft drink industry. Another, more specific, issue was what to do about Pepsi, which was gaining on Coke in recent years. These and other factors meant more intense competition within the soft drink industry.

HISTORY

Coca-Cola, perhaps the world's most renowned trademarked product, was created by Dr. Pemberton in 1886 by stirring various ingredients into a brass pot. His part-

This case was written by Dhruv Grewal, Ph.D. student in marketing at Virginia Polytechnic and State University, under the direction of Larry D. Alexander, assistant professor of strategic management, Department of Management, The R. B. Pamplin College of Business, Virginia Polytechnic Institute and State University, Blacksburg, Virginia 24061.

ner and bookkeeper, Frank Robinson, named the product Coca-Cola, something he felt would be easily remembered by customers. The product was first sold at drugstore fountains for 5 cents a glass, and sales averaged 13 glasses per day during 1886. During that first year, Dr. Pemberton earned $50.00; however, he spent $73.96 on advertising alone.

Later, in 1889, Joseph Whitehead and Benjamin Thomas secured the exclusive rights from the company to bottle and sell Coca-Cola throughout the United States, except for six New England states, Texas, and Mississippi. This contract started the unique relationship that the Coca-Cola Company enjoyed with its largely independent bottlers. By 1894, Joseph Biedenharn started bottling the Coca-Cola product at his own facilities.

The Coca-Cola Company (which replaced the 1892 firm that was incorporated in Georgia) was incorporated in Delaware in 1919. Still, the company's headquarters remained in Atlanta, Georgia. Clearly, several of the most vital assets of the Coca-Cola Company were its trademarks. "Coca-Cola" was registered with the U.S. Patent and Trademark Office in 1893, and the shortened "Coke" was similarly registered much later in 1945. In addition, its unique contoured bottle was registered as a trademark in 1960.

The Coca-Cola Company was best known for manufacturing and distributing soft drink syrups and flavoring concentrates. While the company also operated a separate food division which produced and marketed citrus and other fruit juices, coffee, and plastic products, the focus of this case is on its soft drink division. Some of its products in this category included Hi-C fruit drinks, various Minute Maid juices, and Five-Alive beverages. The Coca-Cola Company significantly diversified its operations when it acquired Columbia Pictures in 1982. That acquired firm was engaged in the production and distribution of motion pictures and television shows. Other entertainment-related activities that Columbia participated in included the publication and distribution of sheet music and song books.

THE PEPSI CHALLENGE

In 1975, Pepsi started its "Pepsi Challenge," aimed directly at Coca-Cola, through its various comparative ads. By 1983, Pepsi was targeting the teenage population, claiming it to be the "Choice of a New Generation." Popular music and television personalities endorsed Pepsi products in the advertisements. Pepsi even agreed to finance partially the Jackson brothers' Victory Tour of 30 cities if they would appear in two Pepsi commercials. Pepsi's name would also be on all the tickets and promotions of the tour and several radio and print advertisements that featured the Jacksons. Other celebrities that signed contracts to endorse Pepsi products in recent years have included singer Lionel Richie, actor Don Johnson, rock musician Glen Frey, actor Michael J. Fox, and comedian Billy Crystal. Clearly, the Pepsi challenge had strengthened the number two soft drink manufacturer, which captured 33 percent of the food store market by 1985.

Pepsi made other changes in its strategy to compete more effectively against Coca-Cola. Pepsi began to acquire some of its largest bottlers. By acquiring its third largest bottler, MEI Bottling Corporation in Minnesota, Pepsi was able to cover

33 franchise markets. Pepsi-Cola also acquired the Alleghany Bottling Company, another major bottler, which served an area stretching from South-Central Pennsylvania to the coastal area of Virginia. The financial statements of PepsiCo, Inc., are presented in Exhibit 29.1.

Pepsi's challenge to Coke's supremacy has been felt the most in recent years. During 1983 alone, Coca-Cola lost both its Burger King and Wendy's accounts to Pepsi. A major aspect of the Pepsi challenge was its comparative advertising in which Pepsi claimed its products were superior to Coke's. Later in 1985, Pepsi reaped benefits when arch rival Coke first discontinued old Coke and later reintroduced it. So happy was Pepsi management that it gave its employees the day off when Coke was discontinued, since management felt it confirmed that Pepsi was superior. Exhibit 29.2 shows that PepsiCo had the dominant share of the caffeine-free market. It also shows that Coke had increased its position in the diet soft drink market with its newly introduced Diet Coke, the most popular diet drink.

Clearly, Coke and Pepsi were locked into a competitive battle for the number one position in the industry. For years, Coke's profit margins had declined while Pepsi's market share increased. To improve its profit margin, Coke replaced weak

---

Exhibit 29.1

PEPSICO, INC. AND SUBSIDIARIES
CONSOLIDATED STATEMENT OF INCOME
AND RETAINED EARNINGS, 1982–1984*
(in thousands except per share amounts)

		1984	1983	1982
Revenues	Net sales	**$7,698,678**	$7,165,586	$6,810,929
Costs and Expenses	Cost of sales	**3,149,940**	3,007,398	2,949,160
	Marketing, administrative and other expenses	**3,853,540**	3,629,509	3,233,050
	Interest expense	**206,956**	176,759	165,270
	Interest income	**(86,131)**	(53,650)	(49,325)
		7,124,305	6,760,016	6,298,155
Income from Continuing Operations Before Unusual Charges and Income Taxes		**574,373**	405,570	512,774
Unusual Charges	Provision for restructuring	**220,000**	—	—
	Reduction in net assets of foreign bottling operations (without tax benefit)	**—**	—	79,400
Income from Continuing Operations Before Income Taxes		**354,373**	405,570	433,374
	Provision for U.S. and foreign income taxes	**147,701**	134,233	220,947
Income from Continuing Operations		**206,672**	271,337	212,427

Exhibit 29.1 (Cont.)

Discontinued Operations	Income from discontinued operations (net of income taxes of $14,915, $6,728, and $5,846 in 1984, 1983, and 1982, respectively)	**20,875**	12,774	11,861
	Loss on disposal (net of $500 tax benefit)	**(15,000)**	—	—
		5,875	12,774	11,861
Net Income		**212,547**	284,111	224,288
	Retained earnings at beginning of year	**1,622,550**	1,489,797	1,412,636
	Cash dividends (per share 1984— $1.65; 1983—$1.62; 1982—$1.58)	**(156,185)**	(151,358)	(147,127)
	Retained earnings at end of year	**$1,678,912**	$1,622,550	$1,489,797
Net Income per Share	Continuing operations	**$ 2.19**	$ 2.88	$ 2.27
	Discontinued operations	**0.06**	0.13	0.13
	Net income	**$ 2.25**	$ 3.01	$ 2.40
	Assets			
	Current Assets			
	Cash	**$ 28,139**	$ 24,434	
	Marketable securities	**784,684**	529,326	
	Notes and accounts receivable, less allowance (1984—$31,966; 1983— $33,738)	**640,081**	647,329	
	Inventories	**451,781**	375,606	
	Prepaid expenses, taxes and other current assets	**242,181**	159,247	
	Net assets of the transportation segment held for disposal	**143,210**	149,504	
		2,290,076	1,885,446	
	Long-Term Receivables and Investments			
	Long-term receivables and other investments	**178,647**	161,283	
	Investment in tax leases	**73,236**	77,941	
		251,883	239,224	
	Property, Plant, and Equipment			
	Land	**218,231**	190,942	
	Buildings	**819,990**	732,999	
	Machinery and equipment	**1,988,112**	1,891,046	
	Capital leases	**191,924**	190,842	
	Bottles and cases, net of customers' deposits (1984—$11,678; 1983— $32,777)	**23,785**	56,550	
		3,242,042	3,062,379	
	Less: Accumulated depreciation and amortization	**1,079,029**	1,019,000	
		2,163,013	2,043,379	
	Goodwill	**163,904**	235,768	

Exhibit 29.1 (Cont.)

Other Assets	81,358	88,919
	$4,950,234	$4,492,736
Liabilities and Shareholders Equity		
Current Liabilities		
Notes payable (including current installments on long-term debt and capital lease obligations)	$ 284,280	$ 276,062
Accounts payable	505,843	406,339
U.S. and foreign income taxes	114,372	80,329
Other accrued taxes	64,338	66,144
Other current liabilities	656,499	521,704
	1,625,332	1,350,578
Long-Term Debt	541,076	668,294
Deferred Income Taxes	621,300	387,000
Capital Lease Obligations	145,218	147,519
Other Liabilities and Deferred Credits	163,932	145,187
Shareholders' Equity		
Capital stock par value 5¢ per share authorized 135,000,000 shares issued (1984—95,164,331; 1983—94,986,557 shares)	4,758	4,749
Capital in excess of par value	251,915	245,030
Retained earnings	1,678,912	1,622,550
Cumulative translation adjustment	(49,426)	(40,976)
Less: Cost of repurchased shares (1984—1,256,768; 1983—1,425,915)	(32,783)	(37,195)
	1,853,376	1,794,158
	$4,950,234	$4,492,736

*Years ended December 29, 1984 (52 weeks) December 31, 1983 (53 weeks), and December 25, 1982 (52 weeks).

Source: PEPSICO, Inc., *1984 Annual Report*, pp. 41–43.

bottlers, bought Columbia Pictures, and introduced Diet Coke, Caffeine-Free Coke, and Cherry Coke. These moves increased Coke's profit margin by 20 percent and doubled Coke's stock price. Still, Pepsi was outperforming Coke in the grocery stores with ads targeted toward the teenage market. Meanwhile, Coke had been concentrating on the baby boomer market, people born after World War II (between 1946 and 1962). By the 1980s the baby boomers were aging, which caused the teenage population to increase.

PepsiCo's attempt to acquire Seven-Up from Philip Morris in 1985 might make the Pepsi challenge an even greater threat. Philip Morris had already agreed to sell Seven-Up to PepsiCo for $380,000,000. All that remained for PepsiCo was to obtain approval from the Antitrust Division of the Department of Justice. If the Seven-Up acquisition was approved, PepsiCo's share of the lemon-lime soft drink market would

Exhibit 29.2

DIET SOFT DRINK AND CAFFEINE-FREE MARKET SHARES, 1980–1984

DIET SOFT DRINK CONSUMPTION

	1980	1981	1982	1983	1984
Coca-Cola	28.5%	28.8%	30.2%	40.9%	43.5%
PepsiCo	23.7	24.3	23.2	22.0	21.4
Seven-Up	8.5	8.4	8.7	8.0	7.6
Dr Pepper	9.2	11.7	10.8	7.2	6.0
Royal Crown Cola	5.4	4.4	3.9	2.6	2.8
R. J. Reynolds	3.1	3.6	3.2	3.2	2.3
Sugar-Free A & W	2.4	2.4	2.4	2.0	1.5
Dad's	0.9	0.8	0.8	0.6	0.5
Others	18.2	17.6	17.5	15.0	14.3
Percentage of total market	12.8	13.8	14.6	17.3	19.2

CAFFEINE-FREE CONSUMPTION

	1983	1984
PepsiCo	43.8%	40.5%
Coca-Cola	20.5	28.6
Dr Pepper	5.5	4.9
Seven-Up	7.7	6.2
Royal Crown Cola	19.8	14.8
Others	2.7	5.0
Percentage of total market	5.6	5.9

Source: Adapted from *Beverage Industry* (March 1985), p. 68.

rise to 60 percent. With Seven-Up's addition, PepsiCo would have two additional soft drinks which accounted for 13 percent of the total industry sales. While Seven-Up suffered losses in past years, PepsiCo believed that its pending acquisition complemented PepsiCo's operations and would help increase its share of the soft drink market to 35 percent, only a few percentage points behind Coke.

COCA-COLA'S FUNCTIONAL AREA STRATEGIES

Marketing/Sales

The major markets for Coke products are vending machines, restaurant sales, and grocery and convenience stores. In 1985, the Coca-Cola Company produced many soft drinks. They included the following:

Classic Coke, New Coke, Caffeine-Free Coke, Diet Coke, Caffeine-Free Diet Coke, Cherry Coke, TAB, Caffeine-Free TAB, Sprite, Diet Sprite, Fresca, Mr. PiBB, Sugar-Free Mr. PiBB, Mello-Yello, Fanta, Diet Fanta, Hi-C soft drinks, Ramblin' Root Beer, Sugar-Free Ramblin' Root Beer, and Santiba.

The firm's product pricing structure worked in the following manner. Coca-Cola USA, which was a division of the Coca-Cola Company, manufactured the beverage syrups and concentrates. They were sold by Coca-Cola USA to bottlers at an established price. The bottlers, in turn, charged a wholesale price to the retailers in their territories, who then sold at a retail price to the ultimate consumers. In recent years, Coke has increased its price discounting in order to increase its market share in the food store segment.

Coca-Cola had always emphasized a strong role for advertising to sell its soft drinks. In 1984 alone, the company spent over $90,000,000 on advertising. In its various advertising campaigns in recent years, Coca-Cola utilized such major slogans as "Things Go Better with Coke," "Coke Is It," "The One You Grow Up With," and others to sell its products. Its ad campaigns seemed to be in line with the tempo of life for the period. Before an advertising campaign was approved, months of work were spent on thorough market research. The campaign was then pretested in one or several target markets, and, if the results proved favorable, final approval was given for it to be undertaken on a full-scale effort.

To increase consumer awareness, Coke refined its popular "Coke Is It" general advertising campaign in 1984. In its place, it introduced a number of commercials targeted at specific consumer groups. Different commercials were aimed at the young and the old and showed Coke as "the one you grow up with." Music video commercials were aimed at the young, and comedian/actor Bill Cosby was used to emphasize the fact that Coke was not as sweet as its competitors products. This campaign was successful since it increased unit sales and market shares in food stores, vending machines, and all other segments. One 1986 advertisement featured William Perry, the football star of the Superbowl Champion Chicago Bears, drinking a whole case of the New Coke.

In April 1985, the company announced the reformulation of the world's best-selling soft drink, Coke. It was a sweeter cola drink—hopefully more appealing to the teen market. Coke had spent four years doing market research before introducing the newly formulated Coke. Taste tests all pointed to the "new" Coke as being more desirable. Once the new Coke was introduced, however, the company soon discovered just how loyal the old Coke customers were. The new Coke was losing ground to old Coke and, more importantly, to Pepsi. After the new Coke had been on the market for only two months, Coca-Cola president David Keough announced that old Coke would be reintroduced as Coca-Cola Classic, but the new Coke would remain Coca-Cola.

The blunder of reformulating Coke had caused several problems. Bottlers had to deal with double inventory and increased production scheduling problems. Coke also faced the problem of limited shelf space from retailers. Many of the retailers did not have space for all of Coke's different products. Fast-food restaurants, which provided a large percentage of Coke's income, likewise lacked enough room for all of

Coke's products. As a result, restaurant owners and retailers let consumer preferences decide what to carry. Still, the market share for Coke products increased since the new Coke and Coca-Cola Classic provided consumers with more choices.

The company's fountain sales continued to grow strongly in the 1980s. Overall, fountain sales represented 33 percent of total U.S. volume. The firm's aggressive marketing of Sprite resulted in McDonald's authorizing its use in all of its 6,500 restaurants. In 1985, Coca-Cola USA managed to obtain the Baskin-Robbins contract to supply Ramblin' Root Beer for its root beer floats. Baskin-Robbins, with over 3,000 stores in the United States and 17 foreign countries, represented over 1,000,000 gallons of soft drink sales annually. Under this agreement, Coke, Diet Coke, Sprite, and Ramblin' Root Beer would all be available to Baskin-Robbins' customers.

Manufacturing/Operations

Coca-Cola USA manufactured the beverage syrups and concentrates which were sold to more than 1,500 bottlers in over 155 countries. These bottlers were generally independent businesses who invested their own capital to purchase the necessary land, buildings, machinery and equipment, trucks, bottles, and cases. These bottlers packaged, distributed, and marketed the products throughout their respective territories. In addition to syrups and concentrates, Coca-Cola USA provided management guidance in such areas as quality control, marketing, advertising, engineering, financing, and personnel to help bottlers maintain product quality and be profitable.

Soft drink syrups and concentrates were manufactured by the company and sold to bottlers and fountain wholesalers. The syrups were a mixture of sweeteners, water, and flavoring concentrate. Bottlers or canning operators combined the syrups with carbonated water, packaged the soft drinks in cans, bottles, and plastic containers, and then sold them to retailers. Fountain retailers purchased the syrups from fountain wholesalers and sold the product in cups and glasses. Major sweeteners that Coca-Cola used included sugar, high-fructose corn syrup (HFCS-55), saccharin, and aspartame.

The company's operations were broken down into geographical subdivisions, each headed up by an area manager. To ensure smooth operations, the company had developed a strong and committed bottling network. In 1984, Coca-Cola sold 68 percent of its soft drink syrup and concentrate to approximately 500 U.S. bottlers. The remaining 32 percent was sold to approximately 4,000 fountain wholesalers, who sold the product to restaurants. The company continued to use multiple sweeteners in its products. It had an agreement from G. D. Searle & Co. to supply aspartame for its diet/low-caloric drinks.

In 1979, Coca-Cola initiated a program to strengthen its bottling network which had high turnover. Company projections estimated that about 50 percent of its franchise ownerships would change hands during a five-year period. The company devoted a great deal of time and money to facilitate transfers or financial restructures of its bottlers, and it invested over $100,000,000 in 1983 alone to strengthen its bottling operations to support the company's ambitious future growth goals.

Finance/Accounting

The consolidated statement of income for the Coca-Cola Company are shown in Exhibit 29.3 for 1982 through 1984. Its net operating revenues for 1984 were $7,363,993,000 and its net income after taxes was $628,818,000. Historically, its net operating revenues had increased from $2,425,000,000 in 1974 to over $7 billionin 1984. Furthermore, its net income increased from $204,000,000 to over $600,000,000 during that same period.

The Coca-Cola Company had recently deemphasized stock financing in favor of long-term debt. For example, in 1984 alone, the company bought back over $6,000,000 worth of shares of common stock, which resulted in higher earnings per share. In turn, the company started utilizing more low-cost debt to finance its investment programs. In total, the company more than doubled its total debt in 1984 alone. The firm's consolidated balance sheets (including its majority owned subsidiaries) are shown in Exhibit 29.4.

In the last five years, sales have exhibited a 10.7 percent growth rate, while net

Exhibit 29.3

COCA-COLA COMPANY CONSOLIDATED STATEMENT OF INCOME, DECEMBER 31, 1982–1984
(in thousands except per share data)

	1984	1983	1982
Net Operating Revenues	$7,363,993	$6,828,992	$6,021,135
Cost and services	3,992,923	3,772,741	3,310,847
Gross Profit	3,371,070	3,056,251	2,710,288
Selling, administrative, and general expenses	2,313,562	2,063,626	1,830,527
Operating Income	1,057,508	992,625	879,761
Interest income	128,837	82,912	106,172
Interest expense	123,750	72,667	74,560
Other Income (deductions), net	5,438	(2,528)	6,679
Income from Continuing Operations			
Before Income Taxes	1,068,033	1,000,332	918,052
Income taxes	439,215	442,072	415,076
Income from Continuing Operations	628,818	558,260	502,976
Income from discontinued operations (net of applicable income taxes of $414 in 1983 and $4,683 in 1982)	—	527	9,256
Net Income	$ 628,818	$ 558,787	$ 512,232
Per Share:			
Continuing operations	$4.76	$4.10	$3.88
Discontinued operations	—	—	0.07
Net income	$4.76	$4.10	$3.95
Average Shares Outstanding	132,210	136,222	129,793

Source: The Coca-Cola Company, *1984 Annual Report.*

Exhibit 29.4

COCA-COLA COMPANY CONSOLIDATED BALANCE SHEET, DECEMBER 31, 1984–1985
(in thousands except share data)

	1984	1983
Assets		
Current Assets		
Cash	$ 307,564	$ 319,385
Marketable securities, at cost (approximate market)	474,575	292,084
Trade accounts receivable, less allowance of $20,670 in 1984 and $20,169 in 1983	872,332	779,729
Inventories and unamortized costs	740,063	744,107
Prepaid expenses and other assets	241,326	195,009
Total Current Assets	2,635,860	2,330,314
Investments, Film Costs, and Other Assets		
Investments (principally investments in affiliates)	334,220	241,780
Unamortized film costs	341,662	252,612
Long-term receivables and other assets	408,324	240,880
	1,084,206	735,272
Property, Plant, and Equipment		
Land	130,883	128,642
Buildings and improvements	645,150	618,586
Machinery and equipment	1,518,264	1,412,697
Containers	337,993	341,597
	2,632,290	2,501,522
Less: Allowance for depreciation	1,009,715	940,716
	1,622,575	1,560,806
Goodwill and Other Intangible Assets	615,428	601,430
	$5,958,069	$5,227,822
Liabilities and Shareholders Equity		
Current		
Loans and notes payable	$ 502,216	$ 85,913
Current maturities of long-term debt	120,300	20,783
Accounts payable and accrued expenses	1,020,807	910,951
Participations and other entertainment obligations	192,537	154,213
Accrued taxes, including income taxes	186,942	219,240
Total Current Liabilities	2,022,802	1,391,100
Participation and Other Entertainment Obligations	175,234	226,129
Long-Term Debt	740,001	513,202
Deferred Income Taxes	241,966	176,635
Shareholders' Equity		
Common stock, no par value		
Authorized: 180,000,000 shares in 1984 and 1983		
Issued: 137,263,936 shares in 1984 and 136,653,676 shares in 1983	69,009	68,704
Capital surplus	532,186	500,031

Exhibit 29.4 (Cont.)

Reinvested earnings	2,758,895	2,494,215
Foreign currency translation adjustment	(234,811)	(130,640)
	3,125,279	2,932,310
Less: Treasury stock, at cost (6,438,873 shares in 1984; 300,588 shares in 1983)	347,213	11,554
	2,778,066	2,920,756
	$5,958,069	$5,227,822

Source: Coca-Cola Company, *1984 Annual Report.*

income has reflected a 12.4 percent growth rate. In 1984, selling, general, and administrative expenses totaled over $2 billion. Of this amount, approximately $5 million in salaries were paid to officers. The highest salaries were paid to Roberto C. Goizueta, the chief executive officer and chairman of the board, and Donald R. Keough, president and chief operating officer. These two officers earned approximately $1.7 million and $1.2 million in salaries, respectively.

Innovation/Research and Development

To maintain its number one position, Coke constantly introduced new products. In recent years this included New Coke, Cherry Coke, Diet Coke, Caffeine-Free Diet Coke, and Caffeine-Free TAB, among others. As Brian Dyson, Coca-Cola's USA president, said to assembled bottlers, "If there's a better product we'll make it . . . if there's a better way we'll find it."[1] In addition to new product development, the company also tried to improve the taste of existing products, like TAB, by using a blend of saccharin and aspartame to sweeten them.

Coke by 1984 had introduced many new drinks. It had come out with new Diet Fanta flavors such as orange, ginger ale, strawberry, grape, root beer, and cherry. All its Fanta products were caffeine free. Its new introduction, Cherry Coke, might result in the emergence of a new soft drink segment. Coke emphasized that its Cherry Coke was not aimed at the Dr Pepper market and that the product had its own light, smooth, and satisfying taste with a slight taste of cherry. This product was targeted at consumers in the 12- to 29-year-old age group. Other introductions included new Minute Maid Orange Soda, which contained 10 percent fruit juice, and a reformulation of Fresca by adding 1 percent grapefruit juice. These drinks were targeted at the growing health-conscious and juice-drinking segments. Fresca was being targeted at the over-25 age group and was being positioned as an alternative to other soft drinks and wine coolers.

Coca-Cola had developed a number of new distributing, vending, and packaging systems over the years. For example, in 1983, the company developed a compact, integrated, and self-contained beverage dispenser (BTS 150) which utilized patented syrup packages. This dispenser was designed for the large untapped office market.

[1]Anonymous. "Coke Foresees New Products, Innovation," *Beverage Industry* (July 1984), p. 1.

During 1985, it was working on the final stages of a futuristic computerized vending machine, which featured a video display screen, voice simulator, and coupon dispenser. When completed, this machine would offer a wide range of Coca-Cola soft drinks for varying container sizes and prices.

Coke always had stressed consumer convenience and had continuously introduced new ways of packaging its product. Examples include the 2-liter bottles and six-packs in plastic bottles, among others. In 1985, Coke was test marketing a 12-ounce plastic can that was made up of uncoated plastic (PET) with an aluminum end.

Human Resources/Personnel

Overall, the Coca-Cola Company and its subsidiaries employed more than 40,500 people. Of this total, 18,200 persons worked within the United States. The company contributed to various pension plans covering the majority of its employees in the United States, and certain foreign employees. Pension expenses incurred in 1984 for its present and retired employees were estimated to be about $36 million. The company also provided health care plans and life insurance benefits to most of its U.S. employees. It even provided health care benefits to most domestic employees who had retired after five or more years of service.

The company introduced a new and more attractive thrift plan for its employees in 1984. SODA, which stood for "Savings on Deferred Accounts," allowed employees to contribute up to 10 percent of their salaries while the company matched the first 3 percent of their salaries. Internal Revenue Service rulings permitted employees to contribute pretax dollars; this money could accumulate tax-free until the employee reached 59.5 years. Furthermore, employees could withdraw money from the plan at any time without penalty by declaring the withdrawn money in the present year as additional income.

Management

The Coca-Cola Company was headed by Robert Goizueta, chairman of the board and chief executive officer. Directly under him, as noted earlier, was Donald Keough, president and chief operating officer. These two top management officials had established (1) growth in annual earnings per share and (2) increased return on equity as the company's two main goals. The firm's various aggressive financial policies helped to support these goals by letting it exploit high-return opportunities.

Under Goizueta's leadership, Coca-Cola's management had followed an aggressive pricing policy combined with new product development to win back market share. It found that this new approach was necessary to respond to changing market conditions and increased competition. The company had changed from being a sleeping giant to an aggressive risk taker.

Goizueta established a guideline that each business segment must satisfy the 20 percent corporate rate of return on investment guideline. In accord with this guideline, the company sold its Wine Spectrum division which could not achieve this return on investment (ROI) level. According to Sergio Zyman, senior vice president of marketing, Coke had experienced a cultural revolution since Goizueta took over as chairman. As Zyman noted, "Before, if you were aggressive, you were out," while to-day, "if you're not aggressive, you're out."[2]

Coca-Cola management began taking a much tougher stance and had started to face competition in a head-on manner. Coca-Cola, which had never put its famous trademark on any other product, used it for the first time on its new product, Diet Coke. Goizueta said this was done because "we didn't have the Coca-Cola trademark on the fastest-growing segment [diet drink market] of the soft drink business."[3] Diet Coke benefited from this brand identification, which made it not only the largest-selling diet soft drink, but also the third largest-selling soft drink product.

International Operations

In its international operations, Coca-Cola Company's key objective was growth. To attract consumers to drink more of its products, Coke made its products more readily available and increased the product variety. The particular types of drinks that the company was targeting for international sales were low-calorie (in some developed countries such as Japan), lemon-lime, and others.

To increase consumption internationally, Coca-Cola tried to increase use of its products through vending machines and fountain outlets. The company had also in-creased the popularity of its products by offering larger package sizes, emphasizing their convenience and economy. The large amount of capital required by bottlers had prevented vending machines from becoming a major factor in penetrating interna-tional markets. Japan was one exception where vending machine sales were a large percentage, some 44 percent, of total company sales. Equipment investment was also a major factor in developing more fountain sales. Recent investments in equipment combined with effective merchandising and advertising had led to substantial gains in this area.

One key factor that contributed to international growth was a strong bottler net-work. In 1984, the company spent $100 million reconstructing its bottler system. Bottling facilities in Japan and Australia were sold to local operators while bottling fa-cilities in South England, which included London, were purchased. The company changed the management at these facilities and participated in ownership changes at other facilities. These changes were made to ensure commitment to its goal for inter-national growth.

In the low-calorie segment, Diet Coke had the most growth potential. Diet Coke's sales averaged 8 percent of Coca-Cola sales in international markets. Particu-lar markets where Diet Coke had been popular included Ireland, Australia, South Af-rica, and Japan. In these markets, Diet Coke sales were greater in volume than those of the primary brand of the company's largest competitor. In Japan, Diet Coke cap-tured 68 percent of the low-calorie carbonated soft drink segment.

Sprite was Coca-Cola's entry in the lemon-lime segment. The company started marketing this product aggressively, focusing on Argentina, the Philippines, and

[2]Thomas E. Ricks, "Coca-Cola's Tough New Ads Take Aim at the Competition," *The Wall Street Journal* July 26, 1984, p. 29.

[3]Eric Morgenthaler, "Diet Coke Is a Big Success in Early Going, Spurring A Gush of Optimism at Coca-Cola," *The Wall Street Journal* December 22, 1982, p. 17.

Mexico. Mexico was the company's second largest market by volume and through this aggressive marketing the company was able to increase Sprite sales volume there by 71 percent.

Coca-Cola sales were approximately 69 percent of the company's international volume. Coca-Cola was first made available in the Soviet Union in 1985, reaching a potential market of 275 million people. Sudan, Congo, and the German Democratic Republic were other possibilities for new markets.

THE SOFT DRINK INDUSTRY

The commercial sale of soda water first began in the United States in about 1806 by Benjamin Silliman. Initially, carbonated drinks were considered to have medicinal values. The industry made great progress with the introduction of the cork bottle cap which enabled carbonated soda to remain inside the bottle. Later, the Painter foot-operated machine allowed syruping, filling, and capping to be done simultaneously.

More recently, the soft drink industry had become a highly competitive one. Major competitors included Coca-Cola, Pepsi-Cola, Seven-Up, Dr Pepper, and Royal Crown Cola. Competitors in the industry included a wide variety of international, national, regional, and private-label producers.

The soft drink industry was influenced by the general economic outlook. Domestic sales increased as the U.S. economy experienced a growing economy in 1984 and 1985. Similarly, sales remained flat during the 1981–1983 recession. Soft drink sales were clearly related to per capita income. Still, the per capita consumption of soft drinks of 19.1 gallons in 1964 increased to 41.5 gallons in 1983 as shown in Exhibit 29.5. Soft drink industry sales were also subjected to seasonal fluctuations due to weather conditions, with higher sales coming in the warmer, summer months and lower sales recorded during colder, winter months.

The U.S. population had become very health conscious. As this trend continued, combined with the aging of the American population, the consumption of beer, wine, and spirits decreased, while the consumption of soft drinks increased. This trend was further accelerated by the raising of legal drinking ages in several states and the growing public sentiment against drunken driving.

Advertising played a major role in the soft drink industry. Soft drink manufacturers spent $367,300,000 collectively on advertising in 1984. Top media expenditures for regular soft drinks of major brands are shown in Exhibit 29.6. The selection of media use depended on a number of factors, including the product, its popularity, the age group at which it was being targeted, and whether it was a new or old product, among others. The amount spent on television promotions had increased in 1984 over the prior year. In 1984, spot advertisements increased 9 percent for regular drinks and 5 percent for diet drinks, whereas network advertisements increased 18.7 percent for regular drinks and 125.5 percent for diet drinks. Radio spot commercials were highly effective for targeting certain audiences such as teenagers and younger people who were devoted radio music listeners. The use of billboard advertising, on the other hand, had decreased in recent years.

Exhibit 29.5

U.S. LIQUID CONSUMPTION TRENDS (GALLONS PER CAPITA), 1964–1984E

	1964	1965	1966	1967	1968	1969	1970	1971	1972	1973	1974	1975	1976	1977	1978	1979	1980	1981	1982	1983	1984E
Soft drinks	19.1	20.3	22.3	23.5	24.8	25.9	27.0	28.6	30.1	31.5	31.4	31.0	33.7	35.9	37.1	38.1	38.8	39.5	40.1	41.5	43.2
Coffee*	38.8	37.8	37.4	37.0	37.0	36.2	35.7	35.3	35.2	35.1	33.8	33.0	29.4	28.0	27.0	29.2	28.7	28.5	27.8	27.0	27.3
Beer	15.9	15.9	16.5	16.8	17.3	17.8	18.5	19.2	19.7	20.5	21.3	21.6	21.8	22.5	23.1	23.8	24.5	24.7	24.4	24.3	24.0
Milk†	25.9	26.0	25.9	25.3	25.6	25.3	23.1	23.0	23.1	22.7	22.0	22.1	21.9	21.5	21.3	21.0	20.7	20.4	20.0	20.9	21.1
Juices	3.5	3.8	4.0	4.8	4.7	4.8	5.2	5.7	6.0	5.2	6.1	6.8	6.8	6.8	6.5	6.7	6.9	6.7	6.8	7.7	6.1
Tea*	6.3	6.3	6.3	6.4	6.6	6.6	6.5	6.7	6.8	7.2	7.3	7.3	7.4	7.7	7.7	7.6	7.3	7.5	7.5	7.2	7.3
Powdered drinks	—	—	—	—	—	—	—	—	—	—	—	4.8	5.5	5.9	6.1	6.0	6.0	6.0	6.0	6.5	6.3
Wine	1.0	1.0	1.0	1.0	1.1	1.2	1.3	1.5	1.6	1.7	1.7	1.7	1.7	1.8	2.1	2.2	2.3	2.3	2.3	2.4	2.5
Bottled water	—	—	—	—	—	—	—	1.1	—	—	—	1.2	1.2	1.3	1.4	1.5	1.6	1.9	2.2	2.7	3.0
Distilled spirits	1.4	1.5	1.6	1.6	1.7	1.8	1.8	1.9	1.9	1.9	2.0	2.0	2.0	2.0	2.0	2.0	2.0	2.0	1.9	1.8	1.8
Subtotal	111.9	112.6	115.0	116.4	118.8	119.6	119.1	123.0	124.4	125.8	125.6	131.5	131.4	133.4	134.3	138.1	138.8	139.5	139.0	142.0	144.6
Imputed water consumption‡	70.6	69.9	67.5	66.1	63.7	62.9	63.4	59.5	58.1	56.7	56.9	51.0	51.1	49.1	48.2	44.4	43.7	43.0	43.5	40.5	37.9
Total	182.5	182.5	182.5	182.5	182.5	182.5	182.5	182.5	182.5	182.5	182.5	182.5	182.5	182.5	182.5	182.5	182.5	182.5	182.5	182.5	182.5

*Coffee and tea data are based on a three-year moving average to counterbalance swings, hereby portraying consumption more realistically. Tea numbers have been restated to reflect this.

†Certain milk figures have been changed based on revisions to USDA data.

‡Includes all others.

Sources: USDA, DSI, MABO, ABWA, and Laidlaw Ansbacher Research estimates, 1985; and "Soft Drinks, Juices, Bottled Water Pace Gains," *Beverage Industry* (February 1985), p. 38. Copyright: John C. Maxwell *Beverage Industry.*

Exhibit 29.6

TOP MEDIA EXPENDITURES OF REGULAR SOFT DRINK BRANDS, 1985
(in thousands)

Product	Four-Media Total	Magazines	Network Television	Spot Television	Outdoor
Coca-Cola	$48,298.3	$252.9	$24,764.9	$20,647.4	$2,633.1
Pepsi-Cola	33,013.5	—	9,028.6	22,845.1	1,139.8
Sprite	23,161.7	72.4	15,399.6	7,669.5	20.0
Seven-Up	22,759.8	95.0	13,317.0	8,926.1	431.8
Canada Dry	9,004.9	—	4,534.9	4,510.0	—
Dr Pepper	8,321.7	—	2,433.5	5,685.8	202.4
Mountain Dew	7,772.9	—	558.3	7,191.7	22.9
Sunkist	4,438.1	—	138.9	4,292.9	6.3
A & W	4,348.7	—	2,273.3	2,075.4	—
Royal Crown	4,103.0	—	—	4,099.9	3.1

Source: Leading national advertisers broadcast advertiser's reports. Copyright *Beverage Industry,* July 1985.

SEGMENTATION

Research demonstrated that the soft drink industry was segmented into six categories on the basis of drink types. The six categories included cola drinks, lemon-lime drinks, pepper drinks, orange drinks, root beer drinks, and all other soft drinks. Among these groups, the cola category had always been the dominant segment. Its staggering 62.6 percent market share in 1981 increased to 63.2 percent in 1984. The market shares for cola and lemon-lime had remained fairly steady, while the pepper-type drinks had increased. The orange and root beer categories, however, had decreased from 1971 to 1984.

There were certain newly emerging segments. Squirt Company introduced Diet Squirt Plus in 1985, which became the first company to use 100 percent Nutra-Sweet in its diet drinks. This use was considered to be partially responsible for the tremendous increase in consumption of diet drinks. Diet Squirt Plus contained 50 percent of the recommended daily dosage of vitamin C and 10 percent of the daily dosage of five important B complex vitamins. In coming years, this new drink could possibly establish a new vitamin-fortified soft drink segment. Other emerging segments may be diet chocolate soda, cherry cola, and carbonated juice.

A more basic way of segmenting the soft drink industry was into full-calorie regular drinks and diet drinks. Back in 1980, diet drinks constituted only 12.8 percent of the market. Their sales rose, however, to 17.3 percent in 1983 and to 19.2 percent of the market by 1984. Their sales were further stimulated in 1984 by the introduction of NutraSweet and the increase in sales of Diet Coke. Thus, diet drinks were the newest and fastest-growing segment in the soft drink industry.

THREATS

One potential problem facing the soft drink industry was the Federal Trade Commission's complaint that the industry participants' exclusive territorial franchise agreements with their bottlers unnecessarily restricted competition. This complaint was still under review in mid-1985.

Another issue was the constant concern about whether the artificial sweeteners used in soft drinks caused cancer, this concern directed especially toward saccharin. The other widely used noncaloric sweetener, aspartame, had an alleged inability to remain stable at high temperatures. This problem caused some health concerns even though it received Food and Drug Administration approval in 1981.

The entrance of Procter & Gamble (P&G) as a small, yet potentially powerful competitor in the soft drink industry posed another threat to Coke. P&G, with 1984 sales of approximately $13 billion acquired Orange Crush for $55 million. P&G was also trying to buy the Lexington, Kentucky-based Coca-Cola Bottling Mideast, Inc., to learn more about how to bottle and distribute soft drinks. Coca-Cola had filed a restraining order to try to prevent this acquisition by its leading competitor. According to Brian Dyson, president of Coca-Cola USA, "The record indicates that they [P&G] have not entered the soft-drink industry in a casual way."[4] Senior Vice President Allen McCusker was even more vocal about the subject and said, "They [P&G] could be our biggest competitor."[5] There were speculations that since P&G did not possess a cola product, it might try to acquire Royal Crown Cola. This would provide it with a strong, well-established bottler network. Another possibility was that P&G might sell its product directly to the supermarkets without even going through bottlers. If successful, this change could have a major impact on the soft drink industry.

The growing sense of awareness against littering posed another potential threat to Coke and the industry. Several states had passed antilitter laws. Various studies had found that disposable package constituted a major portion of the litter. As a result, some states had passed or were considering laws against nonreturnable containers.

A final threat was the aging of the American population. The American population was growing older largely due to the fact that the population birth rate was slowing down, and medical facilities were improving for Americans of all ages. These trends had resulted in a reduction of the number of youths who were the major consumers of regular soft drinks products.

SUBSTITUTES

Soft drinks compete for the consumer dollar spent on all beverages. Major drinks and beverages consumed by the American population were soft drinks, water, coffee, beer, milk, fruit juice, tea, wine, distilled spirits, and others. Soft drinks experienced

[4]"Is P&G Thirsty for Some of Coke's Know-how?" *Business Week* May 30, 1983, p. 62.
[5]Ibid.

tremendous growth from a paltry 9.4 percent in 1960 to 25.5 percent of the beverage consumption in 1984. The overall consumption of beverages increased from 35,200,000,000 gallons in 1960 to 45.1 billion gallons in 1984. The beverage industry expected sales of beverages such as light beer, wine coolers, speciality coffees and teas, decaffeinated and flavored teas, rum, diet and caffeine-free soft drinks, and fruit juices to increase tremendously. The products that increased in popularity were the ones that catered to the largely health-conscious public. Out of the 483,000,000 gallons of increased consumption of soft drinks, 465,000,000 gallons were for diet drinks. Alcoholic beverage sales declined largely due to increased public opinion against alcohol abuse, drunk driving, and increased drinking age laws.

SUPPLIERS

A major material cost incurred by the soft drink industry was the sweetener. The major type of sweeteners used were sugar, high-fructose corn syrup (HFCS-55), saccharin, and aspartame. The increased consciousness among many consumers to be slim had resulted in the growing popularity of diet drinks utilizing noncaloric sweeteners, saccharin and aspartame. As noted earlier, aspartame was a low-caloric sweetening agent produced by a subsidiary of G. D. Searle & Company, the sole supplier of the product in the United States and many foreign countries. Sales of NutraSweet, the trade name for aspartame, had risen from $12 million in 1981 to $110 million in the first half of 1983 alone. Even though aspartame has received FDA approval, certain unanswered questions remained regarding its safety.

FDA proposed a ban against saccharin in 1977, but a congressional moratorium was applied to give further time for testing and researching whether the product was carcinogenic or not. The moratorium was again extended in April 1985. Thus far, this proposed ban seemed not to have had an effect on the sales of saccharin.

Sugar, another raw material utilized in manufacturing soft drinks, was purchased from numerous domestic and international sources and was subject to vast price fluctuations. A large number of major soft drink manufacturers, like the Coca-Cola Company, had been authorized to utilize 100 percent high-fructose corn syrup in their products.

Sugar was the major sweetener used by the soft drink industry to sweeten its products. Quotas on sugar imports resulted in artificially high prices for domestic sugar, causing soft drink manufacturers to switch from sugar to high-fructose corn syrup. With the increase in the consumption of diet drinks, it had resulted in the increased use of noncaloric sweeteners. By 1985, there were some other noncaloric sweeteners, such as Acesulfame K and left-handed sugars, which were awaiting FDA approval.

Another major material cost of the soft drink industry was packaging. The major types of packaging materials used in packaging soft drinks were plastic containers, aluminum cans, glass bottles, and aseptic paper packages. Greatest growth had been experienced by plastic containers, aluminum cans, and aseptic paper packages whereas glass containers application had steadily decreased.

BUYERS

In the soft drink industry, the buyers of the syrups and concentrates were bottlers and fountain wholesalers. Bottlers were the ones who subsequently manufactured the finished product, packaged it, and then sold it to retailers. Still, retailers were the primary customers of the bottlers and wholesalers, not the consumers. To ensure successful sales, the bottlers and wholesalers had to cultivate a positive relationship with their retailers.

Bottlers had broadened the use of various retail outlets to sell their soft drinks in recent years. In 1974, 53 percent of their soft drinks were sold through food stores, while in 1984 they sold 46.2 percent. This shift was a result of the increased competition in the soft drink industry, especially between Coke and Pepsi, which resulted in numerous products being introduced in the markets. This had further resulted in reduced shelf space being available in the supermarkets and food stores to any one soft drink manufacturer. All the bottlers were fighting to increase their sales by various methods, such as increased price discounting, promotions, and maintaining full shelves of their product to consumers in stores. To increase product availability, bottlers resorted to increased distribution through other retail outlets besides food stores. Other retail outlets included convenience stores and general merchandising stores, as well as vending machines.

Expressing market share as a percentage of soft drink sales through retail establishments, convenience stores increased their market share from 17.4 percent in 1974 to 19.6 percent in 1984; food stores decreased their market share from 53 percent in 1974 to 42.6 percent in 1984. An increasingly important success factor was to get the product to the consumers, wherever they wanted it. As the number of two-wage-earner families increased, it resulted in more frequent shopping for just a few items. This trend had resulted in increased soft drink sales through convenience stores and vending machines, where a customer could make a purchase very quickly.

Vending sales clearly were on the increase, a very profitable segment, since it did not include any promotional price discounting. In part, due to the new attractive machines that changed dollar bills, video displays, and voice simulators, sales through vending machines had increased 20–25 percent. Soft drink manufacturers developed minivending machines that dispensed three products for the largely untapped office market.

NEW PRODUCTS/MARKET OPPORTUNITIES

Coca-Cola had introduced new products such as diet drinks, caffeine-free drinks, and juice soda drinks aimed at the health- and diet-conscious market. In anticipation of this new market, Coke had introduced Diet Coke, Diet Sprite, Diet Fanta, Caffeine-Free Coca-Cola, Caffeine-Free Diet Coke, Caffeine-Free TAB, Sugar-Free Mr. PiBB, Sugar-Free Ramblin' Root Beer, Minute Maid Orange Soda, and new improved Fresca.

Other product opportunities that Coca-Cola could take advantage of were the multivitamin juices and multivitamin soda segments, following the lead of the successful introduction of Diet Squirt Plus. Coke started to take advantage of the growing carbonated juice drink market by introducing Minute Maid Orange Soda and new improved Fresca. The juice market in schools and health care institutions might prove to be a good opportunity for market development. This market could be served through recently developed minijuice vending machines. In addition, these mini-vending machines could be used to serve the growing office market.

Another product opportunity, apple-flavored sodas, were gaining tremendous popularity in Australia, Ireland, and most of Europe. Still another fast-growing segment, diet chocolate fudge soda, could capture a portion of the soft drink market and Coke could introduce another new product.

The international markets might provide tremendous opportunities for increasing soft drink sales, for Coca-Cola products had been doing extremely well internationally. Its international soft drink sales volume increased by 4 percent alone in 1984. To increase international sales further, the company was focusing on product availability and product variety. In 1985, Coca-Cola Company products will be available for the first time in Russia, Sudan, Congo, and the German Democratic Republic.

Other important domestic segments might be the black and Hispanic markets. The black population in the United States represented $140 billion in purchasing power, and the U.S. Hispanics represent $50–70 billion in purchasing power. Some marketing efforts in the 1980s were not spending all of their advertising dollars on campaigns designed to reach mass audiences but were being more selective and try-

Exhibit 29.7

SOFT DRINK MARKET SHARE, 1980–1984

	1980	1981	1982	1983	1984
Coca-Cola Co.					
Coca-Cola	24.3%	24.2%	23.9%	22.5%	21.8%
Diet Coke	—	—	0.3	3.2	5.1
Sprite	2.9	2.9	2.8	2.8	3.3
TAB	3.2	3.6	3.8	2.7	1.6
Fanta	1.7	1.5	1.3	1.1	1.6
Cafeeine-Free Diet Coke	—	—	—	0.5	1.0
Mello-Yello	0.8	0.9	0.8	0.6	0.9
Caffeine-Free Coke	—	—	—	0.5	0.6
Diet Sprite	—	—	0.4	0.3	0.5
Mr. PiBB	0.7	0.6	0.5	0.4	0.3
Caffeine-Free TAB	—	—	—	0.2	0.2
Fresca	0.4	0.4	0.3	0.2	0.1
Others	0.4	0.4	0.4	0.4	0.4
Total	34.4	34.5	34.5	35.3	36.4

Exhibit 29.7 (Cont.)

PepsiCo, Inc.					
Pepsi-Cola	17.9%	18.3%	18.1%	16.9%	17.0%
Mountain Dew	2.9	3.0	2.8	2.7	2.7
Diet Pepsi	2.6	2.9	2.9	2.4	2.9
Pepsi Free	—	—	—	1.5	1.4
Sugar-Free Pepsi Free	—	—	0.3	1.0	1.0
Pepsi Light	0.4	0.5	0.5	0.4	0.2
Teem	0.3	0.2	0.2	0.2	0.1
Others	0.3	0.2	0.2	0.2	0.3
Total	24.4	25.1	25.0	25.3	25.6
Seven-Up Co.					
Seven-Up	5.4	5.0	5.2	5.4	5.2
Diet Seven-Up	1.1	1.2	1.3	1.3	1.4
Like	—	—	0.3	0.4	0.3
Sugar-Free Like	—	—	—	0.1	0.1
Dixie Cola	0.2	0.1	0.1	0.1	—
Howdy Flavors	—	—	—	—	—
Total	6.7	6.3	6.9	7.3	7.0
Dr Pepper					
Dr Pepper	5.5	5.4	5.1	4.9	5.1
Sugar-Free Dr Pepper	1.2	1.3	1.3	1.1	1.0
Sugar-Free Pepper Free	—	—	—	0.2	0.1
Pepper Free	—	—	—	0.2	0.1
Welch's	0.5	0.5	0.5	0.5	0.4
Total	7.2	7.2	6.9	6.9	6.8
R. J. Reynolds' Canada Dry Corp.					
Ginger Ale	1.0	1.1	1.1	1.2	1.2
Club soda/seltzer	0.5	0.5	0.6	0.6	0.6
Tonic, Bitter Lemon	0.4	0.5	0.5	0.5	0.4
Barrelhead	0.3	0.2	0.2	0.2	0.1
Wink	0.2	0.1	0.1	—	—
Others	0.5	0.4	0.3	0.3	0.3
Total	2.9	2.8	2.8	2.8	2.6
Sunkist					
Sunkist	1.3	1.5	1.6	1.5	1.5
Diet Sunkist	—	0.1	0.3	0.3	0.2
Total	1.3	1.6	1.9	1.8	1.7

Source: Adapted from *Beverage Industry* (March 1985), p. 17–18.

ing to reach certain segments of the population in the most cost effective manner. Television advertising utilizing certain sitcoms, sport events, and other shows to reach certain targeted audiences had increased. Outdoor advertising was utilized to reach a particular segment of the population without the awareness of other segments. This medium was increasingly used by beverage marketers to reach the black and Hispanic markets.

In considering any product/market opportunity, the Coca-Cola Company should examine the existing soft drink companies, their product offerings, and market shares. Exhibit 29.7 does just this by providing market shares for each soft drink offered by the various manufacturers from 1980 through 1984. Studying these statistics and trends may provide support for whatever new products Coke might introduce.

COCA-COLA'S FUTURE

The Coca-Cola Company, the original inventor of cola drinks, obviously looked forward to a bright future. Facing more vigorous competition within the soft drink industry as a whole in recent years, still, it was the number one soft drink manufacturer in the world. On the other hand, the gains achieved by Pepsi-Cola in recent years were substantial. Just what Coca-Cola would do to counter this growing competitive challenge in coming years remained to be seen as 1985 came to an end.

30

FIDJI

In late 1985, Caroline Batty, age 29, had settled into her new job at L'Oréal. As a result of organizational changes, she had come from England in November 1984 to be product manager for Fidji, the first Guy Laroche perfume, offered for sale in 1966. Fidji had been one of the five leaders on the international perfume market during the 1970s, but sales volume had started to drop around 1980. Caroline felt the challenge of her new responsibilities in France, the hub of the fragrance industry, where she was to perform an in-depth audit of Fidji and recommend corrective strategy to her management. This included Isabelle Avril-Herbillon, recently appointed Guy Laroche marketing manager, Robert Salmon, international general manager of L'Oréal's Perfume and Beauty Division, and Claude Galinier-Warrain, vice president of L'Oréal and managing director of the division.

L'ORÉAL

Parfums Guy Laroche was part of L'Oréal's Perfume and Beauty Division. L'Oréal was the world's leading hair care and coloration products company, one of the largest

This case was prepared by Helen Chase Kimball, Research Associate, under the supervision of Christian Pinson, Associate Professor, INSEAD, as a basis for class discussion rather than to illustrate either effective or ineffective handling of an administrative situation.

cosmetics companies in the world and among the major pharmaceutical groups in France. L'Oréal's activities were divided into five major divisions: hairdresser products, consumer products, hygiene and comfort, pharmaceuticals, and perfume and beauty. The Perfume and Beauty Division consisted of Lancôme (men's and women's perfumes and skin care and makeup products), Jeanne Piaubert (skin care products), Biotherm (hair, face, skin, and sun products), Vichy (pharmacy-sold cosmetics and toiletries), Phas (skin care products), and other prestige perfume brands (e.g., Guy Laroche, Courrèges, Paloma Picasso, and Ralph Lauren).

There were five Guy Laroche perfume products: Fidji, J'ai Osé, and Eau Folle

Exhibit 30.1

GUY LAROCHE PRODUCT LINE

	OLFACTORY MESSAGE	OLFACTORY FAMILY	ADVERTISING MESSAGE
fidji 1966	Refined Exoticism, Escape, Travel. *Ardent. Subtle. Feminine.*	Floral Major Ingredients: Rose, Jasmine, Spices.	Sweetness, femininity, romanticism and always that invitation to escape. *"A woman is an island. Fidji is her perfume."*
Osé 1977	Sensuality for the woman who is not satisfied just keeping up with fashion, so creates it.	Spice (Oriental Chypre Accent) Major Ingredients: Myrthe, Ylang-Ylang, Amber	The woman who fascinates and inspires dreams, she is both beautiful and distant. *"Tender and wild like her perfume."*
eaufolle 1970	Freshness, Humor, Gaiety. *Fresh. Young. Sparkling.*	Fresh. Major Ingredients: Hesperidins, Moss, Wood, Honeysuckle.	A wild, sparkling world full of life, gaiety and fun.
DRAKKAR 1972	Candor, Escape and Wide Open Spaces. *Bold. Frank. Lingering.*	Fresh. Major Ingredients: Galbanum, Wood, Spices.	DRAKKAR was created to reveal the independent exuberant and natural side of a man. *"The calm strength of a man's perfume."*
DRAKKAR NOIR 1982	A modern and powerful accord, it will seduce the man who likes fashion but remains determinedly masculine. *Charmer. A bit Cocky. Present.*	Chypre. Major Ingredients: Lavender, Hesperidins, Spices, Wood, Oakmoss.	The charm and presence of a modern and virile perfume. *"The sweet violence of a man's perfume."*

Source: Company Records.

for women and Drakkar and Drakkar Noir for men (Exhibit 30.1). In 1984, world sales of Guy Laroche perfumes amounted to 655.3 million FF, compared with Groupe L'Oréal's consolidated revenues of 15.8 billion FF and 4.2 billion FF for the Perfume and Beauty Division (Exhibit 30.2). Exhibit 30.3 gives a breakdown of Fidji sales figures by country for the 1977/79–1984 period. Early figures were unavailable due to frequent organizational changes, management mobility, and modified accounting systems over the years as well as L'Oréal's corporate culture, geared to oral rather than written communication.

THE FRAGRANCE INDUSTRY

Estimates varied widely but the world prestige women's fragrance market amounted to approximately $2–3 billion. The fragrance market consisted of a few large leading

Exhibit 30.2

ESTIMATED WORLD AND FRENCH SALES
PERFUME AND BEAUTY DIVISION (P&B) AND GUY LAROCHE (G.L.) PRODUCTS, 1966–1984

YEAR	FRANCE (million FF)			WORLD (million FF)						
	G.L.	Fidji	Other	P&B Division	G.L.	Fidji	J'ai Osé*	Drakkar†	Drakkar‡ Noir	Other§
1966	0.7	0.7			2.4	2.4				
1967	1.5	1.5			8.3	8.3				
1968	2.5	2.0	0.5		13.6	11.4				2.2
1969	3.9	3.2	0.7		17.4	14.8				2.6
1970	5.9	4.5	1.4	161.1	25.3	21.3				4.0
1971	7.8	4.0	3.8	179.6	32.4	22.8				9.6
1972	10.5	5.6	4.9	220.7	45.8	33.0		N.A.		N.A.
1973	13.1	7.1	6.0	360.0	56.6	36.3		N.A.		N.A.
1974	18.1	9.8	8.3	460.5	84.8	53.0		N.A.		N.A.
1975	22.2	12.3	9.9	535.2	102.2	65.3		N.A.		N.A.
1976	26.2	14.9	11.3	617.2	132.3	85.0		N.A.		N.A.
1977	36.5	17.9	18.6	875.3	198.1	125.0	N.A.	N.A.		N.A.
1978	44.8	20.1	24.7	1,143.1	300.0	160.0	N.A.	N.A.		N.A.
1979	48.1	24.9	23.2	1,230.2	340.5	219.2	63.8	46.0		11.5
1980	54.9	28.1	26.8	1,858.8	379.2	239.3	70.6	54.7		14.6
1981	61.3	35.1	26.2	2,096.3	416.1	263.0	73.3	62.6		17.2
1982	82.2	42.2	40.0	2,309.0	460.8	283.1	72.2	43.5	46.5	15.5
1983	91.1	42.0	49.1	3,198.0	520.2	298.9	73.6	41.7	92.7	13.3
1984	107.8	47.7	60.1	4,213.0	655.3	298.3	70.5	40.0	235.1	11.4

*Launched in 1977.
†Launched in 1972.
‡Launched in 1982.
§Douceline (1968); Eau Folle (1970).
N.A. = Not available.

Source: Company Records.

Exhibit 30.3

FIDJI SALES IN FRANCS, 1977–1984, AND UNITS, 1979–1984

A. BREAKDOWN OF FIDJI SALES (million FF),* 1977–1984

Country	1977	1978	1979	1980	1981	1982	1983	1984
France	17.93	20.10	24.93	28.08	35.06	42.19	42.01	47.72
Italy	11.57	15.37	13.44	18.12	22.72	23.05	23.49	25.80
England	10.39	12.60	14.64	17.66	20.30	21.29	29.38	28.43
Belgium	2.94	3.36	4.78	5.32	5.46	5.47	4.81	5.10
Spain	2.22	3.90	4.16	4.86	5.70	7.82	8.83	8.35
West Germany	13.84	14.67	15.11	14.28	18.36	18.87	16.60	16.71
Netherlands	5.90	6.88	8.25	8.68	9.25	6.73	6.17	6.13
Austria	1.80	1.82	2.81	2.46	2.58	2.91	2.32	2.15
Switzerland	2.09	2.04	2.65	2.83	2.45	2.48	2.45	2.55
Scandinavian countries†	1.54	2.00	2.04	2.74	3.18	3.30	3.87	4.44
Total Europe	70.22	82.74	92.81	105.03	125.06	134.11	139.93	147.38
United States	13.90	17.68	8.34	17.28	16.97	25.0	30.70	25.90
Rest of world‡	40.91	59.40	118.00	117.00	121.00	124.00	128.30	125.00
Total world	125.03	159.82	219.15	239.31	263.03	283.11	298.93	298.28

*Pre-1979 figures are gross; 1979–1984 figures are net (including all discounts, adjustments, etc.).
†Pre-1979 = Denmark, Sweden, Finland, and Norway. 1979–1984 = Denmark, Sweden, and Finland.
‡Rest of world: pre-1979 = Canada, Mexico, and P.B.I. (Parfum Beauté International).
Source: Company records.

B. BREAKDOWN OF FIDJI SALES (thousand units),* 1979–1984

Country	1979	1980	1981	1982	1983	1984
France	800	840	909	920	736	754
Italy	618	782	834	709	590	435
England	410	520	540	700	794	689
Belgium	159	159	167	136	130	107
Spain	144	161	205	250	340	272
West Germany	547	512	589	575	467	511
Netherlands	401	368	384	233	207	179
Austria	75	79	80	80	75	72
Switzerland	64	70	70	60	57	54
Scandinavian countries†	147	169	152	129	134	143
Total Europe	3,365	3,660	3,930	3,792	3,530	3,216
United States	N.A.	N.A.	N.A.	N.A.	N.A.	250
Rest of world	3,170	3,620	2,800	2,260	2,300	1,750
Total world	6,535	7,280	6,730	6,052	5,830	5,216

*A unit was any article (bottle, jar, atomizer, vaporizer, etc.) regardless of size.
†Scandinavian countries: Denmark, Sweden, and Finland.
N.A. = Not available.
Source: Company records.

suppliers and numerous small and medium-sized businesses. The leading prestige brand fragrance companies on the French and European markets are given in Exhibit 30.4.

Fragrances were produced in varying concentrations of alcohol, distilled water, and essence, resulting in different generic products. An essence was a substance, or essential oil, that kept in concentrated form the fragrance of the plant or animal from which it was extracted. The grade, or dilution, of alcohol used also varied. (See Exhibit 30.5.)

A tax distinction existed in France between "derived" and "nonderived" product lines. Derived product lines included or were "derived from" an extract. "Nonderived" product lines did not include an extract. The value added tax was substantially higher for derived product lines (33.3 percent of retail price) than for nonderived product lines (18.6 percent). Soft perfumes had been developed in recent years both to avoid the higher French tax and to meet the demands of a consumer trend toward stronger, headier scents. According to Robert Salmon,

---

Exhibit 30.4

LEADING PRESTIGE WOMEN'S FRAGRANCE COMPANIES: EUROPE AND FRANCE, 1976–1984

A. LEADING PRESTIGE WOMEN'S FRAGRANCE COMPANIES— EUROPE,* MARKET SHARES, 1976–1984 AND 1984 SALES (million FF)

Company	1976 MS	1979 MS	1982 MS	1984 MS	1984 Sales
1. Yves Saint Laurent	4.1%	7.1%	8.3%	10.6%	457.20
2. Chanel	5.3	5.6	6.6	7.5	322.89
3. Estée Lauder	6.0	7.1	7.2	6.4	276.52
4. Cacharel	—	2.2	4.9	5.8	248.69
5. Rochas	6.6	6.1	5.0	5.2	223.96
6. Lancôme	5.4	5.2	5.5	5.1	217.44
7. Christian Dior	6.7	5.4	5.1	4.9	212.63
8. Guerlain	6.0	5.2	4.8	4.7	203.35
9. Nina Ricci	4.7	4.2	5.1	4.7	200.26
10. Guy Laroche	4.5	5.7	5.1	4.1	176.56
11. Lagerfeld	1.3	1.3	2.1	3.0	128.47
12. Givenchy	2.0	2.1	2.1	2.8	118.16
13. Hermès	3.3	3.0	2.6	2.6	111.98
14. Lanvin	1.8	1.8	2.1	2.0	86.22
15. Armani	—	—	1.0	1.6	11.50
16. Van Cleef & Arpels	0.5	1.1	1.4	1.5	64.23
Total 16 leaders	58.2%	63.1%	68.9%	72.5%	3,116.58
Total prestige women's fragrances (selective market)	100.0%	100.0%	100.0%	100.0%	4,297.32

MS = Market share.
*France, Germany, Britain, Italy, Spain, and Switzerland.
Source: Company records.

Exhibit 30.4 (Cont.)

B. LEADING PRESTIGE WOMEN'S FRAGRANCE COMPANIES— FRANCE, SALES* (million FF) AND MARKET SHARES, 1976–1984

	1976		1979		1982		1983		1984	
Company	Sales	MS	Sales	MS	Sales	MS	Sales	MS	Sales	MS
1. Y.S.L.	18.0	3.3	56.0	6.6	105.5	7.6	153.5	9.4	184.0	9.7
2. Chanel	27.5	5.1	44.0	5.2	90.5	6.4	101.0	6.2	138.0	7.2
3. Guerlain	41.5	7.7	55.0	6.5	90.5	6.4	106.0	6.5	120.0	6.3
4. Dior	40.0	7.4	51.0	6.1	81.0	5.8	97.0	5.9	105.0	5.5
5. N. Ricci	31.5	5.8	43.5	5.2	82.5	5.9	92.5	5.7	98.5	5.2
6. Rochas	32.0	5.9	45.5	5.4	67.5	4.8	81.5	5.0	97.5	5.1
7. Lancôme	30.0	5.5	39.0	4.6	82.0	5.8	91.5	5.6	93.0	4.9
8. Cacharal	—	—	21.5	2.6	48.0	3.4	64.0	3.9	80.0	4.2
9. G. Laroche	19.5	3.6	40.0	4.7	67.0	4.8	67.0	4.1	70.5	3.7
10. Hermès	22.0	4.1	31.0	3.7	47.5	3.4	58.5	3.6	69.0	3.6
11. Givenchy	10.5	1.9	18.0	2.1	32.0	2.3	35.0	2.1	54.0	2.8
12. Lanvin	17.0	3.1	27.0	3.2	39.0	2.8	46.5	2.8	52.0	2.7
Total	289.5	53.5	471.5	56.0	833.0	59.3	994.0	60.8	1,161.5	61.0

*Sales data cover extracts, eaux de toilette, and perfumed product lines.

Source: Company records.

Exhibit 30.5

BASIC FRAGRANCE CATEGORIES

Product	Concentration of Essence	Grade of Alcohol
Perfume or "extract"	15–30%	90–95°
Soft perfume*	8–15%	80–90°
"Eau de toilette"	4–8%	About 80°
Cologne or "eau de cologne"	3–5%	About 70°
"Eau fraiche"	About 3%	About 80°
Splash cologne	1–3%	About 80°

*Includes "parfum de toilette," "eau de parfum," and "esprit de parfum."

Source: The Haarmann & Reimer Book of Perfume (London: Johnson, 1984).

In 1966, when Fidji was launched, the concentrations were very weak by today's standards: the eau de toilette was 3 percent and the extract 15 percent. The standard criteria today are closer to 10 percent for eau de toilette and 25 percent for extracts.

The number of women using perfuming products was increasing in Europe. Penetration rates ranged from 60 percent in West Germany to 85 percent in France. In the

United States it exceeded 90 percent. The Japanese perfume market was only in the early stages of development: although 80 percent of Japanese women owned a perfume, only 3–4 percent of them actually used the product. Between 1965 and 1980, the proportion of French women using eaux de toilette, in all age brackets, increased from 14 percent to 73 percent while those using colognes dropped from 80 percent to 44 percent. Perfume extract was becoming an elite product: its penetration rate in France had dropped from 30 percent in 1965 to 19 percent in 1980.

FRAGRANCE FAMILIES AND TRENDS

The perfumes on the market in 1985 were associated not only with traditional perfumers (e.g., Guerlain, Molinard, Houbigant) and fashion designers (Chanel, Dior, Yves Saint Laurent) but also with cosmetics firms (Estée Lauder, Helena Rubinstein, Revlon), jewelers (Cartier, Van Cleef & Arpels), luxury leather goods companies (Hermès, Gucci), and even more recently, celebrities (Paloma Picasso, Catherine Deneuve). Although there were still perfume companies that developed their perfume formulas in-house, most resorted to outside firms specializing in fragrance and flavor development.

A prestige perfume could consist of more than 100 ingredients, all with different characters and properties. The essential oils in fragrance formulas were obtained from plants, animals, or chemistry. Since the 1920s the number of fragrances has increased rapidly with the development of synthetic fragrance substances. Not all natural products could be replaced synthetically, however, since most natural blossom and plant oils are extremely complex. Olfactory stimulation is so subjective that a breakdown of fragrances into families was difficult. One of the most respected classifications of women's prestige fragrances is given in Exhibit 30.6. Jean-Pierre Houri, president and managing director of Naarden France (a leading perfume development company) pointed out: "There is no perfect perfume classification. Differences in classifications result from perfumer biases where one element of the formula may be favored over another in the recognition and classification of perfumes."

Fidji was generally classified as a green floral perfume. To quote Jean-Pierre Houri: "For perfumers, Fidji is a L'Air du Temps with a bit of a green note. Charlie and Darling[1] are products that are similar. . . ."

Since the turn of the century there had been a continuous, wavelike movement in perfume trends, vacillating between light and heavy scents (Exhibit 30.7). Naarden felt that current world trends favored semiorientals and chypres. Another trend was to perfumes with provocative, disputatious names like Calvin Klein's Obsession, Matchabelli's Decadence, and Dior's Poison.[2]

In 1985, the best-selling perfumes in the world reportedly included Opium, Chanel N° 5, Anaïs Anaïs, L'Air du Temps, Chloé, Youth Dew, White Linen, Giorgio, Oscar de la Renta, and Shalimar, but exact world sales figures and ranking were not available. Figures on the 1984 best-selling prestige women's fragrances in France

---

[1]Darling was a comparatively high-priced mass market eau de toilette introduced by Elida Gibbs.

[2]Poison could not be classified in a single perfume family but was described as somewhat floral, somewhat oriental and fruity.

Exhibit 30.6

HAARMANN & REIMER GENEALOGY OF PERFUMES

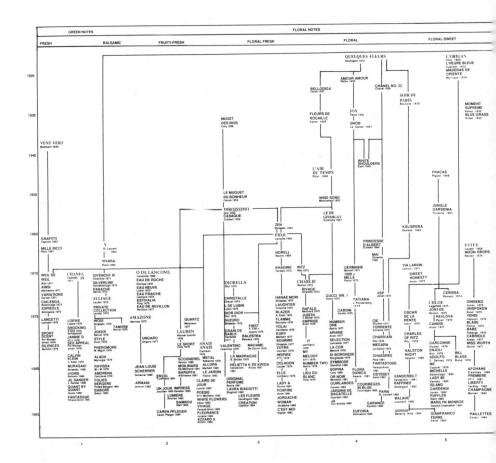

Exhibit 30.6 (Cont.)

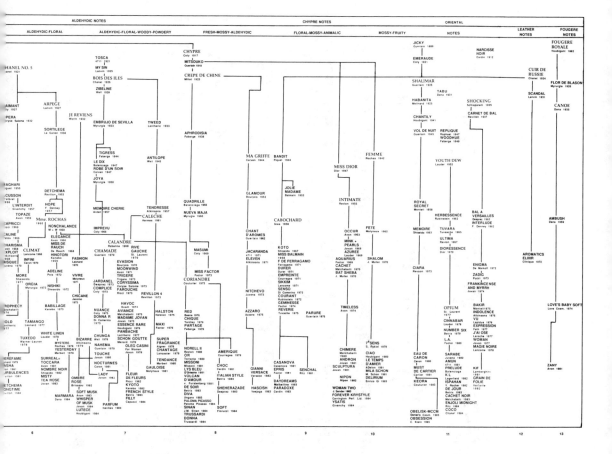

Alphabetic index

The position on the chart is indicated by
Year of appearance
Number of the field in
which the perfume appears

Name	Brand	Position
Adeline	Pola	1972/6
Adolfo	F. Denney	1978/5
Afghane	D'Estrees	1980/5
Ainsi	Atkinsons	1971/1
Alada	Myrurgia	1979/1
Alliage	Lauder	1972/1
Allora	Marbert	1982/2
Amazone	Hermès	1975/2
Ambush	Dana	1959/13
Amérique	Corrèges	1979/8
Amorena	Cantilène Cos.	1979/1
Amour Amour	Patou	1925/4
Amün	4711	1981/11
Anais Anais	Cacharel	1979/2-3
Andron	Jovan	1981/9
An Orig. Perfume	Boots	1981/3
Antilope	Weil	1945/7
Aphrodisia	Fabergé	1938/8
Aquarius	Factor	1969/9
Ariane	Avon	1977/4
Armani	Armani	1982/2
Arpège	Lanvin	1927/6
Aromatics Elixir	Clinique	1972/12
Aviance	Matchabelli	1975/7
Azurée	Lauder	1969/9
Azzaro	Azzaro	1975/8
Azzaro 9	Azzaro	1984/2
Babe	Fabergé	1976/5
Babillage	Kanebo	1973/6
Baghari	Piguet	1950/6
Bakir	G. Monteil	1975/11
Balahé	Leonard	1983/5
Bal à Versailles	Desprez	1962/11
Balestra	R. Balestra	1978/3
Bambou	Weil	1984/2
Bandit	Piguet	1944/9
Baboré	Babor	1983/1
Baruffa	Atkinsons	1981/2
Bat Sheba	J. Muller	1970/9
Bellodgia	Caron	1927/4
Bill Blass	B. Blass	1978/5
Bizarre	Atkinsons	1979/6-7
Blasé	Factor	1975/5
Blazer	A. Klein	1976/3
Blue Grass	Arden	1935/5
Bois des Îles	Chanel	1926/7
Cabochard	Grès	1958/9
Cabriole	Arden	1977/5
Cachet	Matchabelli	1970/9
Chachet Noir	Matchabelli	1983/11
Calandre	Rabanne	1968/7
Calèche	Hermès	1961/7
Câline	Patou	1966/6
Calvin Klein	C. Klein	1978/1
Canoe	Dana	1935/13
Candid	Avon	1977/5
Capricci	Nina Ricci	1960/6
Caren Pfleger	Caren Pfleger	1984/2
Cardin	P. Cardin	1976/4
Carnet du Bal	Revillon	1937/11
Casanova	Casanova	1981/9
Casaque	D'Albret	1956/3
Celadon	Lauder	1978/3
Cerissa	Revson	1974/5
C'est moi	Aigner	1983/3
Chamade	Guerlain	1970/7
Champagne	Monteil	1983/5
Chanel No. 5	Chanel	1921/6
Chanel No. 19	Chanel	1971/1
Chanel No. 22	Chanel	1926/4
Chantage	Lancaster	1979/7
Cant d'Arômes	Guerlain	1962/8
Chantilly	Houbigant	1941/11
Charisma	Avon	1968/6
Charivari	Ritz	1978/4
Charles of the Ritz	Ritz	1978/5
Charlie	Revlon	1973/3-4
Chassres	Pola	1981/4
Chicane	Jacomo	1973/6-7
Chimère	Matchabelli	1980/9
Chique	Yardley	1976/8
Chloé	Lagerfeld	1975/5
Choc	Cardin	1981/8
Chunga	Weil	1978/7
Chypre	Coty	1917/8
Cialenga	Balenciaga	1973/1
Ciao	Houbigant	1981/10
Clara	Revson	1973/11
Cie	Shulton	1977/4
Cinnabar	Lauder	1978/11
Clair de Jour	Lanvin	1983/2
Climat	Lancôme	1968/6
Coco	Chanel	1984/11
Complice	Coty	1973/7
Coriandre	Couturier	1973/7-8
Coryssima	Coryse Salomé	1973/7
Courant	Rubinstein	1972/9
Courrèges in blue	Courrèges	1983/4
Creation	Lapidus	1984/3
Cristalle	Chanel	1974/3
Crêpe de Chine	Millot	1925/8
Cuir de Russie	Chanel	1924/12
Daydreams	Maybelline	1983/9
De Jour	Betrix	1983/11
De Soir	Betrix	1983/8
Delirium	Enrico Gi	1983/10
Detchema	Revillon	1953/6
Detchema Longtime	Revillon	1984/6
Di Borghese	Borghese	1978/4
Dior Dior	Dior	1976/3
Diorella	Dior	1972/3
Dioressence	Dior	1970/11
Diorissimo	Dior	1956/3
Diva	Ungaro	1983/8
Donna R.	R. di Camerino	1975/7
Durer	Durer	1971/9
Eau de Caron	Caron	1980/11
Eau de Roche	Rochas	1970/2
Eau de Revillon	Revillon	1977/2
Eau Fraiche	Leonard	1974/2
Eau Neuve	Lubin	1972/2
Écusson	D'Albret	1956/6
Elégance	Avon	1066/6
Eleven	Atkinsons	1971/8
Elle	Lenthéric	1979/3
Embrujo de Sevilla	Myrurgia	1933/7
Emeraude	Coty	1921/11
Empreinte	Courrèges	1971/9
Emprise	Avon	1976/3-4
Enjoli	Ritz	1978/5
Enjoli Midnight	Ritz	1984/11
Enigma	De Markoff	1972/11
Envol	Lapidus	1980/2
Epris	Factor	1981/9
Espiègle	Atkinsons	1973/1
Essence rare	Houbigant	1976/7
Estée Super	Lauder	1969/5
Estivalia	Puig	1975/2
ESP	Yardley	1983/7
Euforia	Atkinsons	1985/4
Evasion	Bourjois	1970/7
Exploit	Atkinsons	1968/6
Expression	Fath	1977/11
F de Ferragamo	Ferragamo	1971/9
Fantasque	Féraud → Avon	1981/4
Farouche	Nina Ricci	1973/7
Fashion	Leonard	1970/6-7
Femme	Rochas	1942/10
Fête	Molyneux	1962/10
Fidji	Laroche	1966/3
Filly	Capucci	1984/7
First	v.Cleef&Arpels	1976/3
Flamme	Bourjois	1976/3
Fleur de Fleurs	Ricci	1982/7
Fleurance	Juvena	1984/2
Fleurs de Rocaille	Caron	1935/4
Flor de Blason	Myrurgia	1926/13
Flora Danica	Swank	1967/5
Folies Bergère	Folies Bergère	1981/1
Forever Krystle	Carrington Perf. Ltd.	1984/9
Fougère Royale	Houbigant	1982/13
Foxfire	Avon	1981/3
Fracas	Piguet	1948/5
Frankincence+Myrrh	Jovan	1974/11
French Style	Betrix	1983/7
Garance	Kanebo	1984/4
Garconne	Illuster	1978/5
Gauloise	Molyneux	1981/7
Geminesse	Factor	1974/9
Germaine	Monteil	1971/4
Gianfranco Ferre	Ferre	1984/5
Gianni Versace	Versace	1982/8
Ginseng	Jovan	1975/5
Giorgio	Beverly Hills	1984/5
Givenchy III	Givenchy	1971/1
Glamour	Bourjois	1953/8
Gold	Lenthéric	1977/6
Graffiti	Capucci	1963/1
Grain de Folie	Verfaillie	1982/11
Grain de Sable	Verfaillie	1977/3
Gucci No. 1	Gucci	1974/4
Guirlandes	Carven	1982/4
Habanita	Molinard	1934/11
Halston	Halston	1975/7
Halston Night	Halston	1980/5
Hanae Mori	Shiseido	1975/3
Hascish	Veejaga	1983/8
Havoc	Quant	1974/7
Helietta Caracciolo	Caracciolo	1981/3
Herbessence	Rubinstein	1962/11
Hinotori	Kanebo	1969/6
Hope	F. Denney	1957/6
Impress	Kanebo	1983/2
Imprévu	Coty	1966/7
Indolence	Atkinsons	1976/11
Infini	Caron	1970/6
Inoui	Shiseido	1976/1
Inspiré	4711	1978/3
Interlude	F. Denney	1962/11
Intimate	Revlon	1955/9
Island Gardenia	Jovan	1982/5
Ispahan	Y. Rocher	1982/11
It	Lenthéric	1978/3-4
Italian Style	Betrix	1983/8
Ivoire	Balmain	1980/1
JA	Jun Ashida	1983/4
Jacaranda	4711	1971/8
J'ai osé	Laroche	1977/11
Janine D.	4711	1976/1
Jardanel	Desprez	1973/7
Jardins de Bagatelle	Guerlain	1983/4
Jean Louis Scherrer	Scherrer	1980/2
Je Reviens	Worth	1932/6-7
Jicky	Guerlain	1889/11
Jil Sander	J. Sander	1980/1
Joker	Nerval	1978/1
Jontue	Revlon	1975/6
Jolie Madame	Balmain	1953/9
Jurdache Woman	Jordache	1983/3
Joy	Patou	1935/4
Joya	Myrurgia	1950/7
Judith	J. Muller	1975/3-4
Jungle Gardenia	Tuvaché	1957/5
Kalispera	Desses	1962/5
K de Krizia	Krizia	1981/3
Kéora	Couturier	1983/11
Khadine	Yardley	1972/3
Kif	Lamborghini	1981/11
Kiry	Marbert	1975/9
KL	Lagerfeld	1982/11
Koto	Shiseido	1967/9
Kyoto	Kanebo	1982/7
L de Lubin	Lubin	1975/3
L. A.	Factor	1980/11
La Cor	Menard	1978/4
L'Aimant	Coty	1927/6
L'Air du Temps	Nina Ricci	1948/4
Lady	Joran	1983/7
Lady A	Alcina	1981/3
Lady 80	Kanebo	1980/5
La Madrague	B. Bardot	1979/3
Lancetti	Lancetti	1976/1
Laughter	Tuvaché	1975/3
Laura Biagiotti	Biagiotti	1982/3
Lauren	Warner-Lauren	1978/2
Le Dix	Balenciaga	1947/1
Le de Givenchy	Givenchy	1957/4
Le Muguet du Bonheur	Caron	1952/3
Le Jardin	Factor	1982/2
Les Fleurs	Houbigant	1983/3
Le Sport	Coty	1979/2
Le Temps d'Aimer	A. Delon	1981/10
Le Heure Bleue	Guerlain	1912/5
Liberty	Yardley	1982/5
Lieu du blanc	Pola	1979/3-4
L'Interdit	Givenchy	1957/6
L'Origan	Coty	1905/5
Loewe	Loewe	1976/1
Love's Baby Soft	Love Cosm.	1974/13
Lumiere	Rochas	1984/2
Lutèce	Houbigant	1984/6
Lys Bleu	Prince d'Orleans	1981/8
Madame de Carven	Carven	1979/3
Madame Jovan	Jovan	1975/7
Madame Rochas	Rochas	1960/6
Maderas de Oriente	Myrurgia	1918/5
Mademoiselle Ricci	Nina Ricci	1967/1

Name	House	Date
Magie noire	Lancôme	1978/11
Ma Griffe	Carven	1944/8
Mai	Shiseido	1968/4
Marilyn Monroe	Colorkit Cosm.	1983/5
Marmara	Dana	1984/6
Masumi	Coty	1969/8
Maxi	Factor	1976/7
Me	Coparel	1978/5
Megara	Le Galion	1978/4
Mémoire	Shiseido	1963/11
Mémoire Cherie	Arden	1957/7
Mérefame	Menard	1979/6
Metal	Rabanne	1979/2·3
Michelle	Balenciaga	1980/5
Mila Schön	M. Schön	1981/10
Mille = 1000	Patou	1973/4
Mink + Pearls	Jovan	1968/9
Miss Balmain	Balmain	1968/9
Miss de Rauch	M. de Rauch	1968/6
Miss Dior,	Dior	1947/9
Miss Factor	Factor	1973/8
Miss Worth	Worth	1977/5
Missoni	Missoni	1981/6
Misty Tea Rose	Jovan	1983/6
Mitsouko	Guerlain	1916/8
Molinard de Molinard	Molinard	1981/2
Moment Suprême	Patou	1933/5
Moon Drops	Revlon	1970/5
Moonwind	Avon	1971/7
More	Shiseido	1971/6
Muguet des Bois	Coty	1936/3
Murasaki	Shiseido	1980/1
Must de Cartier	Cartier	1981/11
My Melody	4711	1979/3·4
My Sin	Lanvin	1925/7
Mystère	Rochas	1978/6
Nahéma	Guerlain	1979/7
Narcisse noir	Caron	1912/11
Nipon	Nipon	1982/9
Nishiki	Shiseido	1973/6
Nitchevo	Juvena	1973/8
Nocturnes	Caron	1981/7
Nombre noir	Shiseido	1982/6
Nonchalance	Maurer + Wirtz	1960/1
Norell	Revlon	1969/3
Norell 2	Revlon	1980/8
Nuance	Coty	1975/7
Nueva Maja	Myrurgia	1960/8
Number one	Betrix	1977/4
Number six	Betrix	1979/11
Number two	Betrix	1978/3·4
Obelisk-MCM	Daniel's Cosm.	1985/11
Obsession	C. Klein	1985/11
Occur	Avon	1963/9
Ô De Lancôme	Lancôme	1969/2
Odyssey	Avon	1981/4
Oleg Cassini for women	Cassini	1978/7
Ombre Rose	Brosseau	1982/6
Opéra	Coryse Salomé	1932/6
Opium	Yves St.Laurent	1977/11
Orgia	Myrurgia	1973/6
Oscar de la Renta	Stern	1976/5
Or	Torrente	1981/8
Or Noir	Morabito	1981/4
Paillettes	Coveri	1984/5
Panache	Lenthéric	1977/7
Panache	Nerval	1972/1
Partage	Fabergé	1979/8
Paradoxe	Cardin	1983/9
Paris	Yves St.Laurent	1983/4
Parfum	Hermès	1984/7
Paloma Picasso	P. Picasso	1984/8
Parure	Guerlain	1975/9
Pavlova	Payot	1976/5
Phéromone	Miglon	1978/1
Poesie	4711	1983/2
Prelude	Balenciaga	1982/11
Première	4711	1981/5
Princess D'Albret	D'Albret	1964/4
Private Collection	Lauder	1973/1
Prophecy	Matchabelli	1974/6
Quadrille	Balenciaga	1955/8
Quant	Quant	1980/1
Quartz	Molyneux	1977/2
Quelques Fleurs	Houbigant	1912/4
Rafale	Molinard	1975/3·4
Raffinée	Houbigant	1982/4·5
Ravissa	Maurer + Wirtz	1979/1
Red	G. Beene	1976/8
Replique	Raphael	1947/11
Revérie	Tuvache	1975/9
Revillon 4	Revillon	1973/7
Risqué	Juvena	1970/6
Ritz	Ritz	1972/3
Rivage	Shiseido	1974/3·4
Rive Gauche	Yves St.Laurent	1970/7
Robe d'un Soir	Carven	1947/7
Royal Secret	Monteil	1958/11
Ruffles	Stern	1983/5
Sarabé	Juvena	1980/11
Scandal	Lanvin	1931/12
Schön Goutte	Menard	1978/7
Scoundrel	Revlon	1980/2
Sculptura	Jovan	1981/9
Selection	Lancaster	1977/4
Senchal	Ritz	1981/9
Senso	R. di Camerino	1972/9
7e Sens	S. Rykiel	1979/10
Sex Appeal, for women	Jovan	1978/1
Shalimar	Guerlain	1925/11
Shalom	J. Muller	1970/10
Sheherazade	Desprez	1983/8
Shocking	Schiaparelli	1935/11
Shocking you	Schiaparelli	1976/1
Sikkim	Lancôme	1971/9
Silences	Jacomo	1979/1
Sinan	J. M. Sinan	1984/8
Silverline	Gainsborough	1972/1
Snob	Le Galion	1937/4
Soft	Fiorucci	1984/8
Soft Musk	Avon	1983/6
Sophia	Coty	1980/4
Soir de Paris	Bourjois	1929/5
Sortilège	Le Galion	1938/6
Sourire	Shiseido	1977/3
Sport Scent, for woman	Jovan	1978/1
Style	Avon	1978/1
Super Fragrance	Aigner	1978/7
Surreal = Toccara	Avon	1981/6
Suzuro	Shiseido	1976/3
Sweet Honesty	Avon	1973/5
Symbiose	Stendhal	1980/4
Tabu	Dana	1931/11
Tamango	Leonard	1977/6
Tamoré	Nerval	1976/1
Tasha	Avon	1981/6
Tatiana	v. Fürstenberg	1975/4
Tendance	Marbert	1980/7
Tendresse	Atkinsons	1957/7
Tigress	Fabergé	1944/7
Timeless	Avon	1974/9
Toccara = Surreal	Avon	1981/6
Topaze	Avon	1959/6
Torrente	Torrente	1977/4
Tosca	4711	1921/7
Touché	Jovan	1980/7
Trigère	Trigère	1973/7
Trussardi Donna	Trussardi	1984/8
Turbulences	Revillon	1980/6
Tuvara	Tuvaché	1965/11
Tuxedo	Warner-Lauren	1978/6
Tweed	Lenthéric	1933/7
Ultima II	Revlon	1967/11
Ungaro	Ungaro	1977/2
Un Jour	Jourdan	1983/2
Unspoken	Avon	1975/5
Valentino	Valentino	1979/3
Vanderbilt	Vanderbilt	1981/4·5
Variations	Carven	1971/1
Vent Vert	Balmain	1945/1
Via Lanvin	Lanvin	1971/5
Vivage = Jour	Féraud = Avon	1984/2
Vivara	Pucci	1965/1
Vivre	Molyneux	1971/6·7
Volcan d'Amour	v. Fürstenberg	1981/7·8
Vol de Nuit	Guerlain	1945/11
Vôtre	Jourdan	1978/3
VSP	Jovan	1973/4
Vu	Lapidus	1976/11
Weil de Weil	Weil	1971/1
Whisper of Musk	Jovan	1984/6
White Flowers	Astor	1983/2
White Linen	Lauder	1978/6
White Shoulders	Evyan	1945/4
Wind Song	Matchabelli	1953/4
Woman	Jovan	1977/11
Woman Two	J. Sander	1983/9
Woodhue	Fabergé	1949/11
Y	Yves St.Laurent	1964/1
Yendi	Capucci	1975/5
Yesterday	Marbert	1979/6
Yolai	Cantiléne Cosm.	1976/3
Youth Dew	Lauder	1952/11
Ysatis	Givenchy	1984/9
Zadig	Pucci	1973/11
Zany	Avon	1981/13
Zen	Shiseido	1964/3
Zibeline	Weil	1928/7

and Europe are given in Exhibit 30.8. Giorgio, a strong scent with a concentration exceeding current standards, had soared to success (11 percent of American fragrance sales in 1984) through the use of aggressive marketing techniques and direct sales. It was just being introduced in France in late 1985.

FIDJI

In 1974, just after L'Oréal bought Lancôme, Robert Salmon, a recent INSEAD M.B.A., was assigned to its Marketing Department. After studying the perfumes marketed by Lancôme, he felt there was a niche for another perfume like Nina Ricci's L'Air du Temps. Guy Laroche was a French high-fashion designer whose career began in 1949 with his mentor, designer Jean Dessès. His talent was more artistic than commercial and the early years had been tough. The timing of L'Oréal's proposal to launch a prestige perfume bearing his name was right, and the first license agreement of this kind was signed.

Exhibit 30.7

WORLD PERFUME FAMILY TRENDS, 1900–1980

Dates	Fragrance Family	Representative Perfume Brands
1900–1910	Simple floral notes	Quelques Fleurs (Houbigant, 1912)
1910–1920	Chypre notes	Chypre (Coty, 1917), Mitsouko (Guerlain, 1919)
1920–1930	Aldehydic notes	Chanel N° 5 (1921), Arpège (Lanvin, 1927), Je reviens (Worth, 1932)
1930–1940	Oriental notes	Shalimar (Guerlain, 1925), Tabu (Dana, 1931), Shocking (Schiaparelli, 1935)
1940–1950	Green notes	Vent Vert (Balmain, 1945)
	Chypre notes	Femme (Rochas, 1942), Ma Griffe (Carven, 1944), Miss Dior (1947)
1950–1960	Chypre notes	Cabochard (Grès, 1958), Intimate (Revlon, 1955)
	Oriental notes	Youth Dew (Lauder, 1952)
1960–1970	Floral notes	L'Air du Temps (Nina Ricci, 1948), Fidji (Guy Laroche, 1966), Norell (Revlon, 1955)
	Aldehydic notes	Madame Rochas (1960), Calèche (Hermès, 1961)
1970–1971	Chypre notes	Empreinte (Courrèges, 1971), Cachet (Matchabelli, 1970), Sikkim (Lancôme, 1971)
1971–1972	Green notes	Chanel N° 19 (1971), Alliage (Lauder, 1972)
1973–1975	Floral notes	Charlie (Revlon, 1973), Chloé (Lagerfeld, 1975)
1968–1976	Aldehydic notes	Calandre (Rabanne, 1968), Aviance (Matchabelli, 1975)
1975–1977	Oriental notes	Vu (Ted Lapidus, 1976), Opium (Saint Laurent, 1977), J'ai Osé (Guy Laroche, 1977), Cinnabar (Lauder, 1978), Magie Noire (Lancôme, 1978)
1975–1980	Green fruity notes	Amazone (Hermès, 1975)
	Floral fruity notes	Lauren (Warner-Lauren, 1978), Scoundrel (Revlon, 1980)

Source: The Haarmann & Reimer Book of Perfume (London: Johnson Publications Ltd., 1984).

Exhibit 30.8

BEST-SELLING PRESTIGE WOMEN'S FRAGRANCES

A. 1984 BRAND SALES AND MARKET SHARES—FRANCE

Brand	Sales (million FF)	MARKET SHARE FF	MARKET SHARE Volume
1. Opium (Yves Saint Laurent)	88.5	4.7%	5.1%
2. Anaïs Anaïs (Cacharel)	80.0	4.3	5.1
3. L'Air du Temps (Nina Ricci)	71.0	3.8	5.5
4. Chanel N° 5 (Chanel)	70.0	3.8	3.7
5. Fidji (Guy Laroche)	55.0	2.9	2.7
6. Miss Dior (Dior)	52.5	2.8	2.2
7. Paris (Yves Saint Laurent)	51.0	2.7	2.8
8. Shalimar (Guerlain)	45.0	2.4	3.8
9. O de Lancôme (Lancôme)	42.0	2.3	3.6
10. Arpège (Lanvin)	41.0	2.5	2.2
11. Chanel N° 19 (Chanel)	35.5	1.9	2.1
12. Magie Noire (Lancôme)	32.0	1.7	2.4
13. First (Van Cleef & Arpels)	31.0	1.7	2.1
14. Eau de Roche (Rochas)	30.0	1.6	2.4
15. Givenchy III (Givenchy)	28.0	1.5	1.5
16. Rive Gauche (Yves Saint Laurent)	26.0	1.4	3.0
17. Calèche (Hermès)	24.0	1.4	2.1
18. Chloé (Lagerfeld)	24.0	1.3	0.6

Source: Company records.

B. ESTIMATED 1984 MARKET SHARES (FF) OF LEADING PRESTIGE WOMEN'S FRAGRANCES—THREE EUROPEAN COUNTRIES

Fragrance	Great Britain	Italy	West Germany
Anaïs Anaïs	8.4%	7.9%	4.0%
Opium	7.9	3.9	4.5
Chanel N° 5	7.6	1.7	4.2
White Linen	6.0		1.3
Rive Gauche	5.8		
L'Air du Temps	3.7		3.2
Miss Dior	3.2		
Fidji	2.8	4.0	2.8
Chloé	0.2		3.1
K de Lagerfeld	0.1		2.9
O de Lancôme		3.2	2.0
Armani		2.8	2.3
Magie Noire		2.3	2.7
Madame Rochas			2.0
Alliage			1.3
Valentino		4.3	

Source: Company records.

Salmon contracted the renowned perfumer Roudnitzka to develop the fragrance, but Jean Menet, president of Lancôme, and Michel Bedin, the first Guy Laroche advertising manager, created the name, bottle, and package themselves. In 1965, Club Méditerranée was just starting to become fashionable. The idea of "escape" to tropical paradises seemed full of potential as the fragrance image. Menet suggested Fidji after perusing the tropical areas of the globe for short catchy names. The perfume's price was to be positioned slightly below Miss Dior and above L'Air du Temps, with a communication emphasis on the evening and nighttime since L'Air du Temps was associated with the day.

When the first two salesmen set out to take orders, they were horrified to learn from shopowners that the perfume had a very particular odor and would probably never sell. Various new formulas were considered until one by the manufacturer, IFF, closer to the original specifications, was selected and available by Easter 1966. This time it was tested by Salmon's wife on a random sample of friends. Sales were modest during the early years, and the Guy Laroche team was fortunate to be part of Lancôme since seven years passed before the line made a profit.

GUY LAROCHE PRODUCT LINE

The Guy Laroche product line had expanded substantially since 1966 (Exhibit 30.9). Douceline (beauty milk, bubble bath, bath oil, powder) was launched under the influence of the successful Jean Naté line in the United States. The products were perfumed with Fidji but did not bear its name since Fidji wasn't very well known yet and Salmon didn't want to limit its sales to Fidji consumers. The line started slowly but reached more than 30 percent of Guy Laroche perfume product sales at one point. J'ai Osé was launched in 1977, the same year as Saint Laurent's Opium, when the trend was to heady, oriental scents. According to Robert Salmon,

Exhibit 30.9

GUY LAROCHE PRODUCT LINE DEVELOPMENT

Year	Product	Description
1968	Douceline	Perfumed bath products
1970	Eau Folle	Fresh, young splash cologne
1972	Drakkar	Eau de toilette and shaving products for men
1974	Fidji "double concentration"	Concentrated eau de toilette
1977	J'ai Osé	Women's fragrance line
1978	Fidji du Soir	"Double concentration" renamed for evening use
1980	Ambiances Fidji	Fidji air-perfuming products
1982	Eau de Parfum Fidji	Fidji du Soir, renamed
1982	Drakkar Noir	Eau de toilette and shaving products for men
1984	Bain des Iles	Perfumed Fidji bath products

When J'ai Osé was launched, Fidji was number one in France, Italy, Spain, Belgium, the Netherlands, and the Middle East, but we could feel it was running out of steam. When a perfume is not an institution like Chanel, there comes a time when it costs so much to defend one's ground that it is easier to start from scratch, launch a new product, and end up with half the sales of the other. . . . When we realized Fidji's image had slipped, we launched J'ai Osé at a higher price.

As of 1980, under new marketing management and in an effort to increase sales volume, Fidji was marketed in a series of "creative" sizes and shapes: 10-ml atomizers resembling plastic cigarette lighters, ladybug-shaped air-perfuming gadgets, 25- and 30-ml trial sizes, and so on. The Ambiances Fidji line included a series of air-perfuming products, for example, incense sticks and candles. Guy Laroche was the first French designer to enter this market. Ambiances Fidji sales represented 21 percent of Fidji sales volume and 11.4 percent of French franc sales in late 1980. By late 1982,

Exhibit 30.10

**1985 LEADING EAU DE TOILETTE BRAND
RETAIL PRICES (FF) IN EUROPE (100 ml)**

Fragrance	France (1985)	Italy (1985)	Great Britain (1985)	West Germany (1984)
Joy (90-ml vaporizer)	465	475	465	
Opium	400	400	417	411
KL	390	371		402
First	330	338		320
Oscar de la Renta	325		333	311
Armani	295	254	280	247
Paris	285	249	250	268
Parfum d'Hermès	280	235	298	274
Chanel N° 5 and 19	260	254	226	231
Chloé	255	301	262	219
Shalimar/Chamade	255	226	250	235
Magie Noire	255	244	232	213
Courrèges in Blue	250	226		207
Ysatis	250	216	315	265
Arpège	230		208	271
Fidji	225	202	220	183
Miss Dior	210	226	250	231
Rive Gauche	195	193		204
Clair de Jour	175		179	183
L'Air du Temps	160	168	202	177
Anaïs Anaïs	155	183	190	183
Métal	140	135	160	135
Calandre	140	135	160	135
O de Lancôme	130	125		101

Exhibit 30.11

TRENDS IN FIDJI PRICES, 1979–1985

TRENDS IN FIDJI RETAIL PRICES (FF) IN FRANCE,* 1979–1985

	1979	1980	1981	1982	1983	1984	1985
Extract (1 oz)	185	250	280	325	420	490	610
Eau de parfum (115 ml)	90	115	130	145	180	255	310
Eau de toilette (228 ml)	130	170	190	210	260	295	350
Eau de toilette atomizer (100 ml)	82	105	120	136	170	210	260

*Tax included.

Source: Company records.

TYPICAL COST STRUCTURE OF AN EAU DE TOILETTE LIKE FIDJI (100–120 ml), 1985

	FF	% of Full Retail Price
Retail price (including tax)	250.00	100
Tax (33.3%)	62.50	25
Retail price (excluding tax)	187.50	75
Retailer margin	72.50	29
Manufacturer's selling price	115.00	46
Production cost	32.50	13
Overheads and taxes	32.50	13
Advertising and promotion	20.00	8
Sales force	12.50	5
Transport	5.00	2
Manufacturer's profit	12.50	5

Source: Company records.

two more companies, Estée Lauder and Rochas, had entered this new market segment.

Guy Laroche's price policy reflected "middle-of-the-road" alignment with the prices of the other major prestige women's fragrances (Exhibit 30.10). Exhibit 30.11 gives additional information on Fidji retail prices with the typical cost structure for this kind of fragrance.

PROMOTION

Starting in 1983, Guy Laroche management became concerned with Fidji's slipping image, brought on by around ten years of intensive and uncontrolled promotion: larger sizes, trial sizes, lead sizes, discounts, gadgets, gifts with purchase, Christmas gift sets, and so on. "Promotional items" were defined as all items not listed in the catalog. Exhibit 30.12 gives data on the use of promotion by Fidji and competing perfume brands. Reflecting on the early years, Salmon commented,

> In Europe, and especially in France, the major competitors were very snobby and considered Laroche a bit like a poor cousin. I felt that instead of running after image we should treat perfumes like cosmetics, using strong sales tactics. We figured there might be great potential somewhere between the top prestige brands and mass markets. We pushed very hard and it snowballed. From one virtually accidental promotional idea we got to the point where promotion represented close to 40 percent of total sales and the product image suffered considerably.

Jean-Michel Bostroem, Guy Laroche's marketing manager, France, during the 1970s, spoke of parallel importing, that is, transactions between foreign subsidiaries:

> It was a time of restrictions in France. Profitability wasn't good so top management wouldn't allow us to invest in molds or do anything. The foreign subsidiaries had much more liberty, so to beat the system, Guy Laroche management let the English subsidiary develop its own products. They designed a small, 42-gram atomizer, a promotional size that was cheap in price and aesthetically different from the rest of the line. The cost of production was also lower, and it was taxed differently. They sold enormous quantities of it thinking people would be attracted by the low price then come back for standard

Exhibit 30.12

SALES PROMOTION USAGE, 1979–1985

FIDJI PROMOTIONAL SALES AS A PERCENTAGE OF TOTAL SALES IN LOCAL CURRENCY, 1979–1985
(excluding bath product line)

Country	1979	1980	1981	1982	1983	1984	1985*
France	20	21	17	18	18	16	10
Italy	14	26	32	40	34	26	
Great Britain	58†	60†	65†	63†	58	54	17
Belgium	35†	40†	50†	50†	43	37	
Spain	60†	65†	70†	67†	64	71	44
Portugal	15†	15†	30†	30†	28	58	1
West Germany	81	86	82	70	75	60	49
Netherlands	84	81	90	70	90	57	38
Austria	74	79	75	79	37	31	0
Switzerland	58	61	54	77	55	26	28
Denmark	67	83	70	60	7	7	8
Sweden	33	0	30	27	31	31	18
Finland	86	84	79	71			

*1985 percentages indicate the trend for the year.
†Estimated figures.

Source: Company records.

Exhibit 30.12 (Cont.)

PROMOTION AS A PERCENTAGE OF TOTAL SALES—FRANCE, 1983–1985

Brand*	June 1983	June 1984	June 1985
Cardin (Cardin)	39.0	38.2	64.3
Climat (Lancôme)	45.1	26.5	29.7
O de Lancôme	36.5	25.7	27.6
Arpège (Lanvin)	14.7	21.1	26.7
Cabochard (Grès)	24.4	33.8	23.1
Eau de Fleurs (Ricci)	26.4	23.6	23.0
Choc (Cardin)	6.6	17.9	21.8
Quartz (Molyneux)	25.7	36.7	21.0
Charlie (Revlon)	19.4	27.0	19.6
Fleur de Fleurs (Ricci)	24.6	26.9	18.6
Clair de Jour (Lanvin)	13.4	17.6	17.5
Magie Noire (Lancôme)	14.7	16.4	17.4
L'Air du Temps (Ricci)	15.1	17.9	16.6
Envol (Ted Lapidus)	16.7	15.5	14.1
Anaïs Anaïs (Cacharel)	7.4	14.3	12.9
Fidji (Guy Laroche)	16.6	17.1	12.8
Eau de Roche (Rochas)	4.1	11.7	12.7
J'ai Osé (Guy Laroche)	9.1	17.2	11.9
Gauloise (Molyneux)	28.5	33.4	10.9
Nocturnes (Caron)	4.9	5.5	10.7
Eau Folle (Guy Laroche)	5.8	10.3	9.6
Femme (Rochas)	3.7	8.1	9.2
Eau de Courrèges	0.0	0.0	9.1
Farouche (Ricci)	17.9	18.6	7.8
Madame Rochas	4.5	8.0	6.7
Paradoxe (Cardin)	N.A.	0.3	6.7
Fleurs de Rocaille (Caron)	1.5	4.2	6.5
Métal (Rabanne)	6.2	5.3	6.2
Chloé (Lagerfeld)	N.A.	3.3	6.1
Mystère (Rochas)	6.0	9.5	6.1

*Those with less than 6% promotion as of June 1985 are Givenchy 3, Silences (Jacomo), Empreinte (Courrèges), Calandre (Rabanne), Ivoire (Balmain), Courrèges in Blue, KL (Lagerfeld), Diorella, Calèche (Hermès), Rive Gauche (Yves St. Laurent), Eau de Givenchy, Amazone (Hermès), Trophée (Lancôme), First (Van Cleef & Arpels), Y (Yves St. Laurent), Miss Dior, Opium (Yves St. Laurent), and Youth Dew (Estée Lauder).

Source: INTERCOR.

---

sizes. In the end, the other subsidiaries short-circuited Paris and imported this atomizer directly from England. It sold so well that catalog item sales dropped off and the English subsidiary was making all the profit. In certain countries like Holland, these atomizers represented up to 90 percent of sales.

An attempt had therefore been made by the international marketing team to upgrade the image of Guy Laroche products. Prices were raised, the Fidji package changed, the Guy Laroche signature made more prominent, all gadgets eliminated, and pro-

Exhibit 30.13

BREAKDOWN OF 1984 FRENCH FRANC SALES OF FIDJI
IN FRANCE BY TYPE OF PRODUCT

	Extract	EDP*	EDT†	Bath Line	Sets‡
Volume	6%	10%	43%	35%	6%
FF	10%	12%	54%	16%	8.4%

DEVELOPMENT OF FIDJI SALES IN FRANCE
BY TYPE OF PRODUCT, 1981–1984

	Extract	EDP*	EDT†	Bath	Sets‡
Volume	−44%	+ 30%	−22%	+ 6%	+41%
FF	+18%	+181%	+33%	+61%	+62%

*Eau de parfum.
†Eau de toilette.
‡Christmas gift boxes and other sets (two or more products sold together).

Source: Company records.

motional sizes limited to those consistent with the image of catalog items. In 1984, the Fidji bath line was modified and renamed Bain des Iles; standardized "couture" atomizers were launched for both Fidji and J'ai Osé, and a new Fidji advertising campaign was created. Exhibit 30.13 gives the 1984 breakdown and development since 1979 of Fidji sales by type of product.

DISTRIBUTION

There were basically four possible forms of distribution for beauty products: mass distribution, pharmacies, direct sales, and specialized perfumeries" or beauty shops. According to one industry expert, distribution patterns throughout the world fell into three groups: countries where department stores represented approximately 80 percent of sales (United States, Japan, Great Britain), countries where perfumeries represented the majority of sales with department store sales accounting for around 15 percent (France, Italy), and countries where pharmacy sales were predominant (Australia, Israel, Venezuela, New Zealand). Fidji and other prestige fragrances were distributed through selective channels. Special retailing conditions were deemed warranted to both protect the products' prestige/quality image and preserve their international notoriety. In France, requirements such as the aesthetic quality of the store environment, the service and information provided by store personnel, and the attractive display of products and brands had to be met to qualify for selective distribution. Varying percentages of the different kinds of outlet qualified in France as selective distribution channels (Exhibit 30.14).

Exhibit 30.14

PERCENTAGE OF FRENCH OUTLETS CONSIDERED SELECTIVE

Perfume/beauty product shops (perfumeries)	65.9%
Department stores	14.6
Nonfood retailers	6.0
Pharmacies	4.9
Beauty parlors	4.0
Direct sales (e.g., mail order houses)	2.6
Hairdressers	1.7

Source: "Parfumerie" study, CECOD, 1984.

Between 1979 and 1984, French franc sales of beauty products through selective distribution in France had increased 123.6 percent. A general trend among prestige perfume companies was to reduce the number of specialized perfumery shops under license, eliminating those that did not meet the specified qualitative criteria. In 1984, perfume/beauty product shops represented 66–70 percent of Guy Laroche sales in France, department stores 12–14 percent, and duty-free shops 18–20 percent. Exhibit 30.15 gives information on Guy Laroche and its competitors' retail outlets. Eaux de toilettes were purchased increasingly through mass distribution and direct sales. The volume of eaux de toilettes sold in French mass markets increased from 12 percent in 1965 to 32 percent in 1980. Those sold through direct sales jumped from less than 4 percent to 22 percent over the same period. This was particularly spectacular for nonderived eaux de toilettes: in 1982, mass markets and direct sales represented, respectively, 54 percent and 24 percent of sales volume for this category, with only 20 percent for selective distribution. Isabelle Avril-Herbillon recalled the Guy Laroche marketing team's concern over the appearance of upmarket eau de toilette brands in mass markets and direct sales:

> Mass distribution and direct sales were developing rapidly and offered products that were close to Fidji. Our prices were still higher but Fidji, as a product, its package, its appearance and all, was not that different.

COMMUNICATION

Since Fidji's launch, there had been eight major Fidji print ads (Exhibit 30.16). There had also been six different films for television commercials and cinema advertising, the last three of which are illustrated in Exhibit 30.17. Caroline Batty would have no problem obtaining recent advertising expenditure figures for Fidji and a few major competitors, but reproducing the history of advertising spending would imply research and desk work at L'Oréal's Documentation Center to compile the data presented in Exhibit 30.18. Since traditionally agencies were briefed orally, Caroline Batty had considerable trouble finding written documents describing communication

Exhibit 30.15

GUY LAROCHE AND COMPETITORS' RETAIL OUTLETS

NUMBER OF EUROPEAN OUTLETS* CARRYING GUY LAROCHE AND SELECTED COMPETITORS, 1982

Country	Laroche	Chanel	Dior	Guerlain	St. Laurent
France	2,260	1,250	2,300	925	1,800
West Germany	1,322	925	850	850	1,250
Spain	1,013	250	480	525	475
United Kingdom	1,137	1,200	900	550	1,200
Italy	1,852	500	1,300	525	1,100
Switzerland	370	225	440	100	325
Total	7,954	4,350	6,270	3,475	6,150

*Including branch stores.
Source: Company records.

1984 DISTRIBUTION CHANNELS—FRANCE

	NUMBER OF OUTLETS* CARRYING BRAND		
Brand	Total	Shops†	Department Stores
Lancôme	3,172	3,022	150
Cacharel	2,449	2,298	151
Dior	2,428	2,369	59
Ricci	2,066	1,985	81
Laroche	2,059	1,949	110
Givenchy	1,975	1,885	90
Saint Laurent	1,868	1,834	34
Rochas	1,650	1,598	52
Rabanne	1,538	1,518	20
Azzaro	1,550	1,500	50
Chanel	1,533	1,483	50
Lanvin	1,516	1,447	69
Revlon	1,465	1,350	115
Guerlain	1,110	1,110	—

*Excluding branch stores.
†Includes all perfume/beauty shops, duty-free shops, pharmacies, etc.
Source: Company records.

objectives for the earlier campaigns. Positioning objectives for 1977 corresponding to the ad commonly referred to as "the eyes" (ad [f], Exhibit 30.16) were drafted by Michel Bedin, international advertising manager at the time:

Escape—exotic but serene. Escape to a dreamland but not a dream of possessions and elitism (Youth Dew by Estée Lauder), not a dream for romantic young girls (L'Air du

Temps by Nina Ricci), nor of aggressive seduction (Tigress by Fabergé), but a private dream of intimacy and inner richness for a fascinating woman, in love with life, active and sophisticated without being at all ostentatious. This is a woman who has good taste, discrimination, and wants her perfume to be intense, elegant, and feminine.

When the new agency Mirabelle was contracted in 1980, the "Fidji woman" was described by the Guy Laroche team as follows:

Young, active, naturally distinguished, refined, but nonetheless very up-to-date and capable of stepping away from a classic universe to appreciate the unexpected and unusual. (Company records)

Exhibit 30.16

FIDJI MAGAZINE ADVERTISEMENTS

Exhibit 30.16 (Cont.)

Exhibit 30.16 (Cont.)

Exhibit 30.17 **FIDJI ADVERTISING CLIPS**

← 1977

"You could search a thousand islands to find a fragrance as perfect as Fidji. Fidji, warm, exotic, vibrant, with a hidden depth of mystery. Fidji, a little paradise on Earth, discovered by Guy Laroche of Paris. Give her Fidji, the gift the French give."

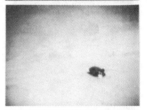

↑
1980

"The Fidji Kiss: In island paradises, lovers gently rub noses as an expression of tenderness. In these island paradises, the women have an instinct for perfumes. Fidji is their perfume. Fidji, the perfume of rediscovered paradises."

↑
1984

"A woman is an island, Fidji is her perfume."

Exhibit 30.18

ADVERTISING EXPENDITURES—FRANCE, 1978–1984
(thousand FF)

	1978	1979	1980	1981	1982	1983	1984
Total women's fragrances	85,505	96,262	97,607	117,523	172,161	202,781	253,345
Armani	—	—	—	—	2,210	2,395	1,569
Balmain (Ivoire)	N.A.	N.A.	774	924	840	1,354	2,319
Cacharel (Anais Anais)	1,582	2,131	711	3,459	5,609	4,001	2,900
Pierre Cardin	1,223	823	22	2,049	1,894	3,326	3,777
(Choc)	—	—	—	1,737	1,894	953	1,262
Chanel	2,662	3,123	3,881	4,431	7,602	8,516	13,555
(Chanel N° 5)	410	1,222	1,779	1,815	2,868	3,736	2,928
(Chanel N° 19)	1,478	1,272	1,515	1,889	3,234	3,449	3,662
(Coco)	—	—	—	—	—	—	5,424
Courrèges	1,265	697	445	151	1,171	4,108	6,409
Dior	889	2,392	2,495	2,957	5,623	7,361	4,958
(Diorella)	—	—	470	835	542	—	—
(Dioressence)	—	2,313	1,955	563	—	—	—
(Miss Dior)	4	19	—	1,558	5,082	7,361	4,958
Estée Lauder	602	962	298	169	86	2,839	2,432
(White Linen)	—	—	298	—	—	2,825	2,110
Givenchy	2,303	2,885	3,647	4,019	3,605	5,822	17,172
(Givenchy III)	2,301	2,210	2,847	1,680	2,576	2,363	4,476
(Ysatis)	—	—	—	—	—	—	8,425
Grès (Cabochard)	N.A.	N.A.	131	—	—	674	189
Guerlain	2,179	5,791	2,150	6,026	6,684	9,420	13,024
(Chamade)	2	290	—	—	1,794	1,329	1,742
(Nahema)	—	4,271	2,150	6,022	1,577	878	390
(Shalimar)	25	191	—	1	2,159	2,127	3,840
Hermès	2,219	2,628	3,364	3,950	5,663	6,947	10,370
(Amazone)	1,134	1,265	1,534	1,636	2,669	2,779	1,743
(Calèche)	1,065	1,325	1,363	1,353	1,748	2,725	3,325
Karl Lagerfeld	735	N.A.	117	264	1,629	2,682	3,726
(Chloé)	735	N.A.	117	264	409	1,732	82
Lancôme	4,221	6,602	6,296	5,623	13,471	13,719	11,498
(Magie Noire)	1,521	4,000	4,100	1,415	4,824	4,421	4,973
(O de Lancôme)	2,396	2,438	2,008	3,218	3,474	2,535	1,384
Lanvin	2,229	3,783	2,245	3,204	3,902	7,860	3,836
(Arpège)	1,903	1,758	2,232	3,204	3,902	2,344	249
Guy Laroche	4,612	N.A.	5,100	8,283	8,538	8,986	7,794
(Eau Folle)	609	N.A.	1,183	—	—	—	—
(Fidji)	1,886	2,526	1,942	3,557	5,132	4,823	6,250
(J'Ai Osé)	2,117	N.A.	1,742	971	3,402	4,004	923
Jean Patou	1,265	1,491	946	408	1,350	934	1,812
(Joy)	110	435	393	408	1,350	910	1,574
Paco Rabanne	694	2,000	1,367	1,982	2,961	5,286	6,462
(Calandre)	675	498	589	397	1,769	3,235	4,873
(Métal)	—	1,473	762	1,561	528	1,932	1,569
Revlon	704	469	1,011	630	1,701	948	1,303
(Charlie)	663	432	942	587	1,701	948	1,303

Exhibit 30.18 (Cont.)

Nina Ricci	2,280	2,707	4,166	5,725	5,028	5,415	7,111
(L'Air du Temps)	1,416	1,912	927	2,073	2,377	3,595	4,199
Rochas	6,298	3,955	2,102	2,057	3,222	4,131	11,699
(Femme)	875	—	—	1,629	516	640	—
(Mystère)	3,131	3,101	1,149	1,426	1,821	2,459	3,866
Sonia Rykiel							
(7ème Sens)	—	N.A.	501	609	471	761	—
Van Cleef & Arpels							
(First)	1,925	2,164	1,504	1,461	1,049	1,135	1,771
Yves Saint Laurent	1,765	1,722	1,889	2,497	5,481	10,950	14,120
(Opium)	543	515	936	1,144	997	1,662	4,256
(Paris)	—	—	—	—	—	4,758	4,083
(Rive Gauche)	392	220	240	791	1,354	4,030	3,294

N.A. = Not available.

Mirabelle was instructed to

> (a) update the Fidji dream by transforming the old advertising message of nature-escape to nature-instinct; (b) capitalize on the connection between Fidji and Guy Laroche ("de la Haute Couture à la Haute Parfumerie"); (c) increase the target age bracket (previously 35–45, add the 18–25 age bracket, and by "process of imitation" also absorb the 25–35 age bracket); and (d) satisfy basic requirements of durability, international adaptation, point-of-sale promotional possibilities, and use of all media.

The resulting ad,[3] called "the snake," is presented in Exhibit 30.16, ad (g).

In 1984, in keeping with the decision to upgrade the image of Fidji, the "snake" ad was abandoned, and the current ad, called "the island," created around the previous concept of "A woman is an island, Fidji is her perfume," was adopted (see ad [h] in Exhibit 30.16). In the course of casual discussion, Caroline Batty learned that the "snake" and "island" ads had been submitted to formal testing by Ipsos, a well-known French media research company (see Exhibit 30.19).

MARKET RESEARCH

Since Fidji bore the Guy Laroche name, Caroline Batty realized that consumer perception of his image was important. According to Alain Charrueau, marketing manager, Chanel Perfumes,

> One of the functions of a brand or designer name is to reassure certain women and allow them to take liberties they wouldn't consider if they weren't protected by a famous

[3]A second version of the ad, without the snake, was designed for countries where snakes were commonly accepted as edible.

Exhibit 30.19

IPSOS TESTS OF TWO FIDJI ADVERTISING CAMPAIGNS IN FRENCH MAGAZINES[1]

| | Total Sample n=300 | Total Sample n=301 | Non Exposed* n=82 | Exposed n=219 | Matching Target† n=231 | Exposed and Matching Target n=174 | Recognized Ad n=173 | Did Not Recognize Ad n=128 | GENERAL IPSOS STANDARD‡ ALL CAMPAIGNS IN MAGAZINES‡ | | IPSOS INDUSTRY STANDARDS§ | |
									3 million FF	1–2 million FF	All Hygiene and Beauty Products	Perfumes
Recognition‖	66%	57%	46%	62%	55%	57%	100%	—	34%	24%	29%	34%
Attribution#	36	36	24	41	36	39	63	—	17	8	11	13
Confusion**	13	6	6	5	4	5	10	—				
Attribution/ recognition	64	63	53	66	67	68	63	—	50	33	37	38
Overall reaction††												
Liked	74	77	67	81	78	81	90	61	48	43	66	43
Disliked	22	20	30	16	20	17	10	34	42	49	31	41
Average frequency‡‡	N.A.	4.78	—	6.58	4.69	6.22	5.83	3.37				

†Number of respondents having target profile (defined as upper/middle class).

‖Respondents were shown a folder containing the test ad plus a few others, with the brand/product or other identification marks blocked out. As they leaved through the ads, they were asked which ones they remembered seeing.

#For each ad and recognized, respondents were asked whether they remembered the (blocked out) name of the brand/product.

**Percentage of respondents incorrectly identifying brand/product.

††Respondents were asked whether they liked or disliked the ad.

*Respondents were presented with a list of periodicals in which the test ad appeared and asked which ones they had read. If they had read the periodical in which the ad appeared, they were assumed to have been exposed to it.

‡‡Defined as the average number of likely exposures to the ad (measured as indicated) for each respondent.

‡Average score of all other IPSOS-Tested campaigns in same media (e.g., magazines) and with similar budgets (e.g., 1 to 2 million FF).

§Average score of campaigns within the same industry.

[1]Dates of tests and costs of campaigns: February 22, 1983, 3 million FF: December 12, 1984, 3.98 million FF.

label. . . . These same women might have rejected Opium if it had been presented in a blind test. . . . What is more, we know that many women purchase as much the brand (e.g., Chanel, Dior, Guerlain) as a particular scent.

A researcher told Caroline Batty that in a Fidji image study conducted in May 1983, Guy Laroche's style was described as very classical, generally for women over 40. His designs were considered less eccentric and "avant-garde," more "wearable" than those of Yves Saint Laurent, who was probably more widely known. Awareness of the Guy Laroche line was considerably higher among women over 30 than among those younger.

Caroline Batty would have to conduct a thorough analysis of competing women's fragrance communication campaigns. The company's competitor tracking service could provide a series of print fragrance ads from women's magazines covering the preceding 5 to 10 years (Exhibit 30.20). Understanding competitor positioning strategy would involve clustering these ads using some simple, qualitative criteria.

It appeared that no international image studies had been performed on the Fidji ads. Caroline Batty understood however that other studies existed elsewhere at L'Oréal, and she hoped she could track them down. These included a 1983 Sofres-Communication study on French consumer motivations and attitudes toward beauty products. It had been conducted over a 12-month period and was based on (1) personal interviews with a dozen experts, (2) four 35-member group interviews, (3) depth interviews with around 10 persons, and (4) a quantitative survey of 819 women, ages 15 to 65. It identified five types of women, each expressing a different degree of involvement with the body and therefore specific attitudes toward beauty products (Exhibit 30.21).

The importance of gift giving in fragrance purchase was reported in a 1980 study conducted by SOFCO (Sofres Communication). That year, 53 percent of perfumes, 42 percent of eaux de toilettes, and 23 percent of colognes had been bought as gifts. In 69 percent of these cases, the gift had been chosen without consulting its recipient. For extracts or eaux de toilettes alone however, this percentage was only 27–29 percent; that is, gift selection was "remote controlled."

In June 1982, the CCA (Centre de Communication Avancée), a French research company specialized in lifestyles, had conducted a comparative study of 18 women's "sociostyles" and reactions to perfume ads. The study was based on interviews with 2000 people over age 15, in their homes, one-third of whom were men, two-thirds women. Extensive factor analyses of these interviews had resulted in a map indicating four basic mentalities (Exhibit 30.22). The horizontal Entropy-Defense axis opposed individuals dominated by open-mindedness, innovation, and adventure (pole: Entropy) and those favoring withdrawal, the need for security and refuge in habits (pole: Defense). The vertical Escape-Positivism axis contrasted mentalities dominated by search for a dream, nature, sensualism, and beauty (pole: Escape) with those stressing realism, pragmatism, and the pursuit of material and moral rigorism (pole: Positivism). The CCA study also measured consumer preferences for 18 different fragrance ads when one or two ads were selected in response to the question, "Which style of ad do you prefer for a women's fragrance?" Based on respondent reactions, the ads were further classified in four major clusters:

Exhibit 30.20

SELECTED FRENCH PRINT ADS

1. Joy

2. Courrèges in Blue

3. Paris

4. Amazone

5. Giorgio

6. Métal

7. First

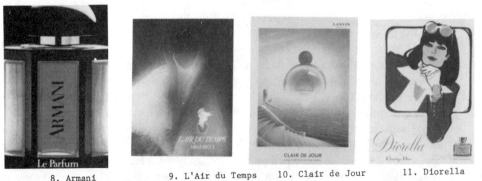
8. Armani   9. L'Air du Temps   10. Clair de Jour   11. Diorella

Exhibit 30.20 (Cont.)

12. Madame Rochas   13. Arpège   14. Chamade   15. Coriandre

16. Nahéma   17. Rive Gauche   18. Sinan   19. Cabochard

20. Ysatis   21. Paradoxe   22. Miss Dior

Exhibit 30.20 (Cont.)

23. Givenchy III

24. Chanel No 19

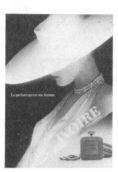

25. Ivoire

26. Silence

27. J'Ai Osé

28. Poison

29. Coco

30. Obsession

31. Magie Noire

32. Shalimar

33. Opium

Exhibit 30.20 (Cont.)

34. Clin d'Oeil   35. Ingénue   36. Ô de Lancôme

37. Eau Folle   38. Eau Jeune   39. Mont St Michel

40. Darling   41. Fleur Bleue   42. Magnolia

Exhibit 30.21

DIFFERENCES IN WOMEN'S ATTITUDES AND BEHAVIOUR TOWARD BEAUTY PRODUCTS SUMMARY OF 1983 SOFRES COMMUNICATION STUDY

TYPES OF WOMEN	ATTITUDES TOWARD BODY	ATTITUDES TOWARD BODY IMPROVEMENT	CONSUMPTION OF BEAUTY PRODUCTS
DETACHED (11% of sample) 62%* over age 35 55% primary school education 70% had rare social contacts Body considered of little importance	Puritanical Body denied, inexpressive Does not want to be noticed Functional body maintenance to remain acceptable	Refuses any effort to improve or preserve the body No physical exercise or diets	**LIGHT** consumer 6.9 Kinds of product 11.5 Different products Use of beauty products implies constraints and a loss of freedom
PERFECTIONISTS (23% of sample) Average age and education level 54% had rare social contacts Body an instrument: source of secondary pleasure, not seduction related	Puritanical Pleasure in disciplining her body Reflection of moral strength and willpower Body maintenance and care a duty	Agrees to make efforts for body improvement Refuses to deprive herself Allows her body to live as it feels without letting herself go, efforts are almost mechanical	**AVERAGE** consumer 10 kinds of products 18.3 products Natural use of beauty products Classic products
SENSUAL (25% of sample) 65% under age 35, secondary school education 57% in work force 60% led active social lives Body very important: source of pleasure for self, not a tool	Takes care of her body Love relationship with her body Observes herself meticulously Hedonist	Makes limited effort; likes her body too much to inflict violence on it Gentle physical activity No mortifications like diets, diet foods, exercise	**HEAVY** consumer 10.5 kinds of product 20.9 products Very open to beauty products and makeup: weapons for reestablishing psychological balance Likes a wide range of products
SOCIAL (12% of sample) 61% over age 35 84% married 53% had rare social contacts Body important as an expression of social status. Tool of social identification → seduction	Cares for the body for functional reasons Obligation to be seen as pleasure Sensation of providing a service	Capitalizes on her assets Agrees to deprive herself to improve appearance; diets Fights against aging	**AVERAGE** consumer 9.2 kinds of product 18.3 products Supports idea of standardizing women with beauty products Uses more skin care than makeup or bath products
SEDUCTRESSES (29% of sample) 18% secondary- or university-level education 60% led active or moderately active social lives Body important as a means of attracting others: a way of conveying an image	Takes care of her body Source of pleasure: to feel beautiful, attractive, admired Only exists through the eyes of others	Will sacrifice anything to improve appearance: strenuous physical discipline, diets, diet foods Constantly striving to improve	**HEAVY** consumer 11.2 kinds of product 20.9 products Beauty products play a major role in creating her personality Heaviest user of makeup products

*Read: 62% of "Detached" women were over age 35.

Source: Fédération Française de l'Industrie des Produits de Parfumerie, de Beauté, et de Toilette (FFIPPBT), 1983.

Exhibit 30.22

1982 CCA STUDY OF SOCIOSTYLES, PREFERENCES FOR, AND MAPPING OF WOMEN'S FRAGRANCE ADS

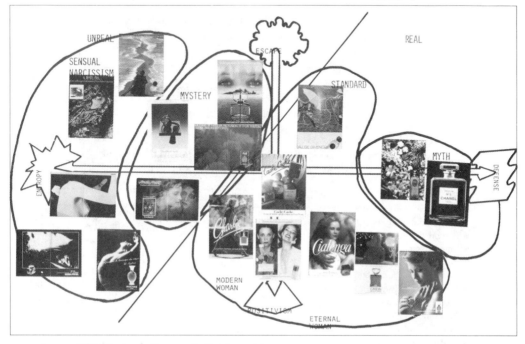

Source: CCA (Centre de Communication Avancée).

- *Cluster 1: Myth.* These were ads in which the brand name was so strong it had the value of a social myth.
- *Cluster 2: Standard.* These were ads showing young women in illustration of positive social roles.
- *Cluster 3: Mystery.* Ads suggesting dream, escape.
- *Cluster 4: Sensual narcissism.* These were ads involving fantasy worlds, metaphors, and placing importance on the senses and pleasure.

The ads, clusters, and their relationships with the four basic mentalities are visualized in Exhibit 30.22. Caroline Batty wondered about the practical implications of this study and how she could use it in her presentations to top management.

Finally, somebody suggested to her that a "Marketing Office" study dated November 1984 might explain some of the mechanisms and consumer motivations behind purchases made in perfume and beauty shops. The study had been conducted in two phases. During the first, 300 buyers and 150 nonbuyers were interviewed as they left a shop. During the second phase conducted 8 days after the first, 150 of the

300 buyers were interviewed in their homes. The findings of the study are summarized in Exhibit 30.23.

Caroline Batty settled back into the armchair at her desk and considered all the information she would have to analyze. A comment Robert Salmon once made about the future of Fidji came to her mind:

> Fidji has become a great classic. The trick now is to make it an institution like Chanel N° 5. If we pull that off, Fidji will last another fifty years.

Exhibit 30.23

MECHANISMS AND MOTIVATIONS OF PERFUME/BEAUTY SHOP PURCHASE: SUMMARY OF NOVEMBER 1984 MARKETING OFFICE STUDY

	Skin Care	Makeup	Fragrances
Intended to buy before entering store* including:	83%†	86%	90%
■ Bought desired product	76	79	87
■ Bought something else	7	7	3
■ Requested a specific product and brand	56	48	71
Reasons for purchase (one or more answers)‡:			
■ Usual product/brand	58	49	60
■ To try product out	23	17	16
■ Fitted desired use	17	14	13
■ Price and/or promotion	3	10	6
■ Salesperson's advice	14	12	6
■ Advertising	8	7	5
Loyalty			
■ Percentage claiming to be loyal to product and brand purchased§	59	40	88
Expectations			
■ Percentage of buyers expecting advice from store personnel	38	42	20

*Of the total, 49% were visiting store for the first time; 68% of the buyers and 34% of the nonbuyers planned to enter the store; 45% of the buyers expected to browse before talking to store personnel.
†Read: 83% of skin care product purchases are made by buyers who intended to purchase before entering the store.
‡Reasons specified by buyers only.
§Percentage of buyers using this same product regularly (for at least 6 months).

31

WESTERN BELL
YELLOW PAGES

The southern California retail scene was changing rapidly, and a number of Korean and Chinese-Americans were opening small businesses. For many of the Western Bell Yellow Pages Directory salespeople, calls on these potential accounts proved difficult. The directories had been modified to include multilingual editions to accommodate people who spoke Chinese, Korean, Tagalog, and Spanish, but sales were not meeting expectations.

Ann Lulan, the area sales manager, thought that if she examined some of the typical sales calls made by her people, she might begin to understand their difficulties. She also hoped to develop some sales techniques for all of her staff. Ann decided she would divide her examination into three questions: what went right, what went wrong, and how are sales to Koreans and Chinese-Americans different (if at all) from other types of sales situations. While Ann felt the changes in the Los Angeles marketplace eliminated the possibility of Western Bell Yellow Pages continuing to do "business as usual," she felt the growing ethnic diversity of the business community represented an opportunity rather than a liability.

Laura Barnes and Todd Tolliver, as well as Western Bell and all the potential clients mentioned in this case, are fictitious. This case was originally developed by John Gould, Associate Professor of Business Communications and Wesley J. Johnston, Associate Professor of Marketing, the University of Southern California, as part of a training presentation for salespeople.

The following sales call itineraries for Laura Barnes and Todd Tolliver were developed for Ann to aid her study of Western Bell sales efforts. They represent some of the problems and issues Western Bell Directory salespeople were encountering in calls to the Asian community's small-business owners in Los Angeles.

LAURA BARNES

Age, 28
Years of experience, 6

Tuesday, 9:00 A.M.—China Imports

Laura Barnes was prospecting along Atlantic Avenue in Monterey Park (see Exhibit 31.1) before going to her 10 A.M. sales appointment when she saw the sign China Imports over the shop and dropped in to talk to proprietor K. C. Wu. She hadn't been on the job very long and wanted to see if she could handle the challenge of selling a page to a Chinese businessman. The weather had been unusually cool, and she was wearing a white woolen sweater over her midnight blue dress.

Mr. Wu and a lady who Laura thought might be Mrs. Wu were the only persons in the shop when she entered. After introducing herself as a representative of Western Bell Directory's sales staff, she proceeded to build rapport by mentioning the beauty of some of the articles on display. These included a number of table lamps and ivory bridges on which miniature elephants were crossing. Mr. Wu thought she might be interested in buying one and hastened to say they were exceptionally good value for the money.

Somewhat taken by surprise at this sudden shift in seller-buyer relationship, Laura hesitated a moment and then seized the opportunity to say that she was offering a service which could materially increase Mr. Wu's sales of beautiful imports such as these although she was not at the moment in a position to buy anything. The soft ringing of the bell indicated that a customer was entering the shop. Mr. Wu clearly wanted to attend to this newcomer but let his assistant handle the prospective buyer. Laura continued to run through her usual practice of proving value and recommending an ad large enough to attract more customers than the current number of 10 to 20 a day. Mr. Wu countered that business wasn't very good and he couldn't afford to do more than run an occasional ad in the neighborhood English and Chinese newspapers.

Their conversation ran on for another 10 minutes, during which Laura, to no avail, did everything she could to show Mr. Wu how much he could gain by running a quarter-page ad in the next Alhambra Directory Intelligent Yellow Pages. Another customer entered the shop and Mr. Wu excused himself to attend to her. Laura thanked him and said she would return on another occasion.

10:00 A.M.—Wolf Sales Company

As Laura entered Wolf Sales Company on North Marianna Street, she determined that the business was a distributor of restaurant equipment and supplies. She was

Exhibit 31.1

LOS ANGELES AREA MAP

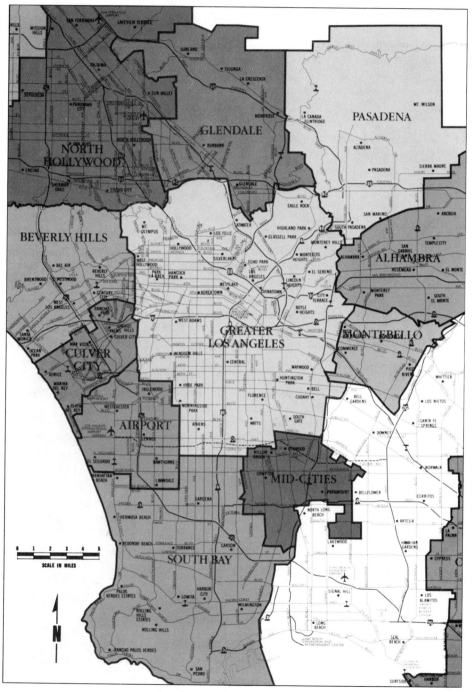

somewhat surprised when she was shown to the office of the owner and found that he was not an American with the surname Wolf but a Chinese immigrant named Steven Lee. When Laura had made the appointment to call on the company she had spoken with a young-sounding woman who spoke flawless English. Steven Lee's was not flawless.

After introducing herself as "Laura Barnes, a sales rep with Pac Bell," she thought it might break the ice to move to first names as quickly as possible. "Steven, I think that I have something that will interest you. My company publishes a telephone directory that represents a great opportunity for expanding your business." At this point, Laura opened a copy of the Los Angeles central area directory and placed it on her prospective customer's desk. She then proceeded to very carefully discuss the sizes and types of display ads, including the prices (see Exhibit 31.2).

Steven seemed very interested and agreeable. Each comment and trial-close question, such as, "Would you like your logo in red instead of black?" met with a strong "Yes!" Laura began to think that this would be an easy sale of a TQHR (triple quarter horizontal with red). After writing up the sales contract, she passed it to her customer and held out her pen. It was at this point that things seemed inexplicably to go wrong. Mr. Lee simply looked at Laura and said, "Advertising is unnecessary for my business. I have only Chinese customers, and they do not read your Yellow Pages. My business is only too little to be so bold. You offer nothing and want very high prices. I like you very much but cannot agree to your offer."

Laura stepped back, stunned. She knew better than to begin to argue with a prospective customer, and yet she really believed that a display ad of the size and type she had suggested would be reasonable for a business this size. She decided to give it another try. As she quickly scanned the open directory she saw the advertisement of an establishment similar to Wolf Sales, Wok King Chinese Restaurant Equipment. "Steven, look at this ad. Here is an example of a business similar to yours that has used our directory to promote itself."

Steven Lee suggested, "Please call next week, Miss Barnes; I will have more time to listen to your company's offer then."

Laura continued to press the issue, however, as the book would close out before then. "Steven, the deadline for placing an ad expires this week. If you wait until next week, you will not be able to get an ad in the book until next year."

"Then, Miss Barnes, I would suggest you come back next year. Goodbye!"

Laura wondered what went wrong in her sales approach to this account. Did she mishandle any of the steps in the sales presentation? She thought her handling of objections and closing techniques would have worked with most potential accounts, but this one was very different.

11:30 A.M.—Byun Realty

Laura could not have been more surprised. When she first asked for an appointment with Byun Realty's owner, Byun Ki Ho, she was told she could stop by anytime she was in the neighborhood. Mr. Byun could not know when a client might drop in off the street, so appointments were out of the question.

Apparently, this was a small firm, Laura thought, so she would take her chances at finding Mr. Byun in the office. The location was a mini-mall in Koreatown. Two rows of desks greeted her eyes as she entered. Several men and women in business attire were working at their desks, three with clients, as she walked back to the low partition which marked off Mr. Byun's space.

"Hello," she ventured as she approached a middle-aged gentleman inside the enclosure, "I'm looking for Mr. Byun. Are you Mr. Byun?"

Exhibit 31.2

**WESTERN BELL YELLOW PAGES RATES FOR GREATER
LOS ANGELES DIRECTORY**
(8–88 Issue, close to advertising: 4-22-88)

	ITEM	MONTHLY RATES
CTM	Custom Trade Mark	$147.00
CTMR	Custom Trade Mark Red	208.00
TM	Trade Mark	73.00
TMR	Trade Mark Red	103.50
TC	Trade Cross Reference	18.50
TN	Trade Name Listing	14.00
TBLN / TNN	Trade Bold Listing Number/Trade Name Listing and Bold Number	18.50
TRL / TNRL	Trade Regular Listing/Trade Name Regular Listing	6.00
TE / TAL	Trade Extra Line/Trade Alternate Call Listing	4.50
TNE / TNAL	Trade Name Extra Line/Trade Name Alternate Call Listing	4.50
TALN	Trade Alternate Call Listing and Bold Number	9.50
TNAN	Trade Name Alternate Call Listing and Bold Number	9.50
6LS	6 Label Space	166.00
6LSR	6 Label Space Red	235.00
6HS	6 Half Space	166.00
6HSR	6 Half Space Red	235.00
5LS	5 Label Space	110.50
5LSR	5 Label Space Red	156.50
5HS	5 Half Space	110.50
5HSR	5 Half Space Red	156.50
4LS	4 Label Space	89.50
4LSR	4 Label Space Red	126.50
4HS	4 Half Space	89.50
4HSR	4 Half Space Red	126.50
3LS	3 Label Space	67.00
3HS	3 Half Space	67.00
2HS	2 Half Space	44.00
1HS	1 Half Space	40.00

Rates subject to change.

"Which Mr. Byun do you want to see? I'm Bong Hwan. My brother is Ki Ho. Do you wish to speak to him?"

"I'd like to speak to the top man," she replied. "Your president, I guess."

"We have no president. My brother and I run the business together. He is not here today. May I help you?"

"Thank you, yes. I'm Laura Barnes. I'm from the telephone company. I called a few days ago to make an appointment to talk with one of you about our Intelligent Yellow Pages directory. I think we can help you increase your sales volume considerably. I must say I think you have a very nice office here. Did you choose the pictures of Korea I see on the walls?"

"My wife did. What is it you said about smart pages?"

"Intelligent Yellow Pages. We have them with both English and Korean headings and can insert some phrases in Korean if you wish."

"Ah, you're talking about the telephone directory," said Byun Bong Hwan. "We already have them. In fact, we have three of them. Would you like to see them?"

"No, that's all right. . . . I know about the directories your newspapers publish. I'm talking about the Western Bell Directory. It goes to over a million people in the L.A. area. Here, I have a copy. Let me show you."

Byun listened intently as Laura proceeded with her approach. "I'm sure you're missing a lot of clients who would come your way if you had an ad in our directory. Statistics show that your ad will be seen many times a day by hundreds of people who would otherwise not know you are located here. And the ads are really quite reasonable. We bill monthly, which makes it easier to pay. It's an investment which brings a measurable return, I assure you."

"Yes, I know, Miss Barnes, but we're really not interested." As he said this, Laura realized that she had done all the talking up to now. Mr. Byun had listened but said nothing in return. She thought it was wise to press further.

"Are your clients mostly recent immigrants from Korea? Or do you cater to people who have been in Los Angeles for a while?"

"Oh, we get all sorts of people. Mostly relatives of those who are already here."

"What's this," she asked, pointing to the figure of a little tiger on his desk.

"That's the symbol of the Seoul Olympics," he replied.

"Oh, how cute. I didn't know you made things like this. Are they available in the stores around here?"

"Yes, I'd give this one to you, but it's the only one left in the office, I'm afraid. You may be able to buy one in Kim's Novelties, down the street. Look, Miss Barnes, I'm really not interested in your directories. I'm sorry. Maybe you'll have better luck with Kim's Novelties. I appreciate your visit. Good luck."

Laura left, determined to return and talk to Byun Ki Ho. On the way out, she observed that all the people she passed were Korean.

1:35 P.M.—Korean Foods

This time Laura had prepared well. She knew that her prospect, Park Joo Young, had developed a good business selling imported Korean canned and packaged foods in

Los Angeles' Koreatown. She had made an appointment and planned to be at the company office a few minutes early. Thinking that her prospect might appreciate an extra one, Laura took with her a copy of the Los Angeles central area community directory. On the way to the office, Laura was delayed by a fire that blocked a section of Olympic Boulevard; nevertheless, she was only 5 minutes late when she walked through the door.

A young woman announced Laura to her employer who directed her to send Laura right in. "How do you do, Mr. Young," Laura began, "I'm glad you can make time to see me. I have what I think is a great way to help you do more business than ever before." With that, she reached into her briefcase and drew out the L.A. community directory, made sure the cover was in a readable position for her host, and handed it across the desk, closing the briefcase meanwhile.

So intent was Laura on doing everything she could to promote a sale, she did not notice the slight flinch in Park's face and sailed into her approach. "That's a great logo you have there, Mr. Young. It's a little like the Olympics rings, only it's triangles instead. That must do its part in contributing to your bottom line, and I've got some suggestions for making your business fly even faster."

Park Joo Young listened intently to all that Laura had to say, giving little indication of how he was reacting to the spiel until she had completed her recommendation. "Miss Barnes," said Park, "what you say is very interesting, but I want to put my advertising in the three Korean directories published by our Korean newspapers. I do not think your American people are so much wanting to buy our Korean foods. Maybe our tastes are a bit spicy for you. So thank you for coming to talk to me, but I'm pretty busy right now. So goodbye. I hope you can find other customers. Goodbye."

Laura left the office. She felt pretty low. "What did I do wrong?" she wondered. After almost a full day of calls on Chinese and Korean small businesses, with little or no result, she began to think that maybe these were impossible sales calls. "Is it my approach? Or is it their attitude toward Yellow Pages advertising?" she thought. She remembered, however, that many of the businesses bought ads in every single one of their own language versions of the telephone directory. But the Western Bell Yellow Pages offered the most value because of its thorough distribution. "Why can't they see that?" she wondered.

TODD TOLLIVER

Age, 30
Years of experience, 3

Thursday, 3:00 P.M.—Hong Kong Fabrics

Todd Toliver made his way along the corridor on the tenth floor of the California Mart. Shop after shop attracted his gaze. It seemed as though every clothing firm in the country had an outlet or sales office here. Perhaps he was right in thinking that it would pay him to drop in on a few firms unannounced. After all, he had to park only once, and there might be two or three good new clients here.

When he came to Hong Kong Fabrics, he checked his central directory. Sure enough, it was not listed in the Yellow Pages, so he walked in.

"Hi," he said in his friendliest tone to the sharp-looking young man behind the table. "Can I have a minute of your time?"

"What are you selling?"

"Western Bell Yellow Pages. The name's Todd Tolliver. Here's my card. And your name is . . .?"

"Everett Lee. And I can tell you right now, we're not buying any."

"Wait a minute. Can I talk to the boss?"

"I *am* the boss."

"Fine, you're just the man I want to see. You say your name is Lee? That's Korean, I thought. Is Lee a Chinese name, too?"

"Has been for centuries. Sometimes people spell it L-i, Li. Same thing. But I'm definitely not Korean."

"It's hard for me to tell the difference sometimes between people from Asia. A person could be Chinese or Japanese or Korean, for all I can tell. Sorry about that. I guess we should do a better job of getting to know the differences while we're in school studying history, or something."

"Yes. Well, look, Mr. Gulliver, I'm really not in the market for Yellow Pages just now. Why not try someone down the hall?"

"Gosh, Mr. Lee, just let me prove to you how much more business you can do if you're in the Intelligent Yellow Pages. We've got evidence that your sales will likely double, even triple, once you've got a half-page ad in our book."

"What's the cost of a half page?"

"Just a few hundred a month. Your new business will cover that 10 times over."

"Sorry, Gulliver, but we're a wholesale company. The number of customers who need our fabrics in Los Angeles is limited, and we know who they are. Ads in a telephone directory aren't going to multiply them. We maintain this showroom for their convenience, not for people who walk in from the street. How did you get in here anyway? Do you know somebody who got you past the guard?"

"No, I just walked in. Nobody stopped me. I guess I look official or something."

"Well, as I said a minute ago, we're not interested. I don't want to be rude, but you're really wasting your time."

"Okay, I'll go. But first tell me, are you from Hong Kong or were you born here?"

"I was born in Hong Kong. I came here with my family when I was fourteen. That was in 1973. My father is in Hong Kong right now, buying fabrics made on the mainland. I get to go to Hong Kong four or five times a year. Ever been there? You should go some time. You might meet some more Lees there. Would you like to buy a few bolts of patterned silk for your lady friend? I can give you a good price, wholesale."

"Nah, my gal doesn't know how to close a safety pin, let alone make a dress. But thanks for the offer. . . . Look, I'm sorry, I guess I came on like the proverbial bull in a china shop. Forgive me."

"That's all right. Come again sometime. But not with Yellow Pages."

"Gee, I see I've really teed you off. I'm truly sorry. I certainly didn't mean to be offensive or aggressive. And how was I to know you were the boss? Isn't your father the boss? I don't understand the way Chinese business works. I thought the father of a family business was the boss until he died. Where can I learn about such things? Are there any courses in the colleges or universities around here?"

"I doubt it. It takes a Chinese to know Chinese culture and business etiquette. Let me tell you something. If you want to sell to a Chinese, you have to *be* Chinese."

"Always?"

"Always, unless you can quote all the sayings of Confucius."

"But what about people like yourself? You're as American as I am. Do I have to be Chinese to convince someone like you that I've got a good deal for him?"

"Being Chinese is something more than being born in China or Taiwan or Hong Kong or Singapore. It's in the blood."

"Now, you've *really* got me worried. What chance is there for assimilation if this is the case? Will we never get to the place where cultural roots become intertwined and the different races are grafted into one vine?"

"My guess is that such a happening would produce sour grapes all around," said Lee. "Let's just be glad for things the way they are. . . . I'll give you credit, though, for being philosophical. That's a Chinese trait."

"See? Maybe you'll consider Yellow Pages after all!"

"So long, Gulliver. Travel on."

5:00 P.M.—The Happy Face Fish Market

Todd was uncertain about the prospects of his next call but thought it was at least worth a try. He had just sold a half-page display ad to what seemed to be a very successful medical practice along Atlantic Boulevard in Monterey Park. The senior partner in the practice, a Dr. Raymond Leung, had suggested that he call on the Happy Face Fish Market and explain the value of advertising to a food business. He said: "Be sure to mention my name and that I sent you."

Upon arriving at the fish market, Todd introduced himself to an elderly woman working in the front of the store, carefully placing various fish on ice in an open display case. The woman did not seem to understand any English and called out to the back of the store in what Todd assumed to be Chinese. A young boy about 15 years old came out from the back and introduced himself to Todd. "Hello, how may I help you?" the boy asked Todd.

Todd explained that he had been asked to come to the fish market and explain the value of advertising in the Yellow Pages to the store owner. The boy then said: "Oh, you want to see my grandfather," and went back into the rear of the fish shop. Todd could hear a conversation taking place in the back of the store in again what he thought to be Chinese. It was several minutes before any one came from the back of the store. In the meantime, Todd mentioned to the elder woman what nice weather it had been lately. She looked at him and smiled a very broad and somewhat toothless grin, but said nothing.

Finally, an elderly man came from the back of store wearing an apron and wiping his hands on a rag. The boy also returned with the man. Todd introduced himself, uncertain whether to bow or shake hands. He informed the Chinese man that he was from the Western Bell Yellow Pages Directory. The man bowed and smiled at Todd. The boy said: "This is my grandfather, Mr. Koh." Todd then told Mr. Koh that Dr. Raymond Leung had suggested he call and explain the value of the Yellow Pages to running a food business. The boy said something very quickly in Chinese to the old man. This seemed to start all three of the Chinese talking at once, none of which Todd understood.

For the next half hour or so the conversation varied from a question-and-answer session on the volume of business and type of customer to a discussion of the importance of advertising and why the Western Bell Yellow Pages were superior to advertising in Chinese language newspapers and other directories distributed through local stores and associations. As a result of the discussion, Todd found out that all Mr. Koh's customers were Chinese, but that the business was wholesale as well as retail. Todd commented that the business seemed rather prosperous based upon the results of his factfinding. To this, Mr. Koh said: "Nali, nali!" The boy said: "Not really."

The interesting part of the entire conversation was that the boy served as an interpreter for Mr. Koh who spoke only Chinese. The owner of the Happy Face Fish Market seemed genuinely interested in what Todd was telling him and the boy translating. The sales call ended when the boy said to Todd: "My grandfather says he finds some value in what you have been telling him, but that he has to get back to work now. He wonders if you could come back at 6:30 A.M. on Saturday to discuss this matter further with him."

Todd felt angry. Hadn't he come at the request of Dr. Leung and spent almost an hour carefully explaining everything about his product? And now he was being asked to come back on the weekend, at 6:30 in the morning. He was barely able to mutter, "Thanks for your time, goodbye" before stomping out of the market. As he burst through the door, almost knocking over a small counter of dried fish, he heard the boy turn to the old man and say: "I have to go home and do my homework now, Grandfather." To which the old man replied: "O.K. I see you later."

"What went wrong?" Todd thought, was there anything he could learn from this sales call to improve future selling efforts within the Chinese community? What should he do now with respect to this account?

Friday, 11:50 A.M.—Che Chu Travel Agency

It had been a good week for Todd with the exception of a few calls in Monterey Park. A higher percentage of calls than he could ever remember were successful, and he thought it might be due to the experiment he had been trying. Instead of planning a number of calls in the same geographical area, Todd had decided to call on similar types of businesses in as close proximity as possible. It meant driving a little farther, but it seemed to improve his overall sales presentation and closing ability. Today it had been travel agencies. This morning he had sold three DHCs (double half columns), one with red.

Now it was just approaching noon and Todd thought, "Maybe one more call and a late lunch on the run." He grabbed a soda while filling up at the gas station and then headed for the next call. It was for a Che Chu Travel Agency on Olympic Blvd. "Uh Oh," thought Todd. "Koreatown!"

Upon arriving at the travel agency, Todd introduced himself to the receptionist, an attractive Korean woman who looked 20 at the oldest, and asked to see the manager or owner of the agency. The receptionist asked him to "sit down, please," and continued her typing. Todd wasn't sure she had heard what he had said, or perhaps she hadn't quite understood. Todd got up, went back to the receptionist, and in a little louder voice this time, said: "I want to see the manager or owner, okay?" To this the receptionist replied in perfect English: "He is busy with a client right now, but I will introduce you as soon as it is convenient."

It was about another 15 minutes. Todd had not seen anyone leave and wondered what had happened to the "client" who had kept him waiting. Upon entering the owner's office he introduced himself. The owner handed him a business card and introduced himself as Mr. Young Bum Kim. The business card, however, said Kim Young Bum on one side and had oriental letters on the other. Todd had been so busy earlier that morning that he had run out of business cards in his wallet. He had some in the back of the car but didn't feel it was necessary to get them now. Instead, he tried to get down to the sales presentation. The owner interrupted Todd to ask if he would like something to drink. Todd wasn't all that thirsty and replied, "No, thanks, I just had a Coke." Mr. Kim, or was it Bum, just grunted and smiled. Todd went back to concentrating on his sales pitch.

"Now, Mr. Young Bum Kim, I'm sure that you'll agree with me that running a travel agency isn't all that easy and that any help you can get is important," said Todd. Mr. Kim said that running a travel agency was important and provided clients with valuable service. He wanted to provide his clients with the best service available from a Korean travel agency.

"Right," said Todd. "Just as I was saying." The rest of the call seemed to go that way, with Todd not on the same wavelength as the owner. Todd pressed on, however, and thought he was doing fairly well until he got to some of Mr. Kim's objections. It seemed that Mr. Kim had no objections to advertising but that he placed all of his with the Korean newspapers and six Korean directories. He really didn't see any value in advertising in the Western Bell/Donnelly Yellow Pages as he described it.

Todd could see that Mr. Kim was confused about the various competing versions of the Yellow Pages. How should he try to counter this objection? Was the sale hopelessly lost anyway? Why not just cut his losses, he wondered, and head for lunch? Forget Koreatown, forget Kim or was it Bum? Forget Che Chu Travel, whatever that stood for anyway!

Monday, 2:00 P.M.—Kim's Beauty Salon

The Monday after Todd Tolliver's call on the Che Chu Travel Agency, he was concentrating on beauty shops and barbers. The next call he had planned was at the Kim Beauty Salon on Vermont Avenue. Once again he had been doing very well up until this call and was filling the book. This time he was prepared. He had business cards and some promotional items to give to the prospective account.

When he entered the beauty shop he told the first beautician he encountered that he wanted to speak to Mrs. or Mr. Kim. The beautician seemed puzzled and uncertain what to do. She hesitatingly asked in very broken English why Todd wanted to see Mrs. or Mr. Kim. Todd explained that he was from Western Bell Yellow Pages and wanted to speak to the owner regarding the possibility of placing a display ad in the book for their area. The beautician still seemed uncertain but suggested that Todd talk to Mrs. Moon at the last chair.

Todd approached Mrs. Moon, who did not have a customer at that time, and introduced himself. He asked to speak to Mrs. or Mr. Kim about the possibility of their advertising in the Western Bell Yellow Pages. Mrs. Moon smiled and said: "There is not Mr. or Mrs. Kim, I am the owner." Todd was now a little bit confused, but continued nevertheless. He handed Mrs. Moon his card and gave her an "Open" and "Closed" sign for the door of her store. Mrs. Moon thanked Todd and began a long discussion of many things including her husband, her son who was attending the University of Southern California, the place they had come from in Korea, and many other nonbusiness-related topics. Todd had trouble both being polite and guiding the conversation toward the issue of advertising in the Western Bell Yellow Pages. He finally got things on track, and then questioned the usefulness of Korean newspapers (well, or so he thought) by indicating that an ad might not appear in the same place from day to day. When it came to Korean directories, Todd indicated that Mrs. Moon spoke very good English and she should think of attracting American as well as Korean customers to use her services during the lunch hours. Mrs. Moon seemed open to Todd's suggestions and let him write up a sales contract on a 5LS type ad. When she saw the price, however, she remarked that it was a little bit high. She wanted to know what kind of discount could Todd give her for the ad. Todd indicated that there was no discount policy for any ads, but that she would get a price break if she placed ads in more than one of the directories. Mrs. Moon hesitated for a moment and then asked how much of a discount Todd could give her if she advertised in his book and the Donnelly Yellow Pages. Todd chuckled a little, and explained that his company had no connection with the Donnelly Yellow Pages, that he had meant two or more of the books his company published. He then explained the selections available to Mrs. Moon. But she thought beauty shops served a very limited geographical area and that advertising in more than the book for her area would not be beneficial.

Todd agreed and pressed for the close again. This time Mrs. Moon told Todd that she would have to discuss this with her husband and that he should call her back the next day. The next day Todd called back several times, to no avail. It seemed each time he called, Mrs. Moon was with a customer and his requests for her to call him went unheeded.

At this point Todd thought Mrs. Moon was avoiding him and that he should quit wasting his time. But he had done a good job in explaining the value of Yellow Pages advertising, hadn't he? He questioned the value of driving over to Vermont Avenue in Koreatown to make a face-to-face sales call. But the phone wasn't working and he did want a higher closing rate with Asian small-business owners. They were taking over the retail scene in Los Angeles and would soon comprise the majority of retail business in many areas. To be unable to understand and to sell to this group of entrepreneurs would eliminate more and more retail display ads in the book. For Todd that would mean a slow and steady decline in sales opportunities.

32

K MART STORES: WHERE AMERICA SHOPS AND SAVES

INTRODUCTION

From the time it opened its first K mart store in 1962, the S. S. Kresge Company had stuck with the same formula. Since then, hundreds of fairly uniform K mart stores had been opened throughout the United States. Each one was a simple boxlike building and sold low- to medium-quality merchandise. Most important, the merchandise was priced lower than any other competitor. This approach proved to be very successful, especially among price-conscious shoppers who left full-service department stores *en masse* to shop at K mart and other discounters. The K mart logo itself became a symbol of low prices in the minds of many shoppers. By 1976, the chain had become the number one discounter in the United States and the second general merchandise retailer behind only Sears, but ahead of J. C. Penney and Montgomery Ward. Exhibit 32.1 shows the top 20 general merchandise chains for 1983, when K mart was still ranked number two, according to annual sales.

By the 1980s, however, the old K mart formula didn't seem to work as well. Younger shoppers had become more discriminating than their parents, and many had

This case was written by John L. Little (Doctoral Student in Strategic Management) and Larry D. Alexander (Assistant Professor of Strategic Management), both from the Department of Management, The R.B. College of Business, Virginia Polytechnic Institute & State University, Blacksburg, Virginia 24061. Copyright © 1987 by John L. Little and Larry D. Alexander greater disposable income. These younger shoppers wanted higher-quality merchandise and were willing to pay for it. Other retailers had moved in to satisfy this new consumer group before K mart reacted. In the process, they helped create a retail environment that had never been more competitive. Furthermore, the successful market penetration of warehouse clubs and specialty stores into the retailing industry meant even more intense competition for discount stores in the future.

Clearly, times were changing which could adversely impact K mart. How these new retail competitors, which emphasized different competitive weapons, would financially impact K mart in the coming years remained to be seen. How K mart would choose to respond to these challenges in the dynamic 1980s was likewise unclear. One issue, however, remained clear. Was the K mart approach, which had been so successful during the 1960s and much of the 1970s, becoming obsolete? Did it need to be changed? And, if so, what would these changes be?

HISTORY

The S. S. Kresge Company was founded in 1899 with the opening of a single store in downtown Detroit, Michigan. Its founder, Sebastian Kresge, who followed a slogan of "Nothing over ten cents," rapidly opened a number of other stores in new locations. He standardized the mix of merchandise, continued to emphasize low prices, and centralized the purchasing function. This last move greatly increased the power that Kresge had over suppliers while reducing administrative overhead. In turn, it made the opening of additional stores easier by spreading overhead costs over a wider base. Kresge soon developed operating procedures that permitted centralized control over a growing number of uniform stores. The lower prices charged by Kresge caused individual store volume to increase substantially. This increased company profits which provided the necessary funds to open still more stores. When the company was incorporated in 1912, Kresge's "five and ten" style stores numbered 85 and had a combined annual sales of more than $10 million.

Variety stores grew in popularity through the 1920s and 1930s as a more convenient means of shopping than earlier established specialty stores. By 1940, a number of variety store chains had been established. The greater buying power available to these chain stores allowed them to underprice specialty stores that concentrated in just one product line. Clearly, the combination of lower prices and wider selection of different product categories was a powerful attraction to customers. Furthermore, since more and more shoppers had their own cars, they were able to travel farther from home to save money.

After World War II, the introduction of shopping centers and supermarkets began to draw customers away from variety stores. To counter this, some variety retailers began to look for new ways to attract customers. In 1954, for example, Marty Chase converted an old mill in Cumberland, Rhode Island, into a discount store and named the new store Ann and Hope. The store sold ribbon, greeting cards, and women's clothing. As other discount stores opened through the 1950s, Harry Cunningham, Kresge's president, began to consider a similar approach. Finally, in 1962, Kresge responded by opening its first K mart discount store in Garden City, Michi-

Exhibit 32.1

TOP 20 GENERAL MERCHANDISE CHAINS, 1982–1983

	1982		1983		
Rank and Chain	Volume (S000)	Total Stores	Volume (S000)	Total Stores	Sales Change (%)
1. Sears	18,778,800	831	20,438,700	813	+ 8.9%
2. K mart	16,772,200	2,370	18,597,900	2,547	+10.9
3. J. C. Penney	11,414,400	2,053	12,078,000	2,014	+ 5.8
4. Federated	6,423,200	831	7,324,059	424	+12.3
5. Dayton-Hudson	5,660,729	980	6,963,300	1,075	+23.0
6. Montgomery Ward	5,584,000	389	6,003,000	375	+ 7.5
7. F. W. Woolworth	5,124,000	5,124	5,456,000	5,276	+ 6.5
8. Wal-Mart	3,376,252	541	4,666,909	646	+38.2
9. May Dept. Stores	3,653,900	1,468	4,211,800	1,584	+15.3
10. Associated Dry Goods	3,188,858	247	3,717,827	318	+16.6
11. Allied Stores	3,215,634	533	3,675,873	570	+14.3
12. Carter-Hawley-Hale	3,054,764	1,026	3,632,662	1,085	+18.9
13. R. H. Macy	2,979,931	92	3,468,144	93	+16.4
14. Melville	2,623,928	5,016	3,169,036	5,234	+20.8
15. BATUS	2,467,135	178	3,145,050	196	+27.5
16. Zayre	2,139,616	617	2,613,667	753	+22.2
17. Tandy Corp.	2,032,555	8,518	2,475,188	8,868	+21.8
18. Wickes	2,638,215	N.A.	2,875,085	2,800	+ 9.0
19. Household Merchandising	2,926,900	3,768	2,872,000	3,664	− 1.9
20. Best Products	1,581,650	202	2,081,328	218	+31.5

N.A. = Not available.

Source: Standard & Poor's *Industrial Survey*, July 4, 1985, p. 115.

gan. In essence, K mart discount stores were nothing more than a large-scale version of the earlier Kresge retail stores. They still emphasized low prices, a wide selection, and low overhead costs which combined to create profits.

The first K mart stores were stocked primarily with Kresge merchandise. A number of licensees, who operated departments within the store, added to the merchandise selection. Over the years, however, top management at K mart replaced these licensees with its own merchandise. Overall, the initial stores were a great success, and, by 1966, they numbered 162 and generated a combined sales of over $1 billion.

The K mart formula remained relatively unchanged for quite a few years. New K mart stores were added by the hundreds each year. Almost all of them were uniform, freestanding stores located away from large shopping centers. By erecting simple freestanding buildings in suburban areas, K mart opened its stores much faster than did its competitors who had to wait for shopping centers to be completed. This also helped to keep overhead costs down since the freestanding stores were not located in expensive shopping malls. K mart stores were placed in almost all major U.S.

metropolitan areas. During the 1960s and 1970s, corporate annual sales grew by an average of 20 percent per year primarily because consumers found K mart's blend of low price and selection so attractive. The company's smaller Kresge stores, unlike its K mart stores, were not as profitable, and many were closed during this period.

By 1976, the Kresge Company had become the second largest general merchandise retailer in the United States behind only Sears. During the next year, the corporate name was changed from the Kresge Company to the K mart Corporation in recognition of the fact that K mart stores accounted for 94.5 percent of all corporate sales.

By the late 1970s, several adverse trends were troubling to K mart. Good locations for new K mart stores were becoming more difficult to find. Other discount chains were drawing away some K mart shoppers. Industry surveys indicated that the needs of the customers were changing. While other discounters started upgrading their stores and started emphasizing brand-name merchandise, K mart continued to sell primarily low-priced unbranded and private-label goods in the same austere-looking stores. As a result of these trends, K mart sales growth started to flatten.

Finally, in 1980, Bernard Fauber was named chief executive officer, replacing an unusual arrangement in which three men shared the office of the president. Fauber quickly moved to refurbish its dated K mart stores and to upgrade the quality of goods that they carried. New display racks, better point-of-purchase displays, and improved traffic flow through the stores helped to make them more attractive to customers.

FUNCTION AREA STRATEGIES WITHIN THE K MART STORES

Marketing

Early on, K mart stores emphasized low prices as an important marketing weapon. However, low prices usually meant that the product being offered was of lower quality. For hard goods such as kitchen appliances, it usually meant just the basic product was carried, without extra features that higher-priced models offered. Still, K mart stores satisfied a real need among its customers who just wanted basic products or who could afford nothing more.

K mart focused on satisfying the needs of low- and middle-income families with limited budgets, who were unwilling to pay higher prices for similar products with extra features. It was estimated that 80 percent of all Americans shopped at K mart sometime during the year.

Promotion of K mart's products was accomplished in several ways. First, sales promotion was emphasized by attractive in-store, point-of-purchase displays. Second K mart's well-known "blue light specials" were used to promote specific products for short periods of time during the day.

K mart relied heavily on newspaper advertising for quite some time to promote it goods. Newspaper inserts were designed at corporate headquarters and sent to newspapers throughout the country for publication. Store managers were sent advertising copy in advance so they could prepare for the sales. The company had placed approximately 120,000,000 inserts in 1,700 different newspapers throughout the United States by the mid-1980s. While the company continued to emphasize newspapers, increasing attention was being given to television advertising. This was relatively economical once K mart numbered some two thousand stores across the nation.

With its high level of market penetration, K mart had initiated a new effort to get customers to buy more goods per shopping trip. Management felt that this would be facilitated by the fact that disposable family incomes of traditional K mart customers had risen. This increase in family income had largely been caused by a significant increase in the number of two-income families. In addition, K mart estimated that 19 percent of it customers were from households with annual incomes of $40,000 or more, but this customer group typically bought only limited items such as tennis balls, batteries, and shampoo at K mart. K mart added more national-brand merchandise and higher-quality private labels and then displayed them attractively. Such brand-name products as Casio, Minolta, Nike, MacGregor, Wilson, and General Electric were increasingly found throughout the store. K mart hoped that these actions would help increase the per sale purchase and attract higher-income customers to other product areas. At the same time, the company hoped to retain the less affluent shopper by continuing to offer an assortment of lower-priced, lower-quality merchandise.

K mart did extremely well in certain departments but performed weakly in others. It was the leader in housewares and the second largest appliance retailer behind only Sears. Many customers were attracted to branded appliances and housewares by K mart's low prices. Unfortunately, these same customers were turned off by K mart's cheap clothing that had a low image among consumers. Its apparel departments, in fact, had been a major shortcoming for K mart through the years. K mart tried to address this problem by upgrading many lines of clothing. The responsibility for ordering apparel was taken away from store managers and given to professional staff buyers at corporate headquarters, who were more knowledgeable about fashion.

K mart had also moved into specialty discount stores through acquisition. The first Designer Depot, which was an off-price specialty apparel store, was started in Detroit during 1982. These stores sold first-quality branded merchandise at discounts of 20 to 70 percent. Some stores also sold shoes, while others sold bedroom and bathroom soft goods. By 1985, there were 64 of these stores in operation, and plans called for 20 new stores to be added each year.

The company also acquired several other impressive specialty chains. Walden Book Company, Inc., another K mart acquisition in 1985, operated 943 stores in all 50 states. Builders Square, Inc., a warehouse-type home improvement center chain, was acquired in 1984. The company had 25 stores located in eight states by 1985. Fredrick Stevens, executive vice president of specialty retailing operations, argued that 400 locations across the country could support the volume requirements of these huge discount builders supply warehouses. Builders Square wanted 25 percent of that business.[1]

[1]"K mart: A Look Inside the Nation's Largest Discounter," *Mass Market Retailers*, December 16, 1985, p. 42.

Pay Less Drug Stores Northwest, another K mart acquisition in 1985, was the tenth largest drug chain in the nation. With sales approaching $1 billion and 176 stores, the chain hoped to expand rapidly, primarily in its present markets in California, Oregon, Washington, Idaho, and Nevada. K mart planned eventually to expand its drug store operations nationwide, possibly through additional acquisitions. In general, Pay Less was a deep discount chain, supported by a very cost-efficient operation and strong management.

Two final K mart acquisitions were in the restaurant industry. Furr's Cafeterias, acquired earlier in 1980, and Bishop Buffets, acquired in 1983, had a combined 162 units by 1985. Growth in this division was expected to be limited to 10 percent per year in new stores because of slow growth of the cafeteria industry.

K mart Corporation had limited involvement in overseas markets. It did have, however, a 20 percent interest in G. L. Coles and Coy Limited, a food and general merchandise retailer in Australia. It also had a 44 percent interest in Astra, S.A., which operated a food and general merchandise chain in Mexico.

Store Operations

During the 1980s, K mart clearly had approached market saturation, with its stores seemingly located everywhere. Its 2,000-plus stores were located in 250 of the United States' 255 Standard Metropolitan Statistical Areas (SMSA). From a record 271 new stores opened in 1976, only 21 new K mart stores were opened in 1984.

K mart switched from opening so many new stores to renovating existing ones. This effort, which was started in the early 1980s, was intended to increase productivity as well as to upgrade the store image. Wider and taller display cases carried more merchandise and made better use of cubic space. This allowed for a wider assortment of merchandise to be displayed within the same square footage. This also reduced the need for additional backroom storage. A new store layout was developed around a wide center aisle which let consumers walk through every department without leaving the aisle. As one K mart store manager put it, "We want to encourage people to go into areas where they would not normally go . . . to pass by merchandise they were not planning to buy!"[2]

All K mart stores were designed around this same basic floor plan, as shown in Exhibit 32.2. As shoppers entered the store, they were no longer assaulted by the smell of popcorn and the sight of gumball machines. Instead they might be greeted by the jewelry department with a wide selection of watches and jewelry of various price ranges. The main aisle down the center of the store separated soft goods from hard goods. On the soft goods side of the store were located women's apparel, then men's apparel, with infants' wear, and children's clothes nearby. Popular crafts and yarn were also located in this side where homemakers were most likely to look for them. In the hard goods half of the store, housewares, sporting goods, automotive supplies, and hardware were located at the rear of the store, drawing men and women past high-impulse, high-margin merchandise in the greeting cards, jewelry and toy sections. The health and beauty items and the pharmacies for those stores that had them were typically located in the right front section of the store.

[2]Ibid., p. 20.

Exhibit 32.2 **K MART'S BASIC FLOOR PLAN**

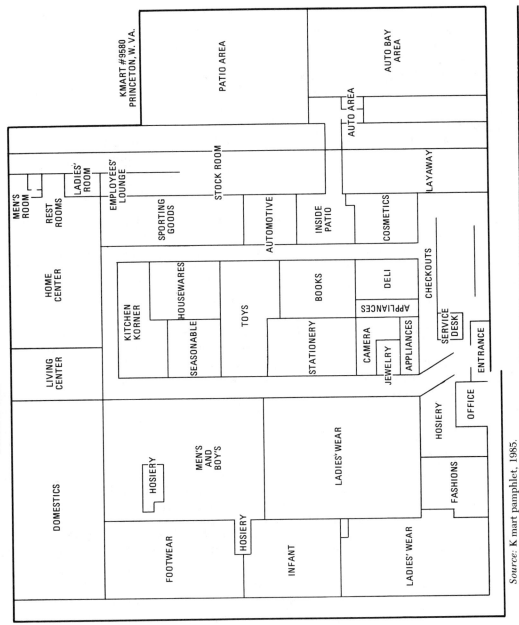

Source: K mart pamphlet, 1985.

539

Electronic communications systems connected all stores to 10 enormous regional distribution centers. These centers were located in Nevada, California, Texas, Kansas, Minnesota, Michigan, Indiana, Ohio, Pennsylvania, and Georgia, as shown in Exhibit 32.3. These highly automated warehouses contained a combined 15 million square feet of warehouse space. Together, they operated a fleet of 250 tractors and 1,000 trailers, which provided weekly delivery to every K mart store which requested it.

Approximately 25 percent of K mart's merchandise was handled by these distribution centers. In contrast, 75 percent of all store purchases were shipped directly from suppliers to the stores themselves to minimize shipping cost. The delivery of products purchased from suppliers was usually fast in order to keep such a large account as K mart satisfied. This also helped reduce inventory level requirements at stores to minimum levels. Significant reductions in reorder time had also been achieved by installing optical scanner registers. Scanning, coupled with a company-wide computer network, also permitted automated replenishment of merchandise and made it possible to differentiate the seasonal needs of each region.

As part of efforts to upgrade its image, K mart was completing a major remodeling program of store interiors to present a stronger fashion appearance to shoppers. This new effort, called "The K mart of the Eighties," incorporated a new color scheme on floors and walls, broader aisles, and more attractive displays. Low-volume lines were dropped or consolidated to achieve a store-within-a-store format. Kitchen Corners, Home Care Centers, and Domestic Centers arranged along the back wall emphasized fashion and style at discount prices. The early success of the plan was helpful. Sales per square foot had risen from $139 in 1980 to $168 in 1984. While this was superior to the $128 per square foot typical among discounter department stores, it was far behind industry leaders such as Target and Wal-Mart.

Product categories no longer in demand were eliminated, such as 360 automotive service departments in rural stores which were closed in 1982. Unprofitable stores were closed altogether, freeing up more than $1 million each in capital for use in other parts of the corporation.

K mart stores were organized into six regions, each of which had from 266 to 422 stores. Each region comprised about 20 districts, and each district had from 10 to 20 stores.

K mart stores came in five basic sizes. The smallest was the 40,000-square-foot sized store, which was placed in smaller markets. At the other end was the jumbo 120,000-square-foot store used in its largest metropolitan markets. These stores were located in suburban areas, as freestanding buildings with large parking lots, and were usually leased rather than owned. Buildings were erected by local contractors for the most part, but a K mart subsidiary built several stores each year and allowed the company to remain knowledgeable about building costs.

K mart's decision to avoid shopping center locations was part of its low-overhead philosophy. Lease costs at shopping centers were very high compared to K mart locations. Shopping centers generally did not want discounters as tenants, because of the negative image associated with them. Also, specialty stores did not want to locate next to a discount store because of the significant price differential between their products and K mart's. Sometimes, K mart would buy existing buildings in shopping

Exhibit 32.3

K MART STORE DISTRIBUTION NETWORK

Store Distribution Network*

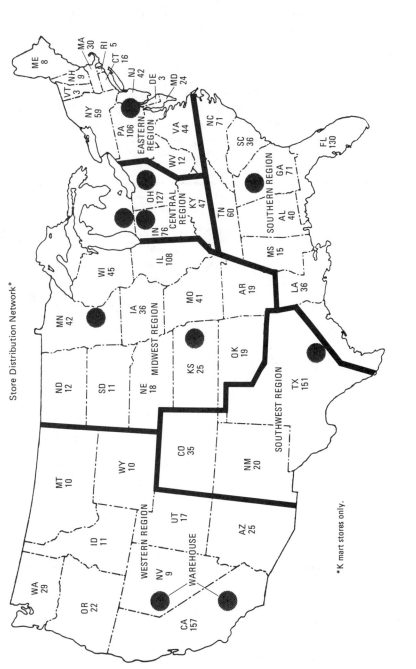

Source: Mass Market Retailers, December 16, 1985, p. 42.

* K mart stores only.

centers or develop properties in good locations and sublease retail space to specialty stores. This trend reflected the strategy to diversify into retail areas of above-average growth potential, where in-house expertise could be used.

Finance

Total sales for K mart Corporation, as shown in K mart's consolidated statement of income in Exhibit 32.4, were $21.1 billion for fiscal year 1984, which ended on January 30, 1985. This represented a 13.4 percent increase over the sales for the previous year. Net income after taxes for that same year was $499.1 million. The consolidated

Exhibit 32.4

K MART CORPORATION CONSOLIDATED STATEMENTS OF INCOME, 1983–1984
(millions, except per share data)

	FISCAL YEAR ENDED		
	January 30, 1985	January 25, 1984	January 26, 1983
Sales	$21,095.9	$18,597.9	$16,772.2
Licensee fees and rental income	207.5	191.3	169.5
Equity in income of affiliated retail companies	58.8	51.7	44.5
Interest income	39.7	38.0	54.6
	21,401.9	18,878.9	17,040.8
Cost of merchandise sold (including buying and occupancy costs)	15,259.8	13,447.4	12,298.6
Selling, general, and administrative expenses	4,427.7	3,880.1	3,602.9
Advertising	554.4	424.6	401.7
Provision for store closings			44.5
Interest expense			
Debt	146.5	84.1	97.7
Capital lease obligations	193.5	189.0	176.5
	20,581.9	18,025.2	16,621.9
Income before income taxes	820.0	853.7	418.9
Income taxes	327.1	366.5	162.0
Income from retail operations	492.9	487.2	256.9
Equity in income of insurance operations	6.2	5.1	4.9
Net income for the year	$ 499.1	$ 492.3	$ 261.8
Earnings per common and common equivalent share	$3.84	$3.80	$2.06

Source: K mart Annual Report, 1985.

balance sheet for fiscal 1984 and 1983 is shown in Exhibit 32.5. Finally, a comparison of sales and various financial data over a 10-year period are presented in Exhibit 32.6.

Retail sales at K mart were extremely seasonal with a high proportion of sales and profits coming during the Christmas shopping season. Some 33 percent of K mart's 1984 sales and 41 percent of its profits came during that fourth quarter alone.

Exhibit 32.5

K MART CORPORATION CONSOLIDATED BALANCE SHEETS, 1984–1985
(millions)

	January 30, 1985	January 25, 1984
Assets		
Current assets		
Cash (includes temporary investments of $294.3 and $762.9, respectively)	$ 492.0	$1,027.7
Accounts receivable	179.0	134.8
Merchandise inventories	4,587.8	3,581.6
Operating supplies and prepaid expenses	52.0	44.4
Total current assets	5,310.8	4,788.5
Investments in and advances to		
Affiliated retail companies	219.2	211.8
Insurance operations	173.1	128.6
Property and equipment, net	3,338.8	2,973.7
Cost in excess of fair value of net assets acquired, net	140.6	14.4
Other assets	79.3	66.1
	$9,261.8	$8,183.1
Liabilities and Shareholders' Equity		
Current liabilities		
Long-term debt due within one year	$ 1.9	$ 3.2
Capital lease obligations due within one year	74.1	70.6
Notes payable	234.9	
Accounts payable—trade	1,916.9	1,717.2
Accrued payrolls and other liabilities	362.5	328.0
Taxes other than income taxes	200.0	172.9
Income taxes	98.8	228.9
Total current liabilities	2,889.1	2,520.8
Capital lease obligations	1,780.1	1,822.3
Long-term debt	1,106.9	711.2
Other long-term liabilities	163.4	127.8
Deferred income taxes	88.5	60.9
Shareholders' equity	3,233.8	2,940.1
	$9,261.8	$8,183.1

Source: K mart Annual Report, 1985.

Exhibit 32.6

K MART CORPORATION 10-YEAR FINANCIAL SUMMARY

	1984	1983	1982	1981	1980	1979	1978	1977	1976	1975
Summary of Operations (millions)										
Sales	$21,096	$18,598	$16,772	$16,527	$14,204	$12,731	$11,696	$9,941	$8,382	$6,798
Cost of merchandise sold	15,260	13,447	12,299	12,360	10,417	9,283	8,566	7,299	6,147	4,991
Selling, general, and administrative expenses	4,982	4,305	4,049	3,810	3,326	2,839	2,503	2,085	1,750	1,409
Interest expense, net	300	235	219	230	200	149	132	116	103	89
Income before income taxes	820	854	419	323	436	625	634	564	484	395
Net income	499	492	262	220	261	358	344	298	262	196
Per Share Data (dollars)										
Earnings per common and common equivalent share	$3.84	$3.80	$2.06	$1.75	$2.07	$2.84	$2.74	$2.39	$2.11	$1.61
Cash dividends declared	$1.24	$1.08	$1.00	$0.96	$0.92	$0.84	$0.72	$0.56	$0.32	$0.24
Book value	$25.87	$23.35	$20.89	$19.81	$18.99	$17.79	$15.68	$13.56	$11.62	$9.69
Financial Data (millions)										
Working capital	$ 2,422	$ 2,268	$ 1,827	$ 1,473	$ 1,552	$ 1,403	$ 1,308	$1,231	$1,074	$ 904
Total assets	9,262	8,183	7,344	6,657	6,089	5,635	4,836	4,489	3,983	3,336
Long-term obligations										
Debt	1,107	711	596	415	419	209	209	211	211	210
Capital leases	1,780	1,822	1,824	1,752	1,618	1,422	1,294	1,266	1,155	989
Shareholders' equity	3,234	2,940	2,601	2,456	2,343	2,185	1,916	1,649	1,409	1,169
Capital expenditures, owned property	622	368	306	361	302	292	217	162	123	112
Depreciation and amortization, owned property	203	168	157	141	119	93	77	65	56	52
Average shares outstanding	126	125	124	124	123	123	122	122	121	121

Source: K mart *1984 Annual Report,* pp. 16, 17.

K mart did not offer a charge card and did not encourage credit sales. By comparison, approximately 58 percent of arch rival Sears' sales were on credit. MasterCard and VISA credit cards were accepted, and limited in-house credit was provided on appliance sales. Most K mart stores, however, did require customers to follow a rigid two-step procedure for writing checks. The customer first had to get approval from the service desk and then wait at a checkout line to pay for the purchased items.

K mart policy for granting exchanges or refunds on merchandise which did not satisfy the customer was quite liberal. Most items could be returned for cash by customers with a minimum of hassle. This policy was inherited from the old Kresge variety stores. Similarly, K mart customers could get a rain check on any advertised item not found in stock at the time of the sale, without any problems.

INNOVATION

The K mart approach to innovation was to adopt new ideas only after they had been developed and proven successful by someone else. This approach avoided risk and had served K mart well through the years. Once a good idea was identified, however, K mart showed its genius in applying and perfecting it. For example, when the discount idea appeared, Kresge was the first to refine the concept with its K mart stores. Rapid expansion followed while other retailers looked on with amazement. The idea of standardizing the store floor plan and layout was another way of borrowing a good idea elsewhere and repeating it many times.

HUMAN RESOURCES/PERSONNEL

K mart Corporation employed more than 290,000 people in 1985, but tried to encourage a small-business feeling within its individual stores. Loyalty among store managers was unusually high and their turnover rate was low. Many K mart managers had never worked for any other employer, and 25-year service pins were common. Furthermore, promotion to managerial positions was almost entirely done from within. For those selected, the management training program consisted of 16 weeks starting in the stockroom. After the program, the trainees became assistant managers with responsibility for several departments. Typically, trainees were rotated through various departments and stores for 6 to 10 years before they were ready to manage their own stores.

The opportunity for promotion was strong in the 1970s when new stores were being opened at the rate of several per week. That changed in the 1980s when K mart greatly curtailed its new store openings. This threatened to increase employee turnover as assistant managers became impatient to move up. At the same time, K mart was reducing the number of assistant managers from three to two per store to cut administrative costs.

K mart relied heavily on part-time employees to operate its stores. The company goal was to have 60 percent part-time and 40 percent full-time employees in each store. This gave the store manager greater flexibility in matching the work force with the amount of traffic during different periods of the day. Also, the labor costs for part-time employees were considerably cheaper because they started at minimum wages and were not paid benefits. The great majority of these employees were women who only wanted to work part-time due to their family obligations. The company, however, did have an employee savings plan in which K mart contributed 50 cents in K mart stock for every one dollar that the employee contributed.

MANAGEMENT

Harry Cunningham designed the basic K mart format and led the company during the rapid growth from 1962 to 1972. When he stepped down in 1972, he appointed K mart's Robert Dewar, Ervin Wardlow, and Walter Tennga collectively to run the company. Dewar, with 32 years of legal and financial background but no store experience, was named chairman. Wardlow, with strong merchandising experience, was named president. Finally, Tennga, a real estate and financial executive, was named vice chairman. These three executives who ran the company for eight years, became known as the troika. Although sales tripled during that period, the three couldn't agree on which direction the company should take.

Finally, in 1980, Bernard Fauber was named the new chief executive officer at the suggestion of Dewar, who felt that K mart needed a store man at the top, rather than a staff man. Since then, K mart has made dramatic changes in its approach to business. As Fauber conceded,

> For 20 years we had been just about the most successful retailer in America, so it was not easy getting our people to admit that some changes were advisable and others were necessary.[3]

In explaining the reasons behind the move to diversification, Fauber added,

> We realized that we must do something else for growth since it was no longer possible to open 100 to 120 K mart stores each year.[4]

Fauber, like all but one previous CEO, was not a college graduate. He first came to work for the company in 1941 as an 18-year-old stockroom boy in a Kresge store. Nine years later, he joined the management training program. Later he gained experience as a store manager and district manager, and in 1968 became vice president of the Western Region. Like nearly all K mart executives, Fauber had never worked for any other company.

The K mart philosophy was to train its store managers as generalists and to give them wide discretion in running their stores. They had an incentive plan based on store profits to avoid the mistake Sears made when it tied its department manager incentive plan to sales volume. The Sears incentive system, which had since been

[3]Ibid., p. 54.
[4]Ibid., p. 54.

changed, caused its managers to focus on low-margin merchandise which boosted sales and their bonuses but hurt overall profits.

Store managers at K mart were encouraged to involve themselves and the store in community activity such as the United Way. One socially responsible effort K mart undertook was its "Lost Child Program" in 1985. The prime exposure available nationally at stores made K mart a good vehicle for the program and enhanced the corporate image at the same time.

THE RETAIL INDUSTRY

Market Segments

The retail industry was fragmented into several general segments which somewhat overlapped one another. There were full-line department stores, discount department stores, discount drugstores, specialty stores, supermarkets, and convenience shops. The trend toward one-stop shopping had blurred the distinctions among these various kinds of stores in recent years. For example, shoppers could find food items in drugstores (or discount stores) and clothing and hardware in supermarkets. Within the discount department store category, the emerging warehouse stores were the fastest-growing segment, along with discount specialty stores.

External Threats

By the mid-1980s, the retail environment had never been so competitive. Retailers were being squeezed by several powerful factors. One was the slower growth in customer demand that general retailing had experienced in recent years. Another one was an excess number of stores that existed in the industry. Finally, several forecasts indicated that a declining proportion of disposable income would be spent on general merchandise in coming years. This was especially true in apparel. These three realities along with several others were making retail merchants somewhat worried about the future.

The decline in the teenage population had decreased per capita spending on apparel. Apparel chains which had expanded so rapidly in the 1960s and 1970s to capitalize on the lucrative teenage market, faced an older customer base with less interest in fashion. As Americans grew older, their spending patterns were shifting toward medical and leisure services and away from general merchandise.

Another source of trouble for retailers was the extremely high level of consumer credit in the mid-1980s. Some industry observers feared this would lead to a decline in consumer spending and increased woes for retailers. Part of this was due to the catch-up spending on consumer durables after the 1981–1983 recession.

COMPETITION

A recent challenge within the retail industry was specialty stores and wholesale clubs. They were at opposite ends of the retailing spectrum. Still, both specialty stores and warehouse clubs were very profitable, and they were making it harder for stores in the middle.

The wholesale club concept was first introduced in 1976 by Sal and Robert E. Price with their first Price Club in San Diego. For a $25 membership fee, small-business owners could buy such diverse goods such as food, office supplies, and appliances at wholesale prices. This membership approach meant that the Price Club got an interest-free loan in advance and locked in the customer with switching costs if he or she decided to move to another such club. By stocking 4,000 items, as compared to 60,000 found in typical discount stores, Price Club stores could turn over their inventory 15 times a year compared to just 5 times for a full-line discount store. The Price Club had 25 stores, but by 1985 the concept was being copied by other retailers.

Specialty stores enjoyed strong growth in the early 1980s. A number of large retailers had established chains of small stores specializing in single product lines such as shoes, women's apparel, and books. Woolworth had found success in its stationery-oriented Harold's Square, Lucky Stores in Minnesota Fabrics, and Allied Stores in Catherine's Stout Shoppes. The attraction of such stores was the much greater depth of choice in a specific line that many consumers seemed willing to pay for.

Between the wholesale clubs and the specialty stores were full-line department stores. Here was where the primary battleground within the retailing industry took place. The saturation of the market with these one-stop shopping stores had caused many changes. For example, both Sears and J. C. Penney had curtailed most of new store openings. Instead, they both were moving to upgrade their existing stores with higher-quality, higher-priced merchandise. Both sought to establish a fashion image to differentiate themselves from the discount chains.

Sears

K mart's greatest competition came from Sears, the world's largest retailer. With 806 retail stores, Sears stores generated sales of $20.4 billion in 1983. That amounted to $25.3 million in sales per individual Sears store annually. Furthermore, Sears breadth of departments was unsurpassed by any competitor, particularly the leaders in the discount segment.

During the 1970s, Sears first moved to higher-priced, more stylish merchandise. This confused many customers who preferred to go to discounters for price and specialty shops for product line depth. Under CEO Edward Telling, who took office in 1978, the company made drastic changes. Twenty percent of the work force was cut, 200 stores were closed, and the remaining stores were renovated. Many Sears clothing labels were replaced by fashion labels with such names as Arnold Palmer, Joe Namath, and Cheryl Tiegs.

With its move into financial services, Sears envisioned the day when a customer could walk into a Sears store and buy a house, insure it, and furnish it before he left. The Sears charge card was held by 57 percent of Americans. By comparison, VISA cards were held by only 53 percent of all households. The potential existed for Sears to convert its ordinary credit accounts into savings and checking accounts quite easily. Furthermore, the deregulated banking environment of the 1980s made possible an integration of multiple financial services into the retail environment, and Sears seemed headed in that direction.

J. C. Penney

While Sears had its strength in hard goods, J. C. Penney was just the opposite with a well-established reputation for quality in soft goods. The company got its initials J. and C. from G. Johnson and T. Callahan who founded the firm back in 1902. During the 1960s and 1970s, Penney tried to move into hard goods to counter Sears' well-established strength there. It did this in several key instances by teaming up with well-known suppliers. For example, it formed an alliance with General Electric to sell its washers, dryers, refrigerators, stoves, and so on in its retail stores.

During 1983, when Penney had total sales of approximately $12 billion, it made a retrenchment of sorts. It renewed its commitment to emphasize its soft goods departments. Conversely, it discontinued its auto accessories department, eliminated children's toys, and even discontinued selling many hard goods such as G.E. appliances. With this move, the firm redoubled its efforts to sell quality clothing for men, women, boys, girls, and even babies. In addition to clothing, Penney's was noted for its underwear, towels, sheets, and so on.

Discount Chains

There were 8,738 general merchandise discount stores in the United States in 1984. Exhibit 32.7 gives a comparison of profitability and growth performance of the top general merchandise retailers. The average discount store had 55,792 square feet of selling space, whose average had been rising in recent years. The average customer transaction was for $12.35. The annual sales per square foot, as shown in Exhibit 32.8, varied from the $603 in the photography department to $132 in men's and boys' wear.

There were a number of regional chains within the discount segment of the retail industry. They included Target in the Midwest, Mervyn's in the West, Caldor in New England, and Richway in the Southeast. For the most part, they had done very well by differentiating themselves from K mart. Some first had accomplished this by appealing to the high end of the discount market. Other discounters sold department-store-quality merchandise at discount prices in attractive stores. As a result, they succeeded in attracting many affluent shoppers who wouldn't normally shop at K mart.

One of the most successful retailers in recent years was Wal-Mart, a discount chain headquartered in Bentonville, Arkansas. Much of its success was based on the locations of its stores. Its 834 discount stores and 19 Sam's Warehouse Clubs were concentrated in small towns in the South and Midwest. By clustering 150 stores within an hour's drive of a central warehouse and stocking only name-brand merchandise, Wal-Mart consistently led the industry in return on investment.

Exhibit 32.7

GENERAL MERCHANDISE RETAILERS: YARDSTICKS OF MANAGEMENT PERFORMANCE, 1985

Company	% in —Segment Sales/Profits	PROFITABILITY						GROWTH				
		Return on equity			Debt as % of Equity	Net Profit Margin	Rank	Sales			Earnings per share	
		Rank	5-Year Average	Latest 12 Months				5-Year Average	Latest 12 Months	Rank	5-Year Average	Latest 12 Months
Department Stores												
R. H. Macy	●/●	1	21.4%	16.3%	14.0%	4.3%	4	14.2%	7.5%	2	21.1%	-15.6%
Lucky Stores	25/13	2	19.2	17.5	61.3	1.1	12	9.5	6.5	12	-0.3	12.8
Dillard Dept. Stores	●/●	3	18.6	19.8	70.4	3.9	1	25.2	49.3	1	40.5	32.0
Mercantile Stores	●/●	4	16.3	15.0	28.0	5.0	7	10.9	6.8	4	17.5	4.2
May Dept. Stores	68/72	5	16.0	17.3	41.2	4.4	10	9.8	10.2	5	14.6	9.3
Federated Dept. Stores	67/89	6	14.6	13.1	27.9	3.3	8	10.8	8.0	10	8.5	11.0
Allied Stores	●/●	7	12.8	15.3	70.9	3.9	5	13.8	5.7	9	9.9	25.5
J. C. Penny	79/N.A.	8	12.7	10.1	54.7	2.9	13	3.0	2.3	8	13.3	-18.6
Strawbridge	●/●	9	12.5	16.0	125.8	3.7	6	11.5	12.5	3	20.1	16.6
Assoc Dry Goods	61/73	10	11.8	12.2	33.8	2.8	2	19.6	9.5	6	13.6	-0.7
Carson Pirie Scott	50/45	11	10.8	13.4	104.2	2.0	3	19.6	23.2	11	4.2	132.5
Sears, Roebuck	67/57	12	10.6	10.7	87.4	2.9	9	10.4	4.6	7	13.5	-19.9
Carter-Hawley-Hale	73/52	13	9.4	7.3	84.6	1.6	11	9.6	-2.0	13	-0.3	-50.0
Equitable of Iowa	41/2	14	7.0	4.3	9.2	2.6	14	2.7	4.9	14	-15.0	-10.2
Alexander's	●/●	15	1.4	7.4	87.0	1.0	15	1.9	0.5		N.M.	24.7
Medians			12.7	13.4	61.3	2.9		10.8	6.8		13.3	9.3

Discount and variety

Wal-Mart Stores	•/•	1	34.9%	30.7%	3.9%	49.6%	1	39.9%	1	32.2%	1	43.0%	24.1%
SCOA Industries	84/•	2	24.8	22.6	2.9	88.5	8	10.4	8	5.1	8	9.3	9.8
Ames Dept. Stores	•/•	3	23.1	19.7	3.1	60.6	2	20.1	2	30.8	5	23.5	19.4
Stop & Shop Cos	48/73	4	19.2	12.8	1.3	52.8	7	11.2	7	12.8	2	33.6	-26.9
Dayton-Hudson	71/73	5	16.8	16.1	3.3	43.2	4	19.0	4	12.2	9	9.1	10.3
Zayre	70/65	6	15.7	19.0	2.6	46.5	5	16.0	5	19.9	3	28.7	22.1
Rose's Stores	•/•	7	15.6	14.2	2.1	16.6	6	14.0	6	9.2	4	28.1	-13.9
K mart	•/•	8	13.2	12.4	1.8	89.3	9	10.0	9	13.4	7	10.5	-23.2
Household Intl	26/8	9	12.0	13.6	2.6	236.0	10	9.1	10	5.3	10	4.7	-4.6
Assoc Dry Goods	38/26	10	11.8	12.2	2.8	33.8	3	19.6	3	9.5	6	13.6	-0.7
Heck's	86/DD	11	9.3	def	def	89.3	11	2.0	11	6.5		N.M.	P-D
F. W. Woolworth	68/39	12	3.5	14.5	2.6	35.4	13	-5.6	13	3.2		N.M.	20.6
Cook United	•/DD	13	def	def	def	N.E.	12	-2.8	12	-47.7		N.M.	D-D
Medians			15.6	14.2	2.6	49.6		11.2		9.5		10.5	-0.7

N.A. = Not available.
N.E. = No estimate.
N.M. = Not meaningful.

Source: Industry survey–retailing, *Forbes*, January 13, 1986, p. 202.

Exhibit 32.8

DISCOUNT STORE SALES BY CATEGORY

Category	Volume ($ billions)	Sales per Store ($ millions)	Annual Sales per Square Foot ($)	Annual Turns	Initial Markup (%)	Gross Margin (%)
Women's apparel	14.3	1,763	176	4.6	48.0%	37.2%
Men's and boys' wear	8.2	1,011	132	3.4	44.6	36.0
Housewares	6.3	777	135	3.2	41.1	30.2
Consumer electronics	5.9	728	316	3.2	31.4	19.4
Health and beauty aids	5.6	691	219	4.5	26.9	20.5
Automobile	5.2	641	279	2.8	34.9	28.7
Hardware	4.8	592	184	2.4	41.9	32.1
Toys	4.1	506	202	3.1	36.5	28.4
Sporting goods	3.8	469	187	2.0	36.9	26.9
Photo camera	3.3	407	603	3.2	24.5	16.6
Domestics	3.2	395	126	2.5	43.4	35.3
Personal care	2.9	358	421	3.3	30.4	20.0
Stationery	2.1	259	140	3.5	46.7	40.1
Paint	1.8	222	175	2.4	43.9	35.2
Electric housewares	1.7	210	238	3.4	33.2	21.4
Jewelry	1.4	166	290	1.8	49.9	37.7
Glassware	0.7	80	129	4.0	40.7	34.9

Source: Standard & Poor's *Industrial Survey*, July 4, 1985, p. 120.

SUPPLIERS

Retailers dealt with thousands of suppliers to stock the wide range of merchandise they carried; most retailers did not manufacture the merchandise. The bargaining power of large retail chains with their suppliers was great. Sears, J. C. Penney, K mart, and others were such large and welcome customers that, at times, suppliers became overly dependent on them. Each year, many new products were introduced by the major chains, replacing old products which were discontinued. Suppliers knew that their products were expected to generate targeted levels of sales. Those that didn't achieve the goal were dropped, with little regard for the supplier. On occasion, suppliers were encouraged to increase production capacity only to find their product dropped a short time later. At times, orders were canceled at the last minute, leaving suppliers in a difficult position. Where possible, chain retailers would take merchandise on consignment, paying for it only if sold, thus shifting the risk to the supplier. Payment to suppliers was at times delayed by retailers in order to enhance cash flow and obtain free short-term financing.

In spite of such treatment by chain retailers, many suppliers were willing to assume the risk and take the abuse. In return, they hoped to get the enormous volume and nationwide distribution which high-volume retailers offered. In response to this somewhat one-sided relationship, a number of general merchandise manufacturers had broadened their product lines. By producing a wide variety of items, a supplier could reduce dependence on a single product and increase its bargaining power with the retailer. In addition, it could turn a cost center into a profit center.

Sears and K mart were good examples of firms making sizable use of private-label merchandise. Often their private-label products were made by a brand-label manufacturer to the same specifications as the brand label. Production of private-label products could then be contracted out to other manufacturers, giving a great deal of leverage to the retailer.

BUYERS—THE NEW CONSUMERS

Several important demographic shifts were affecting retailers during the mid-1980s. Population shifts from the cities to the suburbs were reducing the sales volume of urban stores while helping suburban stores. Population shifts from older industrialized areas of the Northeast to the Sun Belt states had similar effects. The wave of baby boom teenagers of the 1960s was approaching middle age. Better educated than their parents, their perceptions of value, attitudes toward quality merchandise, and responses to promotional techniques were changing the way retailers did business.

Price still remained a key consideration, but quality and brand image had increased in importance. Many consumers were willing to trade dollars for time as was evidenced by the demand for fast-food, microwave ovens, and other time-saving products and services.

The number of households was growing rapidly, although the population growth was slowing. This was causing changes in the kinds of merchandise demanded, their price-quality trade-off, and how it was most effectively marketed. Health-related products, prescriptions, and leisure products were in greater demand reflecting the needs of older customers. At the same time, markets for baby food, toys, and children's clothes had declined.

Women were working in greater numbers than ever before. This contributed to the rise in discretionary income and increased the demand for products needed by working women, such as clothes and cosmetics. A K mart survey showed that the percentage of K mart customers with household incomes from $25,000 to $40,000 had increased from 23.3 percent in 1980 to 28.1 percent in 1984.[5] Some 18.9 percent of K mart's customers in 1984 came from households with incomes greater than $40,000, compared to 8.3 percent in 1980.

With more women working, men were doing retail shopping more than they ever had. Men tended to be less value-conscious and more likely to trust the advertising of national brands. The trend was clearly toward a more mature, affluent customer with a preference for value, quality, and fashion.

[5]K mart Corporation, *K mart 1984 Corporation Annual Report*, p. 3.

K MART AND THE FUTURE

Sales at the average K mart store were good, but could be better. K mart's appliances and housewares were strong areas. Unfortunately, its clothing and other soft goods, which took up almost half of the typical K mart store, had low appeal to many customers. Clearly, K mart needed to address its clothing dilemma by perhaps reducing store space allocated for it or by improving the clothing being offered. Overall, K mart's per-store sales were about one-third that of Sears stores, which left ample room for improvement.

K mart might try to increase its floor space in housewares and furniture departments. To do this, it would require taking some space used by other departments, which remained unclear.

Another possible opportunity might be to add to its existing in-store pharmacies. For in-store K mart pharmacies, it would need to decide what quality and price of such related medicines to carry. K mart's acquisition of Pay Less stores, which had pharmacies, might provide expertise in this area. Less than one-half of K mart stores had pharmacies as of early 1986.

K mart might try to make it more attractive financially for customers to shop at its stores. Whereas 58 percent of Sears' sales were charged to its various Sears credit cards, K mart did not have its own credit card. Still, K mart did accept MasterCard and VISA credit cards. In addition, K mart stores did accept local customer checks if they first were approved at the service desk. Whether a K mart credit card would be helpful remained to be seen. Clearly, it would draw customers in who wanted to buy now, but pay later. But credit cards had added costs for retailers, and that could reduce K mart's ability to compete on the basis of price. These costs might be even higher, relatively speaking, for K mart since its average sale per customer was less than Sears', which had many big-ticket items.

K mart's recent acquisition of Builder's Square, Walden Books, Pay Less, and Furr's Cafeterias might provide ample room for expansion within these markets. Each acquisition was in a segment of the retail industry which was growing more rapidly than overall retail sales. This can be seen in Exhibit 32.9, which compares the growth rates of different kinds of retail merchandise. Furthermore, demographic projections over the next 10 or 20 years favored continued growth in each area.

Since the appointment of Bernard M. Fauber as chief executive officer in 1980, K mart had made a number of substantial changes. By early 1986, the store renovation program was nearly complete, and the move toward higher-quality national-brand merchandise was well underway. Still, as 1986 began, a number of important issues faced K mart. Would the repositioning program succeed in the next five years in attracting more affluent customers to buy its higher-priced name-brand merchandise? What additional steps could be taken to upgrade K mart's stores and its customers? Would the new image result in a substantial loss of lower-income customers which had historically been the backbone of the business? Might K mart customers be confused by the move as Sears customers were in the 1970s? How could K mart really make progress with clothing and soft goods? Would fashion-seeking customers be convinced that K mart was a desirable place to shop? These and other questions came to mind as CEO Fauber looked ahead to the remainder of the 1980s and into the 1990s.

Exhibit 32.9

TOTAL RETAIL TRADE, 1984

	1984 ($ millions)	1983–1984 Change	10-Year Growth Rate
Retail trade total	$1,297,015	+10.5%	+9.0%
Durable goods stores total	464,287	+17.1	+9.6
Nondurable goods stores total	832,728	+7.1	+8.8
General merchandise group	153,642	+10.2	+7.9
General merchandise stores	144,575	+10.6	+8.4
Department stores	129,284	+10.9	+8.6
Variety stores	9,067	+5.1	+1.8
Apparel group	66,891	+10.8	+8.8
Men's and boy's wear stores	8,432	+5.9	+3.1
Women's apparel accessory stores	27,899	+13.9	+9.3
Family and other apparel stores	17,567	+13.8	+11.1
Shoe stores	10,339	+5.6	+9.9
Furniture and appliance group	63,581	+16.3	+8.9
Total general, apparel, and furniture	325,938	+11.7	
Automotive group	277,008	+19.0	+9.5
Gasoline service stations	100,997	+2.2	+10.2
Lumber, building material, hardware	59,304	+15.2	+9.7
Eating and drinking places	124,109	+8.2	+10.8
Food group	269,959	+5.9	+8.3
Drug and proprietary stores	44,165	+10.3	+9.2
Liquor stores	19,494	+2.5	+6.3

Source: Standard & Poor's *Industrial Survey*, July 4, 1985, p. 111

33

GENERAL MOTORS AT THE INDUSTRIAL DIVIDE: A TROUBLED GIANT FACES THE 1990s

As the decade of the 1980s drew to a close, Robert C. Stempel, president of General Motors and heir apparent to the retiring chairman and CEO, Roger Smith, looked to the future with determination and not a little frustration. With a background in engineering, Stempel was a hard-driving "product man" who had risen through the ranks at GM, learning the car business, in his words, "from the roof to the road." When he took charge in 1990, he would break the succession of financial controllers who had run GM in the past.

In 1989, GM is still America's largest industrial corporation, with sales of $127 billion. Yet GM is a troubled giant. The company rose to a position of seemingly unassailable industrial strength by adhering closely to the strategic path of mass production and mass marketing. The world's biggest automaker spreads its product line across five divisions, most of which are comparable in size to other car companies. Since the 1920s, GM has targeted the output of its auto divisions toward big, easily identifiable segments within a stable mass market. This segmentation is based primarily upon relative age and income. As they accumulate years and wealth, GM customers traditionally "trade up" along an ascending scale of divisional offerings from Chevrolet to Cadillac. The selling price—and profit margins—of these models climbs more rapidly than do production costs for many shared components. Thus, in

This case was prepared by Dr. Jerry M. Calton, Assistant Professor of Management, College of Business, Montana State University.

1989, GM spends only $4,000 more to build a $29,000 Cadillac Eldorado than it does to make a $14,100 Pontiac Firebird. Product differentiation is created by adding power, size, styling cues, and luxury features.

Since the 1970s—and especially in the 1980s—environmental turbulence or "chaos" has disrupted the assured pace of industrial giants like GM. Automotive and other product/market segments have fragmented into many narrow, rapidly changing market niches. The ceaseless shift of market sands has forced producers to define their customer needs more precisely and to respond to these needs more quickly. The globalization of competition—epitomized by the aggressive advance of innovative, quality-conscious Japanese challengers—threatens extinction for any U.S. producer that fails to meet the new "world-class" standards for manufacturing and marketing performance. In essence, U.S. automakers have to learn how to cross the "industrial divide" that separates the familiar world of mass production and mass marketing from the unexplored terrain of flexible manufacturing and responsive niche marketing. A successful crossing requires the adoption of radically different product development, manufacturing, and marketing strategies. Even more daunting, the new approach to integrated, team-based problem solving and continuous learning is predicated upon the launching of a profound organizational and cultural transformation.[1]

Despite grandiose plans, massive expenditures, prodigious efforts, and some catchy ad copy, GM in the 1980s has never seemed quite capable of moving in step with the turbulent times. In 1979, GM commanded a 46.3 percent share of all cars, including imports, sold in the United States. By the end of 1989, its share had declined 11.6 percentage points to 34.7 percent of the market. GM sold nearly a third fewer cars in 1989 than it had in 1979. Financially, 1989 was GM's third best year ever, with profits of $4.2 billion on sales of $127 billion. This earned GM the top ranking in the 1989 U.S. *Fortune* 500. However, these healthy numbers concealed a serious internal weakness. In an otherwise good year, GM experienced a loss of $1 billion in its North American automotive operations, which included Canada and Mexico as well as the United States. Strong showings in its truck, European auto, GMAC financing, EDS computer services, and Hughes aerospace/electronics business units masked the weakness of its automotive core. Most disturbing is evidence that the pace of decline seems to be accelerating. From 1980, it took six years for GM's U.S. auto market share to drop 6 percentage points. In the following three years, it has lost nearly another 6 percentage points.

Not surprisingly, the recent Japanese entrants have gained most from GM's stumble. If sales from transplants are included with imports, the Japanese share of the U.S. auto market in 1989 is 25.6 percent, an increase of 10.4 percentage points since 1979. Over the period, Ford has performed best among the domestic automakers. Since 1979, it has gained 1.2 points to reach a 22 percent market share in 1989. Ford, ranking second behind GM on the *Fortune* 500, earned $3.84 billion in 1989 on sales of $96.9 billion. Since 1979, Chrysler has lost nearly 3 points, down to a 10.3

---

[1]The concept of the "industrial divide" is drawn from Michael J. Fiore and Charles F. Sabel, *The Second Industrial Divide: Possibilities For Prosperity* (New York: Basic Books, 1984). See also, Tom Peters, *Thriving on Chaos: Handbook for a Management Revolution* (New York: The Free Press, 1986).

percent share. In 1989, it earned a modest $359 million on sales of $36.2 billion. This still placed Chrysler in the number eight spot of the *Fortune* 500. The remaining 7.4 points of U.S. market share in 1989 is divided between European luxury car importers and Third World (mostly Brazil and South Korea) producers of economy subcompacts. While GM has been the big loser, Detroit's overall share of the U.S. car market over the past decade has fallen from 80.1 percent in 1979 to 67 percent in 1989.[2]

Imports of Japanese cars and light trucks peaked at 2.4 million units in 1986. While Japanese automotive imports began to decline after 1986, the growing output from eight new transplants in North America has more than made up the difference. Production from these transplants is scheduled to reach 2 million units in 1990 and 2.38 million units by 1995. These Japanese-owned transplants pose a severe competitive challenge to the domestic "Big Three." They are virtually immune from the threat of trade restrictions. They enjoy an $800 unit cost advantage—as well as a quality edge—over most Detroit-run plants. Meanwhile domestic producers are experiencing growing excess capacity problems in the mature, saturated U.S. auto market.[3]

Given these sobering statistics, Stempel knew that neither easy excuses nor rosy projections would do:

> Our market share was in the 40s and now we're in the 30s. Those are the facts. We've made those facts and we've got to own up to them. We learned the hard way because we took our eye off the customer. We're not about to [do that] again. The customer is going to get exactly what he wants, and get it in a GM product.

Stempel believed that if GM were to dance more truly to the heartbeat of America, he and other GM employees would have to learn how to implement new organizational approaches to responsive niche marketing and flexible manufacturing. Central to the task of heightening company attention to the shifting array of customer needs would be learning how to integrate the marketing function more fully into short-cycle product development and manufacturing processes.

Stempel decided that this organizational learning should begin with a review of some important initiatives directed by the man he soon would replace as CEO and chairman, Roger Smith. Under Smith's leadership in the 1980s, GM had embarked upon an ambitious, extraordinarily expensive course of product repositioning, technological advancement, and organizational renewal. As a deliberate, hard-working, and loyal team player, Stempel considered the basic thrust of Smith's transformational vision to be sound. Admittedly, the results to date had been mixed or inconclusive. Stempel was convinced that, eventually, Smith's vision could be vindicated by further finetuning, greater attention to detail, and a more dedicated follow-through from all involved. However, as a pragmatist, Stempel was prepared to do whatever

[2]Paul Ingrassia and Joseph B. White, "Losing the Race: With Its Market Share Sliding, GM Scrambles to Avoid a Calamity," *The Wall Street Journal*, December 14, 1989, p. A1, and Alex Taylor III, "The New Drive to Revive GM," *Fortune*, April 9, 1990, pp. 53–54.

[3]Louis Kraar, "Japan's Gung-Ho U.S. Car Plants," *Fortune*, January 30, 1989, pp. 98–108. See also Alex Taylor III, "Japan's New U.S. Car Strategy," *Fortune*, September 10, 1990, pp. 65–77.

was necessary to get GM back in step with the consuming public. He knew that recognizing and responding to past mistakes would be integral to learning how to make the new moves.

Stempel decided that the learning process might be accelerated if, instead of asking for a comprehensive review of GM's North American operations, he initially had an independent consulting firm reassess two of Smith's major product development initiatives: the GM-10 midsize and the Saturn compact car projects. An executive summary of the report appears in Exhibit 33.1.

Exhibit 33.1

EXECUTIVE SUMMARY:
THE GM-10 AND SATURN PROJECTS—LESSONS FOR ORGANIZATIONAL TRANSFORMATION AND COMPETITIVE TURNAROUND AT GENERAL MOTORS

The GM-10 and Saturn programs grew out of radically different approaches to product development and flexible manufacturing. The midsized divisional clones of GM-10 are the progeny of a centralized design and high-tech production system. In contrast, the new compact models of the innovative Saturn Corporation have evolved from a decentralized, largely autonomous product development and manufacturing effort. In their current form, neither can be considered an unqualified success. Indeed, the GM-10 project has been a major marketing and financial debacle. Saturn appears to be positioned not so much for financial success as for a somewhat unlikely role as the model for GM's organizational transformation. Lessons from both GM-10 and Saturn point to the need for more complete integration of marketing information and insights into GM's product development and manufacturing processes. This will require, as well, the breakup and replacement of GM's tall, top-down, control-oriented management structure that grew up to contain and direct the repetitive routines of mass production and mass marketing.

A. THE FAILURE OF GM-10—LESSONS TO BE LEARNED

Background

When Roger Smith took over as GM's new CEO and chairman in 1981, he inherited a company bias toward capital spending on technological "solutions" to market disorder and an organizational rigidity that stifled the competitive impact of the new manufacturing technology. His predecessors, Chairman Thomas A. Murphy and President Elliot M. Estes, had responded to changed market conditions following the second oil shock of 1979 with an ambitious, extraordinarily expensive game plan. They envi-

Exhibit 33.1 (Cont.)

sioned a redesign from scratch of all car models in GM's five divisions. This would be accompanied by a major overhaul or replacement of the factories in which they would be built. GM cars were to be downsized and given front-wheel drive as well as new, more rigid, unitized bodies. Highly automated "factories of the future" were to be constructed. Some, like the Buick City complex in Flint, Michigan, were patterned on the Toyota City layout, with component plants located nearby to facilitate just-in-time deliveries. Numerous delivery doors and robot material-handling carts were installed to move components quickly to assembly lines dominated by computer-controlled robot welders, transfer machines, and painters.

The plan assumed that GM's financial and technological clout would push back the Japanese upstarts and bludgeon domestic competitors back into line. GM's traditional dominance under the stable conditions of mass production was to be restored by imposing a new technological and organizational order that would tame market chaos. Through the 1980s, GM's capital spending (exclusive of acquisitions) totaled $77 billion. This far exceeds the amount invested by any domestic or foreign competitor. GM's weak performance over the decade suggests that technological prowess is an intellectual asset that can best be gained through internal organizational learning rather than by external acquisition.

The massive sums of money that GM has expended on its manufacturing operations over the past decade seem, paradoxically, to have diminished its organizational flexibility and productivity. GM's plant modernization program has been hampered by a preoccupation with lowering direct labor costs and a determination to extend the old paradigm of control. This has been expressed in the wholesale purchase of off-the-shelf automated manufacturing hardware. Mary Ann Keller, the respected auto industry analyst, pointed out that

> the goal of [GM's] technology push has been to get rid of hourly workers. GM thought in terms of automation rather than replacing the current system with a better system.

Improperly utilized, automated hardware can raise fixed costs even as it diminishes quality and flexibility. GM's break-even point has risen 30 percent since 1981. In 1980, GM's unit costs were $300 below those of Ford or Chrysler; by the end of 1986, GM unit costs were $300 higher than those of either domestic competitor.[1] Mazda's new Flat Rock, Michigan, transplant cost 25 percent less than GM's trouble-plagued Hamtramck "factory of the future." Yet Mazda's plant can assemble 240,000

---

[1]Amal Nag, "Tricky Technology: Auto Makers Discover 'Factory of the Future,' Is Headache Just Now," *The Wall Street Journal*, May 13, 1986, p. 1.

Exhibit 33.1 (Cont.)

cars (in several models and body configurations) each year with 3,500 workers. This compares favorably with the 5,000 workers needed to build 220,000 lookalike luxury cars in the Hamtramck facility. GM needs more workers to monitor the quality of delivered components, track inventory, and troubleshoot or substitute for robot equipment that persists in missing welds, dropping windshields into the front seat, and overspraying cars. Production by trial, error, and exception inflates overhead transactions and costs.

Because of a failure to implement a short-cycle production process linked to dealers by a computerized ordering system and to suppliers by a just-in-time materials handling system, the potential for flexibility in GM's new robot hardware cannot be exploited. By purchasing robotic systems off the shelf from independent suppliers, GM factories were filled with the electronic babble of "smart" machines unable to communicate. GM's top-heavy organizational structure and control-oriented management style didn't help in ironing out the prolonged start-up problems of the new plants. Line workers were not broadly trained for multiple tasks; nor were their practical suggestions solicited. One union local representative at the beleaguered Buick City complex complained: "GM is way overloaded with supervision, and they won't listen to people on the floor."[2]

Lesson #1: Short-cycle product development and flexible manufacturing technology requires well-trained, committed employees working together in a nonroutine learning environment.

The trouble-plagued story of the new midsized GM-10 line illustrates the problems Roger Smith has encountered in achieving organizational flexibility via technological acquisition. Smith is fond of quoting his mentor, Alfred Sloan, who developed GM's divisional structure and market segmentation strategy in the 1920s. Sloan wrote in his autobiography, *My Years at General Motors*, that "any rigidity by an automobile manufacturer, no matter how large or how well established, is severely penalized in the marketplace." Smith portrays the four new GM-10 plants, built at a cost of nearly a billion dollars apiece, as the latest in flexible manufacturing:

> Thank God for flexible manufacturing! It's letting us put differentiation back into our lines at a fraction of the cost that we'd have if we had to order individual tooling.

Yet the true flexibility of the programmable automated hardware in these plants is not really being exploited. Each GM-10 plant is dedicated to

[2]"General Motors: What Went Wrong?" *Business Week*, March 16, 1987, pp. 107–110.

Exhibit 33.1 (Cont.)

turning out a single body style with sheet metal and trim variations worked out after consultation with divisional marketing departments. However, once the new flexible hardware has been programmed and debugged, it is utilized very much in the manner of the old, inflexible, special-purpose machinery.

The decision to go with dedicated GM-10 plants has been touted as a bold stroke that will simplify parts procurement, improve quality control, and enhance divisional influence over differentiating styling cues. Yet the GM-10 plants are being run as costly extensions of mass production batch processing, pruned of incremental exceptions. Since each plant is designed to turn out 250,000 units per year, any variance in divisional sales will create either underutilized or strained capacity. This lack of flexibility also inhibits the production of different body styles of the same model. Failing to take into account market information that family-oriented buyers in this segment preferred roomier four-door sedans, GM offered only two-door coupe versions for 1988. It did so to save the extra $2 billion needed to open three more plants that would build four-door sedan and minivan models.[3]

The competitive penalty for continued technological and organizational inflexibility is driven home by the weak market response of such GM-10 models as the Buick Regal, Pontiac Grand Prix, and Oldsmobile Cutlass Supreme. Introduced in 1988 (two years late) to challenge such successful midsized standard and specialty models as Ford's Taurus and Thunderbird, they have languished in dealers' showrooms. In 1984, the Oldsmobile Cutlass was one of GM's (and America's) favorite cars; 334,000 units were bought that year. As of December 1989, only 93,242 of the new GM-10 version of the Cutlass Supreme have moved off dealer floors. At the end of 1989, the four GM-10 plants are running at 60 percent of capacity. Lacking a truly flexible production system, these plants cannot be easily reconfigured to turn out more popular models or to modify existing models. The higher unit costs associated with idle capacity as well as the generous rebates needed to move the cars that were produced mean the company lost over $2,000 for every GM-10 car sold in 1989. Nearly $1 billion was lost on the GM-10 series alone in 1989.[4]

---

[3]Dale D. Buss and Doron P. Levin, "Striking Back: GM Readies New Line Aimed at Regaining Mid-Size Auto Sales," *The Wall Street Journal*, May 1, 1987, pp. 1, 12. See also Melinda Grenier Guiles, "Hazardous Road: GM's Smith Presses for Sweeping Changes, But Questions Arise," *The Wall Street Journal*, March 14, 1985, pp. 1, 13, and Richard Rescigno "Race to the Future: Can Billions and Mr. Smith Make GM a Winner?" *Barron's*, June 30, 1986, p. 30.

[4]Ingrassia and White, "Losing the Race," p. A1; Taylor, "New Drive to Revive GM," p. 57.

Exhibit 33.1 (Cont.)

Lesson #2: Partial decentralization is not true cross-functional integration.

The poor showing of the GM-10 line suggests problems that extend far beyond the inappropriate application of flexible manufacturing technology. Roger Smith's reorganization of GM in 1984 didn't go nearly far enough in decentralizing the company or in promoting the new cross-functional approach to information sharing and cooperative problem solving. This new approach, associated with such concepts as "concurrent engineering" and "semiautonomous, cross-functional project teams," is needed if GM's marketing divisions are to have a real opportunity to exploit the growing consumer preference for customized niche cars. Both these concepts have been applied with great success by Japanese (and some American) companies. Concurrent engineering is a simultaneous, as opposed to a sequential, approach to new product development. It integrates marketing assessment of customer needs, product design, manufacturing, and cost and quality control considerations. This typically takes place within a new, fluid organizational form, the semiautonomous, cross-functional project team. Marketing specialists, design engineers, manufacturing process engineers—even line workers and important customers—share ideas and work together to solve the complex, interdependent problems associated with the product development and manufacturing processes. Top managers are expected to support and give general guidance to these "self-managing teams," not dictate and second-guess their every move. By promoting nonroutine organizational learning, this new approach quickly delivers lower-cost, higher-quality products that are more responsive to customer needs. It builds an internal organizational capability for generating creative response to the forces of "chaos."[5]

Roger Smith recognized that GM's traditional tall, inflexible, control-oriented organizational structure and its centralized, sequential product development processes were badly out of step with the turbulent rhythms of the 1980s. However, his reorganization of the company in 1984 only modified the old system without replacing it. In the 1970s, both product development and manufacturing functions had been centralized into autonomous units. This was done to avoid "wasteful" duplication of resources and to promote scale economies by encouraging the broader application of common components across the five auto marketing divisions. This structure virtually excluded marketing inputs from key design and production decisions. Roger Smith inherited this system, and initially, he

[5]See Robert H. Hayes and Ramchandran Jaikumar, "Manufacturing's Crisis: New Technologies, Obsolete Organizations," *Harvard Business Review* (September–October 1988), pp. 77–85; Tom Peters, "Restoring American Competitiveness: Looking for New Models of Organizations," *Academy of Management EXECUTIVE*, Vol. 2, no. 2 (May 1988), pp. 103–109; and "A Smarter Way to Manufacture," *Business Week*, April 30, 1990, pp. 110–117.

Exhibit 33.1 (Cont.)

did not change it. The first round of model downsizing in the early 1980s was carried out by centralized project centers for each new front-wheel-drive car platform (X-body, J-body, A-body, etc.). The resulting look-alike cars that emerged were shared among the divisions. They failed to generate much market excitement. By seeking scale economies through centralization and standardization, GM homogenized its divisional model lineup at a time when more finely tuned product differentiation and precise market segmentation were needed. GM's proud luxury/big-car divisions, Cadillac and Buick, were particularly hard-hit when affluent customers spurned the premium prices on downsized, front-wheel-drive models that were barely distinguishable from the Chevrolet version of the common corporate platform. Ironically, Ford and Chrysler benefited from having lacked the funds needed to replace all their big, rear-wheel-drive cars in the early 1980s. GM's divisional marketing departments were stung by a clever Ford ad depicting the plight of GM luxury car owners. When parking lot attendants drove up with several look-alike cars, owners had to ask: "Is it a Buick, an Oldsmobile, a Cadillac?" Sales in 1986 of the new Cadillac Eldorado dropped to a dismal 24,000 from the 1983–1984 level of 70,000 units a year for the bigger rear-drive model.

Roger Smith tried to address the model homogenization problem in 1984 with a partial decentralization of manufacturing operations. The five car divisions retained their marketing duties. After 1984 however, design and manufacturing functions were divided between two new groups: the Chevrolet, Pontiac, and GM Canada (CPC) group and the Cadillac, Buick, and Oldsmobile (CBO) group. The rationale behind this corporate restructuring was a desire to reduce excessive model overlap, facilitate differentiation efforts, and increase accountability for meeting cost and quality goals in a timely fashion. Each division was directed to focus on cars appropriate to its market segment rather than offer every body style of a given platform. This would allow a reduction by 25 percent in the number (around 200) of GM model variants built each year. Unfortunately, this new, partially decentralized structure simply added another layer of management without eliminating many of the worst features of the old system. At a time when flexible production and economies of scope were the order of the day, GM was still driven by the old-mass-production/economies-of-scale paradigm. Economies of scope (i.e., breadth) are based on developing the capability for efficiently producing a wider variety of models in smaller lot sizes.[6] Despite the reorganization, GM cars are still designed in a central studio. Cut off from critical design decisions, the marketing divisions are still having difficulty in differentiating their offerings and in developing a coherent and distinct market im-

[6]See Joel D. Goldhar and Mariann Jelinek, "Computer Integrated Flexible Manufacturing: Organizational, Economic, and Strategic Implications," *Interfaces* (May–June 1985), pp. 18–24.

Exhibit 33.1 (Cont.)

age. Jim Perkins, the new vice president of the Chevrolet division, has pointed to the classic 1957 Chevy as an inspiration for recovering "brand character."[7] Product development times have stretched out rather than shortened with the reorganization. The four-door GM-10 Chevy Lumina took six years to bring out. Cars designed by committees have suffered the fate of camels in a horse race. Annual sales volume at Chevrolet has declined from 2.4 million in 1978 to 1.53 million in 1989. Oldsmobile has dropped from 1.1 million in 1984 to 600,000 in 1989. As GM car sales continue to slide, the upper middle divisions—Oldsmobile and Buick—run the risk of failing to maintain the volume needed to support their network of 6,000 dealers. Their rationale for a separate existence is weak so long as 80 percent of their models are virtually indistinguishable from each other.[8]

Lesson #3: Serve your chosen niche well.

Ironically, Cadillac is GM's sole U.S. auto marketing success story for 1989. This success is based on a divisional revolt against the new structure. Stung by sales declines and the blurring of its market identity in the mid-1980s, GM's only profitable North American auto division insisted on having its own engineering design team. Cadillac embarked on a crash body-building course, adding length, weight, and power to its model lineup. A new commitment to quality has caused reported defects on Eldorados and Sevilles to decline by 44 percent since 1986. Cadillac's old, affluent customers have returned in sufficient numbers that plants turning out the big cars are operating at capacity. In 1989, the division sold 267,000 cars, each of which generated an average profit of nearly $4,000. This compares favorably with the estimated average loss of $1,250 on every GM car sold in the United States in 1989.[9]

The message is clear: Business units that successfully differentiate and position products that appeal to a distinct segment can succeed in a very tough marketplace. Of course, the Cadillac formula is hardly transferrable to all GM auto divisions. Government fuel-efficiency CAFE regulations would trigger stiff fines if the traditional "bigger is better" philosophy were applied too freely. The "Big Three" are already straining against the 27.5-mpg CAFE standard. Even tighter fleet standards are in store for the 1990s. Moreover, the average age of a Cadillac buyer in 1989 is 55 years. GM badly needs to develop products that appeal to a younger, somewhat less affluent clientele—the sort that inclines toward buying Japanese imports.

[7]Patrick Bedard, "Two Guys in a Bel Air," *Car and Driver*, July 1990, p. 18.

[8]Taylor, "New Drive to Revive GM," p. 61. See also Jacob M. Schlesinger, "GM Seeks Revival of Buick and Olds," *The Wall Street Journal*, April 12, 1988, p. 41.

[9]"The Boulevard Barge Is Cruising Again," *Business Week*, February 5, 1990, pp. 52–53. See also Taylor, "New Drive to Revive GM," p. 57.

Exhibit 33.1 (Cont.)

B. THE SATURN CORPORATION—CAN IT TEACH GM TO DANCE?

Background

A recent J. D. Power & Associates study found that 42 percent of the new car buyers in the United States simply do not include GM products in their purchase decision. Moreover, customers under age 45 prefer Japanese to GM cars by a 2-to-1 margin. Finally, GM ranks near the bottom, beating out only the hapless Yugo in the percentage of current owners who would recommend their car to someone else. It is for reasons such as these that Roger Smith assigned to the new Saturn Corporation the goal of selling 80 percent of its cars to those who otherwise wouldn't consider buying a GM vehicle.[10]

The physical and spiritual distance between the Saturn Corporation and other GM divisions is both pronounced and deliberate. Saturn has been designated by top GM management as the high-profile learning laboratory that will show the way toward "Saturnizing" the entire company. When he announced the formation of the Saturn Corporation in 1985 as an independent subsidiary, Roger Smith hailed it as "the key to GM's long-term competitiveness, survival, and success."[11] Located in the bucolic setting of Spring Hill, Tennessee, Saturn resembles one of the new Japanese transplants of the Upper South's "Auto Alley" more than it does the typical plants of Detroit's "Big Three."

As a model for continuous learning and organizational transformation, Saturn has, itself, evolved and changed over time. Originally, it was conceived as a home-grown, high-tech manufacturing response to the challenge of Japan's low-cost small-car imports. Ambitious early plans called for the production of 500,000 subcompacts a year, starting in 1989. These subcompacts were to be built on a short, highly automated line from modules assembled off-line by autonomous work teams. GM production planners projected a unit cost reduction of around $2,000 and savings of 50 to 60 percent in direct labor costs. They also anticipated cost savings in new approaches to the utilization of materials and energy in component manufacturing. In addition, they placed the foundry, engine, and transmission production facilities on-site to reduce transportation and holding costs. It was hoped that lessons learned from Saturn eventually could be applied to other GM plants.

In its celestial nomenclature and technological "can do" spirit, the Saturn project drew its inspiration from the massive booster rocket that helped put Americans on the moon. So far, Saturn's shaky takeoff bears a

[10]"Here Comes GM's Saturn," *Business Week*, April 9, 1990, p. 57. See also Ingrassia and White, "Losing the Race," p. A8, and Taylor, "New Drive to Revive GM," p. 57.

[11]"Here Comes GM's Saturn," p. 56.

Exhibit 33.1 (Cont.)

closer resemblance to early U.S. efforts to rise to the *Sputnik* challenge. The first president of Saturn died prematurely. Then the small Saturn Tire and Rubber Company sued GM for trademark infringement. Low-cost subcompacts from South Korea, Yugoslavia, and Brazil preempted Saturn's chosen market niche. The stabilization of gasoline prices, Japan's indefinite extension of export restraints, and the dollar/yen revaluation made the market segments for larger, upscale cars relatively more attractive.

As of early 1990, GM's capital investment in Saturn has been scaled back to $3 billion—still over three times the cost of a typical Japanese transplant of comparable size. Saturn production is scheduled to begin in June 1990. Initially, a single shift will operate at a rate of 120,000 units a year. In the next six to eight months, a second shift will come on line, raising annual output to full capacity at 240,000 units. At this output level, Saturn cannot earn a respectable financial return on its considerable investment. This is particularly the case since Saturn's product planners eventually settled on a hotly contested market niche, the $10,000–12,000 compact car segment. Other models in this range include the Honda Civic, Acura Integra, Mazda 323 Protege, Toyota Corolla, and even GM's NUMMI-built Corolla clone, the Geo Prizm. As it is currently positioned, Saturn's competitive success will have to be measured, not so much in financial as in symbolic terms. If Saturn comes to be seen—in the company as well as in the marketplace—as the prototype of the new slim GM of the 1990s, the competitive payoff could be substantial. However, the payoff on potential organizational learning to aid in coping with the new, chaotic marketplace is by no means a sure thing. GM and Saturn managers must learn how to reconcile two apparent paradoxes if they are to integrate responsive niche marketing successfully with a flexible, short-cycle approach to manufacturing.

Paradox #1: How can Saturn reconcile its need for a voluntary commitment to continuous learning in its "self-managed teams" with an effective form of coordination and control?

Saturn operates according to the tenets of the "commitment model." This management model focuses on facilitating the interaction of highly motivated, intensely trained, cross-functional work teams. These teams are called upon to engage in cooperative problem-solving activities that generate *adaptive, nonroutine, learning behavior*. This model isn't really the antithesis of the traditional management "control model." Rather, it replaces the direct bureaucratic controls of mass production with "indirect modes of control via systems and values."[12]

[12]Paul S. Adler, "Managing Flexible Automation," *California Management Review* (Spring 1988), p. 47. See also Richard E. Walton, "From Control to Commitment in the Workplace," *Harvard Business Review* (March–April 1985), pp. 76–84.

Exhibit 33.1 (Cont.)

For transformation to work, a commitment to continuous learning must be built into the organization. This commitment cannot be forced; yet somehow it must be directed. Managerial exercise of this indirect form of "clan control" requires the constant nurturing of an "organizational culture." Schein has defined this as the "total of the collective or shared learning" about how a group goes about solving internal and external problems. Kilmann, Saxton, and Serpa define it as the "hidden, yet unifying theme that provides meaning, direction, and mobilization" to organization members.[13]

Where rapid, nonroutine responses to shifting consumer needs are called for, the appropriate organizational culture can guide the problem-solving efforts of "self-managed" teams. In this dynamic setting, top managers must take the lead in articulating a transformational vision, providing resources, and developing an organizational culture that will suggest how this vision can be implemented.

Tom Peters, the popular and influential management guru, has argued that a revolutionary new model is needed for companies to develop a capability for "thriving on chaos." Managers must "empower" team-based employees with information and with the vision that will give direction and inspiration to their new power. He portrays the new front-line worker as being controlled

> not by a supervisor, middle management, or a procedure book, but rather by the clarity and excitement of a vision, its daily embodiment by wandering senior managers, an extraordinary level of training, the obvious respect she or he is given, and the self-discipline that almost automatically accompanies exceptional grants of autonomy.[14]

Saturn's flat, nonhierarchical structure and consensus-based decision-making style are consistent with the commitment model. Panels of Saturn employees share in making such decisions as selection of the company's ad agency, suppliers, and dealers. All employees use the same cafeteria, washroom facilities, and parking lot. Hiring decisions are made by a joint union/management committee. Saturn's 3,000 production workers are recruited from within GM's unionized work force. If they are selected, new employees are called upon to embrace a new concept in cooperative industrial relations. The adversarial labor/management posture, buttressed by narrow job classifications, restrictive work rules, and seniority rights,

---

[13]Ralph H. Kilmann, Mary J. Saxton, Roy Serpa, and Associates, eds., *Gaining Control of the Corporate Culture* (San Francisco: Jossey-Bass, 1986), p. ix. See also Edgar H. Schein, "How Culture Forms, Develops, and Changes," in Kilmann, Saxton, and Serpa, pp. 19–20, and William G. Ouchi, "Markets, Bureaucracies, and Clans," *Administrative Science Quarterly* (1980), pp. 129–141.

[14]"Restoring American Competitiveness: New Models of Organizations," 1988, p. 107. See also Tom Peters, *Thriving on Chaos: Handbook for a Management Revolution* (New York: The Free Press, 1986).

Exhibit 33.1 (Cont.)

are to be given up in exchange for the promise of unprecedented decision involvement and job security. The Saturn labor pact holds that workers will be laid off only in the event of "unforeseen or catastrophic events or severe economic conditions." The company hopes that this offer of job security will reduce employee resistance to the introduction of new technology and to flexible, multiple-task work assignments. Greater employee commitment and retention also will enable the company to reap higher long-term returns from its significant investment in human capital. A major difference between GM-10 and Saturn is the emphasis of the latter on investing in people rather than high-tech automated hardware. New Saturn employees receive between 100 and 750 hours of training. This covers not only the basic manual and technical matters, but also information that "empowers" employees to work together in accomplishing their interrelated tasks. Workers are trained at more than one job so that they can trade off tasks and collaborate in designing a simpler, more balanced work flow consistent with the Japanese *kaizen* principle. They are taught how to interpret financial and cost data—which are freely shared rather than hoarded by management—so that all can work to improve productivity and profits. They are given the training necessary to maintain and interpret a statistical process control (SPC) system. Line workers are expected to use SPC in identifying and correcting sources of quality defects in the production process. Team-oriented interpersonal skills are emphasized in the hiring and training process. "Awareness" sessions are an important aspect of training. Employee socialization to the values of Saturn's organizational culture is needed to activate the commitment model. James Lewandowski, vice president of human resources, is pleased to find among Saturn employees a real sense of mission: "It's been described as almost like a cult."[15]

Unfortunately, Saturn's mission, and the transformational vision on which it is based, remains somewhat unfocused and even unremarkable from a marketing standpoint. A preoccupation with industrial relations and production-based concerns has given the new company an inward-looking culture that inculcates employee commitment and empowerment virtually as ends in themselves. Saturn has been slow in getting its products to market and rather inept at identifying and exploiting niche opportunities. Its two- and four-door compacts, available at last in late 1990, may well get lost in the crowd of Japanese contenders. Saturn's avowed goal of building a car that looks and drives like a Honda suggests a derivative rather than a transformational vision. It says more about Honda's secure than about Saturn's tenuous place in the U.S. auto market. If the paradox of commitment and control are to be reconciled in the absence of a strong marketing sensibility, the Saturn model won't get GM back to keeping its eye on the customer and its footwork in tune with the times.

[15]"Here Comes GM's Saturn," p. 60.

Exhibit 33.1 (Cont.)

Paradox #2: How can Saturn retain its autonomy and sense of uniqueness while also offering to GM a sense of continuity within change?

For the commitment model to work, members must feel that their organization's mission is as important as its culture is unique. Expectations of momentous events and revolutionary changes are needed to inspire a commitment to continuous learning. "Business as usual" methods and assumptions are not the stuff of which crusades are made.

If it is to prosper and endure, Saturn must grow and inspire emulation. It will need a production/sales volume of at least 500,000 units a year—twice its current capacity—to be economically viable. To accommodate growth, Saturn's independent dealership network must be expanded beyond the currently planned 70 outlets on the East and West coasts. All of this must be done while GM top management must deal with idle production capacity of at least 1 million cars a year. At least four assembly plants and related component facilities must be shut down. Between 1987 and 1990, GM has already closed 16 plants at a cost of 36,345 jobs.[16]

If GM is to make the transition from the control to the commitment model, its top management must perform radical surgery on the company's "frozen middle." Redundant layers in the hierarchy must be cut away, either by excising or by transforming midmanagers who have served in the past as "cops" to enforce orders from above or as information relays within functionally specialized departments. This is necessary both to cut overhead costs and to free up room for horizontal interaction and semiautonomous problem solving by more cross-functional project teams. Between 1986 and 1990, GM cut 40,000 employees from its white-collar work force. Some industry analysts are recommending further cuts in the 1990s of up to half of GM's remaining 100,000-strong North American white-collar bureaucratic army.[17]

These Draconian measures are hardly consistent with Saturn's promise of job security or with the collaborative rhetoric of GM's "Team Concept." Resentment against Saturn seems to be building in GM's other automotive divisions, both among blue- and white-collar employees. Given Saturn's unimpressive financial prospects at its near-term level of output and the increased threat to other units if it grows, pressure is growing for folding Saturn into GM's traditional manufacturing and marketing operations. The Buick and Oldsmobile marketing divisions and dealership organizations are especially hungry for some exciting new models that might reverse their recent sales declines. This move would

[16]Alex Taylor III, "Can American Cars Come Back?" *Fortune*, February 26, 1990, p. 64.
[17]Taylor, "New Drive to Revive GM," pp. 60–61.

Exhibit 33.1 (Cont.)

diminish the sense of threat posed by Saturn and create for other GM units a greater sense of continuity within change. However, this loss of autonomy might shatter Saturn's sense of uniqueness and destroy its symbolic value as the harbinger of change at GM. It could also undermine the credibility of GM's efforts to reach out to customers in a segment that strongly prefers Japanese cars.

In reviewing the executive summary, Bob Stempel still wasn't sure how he should proceed. His personal style leaned toward hard work, careful preparation, and cautious, incremental change. He recognized the weaknesses in GM's centralized product development system that had led to the GM-10 disappointment. He was less personally involved than his predecessor, Roger Smith, in the Saturn initiative. However, he felt that Saturn was the key to learning how to build small cars for a profit in North America. Stempel had already decided that he would not begin his term as GM's CEO and chairman with a dramatic reorganization or with wholesale layoffs: "One reorganization is enough in anyone's lifetime." He wanted to retain, while improving upon, a system that differentiated models through design and added features and cut costs by using more common parts under the sheet metal. He decided that, initially, GM should "relaunch" its products and push out new cars from the existing development pipeline. Cost cutting and a few hot new models could quicken the pulse of the auto market, bring back the crowds, and make the 1990s the decade of the General. Stempel concluded: "Nothing's for sure. But we think we've got the right things in place to do it. Indeed, we've bet the store on it."[4]

---

[4]Taylor, "New Drive to Revive GM," pp. 60–61, and Ingrassia and White, "Losing the Race," p. A8. See also Jerry Flint, "1990 Will Be the Year of the General," *Forbes*, November 27, 1989, pp. 40–41.

34

LIBERTY NATIONAL BANCORP, INC. AND LIBERTY NATIONAL BANK AND TRUST COMPANY

Liberty National Bank and Trust Company's headquarters city of Louisville, Kentucky, was founded in the latter part of the eighteenth century, when George Rogers Clark's military expedition, aiming to eliminate British and Indian power in the territory northwest of the Ohio River, came to the falls of the Ohio:

> "I observed the little island of about seven acres opposide to whare the town of Lewisville now stands, seldom or never was interely covered by the water, I resolved to take possession and fortify, which I did." In that laconic prose, . . . Clark described the founding of Louisville in the spring of 1778.[1]

Clark had expressed no intention of establishing a town in the locality of the Ohio River rapids, but this restriction to navigation provided opportunities for merchants and others to set up their businesses—including banking—at the site.[2]

> Like the Chemical Bank of New York, which was organized to operate a chemical business; and the Bank of the Manhattan Company, which was established to finance a water

[1]George H. Yater, *Two Hundred Years at the Falls of the Ohio: A History of Louisville and Jefferson County* (Louisville, KY: The Filson Club, 1987) p. 2.

[2]For a supplementary view on Louisville, see Appendix A.

system, Liberty National Bank and Trust Company had its origin in an insurance organi-zation, the German Insurance Company.[3]

In March 1854 when Kentucky's General Assembly vested authority in the German Insurance Company to "invest . . . in any state in the United States," the concept was born that led to German Insurance Bank, which, with a change of name during World War I, became Liberty Insurance Bank.

See Appendix 34B for notes on Louisville's and Kentucky's business environ-ment.

ENTERING THE DECADE OF THE 1990s

Liberty National Bancorp (LNBC) was the largest independent bank holding com-pany headquartered in Kentucky, with assets in excess of $3.7 billion at year-end 1990. Liberty National Bank and Trust Company (LNBL) was the third largest bank in Louisville. Its December 31, 1990 call report showed $2.6 billion total assets and $28.2 million net income.

Second largest First National Bank of Louisville, owned by National City Cor-poration, Cleveland, reported $4.4 billion assets and $18.9 million net income, while the largest banking institution in Louisville, Citizens Fidelity Bank and Trust Com-pany, owned by PNC Financial Corporation, Pittsburgh, reported $5.8 billion in as-sets and net income of $18.1 million.

LNBC was the holding company for its lead bank and eight other Kentucky banks, plus Liberty National Bank and Trust Company of Indiana, with offices throughout southern Indiana. LNBC consummated two mergers in 1985, two in 1986, three in 1988, one in October 1989, and a ninth in January 1990. According to treasurer Carl Weigel, the holding company paid multiples in the range of 1.5 to 2.0 for the acquisitions: cash, exchange of stock, and combinations.

In 1988 LNBC expanded into the Nashville, Tennessee, market with a newly formed subsidiary, Liberty Financial Services, Inc., offering a variety of consumer lending services. Also, Liberty National Leasing Company opened a separate office in Nashville.

Announcement came in February 1991 that LNBC had entered into an agree-ment to acquire Bank of Lexington and Trust Company, sixth largest bank in Fayette County, Kentucky, with assets of $203 million, from its family owners in an all-cash transaction.

Application was filed with regulators in 1991 to merge three of LNBC's affiliate banks in northern Kentucky—Erlanger, Florence, and Fort Thomas—to create a single national bank. Reasons given included more branches for enhanced customer convenience, anticipated increase in lending limits to enable the bank to contribute

---

[3]R. C. Riebel, *Louisville Panorama: A Visual History of Louisville*, Louisville; KY: Liberty National Bank and Trust Co., 1954) p. 198.

more to economic development of its region, and operational efficiencies through an affiliated remote operations processing center in Erlanger.

"Because many newly acquired affiliates are within the lead bank's geographic market area, we moved quickly to include 'Liberty National Bank' in their nomenclature," Frank Hower, recently retired chairman and CEO, said. "This allowed us to capitalize on name recognition established in the region through our highly successful image advertising campaign. Similarly, we changed the majority of affiliated existing product lines to mirror those of the lead bank. We plan to continue introducing selected services suited to each bank's individual market."

Exhibit 34.1 illustrates the geography of LNBC's offices and other service locations in four states. Exhibit 34.2 displays the relationships of affiliates to LNBC and LNB. Corporate objectives are listed in Exhibit 34.3. The bank's planning cycle is portrayed in Exhibit 34.4. And LNBC's multibank philosophy is outlined in Exhibit 34.5.

Exhibit 34.6 presents summaries of selected key financial statistics, with introductory narrative, for Liberty National Bancorp's 1990 performance. Exhibit 34.7 lists principal shareholders and ownership percentages.

Reports of industry financial results reveal that banks in the upper echelon of profitability and growth tend to have one or more ingredients in common: growing noninterest revenues, dependable core deposits or other cheap sources of funds, tight cost controls that compound the dividends from mergers, and consistent strategies championed by a highly visible chief executive and subscribed to throughout the organization.

Reflecting on LNBC's performance in 1990 and looking ahead, President Joseph Phelps remarked, "in an attempt to broaden our base of revenue, we will endeavor to raise the level of noninterest income as a percentage of total revenue. With increased emphasis on trust and investment management services, securities brokerage services, and private banking and insurance services, we hope to raise that level to 30 percent, realizing this goal will allow us to reduce the vulnerability of our earnings as a result of fluctuating interest rates."

The following mission statement was written in 1991:

CORPORATE MISSION

The mission of Liberty is to be the strongest independent financial institution in this region and to be second to none in the excellence and ethical application of our services. In order to achieve this goal, we must be creative in maintaining a full range of financial services on a profitable basis, achieve an excellent rate of return for our stockholders, develop a loyal staff and recognize our responsibilities to them, and maintain a relationship with the community that is beyond reproach.

Source: Corporate document, 1991.

The September 11, 1987 issue of *Keefe Bank Update* reported that

Liberty National Bancorp is a conservatively run organization with very respectable profitability ratios, strong capital, and sound asset quality. We advise investors who cur-

Exhibit 34.1

LIBERTY NATIONAL BANCORP, INC., OFFICES AND OTHER SERVICE LOCATIONS

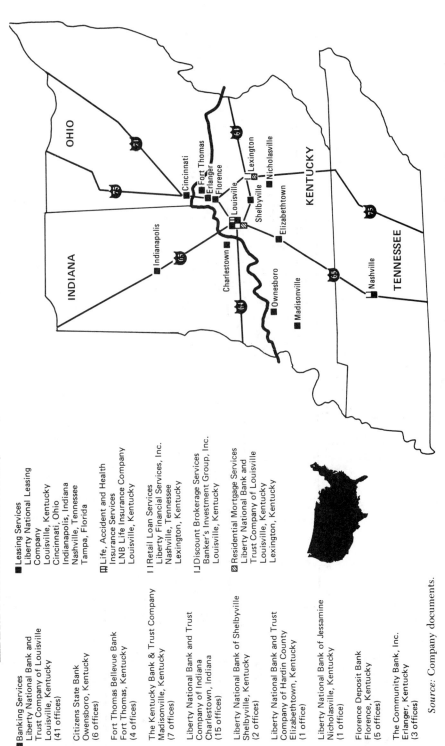

■ Banking Services
Liberty National Bank and
Trust Company of Louisville
Louisville, Kentucky
(41 offices)

Citizens State Bank
Owensboro, Kentucky
(6 offices)

Fort Thomas Bellevue Bank
Fort Thomas, Kentucky
(4 offices)

The Kentucky Bank & Trust Company
Madisonville, Kentucky
(7 offices)

Liberty National Bank and Trust
Company of Indiana
Charlestown, Indiana
(15 offices)

Liberty National Bank of Shelbyville
Shelbyville, Kentucky
(2 offices)

Liberty National Bank and Trust
Company of Hardin County
Elizabethtown, Kentucky
(1 office)

Liberty National Bank of Jessamine
Nicholasville, Kentucky
(1 office)

Florence Deposit Bank
Florence, Kentucky
(5 offices)

The Community Bank, Inc.
Erlanger, Kentucky
(3 offices)

■ Leasing Services
Liberty National Leasing
Company
Louisville, Kentucky
Cincinnati, Ohio
Indianapolis, Indiana
Nashville, Tennessee
Tampa, Florida

⊞ Life, Accident and Health
Insurance Services
LNB Life Insurance Company
Louisville, Kentucky

⎸⎸ Retail Loan Services
Liberty Financial Services, Inc.
Nashville, Tennessee
Lexington, Kentucky

⎸⌋ Discount Brokerage Services
Banker's Investment Group, Inc.
Louisville, Kentucky

☑ Residential Mortgage Services
Liberty National Bank and
Trust Company of Louisville
Louisville, Kentucky
Lexington, Kentucky

Source: Company documents.

575

Exhibit 34.2

AFFILIATE RELATIONSHIPS

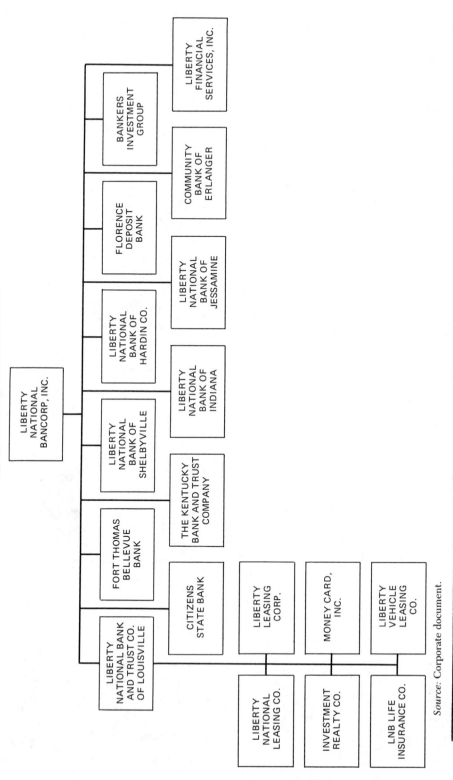

Source: Corporate document.

Exhibit 34.3

LIBERTY NATIONAL BANCORP, INC., AND SUBSIDIARIES: CORPORATE OBJECTIVES

NONFINANCIAL

1. To expand actively the Corporation's independent presence on a regional basis by acquiring additional financial institutions as well as expanding the Corporation's current customer coverage.
2. To increase the Corporation's profits by adding new services while maintaining a high level of quality.
3. To promote increased stockholder and market awareness of the Corporation's profit potential.
4. To attract aggressively, retain, and motivate a high-quality staff.

FINANCIAL

Profitability

1. To achieve an increase of at least 10 to 12 percent in operating earnings per share.
2. To achieve an operating return on average stockholder's equity of at least 14 to 15 percent.
3. To achieve an operating return on total assets of 1 percent or greater.

Capital Adequacy

1. To set primary capital as a percentage of total assets at not less than 6.5 percent.
2. To achieve an internal capital generation rate of 10.5 percent over the next three years.
3. To limit the double leverage ratio, that is, the investment in subsidiaries divided by the equity of the Corporation, for the Corporation to 135 percent.
4. To maintain "risk-based capital" at a level greater than the minimum requirement of 8 percent.

Source: Corporate document.

Exhibit 34.4

LIBERTY PLANNING CYCLE

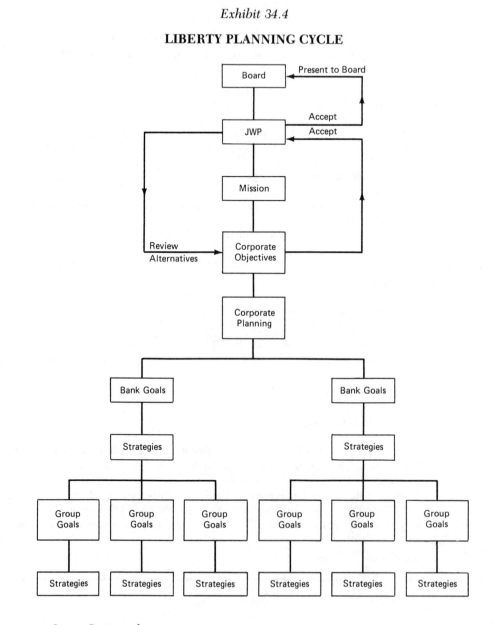

Source: Corporate document.

Exhibit 34.5

LIBERTY NATIONAL BANCORP
MULTIBANK HOLDING COMPANY PHILOSOPHY

1. **Organization.** LNBC will seek to maintain a decentralized business organization wherever possible. Affiliates will have presidents and their own boards of directors. An affiliate CEO is free to utilize organizational resources within defined operational areas as long as the strategy and policies of the affiliate and holding company are adhered to. Performance will be measured against specific goals and targets, to be established annually.

2. **Culture.** LNBC seeks to build a responsive and responsible organization, one that rewards performance and is sensitive to its customers, employees, and community.

3. **Reporting Relationships.** Affiliates will report to an officer of LNBC. All managers and staff within affiliates will have direct reporting relationships to the top of their organization. There will be certain dotted-line reporting relationships to LNBC staff.

4. **Relationships Among Affiliates.** Affiliates will coordinate their activities through LNBC and seek to satisfy customer needs with services available through LNBC prior to contacting outside corporations. The LNBC management is responsible for Affiliate integration and will monitor all integration activities.

5. **Market Territory.** LNBC services the state of Kentucky, southern Indiana, and selected regions of Illinois, Ohio, and Tennessee. Each Affiliate will be assigned an exclusive market territory by product line. There will be little or no overlap, and Affiliates will not compete with one another. Territories will be negotiated by LNBC with each Affiliate but will generally incorporate the county in which the Affiliates is headquartered. Any area not assigned an Affiliate will be the responsibility of LNBL.

6. **Affiliates in the Same Area.** Affiliates operating in the same market area will coordinate product offerings, pricing, and advertising.

7. **Customer Relationship.** All existing customer relationships will remain in place unless two Affiliates and the customer agree to transfer the relationships. New customer relationships developed by officers of another Affiliate or LNBL will be assigned the Affiliate in that territory.

8. **Products and Pricing.** In general, each Affiliate is free to set pricing on the products and services offered. Pricing should be coordinated in overlapping markets. Affiliates are free to offer products and services necessary to remain competitive in their market, but certain products and services will be made available throughout the holding company and the products and services of Affiliates in overlapping markets will mirror one another.

9. **Employee Benefits.** Officers and employees throughout the Holding Company will receive the same, or comparable benefits; be subject to a common review process; and maintain uniform job descriptions, pay grade structures, and officer titles. Compensation may vary among Affiliates due to differences in cost of living and competitive salaries.

10. **Facilities Planning.** It shall be the responsibility of LNBC management to allocate resources throughout the holding company as relates to branch/ATM expansion or remodeling to meet holding company strategic goals.

11. **Performance Measurement.** Each Affiliate, in conjunction with LNBC, will establish annual and long-range financial goals and minimum acceptable perfor-

Exhibit 34.5 (Cont.)

mance levels. In addition some market guidelines (such as market penetration) will be established for specific product or market groups. Such goals are subject to the review and approval of LNBC.

Source: Corporate document.

Exhibit 34.6

Liberty National Bancorp, Inc.
Louisville, Kentucky

LIBERTY NATIONAL BANCORP REPORTS NET INCOME OF $32.8 MILLION

LOUISVILLE, KY (January 31, 1991)—Liberty National Bancorp, Inc. (NASDAQ:LNBC), reported fully diluted net income per share of $2.73 for 1990, a decrease of 6.8 percent from the $2.93 reported in 1989.

Although the 1990 results were below our expectations, 1990 was still the second best earnings year in Liberty's history. The decline was primarily due to the $5.4 million increase, as compared to the previous year, in the provision for loan losses which resulted from the additional charge-offs incurred during 1990.

Liberty continues to support a conservative posture as it relates to the allowance for loan losses, which should minimize the possibility of encountering the unexpected difficulties that other banks have recently reported in these uncertain economic times. The allowance for loan losses was 169 percent of nonperforming loans on December 31, 1990, an increase of six basis points over the 163 percent reported as of September 30, 1990. Nonperforming loans represented only 0.72 percent of outstanding loans on December 31, 1990 compared to 0.76 percent on September 30, 1990, a four-basis-point reduction.

Liberty's capital position ($275.3 million on December 31, 1990) continues to be strong. The percentage of average primary capital (stockholders' equity and allowance for loan losses) to average assets was 8.20 percent for the year ended December 31, 1990, compared to 8.03 percent for the same period in 1989.

On January 16, 1991, Liberty declared a 12.8 percent increase in its quarterly dividend, from 23½ cents per share to 26½ cents per share. The current quarterly dividend reflects an indicated annual dividend of $1.06 per share, up from $0.94 per share in 1990. This marks the 21st consecutive year that Liberty has increased its dividend.

It is our pleasure to present this information for your review. We provide a similar analysis at each quarter end. Any questions about this information should be directed to Carl E. Weigel, treasurer, (502) 566-2510.

Exhibit 34.6 (Cont.)

FIVE-YEAR FINANCIAL SUMMARY, DECEMBER 31, 1986–1990

	1990	1989	1988	1987	1986
Earnings per share					
1st quarter	$0.75	$0.70	$0.61	$0.55	$0.51
2nd	0.74	0.77	0.68	0.61	0.56
3rd	0.56	0.75	0.70	0.63	0.56
4th	0.80	0.85	0.77	0.69	0.62
Primary	$2.85	$3.07	$2.76	$2.48	$2.25
Fully diluted	$2.73	$2.93	$2.63	$2.37	$2.14
Performance ratios					
Return on avg. assets	0.92%	1.03%	1.00%	1.02%	0.95%
Return on avg. equity	12.50	14.51	14.34	14.31	14.50
Equity to assets (avg.)	7.37	7.07	6.96	7.10	6.52
Primary capital ratio (avg.)	8.20	8.03	7.88	8.01	7.41
Book value per share (EOP)	$23.82	$22.17	$20.29	$18.47	$16.62
Market value per share (EOP)	21.50	27.25	24.50	21.75	21.75
Dividends declared per share	0.940	0.820	0.720	0.635	0.570

EOP = End of period.

CONDENSED CONSOLIDATED STATEMENT OF INCOME, 1989–1990
(In thousands except per share data)

	THREE MONTHS ENDED DECEMBER 31		YEAR ENDED DECEMBER 31	
	1990	1989	1990	1989
Interest income	$84,472	$80,263	$330,116	$310,652
Interest expense	51,684	50,734	204,174	195,982
Net interest income	32,788	29,529	125,942	114,670
Provision for loan losses	4,789	3,333	19,157	13,790
Net interest income after provision for loan losses	27,999	26,196	106,785	100,880
Noninterest income	11,246	12,180	44,793	42,404
Noninterest expense	28,286	26,266	111,297	101,641
Income before income taxes	10,959	12,110	40,281	41,643
Income tax expense	1,802	2,701	7,491	8,472
Net income	$ 9,157	$ 9,409	$ 32,790	$ 33,171
Net income per share				
Primary	$0.80	$0.85	$2.85	$3.07
Fully diluted	0.76	0.82	2.73	2.93
Average shares outstanding				
Primary	11,558	11,030	11,525	10,798
Fully diluted	12,434	11,920	12,403	11,696

Exhibit 34.6 (Cont.)

NET INTEREST INCOME, 1989–1990
(In thousands except percentages)

	1990					1989
	Year to Date	Fourth Quarter	Third Quarter	Second Quarter	First Quarter	Year to Date
Average earning assets	$3,184,215	$3,256,839	$3,197,050	$3,153,232	$3,128,183	$2,878,283
Average interest-bearing liabilities	2,747,180	2,813,642	2,751,946	2,714,921	2,706,984	2,486,468
Net interest income*	135,763	35,235	34,298	33,660	32,570	124,483
Net interest spread†	3.25%	3.30%	3.23%	3.24%	3.20%	3.25%
Net interest margin‡	4.26	4.29	4.26	4.28	4.22	4.32

*Taxable-equivalent basis.
†Taxable-equivalent yield on interest earning assets minus rate paid on interest bearing liabilities.
‡Net interest income annualized and stated on a taxable-equivalent basis, divided by average earning assets.

ALLOWANCE FOR LOAN LOSSES AND NONPERFORMING LOANS, 1986–1990
(In thousands except percentages)

	1990	1989	1988	1987	1986
Allowance for loan losses:					
Balance beginning of period	$34,933	$32,019	$24,842	$24,056	$21,445
Balance from acquired banks	602	884	2,200	—	952
Provision for loan losses	19,157	13,790	11,435	8,184	9,017
Net charge-offs	(23,813)	(11,760)	(6,458)	(7,398)	(7,358)
Balance end of period	$30,879	$34,933	$32,019	$24,842	$24,056
Average loans	$2,484,794	$2,272,398	$1,953,641	$1,659,805	$1,471,881
Loans outstanding (EOP)	2,547,582	2,374,934	2,134,951	1,698,434	1,604,408
Ratios:					
Provision for loan losses to average loans	0.77%	0.61%	0.59%	0.49%	0.61%
Net charge-offs to average loans	0.96	0.52	0.33	0.45	0.50
Allowance for loan losses (EOP) to average loans	1.24	1.54	1.64	1.50	1.63
Allowance for loan losses (EOP) to loans (EOP)	1.21	1.47	1.50	1.46	1.50
Nonperforming loans (EOP)	$18,289	$16,528	$10,288	$11,346	$20,650
Allowance for loan losses (EOP) to nonperforming loans (EOP)	169%	211%	311%	219%	116
Nonperforming loans (EOP) to loans outstanding (EOP)	0.72	0.70	0.48	0.67	1.29

Exhibit 34.6 (Cont.)

NONINTEREST INCOME AND EXPENSE, 1989–1990
(In thousands)

	1990					1989
	Year to Date	Fourth Quarter	Third Quarter	Second Quarter	First Quarter	Year to Date
Noninterest income						
Trust income	$12,764	$ 2,958	$ 3,419	$ 3,427	$ 2,960	$10,889
Service charges on deposit accounts	13,395	3,589	3,468	3,212	3,126	11,546
Bankcard income	4,581	1,271	1,102	1,200	1,008	4,212
Insurance premium income	4,801	1,216	1,241	1,279	1,065	4,595
Commissions and trading account profits	1,455	354	354	333	414	1,166
Investment securities gains (losses)	5	9	(4)	—	—	10
Other	7,792	1,849	2,158	1,947	1,838	9,986
Total noninterest income	$44,793	$11,246	$11,738	$11,398	$10,411	$42,404
Noninterest expense						
Salaries and employee benefits	$ 54,483	$13,336	$13,412	$13,613	$14,122	$ 50,669
Net occupancy expense	7,828	1,990	1,975	1,938	1,925	7,006
Equipment expense	9,242	2,336	2,330	2,286	2,290	8,300
Other	39,744	10,624	10,178	10,042	8,900	35,666
Total noninterest expense	$111,297	$28,286	$27,895	$27,879	$27,237	$101,641

LIBERTY NATIONAL BANCORP, INC. AND SUBSIDIARIES
CONSOLIDATED BALANCE SHEET, DECEMBER 31, 1989–1990
(In thousands except share data)

	1990	1989
Assets		
Cash and due from banks	$ 333,793	$ 287,827
Interest bearing deposits with banks	2,100	1,100
Federal funds sold and securities purchased under agreements to resell	20,000	174,400
Trading account securities	253	1,794
Mortgage loans held for sale	967	1,460
Investment securities (market value $699,943 in 1990; $588,256 in 1989)	693,281	585,518
Loans (net of unearned income of $39,216 in 1990; $55,203 in 1989)	2,547,582	2,374,934
Less: Allowance for loan losses	30,879	34,933
Net loans	2,516,703	2,340,001
Premises and equipment	49,556	47,060
Other assets	96,814	96,338
Total	$3,713,467	$3,535,498

Exhibit 34.6 (Cont.)

Liabilities

Deposits

Noninterest bearing, domestic	618,114	$ 634,941
Interest bearing, domestic	2,343,992	2,244,149
Interest bearing, foreign	79,516	90,437
Total deposits	3,041,622	2,969,527
Federal funds purchased and securities sold under agreements to repurchase	264,318	191,234
Commercial paper	7,814	4,936
Other short-term borrowings	49,993	42,088
Other liabilities	37,000	38,657
Long-term debt	37,377	41,268
Total liabilities	3,438,124	3,287,710

Stockholders' equity

Preferred stock

Authorized and unissued 10,000,000 shares — —

Common stock

Authorized 40,000,000 shares in 1990 and 30,000,000 shares in 1989

Issued and outstanding 11,558,175 shares in 1990 and 11,174,838 shares in 1989	25,796	25,379
Surplus	67,916	67,041
Retained earnings	181,631	155,368
Total stockholders' equity	275,343	247,788
Total	$3,713,467	$3,535,498

Exhibit 34.7

PRINCIPAL SHAREHOLDERS
LIBERTY NATIONAL BANCORP, INC.

	Percentage of Shares Owned
All directors emeriti, directors, officers, and certain employees of Liberty and the banks as a group	31.02%
Liberty National Bank & Trust Company of Louisville	23.94
All directors and officers of Liberty as a group (31 in number)	11.30
The Liberty 1987 thrift plan	8.62
Hilliard Lyons (Trust)	5.44

Source: "Notice of 1991 Annual Meeting of Shareholders and Proxy Material," pp. 1–2.

rently own Liberty to continue to HOLD it as part of a portfolio of bank stocks that are fundamentally sound and have a better than even chance of being acquired in the next three years.

Stock analyst Alan Morel of Hilliard Lyons, Louisville, in a buy-recommendation letter (December 4, 1990) observed that

> Liberty National has built its business on traditional values and conservative policies. Lending is restricted to customers located within LNBC's market area with whom the bank is familiar, and to businesses with which LNBC has a level of lending expertise. There are no foreign loans, the energy portfolio is small, real estate construction loans are 4% of loans, and leveraged buyout financing is considered a questionable lending practice. Sound credit policies have guided a diversified loan portfolio, balancing retail and commercial loans funded predominantly by core deposits and enhanced by liquid, short-maturity government securities.

> LNBC's earning power is good, its credit quality higher and its non-performing assets lower than its peers, but current price is at a discount to its peers. . . . Over the next three years we anticipate a combination of banking industry revaluation and recognition of LNBC's particular qualities to result in a stock price . . . exceeding $36 a share.

In a 1988–89 survey of the state's largest publicly held companies, LNBC, with a 10-year compounded annual growth rate of 13.7 percent, ranked as the fastest-growing of the state's 10 largest financial companies and banks. Liberty moved from second place in 1987 to first place in 1988 in the survey's listing of Kentucky-owned banks ranked by asset size.[4]

National status was accorded LNBC when it was listed in 1989 as one of the top 500 publicly held U.S. companies in *Forbes'* annual directory based on assets.[5] Liberty, compared in a group of 23 banks in the Southeast, ranked fifth in the region in 1988 (up from ninth in 1987) with $16,400 in profits for each of its 1,800 employees. Liberty employees represented an average of $164,700 each in sales, ranking fourth in the region. The regional average for all banks was $13,800 profits and $149,800 sales per employee.

CHANGES IN SENIOR MANAGEMENT*

After serving as Liberty's chairman for 17 years, Frank B. Hower, Jr., retired from active management on February 1, 1990, and continues to serve as a director. The board elected Joseph W. Phelps, 62, to succeed Hower, who had worked at Liberty for 40 of his 60 years. Malcolm B. Chancey, 57, was chosen to succeed Mr. Phelps as president.

---

[4]The Wenz-Neely Company, *The Kentucky Forty* (Louisville: The Wenz-Neely Company, 1989).
[5]*Forbes* 500, May 1989.
*See Appendix C for further LNB and Retail Banking Group Organization information.

"Since becoming chairman," Hower stated, "I have seen this organization grow from a $430 million bank to an eight-bank $3.2 billion holding company. Liberty is extremely well positioned for the future." The close relationship among the bank's top leadership was apparent in Phelps's observation, "It's impossible for me to put into words the contribution Frank has made not only to the bank but to this entire community. And from a personal standpoint, I will sorely miss the day-to-day camaraderie we have enjoyed over the years." Both served notably on numerous boards and participated in myriad Louisville and statewide civic activities.

Chancey, who started with Liberty in 1968, became a board member in 1986, while serving as executive vice president and cashier, responsible for all bank administration and the asset and liability management functions. He was founding president of Kentuckiana Automated Clearing House Association and of the Quest Electronic Network. He also served in a public service capacity on numerous boards throughout the state.

Discussion of what the newly elected chairman and CEO hoped to achieve before retiring at age 65 prompted recollections of initiation into the world of banking. William Joseph Phelps (a clerical error dubbed him Joseph William on his birth certificate) remembered having held several different jobs simultaneously in high school, including banking. Billy Joe's father assisted in launching his son's career in the financial services industry by helping him get a messenger's job at Madison National Bank in Richmond, where he later worked as teller, bookkeeper, and, occasionally, substitute janitor when the regular holder of that job took a day off.

In 1950, at 23, he was employed as examiner by the U.S. Treasury Department, a job he performed until joining Liberty as assistant cashier in 1958. He became president of the institution 15 years later, after serving in such positions as head of correspondent banking, secretary to the board of directors, and executive vice president.

Entry-level recruits and seasoned veterans at Liberty are quick to point out that one of the newly appointed chairman's strengths is consideration for every member of the "Liberty family," and an open-door policy for employees. "He loves kids and keeps a box of toys in his office for young visitors whose parents come to conduct business with him," said an assistant. Frank Hower mentioned his replacement's "wonderful sense of humor," remarking that "Billy Joe is not overly impressed with his own position at the bank." They often kidded each other good-naturedly: "He fusses about my dropping pipe tobacco on the carpeting," Hower said, "so I tell him one of his unofficial titles is 'director of sanitary engineering.'" Phelps's penchant for cleanliness is evident in impeccable attire and a spotless office. Traveling, he would readily change hotel rooms when one did not measure up to his standards of neatness. In addition to serving on several other community boards and committees, he was chairman of Louisville's Operation Brightside, a citywide cleanup campaign.

A Liberty executive vice president remarked on Phelps's high energy level, noting that his vigorous results-minded approach to leadership included readiness to step aside and discuss ideas and problems with anyone in the bank. "He is people oriented," commented one. Another: "He sets the tone for our entire organization in relationships inside and outside the bank." "He's tuned in to customer service above all, and preaches it at every meeting," observed a third.

LENDING POLICIES

Comments on the bank's lending policies by lending officers, credit analysts, and others included the following:

> As the largest independent bank holding company based in Kentucky, we focus on the key needs of this region rather than conforming to policies from a distant headquarters. And we do business close to home; we don't try to stretch beyond our reach geographically.

> We have a policy of not lending to Third World countries or to any highly speculative ventures. No national leveraged buyouts; LBOs involve questionable lending practices.

> To avoid many of the more visible problems, Liberty makes a concerted effort to diversify its lending activities—no particular sector of industry accounts for significant portions of our overall portfolio.

> Everyday lending activities do much to foster the quality of life in our region. For example, we financed the reopening of a factory, generating many new jobs in an area where unemployment was well into double digits. We provided funding for sewer system upgrades to meet EPA standards. Through the issue and distribution of tax-exempt municipal bonds, we've assisted in vital projects such as schools, water treatment plants, hospitals, and roads.

> We have been in the forefront in developing a number of special lending programs. In 1988, the lead bank launched an innovative project through the Housing Authority of Louisville that will make low-cost condominum ownership possible for public housing residents—extending the opportunity to make the American dream come true to individuals who otherwise may not have been able to afford their own home. We also continued our successful $5 million West End Loan Program, targeted to businesses located or relocating in an area that has been economically depressed.

> Aggressive efforts to attract new businesses are being made by our affiliates as well. In Dayton, Kentucky, our affiliate has taken the lead in assisting this once dormant city to realize its growth potential by introducing a $1.2 million reduced-interest loan program to attract new and expand existing businesses. Corydon, Indiana, succeeded in landing a major automotive industry supplier that had complex financing needs, thanks in part to an unusual cooperative venture involving our Indiana affiliate and our lead bank with a major Indiana bank and its affiliate.

The Louisville airport business relocation program typified Liberty's focus on local needs, making available $10 million to finance plant, property, and equipment replacement for businesses directly displaced by airport expansion. In announcing the plan, Helm Dobbins, senior vice president of U.S. and regional banking, cited the importance to Liberty of the small- to medium-sized companies, calling them "the bank's primary business clients." "It is a well-documented fact," he said, "that these businesses produce the majority of jobs and most of the economic growth experienced in our region and in the country as a whole." The loans thus provided would carry discounted origination fees and interest rates and extended repayment terms of up to 20 years. Businesses with sales of $40 million or less qualified as applicants for the program.

PRODUCT DEVELOPMENT

Senior Vice President Maria Gerwing, group marketing manager, expressed pride in the bank's historical approach to product development: "Our formula is simple: combine sophisticated market research with plain, old-fashioned listening to customers. Doing both gives us a consistent edge in developing new products and enhancing existing ones."

"In 1989, for example, we began offering 'full-service' brokerage, enabling us to counsel customers more effectively on fixed-income and equity products for investment portfolios and how to tailor them to meet financial objectives."

"Liberty is the most prominent automobile financier in the Louisville market," according to A. R. "Butch" Riddle, senior vice president of the bank's consumer credit administration. "We offer a choice of financing options to customers: fixed-payment, simple-interest, variable-rate loans as well as fixed-rate, simple-interest loans. In other words, we want to offer the customer every conceivable type of product. The fourfold increase in the bank's automobile loan portfolio 1984–1988 was a result of hard work and commitment to customer service. When the prime rate soared to 21.5 percent, we kept our floor plan at 18 percent. Customers remember that and they've rewarded the bank with loyalty." He also cited other contributing factors, including knowledge of a customer's business: "We try to understand our dealers' business as well as we understand the banking business."

Other notes on products and promotions appeared in the bank's 1988 annual report:

> New product and business development was particularly evident in retail banking. Continuing our emphasis on the small-business segment, we entered into a unique arrangement with the national firm, Automated Data Processing, to market payroll processing as a complement to our extensive list of financial services.
>
> Another innovative partnership helped raise our ATM transaction volume in 1988. In cooperation with local fast-food restaurants, we provided a variety of discount coupons on our ATM receipts, which proved to be a highly popular incentive for Quest network users.
>
> We introduced our fixed-rate VISA card with a highly successful summer promotion featuring interest-free purchases through Labor Day.
>
> Private-label credit card merchants reaped the benefits of increased sales through the bank's new "Instant Credit" program, enabling them to provide the convenience of immediate charge privileges to their customers.
>
> Typical of Liberty's dedication to responding positively to our customers' needs, we developed two builder-oriented residential mortgage lending packages. The Forward Commitment Loan gives custom-built home buyers the security of having an approved mortgage waiting when their new residence is completed. Targeted for launch early in 1989, our "Combo Loan" provides a powerful selling tool to area builders. A single-closing, combination construction/permanent mortgage, it allows the buyer to assume the builder's modified construction loan with minimal closing costs.[6]

[6]Liberty National Bancorp, Inc., *1988 Annual Report*, p. 8.

The Asset Management Account (AMA) was another example of a 1989 new product introduction by Liberty. Elements of the service are represented in Exhibit 34.8. AMA realized growth of 11 percent, 1990 over 1989.

Gerwing pointed to the marketing central information file (MCIF) as a crucial tool:

> PROFILE, the in-house MCIF, is completely independent of the data center's central information file. It permits us to analyze all relationships at account, individual, and household levels, to find out profitability for customers and products and to use the findings for direct response marketing, further customer research, and product development.
>
> Research can help us ascertain which products are selling, who the top customers are, how products can be properly priced, and which customers have core relationships at Liberty, and we can do this without delays and costs of hiring a third party to process the data.
>
> The system can automate sales tracking reports and measure cross-sell ratios by employee, branch, and region. All facets of a marketing program—strategy, implementation, and measurement—can be addressed using PROFILE's data.

The following citations from LNBC's *1990 Annual Report* reflect the bank's continuing efforts in developing new products and modifying existing ones:

> Product innovations, undoubtedly catalysts for growth, were plentiful in 1990. In November, we introduced the residential mortgage FastTrack program. FastTrack, which gives customers an answer to first mortgage credit applications within 24 hours, is not only on a holding companywide basis, but also the first program of its kind offered by a major financial institution in our area.
>
> . . . our broker/dealer subsidiary was restructured in 1990. . . . Liberty Investment Services, Inc., is one of the first bank-affiliated broker/dealers in this region to be granted authority to act as an underwriter on certain types of fixed income securities, including tax-free revenue bonds. . . .
>
> Liberty Vehicle Leasing Company was formed in 1990, following Liberty's acquisition of a lease portfolio from one of the state's largest vehicle lessors. Following the acquisition, we launched the Liberty Choice Plan, an innovative new leasing alternative for customers wishing to acquire a new vehicle.
>
> A new insurance agency opened in 1990 in southern Indiana . . . fully licensed to sell property, casualty, life, and health insurance products to Indiana consumers and businesses.

In 1990, LNBL's private banking unit relocated to new quarters at the main office, street-level entrance, with private offices for high-net-worth customers. This unit handles individual loans for first and second mortgages, personal lines of credit, asset management accounts, and checking services.

Exhibit 34.8

PROFILE OF LIBERTY'S ASSET MANAGEMENT ACCOUNT*

Liberty introduces the one account that makes your money work as hard as you do.

The Liberty Asset Management Account, "AMA," is an aggressive concept in personal financial management designed especially for successful people—like you. The Liberty AMA consolidates most aspects of your financial activity into one account.

The Liberty AMA is an unlimited Checking Account earning high money market rates of interest. It is an Investment Account that enables savings dollars to earn even higher rates. It is a discount Brokerage Account providing access to a wide assortment of investment products. It is a premium Line of Credit with Gold MasterCard. It provides access to Federated Money Market Funds and much more.

The Liberty AMA was designed to make it easy to manage your personal assets. To that end, the Liberty AMA provides a single Consolidated Monthly Statement that reports on all aspects of your account.

The Liberty AMA also enhances your flexibility and control by putting you in charge of the investment decisions. We'll execute your orders and provide regular status reports of your investment portfolio.

In the pages that follow, you will learn about these and many other important features and services provided by the Liberty Asset Management Account—the one account that makes your money work as hard as you do.

*1991 asset management, *Liberty National Bank Brochure* (Louisville: 1991), pp. 1, 2.

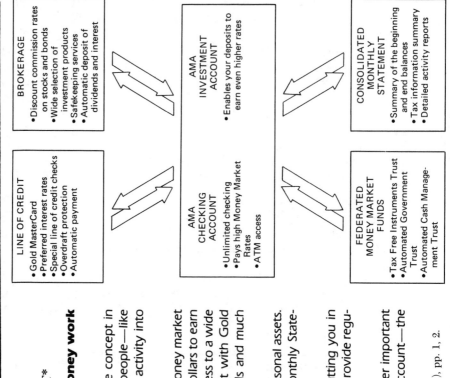

BROKERAGE
- Discount commission rates on stocks and bonds
- Wide selection of investment products
- Safekeeping services
- Automatic deposit of dividends and interest

LINE OF CREDIT
- Gold MasterCard
- Preferred interest rates
- Special line of credit checks
- Overdraft protection
- Automatic payment

AMA INVESTMENT ACCOUNT
- Enables your deposits to earn even higher rates

AMA CHECKING ACCOUNT
- Unlimited checking
- Pays high Money Market Rates
- ATM access

CONSOLIDATED MONTHLY STATEMENT
- Summary of the beginning and end balances
- Tax information summary
- Detailed activity reports

FEDERATED MONEY MARKET FUNDS
- Tax Free Instruments Trust
- Automated Government Trust
- Automated Cash Management Trust

LNBL ADVERTISING

Liberty's market share of deposits increased six percentage points in five years, from 17 percent in 1984 to 23 percent in 1989, and the bank continued the sixth year of its campaign theme, "There are banks. And there is Liberty," developed by its agency of 13 years, Buntin Advertising, Inc., of Nashville. Liberty's unaided slogan identification was 90 percent in 1989, while competitors were in the 14–30 percent range.

Prior to 1977, the bank and its former ad agency were producing commercials featuring heavy product emphasis that few viewers seemed to remember. Shortly after its appointment Buntin produced a humorous, slice-of-life television commercial for a "60-minute loan"—a program designed to get the applicant an answer to a loan application in 60 minutes or less. "The intent was to create an emotional bridge to a viewing audience wider than just potential borrowers—to reach anyone who had ever waited in a long line for anything," said Jeffery Buntin, president and creative director of the 16-year-old, $40 million agency. "Liberty's commercial became one about experiences instead of just bank products. Endless waiting, horrible people, that trapped-at-the-mercy-of-someone-else feeling. These were emotions almost everyone could relate to. This was Liberty's first exposure to what a 'selective perception' commercial could deliver. The viewers tuned in—not necessarily because they were unhappy with their present bank, but because they knew how this loan applicant felt. Within a month, the number of loan openings doubled. If the creative ad hadn't related to the product, then awareness could have been high, but the services would not have sold."

Buntin defined selective perception as a process by which people screen out messages they perceive as not relating to them or their current needs: "We all possess a built-in, automatic, subconscious, very efficient protective device that screens out irrelevant advertising messages. If we don't need it, we don't hear it, and we don't remember it. No participation. No awareness. No market share. Most banks talk about themselves and their products. But Liberty elected to try an oblique, emotional approach on a variety of topics that elicited participation beyond their customers and beyond people who were in the market for banking services. We wrapped the history of the bank and Louisville into service, caring, and commitment. People selectively decided to perceive the message because they had pride in living in Louisville."

As an example, the first 30-second film commercial was set at Churchill Downs. The narrator, an actor well known to the region, commented on the Derby's tradition and how Liberty Bank had been serving Louisville's banking needs for 21 years before the first Derby was run. He concluded with "There are horse races and there is the Derby. There are banks. And there is Liberty."

Rus Zaino, senior vice president, LNBC affiliates marketing, recounted deliberations about competitive advertising: "We concluded that our real competition was not the other banks in town and their bigger ad budgets. It was McDonald's, Pepsi, and Coke. Our challenge was to cut through the ever-increasing clutter of advertising without trying to match spending dollar for dollar. We accomplished that and continue to appeal to the broad audience in Louisville by evoking their pride in the city and all it stands for."

The campaign that began in 1984 swept the local advertising clubs' award competitions in both Louisville and in Nashville. "Quite an honor for a regional bank with a limited media budget," Zaino concluded, "and we can see that image advertising went directly to the bottom line."

LIBERTY'S SALES CULTURE

Executive Vice President Jack Shipman, formerly affiliated with a credit card company, joined Liberty National in 1969, and in 1974 became head of the retail division, which covers any activities and functions for the retail customer with a net worth of less than $500,000. (See Appendix C for LNBL's and retail banking group organizational charts.) "If we identify our central theme," Shipman stated, "the major emphasis is on a team selling effort. We don't promote the notion of superstars, but what all of us can do, working together to achieve sustained results. Equally crucial, we attempt to maintain balance between sales volume and quality of service. Branch managers are evaluated on the basis of calls and results, not just volume. We have business development people who call on customers; that's their sole assignment. They are paid for results. We implemented this approach because branch managers were calling on prospects and customers in a 20:80 ratio, certainly helping to retain existing customers but developing too few new accounts. Cross-sell ratio is the team measure for customer service representatives."

Deregulation posed threats and opened the door to opportunities. Since state law required branch banks to be in the same county as the bank's main office, in Shipman's words, "Louisville became a financial services battleground—too many branches and intense competition for commercial and retail business. Neither Liberty's people nor bankers at other institutions were trained to sell, and branches were ill equipped for selling." The general goal was to make the sales process an integral part of the bank, as formal, organized, and disciplined as the administrative and operational areas had been for years.

In 1980, the average cross-sell ratio of 1.3 was thought to be low, and it was believed that a desirable and achievable ratio would be in the 1.75 to 2.00 range. Cross-sell ratio is based on the number of additional services sold to a new checking account customer. Management thought that 75 additional services could be sold for each 100 checking accounts opened.

In the autumn of 1980, the marketing group undertook a study of retail banking at branch level, matching branches against neighborhood competitors, inaugurating a mystery shopper program, and sending questionnaires to all checking account customers, asking their opinions of the bank's service and products. The bank's 33 branches were shopped three times, checking accounts were opened, and deposits were made to existing accounts with lobby and drive-in tellers. This project helped management learn about the physical state of the branches, their appearance, and maintenance. More important, data were collected on employees' demeanor and skills in dealing with customers—speed, efficiency, appearance, courtesy, enthusiasm, product knowledge, and cross-selling approaches. An outside research firm supplied the shoppers, Liberty trained them for the assignment. From this study, specific training needs were identified and performance measures devised to help management track progress toward developing a sales culture at Liberty.

Shipman believed, "We have become like any other major sales organization, not order takers waiting for customers to come to us, but a professional sales team actively developing new business. We've been at this almost a decade and are still searching for ways to sustain and deepen everyone's commitment to becoming a sales-oriented, service-driven bank in each and every one of our organizational units."

SHAPING THE SALES CORPS

Many sales training packages were available, but few were suitable for Liberty's needs. To integrate product knowledge with sales skills training specific to the bank, Liberty decision makers leaned toward developing their own. This decision was made to seem even more desirable when they realized that the ultimate goal of training some 375 branch personnel in 42 branches would be extremely costly using outside materials. The marketing department was assigned to develop an in-house program and to plan and conduct the training.

Branch managers received training first, learning about products and how to perform consultative selling. Throughout 1982–1983, training was expanded to include branch staff members responsible for customer contact in the branch. New accounts personnel took on the title of customer service representative (CSR). Follow-up clerical paperwork was shifted to the newly created position of branch operations coordinator.

An additional organizational change responded to the expectation that branch managers could develop new business by making outside calls. They found this difficult, given demands on their time for processing loans, so a retail consumer credit department was created in the central office to relieve branch managers of the time-consuming investigative work of checking credit reports.

The third phase of training, started in 1984, covered product knowledge and sales/referral skills for tellers. "We recognized early on," Shipman remembered, "that the real sales force at Liberty, from the customers' viewpoint, was the tellers. But given their responsibilities for handling transactions speedily and efficiently, they could scarcely spare the time actively selling each customer. So we trained them to spot prospects and refer them to the desk staff." A marketing department sales training officer taught sales skills to 265 tellers over a three-month period.

To reinforce a team philosophy, sales and other related meetings were held at least monthly but more often if required. Management conducted regular monthly meetings as open forums to discuss and exchange information, as well as to communicate sales and incentive results. Specialists from various areas in the bank often attended and provided information on particular products or services. Pep-rally approaches were shunned in favor of substance that contributed to individual development. Branch managers held monthly sales meetings with their own branch employees to share information obtained in the sales management meetings, plus information of specific relevance to the branch team. In addition to these sessions, assistant managers, CSRs, and tellers met quarterly.

Incentives, Support, and Reinforcement

Branch teams were divided into three groups, each with different measurement standards:[7]

- *Group I:* branch manager, who manages the branch sales team, expected to make outside calls to attain a point quota established for each branch. (Branches grouped into several categories: moderate to high growth, low to moderate growth, no growth, and metro/downtown. The number of points attributed to each depository and fee-income product and service is scaled according to its value to the bank.) In addition, the branch manager is responsible for all branch sales and service activity and is rewarded on the basis of the branch's success.
- *Group II:* assistant managers and CSRs, with a goal of achieving a 1.80 cross-sell ratio monthly, based on at least 15 new demand deposit accounts sales which provide the cross-selling opportunities, and certain service criteria interwoven.
- *Group III:* tellers and branch operation coordinators; periodic product referral programs and quality of service criteria. Team emphasis requires that all team members' efforts combine to bring the overall branch team cross-sell ratio to 1.65.

Examples of Incentive Award Program

A limited assortment of examples from the incentive award program will serve to illustrate selected aspects of the incentive award program:[8]

District sales coordinators: DSC's quarterly incentive compensation will be directly proportionate to the percentage of the district sales goal achieved (the sum of branch manager quotas within the district) for the quarter. To be eligible, the DSC must complete 180 prospect calls in his or her district during the quarter, the district must reach 80 percent of its sales point goal, and a minimum number of branches must meet their sales and call point quotas. Incentive compensation will be computed by $8.00 times the total percentage of the goal earned with $800 per quarter being the maximum amount that is possible to earn. (Example: $8.00 × 100 percent of district goal = $800.)

District managers: These personnel receive incentive compensation equal to 25 percent of pool incentives paid to Group I officers in the district for the quarter. The award is divided into general sales and credit life sales categories, the general sales appropriation equal to 13 percent and credit life, 12 percent, of pool incentives paid to Group I officers. The district's cross-sell ratio average must be at least 2.0, with all branches in the district producing at least a 1.65 cross-sell ratio. Average branch score within the district must be at least 80 percent on customer service mystery shops. For every percentage point the district is below the 80 percent target, district managers' *general sales* entitlement will be reduced one percentage point.

Branch Employees: All Group II employees will be paid cash incentives directly exclusive of any other requirements, an amount equal to 5 percent of the life insurance premiums they generate and 3 percent of A & H premiums they generate up to a maximum incentive of $275 per quarter. "Teamwork is the cornerstone of any excellent organization and will play a key role in determining incentives to be paid," the introduction to this bulletin reminds employees.

---

[7]Adapted from LNBC corporate document.
[8]Adapted from LNBC corporate document.

Branch sales support systems included detailed product profiles kept current by marketing with update binders. Product sections identified likely prospects; listed features and corresponding benefits, costs, and comparisons to competitors' products; suggested cross-sell opportunities and answers to common customer questions; and provided names and telephone numbers of product specialists. An indexed looseleaf format allowed quick and easy revisions.

By 1990, most branches also had "Liberty Banker," an integrated on-line microcomputer and software system that enabled branch personnel to provide customers prompt, accurate information on all bank products and services.

In December 1989, the retail customer service department changed its name to "customer service center," complete with new logo and expanded service capacity. At the core of the change was an automated inquiry system, the first such installation in a Louisville bank. Service capacity quadrupled with the system's ability to handle up to 24 customers simultaneously. With the computerized setup, a touch-tone telephone enabled customers to obtain information about their checking and bankcard accounts and about CD (certificate of deposit) and DDA (demand deposit account) rates, 24 hours daily. A recorded voice guided callers through the extensive menus, providing instructions about which buttons to use. Personal checking customers, for example, could obtain account balance, the last four withdrawals (checks, ATM or money card, and service charges), and find out if a specific check had cleared. Credit card information included account balance, amount of finance charges paid last year, and year-to-date finance charges. Merchants also had access to the system, verifying up to four checks in a single call. During banking hours, system users could touch a key and connect themselves with a customer service representative. Average installment loan outstandings grew almost 10 percent in 1990.

Executive Leadership for Sales and Service

Termed "a marathon, not a wind sprint" by one sales team member, Liberty's attempts to sustain and enhance its sales culture were continuous and tenacious. Several participants in Liberty's marketing and sales activities saw Billy Joe Phelps also as "chief of the sales culture" and "president of customer satisfaction."

The casewriter was invited to a regularly scheduled sales recognition luncheon in November 1989 (the "Presidents Club") hosted by Billy Joe Phelps and honoring eight employees from different areas of the bank. His pride in these achievers was apparent; he knew them all by name and why they were being honored. Along with Lawrence W. Fox, senior vice president for retail sales and customer service, Phelps presented framed certificates of commendation. "As you could see," said Fox afterward, "the quality service connection at Liberty is kept alive by all of us, especially the president. He makes it thrive."

Following the luncheon, one of those being recognized for achievement, James Tilford, vice president of Riverfront branch, expressed his thoughts about the sales emphasis at Liberty:

> Being a competitive person by nature I enjoy meeting and exceeding goals which are established by bank management. It makes my job fun and rewarding to come up with my

own ideas to enhance the sale of the bank's services and successfully compete against the other banks. Occasionally, we will have incentives within the bank to sell certain services, for example, MasterCard, VISA, and safety deposit boxes. To use our own creativity in competing against the other branches adds another dimension to the normal day-to-day operations of the branch. In addition, morale of the entire branch is noticeably increased by making it a team effort.

"It is not at all unusual," a teller exclaimed, "for us to get thank you notes from the president." One such note is reproduced in Exhibit 34.9.

Exhibit 34.9

PRESIDENT'S COMMENDATION LETTER TO EMPLOYEE

Date: November 8, 1989

TO: PENNIE CUMMINS

FROM: J. W. PHELPS

Dear Pennie:

This past Friday night I was sitting at home when my son answered the phone and told me that a customer was calling. Naturally, I thought it would be a complaint and on Friday night was not quite ready for this.

Fortunately, however, a gentleman by the name of Mr. Hodge called me to commend you on the outstanding job you had done for him, and he could not have been more complimentary in praising you.

I can assure you, it is most refreshing to receive a call such as this, and I, too, join him in commending you on the outstanding job you do for the Liberty Bank. With wonderful people such as you, the Liberty Bank is a tremendous success.

Thanks for being part of our Liberty family and, again, my sincere congratulations.

JWP

JWP/jlh

Source: Corporate document.

An annual retail awards banquet provides yet another regularly scheduled occasion to recognize employees' accomplishments. Senior vice president Lawrence Fox proclaimed the 1989 meeting "a night of exaltation for the retail population."

REINFORCEMENT FROM BANK PUBLICATIONS

The bank and holding company publish two magazines: *Alliance,* a quarterly magazine targeted to employees, retirees, and directors of LNBC's subsidiaries, the first edition appearing in the fall, 1989, and *Assetera,* a monthly magazine, principally for LNBL employees. *Assetera* is partly a medium of recognition and reinforcement for sales achievements, usually carrying two such anecdotes in each edition, along with pictures of the achievers. Two selected narratives are reproduced here as examples:

> *Example 1:* Sales Successes. "It Pays to Care." Mary Littrell always gives top-quality service in her quiet and caring way. Every Middletown customer has experienced her courteous, efficient, personal attention. Recently an area newcomer sought Mary's advice. Initially the deposit was to be $74,000, but after listening to a careful explanation of our AMA and its many benefits, she presented Mary with a second check for $80,000 and signed on the dotted line. Next came $5,000 representing proceeds from an IRA, which was promptly rolled over into a Liberty account. Her customer then confided that a considerable sum was being wired, the management of which was of great concern to her. Our "salesperson" explained Liberty's money management and trust services in great detail. When the wired funds were received (totaling $280,000), Mary wisely divided them among certificates of deposit, a money management account, and trust services. During the whole process, she gained another grateful customer and, excluding the trust, sold seven Liberty services! Fitting customers' needs to specific bank products is a special talent Mary has, along with the ability to truly communicate and relate to their needs.[9]
>
> *Example 2:* Sales Successes. "Karen Sweeps the Shops." With her heart-warming smile and bubbly personality, Karen Mingis exhibits a special friendliness to every customer at the Chenoweth branch. Recently, Karen's consistently courteous service was spotlighted after several "mystery shoppers" visited the branch. Four "shoppers," posing as customers, came on different days to cash checks, and each was waited on by Karen. The result was astounding—all four rated Karen's customer service skills with a 100 percent score! It's not often that an individual is shopped four times in one quarter, but it does happen. However, never before has anyone ever scored four 100 percent ratings in a single quarter. This is a truly outstanding accomplishment which shows the quality and consistency of this young woman's customer service skills.[10]

Assetera publicizes not just sales news, but also other events, programs, and Liberty National Bank employee news items, such as, for example, residential mortgage loan officer Deborah Cummings congratulated on being chosen as "Mrs. Kentucky of the Year" for 1989, 25-year employee (17 in the financial institutions division) Pat Ackerman's winning the $2 million Kentucky Lotto jackpot in October 1989, and myriad other items of personal or business import.

---

[9]Adapted from *Assetera,* October 1989, p. 10.

[10]*Assetera,* December 1989, p. 14.

Balancing Selling and Quality of Service

In referring to Liberty's unrelenting emphasis on quality of service, Shipman's pride was apparent: "Focus on quality is evident throughout the bank, from one-on-one private banking relationships to the friendly smiles of our tellers. Quality people make it possible, and the bank's stress on continual training and development of all employees provides an important stimulus. The number of in-house workshops is increasing, and many receive the benefits of Liberty's tuition reimbursement program.

"In 1988, introducing the branch banking G.U.E.S.T. program reemphasized our high priority on polishing platform and teller personnel's customer relations skills. This effort is designed to complement our existing product knowledge and sales skills training programs. Employees are expected to perform at a level of proficiency that meets lofty and exacting standards."

Lawrence Fox expressed a strong belief that "customer service for the 1990s means getting back to the basics. We've got to make certain things are done right, with quality service. Management commitment is absolutely necessary. Careful and continuous monitoring is one of the keys, because people tend to forget and lapse into unacceptable habits unless reminded in various ways. There's always a tendency to do what is inspected, not necessarily what is expected."

Mystery shops were implemented in the branch banking system to inspect and measure the level of service being delivered. The shops included four teller surveys and two platform surveys conducted quarterly in each branch. The incentive program commenced after the second wave of the first year. If a branch score exceeded 80 percent, each teller received $100. Platform employees were entitled to their pool allocation after meeting the expected customer service criteria. Each person receiving 100 percent when shopped the first time got six roses; the second time, a dozen roses; the third and fourth times, a dozen roses with helium balloon attached. As with all Liberty's incentive efforts, the goal is to reward excellent performance.

Exhibit 34.10 lists the components of G.U.E.S.T. printed on a laminated card given to each employee.

AUTOMATION: KEY INGREDIENT IN SERVICE QUALITY

In 1987, a committee comprising representatives from retail banking, operations, customer service, and marketing investigated ways of replacing aging teller machines, relying considerably on feedback from branch and customer service users in designing a branch automation system. Software development and testing got underway in March 1989. Dubbed "PASS KEY" (Professional And Simplified Service), the system would provide, for each workstation, CRT access for central information file or account transaction journal inquiries so personnel could stay with the customer, access to the audio system so inquiries and holds could be made by keyboard so tellers could check out the customer unobtrusively, a link to each branch's printer, thus eliminating handwritten forms, and color display screens at platform workstations for augmenting sales presentations with attractive visuals. As a result of offering more information, speedily available, higher levels of service could be delivered. Pilot loca-

Exhibit 34.10

THE QUALITY SERVICE CONNECTION
"Every Customer Is our *GUEST*"

Greet the customer:

- Acknowledge customer immediately.
- Stand to show respect.
- Smile to show friendliness.
- Introduce self and use customer's name.
- Establish eye contact.
- Shake hands.
- Offer assistance by saying "May I help you?"
- Offer the customer a seat.

Understand the customer's feelings:

- Listen attentively.
- Ask questions to probe and clarify.
- Rephrase so that understanding occurs.
- Maintain a friendly tone of voice.
- Maintain confidentiality.

Empathize with the customer:

- Put yourself into the customer's shoes.
- If the customer complains, seek out something to agree with.
- Demonstrate genuine concern.

Solve the customer's needs yourself:

- Take responsibility.
- Offer additional support, if needed.

Thank the customer:

- Offer business card.
- Thank the customer.
- Invite the customer back.

Remember, every customer is our GUEST. Be a professional at all times in appearance and dress. Always keep your work area neat. Be cautious not to eat, drink, smoke, or chew gum in front of the customer, because to the customer, YOU ARE THE BANK!

tion test sites and subsequent rollout were successful, and the system was active in all lead-bank branches using personal computers in 1991.

Prior to 1985, Liberty's central retail credit area searched and documented, and accepted or declined, all consumer credit applications for direct loans from branches, credit card, and indirect dealer loans. Branch loan officers, however, retained the authority to make a final decision. Butch Riddle remembered, "As we grew and demand increased, we knew that specialization was needed; otherwise, the volume would swamp us. Although spinning off MasterCard decision making to retail revolving credit staff helped somewhat, indirect loan volume from automobile dealers was growing significantly."

Expense of adding to staff grew increasingly prohibitive, both in salaries and physical space. "The problem was obviously one of either processing the same number of applications with fewer people or—and this was the preferred alternative—processing more applications with the same number of people," said Douglas Meredith, senior vice president, retail collections, "that implied thinking about adding some form of computer-based credit scoring system. We wanted something that would combine application processing and scoring, which meant customizing a workable off-the-shelf program to meet our specifications and requirements."

The credit application scoring system (CASS) was built to maintain two separate data base files: a bad account file, containing frauds, charge-offs, bankruptcies, and other data—any negative information on previous Liberty accounts—and a file for detecting duplicate applications, in case a customer applied for a credit card at one branch and a car loan at another. With 37,000 records, developing the bad account data base proved to be a substantial task. The scoring program took 17 variously weighted characteristics into account (for example, type of residence, length of time with current employer, and income level). The scoring algorithm—factors considered and weights attached to them—was based on collective experience of Liberty's lenders over the years. Revolving credit applications were added to CASS in 1988, which led to a reduction in turnaround time for processing credit card applications from 10 days to 1 or 2 days. Decline letters are automatically generated, while approved applications are routed to effect issuance and mailing of cards to customers.

Smaller banks in Kentucky were also seeking efficiency and profitability through use of software aids for lending. Bank of Louisville, a unit of Ohio-based Mid-America Bancorp, in 1991 announced plans to put personal computers on the desks of its 25 commercial loan officers. The bank expected the system to help it compete with larger local competitors. Such systems usually gather customer and product data from a main processing unit and automate several lending tasks, also helping to satisfy regulators' demands for documentation.

1991 PLANNING CONSIDERATIONS

Lending, operations, sales, and marketing seemed confident of the bank's ability to conquer the challenges and seize the opportunities of 1991. As Maria Gerwing put it, "We will focus on Liberty's independence by enhancing our level of personal service and continuing to offer consistent delivery of sound, traditional banking products that have a unique competitive advantage."

Market Overview

In developing marketing strategies, many factors must be considered: economic conditions, competitive positioning, industry trends, demographic forecasts, political and legislative issues, and any other matters that might affect the planning process. Some of the issues facing us in 1991 are as follows:

- A sluggish economy with modest inflation and relatively low interest rates
- An increased rate of savings translating into steady deposit growth
- Increased competition for loan volume, especially on the consumer side
- Growth in promotions directed toward the "senior" category
- Continued pressure from nontraditional banking competitors
- Further blurring of distinctions between banking and savings and loans, with a great deal of merger activity taking place

Source: Corporate document.

Appendix 34D contains bank performance statistics, Eighth District, for Kentucky banks of $1–$10 billion assets.

Appendix 34A

EXCERPTS FROM *BUSINESS FIRST*, FIFTH ANNIVERSARY ARTICLE

Our community's accomplishments over the past five years have been so many and so varied that it is impossible to point to any one as the most significant. . . .

Some of our outstanding accomplishments trace their beginnings to much earlier years: the revitalization of the downtown area, for example, had its roots in the late 1960s and early 1970s, as did preservation of our historic neighborhoods.

Others are more recent: the city/country "compact" of 1987, which eliminated frustrating and divisive competition between our local governments, the phenomenally successful business/education partnership which has made our school district a much-lauded model at a time of both statewide and national educational crisis, medical facilities that have earned us national and international attention, and arts and cultural programs that are unrivaled even by cities many times our size.

Still others can be interpreted as first steps toward solving existing problems and ensuring continued progress: the exciting beginnings of long-

Appendix 34A (Cont.)

term waterfront development plans, the $10 million plus raised by the Campaign for Greater Louisville to spur economic development, the completion of new landside and airside terminals at Standiford Field, and the announcement of a major airport expansion that should meet our needs for at least the next 40 years.

Perhaps the accomplishments of the last five years can be best described by saying that we have developed a new attitude and spirit of cooperation. The city, the county, the business community, and the citizens of the area have begun to work together, boldly setting aside past differences for the sake of the common good. It is this attitude that is responsible for the computerization of our schools, the relocation of the Presbyterian headquarters, the creation of economic enterprise zones, the building of new low-cost housing, and rehabbing of old housing. We are a community that is reinvesting in itself. Working together, we have built a quality of life that is the envy of not only comparably sized cities, but also many much larger ones. . . .

The proposed airport improvement program, which includes the construction of two new parallel runways, can provide the spark that will bring new jobs and greater economic diversity to our community. Not only will it increase our competitive edge with other nearby airports (Indianapolis, Cincinnati, and Nashville are building new parallel runways), but it is our only chance of getting an airline hub, a major attraction for new businesses. . . .

Source: Frank B. Hower, Jr., chairman, Liberty National Bancorp, Inc., June 22, 1989.

Appendix 34B

BUSINESS ENVIRONMENT

U.S. AND REGIONAL ECONOMY[1]

Real GNP, a comprehensive measure of U.S. production, declined 2.1 percent in the fourth quarter of 1990—its first decline since a 1.8 percent drop in the second quarter of 1986.

The price index (fixed weights) for gross domestic purchases increased 6.3 percent in the fourth quarter, 1.2 percentage points more than in the third. For many applications, this index is preferable to the GNP

[1]U.S.D.C., *Survey of Current Business*, January 1991, pp. 1, 3, and 40.

Appendix 34B (Cont.)

price index as a measure of U.S. inflation because it measures prices of goods and services *purchased;* the price index for GNP measures prices of goods and services *produced.* The GNP price index increased 4.1 percent in the fourth quarter, about the same as in the third.

In the Southeast personal income grew 1.3 percent in the third quarter after increasing 1.1 percent in the second . . . and 2.7 percent in the first. The third quarter growth reflected payroll gains in retail trade, in the finance-insurance-real estate group, and in services. . . . payrolls in construction declined for the second consecutive quarter. By state, personal income growth was above the U.S. average in Florida, South Carolina, Tennessee, Louisiana, and Virginia and below the average in Arkansas, West Virginia, Kentucky, Mississippi, Georgia, Alabama, and North Carolina.

1991 ECONOMIC OVERVIEW[2]

During the last decade, the United States has become a more integral part of the world economy, making it much more difficult to make economic projections. We as a nation have less control over our economic and trade policies than we had in the past. This will continue and accelerate with the economic unification of Europe beginning in 1992.

Economic cycles will continue to exist, the severity of which is the only question.

Delinquency rates on consumer borrowing in the banking industry, both installment and mortgage loans, have increased and will continue this trend in 1991.

With this economic scenario in mind, 1991 is anticipated to suffer from a weak economy, especially during the first half of the year, but with economic activity picking up somewhat during the second half. Inflation will probably be about the same as in 1990. Interest rates, especially short-term rates, should remain steady during the first six months or so and then rise gradually.

The decline in consumer spending, especially relating to automobiles, and the higher delinquency rates on installment loans have been anticipated in the 1991 plan by continuing low rate of growth in installment loans. This is especially the case in Liberty-Louisville, where much of the installment loan portfolio consists of automotive-related loans. Commercial lending is expected to remain strong, and mortgage lending is believed to offer some selected opportunities for growth in the commercial real estate area, as well as continued growth in the residential sector.

As has been the case for the last several years, the 1991 budget is not built around an absolute level of interest rates. Rather, the emphasis in

[2]Internal LNBC document.

Appendix 34B (Cont.)

the planning process is on managing the net interest spread and net interest margins. The interest rate forecast was presented to provide an atmosphere within which the loan portfolio and fund managers were to develop both their tactical and strategic plans.

NOTES AND STATISTICS ON LOUISVILLE AND KENTUCKY

The following table summarizes population projections for the state of Kentucky and Louisville's MSA:

POPULATION PROJECTIONS*

	1990	1995	2000	2010	2020
Kentucky	3,847,018	3,959,645	4,053,537	4,185,811	4,252,057
Louisville MSA†	790,246	797,095	801,836	800,459	786,594

*University of Louisville, Urban Studies Center, "Louisville Summary."
†Kentucky portion only. The MSA population approaches 1 million.

LOUISVILLE ECONOMIC OUTLOOK

In some geographic areas, the local economy was expected to thrive in the early 1990s, but other parts showed signs of turning downward. "*The Courier Journal*/University of Louisville indicators are looking as sluggish as the national ones, and the news of national auto industry woes is matched by shutdowns in the local Ford factory."[3]

The report on which this section is based pointed out that "even if the unemployment rate rose from 5 percent to 7 percent, 93 percent of the labor force would still have the same spending power."

Local hours worked in manufacturing has been declining (cited as a customary sign that orders had slowed, reducing overtime), and the help-wanted advertisements had leveled off after fairly consistent growth since the bottom in 1982.

Growth in health services, including spinoffs attached to that industry, was expected to continue. Dominated by UPS in Louisville, air transportation showed a continuing upward trend, although plateauing seemed inevitable. Louisville and Kentucky distillers were replacing losses in domestic demand by cultivating international markets.

[3]University of Louisville, *Economic Outlook for the Louisville Metropolitan Area*, Vol. 2, no. 3 (September 1989).

Appendix 34B (Cont.)

LOUISVILLE MSA EMPLOYMENT DATA, 1988–1989

	1988 Average	August 1989
Total nonagricultural employment	450,713	458,432
Total manufacturing	87,909	87,275
Nondurable goods	38,646	38,643
Food and kindred	9,760	9,436
Tobacco	4,531	4,560
Apparel	2,735	2,992
Printing and publishing	7,906	8,048
Chemical and allied	7,524	7,411
Other nondurables	6,189	6,196
Durable goods	49,264	48,032
Lumber and wood	4,040	4,123
Furniture and fixtures	2,119	1,848
Stone, clay, glass products	2,732	2,814
Fabricated metals	8,526	7,677
Machinery	20,705	20,479
Transportation equipment	7,472	7,826
Other durables	3,670	3,865
Total nonmanufacturing	362,803	371,157
Mining	821	1,234
Construction	21,585	21,945
Transportation, communication, public utilities	28,440	29,135
Trade	112,124	111,333
Finance, insurance, real estate	26,792	26,560
Services	111,660	120,544
Government	61,382	60,406
Unemployment rate, August, 1989: 5.2%		

Source: U.S. Bureau of Labor Statistics, 1989.

LNB AND RETAIL BANKING GROUP ORGANIZATION CHARTS

Exhibit 34C.1

LIBERTY NATIONAL BANK ORGANIZATION CHART

Board of Directors

Chairman of the Board

President

Executive Committee*

Executive Committee — — — Audit — Loan Review

Staff	Staff	Staff	Staff	Staff	Line	Line	Line	Line	Line	Line	Line	Line	Line	Line
Legal Group	Corporate Planning Group	Operations Group	Comptroller Group	Admin. Services Group	Marketing Group	Treasury Group	Lib Life Insurance Company	Leasing Group	Corporate Group	Commercial Mortgage Group	Residential Mortgage Group	Private Banking Group	Retail Group	Trust Group

Corporate Planning Group: Budgeting

Operations Group: Computer Division; Operation Planning & Research; Prof. Admin. II; Deposit Services Division

Comptroller Group: General Accounting; Tax

Admin. Services Group: Cashiers Division; Human Resources; Development; Security; Remedial Services

Marketing Group: Training and Development; Public Relations; Word Processing; Adv/Comm Relations; Marketing Research; Financial Relations; Product Development; Liberty Gallery

Treasury Group: Bank Investment; Money Mgmt.

Leasing Group: Admin.; Sales

Corporate Group: Special Services; Loan Services Dept.; Affairs & Economic Develop.; Cash Mgmt.; Comm. Lending; Financial Instit.; International Banking

Residential Mortgage Group: Loan Orign.; Loan Admin.

Private Banking Group: Prof. Banking Division; AMA Division; Perts. Loan Division; Fin. Plan Division

Retail Group: Consumer Credit; Retail Consumer Services; Retail Collect; Retail Sales; Branch Admin.

Trust Group: Pers. Trust; Trust Opns.; Pers. Trust Admin.; Trust Invest.; Corp. Trust; Corp. Trust Admin.; Employ. Benefits; Instit. Trust; Bus. Dev.

*The executive committee is composed of Joseph W. Phelps, chairman and CEO of LNBC and LNB; Malcolm Chancey, president of LNBC and LNB; and Raymond Guillaume, executive vice president and chief credit officer (loan policies, loan operations, and loan recovery).

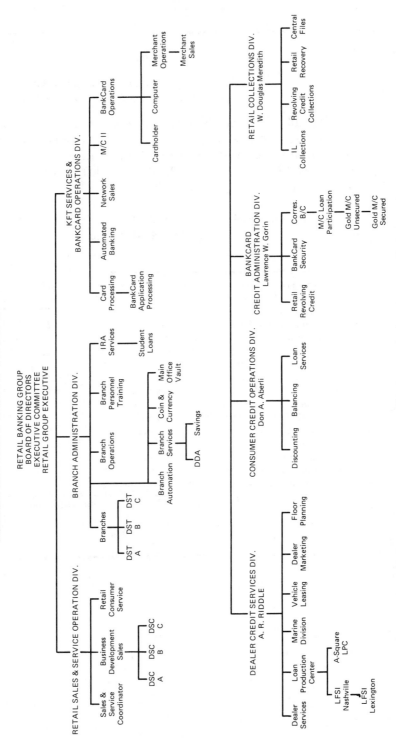

Exhibit 34C.2

RETAIL BANKING GROUP ORGANIZATION CHART

Appendix 34D

BANK PERFORMANCE STATISTICS,
EIGHTH DISTRICT KENTUCKY BANKS

Kentucky counted 332 banks at December 31, 1990, 4 of them in the $1–10 billion asset size range. For the four, return on average assets was 0.52 in 1990, down from 0.93 in 1989, which was three basis points off the 1988 ROA of 0.97. Annualized return equity in 1990 was 7.83 versus 14.33 in 1989 and 14.76 in 1988.

SELECTED STATISTICS, BANKS $1–10 BILLION ASSETS,
DECEMBER 1988–1990

	1988	1989	1990
Provision for loan losses/average assets	0.50	0.61	1.13
Loan loss reserve/total loans	1.45	1.41	1.61
Net loan losses/total loans	0.77	0.87	1.57
Agricultural loan losses/total agricultural loans	0.56	0.00	−1.99
Consumer loan losses/total consumer loans	0.41	0.58	0.87
Real estate loan losses/total real estate loans	0.32	0.28	1.44
Commercial loan losses/total commercial loans	1.23	1.61	2.41
Nonperforming loans/total loans	1.53	1.88	2.78
Nonperforming agricultural loans/total agricultural loans	0.83	0.89	0.38
Nonperforming consumer loans/total consumer loans	0.34	0.58	0.66
Nonperforming real estate loans/total real estate loans	1.38	2.49	5.38
Nonperforming commercial loans/total commercial loans	2.45	1.81	3.00
Primary capital	7.48	7.34	N.A.*
Total capital ratio	7.49	7.35	N.A.*
Total capital/total risk-weighted assets			9.56
Tier 1 capital/total risk-weighted assets			8.28

*N.A. = not available. No longer used; replaced by risk-based capital ratios.

Source: Data prepared for case study by Robin C. Miller, senior statistical analyst, Federal Reserve Bank, St. Louis, Missouri.

─── 35 ───

BOLTER TURBINES, INC. (A): PRODUCT DEVELOPMENT IN INDUSTRIAL MARKETING

INTRODUCTION

It's January 15, 1975. Mr. Harland Miller, vice president of marketing and sales for Bolter Turbines, Inc., is sitting at his desk, mulling over a most troublesome problem. He's reviewed the original "S-Engine Report," which is the basis of Bolter's investment in the development of a new product. So far, the company has spent $8 million in the early phases of the seven-year development plan. The total development investment will be more than $45 million (1972–1978), and the first prototype is scheduled to be produced and sold in 1976.

Miller is feeling very uncomfortable because the plan was developed and acted upon in late 1973—before the emergence of OPEC's strength as a worldwide cartel. He's recently read *Business Week's* analysis of the current situation and future prospects for OPEC and world oil prices. (See page 644.) The company is presently enjoying an extraordinary boom in its oil field business—much better than that forecasted in the 1973 report. The higher oil prices are supporting an unprecedented level of new exploration for oil worldwide, and the associated orders for production equipment. Most executives in the firm are feeling euphoric about the burgeoning backlog of orders and the premium prices clients are willing to pay. And this euphoria is reinforced because Bolter is having its best year ever while the rest of the U.S. economy is headed toward a deep recession.

However, Mr. Miller is concerned with the long run. The S-Engine product development is a long-term investment that will not generate revenues for more than five years. He's wondering what the marketplace will look like in 1980. He's pondering the wisdom of continuing the S-Engine development.

What would be your recommendation to Mr. Miller? The "S-Engine Report" and excerpts from the *Business Week* article are outlined for your information.

THE S-ENGINE REPORT:
A MARKETING ASSESSMENT FOR NEW PRODUCT OPTIONS
Strategic Planning Group
Bolter Turbines, Inc.

Table of Contents

Summary

Background

The Decision-Making Process

Market Analysis

    A. Field Sales Force Survey

    B. Engineering-Marketing Survey Team Assessment

    C. Assessment of the Current Market and Competition

    D. Analysis of Energy Demand Requirements

    E. Sales Management Assessment

List of Exhibits

Exhibit	Title
35.1	Charter—Strategic Planning Group
35.2	1970 Field Sales Force Survey Results
35.3	Recent Distribution of Neptune and Apollo Sales by Market Segment
35.4	Next Engine Market Assessment Survey Checklist
35.5	Next Engine Market Assessment Survey Interview List
35.6	Next Engine Market Assessment Survey Summary of Engineering-Marketing Team Interview Activity
35.7	Estimated Market Segments Beginning in 1976
35.8	Estimated Market Size Beginning in 1976
35.9	Estimated Market Penetration
35.10	Total 8,000–40,000-HP Prime Mover Market in 1973—Summary
35.11	Total 8,000–40,000-HP Prime Mover Market in 1973—Detail Information

35.12   S-Engine Market Size in 1973—Lower Limit

35.13   S-Engine Market Size in 1973—Upper Limit

35.14   Relative Importance of Customer Buying Influences

35.15   Required Product Characteristics by Market Segment

35.16   S-Engine Comparative Economic Analysis

35.17   Forecast of Gross National Product

35.18   Total World Energy Demand

35.19   World Energy Consumption as a Function of Population

35.20   Total World Energy Supply

35.21   World Oil Reserves

35.22   Crude Oil Production and Horsepower Increases, 1975–1980

35.23   Natural Gas Production and Horsepower Increases, 1970–1980

35.24   1978 Oil and Gas Industry Horsepower Market

35.25   1981 Potential Oil and Gas Market in Dollars and Units

35.26   S-Engine Planned Sales Schedule

35.27   S-Engine Forecast of Revenues

SUMMARY

Bolter Turbines, Inc., has identified a potential new product through which the division will capture a significant share of a dynamically growing market. This product, the S2 high-performance, simple-cycle, industrial turbine, was determined to be the best alternative available to Bolter through a step-by-step decision process followed by the division's Strategic Planning Group. The data used to support this decision process were supplied by the Engineering, Manufacturing, and Financial departments and by a five-pronged analysis of the market conducted by Market Development. This analysis, in Sections A through E, included:

1. Survey of the field sales force
2. Marketing-engineering team field survey
3. Survey of the current market and competition
4. Survey of the primary demand for the proposed new turbine in the oil and gas industry
5. Evaluation by Bolter sales management personnel

The analysis to support the market forecast portion of the product plan will be updated on a regular basis throughout the product development effort.

BACKGROUND

Bolter's two major turbine product introductions, the Neptune and Apollo engines, now account for about 80 percent of the total division revenues. The smaller Hercules and Trojan engines and contract research account for the remaining 20 percent. Bolter has reached an estimated aggregate market share of about 30 percent in both the Neptune and Apollo markets. This share has been obtained by capturing new business in a growing market and by capturing some business that had previously gone to competitors.

Based on a conservatively estimated growth rate in Bolter's markets of over 7 percent per year, the dollar value of this 30 percent market share should double by 1983 and double again by 1993. The message is that an investment in market share today will produce an even larger dollar return in a growing market. Thus, Bolter should plan to expand its product line, deepen its market penetration, or enter new segments of this market as soon as possible in order to increase market share when the cost is low relative to the value of the share which will result from market growth. The questions are: How should Bolter plan to increase its market share, and where should Bolter concentrate the division effort in the future?

THE DECISION-MAKING PROCESS

The issue of Bolter's future was put before the Strategic Planning Group. The purpose, membership, function, and responsibilities of this group are outlined in the charter included as Exhibit 35.1. The decision-making process followed by this group involved, first, an identification of the basic options available, and, then, an evaluation of each option. The evaluations included an analysis of Bolter's strengths and weaknesses and led to specific recommendations and actions for the division to follow.

The basic options identified were internal growth through new products and/or markets, external growth through acquisition of a company or product, and an intermediate position in which Bolter would purchase or license and manufacture the product.

The capabilities in each of Bolter's functional areas were analyzed and the limitations identified. In the engineering area, the strengths are a proven design concept of a compact, lightweight industrial turbine, a gas compressor design concept to match, and an integrated package design. The state of the art in small turbine design at Bolter is well above that of the other small industrial turbine manufacturers; however, Bolter lags the state of the art relative to the aircraft engine technology. For Bolter to develop a new turbine to compete with the performance of the aircraft derivatives will require an upgradiing of the technical base at Bolter.

Bolter has established itself as a major supplier of prime mover horsepower to the oil and gas industries within the Neptune and Apollo equipment size range. In addition, Bolter is becoming an increasingly important supplier of gas-turbine-powered electrical generator packages for both standby and continuous-duty applications. To support these markets, Bolter has developed a worldwide sales force.

Bolter's sales coverage of its markets is relatively complete. The primary focus of the sales force has been the oil and gas markets where Bolter has been most successful.

Bolter's strengths are summarized as a modern, industrial design turbine package which has gained wide acceptance in the oil and gas market and in the electric generator market, the engineering and manufacturing capabilities required to produce this equipment, and the sales force required to sell the product. Limitations include a technical capability slightly behind the state of the art in aircraft-engine technology, a manufacturing plant and philosophy limited primarily by the maximum diameter of the parts, and a sales force whose primary contacts are in the oil and gas industry.

The available options were evaluated by the Strategic Planning Group in the light of strengths and weaknesses identified. The conclusion was reached that the best growth opportunity for the division, both in terms of sales and profits, was through the utilization of Bolter's experience to develop a new industrial gas turbine engine. Six potential alternatives were initially identified.

1. A 600-KW radial inflow turbine packaged as a standby, intermittent and continuous-duty turbine generator sets.
2. An axial flow engine in the 5,000- to 15,000-HP range. Five turbine alternatives were identified with this category.
   a. S1: a scale-up of the basic Apollo design
   b. S2: a high-performance, simple-cycle industrial turbine
   c. S3: a low-compression-ratio industrial turbine capable of being recuperated
   d. Stretching the existing Apollo design employing as much commonality of parts as possible
   e. Purchasing an aircraft derivative gas producer and packaging it with a Bolter-designed power turbine and driven equipment

These alternatives were analyzed in terms of their potential sales and profits and the degree to which they could utilize existing capabilities at Bolter, thereby reducing both the risk and the cost of the new venture. The information used in this analysis was obtained from Manufacturing and Engineering and from the field sales force as discussed in Section A. The initial evaluation reduced the field to two viable alternatives as discussed next.

The first turbine alternative, the 600-KW radial engine, was planned to provide a rapid introduction into the standby power market. This approach was rejected because

1. The major market is in an area where Bolter does not have marketing strength.
2. The 600-KW rating was in the market presently controlled by high-speed automotive engines manufactured by GM, Caterpillar, and Cummins, all of which have extensive market and service coverage through their dealer network.
3. The market is extremely cost sensitive with relatively low profit margins. It was determined that Bolter could not develop a design under the cost target of $75 per kilowatt within the time frame required to bring the product to market.

This led to consideration of a larger gas turbine in the 5,000- to 15,000-HP size class. The lower limit of this range was set by the Apollo potential, and the upper limit was set by logical extension of Bolter's present capabilities. The first large turbine alternative, the S1 Apollo scale-up, was basically Apollo technology in a larger rated turbine. This alternative was rejected because it resulted in a noncompetitive selling price at the larger rating.

The second large turbine alternative, the S2 high-performance industrial turbine, represents an advancement in the state of the art in industrial turbine design, yet is conservatively below the state of the art existing in aircraft turbine design. This approach results in the best simple-cycle efficiency available today in industrial turbines and the lowest dollars per horsepower selling price. This alternative was retained for future evaluation.

The next alternative was the S3 engine, a low-compression-ratio turbine capable of being recuperated. The simple-cycle turbine is only slightly larger than the S2 and slightly more expensive to build. It fits market conditions where fuel cost is not of paramount concern. Recuperation results in additional size and maintenance requirements as well as initial cost. However, the resulting fuel rate is most attractive. This alternative was retained for future evaluation because of the potential fuel economy, although it entails a *higher technological risk.*[1]

The Apollo stretch to a 7,500-HP rating by adding two compressor stages and increased temperature capability appeared to be an attractive alternative, but close scrutiny indicated that less than 40 percent commonality with existing Apollo parts could be achieved. The result was a compromise turbine that was neither cheap to manufacture nor particularly good in fuel economy. This alternative was therefore rejected.

The final alternative considered was the use of a purchased aircraft derivative gas producer coupled with a Bolter-designed power turbine and compressor. This would allow Bolter to enter the large horsepower segments of the market relatively quickly. These engines offer excellent fuel economy. The disadvantages of these engines are

1. The use of antifriction bearings which require relatively frequent overhauls and which can occasionally lead to a catastrophic failure of the engine.
2. The high maintenance and parts costs associated with an engine designed for high-performance applications.
3. The long-run potential uncertainty which can result as the aircraft applications are phased out of the production line leading to significantly higher engine costs.
4. The high level of dependency placed on the jet engine manufacturer by Bolter or an end user, while having very little leverage to command attention in the event that a problem were to occur.
5. Reduced profit potential from this approach because of the reduced fraction of the product directly manufactured by Bolter.

These five points directly conflict with the philosophy successfully followed with both the Neptune and Apollo engines. Thus, the aircraft derivative approach was rejected because of the inconsistency with Bolter's present design, manufacturing, and marketing strategies.

[1]Engineering Department.

The two alternatives remaining after the initial evaluation, the S2 and S3 turbines, were further evaluated by a field survey team composed of Marketing and Engineering management personnel. The purpose of this survey was to determine the market size and requirements for a turbine in this size class. The details of this survey are discussed in Section B. An evaluation by the Strategic Planning Group of the findings of the survey team led to the recommendation to pursue a 12,000-HP simple-cycle, high-performance S2 turbine.

As part of the further evaluation of the S2 turbine, three additional approaches were taken to estimate the size of the potential market. These included an evaluation of the current market and competition discussed in Section C, an evaluation of the primary demand for prime mover horsepower based on the world growth in oil and natural gas production discussed in Section D, and an evaluation of the market by Bolter sales management to develop a cohesive picture based on the other approaches as discussed in Section E. This evaluation by Bolter sales management let to the establishment of the forecast upon which the formal marketing and financial plans are being developed. This planning forecast is included in Section E.

Exhibit 35.1

CHARTER—STRATEGIC PLANNING GROUP

PURPOSE

To assist the division president in planning the future of the division.

MEMBERSHIP

The group shall consist of the key executives who will be most responsible for assuring the achievement of the division's future aims and objectives. The division president may, for any particular matter or subject, assemble only those people whose direct involvement is required. The Strategic Planning Group is currently made up of

President
Executive Vice President
Vice President, Engineering and Research
Vice President, Turbomachinery Sales
Director, Administration
Director, Product Management
Comptroller
Division Counsel
Manager, Manufacturing Operations

Exhibit 35.1 (Cont.)

Director, Research
Manager, Marketing Development—Turbomachinery
Manager, Aerospace and Industrial Products
Senior Divisional Planner

FUNCTIONS AND RESPONSIBILITIES

1. Continually evaluate and adjust when necessary the stated mission of the division.
2. Continually assess the strengths and weaknesses of the division from both an internal and external point of view and evolve actions necessary to overcome weaknesses and fully exploit strengths and opportunities.
3. Fully evaluate previously identified areas of potential for the division and establish specific plans of action. Continually identify new potentials resulting from internal and external change and events.
4. Monitor accomplishment of previously identified division goals and change or establish new objectives and goals as the result of strategic planning evaluations.
5. Establish strategic planning study groups as required to thoroughly evaluate specific strength, weaknesses, opportunities, threats, and potentials and present findings and recommended courses of action to the Strategic Planning Group. Individual study groups will be composed of those people within the division who are most knowledgeable and qualified to evaluate specific areas of interest. The president may elect to establish an executive management steering group to provide intensive guidance for individual study groups.
6. The group will meet on a very frequent basis, on call by the president.

RELATIONSHIPS

Implementation and documentation of decisions resulting from strategic planning activities will be coordinated by Product Management/Divisional Planning.

A. Field Sales Force Survey

One of the early steps taken to determine what type of turbine Bolter should undertake next was to survey the field sales force by questionnaire. The results of this survey, performed in 1970, indicated that a turbine in the 12,000-HP range was the overwhelming choice of the sales force.

The field sales force was asked to select both the size of the next turbine and the number of units of that size that could be sold per year. Thus, sales personnel were forecasting exclusively the size range of their choice. In analyzing these data, the horsepower spectrum was first divided into 1,000-HP increments, and the combined forecasts of all the salesmen were totaled within these horsepower increments. To facilitate easier understanding of the data, the total forecast of units within each horsepower increment was then converted to a percentage of the total number of units forecast within the 4,000- to 15,000-HP range. These results are displayed in graphical form in Exhibit 35.2.

Exhibit 35.2 does not contain all the data obtained from the survey. Some interest was shown by the sales force for smaller turbines for generator applications and also for much larger turbines. The level of this interest was actually quite small, and these alternatives were rejected by the Strategic Planning Group as part of its decision-making process.

Within the range of viable turbine alternatives for Bolter, the data presented in

Exhibit 35.2

1970 FIELD SALES FORCE SURVEY RESULTS

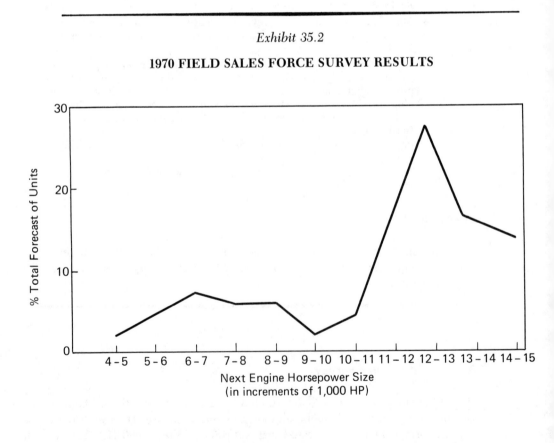

Exhibit 35.2 clearly demonstrated that the 12,000-HP turbine is the most preferable alternative in the opinion of the field sales force. Those respondents who recommended 12,0000 HP as the size to pursue for Bolter's next engine estimated that Bolter should be able to sell between 40 and 50 units per year. This offered much of the encouragement to pursue a 12,000-HP turbine development program.

Since this initial survey, considerable contact has been maintained with the field sales force. This continuing contact has taken the form of discussions during the quarterly regional managers meeting in Houston, questioning of individual salesmen on their visits to Houston, interviews by marketing development personnel on location in the sales regions, and discussions at conventions and trade shows. This information, obtained only a piece at a time, is constantly being factored into the current opinion of the potential S-Engine market. This line of communication with the field sales force will be utilized continually as a source of information about any potential changes in the marketplace.

B. Engineering-Marketing Survey Team Assessment

As planning progressed on Bolter's next engine and the viable turbine alternatives became more clearly defined, it became necessary to take a harder look at the market. First, it was necessary to evaluate the preliminary studies being undertaken by the Engineering Department in light of the projected requirements of the marketplace. Second, it became necessary as part of the economic evaluation of the next engine program to determine the size of the total market and to obtain a reliable estimate of the number of units that Bolter could potentially sell.

Recent internal analyses have identified the continued high level of dependence of Neptune and Apollo sales on the oil and gas industries. This is adequately shown in Exhibit 35.3. Further, this trend is likely to intensify for the large turbine alternatives proposed as Bolter's next engine. Thus, the most important market data would be expected to come from this segment. It was determined that the most effective way of obtaining the necessary information about the oil and gas segment would be through a personal interview survey conducted by a team composed of both engineering and marketing personnel. A team was formed, and a worldwide list of influential companies and people was compiled. From this list, interviews were arranged, and a three-month itinerary was prepared for the team.

To ensure that all the important questions were covered with each interviewee and to ensure some degree of uniformity among interviews, a checklist was prepared for the use of the interviewers. This checklist identified the basic assumptions inherent in the S-Engine effort, the market requirements and the type of market information needed, the format in which the market size data were to be collected, and a list of questions about the world economic and political situations. These world political situations are considered to be extremely important factors in the F-Engine market environment and include items such as duties and tariffs, English versus metric systems, nationalistic restrictions, buy-local restrictions, and so on. A copy of this complete checklist is included in Exhibit 35.4.

The interviews were conducted primarily by the three-person Engineering-Marketing survey team. This included the manager of Market Development, the

Exhibit 35.3

RECENT DISTRIBUTION OF NEPTUNE AND APOLLO SALES
BY MARKET SEGMENT
(percentage of total units)

	FISCAL YEARS				
Market Segment	1969	1970	1971	1972	1973 Est.
Apollo					
Gas and oil	—	100	100	95	88
Utilities*	—	—	—	5	10
Other	—	—	—	—	2
Neptune					
Gas and oil	70	74	63	70	66
Utilities*	16	23	26	21	23
Government	6	2	3	3	5
Other	8	1	8	6	6

*Utilities includes generator drive applications outside of oil and gas industry.

Exhibit 35.4

NEXT ENGINE MARKET ASSESSMENT SURVEY CHECKLIST

A. ASSUMPTIONS
   1. The next turbine rating is to be in the range of 7,000- to 15,000-HP ISO.
   2. The principal market is the worldwide oil and gas industry; others are secondary, and compromises will be made to reach some share of these markets.
   3. Six years will be required to begin production, and therefore we are assessing a worldwide market beginning in 1978–1980.
   4. Price, performance, and packaging characteristics of turbine alternatives S2 and S3 are the bases for market assessment.

B. MARKET REQUIREMENTS
   1. *Size.* Horsepower rating: consider a range of 7,000 to 15,000 ISO (International Standards Organization).
   2. *Cycle.* High performance, simple cycle, recuperated, combined cycle, based on reference turbine characteristics for S2 and S3.
   3. *Duty.* Continuous duty (8,760 hours per year), intermittent duty, part load, cyclic operation.
   4. *Fuel.* Fuel range requirement: gaseous and liquid, dual fuel, fuel-cost consideration.
   5. *Construction.* Vertical stacked, horizontal flanged, steam turbinelike, light aircraft, intermediate height, quick removal, repair in place, metric system.
   6. *Maintainability.* Fast change-out characteristics, time between overhauls, in-country overhaul, package configuration for accessibility versus excess cost.
   7. *Package Configuration.* Compressor set, mechanical drive, generator set, maintainability, and accessibility versus excess cost versus size and weight.

Exhibit 35.4 (Cont.)

8. *Output Speed Ranges.*
9. *Two Shaft Only versus Two Shaft and Single Shaft.* Power characteristic for intended applications.
10. *Applicable Codes Worldwide.* Requirements and restrictions: API, NEMA, NEC, CSA, ASME, SAE, etc.
11. *Environmental Considerations—Worldwide.* Exhaust emissions, noise, safety, heat release.
12. *Driven Equipment.* What is available and what is needed—pumps, compressors, generators.
13. *Accessory Equipment.* Intake air filters, intake air coolers, intake exhaust silencers, heat boilers, generators, starters, control, remote controls.
14. *Price.* Equipment first cost, installed cost, owning and operating cost, present worth economics, return on investment economics, payback economics.
15. *Shipment.* Delivery cycle, airfreightable, containerized shipment, truck shipment, heavy lift restrictions.
16. *Financial Arrangements.* Deferred payments, lease, rental, conditional sale.

C. MARKET SIZE—SEGMENTS

1. *Natural Gas.* Gathering, transmission, processing, refrigeration, reinjection, storage, gas lift, fuel gas compression, distribution.
2. *Petroleum.* Crude oil pumping, production pipeline pumping, water-flood, crude storage boil-off compression, drilling, well fracturing and servicing, platform and remote location power generation, refinery compressor and pump drives, standby power, continuous power generation.
3. *Chemical—Petrochemical.* Production and pumping and compression, refrigeration, continuous power generation, standby power.
4. *Generator Drive.* Continuous-duty power generator, standby power, oil well drilling drive applications, DC power generator, peak shaving, utility, industrial, government/institution.
5. *Marine.* Main propulsion, main power generation, auxiliary power generation, standby power, emergency power, hotel facilities power, cargo loading and unloading.
6. *Industrial.* Steel-aluminum-nonferrous, pump and paper, textile, food processing, automotive, communications, transportation, etc.

D. WORLD POLITICS

1. Individual country tariff and duty barriers.
2. Economic community tarriff and duty barriers (EEC).
3. National and international customs.
4. Monetary exchange barriers or problems.
5. Border or boundary restrictions preventing free movement in and out (i.e., Iran and Pakistan).
6. Prejudicial barriers (i.e., Arab world versus Israel).
7. Measurements—English system versus metric.
8. Controls—what measurement system?
9. Prejudice—such as electronic or pneumatic.
10. Nationalism—preferential treatment for national products. What constitutes national products? (% value added, etc.)
11. Representation—nationals, language, ethnic, engineering qualifications.
12. Package configuration—applicable labor codes and labor union restrictions, accessibility, maintainability.

manager of Product Engineering, and the vice president of Engineering and Research. In addition, local field sales and field sales management personnel who arranged the interviews were also present. In several cases, the local field sales personnel were called on to act as translators and to explain particular local situations to the survey team.

The interviews were begun in the United States in October 1972 and concluded in the Middle East and Europe in January 1973. During this period, the survey team visited four states within the United States and nine foreign countries, contacted 48 organizations and interviewed 75 individuals in a broad spectrum covering presidents and vice presidents down through operating managers of small subsidiaries. The interviews covered almost the entire spectrum of company types within the oil and gas industry with which Bolter deals. A detailed list of the organizations contacted is included in Exhibit 35.5 and summarized in Exhibit 35.6.

As anticipated, the survey produced a wealth of information about the type of product that will be required to compete in the oil and gas industry in the future and the expected size of the market for this equipment. (See Exhibit 35.7 for estimates.) With respect to the product definition, the interviews conducted by the survey team provided the input for the following recommendations made by the team:

Rating	The 12,000-HP ISO rating fits a large range of oil and gas industry applications. No highly qualified industrial turbine now exists at this rating, and the derate caused by high ambient temperatures and altitudes in many production areas will still leave this size engine with substantial output to meet production duties.
Performance	The survey team evaluated the relative importance of initial cost, size, weight, fuel consumption, maintainability, service requirements, and so on. The survey team recommend a small, lightweight, high-performance, simple-cycle engine as the best compromise. Thus, the S2 became the recommended turbine.
Fuel	One of the very important concepts to result from the survey was the future importance of the wide-range fuel capability for turbines sold in both the domestic and export markets. The uncertainty about the availability of natural gas for turbine fuel makes the wide-range fuel capability mandatory. Future fuels that are expected to be encountered, range from "sweet," low-sulphur natural gas to the "sour," high-sulphur crude oil of the Middle East.
Timing	Time is of the essence. The increased growth in the oil and gas industry is coming faster than previously anticipated. Thus, the earlier that Bolter can introduce the next engine, the larger accumulated share that can be expected.

Additional recommendations of the survey team covered such topics as duty cycle, package configuration, output speed ranges, applicable codes, and specifications to comply with environmental considerations, driven equipment availability, accessory equipment, price, and required financial arrangements.

Drawing on the information obtained in the interviews, the survey team developed estimates of the total, worldwide market for the S-Engine. Based on the design characteristics of the recommended S2 engine, particularly the low initial cost per horsepower and superior fuel consumption, the total market is expected to cover all

Exhibit 35.5

NEXT ENGINE MARKET ASSESSMENT SURVEY
INTERVIEW LIST

Interview Location	Organization Visited	Organization Category
Algeria	Sonotrach	State oil and gas company
Libya	Mobil Oil Corporation	Integrated oil company
	Esso-Libya	Integrated oil company
	American Overseas Oil Co. (AMOSEAS)	Oil production company
	Oasis Oil Company	Oil production company
	Occidental Petroleum Co.	Oil production company
	Sahara Oil Field Service Co.	Manufacturers agent
Beirut	Trans Arabian Pipeline Co. (TAPLINE)	Crude oil pipeline company
Iran	Iranian Oil Producting (IOP)	Private production consortium
	Iranian Oil & Exploration Petroleum Co. (IOEPC)	Private production consortium
	National Iranian Oil Co. (NIOC)	State oil and gas company
France	ELF	State-owned petroleum company
	Gaz de France	State gas utility
Italy	SNAM, Gas Dotti	State oil and gas company
Brussels	Distrigaz	State gas utility
Hague	Arabian American Oil Co. (ARAMCO)	Oil production company
	Royal Dutch Shell Company	Integrated oil company
	Bechtel	Consulting engineer
London	AMOCO International	Integrated oil company
	British Petroleum	Integrated oil company
	Continental Oil Company	Integrated oil company
	Gulf Oil Corporation	Integrated oil company
	Phillips Petroleum Company	Integrated oil company
	Iraq Petroleum Company	Oil production company
	British Gas Council	State gas utility
	Fluor Corporation	Consulting engineer
	Brown & Root	Consulting engineer
Texas	Columbia Gulf Transmission Co.	Gas transmission company
	El Paso Natural Gas Company	Gas transmission company
	Texas Eastern Transmission Co.	Gas transmission company
	Tennessee Gas Transmission Co.	Gas transmission company
	Trunkline Gas Company	Gas transmission company
	Texaco	Integrated oil company
	Creole Engineering Company	Engineering and service company
Louisiana	Texas Eastern Transmission Co.	Gas transmission company
	United Gas Pipeline Company	Gas transmission company
	Shell Oil Company	Integrated oil company
	Texas International	Integrated oil company
	Texaco Offshore	Integrated oil company
Oklahoma	Phillips Petroleum Company	Integrated oil company
	Williams Brothers Pipeline Co.	Products pipeline company
	Williams Brothers Engineering Co.	Consulting engineer
	Global Engineering Company	Consulting engineer

Exhibit 35.5 (Cont.)

California	Standard Oil of California	Integrated oil company
	Union Oil Company	Integrated oil company
	Pacific Gas & Electric	Investor-owned utility
	Bechtel Incorporated	Consulting engineer
	Fluor Corporation	Consulting engineer

Exhibit 35.6

NEXT ENGINE MARKET ASSESSMENT SURVEY SUMMARY OF ENGINEERING-MARKETING TEAM INTERVIEW ACTIVITY

Countries visited	10
Organizations contacted by category	
Integrated petroleum companies (public and private)	17
Oil production companies	9
Gas transmission companies	7
Gas utilities (public and private)	4
Liquid pipeline companies (including crude)	2
Engineering and service companies	8
Manufacturers agents	1
Total	48
Individuals interviewed	75

applications within the 8,000–30,000-HP ISO range. Separately looking at the projected applications in the natural gas, oil, generator, margin, and process industries beginning in 1976, the size of each geographic and industry segment was estimated. This market breakdown is displayed in Exhibit 35.8. A concise summary of these data is also tabulated in Exhibit 35.8. This worldwide market is expected to total 120–12,000-HP equivalent units per year in 1976.

Based on this estimate of the 1976 world market, the expected competitive strength of the S2-Engine in this market, and Bolter's experience with Apollo regarding the rate of acceptance of a new engine, the expected levels of market penetration were determined. This forecast begins with 2 units in the first year, 1976, and grows to 75 units per year in 1981. The 1981 figure is assumed to represent a mature penetration. The details of the market penetration forecast by the survey team are included in Exhibit 35.9.

The persons contacted in this survey are considered to be key decision makers with regard to oil and gas industry prime mover purchases. Thus, within the limits of their visibility estimated at about five years ahead, the reliability of their opinion is probably quite high. Since the survey team market forecasts are based on these opinions, a relatively high level of confidence is placed on these forecasts for 1976.

C. Assessment of the Current Market and Competition

The purpose of this assessment was to obtain an independent check on the market estimate of the Engineering-Marketing team. Because of the inertia inherent in the marketplace created by the very long life cycles of this type of product, the present market is expected to be very similar to the forecast for 1976. By 1976, the size of the market is expected to increase, the relative importance of fuel economy is expected to increase, and certain competitors' market shares will certainly change. However,

Exhibit 35.7

ESTIMATED MARKET SEGMENTS BEGINNING IN 1976*
(12,000-HP equivalent units within the 8,000–30,000-HP ISO Range)

Region	INDUSTRY CATEGORY				
	Natural Gas	Oil	Generator	Marine	Process
U.S. domestic	2	1	5	3	
Offshore					
United States	8	3	2		
Canada	5	2			
North Sea	5	1	1		
Persian Gulf	4	2	1		
North/West Africa	2	1			
Indonesia	2				
Australia	2	1			
South America	1	1			
Field production, onshore					
United States	1	2			
Canada	2	2	2		2
South America	1	1	1		
Middle East	8	4	4		
North/West Africa	5	2	1		
Indonesia	2	2			
Australia	3	1	1		
Europe, distribution	3			1	
Japan				5	
Russia	5	3	2		
China					
Total	61	29	20	9	2
Grand total			120		

*At sea level and 59°F.

Exhibit 35.8

ESTIMATED MARKET SIZE BEGINNING IN 1976*
(12,000-HP equivalent units within the 8,000–30,000-HP ISO range)

	United States and Canada	Export	Total
Natural gas industry	15	40	55
Petroleum	8	17	25
Process (refrigeration)	2	—	2
Power generation	8	11	19
Marine	3	6	9
Total	36	74	110

*At Sea level and 59°F.

Exhibit 35.9

ESTIMATED MARKET PENETRATION, 1976–1981
(UNITS)

	PACKAGE TYPE			
Year	Compressor Sets	Mechanical Drives	Generator Sets	Total
1976	2			2
1977	10	2		12
1978	15	5	2	22
1979	25	8	3	36
1980	30	12	6	48
1981	35	15	10	60
	117	42	21	180

for the level of detail required in this assessment, the current market will provide an adequate basis for comparison.

The first step of this approach is to define the scope of the market in which the S-Engine will be a viable competitor. The initial assessment said that, because of the superior performance of the S-Engine, it will compete effectively as a single unit in 8,000–15,000-HP applications and with multiple units in applications requiring up to 36,000 HP. A large amount of horsepower is also supplied by the relatively old and inefficient General Electric Frame 5 industrial turbine in the 30,000–40,000-HP range. This turbine is produced by both General Electric in the United States and by the General Electric Manufacturing Associates overseas. The poor fuel economy and high initial cost of the Frame 5 unit make some fraction of the sales vulnerable to substitution by multiple S-Engines. The total picture of the 1973 market in the 8,000–30,000-HP range plus all G.E. Frame 5 units is estimated to be almost 200 units per year or the equivalent of 400 S-Engine (12,000-HP size) units per year. A summary of this market is shown in Exhibit 35.10, and the detail composition is shown in Exhibit 35.11. These data regarding the relevant competition and market share estimates were obtained from the following independent sources.

1. *Sawyer's Gas Turbine Catalog,* 1973
2. *1973 Diesel and Gas Turbine Worldwide Catalog*
3. Bolter's turbomachinery sales "competitive information files" on individual competitors containing field reports, magazine articles describing specific installations, competitive proposals, and so on
4. Installation lists and product bulletins published by potential S-Engine competitors

Bolter cannot expect to be a viable competitor against the G.E. Frame 5 engine in all applications. Only about one-third of the Frame 5 units are two-shaft machines used in mechanical drive applications. These are the gas compression and oil pumping applications which will be the heart of the S-Engine market. In that one-third

Exhibit 35.10

TOTAL 8,000–40,000-HP PRIME MOVER MARKET IN 1973—SUMMARY*

Company	Number of Units Sold per Year	12,000-HP Equivalents	Total Horsepower per Year $(\times 10^{-3})$	Dollars per Horsepower	Total Revenue ($ millions)	Market Share by Horsepower (%)
G.E.—U.S.	51	138	1,665	80	133.2	33.5%
G.E. Manufacturing Associates	105	225	2,700	80	216.0	54.3
Ingersoll-Rand	7	10	125	80	10.0	2.5
Cooper-Bessemer	11	14	173	80	13.84	3.5
Dresser-Clark	7	9	105	80	8.4	2.1
De Laval	3	3	45	80	3.6	0.9
Brown-Boveri-Sulzer (BST)	10	8	100	80	8.0	2.0
United Aircraft Turbomarine	0	0	0	80	0	0
Orenda	0	0	0	80	0	0
Cooper-Recip	3	2	30	150	4.5	0.6
Clark-Recip	3	2	30	150	4.5	0.6
Total	200	414	4,973	—	402.0	100.0%

*Includes all G.E. Frame 5 business.

Exhibit 35.11

TOTAL 8,000–40,000-HP PRIME MOVER MARKET IN 1973—DETAIL INFORMATION

Company	Model	Horsepower	Number of Units Sold per Year*	12,000-HP Equivalents per Year	Total Horsepower per Year ($\times 10^{-3}$)	Dollars per Horsepower (avg.)	Total Revenue ($ millions)
General Electric	Frame 1	5,000	0	—	—	—	—
	Frame 3	14,600	15	19	225	80	18.0
	Frame 5	40,000	36	12	1,440	80	115.2
AEG-Kanis Turbinefabrik	Frame 1	5,000	0	—	—	—	—
	Frame 3	14,600	10	12	150	80	12.0
(G. E. Manufacturing Associate)	Frame 5	40,000	5	17	200	80	16.0
Alsthom	Frame 1	5,000	0	—	—	—	—
(G. E. Manufacturing Associate)	Frame 3	14,600	15	19	225	80	18.0
	Frame 5	40,000	10	34	400	80	32.0
Hitachi	Frame 1	5,000	0	—	—	—	—
(G. E. Manufacturing Associate)	Frame 3	14,600	5	6	75	80	6.0
	Frame 5	40,000	10	34	400	80	32.0
John Brown Engineering	Frame 1	5,000	0	—	—	—	—
(G. E. Manufacturing Associate)	Frame 3	14,600	15	19	225	80	18.0
	Frame 5	40,000	15	50	600	80	48.0
Kvaerner Brug	Frame 1	5,000	0	—	—	—	—
(G. E. Manufacturing Associate)	Frame 3	14,600	5	6	75	80	6.0
	Frame 5	40,000	0	—	—	—	—

		7,000–30,000					
Mitsui (G.E. Manufacturing Associate)	Electric only						
Nuovo Pignone (G.E. Manufacturing Associate)	Frame 1	5,000	0	—	—	—	—
	Frame 3	14,600	10	12	150	80	12.0
	Frame 5	40,000	5	17	200	80	16.0
Ingersoll-Rand	LM1500	15,500	5	6	75	80	6.0
	LM2500	24,000	2	4	50	80	4.0
Cooper Bessemer	Avon	12,500–18,000	10	12	150	80	12.0
	LM2500	23,300	1	2	23	80	1.84
	PW	15,000	0	—	—	—	—
Clark	Avon	15,000–17,000	5	6	75	80	6.0
	LM2500	23,300	0	—	—	—	—
	LM1500	15,000	2	2	30	80	2.4
	PW	15,000	0	—	—	—	—
DeLaval	Avon	16,000–18,000	3	4	45	80	3.6
	LM1500	15,100	0	—	—	—	—
	LM2500	23,700	0	—	—	—	—
Brown-Boveri-Sulzer (BST)		5,000–12,000	10	8	100	80	8.0
United Aircraft TMP		18,000	0	—	—	—	—
Orenda	Misc.	9,000–13,000	0	—	—	—	—
Cooper-Recip.	Z330	8,000–13,500	3	2	30	150	4.5
Clark	TCVC-1	8,000–11,000	3	2	30	150	4.5
Total			200	414	4,973		402.0

*The number of units sold per year by each manufacturer, particularly by G.E., are preliminary estimates only. This information will be further refined through more in-depth analyses in the future. However, in performing the initial appraisal of the market, these estimates are adequate.

of the Frame 5 sales that are two shaft, the customers, often because of historical preferences and other reasons, will accept only the G.E. unit in the majority of applications. On this basis, it was established that the total market for the S-Engine would cover the entire 8,000- to 36,000-HP range and would also include between 0 and 25 percent of the market currently dominated by the G.E. Frame 5 turbine. Rather than defining the total market by a single number, a range was considered. The lower limit, without any Frame 5 units, was estimated to be 144 S-Engine equivalent (12,000-HP) units per year. The upper limit, including 25 percent of the G.E. Frame 5 sales, was estimated to be about 200 S-Engine equivalent units per year. The detailed distributions of the two limits of the market are included in Exhibits 35.12 and 35.13.

The next step was to estimate the share of the market that Bolter could reasonably expect to capture with the S-Engine in today's market. The approach used was to compare Bolter's present share in both the Neptune and Apollo markets with the characteristics of the S-Engine and the corresponding markets.

Previous analyses of Bolter's current business have produced estimates of the important factors in the marketplace, particularly the relative importance of the customer buying influences. A summary ranking of the customer buying influences by

Exhibit 35.12

S-ENGINE MARKET SIZE IN 1973—LOWER LIMIT
(8,000–30,000-HP without G.E. Frame 5)

Company	Number of Units Sold per Year	12,000-HP Equivalents	Total Horsepower per Year $(\times 10^{-3})$	Dollars per Horsepower	Total Revenue ($ millions)	Market Share by Horsepower (%)
G.E.—United States	15	19	225	80	18.0	13.0%
G.E. Manufacturing Associates	60	85	900	80	62.0	51.9
Ingersoll-Rand	7	10	125	80	10.0	7.2
Cooper-Bessemer	11	14	173	80	13.84	10.0
Dresser-Clark	7	8	105	80	8.4	6.1
De Laval	3	4	45	80	3.6	2.6
Brown-Boveri- Sulzer (BST)	10	8	100	80	8.0	5.8
United Aircraft Turbomarine	0	0	0	80	0	0
Orenda	0	0	0	80	0	0
Cooper-Recip	3	2	30	150	4.5	1.7
Clark-Recip	3	2	30	150	4.5	1.7
Total	119	144	1,733	—	142.8	100.0%

industry and application is included in Exhibit 35.14. Bolter's ability to respond to these demands of the market has produced approximately a 30 percent aggregate market share for both Neptune and Apollo engines.

The applications of the S-Engine are generally scale-ups of Apollo applications, particularly in the oil and gas industry. Thus, by analyzing those features that are expected to be different for the S-Engine market, a table of required product/market characteristics was prepared by industry segment. The percentage of each segment in which the particular requirement is expected to apply has been estimated on the basis of both the present requirements and predicted changes. These product/market requirements are shown in Exhibit 35.15.

Each competitor's strengths and weaknesses were then evaluated in light of these product/market requirements. The major competitors were analyzed as follows:

1. In the case of General Electric, G.E.and its equipment represent the dominant force in the marketplace. G.E. itself competes primarily with its horizontally split-steam turbine-type industrial engine, Frame 3 and Frame 5 in this market. In addition, G.E. "sells" both Frame 3 and Frame 5 units through its nine manufacturing associates throughout the world. G.E.'s strengths are a worldwide manufacturing capability, reliability, excellent reputation, and a strong marketing organization. Its weaknesses include high first cost, high fuel consumption, and large size and weight. These two engines are quite old designs; however, they account for between 60 and 75 percent of the worldwide market.

Exhibit 35.13

S-ENGINE MARKET SIZE IN 1973—UPPER LIMIT
(8,000–30,000-HP plus 25% of G.E. Frame 5 business)

Company	Number of Units Sold per Year	12,000-HP Equivalents	Total Horsepower per Year $(\times 10^{-3})$	Dollars per Horsepower	Total Revenue ($ millions)	Market Share by Horsepower (%)
G.E.—United States	24	49	585	80	46.8	23.0%
G.E. Manufacturing Associates	71	11	1,350	80	108.0	53.1
Ingersoll-Rand	7	10	125	80	10.0	4.9
Cooper-Bessemer	11	15	173	80	13.84	6.8
Dresser-Clark	7	9	105	80	8.4	4.1
De Laval	3	4	45	80	3.6	1.8
Brown-Boveri-Sulzer (BST)	10	8	100	80	8.0	3.9
United Aircraft Turbomarine	0	0	0	80	0	0
Orenda	0	0	0	80	0	0
Cooper-Recip	3	2	30	150	4.5	1.2
Clark-Recip	3	2	30	150	4.5	1.2
Total	139	212	2,543	—	207.6	100.0%

Exhibit 35.14

RELATIVE IMPORTANCE OF CUSTOMER BUYING INFLUENCES

Industry/application	TYPICAL CUSTOMER BUYING INFLUENCE (Rated 0–10 in Proportion to Importance)						
	Initial Cost	Ownership Economics	Reliability	Size/ Weight	Service	Delivery	Local Manufacturing Content
Oil and Gas							
Exploration (domestic)	7	6	8	7	7	5	1
Exploration (foreign)	7	6	8	7	7	5	5
Production (domestic)	9	7	8	7	8	6	1
Production (foreign)	10	7	8	7	8	6	6
Processing (domestic)	6	7	10	6	8	6	1
Processing (foreign)	6	7	10	6	8	6	6
Transmission (domestic)	8	7	8	6	8	7	1
Transmission (foreign)	7	6	8	6	8	7	5
Utilities							
Power companies	9	7	8	5	8	6	1

Exhibit 35.15

REQUIRED PRODUCT CHARACTERISTICS BY MARKET SEGMENT

Industry	PRODUCT CHARACTERISTICS (5 of Each Market Segment Where Characteristic Is Required)								
	Continuous Duty	Intermittent Duty	Low First Cost	Fuel-Cost Sensitive	Not Fuel-Cost Sensitive	Fast Turbine Change-out	Natural Gas Fuel	Dual Fuel	Liquid Fuel (wide range)
Natural gas industry	100	14	57	43	57	100	100	0	40
Petroleum	100	0	72	17	83	100	83	0	40
Process	100	0	100	0	100	100	100	0	10
Power generation	57	43	89	11	89	100	57	0	43
Marine	100	0	50	100	0	100	0	0	100
Total	88	15	78	26	74	100	77	0	28

In addition to these machines, G.E. also manufactures industrial versions of its commercial aircraft engines. The two most important of these aircraft derivatives are the LM 1500 and LM 2500 gas producers which are sold to other manufacturers who package these turbines with their driven equipment.

2. Ingersoll-Rand, also a strong competitor of the Apollo engine, competes in the 8,000–30,000-HP market using G.E., Rolls-Royce, and Pratt & Whitney aircraft gas producers coupled with Ingersoll-Rand–produced power turbines, compressors, and pumps. Ingersoll-Rand's strengths lie in an excellent reputation and a complete product line of compressor and pump packages, blowers, and other equipment used in the oil and gas process industries. In addition, it has an effective marketing organization with strong contacts with its customers. Its weakness lies primarily in the uncertainty inherent in an aircraft derivative turbine. Fuel consumption of the LM 2500 is comparable to that of the S-Engine; however, the LM 1500, rated at about 15,000-HP, has considerably higher fuel consumption. It is estimated that Ingersoll-Rand controls between 3 and 8 percent of this market segment.

3. Cooper-Bessemer also utilizes aircraft derivative gas producers in the same manner as Ingersoll-Rand. However, Cooper-Bessemer does not offer the broad product line that Ingersoll-Rand does and would compete with the S-Engine mainly in gas transmission applications. In addition, Cooper-Bessemer recently reduced the effort on its Coberra 30, a rival to Apollo. Thus, its total power within the marketplace is diminished with the reduction in the product line.

4. Dresser-Clark operates in the same markets as Cooper-Bessemer with a similar aircraft-derivative–based product line; however, it enjoys a smaller market share.

5. Rising fuel prices have given reciprocating competitors a new lease on life. These engines are large, heavy, and expensive and require high maintenance. However, they have significantly lower fuel consumption that, when combined with the increased efficiency of reciprocating gas compressors, makes them viable competitors in large gas transmission applications. The two most significant competitors in this segment of the market are Cooper-Bessemer and Dresser-Clark.

Very little visibility can be obtained regarding the remaining competitors in the potential S-Engine market. However, the following potential developments have been identified which could change the composition of the market in the future.

1. Brown-Boveri-Sulzer has just announced the development of a lightweight gas turbine rated at 12,500-HP ISO. Six of these units have been sold in the Middle East.

2. DeLaval Engine and Compressor Division (Enterprise) has just announced availability of a new 20-cylinder, V-type version of its RV series diesel engine rated at 12,500 HP. This is a 450-RPM engine which appears to be aimed at the gnerator-drive market at a 9,000-KW rating.

3. Ruston Gas Turbines Ltd. is rumored to be developing a new turbine in the 8,000–12,000-HP size class.

4. Rolls-Royce intends to industrialize the Spey aircraft engine. This will produce a state-of-the-art aircraft-derivative industrial turbine in the 15,000–18,000-HP range.

5. The Allison Division of Detroit Diesel is considering industrializing the uprated version of the T-56 helicopter engine. This engine would arrive at the market in 1979 at a 9,000-HP rating.

All these developments which could affect the S-Engine market are being monitored very closely.

A significant fraction of the potential market places a great importance on ownership economics in the purchase decision. Thus, another step in the evaluation of how the S-Engine would fit into today's market was an analysis of the total ownership economics of the S-Engine with respect to the expected competition. The two engines chosen as representatives of the competition were the G.E. Frame 3 and the Cooper-Bessemer Z330 integral reciprocating gas compressor. These engines were analyzed for a main line natural gas transmission application. Four economic methods, those generally employed by Bolter's customers in evaluating our equipment, were used in this analysis. These were the simple payback, net cash flow, discounted net cash flow, and levelized annual savings methods. Different fuel prices and load factors were considered in the analysis. To arrive at the total ownership cost, historical information from the competitive information files was used to establish installation costs, fuel rates, and maintenance costs. These data are summarized in Exhibit 35.16.

The results of the analysis indicated that the S-Engine was superior to both the simple-cycle and reciprocated versions of the G.E. Frame 3 unit. However, the S-Engine was at a disadvantage with respect to the Cooper-Bessemer Z330 reciprocating engine compressor set at high fuel costs and high load factors for three of the four economic methods. The simple payback method shows the S-Engine to be superior only at fuel costs below $1.25 and load factors below 85 percent.

This economic disadvantage relative to the reciprocating compressor package is not of overriding concern because of the relatively small number of applications in which the reciprocating packages will be truly viable competitors. Factors adversely affecting the competitiveness of reciprocating equipment include environmental restrictions, the large size and weight of the units, and customer prejudices favoring turbines.

Having analyzed the nature of the market in which Bolter currently operates with Neptune and Apollo, the shares that these engines command in those markets, the expected characteristics in the S-Engine size market, the organizations and products currently competing in that market, and the relative economics of the situation, there is no reason to expect Bolter to have any less share than it commands in its present markets. As the customers become more familiar with Neptune and Apollo

---

Exhibit 35.16

S-ENGINE COMPARATIVE ECONOMIC ANALYSIS INPUT DATA*

Unit	Horsepower	Heat Rate (Btus/HP-hr)	Total Installed Cost ($/HP)	Maintenance Cost ($/HP-year)
Solar S-Engine	12,000	9,552	$125	$4.00
G.E. Frame 3S	10,000	10,000	160	4.00
G.E. Frame 3R	10,000	7,140	210	4.50
Cooper-Bessemer Z330	8,800†	5,900	220	5.00

*In addition, fuel costs were varied between $100 and $150 per million Btu and load factor varied between 70 and 100%.

†Because of the higher efficiency (12% greater) of the associated reciprocating compressor, less horsepower is required to move the same amount of gas.

in the oil and gas markets and also in the generator market, Bolter's position should be considerably stronger. For the purpose of this assessment, a mature share was expected to be in the range of one-fourth to one-third of the market. On the basis of this share and the limits of the market size estimated in Exhibit 35.12 and 35.13 of between 173 and 254, Bolter could reasonably be expected to sell between 43 and 84 units per year. The most likely or expected value would be expected to fall at the midpoint of this range or between 60 and 65 units per year.

The results of this assessment agree quite well with the results of the two previous methods. Although this method would not be appropriate as a sole means of forecasting a project of the size and importance of the S-Engine, it does provide a useful independent evaluation of the markets for comparison with other forecasting techniques.

D. Analysis of Energy Demand Requirements

The three preceding approaches to determine the size of the S-Engine market were focused on a relatively short-range view of that market. This is because the visibility of the sources used and the people contacted is limited to perhaps a five-year time horizon. For a product with a life cycle of 15 to 20 years, a much longer view of the market must also be taken. The approach chosen for this forward look was to examine the primary demand for Bolter products which is created by a buildup in oil and gas production throughout the world. The year 1981 was chosen for evaluation as it is the year in which the engineering/marketing team forecast that a relatively mature level of 70 S-Engines would be sold. It is this level of sales that this approach to the market is intended to evaluate and confirm or disconfirm.

Looking at Bolter's product lines in terms of the customers needs that they satisfy, two general functions performed by the products are identifiable. First, Bolter turbines are used to supply electrical energy to people in both continuous and stand-by modes. In 1973, generator sets will comprise 44 percent of Neptune sales and 17 percent of Apollo sales. The demand for this equipment will depend on the relative costs of electricity versus other forms of energy and on the importance that the customer places on not being without electricity during utility power outages. Thus, a strong correlation could be expected between the demand for Bolter generators and the demand for electricity within the economy.

Second, and most important, Bolter turbine packages provide the power necessary to support the production and transmission of oil and gas throughout the world. In 1973, 65 percent of all Bolter product sales will be to the oil and gas industry. This is composed of about 85 percent compressors and pumping units and 15 percent generators.

The demand for this type of equipment directly follows the demand for oil and gas with minor adjustments made for the timing and location of the supplies. Thus, Bolter's market and demand for this equipment is very closely related to the world energy growth and, more particularly, gas, oil, and electricity.

Forecasts of energy demand are generally constructed by aggregating the demands from the individual consuming sectors such as residential, commercial, industrial, transportation, and so on. Within these sectors, demands are highly dependent on projections of economic and population growth rates. This results in aggregate energy demand forecasts which are closely related to economic growth forecasts as measured by GNP. Thus, the first step is to look at a forecast of economic growth in both the United States and in the balance of the world. This is shown in Exhibit 35.17 and indicates a fivefold increase in the world economy in 30 years, an aggregate annual growth rate of approximately 5.5 percent. The growth in the United States will be somewhat less, with the result that the U.S. economy will become a decreasing fraction of the total world economy in the future. The geographic distribution of the world energy demand forecast shown in Exhibit 35.18 closely parallels the economic forecast. The decreasing share of the energy consumed within the United States follows the same pattern as the GNP forecast. This fact is easily understandable. The United States contains approximately 6 percent of the world's population, but consumes approximately 30 percent of the world's energy as shown in the breakdown of the world per capital energy consumption in Exhibit 35.19. This distribution is not expected to continue, and considerable leveling out is expected over the next 20 years. Accordingly, the major emphasis in the world will be on supplying the energy

---

Exhibit 35.17

FORECAST OF GROSS NATIONAL PRODUCT (1970 dollars)

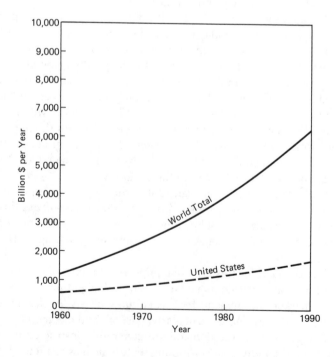

Exhibit 35.18

TOTAL WORLD ENERGY DEMAND

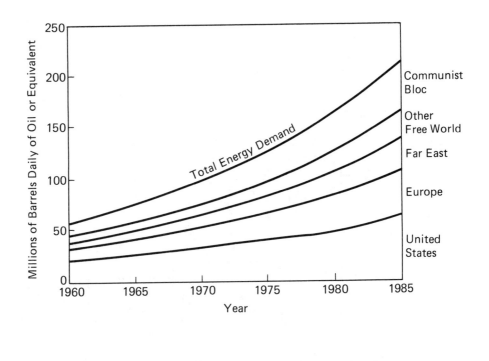

needs of countries outside of the United States. Thus, the United States will face severe competition in its search for the world's energy reserves.

The corresponding world energy supply picture by source is shown in Exhibit 35.20 through 1985. The major point to note is the high level of dependence on both natural gas and oil. The fraction of energy requirements to be met by gas and oil are projected to increase from 60 to 67 percent of the total, such that 75 percent of the total increase in energy is to be supplied by oil and gas. Again, most of this will occur outside of the United States because of the locations of oil reserves within the world, as shown in Exhibit 35.21.

Thus, not only is Bolter a participant in the energy picture, but also a key figure in the sector that is expected to experience the most significant worldwide growth in the next 15 to 20 years.

The total world gas and oil supply figures shown in Exhibit 35.20 were broken down into regions of the world. By compiling these oil and gas supply forecasts by region, the current production and reserve levels within these regions, the geography

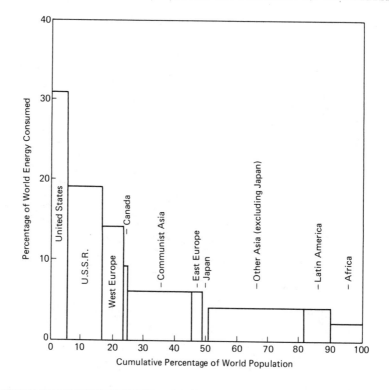

Exhibit 35.19

WORLD ENERGY CONSUMPTION AS A FUNCTION OF POPULATION

of the supplies, the economics of transportation, and the political situations, forecasts of oil and gas production levels in 1975 and 1980 were made. Sources of data used in these forecasts included the 1973 *International Petroleum Encyclopedia*, the *U.S. Energy Outlook* published by the National Petroleum Council, and numerous magazine and journal articles. The resulting 1975–1980 average annual oil and gas production capacity increases within each region are shown in Exhibits 35.22 and 35.23.

After examining Bolter's applications experience as well as published historical Federal Power Commission data, estimates were made of the aggregate pumping horsepower required to produce and transport a barrel of oil and the compression horsepower required to move a standard cubic foot of natural gas. By taking into account such factors as oil and gas field decay rates and estimates of the distribution of associated and gas well gas, total production and transportation horsepower buildups were calculated. These data for oil and gas are also displayed in Exhibits 35.22 and 35.23, respectively. The total horsepower was then divided into segments by equipment size classes to correspond with the projected markets for the Neptune, Apollo,

Exhibit 35.20

TOTAL WORLD ENERGY SUPPLY

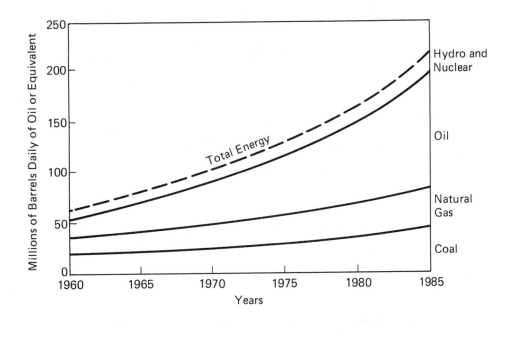

and S-Engine, respectively. The Neptune is expected to compete in the 800–3,000-HP size class, the Apollo in the 3,000–10,000-HP size class, and the S-Engine up to 30,000 HP. Bolter does not participate in the market below 800 HP dominated by reciprocating engines or in the market above 30,000 HP dominated by large industrial gas turbines. The distribution of horsepower into these segments and the corresponding numbers of equivalent Bolter units are shown in Exhibit 35.24.

Since the goal of this market approach is a comparison of these unit forecasts with those obtained by the other methods, it is necessary to extrapolate these data to 1981. The number presented in Exhibit 35.24 effectively represent the market size for 1978. The growth of the market between 1978 and 1981 was estimated to parallel the growth of the oil and gas supply during the 1970s at 7.25 percent per year. The corresponding market numbers for 1981 are indicated in Exhibit 35.25.

The S-Engine market obtained from an analysis of the primary demand for the equipment, includes only gas compression and crude oil and product pumping units.

Exhibit 35.21

WORLD OIL RESERVES

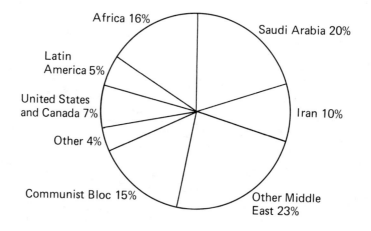

Total reserves: 667 billion barrels

Africa 16%

Saudi Arabia 20%

Latin America 5%

United States and Canada 7%

Iran 10%

Other 4%

Communist Bloc 15%

Other Middle East 23%

Exhibit 35.22

CRUDE OIL PRODUCTION AND HORSEPOWER INCREASES, 1975–1980

Region	PRODUCTION LEVEL (MMB/D)			Production Buildup per Year, 1975–1980	Required Horsepower per Year*
	1972	1975	1980		
United States	9,465	11,080	11,800	144	40,000
Canada	1,517	2,350	3,000	130	36,000
U.S.S.R., China	8,750	11,450	18,900	1,490	414,000
Mideast/Africa	24,334	31,690	39,510	1,564	435,000
NSEA/Europe	373	500	1,500	200	56,000
South America	4,830	4,170	5,000	166	46,000
Asia/Pacific	1,187	4,260	6,000	348	97,000
Total					1,124,000

MMB/D = Millions of barrels per day.
*Includes gathering and transportation applications.

Exhibit 35.23

NATURAL GAS PRODUCTION AND HORSEPOWER INCREASES, 1970–1980

Region	PRODUCTION LEVELS (TCF/Y)			Production Buildup per Year, 1975–1980*	Required Horsepower per Year†
	1972	1975	1980		
United States‡	22.30	21.8	22.0	1.13	737,500
Canada	2.86	3.4	4.8	0.45	264,000
U.S.S.R., China	9.46	13.0	20.0	2.05	563,400
Mideast/Africa	2.32	3.0	5.0	0.55	355,600
NSEA/Europe	4.37	4.37	5.37	0.42	295,200
South America	3.27	3.4	4.0	0.29	141,400
Asia/Pacific	0.67	0.7	1.0	0.096	95,145
Total					2,452,245

TCF/Y = Thousands of cubic feet per year.
*Includes amounts required to recover field depletions.
†Includes production and transportation gas compression applications.
‡United States uses about half the gas consumed in the world, but will add about ⅓ horsepower per year.

However, the forecast for this portion of the market at 215 units per year indicates that selling the planned 70 units in 1981 could be accomplished with 31 percent market share. Thus, without including any generator sales, Bolter should be able to achieve its historical market share. Because of the superior nature of this product in the market, even this would be a conservative share estimate.

The result of this longer-range look at the market would tend to indicate that the total market potential for the S-Engine could be considerably larger than estimated by other methods. This implies a greater level of confidence that the other forecasting techniques indeed represent a conservative view of the market as appropriate for planning purposes.

E. Sales Management Assessment

The previous sections discussed four independent analyses used to establish the size of the potential market for Bolter's next turbine. The use of multiple approaches was adopted to increase the level of confidence in the forecast. However, it is the responsibility of sales management to establish a single forecast for use by the division in planning for the project. Because the Engineering-Marketing field survey contacted individuals who would be making the buying decisions for the new turbine, it was decided that the resulting forecast would be the most accurate for the five- to seven-year planning horizon. The forecast sales schedule to be used for planning purposes was obtained from the Engineering-Marketing team field survey in Section B and is shown in Exhibits 35.26 and 35.27.

Exhibit 35.24

1978 OIL AND GAS INDUSTRY HORSEPOWER MARKET*

Application	Horsepower	% of Application	SIZE RANGE							
			0–800		800–3,000		3,000–5,000		5,000–30,000	
			%	HP	%	HP	%	HP	%	HP
Crude oil										
Gathering	124,000	11.1	75	93,000	25	31,000	—	—	—	—
Transmission	1,100,000	88.9	5	50,000	35	350,000	40	400,000	20	200,000
Natural gas										
Gathering										
Gas plant boost	1,178,000	47	30	353,400	35	412,300	25	294,500	10	117,800
Transmission	1,274,000	53	0	0	5	63,700	5	63,700	90	1,146,600
Other oil and gas applications†	1,192,000	100	35	417,200	30	357,600	25	298,000	10	119,200
HP—all applications	4,767,000	100		913,600		1,214,600		1,056,200		1,583,600
% by size class				19.2		25.5		22.2		33.1
No. solar equivalent units by size class				None		972 Saturns		302 Centaurs		132 S-Engines

*Excluding all generator horsepower. Also excludes process and liquid natural gas applications with load requirements greater than 30,000 HP.
†Secondary recovery (gas lift and water flood), conservation (gas injection and arctic refrigeration), and product pumping and tanker loading. This segment estimated to be 25% of total oil and gas horsepower market.

Exhibit 35.25

1981 POTENTIAL OIL AND GAS MARKET IN DOLLARS AND UNITS

	MARKET SEGMENT SIZE BY HORSEPOWER RANGE				
	0–800	800–3,000	3,000–5,000	5,000–30,000	Total
Total Market					
HP (1978)	913,600	1,214,600	1,056,200	1,583,000	4,767,000
$ (1978)*	$54,800,000	$133,500,000	$105,600,000	$126,700,000	$420,000,000
HP (1981)	1,126,000	1,498,000	1,302,000	1,952,000	5,878,000
$ (1981)*	$67,568,000	$164,600,000	$130,200,000	$156,200,000	$518,610,000
Solar product	None	Saturn	Centaur	S-Engine	—
Potential market					
HP (1981)	0	1,498,000	1,302,000	1,952,000	4,752,000
$ (1981)*	0	$164,600,000	$130,200,000	$156,200,000	$451,000,000
Units (1981)	0	1198 Saturns	372 Centaurs	162 S-Engines	—

*In 1973 dollars.

Exhibit 35.26

S-2 ENGINE
PLANNED SALES SCHEDULE, 1976–1981

	PACKAGE TYPE			
Year	Compressor Sets	Mechanical Drives	Generator Sets	Total
1976	2			2
1977	12	2		14
1978	18	5	2	25
1979	24	10	4	38
1980	30	15	8	53
1981	36	20	12	68
Total	122	52	26	200

Exhibit 35.27

FORECAST OF REVENUES S2-ENGINE PROJECT, 1973–1981
($ millions)

	1973	1974	1975	1976	1977	1978	1979	1980	1981
Sales units	0	0	0	2	14	25	38	53	68
($000,000)*				3†	21	37.5	57	79.5	102
Less: Variable costs, 60%	0	0	0	1.8	12.6	22.5	34.2	47.7	61.2
Contribution to overhead	0	0	0	1.2	8.4	15.0	22.8	31.8	40.8
Less: Development costs	4	4	20	15	12	0	0	0	0
Contribution of S-Engine project	(4)	(4)	(20)	(13.3)	(3.6)	15.0	22.8	31.8	40.8
Total									65

*Constant dollars.
†Sale price = $1,500,000 per unit.

OPEC THE ECONOMICS OF THE OIL CARTEL*

In the past 13 months, the oil cartel has succeeded in doing what it could not do in the previous 13 years of its existence: fundamentally alter the structure of world economic power. Since its creation in 1960, the Organization of Petroleum Exporting Countries (OPEC) has had two main goals: to raise the taxes and royalties earned by member governments from crude oil production and to assume control over production and exploration from the major international oil companies. With government revenue now well above $10 a barrel—a ninefold increase over the last four years—and Saudi Arabia moving to complete 100 percent acquisition of the companies' producing properties, these goals are close to achievement.

The OPEC cartel now holds unprecedented power over a commodity vital to the health of the world's economies, and there is little reason to expect that power to disappear quickly. Reversing previous administration optimism, Assistant Treasury Secretary Gerald Parsky now says, "I believe the cartel can and will be maintained on economic grounds for about three years no matter what we do economically."

And Shell Oil Co.'s President Harry Bridges is impressed by the deeper strengths of the cartel. "I just don't see any weakness in OPEC," he says. "Tell me of another organization that has two nations like Iran and Iraq, which are at war with each other and yet sit together in OPEC and show no signs of breaking the cartel up or quarreling over oil prices. That indicates to me that these countries have found the mechanism they need to achieve their goals, and their loyalty to it transcends traditional political enmities."

However, looking beyond the next two or three years, OPEC's continued cohesion will depend on how well it handles the changing supply and demand trends that its own success in increasing prices has unleashed. OPEC will have to find and enforce a price structure that maximizes revenue without generating such huge new sources of petroleum and other forms of energy that its control over the market is destroyed. At the same time, that price structure will have to reconcile the often conflicting economic and political requirements of the member nations.

Business Week, January 13, 1975, pp. 77–81.

Most oil industry authorities think these requirements will be more and more difficult to achieve, the longer the present real price of oil persists. They, therefore, question whether the current high price level can be maintained indefinitely.

Several countries, including Kuwait and Libya, have indeed cut output as world consumption of crude oil in 1974 dropped 4 percent from the 1973 level. Shell's Bridges says: "I would not be surprised if in 1975 OPEC adopts a prorationing scheme to formally assign each producing country a rate of production that is a certain percentage of capacity. The scheme would relate population and infrastructural needs of each producing country to its available crude supplies. Venezuela has been suggesting such a mechanism for 10 years."

The purpose of any cartel is to maximize the earnings of its members. It does so when the cartel ignores its internal differences and sets the same price that a monopolist would in the same circumstances. If consumers are unable to substitute readily for a given commodity or do without it, the price can be raised quite high without—in the short run—a great loss in volume of sales, so total revenue will increase.

Edward Hudson of Data Resources, Inc., and Dale Jorgenson of Harvard University have calculated in an oft-cited study of U.S. energy demand, that, in the short run, a 100 percent increase in the price of crude oil leads to only a 15 percent reduction in consumption—what economists call a price elasticity of -0.15. So OPEC price hikes are very profitable.

But over a longer period, such as five to ten years, consumers have a better opportunity to substitute other forms of energy, and the price elasticity of petroleum will be higher, perhaps even approach -1.0, where higher price is completely offset by loss of sales volume. In a longer time perspective, a still greater threat to OPEC comes from the supply side of the equation: High prices and profits induce a worldwide expansion of exploration and production of crude oil, perhaps creating alternative supply sources that undercut OPEC's control of the market.

The Forces of a Surplus

Several recent studies see these demand and supply adjustments coming together strongly in the early 1980s to force OPEC either to allow prices to fall (in real terms) in a managed way or else risk a breakup of its group. Hollis Chenery, former economics professor at Harvard and now vice-president for development policy at the World Bank, writes in *Foreign Affairs* that if OPEC holds to the present real price until 1980, in that year it will have 16 million barrels a day of idle productive capacity out of total capacity of 40 million barrels and will have great difficulty in allocating that much shut-in capacity among its members.

MIT's Energy Laboratory Policy Study Group, relying chiefly on Adelman for guidance on the world oil market, calculates that OPEC will face a surplus of 10.6 million barrels a day of producing capacity by 1980. It argues that "the price could fall, due to the personal gulf countries' perceptions of their own long-run interest or to a succession of price shadings and a failure of understanding, powerfully aided by attempts of buyers to obtain long-run contracts at lower prices."

Equilibrium by 1980?

That still leaves a wide range within which to set the price, and OPEC has commissioned several studies to help it to determine the profit-maximizing price level and price sequence. The most important of these reports will be coming from the Geneva office at Battelle Institute in 12 to 18 months, examining the long-term effects of oil prices on investment in alternative energy sources. A dozen major research institutes and think tanks in Europe are reported working on related problems, under contract to OPEC countries, along with several in the United States.

While OPEC awaits the result of its own research, Western experts are busy with major studies to determine the strains that the cartel would experience if the oil price stayed at its current level. Generally, they use a four-step analysis:

- First, world demand for oil must be predicted for the reference year, usually 1980 but sometimes 1985.
- Next, it is necessary to estimate how much oil will be added from non-OPEC sources by the reference year. This can include increased production within consuming nations, such as oil from offshore United States and the North Sea, as well as supplies from new or expanding exporters that stay outside OPEC.
- Subtracting estimated non-OPEC supply from estimated world demand gives a figure for the world market open to the OPEC countries. This in turn can be compared with the total productive capacity that OPEC nations will have in place by the reference year. The comparison gives an indication of how great a problem OPEC will face in allocating output among its members.
- Not to be overlooked are the internal differences within OPEC in terms of oil reserves, population, revenue needs, and military ambitions. These will determine whether the members can achieve a mutually acceptable scheme of prorating production or will break up, with each country paring the price to reach its desired market share.

Estimating future worldwide oil consumption is especially chancy now that prices have skyrocketed far outside the range of previous experience, but a number of experts have made the attempt. The World Bank's Chenery suggests that total energy demand for the major noncommunist industrial countries will grow at 3.8 percent a year, on the average, for the rest of the decade. That is well below the 5 percent annual rate of the past few years. Gulf Oil's director of energy economics, Warren Davis, expects demand to grow at only 2 percent to 3 percent a year in the period.

If consuming countries themselves can step up their own oil production to match a 2 percent to 4 percent rate of growth in consumption, OPEC's expert market will obviously be frozen at its present level. In 1973, OPEC produced an average of 30.2 million barrels a day, almost all for export. Chenery figures that if oil stays at about $9.60 a barrel in 1974 dollars, OPEC's 1980 production will be 33 million barrels a day. The MIT group puts OPEC's 1980 output at 32.2 million barrels a day—a remarkable coincidence for two completely independent studies.

Much worse prospects for OPEC can be foreseen if non-OPEC production, such as the North Sea Fields, increases as some experts feel it will. Rotterdam University economist Peter Odell thinks that by 1990, North Sea Oil and Gas will satisfy 75 percent of Western Europe's total demand. Other experts tend to be less ebullient.

HOW THE CARTEL HAS BOOSTED ITS PURCHASING POWER

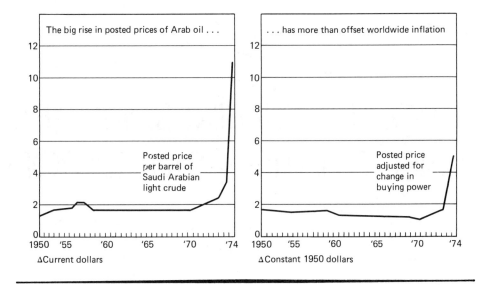

36

BOLTER TURBINES, INC. (B): NEGOTIATION SIMULATION

Negotiation is the most frequent means of resolving conflicts between organizations. Particularly in industrial marketing, when "big-ticket" and/or high-technology products are involved, sales are most often negotiated. Yet principles of effective negotiation and negotiation skills are seldom part of the curriculum in business schools. The Bolter Turbines, Inc. (BTI), negotiation simulation has been developed specifically to provide a context for experiential learning and practical discussion of business negotiations. Through the simulation and associated debriefing, participants are familiarized with the complex bargaining issues, strategies, and pressures typical of relationships between industrial firms.

The presentation of the BTI negotiation simulation that follows is divided into five parts. First, the simulation is briefly described. Next, instructions for participation and administration are detailed. Third, instructions for debriefing are outlined. Fourth, variations in the use of the game are suggested. The last section, contained in the Instructors manual and the appendix, consists of the student materials.

A BRIEF DESCRIPTION OF THE SIMULATION

The simulation and debriefing can be accomplished during a four-hour period. Two two-hour sessions are ideal. The BTI negotiation simulation involves a final sales negotiation between two industrial companies. The product is a $3 million natural gas compressor set for installation on an off-shore gas platform.

Six representatives of three firms are participating in the discussions: (1) a sales representative, a regional sales manager, and an applications engineer from Bolter Turbines, Inc.; (2) a purchasing agent and a production engineer from the client firm, Maverick Natural Gas, Inc.; and (3) a consulting design engineer working with the Maverick group, but employed by PARTEX and Associates Construction Company. Each participant has somewhat different (and in some cases conflicting) personal and professional motives regarding the deal. For example, the PARTEX consultant believes the recuperator, a Bolter product option, to be very important. Alternatively, the Maverick production engineer considers it to be an unnecessary frill.

Previous to the negotiation, BTI has submitted a price quotation for the gas compressor set, including several product options and Bolter's standard terms and conditions (Exhibit 36.1). The Maverick purchasing agent has established certain purchasing objectives which would require substantial concessions from BTI. Both sides are supplied with similar amounts of information about various environmental constraints (e.g., time schedules, market conditions). Additionally, each side has been instructed to come to an agreement during this meeting. The final agreement will consist of a completed purchase agreement, signed by representatives of both companies (Exhibit 36.2).

Exhibit 36.1

PRICE QUOTATION AND STANDARD TERMS AND CONDITIONS

FOR MAVERICK NATURAL GAS, INC. 7 EUWING AVENUE DALLAS, TEXAS	INSTALLATION: OFFSHORE PRODUCTION PLATFORM #6 GULF OF MEXICO
Model JR2000 natural gas compressor set	$2,500,000
Product options	
Custom-built marine shelter	400,000
Recuperator	500,000
Salt spray air filters	100,000
Service contract (2 years normal maintenance, parts and labor)	150,000
Total price	$3,650,000
Standard terms and conditions	
Delivery	6 months
Penalty for late delivery	$10,000/month
Cancellation charges (if client cancels order)	10% of contract price
Warranty (for defective machinery)	parts, one year
Terms of payment	COD
Inflation escalator*	15% per year

*In the event that delivery is delayed by client, the quoted price will be increased at a rate of 15% per year, computed on a monthly basis.

Exhibit 36.2

FINAL CONTRACT TERMS

JR2000 compressor set
Product options (circle those selected)
Shelter
Recuperator
Filter

Total price $ _____

Service contract (list conditions)

_____

_____

Price $ _____

Terms and conditions
Delivery   _____
Penalty   _____
Cancellation charges   _____
Terms of payment   _____
                                            _____

Inflation escalator   _____
Warranty   Parts _____   Labor _____   Years _____
Arbitration clause   Yes _____   No _____

Signatures

_____   _____
Maverick representative   Bolter representative

INSTRUCTIONS FOR PARTICIPANTS

There are six roles to be played in the simulation: three for the Bolter sales team and three for the Maverick purchasing team. Groups of six students (smaller groups also work) are given the appropriate materials, and the three Bolter representatives are sent to a different location to plan bargaining strategies. The role-playing instructions are self-explanatory; however, a few questions of clarification should be anticipated. The Bolter team is instructed to return at the end of the 30 minutes *(30-minute time limit for negotiation preparations)* and begin the sales discussions.

The bargaining session is limited to 1 hour. If facilities allow, private intrateam conferences are permitted. In any case, the *60-minute time limit for bargaining* is strictly adhered to. The simulation is complete when the final contract terms are specified and approved by the appropriate representatives of both firms (the form is included in the Bolter sales representative's materials). Usually bargaining is concluded very near the end of the time limit.